SAP PRESS Books: Always on hand

Print or e-book, Kindle or iPad, workplace or airplane: Choose where and how to read your SAP PRESS books! You can now get all our titles as e-books, too:

- ▶ By download and online access
- ▶ For all popular devices
- ▶ And, of course, DRM-free

Convinced? Then go to **www.sap-press.com** and get your e-book today.

Universe Design with SAP® BusinessObjects™ BI

 **PRESS**

SAP PRESS is a joint initiative of SAP and Galileo Press. The know-how offered by SAP specialists combined with the expertise of the Galileo Press publishing house offers the reader expert books in the field. SAP PRESS features first-hand information and expert advice, and provides useful skills for professional decision-making.

SAP PRESS offers a variety of books on technical and business-related topics for the SAP user. For further information, please visit our website: *www.sap-press.com*.

Christian Ah-Soon, Didier Mazoué, and Pierpaolo Vezzosi

Universe Design with SAP® BusinessObjects™ BI

The Comprehensive Guide

Galileo Press

Bonn • Boston

Galileo Press is named after the Italian physicist, mathematician, and philosopher Galileo Galilei (1564–1642). He is known as one of the founders of modern science and an advocate of our contemporary, heliocentric worldview. His words *Eppur si muove* (And yet it moves) have become legendary. The Galileo Press logo depicts Jupiter orbited by the four Galilean moons, which were discovered by Galileo in 1610.

Editor Emily Nicholls
Acquisitions Editor Kelly Grace Weaver
Copyeditor Julie McNamee
Cover Design Graham Geary
Photo Credit iStockphoto.com/16923094/© sharply_done
Layout Design Vera Brauner
Production Graham Geary
Typesetting Publishers' Design and Production Services, Inc.
Printed and bound in the United States of America, on paper from sustainable sources

ISBN 978-1-59229-901-0
© 2014 by Galileo Press Inc., Boston (MA)
1st edition 2014

Library of Congress Cataloging-in-Publication Data
Ah-Soon, Christian.
Universe design with SAP BusinessObjects : the comprehensive guide / Christian Ah-Soon,
Didier Mazoue, and Pierpaolo Vezzosi. — 1st edition.
pages cm
Includes bibliographical references and index.
ISBN 978-1-59229-901-0 (print : alk. paper) — ISBN 1-59229-901-6 (print : alk. paper) — ISBN 978-1-59229-902-7 (e-book) — ISBN 978-1-59229-903-4 (print and e-book) 1. BusinessObjects. 2. Business intelligence—Data processing. 3. Business intelligence—Computer programs. I. Mazoue, Didier. II. Vezzosi, Pierpaolo. III. Title.
HD38.7.A386 2014
658.4'038028553—dc23
2013037969

Contents at a Glance

Dear Reader,

By the time his first book arrived in the mail, Christian Ah-Soon was already putting together his next SAP PRESS book proposal: a comprehensive guide to designing universes to best represent business data in SAP BusinessObjects BI. Having worked with Christian on *SAP BusinessObjects BI Security*, I was excited to see the proposal for a universe book get approved and the writing begin.

Now, almost a year later, I can again say that it has been a sincere pleasure to work with Christian and his coauthors, Didier Mazoué and Pierpaolo Vezzosi. With humor, grace, and an acute understanding of what information their readers need, these three redefined what it means to be a hands-on author team. Throughout the months of editorial preparation and the late nights of production processes, they exceeded expectations for content quality and stayed involved in copyediting style, image design, and title verbiage conversations. Perhaps I shouldn't have expected anything different from universe designers!

Your comments and suggestions are the most useful tools to help us improve our books (and to spur Christian's next proposal!). We encourage you to visit our website at *www.sap-press.com* and share your feedback about *Universe Design with SAP BusinessObjects BI: The Comprehensive Guide*.

Emily Nicholls
Editor, SAP PRESS

Galileo Press
Boston, MA

emily.nicholls@galileo-press.com
www.sap-press.com

Contents

10 Securing Universes 571

12 Connecting to SAP ERP, SAP NetWeaver BW, and SAP HANA 635

Preface

Business intelligence finds and exposes useful information from raw data. A successful business intelligence project requires multiple skilled people working on the various steps, which range from finding the data in the sources, modeling it, exposing it in business terms, and securely providing it to the final users. This book is for them.

Book Objectives

This book presents the SAP BusinessObjects Business Intelligence 4.x semantic layer technology and guides you in the creation of universes with Information Design Tool. The goal of the book is to provide detailed information, examples, best practices, and step-by-step procedures that can help you successfully work with the technology.

This book is complementary to the existing official product guides. The official guides and product help systems explain how to do things, whereas this book shows how the products work but also why you should take certain actions, what to avoid, and what the possible alternatives are. With a more global view and understanding, you can be more autonomous and drive better SAP BusinessObjects BI projects to get the most out of the technology.

This book can be a first read for those who don't know how to build universes because it explains the basic functionalities and provide detailed step-by-step workflows to follow with sample screenshots.

More experienced universe designers can read this book to find information that helps them update their knowledge of previous versions of the semantic layer technology to the SAP BusinessObjects BI 4.x version, which has been greatly enhanced and exposes new interfaces to be learned.

The most important innovations (Information Design Tool, multisource universes, multidimensional universes, new access methods to SAP sources, new security model, etc.) are discussed in detail so that both new and experienced users can fully understand their usage and how to benefit from them.

Target Audience

If you are in any way involved in an SAP BusinessObjects BI project, you'll find useful information in this book. If you are tasked with designing a universe, you can find all of the necessary information to complete the task included in this book.

The presented information can also be useful for business analysts, data artisans, data scientists, translators, security managers, or any other roles that require working with data and extracting business meaning out of it. The book provides best practices for exposing good information out of data.

Database administrators and ETL experts can also find useful insights by understanding the load that an SAP BusinessObjects BI project can have on their data and how they can better prepare the data for the project.

Finally, anyone managing or working in a business intelligence center of excellence or business intelligence department can use this book to understand the benefits and challenges of a well-designed SAP BusinessObjects BI project.

Book Roadmap

The book contains 13 chapters:

▶ **Chapter 1**, Introduction to the Semantic Layer, is an introduction to the concept of the semantic layer and to the implementation of this technology in the SAP BusinessObjects BI solution.

▶ **Chapter 2**, Introduction to Information Design Tool, introduces Information Design Tool, which is the application used to build universes—the fundamental component of the semantic layer. You can find a description of the user interface and of some functionality that is commonly used when working with the application.

▶ **Chapter 3**, Local and Shared Projects, provides information about the local and shared projects. The chapter provides fundamental information about authoring your resources in a local project. It also describes how to share a project with others when working in a team.

▶ **Chapter 4**, Connecting to Data Sources, explains the first technical step of any SAP BusinessObjects BI project: connecting to data sources. With SAP BusinessObjects BI 4.x, there are many supported sources, and it's important to understand the best ways to connect to them. The chapter explains how to work with connections defined locally or on a server and how to connect to relational and OLAP sources.

▶ **Chapter 5**, The Data Foundation, describes the data foundation, which is the data model used to define the SAP BusinessObjects BI project. A lot of the intelligence of your project resides within the data foundation. This chapter provides deep insights into the data foundation functionality such as joins, derived tables, contexts, traps resolution, and so on.

▶ **Chapter 6**, Multisource Data Foundations, builds from the content of the previous chapter and extends it to the ability to build a data foundation on top of multiple data sources. You can find information on how to federate data from various sources in real time for your SAP BusinessObjects BI project. The chapter introduces the concept of federated tables and gives an overview of the Data Federation Administration Tool, which can be used to optimize multisource queries.

▶ **Chapter 7**, The Business Layer, explains how to build a business layer. This layer is the business representation of your data. The chapter shows in detail how to define the various business objects such as dimensions, measures, hierarchies, and so on, and it explains how to successfully expose those objects to the end users.

▶ **Chapter 8**, Universe Query Panel, shows how to execute queries on a universe using a query panel. The Information Design Tool query panel is described in depth, along with examples showing how to build simple to very sophisticated queries.

▶ **Chapter 9**, Publishing and Retrieving Universes, talks about the publication of a universe. When a universe is published, all SAP BusinessObjects BI client tools can access it to run queries. The chapter explains the publication workflow and its reverse operation: retrieving a published universe.

▶ **Chapter 10**, Securing Universes, covers the security that can be put on a universe. It describes the security editor interface and the various options of security on the database objects and on the business objects to make sure that data is accessed only by authorized users.

▶ **Chapter 11**, Working in Multilingual Environments, explains how to create universes with multilingual requirements. In multilingual environments, universes must be able to support data and metadata in different languages and return that data in a user's language. This chapter also introduces the Translation Management Tool.

▶ **Chapter 12**, Connecting to SAP ERP, SAP NetWeaver BW, and SAP HANA, is specific to SAP systems and their interactions with the semantic layer. It deep dives into the connections to SAP ERP, SAP NetWeaver Business Warehouse (SAP NetWeaver BW), and SAP HANA, and it explains how to expose those sources to the SAP BusinessObjects BI client tools through universes or a direct access methodology.

▶ **Chapter 13**, Comparing the Universe Design Tool and Information Design Tool, compares the functionalities of Information Design Tool and its predecessor, the Universe Design Tool. This chapter is targeted mainly to users of previous versions who are upgrading to SAP BusinessObjects BI 4.

So let's jump right in and start our journey into the semantic layer and the definition of universes with Information Design Tool.

Acknowledgments

We would like to collectively thank the following people who, directly or indirectly, helped in the writing of this book: David Mobbs, Jean-Pierre Montu, Nicolas Dieu, Mokrane Amzal, Ayhan Ulusoy, Olivier Tsoungui, Jérôme Ivain, Janet Richards, Makesh Balasubramanian, Ranganathan Natarajan, Abdellatif Astito, Nicolas Mourey, Olivier Duvelleroy, Emmanuel Zarpas, and everyone on the semantic layer team.

We also thank Kelly Grace Weaver, who believed in this book, and Emily Nicholls for her patience and her great help throughout the writing process.

Christian Ah-Soon

My first thoughts are for Claire, Inès, and Elisabeth. I'd also like to thank my family, my friends, and my colleagues for their support during these last months.

Didier Mazoué

I want to thank my wife, Valerie, and my beautiful daughters, Mathilde and Julie. Thank you for your support and patience during this long journey. I also want to thank the people who have been my mentors at Business Objects and SAP, Roxane Edjlali and Pierre Charmoille. Finally, I want to thank all of the people I used to work with in the product group and the sales and presales teams, both in France and abroad.

Pierpaolo Vezzosi

This book is for Tamara, my wife, and Gaia, my daughter. Thank you for being patient with me and so enthusiastic about this adventure. I want to thank my parents, Celestino and Vanna, who gave me the freedom to make my choices. A big thank-you goes also to my American family: Sam, Elaine, Kyle, Amy, and John, without whom this book could not even have been conceived. Thanks to Roxane for believing in me and taking me on her team.

The semantic layer is the SAP BusinessObjects technology that enables the content of a data source to be exposed in simple business terms for end users. This chapter introduces the concepts of the semantic layer, its purpose, its architecture, and the different business intelligence tools that use it.

1   Introduction to the Semantic Layer

At the beginning of the 1990s, the French startup Business Objects successfully entered the business intelligence (BI) market relying on a technology known as *semantic layer*. The founding idea of that technology was so useful that, after more than 20 years, many companies still rely on it for making everyday decisions on how they want to run their business.

In SAP BusinessObjects Business Intelligence (BI) 4.x, the latest major release of the SAP BusinessObjects BI suite, the semantic layer has become a central component that most SAP BusinessObjects BI tools can benefit from.

This chapter presents the basic concepts of the semantic layer technology and its implementation in the SAP BusinessObjects stack. It describes its main objectives and advantages, its architecture, the components that compose the technology, and the SAP BusinessObjects BI tools that benefit from it.

1.1   What Is a Semantic Layer?

In the business intelligence area, the main goal of a semantic layer is to enable any user to ask questions to any kind of data source without worrying about the technical details of how the request is physically run. A semantic layer is an abstraction layer that hides the complexity of a data source and enables users to use well-known business terms when asking questions, without knowing the specific data source query language.

As an example, a business person is able to run a query about customers by selecting a "Customer" object in a BI client tool. This object, via the semantic layer technology, retrieves actual data from a specific column of a specific table in a given relational database. The semantic layer takes care of translating the business question to the relative SQL sentence, which retrieves the data as shown in Figure 1.1.

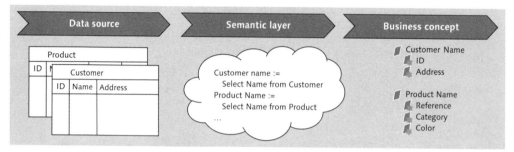

Figure 1.1 A Basic View of a Semantic Layer Main Functionality

In addition to the ability to translate business questions to database language queries, a semantic layer also provides multiple functionalities that greatly simplify and enhance the experience for the final user. Some of those functionalities include the following:

► **Business language for technical choices and filters**
  If a choice has to be given to the business user when running a query, the semantic layer exposes it in business terms, not in technical terms. For some business questions, it might be necessary to specify which tables are to be used when running the query. The semantic layer technology is able to ask the question in business terms instead of exposing the table names (e.g., the question might be related to choosing a "bookings" or a "sales" information, and the answer is translated in the choice of a specific set of tables in the source).

  Similarly to the choices in business terms, some questions might require filtering the data. Here again, the semantic layer can expose the filter question in business terms and not technical terms. Instead of asking values for a table and column, the values are asked for the business concept related to that column—for example, "Please select the Customer name."

► **Homogeneous experience**
  In a company, there are often multiple kinds of data sources. If relational databases are the most frequent kind of source for governed production usage, it's usually possible to find Online Analytical Processing (OLAP) cubes, spreadsheets, XML files, web services providers, and so on. The semantic layer technology is

able to connect to any and all of those different kinds of data sources and expose them with a homogeneous interface. The final user should not have a different experience when connecting to different sources from the semantic layer; a single user experience avoids having to learn how to use each different source, and the final user is able to concentrate on the question to ask rather than on the possible ways to ask it.

▶ **Simplified connectivity**

A semantic layer takes care of all of the technicalities related to the physical connection to the data source. The final user just selects a semantic layer object, and all details of connectivity, such as knowing the database server name or IP address, configuring the client machine middleware, setting users and passwords, and initializing the database session with the correct parameters, are automatically and transparently managed by the semantic layer technology.

▶ **Multisource**

A semantic layer can be built on top of multiple sources. When using a multisource semantic layer, the final user doesn't perceive any difference from accessing a single source. The semantic layer technology enables the definition of a model with multiple query languages and supporting relationships of information (as table joins) between different data stores. A multisource query algorithm analyzes the question of the final user, and then optimizes and splits it into specific questions for each data source. The data is retrieved from each source, synchronized, and returned as a single data set to the calling BI tool. A semantic layer can even enable the sources to be a mix of data on premise and data in the cloud. The final goal is to define the best possible virtual view of data based on the business users' needs, independent of where the data sits.

▶ **Additional security layer**

A semantic layer can also provide a security layer that sits on top of the database security mechanisms. Security at the semantic layer level can be added directly on the source data (e.g., row-level security) or defined at the semantic level. Security on the semantic level enables you to secure the business concepts that are being manipulated, independently of their definition. A "Revenue" object can, for example, be made non-accessible to a group of people while its definition or its source of data might change with time.

▶ **Query optimization**

When the IT team defines a semantic layer, it provides a description of the data source and of how the data is stored. This information is used at query time to calculate the optimal query to execute. The final user doesn't have to know advanced query language techniques nor the physical implementation of the source because the semantic layer technology adapts and optimizes the query syntax to the business question.

▶ **Master definitions**
The semantic layer can also be the place where a company provides a master definition of its data. It's common to see the same data stored in multiple places. This situation causes the following:

 ▶ A decreased level of trust in the data because users don't know which is the "best" data to use.

 ▶ An increased complexity in finding the data because users must know where the correct data is among different places.

A company can standardize the access to its data via a well-defined semantic layer that takes into account this multiplicity of sources and uses it as an advantage.

The team or person designing the semantic layer, knowing the various places where information can be found, has to make sure that the most appropriate and optimal information is always used at query time.

Thus, the semantic layer provides the ability for a non-technical user to ask complex questions to multiple data sources with a simple experience. The lifecycle of a semantic layer project is usually as follows:

▶ The IT team builds the semantic layer model once and maintains it.

▶ The business users (or IT report designers) make use of the semantic layer model to create all of the needed reports.

▶ If any kind of information is missing, the IT department adds it to the semantic layer model for all business users, rather than creating a new report that is beneficial only to the requester.

This model on one side makes the business user more independent and productive, and, on the other side, makes the IT team less charged with business users requests for reports. But to achieve this objective, it's important to pay attention to the semantic layer content and make sure it's well designed.

1.2   A Well-Designed Semantic Layer

One frequently asked question regards best practices for successfully running a BI project involving a semantic layer. The persons designing a semantic layer must have knowledge in different areas—both technical and non-technical. Their main difficulty is to find the balance between the technical implementation of the model and the business abstraction that must be exposed.

Many local factors such as the context, the business users' knowledge, the clarity of the requirements, or the final expectations can influence the success of a BI project. Some items, however, recurrently appear in a successful deployment, and they can be used as the foundation for a good project. Those items are just a starting point or a list of common-sense advice not to forget when starting a new project.

1.2.1   Characteristics

There are three must-have characteristics and three nice-to-have characteristics, listed here in order of priority:

▶ **Correctness (must-have)**
The semantic layer must return correct information; this is its first and most important requirement.

▶ **Security (must-have)**
The semantic layer must enable only authorized persons to see the data. Unsecured projects either are closed down immediately or generate a risk for the company.

▶ **Beneficial (must-have)**
The project request has to be initiated by the business, and its definition and outcome have to be validated by the business team. If the business finds benefits in using the solution, then the IT team has invested time and resources successfully. Projects that start as IT technological opportunities have fewer chances to be successfully adopted by the business team. If an IT team initiates the project, then the first step is to convince the businesspeople of the usefulness of the development.

▶ **Performance (nice-to-have)**
The semantic layer and the BI toolset should return information in a reasonable time frame. Many projects get abandoned because the long response times result in bad usability for the business users.

▶ **Ease of use (nice-to-have)**
A business user should be able to find its way easily into a semantic layer. The location of business concepts, naming choices, detailed information related to the business concepts, and requested workflows should reflect the business user's mind and expectations, not the technical implementation or IT processes.

▶ **Easy maintenance (nice-to-have)**
The IT team should be able to maintain the semantic layer with a limited effort.

These six characteristics are the basis of a well-designed semantic layer, even if many more characteristics are to be considered for each specific project.

1.2.2 Designing a Semantic Layer

For SAP BusinessObjects, the semantic layer is based on a model called a universe. The persona creating a universe is usually called a *designer* or *universe designer* (see Section 1.3). The designer is often working for the IT department or for the chief data officer's department. A designer should have a good understanding of the data source technology and also of the way the enterprise data is stored and organized on it. This person works with the business teams to define exactly what concepts they need surfaced for their queries and how they want them to appear. The business defines the requirements of a universe, not IT. IT's task is to find the most optimal implementation of the business user's requirements.

The designer's goal is to balance completeness and complexity of a universe:

▶ The universe should be complete enough to expose all necessary concepts.

▶ It must still be small enough to be understandable by the average business user. Business users might get confused when dealing with more than a hundred business concepts in a universe, but universes containing thousands of objects are often found in production.

▶ If it's not possible to keep it small, a universe must—in all cases—be well organized.

▶ The organization of a universe should follow the business user's experience expectations, not the data source implementation. For example, it's usually not recommended to expose all fields of a table as they are found in the database; it's usually better to organize the business objects by theme and expose together fields from various tables that talk about the same theme.

▶ Most importantly, the universe model must return correct results as a prerequisite. Any optimization, organization, or simplification consideration must be taken into account only after making sure that the results of queries are correct.

▶ Some data sources, such as OLAP sources, contain enough metadata information in themselves to provide an automatic, partial, or complete creation of a universe model. The designer should take advantage of this information by using the different wizards proposed by Information Design Tool.

1.3 Semantic Layer Components

The SAP BusinessObjects implementation of a semantic layer is made up of four main parts, as shown in Figure 1.2:

▶ **Universe**
The semantic layer persisted model.

▶ **Interface**
Method for client tools to connect to the universe, run queries through it, and retrieve the data.

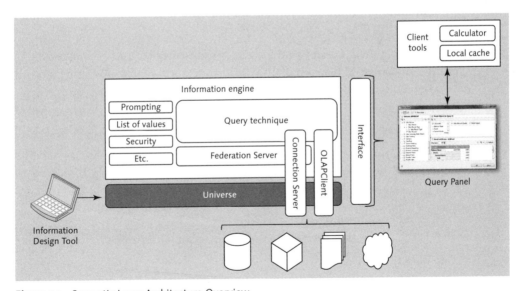

Figure 1.2 Semantic Layer Architecture Overview

- ▶ **Information engine**
  Internal component that processes user's queries sent through the query panel.

- ▶ **Information Design Tool**
  Metadata tool used to create universes.

In addition, client tools that support the semantic layer and can implement some capabilities to interact with universes include the following:

- ▶ A *query panel* graphical interface exposes universe content for query creation. Traditionally, client tools have implemented a query panel to connect to the semantic layer interface.

- ▶ Data providers, calculators, and caching mechanisms process the data returned by the semantic layer.

The semantic layer can be seen as a consistent set of components (model, algorithms, interfaces and tools) working together to expose the data to the end user. Rather than saying that the universe *is* the semantic layer, it's more appropriate to say that the universe *is part of* the semantic layer.

Let's start by examining the universe, since it's probably the most known component.

1.3.1 The Universe

The universe is a model of one or more data sources that exposes them in business concepts. The universe file contains all of the necessary information to connect to the underlying sources and query them using business terms in an optimized manner. The information in the universe is used by the information engine to translate the business question into the data source query language (e.g., SQL or MDX).

To develop a universe, the designer has to build a set of *resources* that define how the universe works, and that must be compiled or rather *published* into a universe file, as shown in Figure 1.3. The resources of a universe are listed here:

- ▶ **One or more connections**
  Define the connection information to the data source (see Chapter 4).

- ▶ **One data foundation**
  Defines the physical model of the source being connected. Data foundations are used only on relational data sources, and they can be single-source (see Chapter 5) or multisource (see Chapter 6).

▶ **One business layer**

Defines the business model that has to be exposed to the business users (see Chapter 7). The business layer is built on the data foundation for relational sources or directly on the connection for OLAP sources.

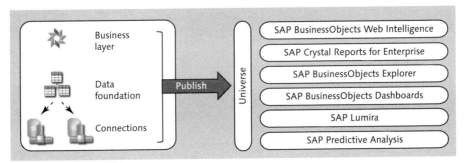

Figure 1.3 Publishing SAP BusinessObjects BI Resources into a Universe File

The goal of the business model is to expose the content of the source in plain business terms that can be understood by any user. In the universe, each business concept is a mapping to a specific object of the data source, such as a table field in a relational database or a dimension in an OLAP cube (see Figure 1.4) or is a calculation on top of one or multiple data source objects (see Figure 1.5).

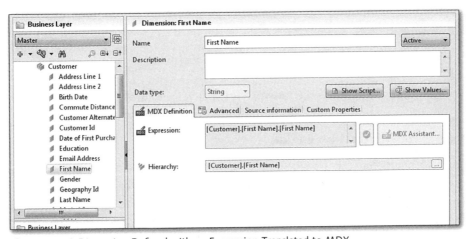

Figure 1.4 A Dimension Defined with an Expression Translated to MDX

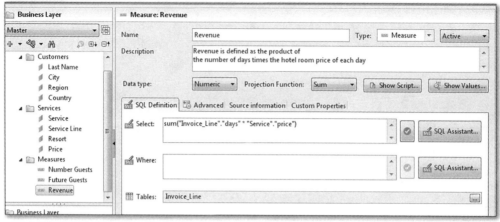

Figure 1.5 A Measure Defined as a Calculation on Multiple Database Fields

OLAP cubes such as Microsoft SQL Server Analysis Services, Oracle Hyperion Essbase, or SAP NetWeaver BW define business concepts. When creating a universe on those cubes, the business concepts are automatically detected, and the universe can be defined with a shorter and mostly automated workflow.

When connecting to SAP NetWeaver BW or SAP HANA (see Chapter 12), the designer has the choice to either manually build a universe or let the semantic layer build a model on the fly, which is immediately consumed by an SAP Business-Objects BI client tool. In this second scenario, it's possible to connect to the data source directly from a client tool, without the need to create a universe because the tool sees the source as if a universe was modeling it. This mechanism is known as a *direct access* connection.

The client interaction with the universe is usually done through a query panel.

1.3.2 The Information Engine

The information engine is a whole set of algorithms, services, interfaces, and APIs that enables the manipulation and the consumption of a universe. The information engine's task is to show the universe content to the user in a client tool, receive the questions from the user in business terms, rephrase the question in the source query language, retrieve the data from the source, and send it back to the BI client tool, as depicted in Figure 1.6.

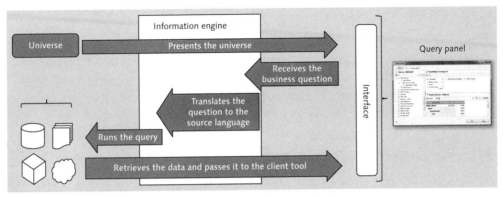

Figure 1.6 The Typical Workflow Performed by the Information Engine

At the core of the information engine is the service that translates the business question into the specific query language. This service is called the *query technique*, which you'll recall from Figure 1.2.

On one hand, the query technique knows the exact definition of a universe and its mappings onto the underlying data source; on the other hand, it analyzes the business question asked by the final user. From this analysis, the query technique identifies the best syntax to produce to run the query in a correct and optimal way.

To support the query technique and processes the query it generates, the information engine relies on additional services:

▶ Some questions require user interactions to answer prompts before running the queries. In such cases, the engine invokes a set of services which surface *prompts* in conjunction with *lists of values* to let the final user filter the query.

▶ Another important task of the information engine is to enforce the security put in place at the semantic layer level. If a user isn't entitled to see specific objects for the query, the information engine takes care of hiding them. If a user isn't entitled to see a specific set of data, the information engine makes sure that the data is taken away from the data set before being sent back to the user.

▶ The information engine also takes care of data source access through the *Connection Server* service for relational data sources and the *OLAPClient* service for OLAP data sources. These services simplify the access to the data by standardizing the calls across various middleware and vendor-specific languages. Some client tools use the Connection Server independently of the semantic layer to run freehand SQL queries onto a database and avoid implementing their own connectivity layer.

As suggested by its name, the information engine is really the service that processes and operates the semantic layer. To enforce these behaviors, the information engine relies on the definitions found in the universe that universe designers create in Information Design Tool, described in the next section.

1.3.3 Information Design Tool

Information Design Tool (IDT) is the new metadata design tool delivered in SAP BusinessObjects BI 4.x. IDT is installed from the SAP BusinessObjects BI 4.x client tools installer, and it can be used by universe designers to create and edit all resources required to create a universe: connections, data foundations, and business layers. It can also manage all workflows related to the lifecycles of these resources: publication, security, and sharing.

IDT is the successor of the Universe Design Tool, which is still available and supported in SAP BusinessObjects BI 4.x. Existing universes created in previous releases with Universe Designer (the Universe Design Tool's former name) can still be modified and enhanced in SAP BusinessObjects BI 4.x Universe Design Tool. When upgrading your deployment to SAP BusinessObjects BI 4.x, you can immediately use these universes in client tools.

Existing universes in the Universe Design Tool's format can also be converted to the new universe format supported by IDT and benefit from its new capabilities. More generally, for new projects in SAP BusinessObjects BI 4.x, we recommend that you create new universes directly with IDT. We'll describe IDT in detail in upcoming chapters of this book.

1.3.4 Client Tool Technology

SAP BusinessObjects BI client tools can have different purposes, such as data discovery, reporting, dashboarding, analysis, and so on. They can all access the semantic layer in different ways that are well suited for their usages. There is no strict enforcement from the semantic layer on how it has to be accessed and used; the objective is to keep the technology open to serve multiple use cases.

Query Panel

Client tools connecting to a universe usually implement a *query panel*. This query panel is an easy-to-use graphical interface displaying the business model exposed by the universe. In the query panel, the user defines the business question to be asked by a simple selection of the objects in the universe. Depending on the client tool, the question can be fine-tuned with prompts, selections from lists of values, mandatory filters, or other specific options.

The query panel interface and workflows implemented in IDT are described in detail in Chapter 8. SAP BusinessObjects Web Intelligence and SAP Crystal Reports for Enterprise implement very similar query panels, whereas other client tools implement query panels that better fit their needs. After the query has been created and validated, it's sent to the information engine for processing.

Data Provider

Client tools access the semantic layer information engine from an interface called a *data provider*. The data provider exposes the list of business concepts through the query panel interface, takes the business questions, and then manipulates the information engine to get a response back.

When the response (the data) is available, the client tool takes it, and the role of the semantic layer is completed. What happens afterwards is managed by the client tool itself. In many situations, the manipulation of the data set in the client tools results in new calls to the data provider, and hence the use of the semantic layer, but the responsibility of the tasks is owned by the client tool.

Calculator

Some client tools cache the data set locally to perform additional calculations that are necessary for the tool experience. Those tools embed a *calculator* technology, which can greatly vary from application to application. Even the way the data is cached locally (if it is) changes in different clients.

With some *slow* data sources or when working offline, for example, some client tools offer the ability to retrieve the necessary quantity of data to work locally, without charging the database any more or being connected to a network. This kind of workflow is often, but not always, associated with a scheduled refresh of data. On the other hand, with some very *fast* data sources, the client tools push each calculation to the database and have each manipulation of data generate a request on the data source itself. The semantic layer technology adapts to both kinds of workflows.

The information engine and the data providers are internal services (not exposed externally) that enable the consumption of the semantic layer by client tools. As said before, the most important task at hand for the designer is to define a good universe, which is the model of the data sources to be queried.

The capabilities implemented by the client tools that connect to the semantic layer depend on semantic layer deployment, as discussed next.

1.4 Deploying the Semantic Layer in SAP BusinessObjects BI 4.0

The SAP BusinessObjects BI 4 solution contains various SAP BusinessObjects BI client tools (described in Section 1.5) and server components. In a server deployment, these tools and components are hosted in a framework called the *BI platform* that provides them the general services, including:

- ▶ Resources and system administration
- ▶ Authentication and security
- ▶ Central repository where documents, universes, connections, and so on can be stored and shared among the platform users
- ▶ Scheduling and publishing
- ▶ Audit and monitoring

BI platform services are orchestrated by a specific server called *Central Management Server* (CMS) that also maintains the central repository, which by extension is called *CMS repository*. In the CMS repository, all resources and objects are stored using generic objects called *InfoObjects*.

The semantic layer is a core component in the SAP BusinessObjects BI 4 architecture because it enables the BI client tools to connect to the data sources and use them easily.

Still, the semantic layer is optional; not all client tools use it to connect to their data sources. In general, they use it when they need to connect to multiple kinds of data sources using a unified experience. When they need a dedicated user experience or when the usage of very specific data source functionalities is necessary (such as SAP NetWeaver BW), some client tools don't use the semantic layer and have developed their own source-specific interfaces.

There is no license fee for using the semantic layer. Licenses fees might apply to the SAP BusinessObjects BI platform itself or to client tools that make use of the semantic layer.

The semantic layer supports the two deployment scenarios shown in Figure 1.7:

▶ **Server deployment (❶)**
The semantic layer fully resides on the BI platform where a client tool can connect to access a universe and use the information engine as a platform service. In this scenario, all of the connections to the database and all of the data transit via the machine running the SAP BusinessObjects BI platform before reaching the client tool. This configuration is used both by browser-based clients and thick clients.

▶ **Client-only deployment (❷)**
The semantic layer can also be completely embarked in a client tool. In this scenario, the client tool uses a universe stored on the file system and manipulates it with the information engine embedded in the client. Thus, there is no intermediary, and the client tool directly connects to the database.

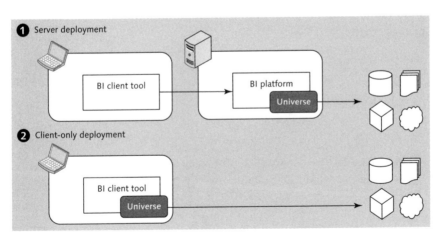

Figure 1.7 Possible Semantic Layer Deployments: Server or Client-Only Deployment

In both scenarios, the semantic layer is automatically installed whenever the BI platform or the client tools are installed. These two deployments aren't necessarily supported by all client tools because each tool has its own policy and architecture.

1.5   SAP BusinessObjects BI Applications that Consume the Semantic Layer

The semantic layer technology was historically used by two SAP BusinessObjects tools: SAP BusinessObjects Desktop Intelligence, retired after the SAP Business-Objects XI 3.1 release, and by SAP BusinessObjects Web Intelligence.

With the acquisition of Crystal Decisions by Business Objects and the subsequent acquisition of Business Objects by SAP, the semantic layer has become a shared and common component used by most SAP BusinessObjects BI products and tools. As of SAP BusinessObjects BI 4.1, this list includes the following:

▶ SAP BusinessObjects Web Intelligence

▶ SAP BusinessObjects Dashboards

▶ SAP Crystal Reports for Enterprise

▶ SAP BusinessObjects Explorer

▶ SAP Lumira

▶ SAP Predictive Analysis

Some client tools that are specialized on a few sources with a dedicated interface can use the semantic layer technology to reach all other sources. The semantic layer, which supports hundreds of combinations of data sources and middleware, is the entry point for these client tools to the breadth of data sources available in the market.

The following sections briefly describe how each of those tools consumes the semantic layer. You may find more detailed, additional information online, especially at *http://help.sap.com*.

1.5.1   SAP BusinessObjects Web Intelligence

SAP BusinessObjects Web Intelligence is an application used to let business users create reports with a high level of interoperability and with an ad hoc mindset. In ad hoc reporting, a business user is left with the choice to define the query and change it as needed depending on the requirements. The report isn't a fixed-format document provided by the IT department.

SAP BusinessObjects Web Intelligence can connect to a universe either via the BI platform or the file system through its Rich Client version that embeds the semantic layer technology.

When connecting to a universe, SAP BusinessObjects Web Intelligence displays its query panel as in Figure 1.8.

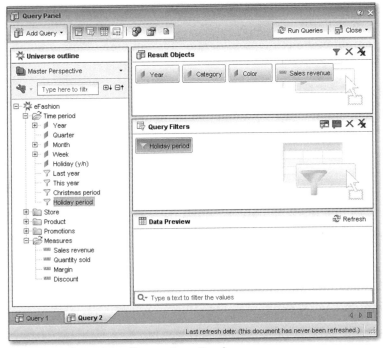

Figure 1.8   The Web Intelligence Query Panel

In the query panel, the final user defines the business question to be asked by a simple drag and drop of objects. The question can be fine-tuned with prompts, selections from lists of values, mandatory filters, or other specific options. After the query is executed, the result is received by the SAP BusinessObjects Web Intelligence application and remains in its memory to be used for further calculations.

SAP BusinessObjects Web Intelligence has a calculator technology that gets information from the universe model and uses it to provide complex manipulations of the local data. This technology is also called *microcube*.

Some SAP BusinessObjects Web Intelligence and semantic layer functionality such as *query drill*, *database delegated measures,* and *query stripping* enable the user to minimize the size of data returned from the database and work on the most updated information from the source with a small local cache.

SAP BusinessObjects Web Intelligence provides a direct access technology to SAP NetWeaver BW. There is no need to build a universe in IDT when connecting to an SAP NetWeaver BW data source. The query panel exposes the SAP NetWeaver BW BEx queries information through a universe automatically generated on the fly (see Chapter 12, Section 12.1).

1.5.2 SAP Crystal Reports for Enterprise

SAP Crystal Reports for Enterprise is a reporting application targeted at creating pixel-perfect report documents. The end user has a limited interoperability with the document, but all of the information is presented in a very well-defined, precise, and standardized way. Such reports are often printed or exported as read-only documents.

The designer of an SAP Crystal Reports for Enterprise document is often part of the IT department, and the business user asks the IT team to build a report. The designer of the report has access to a query panel to define the query to the database. After the query is completed, a basic document is built as a starting point for the designer, as shown in Figure 1.9. In the report interface, the designer or the final user can refresh the data and change the values of prompts.

In SAP Crystal Reports for Enterprise, the semantic layer is the main access method to data. Since SAP BusinessObjects BI 4.0 Support Package 4, the application provides a freehand SQL access technology based on the semantic layer's Connection Server. Like SAP BusinessObjects Web Intelligence, SAP Crystal Reports for Enterprise also supports direct access for SAP NetWeaver BW and, additionally, for SAP HANA.

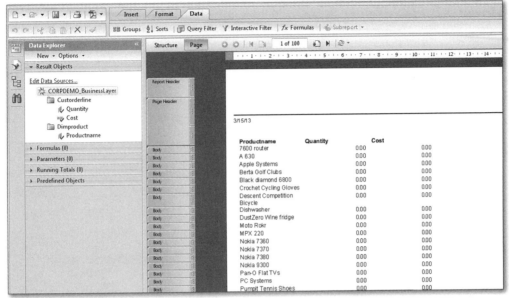

Figure 1.9 An SAP Crystal Reports for Enterprise Document Based on a Universe

For SAP Crystal Reports for Enterprise, the access to the semantic layer is provided via the BI platform only.

SAP Crystal Reports 2013

SAP Crystal Reports 2013 is a version of the product mainly targeted at the community of developers who might not have access to the SAP BusinessObjects BI platform or prefer not to use it. The tool is able to connect to many external data sources using its own technology.

Both SAP Crystal Reports 2013 and SAP Crystal Reports for Enterprise propose a pixel-perfect reporting style. SAP Crystal Reports 2013 doesn't support universes created with IDT, but it does support universes created by IDT's predecessor, the Universe Design Tool.

1.5.3   SAP BusinessObjects Dashboards

SAP BusinessObjects Dashboards is a tool used to build eye-catching representations of data, usually highly aggregated and designed to quickly highlight a message. Typical end users of SAP BusinessObjects Dashboards are C-level executives or users who are interested in a very specific detail and need an immediate and visual representation of its status.

The designer of SAP BusinessObjects Dashboards documents can connect to the semantic layer via the BI platform only. The query definition is done using a query panel, and the resulting objects are attached to components of the dashboard (see Figure 1.10).

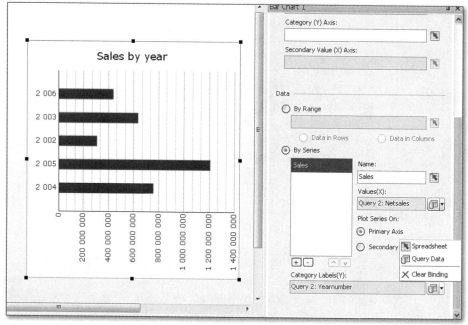

Figure 1.10 A Dashboard Built on the Results of a Universe Query

The application enables you to set an automatic refresh rate of the query so that the published dashboard is automatically updated with the latest data from the data source via the universe.

Like SAP BusinessObjects Web Intelligence, SAP BusinessObjects Dashboards also supports direct access to SAP NetWeaver BW.

1.5.4 SAP BusinessObjects Explorer

SAP BusinessObjects Explorer is a web-based application that lets users easily discover information in a large data set by means of a faceted navigation, good visualizations, and slice-and-dice capabilities. SAP BusinessObjects Explorer allows quick navigation and analysis of data that have been retrieved directly from the data sources and then saved and indexed in data sets called *information spaces*.

Information spaces are created from a query that has been indexed by the internal BI platform engine. When designing a new information space, SAP BusinessObjects Explorer can connect to a relational universe on the BI platform. After the universe is selected, the tool provides a query panel where the objects to index can be selected, as shown in Figure 1.11. All prompts and questions have to be answered when the information space is designed.

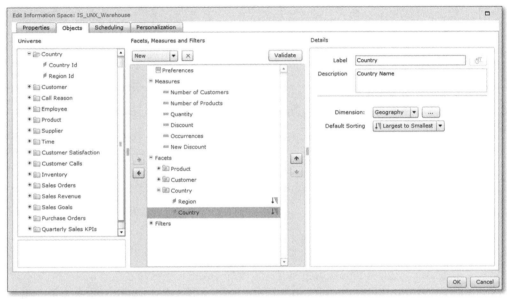

Figure 1.11 Universe Query Panel Used to Generate the Information Space

After the query is completed and executed, the data is transferred into the BI platform to be indexed by the local engine. When the index is complete, the data can be browsed via the Explorer interface shown in Figure 1.12.

SAP BusinessObjects Explorer provides its own connectivity to access SAP HANA. Because SAP HANA already stores its data in memory, the data is not extracted from SAP HANA for indexing. SAP BusinessObjects Explorer also provides its own connectivity to access SAP NetWeaver Accelerator (SAP NetWeaver BWA).

Figure 1.12 An Information Space Created with a Universe Connection

1.5.5 SAP Lumira

In the SAP portfolio, SAP Lumira is the brand that covers the new self-service, discovery, and visualization products. SAP Lumira comes in different deployments: Cloud and Desktop. These applications enable users to quickly discover information in their data, enrich that information, and create powerful visualizations. They are designed mainly for data artisans, but also developers and business users can find value in their use.

SAP Lumira Desktop supports relational universes created with IDT. It can retrieve data from the different sources that semantic layer supports through a query panel that presents the list of available business objects, as shown in Figure 1.13.

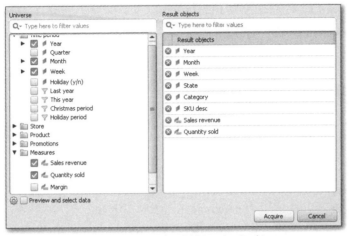

Figure 1.13 Universe Query Panel in SAP Lumira Desktop

After the query is executed by selecting objects from the list, the data is retrieved on the machine where SAP Lumira sits and can be further manipulated from there, as shown in Figure 1.14.

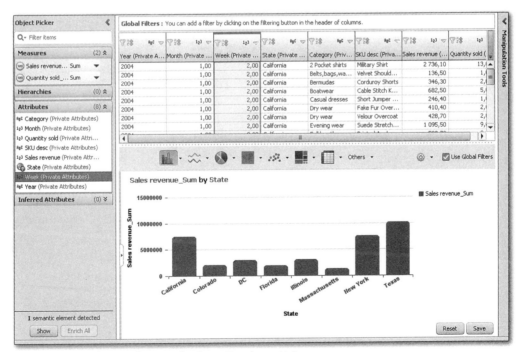

Figure 1.14 Results Visualization of a Query Based on a Universe

SAP Lumira also provides a freehand SQL interface to multiple data sources. This interface uses another semantic layer's component: the Connection Server. Finally, SAP Lumira also provides its own connectivity to SAP HANA.

1.5.6 SAP Predictive Analysis

SAP Predictive Analysis is an application that enables data analysts to understand historical information and forecast possible future evolutions or see what the major influence factors of a given situation are. The SAP Predictive Analysis solution can use universes as the source of the historical data to be analyzed. SAP Predictive Analysis is built on the SAP Lumira framework for data provisioning, so it presents the same experience as SAP Lumira when connecting to a universe.

After the query has been executed, the tool's predictive algorithms can be run on the result set, and the resulting information is returned as tables or graphical summaries, as shown in Figure 1.15.

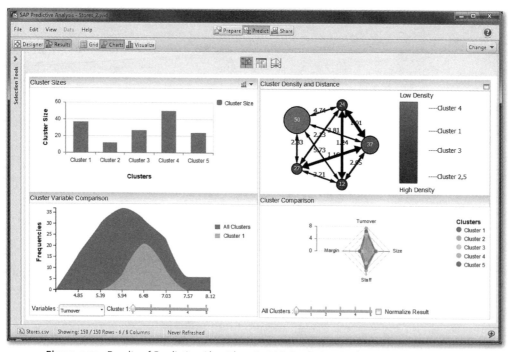

Figure 1.15 Results of Predictive Algorithms in SAP Predictive Analysis

1.6   Summary

In SAP BusinessObjects products, the semantic layer has always been a central component. Through an intuitive abstraction, it exposes an interface that hides a data source's technical details and provides business concepts, a security layer, connectivity abstraction, multisource access, homogeneous experience, and shared metadata.

When designing the semantic layer, the designer must take into consideration the business requirements and underlying data sources so that it's correct, secure, beneficial, performs well, and is easy to use and to maintain. The following are the semantic layer's main artifacts:

- The universe, a persisted file that contains the metadata definition
- Information Design Tool (IDT), the metadata design tool used to create universes
- The information engine, which provides services to process the queries sent by client tools
- An interface, which enables client tools to connect to the universe, usually via a query panel where users may create queries by selecting objects defined in the universe and named from their business vocabulary

In SAP BusinessObjects BI 4.x, most products and tools support semantic layer universes created with IDT, including SAP BusinessObjects Web Intelligence, SAP BusinessObjects Dashboards, SAP Crystal Reports for Enterprise, SAP BusinessObjects Explorer, SAP Lumira, and SAP Predictive Analysis.

Universe designers use Information Design Tool to build universes. This chapter provides a description of the tool interface and its main concepts.

2   Introduction to Information Design Tool

Information Design Tool (IDT) is the new application introduced in SAP Business-Objects Business Intelligence (BI) 4.0 to author universes. It's the successor of the Universe Designer, the metadata design tool application from previous releases and available in SAP BusinessObjects BI 4.x under the name Universe Design Tool.

A first difference between the two tools is that in the Universe Design Tool, the designer works always with a single universe file; whereas IDT deals with multiple files such as connections, data foundations, business layers, and universes. This impacts the IDT interface that presents a metadata definition-oriented interface with project file trees, views, and editors that can be easily customized based on the user needs.

These new resources introduce many new concepts and workflows in IDT that make its interface richer than the Universe Design Tool. The two applications are compared in Chapter 13.

Fortunately, IDT proposes different helpers to get you started and in fact, a person who knows the Universe Design Tool needs a very little training to be productive on IDT. Furthermore, the user interface is rich in context-sensitive menus and in right-click context-sensitive actions. Those functionalities increase the productivity of a designer by minimizing menu and submenu navigation for any given action.

> **IDT Ease of Use**
>
> User experience tests with real customers have shown that designers familiar with the Universe Designer application were able to successfully create a new universe from scratch with contexts, prompts, and lists of values after just a five-minute training session on IDT.

This chapter guides you through your first steps in IDT. It presents the WEL-COME page and the NEW UNIVERSE wizard, which are two new additions in SAP

BusinessObjects BI 4.1 to help you ease into using IDT. The chapter then presents the general interface framework and the different helpers that are available. Finally, the chapter concludes by discussing two important components: the PREFERENCES dialog box where you can set parameters for the tool and the DATA PREVIEW panel that is regularly used to display data.

But before using the application, you need to download and install it, which is covered in the first section.

2.1 Installing Information Design Tool

IDT is installed from the SAP BusinessObjects BI 4.x client tools installer. This installer can be downloaded from the SAP Support site (*http://service.sap.com/support*) under the SOFTWARE DOWNLOADS tab.

As shown in Figure 2.1, the software can be found by browsing the download catalog under ANALYTICS SOLUTIONS • INSTALLATION AND UPGRADE • SBOP BI PLATFORM • SBOP BI PLATFORM 4.1.

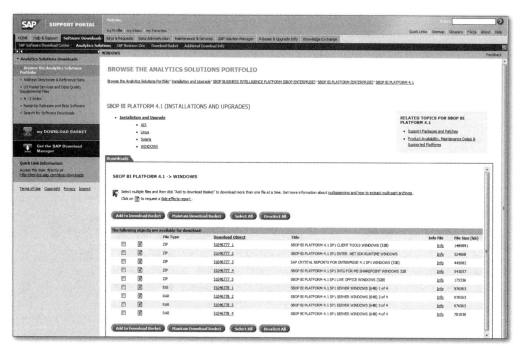

Figure 2.1 SAP BusinessObjects BI 4.1 Installers on the SAP Service Website

Alternative Packages

IDT can also be found in other packages, such as the Edge package and the Crystal Server package. In general, IDT is available in all packages that contain client tools that might use universes to connect to data.

The installer contains other client tools that are used both for reporting and for managing the SAP BusinessObjects BI deployment and projects from a local machine.

The SAP BusinessObjects BI 4.1 installer does not require an existing installation of any previous version of SAP BusinessObjects BI 4.x.

Upgrading from a Previous BI 4.0 Version

You can download an upgrade installer that updates an existing installation of SAP BusinessObjects BI 4.0 or any one of its support packages from *http://service.sap.com/ support*. Browse the catalog to ANALYTICS SOLUTIONS • SUPPORT PACKAGE AND PATCHES • SBOP BI PLATFORM • SBOP BI PLATFORM 4.1.

After the installer file has been downloaded, double-click on it to start the setup process. If you don't run the default installation and choose the custom installation procedure, make sure that in addition to IDT, you've selected the following components and products for installation:

▶ **SAP BusinessObjects Web Intelligence Rich Client**
This is a reporting client tool you can use to quickly test a universe on the local machine.

▶ **Universe Design Tool**
This is the predecessor of IDT that is useful when some work has to be done on universes imported from an SAP BusinessObjects XI 3.x release (*see* Chapter 13).

▶ **Universe Landscape Migration**
This is an IDT plugin that converts existing universes based on external data sources into universes based on SAP HANA (see Chapter 12).

▶ **Translation Management Tool**
This tool is used to localize SAP BusinessObjects BI resources, including universes (see Chapter 11).

▶ **Data Federation Administration Tool**
This administration tool audits and optimizes queries on multisource universes (see Chapter 6).

Furthermore, you also need to install the drivers needed to connect to the data sources or databases you use and from which you plan to base your SAP Business-Objects BI solution.

When the installation is complete, IDT can be found in the Windows START menu under the SAP BUSINESS INTELLIGENCE program group, as shown in Figure 2.2. After you correctly install the program, you can launch it and explore its interface.

Figure 2.2 Information Design Tool in the Windows Start Menu

2.2 Getting Started

In SAP BusinessObjects BI 4.1, it's much easier to get started with IDT thanks to a WELCOME page and a NEW UNIVERSE wizard that can guide you in your first steps.

2.2.1 Welcome Page

Starting SAP BusinessObjects BI 4.1, IDT opens on a WELCOME page, as shown in Figure 2.3.

The two main objectives of this Welcome page are to let experienced users quickly start a new project or modify an existing one, and to let new users quickly access wizards and tools to speed up both the learning curve and the creation of their first universe.

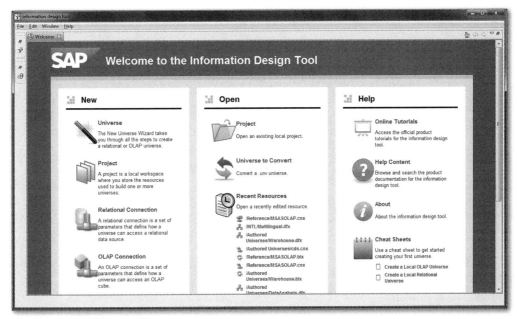

Figure 2.3 The Welcome Page

The Welcome page is structured in three sections: New, Open, and Help.

▶ The New section provides shortcuts to create new projects or new resources in an existing project using a wizard interface. The New Universe wizard is described in detail in Section 2.2.2.

▶ The Open section contains commands to open projects, convert universes, or quickly go to the latest used resources.

  ▶ The Recent resources functionality is useful because usually many resource files (connections, data foundations, business layers) are used in a project. Instead of keeping them all open, the links allow you to get to them quickly.

► The UNIVERSE TO CONVERT link opens a wizard to create a UNX version of a universe (UNV) developed with the Universe Design Tool or imported from a previous SAP BusinessObjects XI 3.x version. More details about universe conversion are provided in Chapter 13.

► The HELP section contains links to the help system, which include online tutorials, online help, and the CHEAT SHEETS wizards (see Section 2.4).

If the WELCOME page has been closed, you can re-open it from the HELP • WELCOME menu.

In addition to this WELCOME page, SAP BusinessObjects BI 4.1 also proposes a NEW UNIVERSE wizard that can help you get started with IDT.

2.2.2 New Universe Wizard

The NEW UNIVERSE wizard allows you to create a new universe either from scratch by adding all new resources or by reusing existing resources in a project. The goal of this wizard is to quickly let you go over some repetitive steps in the creation of a new project. The wizard can be launched from three different places:

► In the WELCOME page, by clicking the NEW • UNIVERSE hyperlink

► In the main toolbar, by clicking the UNIVERSE WIZARD button (🔩)

► In the menu bar, by selecting the FILE • NEW UNIVERSE command

The different steps of the wizard include the following:

1. In the first page, select an existing project or create a new one. If you want to create a new project, enter the name of the project.

2. Select to work either from a relational data source or from an OLAP data source.

3. Select an existing connection or create a new one. The wizard scans the selected project for existing relational or OLAP connections (depending on your previous selection) and proposes them, as shown in Figure 2.4.

4. If you've selected to create a connection, then the connection wizard opens and lets you go through the steps of the connection creation.

5. If you've selected a relational connection, you must select an existing data foundation or build a new one. When creating the new data foundation, you can select an automated detection of joins and cardinalities, as shown in Figure 2.5.

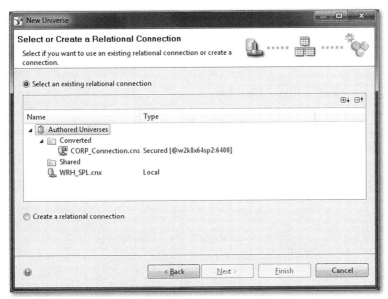

Figure 2.4 Selecting an Existing Connection or Creating a New One

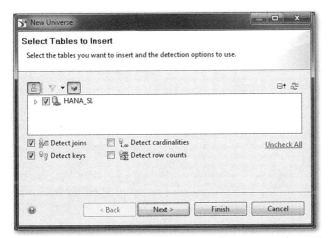

Figure 2.5 Automatic Detection Selection for Data Foundation Creation

6. Finally, you create a business layer or let the wizard define one automatically with an automated detection on the tables and fields of the data foundation (for a relational universe) or an automatic creation of classes and objects (for a multidimensional universe or SAP HANA universe).

After the connection, data foundation, and business layer are created, they are opened in different IDT editors.

2.3 Information Design Tool Interface

As shown in Figure 2.6, IDT has two main kinds of visual containers that appear on the screen: views and editors.

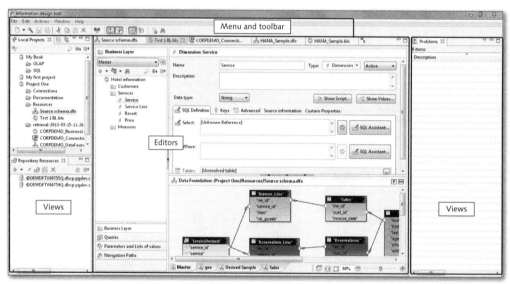

Figure 2.6 Views, Editors, and Toolbar in the Information Design Tool Interface

Views and editors can be moved around the screen and locked in other positions that better fit user preferences or the workflow to be accomplished. In addition to views and editors, the menu bar and the main toolbar also appear in the user interface. The following sections explain the usage of views, editors, and the toolbar.

2.3.1   Menu and Toolbar

The menu bar and toolbar are positioned on the top part of the screen, as shown in Figure 2.6. The menu bar follows the general applications standards:

▸ The FILE menu contains the commands related to the files and resources management and their lifecycle in IDT.

▸ The EDIT menu contains actions useful during the authoring: undo, redo, cut, copy, paste, delete, search, and so on.

▸ The ACTIONS menu is available only when working with data foundations and business layers. It contains specific commands enabled only on those resources.

▸ The WINDOWS menu lets you open and close various views and editors and gives access to the tool preferences.

▸ The HELP menu gives you access to the different documentation and help capabilities, as described in Section 2.4.

The main toolbar provides a quick access to the most common actions performed in IDT. Table 2.1 lists and describes them.

Button	Name	Description
	NEW	Create a new resource (a dropdown list lets the user specify what has to be created).
	NEW UNIVERSE	Launch the NEW UNIVERSE wizard.
	SAVE, SAVE ALL	Save the resource being edited or save all modified resources that are opened in the editors.
	CUT, COPY, PASTE	Cut or copy the selected item (a resource, an object, etc.) and paste it at the selected location.
	DELETE	Delete the selected items.
	PROJECT SYNCHRONIZATION	Show/hide the PROJECT SYNCHRONIZATION view.
	CHECK INTEGRITY PROBLEMS	Show/hide the CHECK INTEGRITY results view.

Table 2.1 Main Toolbar Buttons

Button	Name	Description
	LOCAL PROJECTS	Show/hide the LOCAL PROJECTS view.
	REPOSITORY RESOURCES	Show/hide the REPOSITORY RESOURCES view.
	SECURITY EDITOR	Launch the Security Editor.
	CHECK INTEGRITY	Launch the CHECK INTEGRITY process on the active resource. The icon is enabled only when working with data foundations or business layers.
	SEARCH	Search for a string in the active resource.

Table 2.1 Main Toolbar Buttons (Cont.)

These buttons are context sensitive and are accessible or disabled depending on the items being selected in the view or editor and on its status. As an example, the SAVE and SAVE ALL icons are enabled only when working on a resource that has been modified and needs to be saved.

Apart from the main toolbar, some editors have specific toolbars that appear within the editor's interface itself. Those toolbars are described in the chapter dedicated to the edited resources.

2.3.2 Working with Views

There are four views in which a project can be managed, synchronized, and audited:

▶ LOCAL PROJECTS
You can access and work with local resources in this view.

▶ REPOSITORY RESOURCES
You can access connections and universes published on a server in this view.

▶ PROJECT SYNCHRONIZATION
You can share and synchronize projects from the local workspace with the server shared workspace in this view.

▶ CHECK INTEGRITY PROBLEMS
You can log all information returned by a check integrity action (described in Section 2.5) in this view.

The views can be moved around the screen by dragging and dropping, or they can be grouped one behind the other to appear stacked. When they are stacked, a tab enables you to pass from one view to the other, as shown in Figure 2.7. To stack views one on top of another view, you just need to drag the title of a view on top of the title of the other view.

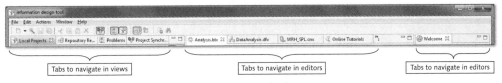

Figure 2.7 Tabs to Navigate between Stacked Views and Editors

You can always return to the default position of the various views and editors by selecting the menu command WINDOWS • RESET TO DEFAULT DISPLAY. Also, any closed view can be opened and accessed with the WINDOWS menu command or via the menu icon bar.

2.3.3 Working with Editors

Editors are windows in which it is possible to create or modify resources. They are positioned in the central top part of the screen, and, if multiple editors are opened, can be accessed via a tabbed navigation, as shown in Figure 2.7.

Authoring Editors

There are three types of editors:

▶ **Connection editor**
Defines and modifies connections to data sources

▶ **Data foundation editor**
Defines and modifies single-source and multisource data foundations

▶ **Business layer editor**
Creates or changes business layers

Those editors have a specific interface that changes based on the resource being used. Within each editor, subsections enable you to work on a specific part of the resource. The subsections are found on the bottom-left part of the editor screen. Clicking on a subsection title opens the appropriate panel.

As an example, Figure 2.8 shows the subsections of the business layer editor where the designer can work with the BUSINESS LAYER, the QUERIES, the PARAMETERS AND LISTS OF VALUES, and the NAVIGATION PATHS.

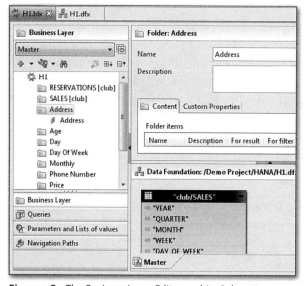

Figure 2.8   The Business Layer Editor and Its Subsections

When multiple editors are opened or when working with a lot of resources in local projects, it's practical to synchronize the LOCAL PROJECTS view with the selected editor by clicking the LINK OPENED EDITORS toggle button (🔄) located at the top of the LOCAL PROJECTS view. When this button is selected, the resource whose editor has the focus is highlighted in the LOCAL PROJECTS view.

Security Editor

In addition to the three editors just mentioned, the Security Editor manages the security of a universe published in a CMS repository and can be launched via its icon on the top menu bar. This editor and its functionality are discussed in detail in Chapter 10. From this editor, you can manage access restrictions with business security profiles and data security profiles and assign those profiles to users or groups.

Access to the Security Editor requires a specific user right; therefore, it's possible to have users who design universes and users who manage the security of universes with different rights (and only security administrators are allowed to access the security editor).

The IDT interface contains many parts, and the workflow to build a new universe might not be straightforward for a new user. For this reason, a set of assistants has been added in the IDT embedded documentation to help you quickly find information on the application.

2.4   Help

In addition to the IDT User Guide that can be downloaded from *http://help.sap.com*, IDT proposes different ways to get immediate information about the tool and its workflows.

2.4.1   Context-Sensitive Help

In the menu bar, you can select the HELP • CONTENT command to open the online version of the User Guide and navigate in it. In addition, you can use context-sensitive help to open the User Guide online version exactly at the page describing your current workflow or interface. Context-sensitive help is available in any places showing the HELP button (). When you click on this button in a dialog box, the dialog box is extended to include the context-sensitive help, as shown in Figure 2.9. Otherwise, the context-sensitive help is displayed in a view that opens in the IDT interface.

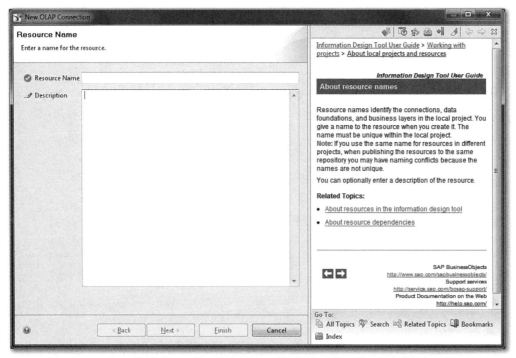

Figure 2.9 New OLAP Connection Dialog Box with Context-Sensitive Help Displayed

2.4.2   Cheat Sheets

The cheat sheet concept is similar to a wizard, but its goal is to let the user understand the steps to take to create a new universe. The designer learns the workflow by using the cheat sheet and then can repeat the workflow without help. Cheat sheets can be very useful for designers who know the Universe Design Tool well and want to move to the new IDT.

You can launch cheat sheets in two ways:

▶ Choose the HELP • CHEAT SHEETS menu command.

▶ Click a link in the CHEAT SHEETS section of the WELCOME page to open the CHEAT SHEET SELECTION dialog box, as shown in Figure 2.10.

When launched, the cheat sheet interface proposes a detailed and guided process to create a new relational or multidimensional universe from scratch.

Figure 2.10   Selecting One Cheat Sheet

Selecting the relational universe cheat sheet, for example, opens a new page that lists step by step the procedure to follow to create a new relational universe, as shown in Figure 2.11.

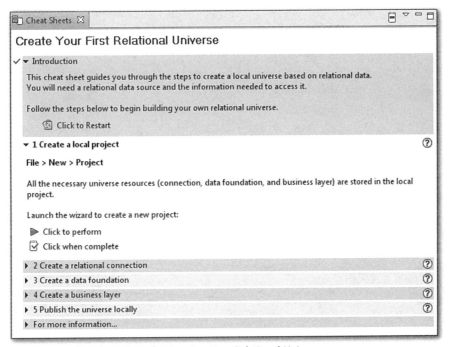

Figure 2.11   The Cheat Sheet for Creating New Relational Universes

69

While reading the scripted workflow, you can either manually run the commands listed in the page or have the tool automatically perform the task. When a task is completed and you understand what was done, clicking on the CLICK WHEN COMPLETE action moves the cheat sheet to the next step.

The cheat sheet gives the designer more freedom to test and understand what is happening behind the scenes. It can be used as a tool to get familiar with the environment before starting a brand new project independently.

2.4.3   Online Tutorials

You can learn how to use IDT and how to perform very specific actions with a series of public videos available on the web. The videos are continuously updated to show the newest functionalities of IDT. They can be easily accessed from the WELCOME page or with the command HELP • ONLINE TUTORIALS. As shown in Figure 2.12, a browser page opens inside IDT and you can scroll and select the necessary tutorial. The same web page can also be accessed from any other browser outside of IDT.

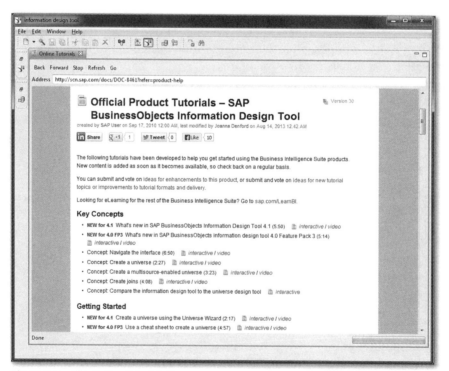

Figure 2.12   The Online Tutorials Page

The tutorials can be watched as plain videos or as interactive videos where you have to click on the appropriate part of the screen and fill in information to successfully complete the workflow. Most of the key concepts and most of the common and seldom-used workflows can be found on this page. The tutorials are the first place to go when in doubt about how to use a specific functionality or how to perform a given workflow.

2.5 Preferences

To open the PREFERENCES dialog box, in the menu bar, select WINDOWS • PREFERENCES. This dialog box contains three main sections in its left panel, as shown in Figure 2.13:

▶ GENERAL
Fine-tunes both general parameters related to the IDT framework, such as its appearance and behavior.

▶ HELP
Defines how the online help is displayed and the default URL for online tutorials.

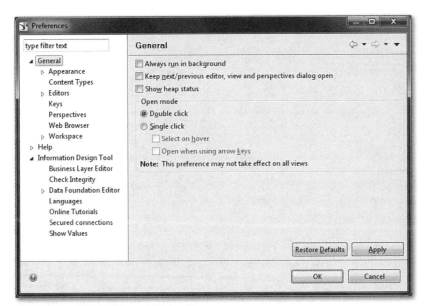

Figure 2.13 The Preferences Dialog Box

▸ INFORMATION DESIGN TOOL
Provides more specific settings for IDT behavior, algorithms, and default values.

The INFORMATION DESIGN TOOL section presents the most important settings for a universe designer, which we describe next.

2.5.1 Business Layer Editor

In the BUSINESS LAYER EDITOR tab, the only setting specifies how to automatically create object names. The objects are created automatically both when using a wizard and when dragging and dropping table columns into the business layer editor.

By default, the object name is a user-friendly version of the table column name: All words are set with an initial in caps, and special symbols and characters (such as "–" or "_") are substituted with space characters. For example, a column "customer_name" generates an object labeled CUSTOMER NAME.

The setting in the PREFERENCES page enables the automatic creation algorithm to use the name of the column as-is without making it user friendly. This setting is useful in situations where a company policy is very strict on the name of business intelligence items or where the correct names are enforced down into the data source.

2.5.2 Check Integrity

The integrity check functionality is used to run a set of automated tests on the data foundations and business layers to make sure that some rules of correctness are respected. The details about the rules are exposed in Chapter 5 for the data foundation and in Chapter 7 for the business layer.

From the CHECK INTEGRITY page of the PREFERENCES dialog box, it's possible to set a list of check integrity rules to automatically control a resource each time it's saved.

The automatic check execution on save is set by checking the ENABLE BACKGROUND CHECK INTEGRITY ON SAVE checkbox at the top of the screen and selecting a list of integrity rules, as shown in Figure 2.14.

From this interface, it is possible to modify the default severity of an integrity rule. As an example, based on your project and your environment, rules which return a warning by default can be considered only as information. Or, vice versa—if you want to enforce a specific constraint in your project, rules that are by default considered as information can be turned into errors.

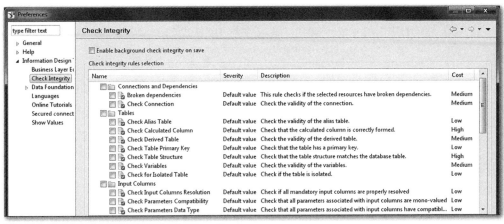

Figure 2.14 The Check Integrity Preferences Page

2.5.3 Data Foundation Editor

Many preference settings are available for the data foundation editor. This section highlights the most important ones.

Data Foundation Editor

The SHOW QUALIFIERS/OWNERS setting, checked by default as shown in Figure 2.15, controls what tables are visible when looking at the data source connection from the data foundation editor.

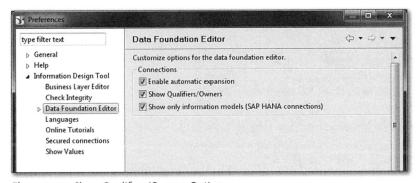

Figure 2.15 Show Qualifiers/Owners Option

By default, this option is selected and all owners are visible, as shown in Figure 2.16 (❶). When this setting is unchecked, only the tables owned by the user defined in the data source connectivity are visible (❷).

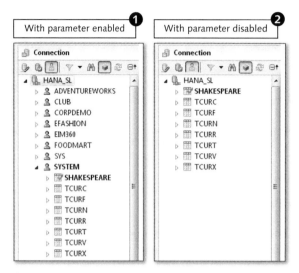

Figure 2.16 Impact of the Show Qualifiers/Owners Option

This setting can be overridden at any time by clicking the QUALIFIERS/OWNERS toggle button in the CONNECTION section toolbar in the data foundation editor, as shown in Figure 2.17.

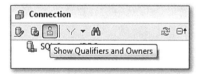

Figure 2.17 The Show Qualifiers/Owners Button

It's important to know about this setting because in some situations, you might think that some tables aren't available for selection in the data foundation, when they are actually just hidden. Modifying this setting makes them visible again.

Detection

Under the DATA FOUNDATION EDITOR • DETECTION section, you can set the automatic detection of information related to joins, keys, and cardinalities when a table is added to the data foundation (see Figure 2.18). By default, all automatic detection mechanisms are disabled. If you enable the automated detections, then each time a table is added to the data foundation, the system searches for key information in the data source, then proposes joins to tables already in the data foundation, and automatically calculates the cardinality of those joins. All of those actions have an impact on the performance because many calls are performed on the data source.

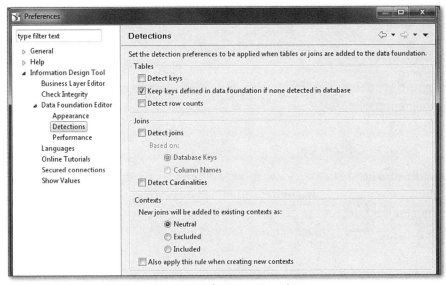

Figure 2.18 Automatic Detection Settings for a Data Foundation

Best Practice

We recommend that you leave the automatic detection mechanisms disabled. Those mechanisms provide a best guess for joins and cardinalities, so you have to go back and check if the proposals are correct. In general, it takes less time to manually define joins and cardinalities than it does to check the automatically detected ones for possible errors. The detection mechanism works well on well-formed databases where the information can be retrieved without errors, such as data sources where all primary and foreign key information is well-defined in the source tables.

Performance

Under the DATA FOUNDATION EDITOR • PERFORMANCE tab, you can disable some graphical enhancements to the editor that might slow down the refresh of the screen for very large data foundations (with many tables) and on slow workstations.

2.5.4 Languages

The LANGUAGES section contains parameters to set product language and preferred viewing locales (see Chapter 11).

Modifying the product language in the LANGUAGES preference settings requires you to restart IDT.

2.5.5 Online Tutorials

The ONLINE TUTORIALS section contains only the parameter to set the default URL for online tutorials.

2.5.6 Secured Connections

From the SECURED CONNECTIONS section, you can define whether a query sent to a relational connection must, under certain conditions, be processed server side or through local middleware. This very important option to run tests locally or remotely is described in more detail in Chapter 4.

2.5.7 Show Values

The SHOW VALUES section defines where IDT displays the results of any action related to viewing data. This choice lets you decide if the data is going to be visible on the same screen as the resource from which it was requested, for comparison reasons, or if it takes the whole available space for better visibility. The values are displayed in a panel called DATA PREVIEW, described in the following section.

Whenever you modify a setting in the PREFERENCES window, remember to click the APPLY or OK buttons to enable the changes.

2.6 Data Preview

The DATA PREVIEW panel is the common display area for results from all data requests. With this panel, you can check in any step of universe creation and deployment to determine whether your data sources are working properly and see what data they return.

Depending on your choice in the PREFERENCES settings (see Section 2.5), the DATA PREVIEW panel can either be displayed in a specific editor, a view, or a pop-up window.

The DATA PREVIEW panel is displayed for any of the following situations:

▶ In a connection editor SHOW VALUES tab, when displaying information retrieved directly from the data source tables and columns or via a free-hand SQL sentence (in this case, the panel is embedded within the editor, independently of the preferences settings).

▶ In a data foundation editor, when running any of the following commands:

   ▶ SHOW TABLE VALUES on one or more tables

   ▶ SHOW COLUMN VALUES on one or more columns from single or multiple tables

   ▶ When previewing data from a list of values defined in the list of values editor

   ▶ When previewing data from a federated table in the federation editor

▶ In a business layer editor, when running any of the following commands:

   ▶ VIEW DATA on one or more business objects

   ▶ When previewing data from a list of values defined in the list of values editor

   ▶ Clicking the EXECUTE QUERY button on a pre-defined query

▶ In the query panel, when clicking the ADVANCED PREVIEW button after the query has been run. In this case, the DATA PREVIEW panel always opens in a pop-up window.

When retrieving data from any of the preceding places, the DATA PREVIEW panel always presents the same interface, as shown in Figure 2.19.

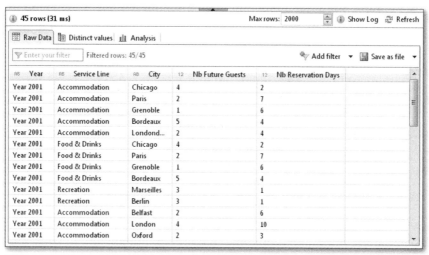

Figure 2.19 The View Data Panel

From the top bar of the panel, you can see how many rows have been returned by the query and how long the execution has taken.

▸ The Max rows box lets you limit the maximum number of rows to retrieve at the following query or the following refresh. This limit is very useful for testing large data sources or when testing across a slow connection. A small sample of data might already provide good information on its correctness and pertinence.

▸ The Show Log button provides the list of all queries executed (in the open Data Preview panel). This list lets you compare execution times and see the exact SQL (or MDX) sent to the underlying database. Many errors in modeling can be found by analyzing the query text found in this log.

▸ The Refresh button runs the same query again, taking into account the limits set in the Max Rows box.

As shown in Figure 2.19, the Data Preview panel is divided into three tabs: Raw Data, Distinct Values, and Analysis. The following sections provide details about each panel.

2.6.1   Raw Data Tab

The RAW DATA tab presents the results of the query in a detailed text format. Depending on the data source capabilities, the result is displayed in tabular or hierarchical mode. If the query is run against a relational source, the result is a simple table, as shown previously in Figure 2.19. If the query is run against an OLAP data source, you can have a display format with indented labels that shows the hierarchical relationships in the data (see Figure 2.20).

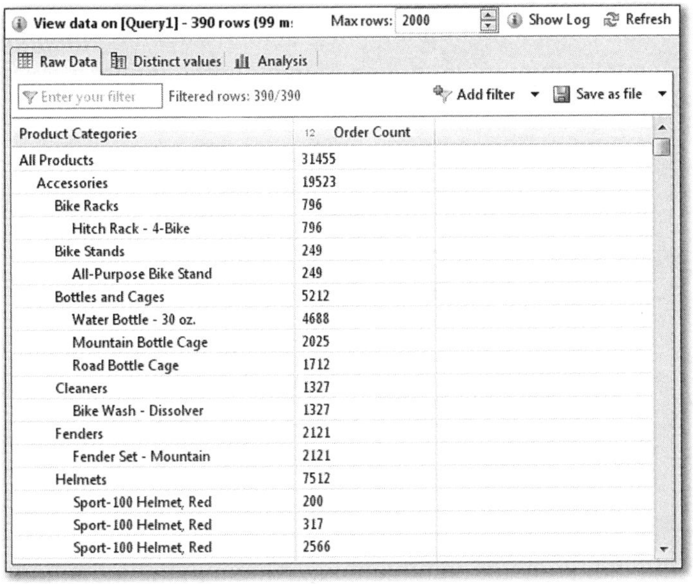

Figure 2.20   An Example of Hierarchical Query Output

In the RAW DATA tab, you can search for specific data very easily and export the query result in a reusable format. To search for data, you can type some text in the search box at the top-right part of the screen. Only lines containing that text in the data are shown, and the text is highlighted as in Figure 2.21. This functionality allows you to find a record containing a known value very quickly.

The ADD FILTER button lets you choose a specific field and displays an interface from which values can be dynamically filtered. Figure 2.22 shows that multiple filters can be added to the result set (they have an AND relationship) and that it's possible to choose from a wide range of filtering mechanisms to restrict the data set view to only the required records.

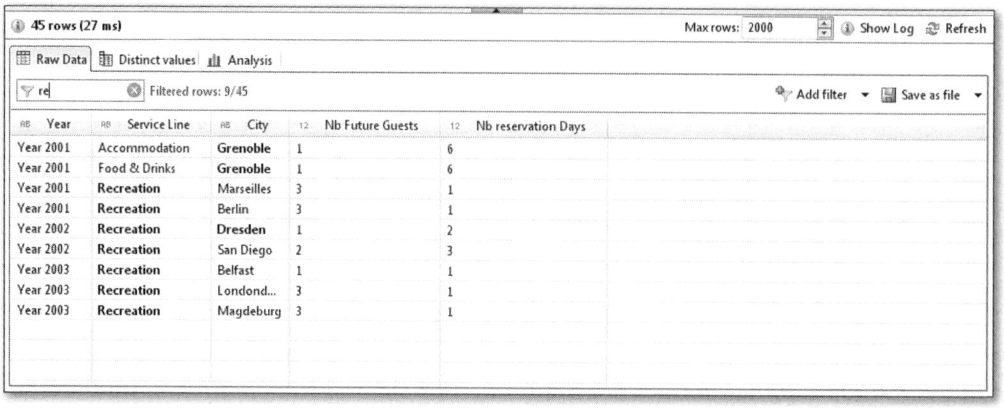

Figure 2.21 The Search Functionality in the Data Preview Panel

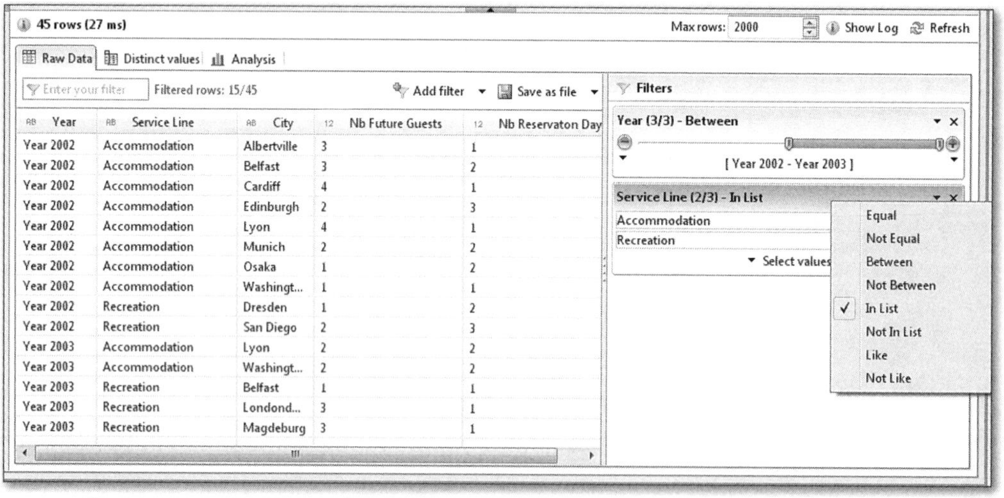

Figure 2.22 Data Preview Filters

Finally, from the RAW DATA tab, you can export the result into a text file, an *.html* file, or an *.xml* file by selecting the SAVE AS FILE button on the top-right part of the panel. Saving a result as a file is useful, for example, to check if the results are always correct over time.

After retrieving the data and seeing the details in the RAW DATA tab, it's possible to see a graphical visualization of the content from the DISTINCT VALUES or the ANALYSIS tabs.

2.6.2 Distinct Values Tab

The DISTINCT VALUES tab provides useful information on the content of each column of the result set. As shown in Figure 2.23, when you select a result column, the page displays multiple kinds of information about it: the number of distinct items and their values, how many times each item appears in the result, some statistics around the values distribution, and whether the values are unique in the column.

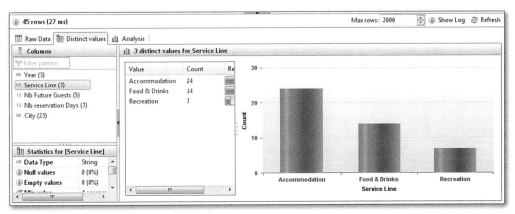

Figure 2.23 The Distinct Values Tab

You can use this information in multiple ways:

▸ When selecting a column that should be a unique key, such as primary IDs, you can check if there really are single instances of each value (and check that the ALL VALUES ARE UNIQUE statistics appear).

▸ For an enumerated field (such as Month whose values should be only between 1 and 12), it's easy to see whether the boundaries are respected or if there is some wrong value.

▸ In other situations, it's possible to see if a specific dimension or measure value has an outlying number of occurrences that might represent an error (e.g., if on average only 2 or 3 occurrences of a dimension appear and for a certain value there are more than 10, then it's possible to go back to the data source and check whether the data entry is correct).

The DISTINCT VALUES tab is helpful in checking the correctness of the data distribution, and the ANALYSIS tab is helpful to get an immediate understanding of the possible results that can be obtained out of the data set.

2.6.3   Analysis Tab

In the Analysis tab, you can quickly see aggregated information coming from the result set. All the fields of the result set can be dragged and dropped in the Labels or Values boxes. Depending on your choice, a graphical representation appears in the panel, as shown in Figure 2.24.

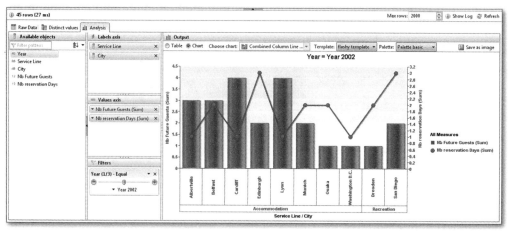

Figure 2.24   The Analysis Tab

You can choose from more than 30 types of visualizations. Only the ones applicable to the selected data are enabled in the dropdown list.

The fields added to the Values box are automatically aggregated before being visualized. By default, numeric fields are aggregated by Sum and other fields by Count. You can choose what aggregation method has to be used directly in the interface by clicking on the downward arrow in the field label as shown in Figure 2.25.

You can save the visualization as an image file by selecting the Save as Image button on the top-right part of the panel.

The goal of the Analysis tab isn't to substitute any SAP BusinessObjects BI tool but rather to let the designer of BI project see, while developing the solution, what an SAP BusinessObjects BI application might expose when the project is published.

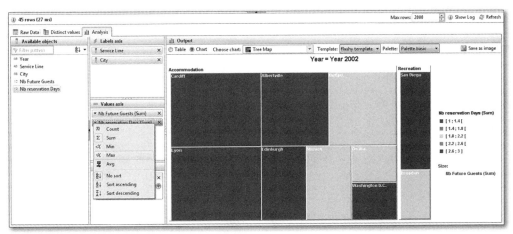

Figure 2.25 The Choice of the Aggregation Function for Values Fields

Visualizing the results (even if in a different way than what actually appears in the final client) provides good insights and, most importantly, lets the designer more quickly identify errors in the design or in the data. The data preview can also be used by the designer to have a validation of a universe and of its queries from the final user in the early stages.

2.7 Summary

You can install Information Design Tool, which is used for authoring universes, with the SAP BusinessObjects BI 4.x client tools installer. Once installed and started, IDT proposes different ways to get familiar with its interface or learn how to use it: the WELCOME page, NEW UNIVERSE wizard, cheat sheets, online tutorials, and context help. The interface relies on a framework based on views and editors that you can move and arrange at will.

You can use the PREFERENCES dialog box to customize IDT behavior or fine-tune its framework. The DATA PREVIEW panel is a graphical component available in different locations in the tool. It allows you to display and analyze data retrieved from any means or data sources, which can be helpful when creating your universes.

Information Design Tool is an authoring tool for creating universes. The different resources can be organized in local or shared projects, whereas the universes and connections in the Central Management Server repository are used for enterprise consumption.

3 Local and Shared Projects

To create a universe in Information Design Tool (IDT), you need to create several different resources:

► For a relational universe: One or several relational connections, a data foundation, and a business layer.

► For a multidimensional universe: An OLAP connection and a business layer.

These resources, created in IDT, are stored in a space called *local project*, which is used to group these resources. This local project is stored locally on the file system of the machine running the application.

In a large deployment, IDT, like other SAP BusinessObjects Business Intelligence (BI) 4.x tools, can take advantage of another space: the BI platform CMS repository, where universes and connections are published for consumption. For the different workflows involving the CMS repository—publishing and retrieving universes, editing secured connections, and so on—you must connect and authenticate to the CMS repository to open a session in IDT.

The CMS repository also offers you the ability to share your authored resources. In some organizations, an entire team of designers may work together to create universes. To ease the exchange of collaborative work and resource exchange, you may create a *shared project* in the CMS repository. The team members can then synchronize this shared project with a local project on their computers.

This chapter covers these three different spaces, as shown in Figure 3.1:

- ▸ Local projects and the workflows to manage them
- ▸ CMS repository, its different authentication modes, and how to manage sessions with the CMS repository in IDT
- ▸ Shared projects and how they can be used to share authored resources

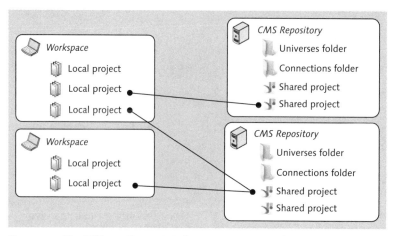

Figure 3.1 The Different Spaces in Information Design Tool

3.1 Authoring Resources in Local Project

Whatever universe you intend to create in IDT, you first need to create a local project—your authoring workspace. In this local project, you create and store the different resources that make the universe:

- ▸ The connection and connection shortcut used to reference the data source to query (see Chapter 4)
- ▸ The data foundation used by relational universes to define the relational model (tables, joins) to query (see Chapter 5 and Chapter 6)
- ▸ The business layer that exposes the objects of the universe in the different client tools through the query panel (see Chapter 7)

3.1.1 Local Project and File System

Local project content is saved on the file system of your machine. The resources contained in your local project are indirectly mapped to the folder used to represent objects saved in the local file system. As shown in Figure 3.2 and Figure 3.3, each resource and folder of a local project is mapped to a corresponding file or folder in the file system.

Figure 3.2 Local Projects View

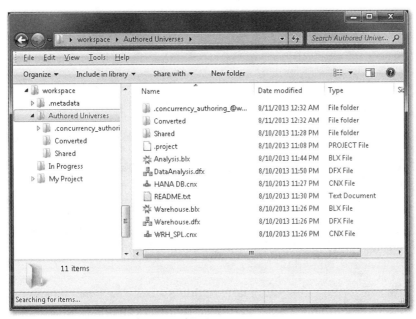

Figure 3.3 Folder Mapped to a Local Project

You may organize a local project by creating folders and subfolders and using them to organize the project resources. These folders are directly saved as folders in the folder storing the local project in the file system.

In the local project, resources are displayed with their name on the file system. It especially keeps the Windows file extension. The icons and extensions listed in Table 3.1 are used to identify the resource type.

Icon	Extension	File Type
	.cnx	Relational connection
	.cnx	OLAP connection
	.cns	Relational connection shortcut
	.cns	Relational connection to SAP NetWeaver BW or SAS shortcut
	.cns	OLAP connection shortcut
	.dfx	Data foundation
	.blx	Business layer
	N/A	Folder

Table 3.1 Icons and File Extensions in Local Projects

Local projects can also contain files that aren't universe resources: text files, pictures, and so on. This ability to support agnostic files can be used to add complementary documentation for the authored resources in a local project.

If you access the file system and go to the folder where the local project is saved, you recognize the same file structure that is in the local project. If you add a file in this folder, after you refresh the LOCAL PROJECTS view, this file appears in the local project in the corresponding folder.

It's possible to add some resources in a local project by dragging and dropping the corresponding files from a file into a local project in the LOCAL PROJECTS view. The files are copied and displayed in the local project.

Local Project Backup

You can back up a local project by copying the folder containing it. This folder location is available in the PROJECT LOCATION text field when you right-click the local project and select PROPERTIES. To restore this local project backup, create a new local project and enter the path of this folder.

Another method for backing up local project content is to go into the folder used to save it and manually copy the files to the backup. If you need to restore them, return to the folder and re-copy these files in the folder.

3.1.2   Local Project Lifecycle

When you create a new local project, IDT proposes that you create it in its default local folder, but you may change the location. The local project is the central location from where you perform your authoring and design tasks in IDT. You may create different local projects in IDT, which allows you to organize your resources.

When a resource is created locally in a local project, you can perform any operation on this resource because no security right controls what you can perform, except the databases privileges when you access it. Except for connections and connection shortcuts that are scrambled when saved in the file system, the other resources created in a local project (data foundation and business layer) are saved without any encryption.

After you've authored the resources that make the universe, you may generate this universe so it can be consumed by client tools. To publish this universe in a CMS repository (see Chapter 9, Section 9.2), you need to link these resources to data sources saved in this repository through connection shortcut(s) (see Chapter 4, Section 4.2). The same resources can be used to generate the same universes in different folders in the file system or in different CMS repositories, as long as you properly attach them to the appropriate connections.

A local project is intended to display only authoring resources. It doesn't display the published universes, even if they have been published locally. Local projects are known and accessed only by IDT. Other tools of the SAP BusinessObjects BI 4.x suite do not know these local projects and access only the artifacts.

As long as you're working on a local project, we recommend that you regularly back up your work and the files containing your local projects. This can be done manually by using shared projects (see Section 3.5), or simply by copying directly the folder mapped to your local projects (see Section 3.1.1). Some applications can be used to schedule such backups.

When you plan to stop using a local project, you have several options:

▶ **Closing the project**
The local project is still available in the LOCAL PROJECTS view, but you can't access its resources anymore. To access them, you need to explicitly reopen the project.

▶ **Removing the project**
The local project is removed from the LOCAL PROJECTS view but its content is still kept in the file system.

▶ **Deleting the project**
The whole folder used to save the local project is deleted, including all files (authored resources or agnostic files) contained in the file system.

3.1.3   Resource Dependencies

Some resources depend on other resources, so when you create them, you need to define on which resources they depend:

▶ A data foundation depends on a relational connection or one or more connection shortcut(s).

▶ A business layer relies on a data foundation or an OLAP connection.

For organizational purposes, a resource can only depend on resources saved in the same project; that is, when you create or edit a resource that depends on another resource, you can only select the resources of the same project. To comply with this constraint, dependencies between resources are saved as relative—and not absolute—paths. Thus, when you move or copy a resource, it looks for its dependencies based on its new location.

> **Relative Dependency Example**
>
> A business layer saved in *Project1* depends on a data foundation saved in *Project1* in the *database* folder. If the business layer is copied or moved in *Project2* in the *Final* folder, then it expects to find its data foundation in *Project2* in the *Final/database* folder.

> If this isn't the case, you can either copy this data foundation in this folder or relink the business layer to the version of this data foundation saved in this project.

To help you keep track of the dependencies between your resources, IDT can show you the following for a local resource in a local project:

▸ The resources that depend on this resource

▸ The resources this resource depends on

Furthermore, as shown in Figure 3.4, this impact analysis is automatically run by IDT before deleting an authored resource to warn you if this operation impacts other objects that may reference this resource.

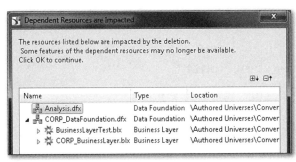

Figure 3.4 Dependent Resources Warning

3.2   Managing Local Projects

In IDT, the Local Projects view is used to display and manage local projects and the folders and resources they contain.

3.2.1   Creating a Local Project

To create a local project, follow these steps:

1. Open the Local Projects view. Then, to open the New Project dialog box, you can use one of the following methods:

   ▸ In the menu bar, select File • New • Project.

   ▸ In the toolbar, select the New button ( ), and in the context menu, select Project.

▶ Right-click in the Local Projects view. In the context menu, select New •
Project.

2. In the Project Name text field, enter a name for the project.

3. The Project Location text field contains the folder in the file system where
this local project is saved. To change this default folder, click the (...) button
located in this text field, and select another folder in the Browse for Folder
dialog box.

   If you enter a folder containing an already saved local project, this local project
   is reopened if it isn't yet listed in the Local Projects view.

4. Click OK to create or open the project. If you've used the default folder set in
the Project Location text field, then the local project is saved in a subfolder
created in this default folder. If you've provided another folder, then this folder
is used to save the local project content.

3.2.2 Closing and Opening a Local Project

When you deal with several local projects, it can be useful to close the ones you
don't use often to focus only on the important ones. To close a local project,
right-click it and select the Close Project command in the context menu. Once
closed, the local project is still displayed in the Local Projects view, but you can't
navigate in it and see its content. To reopen it, right-click it and select the Open
Project command.

3.2.3 Managing Resources and Folders

In the Local Projects view, the local project displays the folders and resources it
contains. It's the main entry point for most actions on the projects, folders, and
resources management. For example, the context menu contains these commands
if you right-click a project, folder, or resource:

▶ New
Creates a new resource or a new folder. For example, in the submenu, select
the following:

   ▶ Folder to create a new folder

   ▶ Relational Connection to launch the New Relational Connection wizard

▶ Copy and Paste
Copies and pastes, respectively, the selected object(s). Copying a folder or a project also copies the content.

▶ Move
Moves the selected object(s) into another location. This operation can also be done by drag and drop in the Local Projects view. This command isn't available for projects.

▶ Refresh
Refreshes the selected object(s). For example, if you've directly added some files in the file system in the folder storing a local project, refreshing the project displays these added resources in the local project.

▶ Delete
Deletes the selected object(s) or folder(s) and all of the objects it contains.

▶ Rename
Renames the selected object or folder.

Cut, Copy, and Paste Shortcuts

Copy, cut, and paste actions can also be called from the standard keyboard shortcuts by pressing `Ctrl`+`C`, `Ctrl`+`X`, and `Ctrl`+`V`, respectively.

If you select a resource, the right-click menu contains additional commands:

▶ Open
Opens the resource(s) in its editor so you can modify it. This can also be done by double-clicking it.

▶ New Data Foundation
Creates a data foundation based on the selected resource. This command is available only if the selected resource is a relational connection or relational connection shortcut.

▶ New Business Layer
Creates a business layer based on the selected resource. This command is available only if the selected resource is a data foundation or an OLAP connection.

▶ Save As
Generates a report—text file, *.pdf*, or *.html*—describing the selected resource.

▶ PRINT
Prints a report describing the selected resource.

▶ CHECK INTEGRITY
Runs an integrity check on the selected resource.

▶ SHOW LOCAL DEPENDENCIES
Opens the LOCAL DEPENDENCIES FOR dialog box and displays the selected resource dependencies (see Section 3.1.3).

Other commands available for the resources are described in the next chapters.

3.2.4   Filtering Resources in Projects

When you navigate in local projects and their folders, you can select the resources type to display:

1. In the LOCAL PROJECTS view toolbar, click the FILTER button (⚲).

2. In the dropdown menu, as shown in Figure 3.5, select a command to toggle a resource type display:

   ▶ RELATIONAL CONNECTION: For relational connections and connection shortcuts

   ▶ OLAP CONNECTION: For OLAP connections and connection shortcuts

   ▶ DATA FOUNDATION: For data foundations

   ▶ BUSINESS LAYER: For business layers

3. If a filter already exists, select the SHOW ALL command to remove all filters and display all resources.

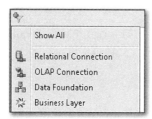

Figure 3.5   Filters List

To search a specific resource in a local project, follow these steps:

1. In the LOCAL PROJECTS view toolbar, click the SHOW/HIDE SEARCH BAR button (🔍). The search text field opens below the toolbar.

2. Enter the name of the resource to find. You may use the "?" character to replace one character or the "*" character to replace several characters.

3. Press ⌷Enter⌷ to put the focus on the first resource that matches the name. Press this key again to move the focus to the next found resources.

3.2.5   Viewing Local Dependencies

IDT can show the dependencies between resources of the same project (see Section 3.1.3):

1. In the LOCAL PROJECTS view, select a resource.

2. Right-click it, and select the SHOW LOCAL DEPENDENCIES command in the context menu.

3. As shown in Figure 3.6, in the LOCAL DEPENDENCIES dialog box that opens, the DEPENDENT RESOURCES tab lists the resources that use this resource, whereas the REFERENCED RESOURCES tab lists the ones it uses.

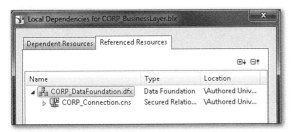

Figure 3.6   Local Dependencies Dialog Box

3.2.6   Deleting a Local Project

Deleting a project can either just remove the project from the list managed in IDT or actually delete it and all of its contents. To do so, follow these steps:

1. In the LOCAL PROJECTS view, select a project.

2. From the EDIT menu, the right-click menu, or the toolbar, select the DELETE command or button (✖). You can also select it and press the ⌷Delete⌷ key.

3. In the CONFIRM PROJECT DELETE dialog box, click the DELETE PROJECT CONTENTS ON DISK checkbox before validating to definitively delete the project and all of its contents as well. If you don't click this checkbox, the project is only removed from the LOCAL PROJECTS view. Its content isn't deleted, and you can reopen this project later by providing its folder in the file system (see Section 3.2.1).

3.3   CMS Repository

In an SAP BusinessObjects BI 4.x deployment, the Central Management Server (CMS) repository is used to centralize all corporate BI resources so they can be used and shared by different people. IDT can take advantage of this framework to manage secured connections and universes in the following workflows:

▶ Using shared projects (see Section 3.5)

▶ Managing a secured connection or retrieving data from the data source it identifies (see Chapter 4, Section 4.6 and Section 4.7)

▶ Publishing a universe or a connection in the CMS repository (see Chapter 9, Section 9.2)

▶ Opening retrieved data foundations and business layers that haven't been saved for all users (see Chapter 9, Section 9.4)

▶ Managing universe security through security profiles (see Chapter 10, Section 10.3)

To connect to a CMS repository, IDT needs to open a session and manage its lifecycle. The following sections start with the session definition and then cover different aspects of session management: predefined sessions, authentication, security, and so on.

3.3.1   Session to CMS Repository

To open a session, you need to provide the following parameters given to you by your administrator:

▶ **System name**
The system to use for authentication. This system name is made of a hostname and the port used by the CMS. The hostname can be provided as any of the following:

- ▸ A simple hostname (e.g., `mymachine`)

- ▸ A fully qualified hostname (e.g., `mymachine.mydomain.com`)

- ▸ An IP address (e.g., 10.10.10.10) supporting both IPv4 and IPv6 protocols

You can also enter a cluster name (e.g., `@mycluster`) if it's already registered in IDT.

▸ **User name**
The account used to authenticate you in the CMS repository.

▸ **Password**
The password associated to the user name.

▸ **Authentication**
The authentication mode (see Section 3.3.3).

The first time you enter a hostname in IDT and successfully log on, the name of the cluster containing this hostname is retrieved. This cluster name is even used to display and identify the new open session. Later, you can open a session by providing only the cluster name because the registration has saved both the cluster name and the hostnames it contains.

Default Cluster Name

If your cluster contains only one machine, by default, the cluster name is the name of the single machine of the cluster and its port name, prefixed by the "@" character (for example, `@mymachine:6400`). This cluster name can be modified later using the Central Configuration Manager (CCM) tool.

Several sessions to different clusters can be opened at the same time. But only one session to the same cluster can be opened at the same time. If you try to open a session through another hostname of the same cluster, the cluster IDs are compared and, because they are identical, it's considered as a similar cluster.

When you open a session, if it doesn't yet exist as a predefined session, then it's saved as a predefined session (see Section 3.3.2). When a session is opened, as shown in Figure 3.7, you can navigate in the system's *Universes* and *Connections* folders, where you can manage the resources they contain, as long as you have the appropriate security rights (see Chapter 10, Section 10.1).

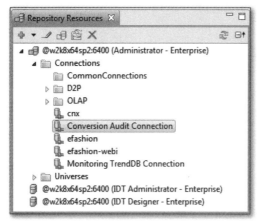

Figure 3.7 Repository Resources View

IDT keeps all open sessions in the REPOSITORY RESOURCES view that lists them. If, for a specific workflow, you need to connect to a CMS repository, IDT tries to reuse a session to this CMS repository that is already open.

A session can be closed only if all other views or editors that may use it are closed: SECURITY EDITOR, PROJECT SYNCHRONIZATION, and so on. When you close IDT, all open sessions are closed.

3.3.2 Predefined Sessions

To avoid retyping the session parameters each time you open the same session, IDT can save the following parameters used to connect to CMS repositories:

▶ The cluster ID and name to connect. As described in Section 3.3.1, even if you provide a hostname when creating a predefined session or opening a session, the corresponding cluster ID and name are in fact saved in the predefined session.

▶ The user name to use to open the session.

▶ The authentication mode (see Section 3.3.3) used to authenticate the user.

These parameters are saved in a predefined session. Thus, if you need to reconnect to the same system with these parameters, you may just select the corresponding predefined session and open it. However, the password associated to the session isn't stored in the predefined session, so to actually open it, you need to retype it.

IDT allows you to create several predefined sessions that are listed in the REPOSITORY RESOURCES view. To create a predefined session, you can explicitly create it in the REPOSITORY RESOURCES view. Opening a session automatically creates a predefined session with its parameters, if it doesn't yet exist.

It's possible to create different predefined sessions to the same CMS repository with a different user name or authentication mode. But only one session to the same CMS repository can be opened simultaneously at the same time. IDT is able to open different session simultaneously, but they must reference different CMS repositories.

Storing the cluster ID instead of a CMS repository hostname doesn't impact the predefined sessions if the hostname is removed from the cluster or renamed, or if the cluster name is modified. In these two cases, the cluster ID isn't modified, and the predefined session remains valid.

> **Cluster ID**
>
> To open resources retrieved from the CMS repository that haven't been saved for all users, you must also be authenticated to the CMS repository (see Chapter 9, Section 9.4). To be independent of cluster changes, these resources also store the cluster ID to identify the cluster they come from.
>
> Saving cluster IDs in a predefined session has been introduced in SAP BusinessObjects BI 4.0 SP5. So if you migrate from a prior release and have removed the referenced hostname from the cluster or modified your cluster name, your predefined sessions are no longer valid after a migration to an SAP BusinessObjects BI 4.1 release.

3.3.3 Authentication Modes

Authentication defines how users authenticate to log on to SAP BusinessObjects products. The SAP BusinessObjects BI 4.x platform supports different authentication modes. The main difference between these authentication modes is the external authentication system they use, if any. IDT supports the following authentication modes:

▶ **Enterprise**
In this authentication mode, all authentication parameters (user name and password) are stored in the CMS repository.

▸ **SAP**

In this authentication mode, user authentication is done with an external SAP system.

▸ **Active Directory**

In this authentication mode, user authentication is done with an external Active Directory system.

▸ **Lightweight Directory Access Protocol (LDAP)**

In this authentication mode, user authentication is done with an external LDAP system.

In all these modes, the user needs to type a password to log on to the SAP Business-Objects BI 4.x platform. SAP, Active Directory, and LDAP are external authentications that require the CMS to be configured to authenticate to these external systems. The use of external sources allows you to enforce an existing security system without having to duplicate it in the SAP BusinessObjects BI 4.x system and maintain it in two locations. It's updated in one location: the external source.

Active Directory enforces the Kerberos protocol — an authentication protocol that relies on the use of tickets and secret keys to allow secure communication between systems. However, because IDT is written in Java, it requires some additional configuration steps to support Active Directory. Ask your administrator to configure the *krb5.ini* and *bscLogin.conf* files.

Windows Single Sign-On

Although IDT can authenticate with Active Directory, it doesn't support Windows Single Sign-On (SSO), and you need to enter your user name and password to log in to a CMS repository. But IDT supports SSO to databases (see Chapter 4, Section 4.3.3).

3.3.4 Folders and Objects

In the CMS repository, all objects are organized in folders. This is also the case for universes and connections that are stored in two root folders, displayed in IDT:

▸ *Connections* folder that contains the secured connections

▸ *Universes* folder that contains the universes published for consumption

These two root folders can contain subfolders for easier resource organization. These subfolders can be managed in the IDT REPOSITORY RESOURCES view (see Section 3.4.2).

Some other resources used by IDT are also saved in the CMS repository and its subfolders:

▶ Shared project (see Section 3.5)

▶ Universe security, with the security profiles (see Chapter 10, Section 10.3)

But these folders and resources can't be directly accessed in IDT or the CMC. IDT proposes dedicated editors to manage them.

3.3.5 Predefined Groups

When you connect to the CMS repository, rights assigned to you for resources (universes and connections) saved in this repository are enforced by IDT. Typically, if you don't have the view rights for the *Connections* or *Universes* root folders, you don't see these folders. After the installation, the CMS repository contains several *predefined groups* that have predefined rights assigned.

Among these groups, the Universe Designers group has the Full Control access level on the *Universes* and *Connections* folders. It has also granted the following rights for IDT:

▶ SAVE FOR ALL USERS

▶ COMPUTE STATISTICS

▶ PUBLISH UNIVERSES

▶ RETRIEVE UNIVERSES

▶ CREATE, MODIFY, OR DELETE CONNECTIONS

▶ SHARE PROJECTS

Another group, the Administrators group, has granted the ADMINISTER SECURITY PROFILES right to IDT.

You can use these groups to quickly give IDT rights to users by adding them to these groups. Through rights inheritance, these users inherit the rights or access levels assigned to the predefined groups. Once you've better defined your security model, you may prefer to create your own groups and assign them your own explicit security, but these predefined groups are a good start to defining security.

3.4 Managing Sessions

In IDT, session management is mainly done in the REPOSITORY RESOURCES view. But before covering the different tasks you can perform in this view, this section first details how sessions are opened.

3.4.1 Opening a Session

In any workflow where you need to access a CMS repository, IDT prompts you with the OPEN SESSION dialog box to open a session.

Depending on your workflow, the OPEN SESSION dialog box may differ:

▶ If you're creating a predefined session, and thus indirectly open a session, you're prompted for the system name, user name, password, and authentication mode (see Section 3.3.3), as shown in Figure 3.8.

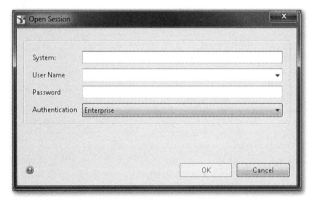

Figure 3.8 Open Session Dialog Box

▶ If you're opening the SECURITY EDITOR or the PROJECT SYNCHRONIZATION editor, you can select any CMS repository. As shown in Figure 3.9, the OPEN SESSION dialog box contains a SESSIONS dropdown menu where you can choose to do one of the following:

► Open one of the predefined sessions already created. If you select a session that is already open, then you can simply click OK to use this session. If the selected predefined session isn't yet open, enter the password for the user of this predefined session to open it.

► Create a new predefined session if there is no predefined session for the CMS repository to access. In this case, select the NEW SESSION option in the dropdown menu, and then enter the parameters required to create a predefined session: system name, user name, password, and authentication mode. Click OK to create this predefined session and open it.

By default, the dialog proposes an already open session if one is available.

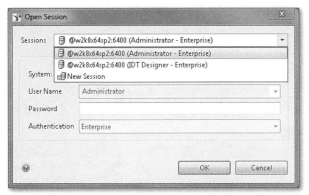

Figure 3.9 Open Session Dialog Box with Predefined Session Selection

► If you're opening a session in which the CMS repository is already known (e.g., to access a secured connection through a connection shortcut), the OPEN SESSION dialog box already contains the name of the system to connect.

In all cases, if your credentials are valid, after you've validated your choice, a predefined session is created if it doesn't yet exist. This session is displayed as open in the REPOSITORY RESOURCES view and can be reused if you need to access this CMS repository for another task.

3.4.2   Using the Session

After a predefined session is created, you can open it to display the contents of the *Universes* folder and the *Connections* folders and perform additional tasks described in the next chapters. As shown earlier in Figure 3.7, you can expand these folders to navigate in their subfolders.

Table 3.2 lists the commands available in the REPOSITORY RESOURCES view toolbar.

Button	Description
✚ ▾	INSERT opens a menu containing the commands to create a new session, folder, secured relational, or OLAP connection.
✏	OPEN opens a secured connection editor.
▤	OPEN SESSION opens the selected predefined session.
▣	REFRESH FOLDER refreshes only the selected folder.
✕	DELETE deletes the selected predefined session, folder, connection, or universe.
↻	REFRESH refreshes the entire REPOSITORY RESOURCES view.
⊟↑	COLLAPSE ALL collapses all sessions and folders in the REPOSITORY RESOURCES view.

Table 3.2 Buttons in the Repository Resources View Toolbar

Through this toolbar or the right-click menu, this view allows you to perform some tasks on the resources saved in the CMS repository:

▸ Manage secure connections, described in Chapter 4, Section 4.6.

▸ Manage published universes, described in Chapter 9.

▸ Create, rename, and delete folders in the *Universes* and *Connections* folders by clicking the corresponding button in the toolbar or selecting the corresponding command in the right-click context menu.

3.4.3 Creating a Predefined Session

A predefined session is usually explicitly created from the REPOSITORY RESOURCES view, as described in the following steps:

1. In the REPOSITORY RESOURCES view toolbar, select INSERT, and then select INSERT SESSION from the dropdown menu.

2. In the OPEN SESSION dialog box that opens, in the corresponding fields, enter the system, user name, password, and authentication mode.

3. Click OK. The predefined session is created and opened. It's displayed in the REPOSITORY RESOURCES view with the following format:

```
<Cluster name> (<username> - <Authentication mode>)
```

However, the predefined session isn't created in the following cases:

▶ A session to the same system is already open; before creating the predefined session, it tries to open it.

▶ A predefined session with the same system, authentication mode, and user name already exists.

▶ IDT can't open the session to the CMS repository.

It's also possible to indirectly create a predefined session when opening a new session. In fact, if you enter some parameters that don't fit an existing predefined session in the OPEN SESSION dialog box, then a new one is automatically created and added to the REPOSITORY RESOURCES view (see Section 3.4.1).

Modifying a Predefined Session

When a predefined session is created, it isn't possible to modify its parameters, except the password that is requested each time you open the session. To modify a predefined session, you actually need to delete it, as described in Section 3.4.6, and then recreate it with the new updated parameters.

3.4.4 Opening a Predefined Session

To open a predefined session, follow these steps:

1. Open the REPOSITORY RESOURCES view.

2. Select the predefined session to open, and choose one of these methods to open it:

▶ Double-click it.

▶ Right-click it, and select the OPEN SESSION command.

▶ In the REPOSITORY RESOURCES view toolbar, select the OPEN SESSION button ( ).

3. The OPEN SESSION dialog box opens. Enter your password in the PASSWORD field and click OK to open the session.

3.4.5 Closing a Session

To close a session, go in the REPOSITORY RESOURCES view, and right-click the open session. In the context menu, select the CLOSE SESSION command. If no other editor or view using this session is still open, then the session is closed, and you can't access its resources unless you reopen it. If the session doesn't close, you need to close any remaining editor or view that keeps the session open. In the worst case, you may simply close IDT, which closes all open sessions.

3.4.6 Deleting a Predefined Session

To delete a predefined session, follow these steps:

1. Open the REPOSITORY RESOURCES view.

2. Because IDT doesn't allow you to delete an open session, close the session if it's open.

3. Select the predefined session and use one of these methods:

   ▶ Right-click it, and select DELETE SESSION.

   ▶ Click the DELETE SESSION button (✖) in the REPOSITORY RESOURCES view toolbar.

   ▶ Select it and press the ⌷Delete⌷ key.

   After you confirm, the predefined session is deleted and removed from the REPOSITORY RESOURCES view.

3.5 Shared Projects

In deployments that involve several universe designers working together on different universes, IDT allows these designers to collaborate and share authored resources through the shared projects.

3.5.1 Shared Project Definition

A shared project is a folder in a CMS repository that can contain any objects contained in a local project: connection, connection shortcut, data foundation, business layer, or agnostic resources (see Section 3.1).

After a local project has been shared in a shared project, other designers can retrieve this shared project content and make it a local project on their machine to work on these resources in their IDT installation. Thus, designers can exchange their resources and collaborate on the same universes.

A shared project is only intended to share files saved in the local project, that is, authored resources or agnostic files. Here are a few things for which a shared project is not intended:

▶ The shared project isn't an authoring space. You can't edit a resource directly in a shared project. You must retrieve it locally first, edit it, and then resynchronize it.

▶ The shared project isn't a consumption space. You can't store universes published for consumption in a shared project.

▶ The shared project isn't a direct publishing space. You can't directly publish a universe from resources located in a shared project. You first need to synchronize your resources from your shared project. After the resources that make the universes are in a local project, you may publish them to generate the universe.

Even if saved in the CMS repository, a shared project can be accessed only in an IDT dedicated editor: the SYNCHRONIZATION PANEL.

3.5.2 Synchronizing

After a local project has been shared into the CMS repository as a shared project, other designers can get a local copy of this shared project as a local project in their IDT workspace. Collaboration between designers is possible through *synchronization*, which allows you to do the following:

▶ Get a version of a resource from a shared project to create it in a local project, or get the latest version of this resource from the shared project, if it has been updated by another designer, to update the local version.

▶ Save in the shared project the local version of the resource you've modified in the local project associated to the shared project so other designers can benefit from it.

The first time a designer synchronizes a shared project, the entire shared project is retrieved. A designer can see if there are differences between the local version of a resource and the shared version and know who has made the changes on the server version and when. You have the choice, resource by resource, to push the local changes to the server shared project or, on the contrary, pull the changes from the server to the local authoring workspace. Each time a new version of a resource is synchronized in a shared project, its version number is incremented in the shared folder.

A local project that has been shared on a CMS repository is identified by its name. Thus a local project can only be shared once in a CMS repository, unless you've renamed it. In this case, if you resynchronize the renamed local project, a new shared project is created in the CMS repository.

3.5.3 Security

Shared project security is managed only by the IDT security right SHARE PROJECTS (see Chapter 10, Section 10.1.1).

A designer who has this right granted in a CMS repository can do the following:

▶ Create a shared project in this CMS repository.

▶ Share any resources in any shared projects of this CMS repository.

▶ Synchronize objects from any shared project saved in this CMS repository.

▶ Open the PROJECT SYNCHRONIZATION editor to manage shared projects.

There is no other right to more precisely define security for each resource in the shared folder or at the shared project level. If the SHARE PROJECTS right is granted to you, then you can access all shared projects in this repository and all folders and resources it contains that have been shared in the local project.

Shared Project Scope

This resource synchronization is rather recommended for small or mid-size deployment due to its limitations:

▸ Security is applied at the application level.

▸ There is no way to compare a local and a shared resource and to merge them.

Thus, it can be seen as a commodity to back up resources or exchange them between different designers.

3.5.4 Locking and Unlocking Resources

When you work on a local resource shared in a shared project, you want to prevent other designers from editing or deleting the version of the resource stored in the shared project. In such cases, you may lock this resource to warn other designers that you're still editing it. After it's locked, a resource appears with a specific icon in the SHARED PROJECT panel to show that it's locked.

This lock is a soft lock because any user can unlock it and it doesn't prevent from synchronizing the resource to the shared project. However, along with signifying that someone is working on it, the lock also indicates who locked it and the date when it was locked.

You usually lock a project after you've synchronized your local version of the resource with the version saved in the shared project to get its latest changes.

3.6 Managing Shared Resources

IDT proposes a dedicated editor, the Project Synchronization editor, for shared project management and resource synchronization. This panel can display only the resources of one shared project at once.

3.6.1 Creating a Shared Project

To create a shared project in the CMS repository to share authoring resources among different designers, follow these steps:

1. In the LOCAL PROJECTS view, select the local project to share.

2. Right-click the project, and select the NEW SHARED PROJECT command in the context menu.

3. In the OPEN SESSION dialog box, select a predefined session or open a new one, as described in Section 3.4.1.

4. After the session is open, IDT connects to the CMS repository to create the shared project. The Project Synchronization editor opens and displays the new shared project, as shown in Figure 3.10.

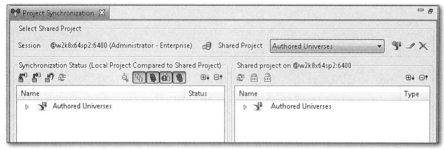

Figure 3.10 Project Synchronization Editor

You use this Project Synchronization editor to synchronize resources between your local projects and the corresponding shared projects. This editor has three panels:

▶ The SELECT SHARED PROJECT panel, which enables you to select the shared project to open.

▶ The SYNCHRONIZATION STATUS panel, which displays the shared resources of the local project corresponding to the open shared project. For each resource, the synchronization status between the local resource and its shared version in the shared project is provided, as shown in Figure 3.11. These different synchronization statuses are listed in Table 3.3.

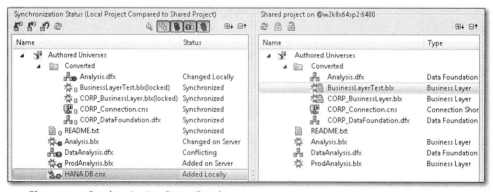

Figure 3.11 Synchronization Status Panel

Icon	Description
	The local version of the resource is more recent than the one in the shared project, or it has never been shared in the shared project. It is a candidate for being synchronized from the local project to the shared project.
	IDT isn't able to determine the version that should be taken as a reference because both versions have evolved independently. You must manually review these files to resolve this conflict and define how the synchronization must be done.
	The version of this resource shared in the shared project is more recent than the one in the local project, or it has never been retrieved locally. It is a candidate for being synchronized from the shared project to the local project.
	The local and shared versions of the resource are synchronized.

Table 3.3 Synchronization Status Icons

▶ The SHARED PROJECT ON <system name> panel, which lists the resources of the shared project, as well as additional details about each resource:

- ▶ TYPE: Connection, shortcut, data foundation, or business layer.

- ▶ VERSION: The version number from the SYNCHRONIZATION panel point of view.

- ▶ MODIFIED BY: The user who has last saved it in the shared project.

- ▶ DATE MODIFIED: The last modification date.

- ▶ LOCKED BY: If the resource is locked, the user who has locked it.

- ▶ DATE LOCKED: If the resource is locked, the date when it was locked.

The SYNCHRONIZATION STATUS toolbar contains the buttons described in Table 3.4. The SHARED PROJECT ON toolbar contains the ones described in Table 3.5.

Button	Description
	GET CHANGES FROM SERVER updates local resources with their latest version saved in a shared project.
	SAVE CHANGES ON SERVER saves the last version saved locally in the shared project.

Table 3.4 Commands in the Synchronization Status Panel Toolbar

Button	Description
	REVERT CHANGES reverts to the previous synchronization state.
	REFRESH retrieves the resources status with the shared project on the server.
	SHOW ALL RESOURCES sets all filters to display all resources, whatever their status is.
	SHOW/HIDE SYNCHRONIZED RESOURCES filters the resources that are synchronized.
	SHOW/HIDE LOCAL ADDITIONS, DELETIONS, AND CHANGES filters the resources that must be pushed on the shared project.
	SHOW/HIDE CONFLICTING RESOURCES filters the resources that have conflicting status.
	SHOW/HIDE SERVER ADDITIONS, DELETIONS, AND CHANGES filters the resources that must be retrieved from the shared project.
	EXPAND ALL expands the resources list in the SYNCHRONIZATION STATUS panel.
	COLLAPSE ALL collapses all resources in the SYNCHRONIZATION STATUS panel.

Table 3.4 Commands in the Synchronization Status Panel Toolbar (Cont.)

Button	Description
	REFRESH retrieves the version of the shared project.
	LOCK locks the selected resource in the shared project.
	UNLOCK unlocks the selected resource in the shared project.
	EXPAND ALL expands the resources list in the SHARED PROJECT panel.
	COLLAPSE ALL collapses all resources in the SHARED PROJECT panel.

Table 3.5 Commands in the Shared Project Panel Toolbar

Project Synchronization User Interface

To properly display all commands and buttons of the Project Synchronization editor, maximize the IDT window.

3.6.2   Opening a Shared Project

To open an existing shared project, follow these steps:

1. To open the Project Synchronization editor, click the SYNCHRONIZATION button (⬛) in the IDT toolbar, or select PROJECT SYNCHRONIZATION in the WINDOW menu.

2. In the Project Synchronization editor, click the CHANGE SESSION button (⬛).

3. In the OPEN SESSION dialog box, select a predefined session or open a new one, as described in Section 3.4.1.

4. When connected to the CMS repository, in the SHARED PROJECT dropdown menu, select one shared project in the list of shared projects saved in this CMS repository.

The shared project content is displayed in the SHARED PROJECT ON panel, whereas the SYNCHRONIZATION STATUS panel displays the list of resources and whether they must be synchronized between the local and shared project. Before the resource's name, an icon gives its synchronization state, as described in Table 3.3.

You may display such resources by toggling the corresponding button in the SYNCHRONIZATION STATUS toolbar (refer to Table 3.4). Synchronization is based only on the resource's last modification date.

3.6.3   Synchronizing Resources

To get a shared resource's latest version from the server, follow these steps:

1. Select the resource in the SHARED PROJECT ON panel.

2. In the SYNCHRONIZATION STATUS panel toolbar, click the GET CHANGES FROM SERVER button.

Identically, to share a local resource's last version into a shared project, follow these steps:

1. Select the resource in the SYNCHRONIZATION STATUS panel.

2. In the SYNCHRONIZATION STATUS panel toolbar, click the SAVE CHANGES ON SERVER button.

In both cases, it's possible to select several resources with the Ctrl key to synchronize them at once.

3.6.4 Locking and Unlocking Resources

To lock or unlock a resource in a shared project, follow these steps:

1. Open your shared project in the Project Synchronization editor, as described in Section 3.6.2.

2. In the SHARED PROJECT panel, navigate in the resources tree and select the resource to lock or unlock.

3. If the resource isn't yet locked, click the LOCK button (🔒) in the toolbar to lock it. If it's already locked, click the UNLOCK button (🔓) to unlock it.

When a resource is locked in the shared project, it's displayed with a specific icon (🔒), as shown in Figure 3.12.

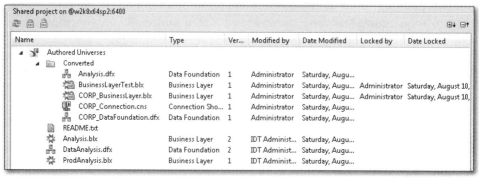

Figure 3.12 Locked Resources

3.6.5 Deleting a Shared Project

To delete a shared project, follow these steps:

1. In the Project Synchronization editor, after you're logged on to the CMS repository that contains the shared project, go to the SELECT SHARED PROJECT panel.

2. In the SHARED PROJECT dropdown menu, select the shared project to delete.

3. Near the SHARED PROJECT dropdown menu, click the DELETE SHARED PROJECT button (✗).

After your confirmation, the shared project is actually removed from the CMS repository, with all the objects and folders it contains.

The resources from the shared projects that other designers may have retrieved or synchronized locally aren't deleted and are still available in their local projects. However, they can't be shared anymore, unless a new project is recreated in the CMS repository.

3.7   Summary

Information Design Tool is the authoring tool you use to create resources that generate universes: connections, connection shortcuts, data foundations, and business layers. These resources are saved in a local project—the workplace stored on your disk folder.

Several workflows require you to connect to the CMS repository (for example, managing corporate connections and universes). In this case, authentication to the CMS repository can be done through any authentication mode supported by the BI platform.

To ease CMS repository connection, IDT can save predefined sessions that keep you from retyping all session parameters, except the password.

For collaborative work, local authored resources can be shared in the CMS repository in shared projects. With shared projects, several designers can share their authored resources and synchronize their local versions of these resources with the versions saved in CMS repository.

Connections are the keys to the database containing your production data. Different client tools support different types of connections and their authentication modes.

4 Connecting to Data Sources

In the SAP BusinessObjects BI 4.x system, a connection is a resource used to connect to the source containing the data to query. This connection contains the parameters requested to access and connect to the source and, for this reason, a connection is mandatory for any workflows where a data source is involved.

Because of the evolution of SAP BusinessObjects releases over time, different types of connections exist in SAP BusinessObjects BI 4.x based on different components. Some connection types have existed for several releases and some others have been introduced to support new technologies.

This chapter focuses on the connections in Information Design Tool (IDT):

▸ The different types of data sources that can be accessed through them

▸ The differences between secured and local connections and why connection shortcuts are needed

▸ The authentication modes used to connect to the database

▸ Some deployment details required to understand connections workflows

▸ The definition of some connections parameters

▸ The workflows to manage connections in IDT and to preview data

Let's begin by exploring the various types of data sources supported by IDT.

4.1 Data Sources Typology

Since its origins, the semantic layer has always supported multiple data sources. IDT has inherited this heterogeneous nature and is able to access a wide range of data sources. Because of this variety, the connections and the engines used to access these data sources rely on three different technologies that represent the three connections categories in IDT:

▶ Relational connections processed by the Connection Server.

▶ Relational connections to SAP NetWeaver BW and SAS processed by the Federation Query Server. Federation Query Server also supports other RDBMSs that you can use in multisource universes.

▶ OLAP connections processed by the OLAPClient.

Connections to SAP Systems

Some SAP systems (SAP NetWeaver BW and SAP HANA) can be accessed either through a relational or an OLAP connection.

However, the IDT version distributed in the SAP Crystal Server 2013 package doesn't support connections to SAP NetWeaver BW and SAP ERP.

Connections to SAP systems aren't covered in this chapter but are discussed in Chapter 12.

4.1.1 Relational Connections

Relational connections are handled by the Connection Server component and are historically used to access a wide range of relational databases. The Connection Server has been extended to support new types of data sources such as SAP ERP, Web Services, Hadoop, Open Data Protocol (OData), and others. These data sources are exposed with a relational interface by the Connection Server. Relational universes can be created on top of them as if they were relational databases.

In SAP BusinessObjects BI 4.x, these relational connections are common to the Universe Design Tool and IDT. Interoperability of connections between these two tools is supported; they can be created in either IDT or the Universe Design Tool and subsequently used by a universe in either tool.

There are, however, some slight differences between the database vendors and versions supported by the two tools:

▶ In the Universe Design Tool, you can create connections based on Connection Server that refer to OLAP databases. But universes created in the Universe Design Tool are relational only and the data returned by these connections are flattened to match a relational format. These connections aren't supported by IDT, which proposes its own OLAP connections (see Section 4.1.3).

▶ New connection types, such as Hadoop, Web Services, and so on, are only supported by IDT, and not by the Universe Design Tool.

From one release to another, new database versions or types become supported to follow the evolution of the technology. It also happens that older database versions or types are no longer supported:

▶ When a connection created in a previous release of SAP BusinessObjects BI references a database version that is no longer supported, Connection Server tries to connect to it with the newer version of the middleware it supports. If the database is forward compatible, this should allow you to continue to access it.

▶ It's very unusual that a connection type becomes no longer supported. In this case, you may still continue to access your database by connecting with a generic ODBC, JDBC, or OLE DB driver.

Table 4.1 displays the list of vendors and databases supported by IDT in SAP BusinessObjects BI 4.1. Since this list may evolve with releases of new support packages, you should check the latest status by referring to the Product Availability Matrix (PAM), available at *http://service.sap.com/pam*. These relational connections can be used for both single-source and multisource data foundations, except some cases also listed in Table 4.1.

Vendor	Database	Support Multisource
Apache	Amazon EMR Hive 0.7, 0.8	Yes
Apache	Apache Hadoop Hive 0.7, 0.8, 0.9, 0.10	Yes
Apache	Derby 10 Embedded	Yes
Generic	JDBC data sources	Not supported
Generic	OLE DB Provider	Not supported
Generic	ODBC, ODBC3	Not supported
Generic	OData 2.0	Yes
Generic	Text Files	Not supported
Generic	Web Service (WSDL 1.1)	Yes

Table 4.1 Supported Relational Databases and Their Multisource Support

Vendor	Database	Support Multisource
Generic	XML files	Yes
GreenPlum	GreenPlum 4	Yes
IBM	DB2 9 and 10 for LUW, DB2 9 and 10 for z/OS, DB2 5, 6, and 7 for iSeries	Yes, some exceptions for DB2 for iSeries on UNIX
IBM	Informix Dynamic Server 11	Yes
Ingres	Ingres Database 9	Not supported
Microsoft	MS SQL Server 2008, 2012	Yes
Microsoft	MS Access 2007, 2010, 2013	Not supported
Microsoft	MS Excel 2007, 2010	Not supported
Microsoft	Text files (ODBC drivers)	Not supported
Netezza	Netezza Server 4, 5, 6	Yes
Oracle	MySQL 5	Yes
Oracle	Oracle 10, 11	Yes
Oracle	Oracle EBS	Yes
Oracle	Oracle Exadata	Yes
PostgreSQL	PostgreSQL 8, 9	Not supported
Saleforce.com	Saleforce.com	Not supported
SAP	MaxDB 7.7	Yes
SAP	SAP R/3 Release 4, mySAP ERP 2004, SAP ERP 6	Yes
SAP	SAP HANA 1.0	Yes
SAP Sybase	Sybase Adaptive Server Enterprise 15.5	Yes
SAP Sybase	Sybase IQ 15	Yes
SAP Sybase	Sybase SQL Anywhere 11, 12	Yes
Teradata Corporation	Teradata 12, 13, 14	Yes

Table 4.1 Supported Relational Databases and Their Multisource Support (Cont.)

4.1.2 Relational Connections to SAP NetWeaver BW and SAS

Relational connections to SAP NetWeaver BW and SAS rely on a new connection type introduced in SAP BusinessObjects BI 4.0 with the integration of a new federation engine into the BI platform.

> **SAP BusinessObjects Data Federator Data Source**
>
> The federation engine, referred to in this book as Federation Query Server, is based on a previous product (not distributed anymore) called SAP BusinessObjects Data Federator.
>
> The relational connections to SAP NetWeaver BW and SAS based on the federation engine are called Data Federator data sources, for example, in the Central Management Console (CMC).

These relational connections are used to access some relational databases that require the use of the Federation Query Server to access them. As shown in Table 4.2, the supported databases are SAP NetWeaver BW (this connection and its specificities are described in detail in Chapter 12, Section 12.1) and SAS.

Vendor	Database
SAP	SAP NetWeaver BW 7.x
SAS	SAS 9

Table 4.2 Supported Data Sources

These connections can be used only for relational universes created in IDT. These connections rely on the Federation Query Server; to create a universe on top of them, you need to explicitly choose to create a multisource data foundation (see Chapter 6, Section 6.2).

Furthermore, in contrast to the other connections you can create in IDT, these connections can be created only in the CMS repository, and not locally on your file system.

4.1.3 OLAP Connections

OLAP connections, handled by the OLAPClient component, are used to access and to manage OLAP databases. As shown in Table 4.3, in SAP BusinessObjects BI 4.1, except Microsoft SQL Server Analysis Services and Oracle Hyperion Essbase, most of these data source types are used to access SAP systems.

Vendor	Database
Microsoft	Microsoft SQL Server Analysis Services 2008, 2012
Oracle	Hyperion Essbase 11.x
SAP	SAP HANA
SAP	SAP NetWeaver BW 7.x
SAP BusinessObjects	Financial Consolidation 10 for Microsoft platform
SAP BusinessObjects	Planning and Consolidation 10 for Microsoft platform
SAP BusinessObjects	Planning and Consolidation 7.5 for Microsoft platform
SAP BusinessObjects	Profitability and Cost Management 10

Table 4.3 Supported OLAP Data Sources

The OLAP connections can be created both in IDT and CMC. They are interoperable, even if some differences exist:

▶ The list of OLAP databases they support slightly differs. For example, SAP BusinessObjects Analysis, Edition for OLAP, doesn't support Oracle Hyperion Essbase. Refer to the PAM (*http://service.sap.com/pam*) for more details.

▶ The authentication modes (see Section 4.3) supported by the connections created in the two tools are different:

  ▶ In the CMC, you can set the prompted authentication but not the credential mappings authentication.

  ▶ In IDT, you can set the credential mapping authentication but not the prompted authentication.

An OLAP server usually contains several cubes. The OLAP connection offers you the flexibility to either reference a cube on this server or just reference the server and let the choice of the cube fall to the final user:

▶ If the connection refers to a cube, then the connection is self-sufficient, and client tools can directly query the cube referenced by the connection, and only this one. Client tools can't query other cubes in the server.

▶ If the connection refers to the server, then when the connection is used in IDT or any client tool that supports it, users must explicitly select the cube to access on this server before creating their reports, dashboards, or analyses.

The connections to non-SAP systems are used by SAP BusinessObjects Analysis, Edition for OLAP, and multidimensional universes created in IDT (see Chapter 7, Section 7.2.3).

Regarding the connections to SAP systems:

▸ **SAP NetWeaver BW**
This connection, based on the SAP Java Connector (SAP JCo) driver, can be used only for direct access from client tools (SAP BusinessObjects Web Intelligence, SAP Crystal Reports for Enterprise, SAP BusinessObjects Analysis, Edition for OLAP, SAP BusinessObjects Dashboards) to a BEx query. You can't create a multidimensional universe on top of it, but you can create a relational universe through a relational connection based on the Federation Query Server (see Chapter 12, Section 12.1) that references the same system to access an InfoProvider.

▸ **SAP HANA**
This connection can be used only for direct access from SAP Crystal Reports for Enterprise. You can't create a multidimensional universe on top of it. However, you can create a relational universe through a relational connection (see Chapter 12, Section 12.3) that references the same system.

▸ **SAP BusinessObjects**
These connections reference SAP BusinessObjects products that store their data in a Microsoft SQL Server Analysis Services database. These connections are in fact connections to the underlying cube and behave like OLAP connections on the database. Typically, they can be used to create a multidimensional universe.

Whatever data source you access through a connection, the connection you create is a resource that can be saved either in a local project or a CMS repository. Both options have some impacts that are described in next section.

4.2   Connection Persistence

Connections can be created in IDT and saved either in a CMS repository (a secured connection) or in an IDT local project. When a connection is in the CMS repository, it can be referenced in a local project through a connection shortcut.

Let's discuss the impact of these two options and consider how the different connections can be used.

4.2.1 Secured Connections

A secured connection is a connection saved in a CMS repository. After it's saved in the repository, the connection becomes public and can be used across your organization through universes also saved in the CMS repository and through any resource created with SAP BusinessObjects tools. Except for specific tasks related to administration, a resource in a CMS repository can't reference resources in another repository. A secured connection can only be used to create resources stored in the same repository.

In the CMS repository, the connection benefits of the SAP BusinessObjects BI 4.x security rights framework (see Chapter 10, Section 10.1) and it is possible to control who can view it and use it to query the database. Furthermore, its access is more secure than if it were saved locally on a file system because the connection is stored on the server side and can be protected from external access.

The three connections categories described in Section 4.1 can be stored in the CMS repository:

▶ Relational connection used for relational universe and created with the Universe Design Tool or IDT

▶ Relational connection to SAP NetWeaver BW and SAS, and created with IDT

▶ OLAP connection created by IDT or the CMC

In SAP BusinessObjects BI 4.x, these connections are all located under the same *Connections* top-root folder. Subfolders can be created in this folder to ease connection management.

Specific Connections

Some tools enforce their own version of connections and don't store them under the *Connections* top-root folder in the CMS repository. For example:

▶ SAP Crystal Reports 2013 still manages its own connections in the CMS repository.

▶ SAP BusinessObjects Explorer saves its parameters to connect to SAP NetWeaver BW Accelerator (SAP NetWeaver BWA) or SAP HANA in the CMS repository as application parameters.

These connections are available only from their respective products.

A secured connection may have been created directly in the CMS repository or published in the CMS repository from a local connection (see Section 4.2.3). In the latter case, the secured connection is created with the same parameters as the local connection. It can be seen as a copy because after it's created, this secured connection no longer has a link with the local connection.

The secured connection is identified by the name of the InfoObject that contains it. By default, when a local connection is published, the created secured connection is named with the local connection's business name.

4.2.2 Connection Shortcuts

When you publish a universe in a CMS repository, it must rely on a secured connection of the same repository. For security reasons, a secured connection must remain in the CMS repository, and its parameters must not be retrieved from the server. Hence, the *connection shortcut* has been introduced to reference a secured connection when you're working in local projects.

The connection shortcut is an object created in the local project and it references a secured connection on the CMS. When created, the connection shortcut contains the ID and the path in the CMS repository of the referenced secured connection.

> **Synchronization**
>
> When a connection shortcut is created, it's filled with some properties of the secured connection. These properties are only displayed for information and aren't updated if the secured connection is modified in the CMS repository.

Before publishing the universe in the CMS repository, its data foundation (if it's a relational universe) or its business layer (if it's a multidimensional universe) must be linked to a connection shortcut pointing to the secured connection the universe must use when published in the CMS repository (see Chapter 9, Section 9.2). When the universe is published, it embeds a copy of this connection shortcut. Thus, a universe is linked to the secured connection through the connection shortcut and the link between InfoObjects in the CMS repository.

A multisource universe embeds all connection shortcuts pointing to all the used secured connections.

In the file system, the connection shortcut has the *.cns* file extension. Like any resource in a local project, a connection shortcut can be shared in a shared project (see Chapter 3, Section 3.5).

4.2.3   Local Connections

With IDT, you can create connections in a local project stored in your file system. Local projects in IDT are used only for authoring the different resources that are merged to create the universe: data foundation and business layer (see Chapter 5, Chapter 6, and Chapter 7, which cover these resources in more details).

In local projects, you can create only two kinds of connections:

▶ Relational connections based on the Connection Server

▶ OLAP connections

You can't create locally relational connections to SAP NetWeaver BW and SAS because they need a Federation Query Server running on the server to be defined and require an open session to the CMS repository.

When you create a local connection, you can select any authentication mode among those supported by IDT for the database (fixed credentials, credentials mapping, or Single Sign-On). Credentials mapping and Single Sign-On require you to have an open session to a CMS repository to validate credentials entered by users. In IDT, to use a connection based on credentials mapping and Single Sign-On, you need to open a session to an SAP BusinessObjects BI 4.x system.

Local Connection Security

Although scrambled on the file system, a local connection is less secure than a connection saved in the CMS repository. We recommend that you do not use local connections to store references to production databases, and instead use them only in development or test environments, especially if they are defined with the fixed credentials authentication mode.

A local connection created in IDT can only be used in IDT. It can be used to publish a universe locally from the resources—connection, data foundation, and business layer—that make it (see Chapter 9, Section 9.1). When you publish a universe locally, the connection is embedded in the generated universe that is directly consumed by SAP BusinessObjects Web Intelligence Rich Client. A local connection can't be used to publish a universe to the CMS repository; to publish a universe to the repository, the connection must have been published and the data foundation, or the business layer, must point to its local shortcut.

In a local project, a connection is identified by the file name and the resource name. By default, the file name is the name of the resource connection, with the *.cnx* extension, but you can modify them later. In one folder of a local project, two connections can't have the same file name. Like any resource created in a local project, it's possible to share a local connection through a shared project (see Chapter 3, Section 3.5).

4.2.4   Connection Usages

The capabilities of the three connection types differ because of the various components and technologies on which they are built. They are not used in the same way by all SAP BusinessObjects BI client tools.

As of SAP BusinessObjects BI 4.1, the connections support the following:

- ▶ Relational connections, based on Connection Server
    - ▶ Relational universe created by IDT
    - ▶ Relational universe created by the Universe Design Tool
    - ▶ Relational multisource universe created by IDT
    - ▶ Direct access from SAP Crystal Reports for Enterprise
- ▶ Relational connections to SAP NetWeaver BW and SAS, based on Federation Query Server
    - ▶ Relational multisource universe created by IDT
- ▶ OLAP connections, based on OLAPClient
    - ▶ Multidimensional universes created by IDT
    - ▶ Direct access from SAP BusinessObjects Analysis, Edition for OLAP
- ▶ OLAP connections, based on the Connection Server
    - ▶ OLAP universe created by the Universe Design Tool (cannot be created or used in IDT)

4.3   Authentication Modes

In most cases, the connection refers to a database that enforces its own security repository. The connection authentication mode defines how the user running a query via the universe is going to be identified by the database. This section describes the authentication modes you can set in IDT:

▸ Fixed credentials, supported by all connections

▸ Credentials mapping, supported by all connections, except in the CMC and SAP BusinessObjects Analysis, Edition for OLAP

▸ Single Sign-On, supported only by a limited set of databases

▸ Credentials mapping used for Single Sign-On

Prompted Authentication

The prompted authentication mode can only be set in the CMC when you create an OLAP connection, and only SAP BusinessObjects Analysis, Edition for OLAP supports this authentication mode. IDT and SAP BusinessObjects Web Intelligence don't support the prompted authentication mode.

The account used to connect should have read-only rights at the database level because for reporting use, it doesn't require the right to write in the database. For a multisource universe, each connection authentication is computed independently of the others. It's possible to have one connection with fixed credentials and another one defined with Single Sign-On.

Let's begin with the most basic authentication mode—fixed credentials.

4.3.1 Fixed Credentials

This is the simplest authentication mode because the credentials used to connect to the database are stored in the connection. The fixed credentials authentication mode uses these credentials to connect to the database, whatever the context, product, or connected user. For this reason, it doesn't allow you to trace who actually has sent requests to the database, except through some workarounds based on ConnectInit, if it is supported.

This authentication mode is the least secure because the connection explicitly stores the credentials. Especially if saved locally, it can be seen as vulnerable and, for this reason, should contain only parameters to access test databases rather than production databases.

When it's published in the CMS repository, it can be secured with the CMS security framework. For relational connections stored in the CMS repository, you can deny the DOWNLOAD CONNECTION LOCALLY connection right to force database queries to be run on the server and prevent the connection credentials from being retrieved on client machines.

The fixed credentials mode can't have a dynamic user name and password through the use of the built-in function @variable, as opposed to the Universe Design Tool that supports it. In IDT, this mode can be replaced by credentials mapping, described in the next section.

4.3.2 Credentials Mapping

This authentication mode is available only when the connection is used with a session opened on the CMS repository. The connection doesn't store any credentials to connect to the database. They are saved in the CMS repository as the user's properties.

You can define a different set of credentials for each user. However, only one set of database credentials can be assigned to a user. The same credentials are used for the user by all connections that use this authentication mode.

Alternate Names

Depending on the context, credentials mapping is also called secondary credentials, SAP BusinessObjects credentials mapping, user's database credentials, or user's data source credentials.

With this mode, when the connection tries to connect to the database, it retrieves database credentials saved as properties of the logged on user. These credentials are used by the connection to authenticate to the database.

You can define this authentication mode for any relational or OLAP connections in IDT. It is not possible to set this authentication mode when you create an OLAP connection in the CMC because it's not supported by SAP BusinessObjects Analysis, Edition for OLAP. On the other hand, even if you set this authentication mode for an OLAP connection in IDT, it's not supported by SAP BusinessObjects Analysis, Edition for OLAP.

Defining a User's Database Credentials

You can enable or disable credentials mapping for each different user. If credentials mapping is disabled for a user, then the user can't use connections whose authentication mode is credentials mapping.

To define credentials mapping for a user, you need to go in the CMC and edit the user's properties. In the DATABASE CREDENTIALS section, as shown in Figure 4.1, you can set the following parameters:

▶ The ENABLE checkbox, to enable or disable credentials mapping for this user

▶ The ACCOUNT NAME text field, to set its database user name

▶ The PASSWORD and CONFIRM text fields, to set the database password

These steps must be done for each user who needs to authenticate with credentials mapping.

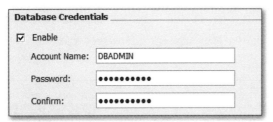

Figure 4.1 Database Credentials Parameters in User's Properties

4.3.3 Single Sign-On

This authentication mode is also called *Single Sign-On to database*. It goes beyond the Single Sign-On used to log on to SAP BusinessObjects BI 4.x products because the authentication is also used to connect to the database. If the connection authentication mode is Single Sign-On to database, then the credentials used to connect to the SAP BusinessObjects BI 4.x are reused by the connection to authenticate to the database and query data from it. It means that the database and the SAP BusinessObjects BI 4.x system must share the same authentication information.

Single Sign-On is supported only for a limited set of databases and in specific configurations. Table 4.4 lists the different combinations that support Single Sign-On. It especially details the external authentication system for which the SAP BusinessObjects BI 4.x system must be configured for authentication.

Data Source	Platforms	Drivers	SAP BusinessObjects BI 4.x External Authentication
Microsoft SQL Server Analysis Services	Windows	XMLA	Active Directory/Kerberos
Microsoft SQL Server	Windows	ODBC, OLE DB	Active Directory/Kerberos
Oracle	Windows	OCI	LDAP
Oracle EBS	All	OCI	Oracle EBS system
SAP NetWeaver BW	All	OLAP BAPI	SAP NetWeaver BW
SAP ERP	All	SAP JCo	SAP ERP
SAP HANA (relational)	All	ODBC	Active Directory/Kerberos
SAP HANA (relational)	All	JDBC	SAML or Active Directory/ Kerberos
SAP HANA (OLAP)	Windows, Linux, AIX	SAP HANA Client	Active Directory/SAML
Sybase IQ	Windows	ODBC	Active Directory/Kerberos
Teradata 13, 14	Windows	ODBC	Active Directory/Kerberos

Table 4.4 Single Sign-On Support

Single Sign-On requires the SAP BusinessObjects BI 4.x system and the database to be configured with the same external authentication system. When the user logs into the CMS and uses a connection defined with Single Sign-On authentication to query a database, the authentication used to connect to the CMS is passed to the database (through a token, for example) and reused to authenticate to the database.

Single Sign-On doesn't work in workflows where no session to an SAP Business-Objects BI 4.x system is available:

▶ In scheduling: If the schedule is run when you're no longer connected, then the refresh can't happen because authentication information is no longer available.

► In publishing: If the report bursting option requires the recipient credentials to run the publication in its name, then the credentials for the recipient are also not available.

4.3.4 Using Credentials Mapping for Single Sign-On

For the different data sources that don't support Single Sign-On and for the scheduling workflow that requires the user to be connected, an option based on credentials mapping authentication can be used to achieve Single Sign-On. This option requires the following:

► The connection to the database is defined with credentials mapping authentication. Hence, this option works only for products that support this authentication mode.

► The CMS repository and the database share the same authentication information, which can be achieved in one of two ways:

  ► Through a replication process that synchronizes the users and passwords between the two systems, if the authentication mode to the CMS repository is Enterprise

  ► Through a common authentication system, which is the case if the CMS repository authenticates with Active Directory or LDAP

► In the CMC, in the tab that defines your SAP BusinessObjects BI 4.x system authentication mode (Enterprise, LDAP, or Windows Active Directory), you select the ENABLE AND UPDATE USER'S DATA SOURCE CREDENTIALS AT LOGON TIME checkbox.

After this option has been set, two things happen when a user logs on to the system using authentication mode where this option has been selected:

► The user's ENABLE DATABASE CREDENTIALS parameter is enabled.

► The user name and password the user has provided to log on are saved in the user's DATABASE CREDENTIALS ACCOUNT NAME and DATABASE CREDENTIALS PASSWORD parameters.

Then, the connection defined with credentials mapping authentication can reuse the user name and password that have been saved to authenticate to the database, which simulates Single Sign-On.

Even if the user logs off the SAP BusinessObjects BI 4.x system, the credentials remain saved in the database credentials settings. Thus, they can also be used for scheduling or publication workflows when the user is no longer logged on. However, if the user hasn't logged on to the system after the option was set, then the credentials haven't been saved yet and the scheduling or publication workflows fail.

4.4   Client and Server Deployment

To better understand how connections are managed in IDT, it's useful to have some insights about how the components that support connections work and how they are deployed.

4.4.1   Middleware and Drivers

When a database is released by a vendor, it comes with a set of middleware. This set of components is used by client applications to exchange data with this database. The middleware components have an interface defined in different technologies:

▶ Standard interfaces: JDBC, ODBC, OLE DB, XMLA, and so on

▶ Proprietary interfaces: Oracle OCI, SAP JCo, and so on

SAP can't redistribute the database middleware components and they aren't installed with SAP BusinessObjects BI 4.x installers. You must install them independently from the SAP BusinessObjects BI 4.x products, except for specific cases such as SAP NetWeaver BW or SAP HANA. The middleware must be installed on all machines running components, products, or tools that must access the databases. Middleware must be present on the client installation for desktop applications and on the server installation for server components. Depending on your database vendor, you may have one or several middleware sets per database, or database version.

32-bit versus 64-bit

Middleware comes usually in 32-bit or 64-bit versions. As SAP BusinessObjects BI 4.x client tools are available in 32-bit, you need to install 32-bit versions of the middleware to be used with client tools. SAP BusinessObjects BI 4.x servers are available in 64-bit, you need to install 64-bit versions of the middleware to be used with servers.

To contact the database through the middleware, SAP BusinessObjects BI 4.x has dedicated components (namely Connection Server, Federation Query Server, and OLAPClient) that are released with some drivers, usually one per middleware. The drivers manage the data exchanges with the database middleware. These drivers must be installed on all machines where you have installed the middleware. During SAP BusinessObjects BI 4.x installation, you may unselect the drivers to databases that you don't use.

4.4.2 Connection Server

Relational connections are managed by the Connection Server, except for the relational connections to SAP NetWeaver BW and SAS. The Connection Server is historically the component that supports the most data sources types. It also supports different deployment options to address requirements from all the client tools that use it. The Connection Server is available in different modes:

▸ **As a library embedded in other applications**
This mode is typically used for applications that directly embed the Connection Server library. Desktop applications first try to use the Connection Server in library mode before trying any available server mode. They can also be used by server components such as SAP BusinessObjects Web Intelligence servers that embed the Connection Server as a library.

▸ **As a service running on the server and answering requests from other clients and servers components**
This mode includes different flavors:

   ▸ ConnectionServer64, available on all platforms: In SAP BusinessObjects BI 4.x, server components are provided only in 64-bit. This version of the Connection Server is the one to use by default because it's dedicated to handling 64-bit middleware that most databases provide.

   ▸ ConnectionServer32, available only on Windows platforms: This version of the Connection Server is used for databases that use middleware only available in 32-bit. This is the case for Microsoft Access and Excel 2007, Ingres, and the OLAP connections managed by the Connection Server but used only by universes created with the Universe Design Tool.

   ▸ Adaptive Processing Server: This generic server hosts most SAP BusinessObjects BI 4.x services and is used to process users and internal requests. It especially hosts a version of the Connection Server that can support Java middleware, such as JDBC. Thanks to this server, it's possible to support the SAP BusinessObjects Web Intelligence HTTP deployments with Java middleware.

Both ConnectionServer32 and ConnectionServer64 can run on a server and to avoid ambiguity between 32-bit and 64-bit middleware, we recommend that you do not install SAP BusinessObjects BI 4.1 client tools on a 64-bit server running an SAP BusinessObjects BI 4.x server. In such cases, 32-bit requests may be improperly sent to 64-bit middleware, and vice versa.

If you need to use both 32-bit and 64-bit middleware, you should install a dedicated Windows server for only 32-bit drivers and middleware; other servers answer only requests to 64-bit middleware.

4.4.3 Download Connection Locally

With SAP BusinessObjects Web Intelligence Rich Client, you can work offline on documents retrieved from the CMS repository. When you connect to the CMS repository, SAP BusinessObjects Web Intelligence stores the report, the universe and the connection on caches in your machine. Of course, offline work isn't supported with multisource universes because it requires access to the Federation Query Server.

Since SAP BusinessObjects BI 4.0 Feature Pack 3 (FP3), to retrieve connection parameters of a relational connection based on the Connection Server, you need to explicitly grant to the users the DOWNLOAD CONNECTION LOCALLY right for the connection. If this right is denied, the connection-sensitive parameters are kept on the server and are never downloaded on the desktop, which results in the following consequences:

► In online mode, even if you are using any desktop applications (SAP BusinessObjects Web Intelligence Rich Client, IDT), queries to the database through this connection aren't processed by the local middleware but are always run on the server side by the Connection Server in server mode.

► In SAP BusinessObjects Web Intelligence offline mode, it's not possible to use this connection because its parameters haven't been saved in the cache. To use this connection in offline mode, you need to explicitly grant the download right. When the right is granted the connection can be saved in the cache and the desktop interface can use it and run queries with the local middleware.

▶ In IDT, the connection parameters can't be retrieved from the CMS repository and it's not possible to display and identify them. If you have this right granted for a connection, you can choose the queries to be run through local middleware or server side with middleware installed on the server. See Section 4.6.6 for more details.

This right isn't implemented for OLAP connections and relational connections to SAP NetWeaver and SAS based on the Federation Query Server for different reasons:

▶ You can't use offline mode for relational connections to SAP NetWeaver BW and SAS because it needs access to a Federation Query Server.

▶ You can always use offline mode with an OLAP connection through SAP direct access or universes created with IDT.

4.4.4 Relational Connections to SAP NetWeaver BW and SAS

In contrast to relational connections processed by the Connection Server, relational connections to SAP NetWeaver BW and SAS can only be created and used on the CMS server because they are based on the Federation Query Server. For this reason, it's also not possible to create a local universe based on a relational connection to SAP NetWeaver BW or SAS.

Multisource universes use the Federation Query Server for running their queries and hence can be created and used by SAP BusinessObjects BI tools only in a server mode environment.

The Federation Query Server relies on the same middleware and drivers as the Connection Server. Thus, to create a multisource universe, you must install server side the corresponding middleware and drivers (when they are supported for multisource universes, as listed in Table 4.1).

4.4.5 OLAP Connections

OLAP connection created by IDT can be created locally or on the server. They are processed by the OLAPClient that is available only as a library. This library is directly embedded in client or server components.

4.5   Connection Parameters

When defining a connection, you have to set different compulsory or optional parameters:

▸ The parameters requested by the corresponding middleware to access the data source

▸ Configuration and custom parameters for connections based on the Connection Server

These parameters are defined in the connection creation wizard.

There are other advanced parameters that modify the product behavior when connecting to a data source that don't appear in the connection wizard. Those parameters are set in configuration files, as described in Section 4.5.4.

4.5.1   Authentication and Data Source Parameters

Some parameters are mandatory for all connections that reference a relational or OLAP database. You always have to provide the following information, at minimum:

▸ An authentication mode and some credentials if the authentication mode is fixed credentials.

▸ Some parameters to identify the server, database, or instance to access. These parameters are quite similar, but they may be specific to vendors, especially if the vendor middleware you use doesn't follow the OLE DB, ODBC, or JDBC standards.

Table 4.5 lists these most common parameters, but it's not an exhaustive list.

Parameter	Description
AUTHENTICATION MODE	The authentication mode is one of three supported in IDT—FIXED CREDENTIALS, CREDENTIAL MAPPINGS, or SINGLE SIGN-ON—if it's supported (refer to Table 4.4).
USER NAME	If AUTHENTICATION MODE is FIXED CREDENTIALS, then a user account and password are used to connect to the
PASSWORD	system.

Table 4.5 Mandatory Parameters for Database Connections

Parameter	Description
SERVER	For most databases, this is the server that hosts the database to query. Depending on the databases, it can be one of the following: ▶ A server name ▶ A server name and a port (e.g., for Oracle Hyperion Essbase or SAP HANA) ▶ A URL to a library (e.g., for Microsoft SQL Server Analysis Services)
DATABASE	For most databases, this is the name of the database or database instance on the specified server.
DATA SOURCE NAME	For ODBC middleware, this is the system data source (DSN) defined in the machine ODBC manager.
ALIAS	For IBM DB2 databases, when using IBM DB2 Client middleware, the alias is used to identify a table or a view.
SERVICE	For Oracle databases, this parameter is used to define the service to access when using Oracle Client middleware.
LANGUAGE	For SAP NetWeaver BW, SAP HANA, Oracle Hyperion Essbase, or Microsoft SQL Server Analysis Services, the language is used to retrieve data and metadata (see Chapter 11, Section 11.5).
INSTANCE	For SAP HANA, the instance is used to define the port in the format 3xx15, where xx is the instance number.

Table 4.5 Mandatory Parameters for Database Connections (Cont.)

Connections to data sources that aren't plain relational or OLAP databases require parameters that are more specific to the data source nature. This is the case for the connections to text files, XML files, or Web Services. Refer to the SAP Business-Objects BI 4.1 Data Access Guide for more details on these connections.

4.5.2 Connection Server Configuration Parameters

In addition to the previous mandatory parameters to identify and to connect to the data source, it's possible to set configuration parameters that define how the Connection Server manages the session to the database it opens. These parameters, listed in Table 4.6, can be set when creating the connection or editing it.

Parameter	Description
CONNECTION POOL MODE	This defines whether the Connection Server can reuse a connection when it opens to a database. There are several possible options: ▶ DISCONNECT AFTER EACH TRANSACTION: To disconnect from the connection after the query has been run. ▶ KEEP THE CONNECTION ACTIVE FOR: To keep the connection open after the query has been run. The connection remains available in a pool and can be reused by any user that requests a similar connection. ▶ KEEP THE CONNECTION ACTIVE DURING THE WHOLE SESSION: To close the connection to the database only when the application terminates. This option is not recommended especially for server application since the connection may remain open forever.
POOL TIMEOUT	If the connection pool mode is KEEP THE CONNECTION ACTIVE FOR, then this is the number of minutes the connection remains open and can be reused before it's closed.
ARRAY FETCH SIZE	This is the number of rows of data retrieved per slice. When setting this parameter, you must find a balance between performance and memory. A high value reduces the number of call over the network, but has a large memory footprint.
ARRAY BIND SIZE	This is the number of rows that can be exported with each INSERT query for parameterized SQL. In practice, parameterized SQL isn't used in SAP BusinessObjects BI 4.x.
LOGIN TIMEOUT	This is the number of seconds the Connection Server waits for an answer from the database before canceling the request. This parameter is passed to the middleware that manages this timeout.
JDBC DRIVER PROPERTIES	This is used to pass JDBC-specific parameters that the middleware supports.

Table 4.6 Connection Server Configuration Parameters

4.5.3 Connection Server Custom Parameters

The Connection Server gives you the flexibility to enter custom parameters, which are passed to the database. The most common parameters are listed in Table 4.7.

Parameter	Description
CONNECTINIT	Supported by most relational connections, except for JDBC drivers. Each time a connection is created to access the database, the statement contained in this parameter is sent to the database. The following are typical use cases for this parameter: ▶ Query banding on Teradata ▶ Stored procedure call to initialize a context ▶ Language settings ▶ Choice of database options
HINT	Used for Oracle databases to pass some indication to its query optimizer to choose an execution plan.

Table 4.7 Connection Server Custom Parameters

4.5.4 Configuration Files

Customizing configuration files for the Connection Server or the OLAPClient to set advanced parameters is reserved for administrators only. Their description goes beyond the scope of this book; however, it's useful to know about these files and their usage:

▶ *cs.cfg*
This XML file, located in the *<Install directory>\dataAccess\connectionServer* folder, is used to modify global settings that impact the Connection Server behavior: logging, supported modes, and so on.

▶ *.prm*
These files, used by the Connection Server, are located in the folders *<Install directory>\dataAccess\connectionServer\<RDBMS>* where *<RDBMS>* is the network layer or middleware name. There is one *.prm* file for each database or driver. For example, the data access parameters file for Microsoft SQL Server is named *sqlsrv.prm*, and the data access parameters file for Oracle is named *oracle.prm*.

These files define the data source SQL capabilities and indirectly the client tools' capabilities through universes. These files are XML files containing the following sections:

▶ `<Configuration>`: Parameters used to describe capabilities of databases used as the source of data for universes, for example, `GROUP_BY`, `INTERSECT`, and `INNER_JOIN`. These parameters can be edited to optimize query execution on the target data source.

▶ `<DateOperations>`: Available date operators and how they are computed. For example: `YEAR`, `QUARTER`, `MONTH`.

▶ `<Operators>`: Available operators and how they are computed. For example: `ADD`, `SUBSTRACT`, `MULTIPLY`.

▶ `<Functions>`: Database functions visible in the Universe Design Tool and IDT editors. For example: `SUM`, `MINIMUM`, `COUNT`.

In case of conflicts, a setting defined in the data foundation or business layer overrides the one defined in the *.prm* file.

▶ *.sbo*
These files, used by the Connection Server, define the parameters supported by the data source. They are located in the *<Install directory>\dataAccess\ connectionServer\<RDBMS>* folders where *<RDBMS>* is the network layer or middleware name.

▶ *OlapClient.cfg*
This XML file, located in the *<Install directory>\win32_x86* folder, is used to modify global settings that impact the OLAPClient behavior, such as logging, and so on.

It can also be used for Microsoft SQL Server Analysis Services on Microsoft Windows platform to use OLEDBO driver instead of XMLA. To do so, in this file, search for the `SwitchToOdbo` parameter and set it to 1, for example:

```
[OlapClient]
SwitchToOdbo=1
```

4.6   Managing Connections

IDT allows you to manage both local and secured connections; to manage secured connections, you must have the IDT CREATE, MODIFY, OR DELETE CONNECTIONS right granted. As shown in Chapter 3, Section 3.2.3 and Section 3.4.2, you can also create, rename, or delete connections folders in LOCAL PROJECTS and PUBLISHED RESOURCES views.

Table 4.8 shows the icons displayed in IDT to represent connections and connection shortcuts.

Connection Type	Connection	Shortcut
Relational connection		
Relational connection to SAP NetWeaver BW or SAS		
OLAP connection		

Table 4.8 Connection Icons in Information Design Tool

4.6.1 Creating a Connection in a CMS Repository

To create a secured connection, you also need the ADD OBJECTS TO THE FOLDER right for the folder where you create the connection.

To create a secured connection in IDT, follow these steps:

1. In the REPOSITORY RESOURCES view, open a predefined session to the CMS, or, if it doesn't exist, create and open one (see Chapter 3, Section 3.4).

2. In the CONNECTIONS tree folder, select the folder where the connection must be created.

3. In the REPOSITORY RESOURCES toolbar:

   ▸ Select INSERT RELATIONAL CONNECTION to open the NEW RELATIONAL CONNECTION dialog box and create a relational connection.

   ▸ Select INSERT OLAP CONNECTION to open the NEW OLAP CONNECTION dialog box and create an OLAP connection.

4. In this dialog box, in the RESOURCE NAME text field, enter the name of the connection.

5. Click NEXT to display the DATABASE MIDDLEWARE DRIVER SELECTION page as shown in Figure 4.2. This page displays the list of databases, versions, and middleware supported by IDT and available on the server.

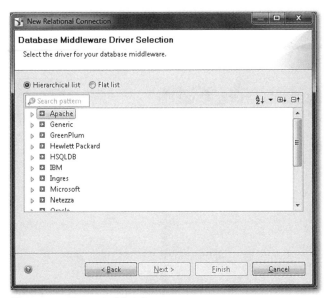

Figure 4.2 Supported Databases

6. In the DATABASE MIDDLEWARE DRIVER SELECTION panel, select the driver for the database to access among the ones supported by IDT. Use the HIERARCHICAL LIST or FLAT LIST radio buttons to display these drivers as a tree or as a list.

7. Click NEXT to open the screen that displays the list of mandatory parameters required to identify the data source and, if needed, to authenticate to it. These parameters depend on the connection (refer to Section 4.5.1).

8. Enter the different parameters. For example, if it requires authentication, in the AUTHENTICATION MODE dropdown list, select the following:

   ▶ USE SPECIFIED USER NAME AND PASSWORD for fixed credentials

   ▶ USE SINGLE SIGN-ON WHEN REFRESHING REPORTS AT VIEW TIME for Single Sign-On

   ▶ USE BUSINESS-OBJECTS CREDENTIALS MAPPING for credentials mapping

9. Click NEXT. Depending on the connection to create, you may have additional parameters to enter.

10. If you're creating a relational connection then you may enter the Connection Server configuration parameters and the custom parameters, as shown in Figure 4.3 and Figure 4.4.

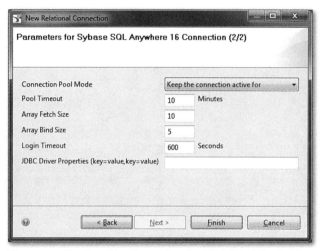

Figure 4.3 Configuration Parameters for a Relational Connection

Figure 4.4 Custom Parameters for a Relational Connection

11. If you're creating an OLAP connection, in the CUBE SELECTION page, select the DO NOT SPECIFY A CUBE IN THE CONNECTION radio button if you want the connection to refer to the database server. Otherwise, select the SPECIFY A CUBE IN THE CONNECTION radio button, and, in the tree list, navigate in the server content to select the cube the connection must refer, as shown in Figure 4.5.

12. Click FINISH to close the connection wizard and create the connection in the selected folder. The connection is displayed in the REPOSITORY RESOURCES view, and the editor for the newly created connection opens in the right pane.

Figure 4.5 Cube Selection Page for the OLAP Connection

4.6.2 Creating a Local Connection

To create a local connection, follow these steps:

1. Open the LOCAL PROJECTS view.

2. Select the project and the folder where the connection must be created.

3. Right-click the project or the folder where the connection must be created and in the context menu, do one of the following:

   ▶ Click NEW • RELATIONAL CONNECTION to open the NEW RELATIONAL CONNECTION wizard and create a relational connection.

   ▶ Click NEW • OLAP CONNECTION to open the NEW OLAP CONNECTION wizard and create an OLAP connection.

4. The wizard that opens is similar to the one used to create the similar connection in the CMS repository (refer to Section 4.6.1). Follow the same workflow to enter the connection parameters.

The list of proposed drivers (and thus the databases and versions you can access) are the ones installed on the local system. If a session to a CMS repository has been opened, the list of drivers installed on the server is also proposed in addition to the list of local drivers.

5. Click FINISH to close the connection wizard and create the connection in the selected project or folder. The connection is displayed in the local project, and the editor for the newly created connection opens in the right pane.

> **Warning**
>
> The relational connections to SAP NetWeaver BW and SAS can only be created on the server side. Thus, they aren't proposed when you create a local connection.

4.6.3 Publishing a Connection

You can also create a secured connection by creating it locally and then publishing it in a CMS repository. The published connection is created with the same parameters as the local one. To do so, follow these steps:

1. In the LOCAL PROJECTS view, select and right-click a local connection.

2. In the context menu, select the PUBLISH CONNECTION TO A REPOSITORY command.

3. In the PUBLISH CONNECTION dialog box, select a predefined session or open a new one, as described in Chapter 3, Section 3.4.

4. Click NEXT.

5. In the CONNECTIONS tree folder, select a folder. You must have the ADD OBJECTS TO THE FOLDER right granted for this folder.

6. Click FINISH to publish the connection in the selected folder.

7. When you're asked whether to create a shortcut, click YES to create it in the local connection's folder or No to not create it.

You can also publish a local connection by dragging and dropping from the LOCAL PROJECTS view to the destination folder in the REPOSITORY RESOURCES view.

4.6.4 Creating a Connection Shortcut

At the end of the connection publication, IDT asks you to create a connection shortcut to this connection. You can also explicitly create it by following these steps:

1. In the REPOSITORY RESOURCES view, open a session to a CMS repository.

2. Right-click a secured connection and select CREATE CONNECTION SHORTCUT.

3. In the SELECT A LOCAL PROJECT dialog box, select a local project. You can also select a folder in this project.

4. Click OK to create the connection shortcut that appears in the LOCAL PROJECTS view. Double-click this shortcut to open the tab with these connection shortcut parameters, as shown in Figure 4.6.

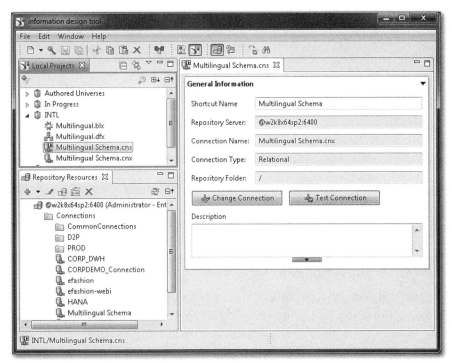

Figure 4.6 Connection Shortcut Editor

You can use this connection shortcut to create a data foundation or a business layer based on the secured connection it references.

4.6.5 Editing a Connection

Editing a local or secured connection is done identically through the same wizard used to create the connection (refer to Section 4.6.1). For a secured connection, you must have the following rights granted:

▶ IDT CREATE, MODIFY, OR DELETE CONNECTIONS.

▶ The connection EDIT OBJECTS.

▶ If the connection is relational, then the connection DOWNLOAD CONNECTION
LOCALLY. If this right is denied, then the following are true:

    ▶ Only a limited set of parameters that are considered as not sensitive (AUTHEN-
TICATION MODE, DRIVER, DATABASE) are displayed in the CONNECTION tab;
the other parameters (USER NAME, PASSWORD, etc.) remain on the server.

    ▶ You can't edit this connection.

To launch the wizard to edit a local or secured connection, follow these steps:

1. In the PUBLISHED RESOURCES or LOCAL PROJECTS views, double-click the connection to open this CONNECTION tab in the right pane.

2. In this tab that lists the connection parameters, click EDIT to open the connection wizard.

3. Go through the wizard and modify the connection parameters. This wizard is
the same wizard used to create the connection.

4. Click FINISH to close the connection wizard. The modified parameters are updated
in the CONNECTION tab.

5. In the toolbar, click SAVE to save your changes.

4.6.6 Switching Server/Client Middleware

In IDT, if the right DOWNLOAD CONNECTION LOCALLY of a relational secured connection is granted to you, you can use either the local or server middleware to access
the data source. To set this global option in IDT, follow these steps:

1. In the menu bar, select the WINDOW • PREFERENCES command.

2. In the PREFERENCES dialog box, select the INFORMATION DESIGN TOOL • SECURED
CONNECTIONS section, as shown in Figure 4.7.

3. Click the LOCAL MIDDLEWARE radio button to select the middleware installed on
the client side or the SERVER MIDDLEWARE radio button to select the middleware
installed on the server side.

4. Click OK to close the PREFERENCES dialog box and save your changes.

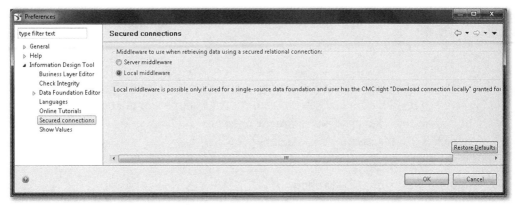

Figure 4.7 Secured Connections Preferences

4.6.7 Testing a Connection

You may find it useful to test a connection when you create it or after it has been created in order to check that its parameters are valid. You can test a connection via two paths:

▶ In the connection editor or in the connection wizard, click TEST CONNECTION.

▶ In the LOCAL PROJECTS view, right-click a connection, and select TEST CONNECTION.

This test uses the parameters that define the connection to connect to the data source (for example, it uses ConnectInit parameter, if it has been defined) and check whether it's available:

▶ For a database, a session using the authentication mode and the credentials is tentatively opened and IDT checks that the middleware answers.

▶ For a specific data source text file test, the test checks that the data source is properly available.

If the test fails, use the details of the error message to troubleshoot the root cause of the error. This test can be used to identify the most common errors, which are middleware configuration issues and invalid credentials.

4.7   Data Preview

After you've created a connection to a data source, IDT allows you to navigate in the data sources, display the data, and even analyze the data it contains. Although they are quite similar on the principles, these capabilities are slightly different between relational and OLAP connections. For example, for relational connections, the same DATA PREVIEW panel already presented in Chapter 2, Section 2.6 is used, which is not the case for OLAP connections.

4.7.1   Relational Database

In IDT, the connection editor allows you to navigate in the database to get samples of the data it contains and even to type some SQL scripts and send them directly to the database. For relational connections stored in the CMS repository, this capability is available only if you have the DATA ACCESS right.

In the relational connection editor, select the SHOW VALUES tab, which has the following three sections:

▶ The CATALOG browser allows you to navigate in the databases, tables, and columns.

▶ The SQL editor in the SHOW VALUES panel enables you to edit an SQL script to send to the database. You can hide or unhide this editor by clicking SHOW EXPRESSION.

▶ The DATA PREVIEW panel is displayed in the SHOW VALUES pane.

The SHOW VALUES and DATA PREVIEW panels aren't displayed if the DATA ACCESS right is denied.

In the SHOW VALUES panel, you can do the following:

▶ Navigate in the database using the CATALOG browser. You can double-click the name of a table or different columns of the same table. The SQL to query the selected table or columns is then automatically added into the SQL editor where you can edit it.

▶ Directly type an SQL script in this SQL editor.

▶ Right-click a table or a column and select SHOW VALUES to view the content of a table or a column.

▶ Right-click a column and select SHOW DISTINCT VALUES to view the distinct values of a column.

When the SQL script is ready, click the REFRESH button to send it to the database. The result set returned by the database is then displayed under the SQL editor, in a DATA PREVIEW panel, as shown in Figure 4.8.

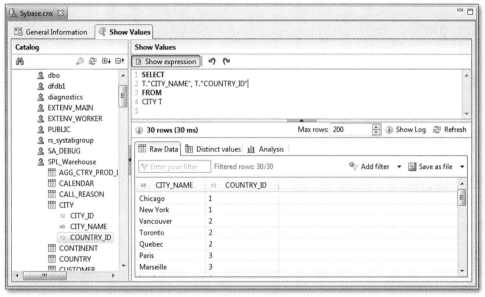

Figure 4.8 Show Values Tab for a Relational Connection

This functionality is useful to quickly analyze data by sending the query directly to the database. For this reason, you must carefully choose the database accounts dedicated to SAP BusinessObjects BI 4.x. To avoid user making changes in the database use only accounts that have read-only privileges on the database. Additionally, check that the security defined at the database level allows these accounts to see only the data they are allowed to see.

You can also view the properties of a table or an SQL view. Right-click a table and select VIEW PROPERTIES to display the PROPERTIES dialog box, as shown in Figure 4.9.

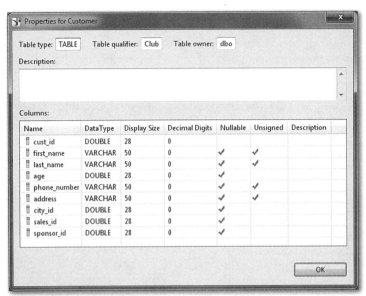

Figure 4.9 View Table Properties

Some equivalent capability is also available for OLAP connections, as described in the next section.

4.7.2 OLAP Connections

For an OLAP connection, you also have some data preview capabilities, although they are less evolved than for relational connections. In addition to the GENERAL INFORMATION tab, the OLAP connection editor contains the BROWSE METADATA tab, and for connections that support MDX, the QUERY tab. The preview capability isn't available to OLAP connections to an SAP NetWeaver BW system because they don't use MDX. For these connections, the BROWSE METADATA tab isn't displayed.

In the BROWSE METADATA tab, you can navigate in the server in the OLAP METADATA browser (see Figure 4.10). After you select a metadata in this browser, properties are displayed in the PROPERTIES FOR panel.

You can also right-click a hierarchy in the browser and select SHOW MEMBERS to display the members in a hierarchical tree (see Figure 4.11). The properties of the selected member are displayed on the right side of the hierarchy browser.

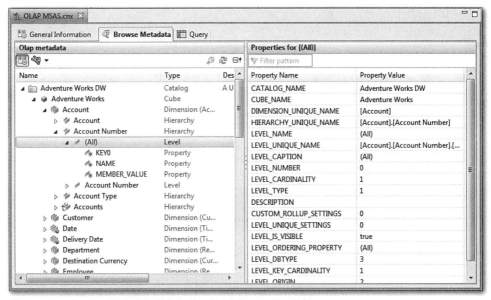

Figure 4.10 Browse Metadata Tab in the OLAP Connection Editor

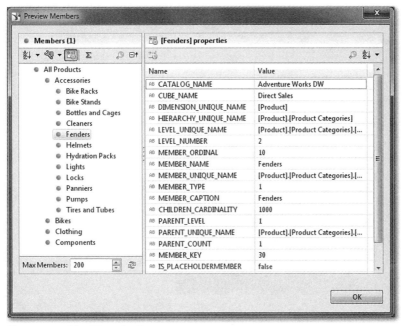

Figure 4.11 The Hierarchy Browser

As in the relational connection's SHOW VALUES tab, the OLAP connection QUERY tab is made of three sections:

▶ The OLAP METADATA browser allows you to navigate in the database server, its cubes, and its metadata.

▶ The MDX QUERY pane enables you to edit an MDX script to send to the database.

▶ The result pane displayed under the MDX QUERY pane.

In this QUERY tab, you can do the following:

▶ Directly type an MDX command in the MDX editor.

▶ Navigate in the database using the OLAP METADATA browser. If you double-click an object, its name is automatically added to the MDX editor. As opposed to the relational connection, the full MDX statement to query this object isn't generated, but you can enter it.

After you click the RUN button, the query is sent to the database using the connection parameters. The result set is then displayed under the MDX QUERY pane shown in Figure 4.12.

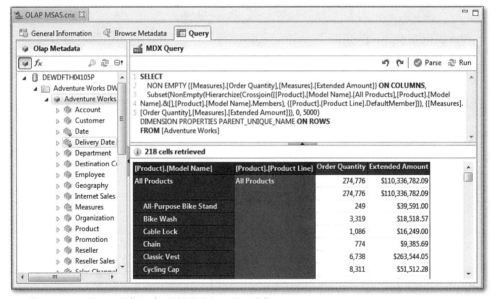

Figure 4.12 Query Tab in the OLAP Connection Editor

4.8 Summary

Information Design Tool can connect to a wide variety of data sources: classical database (relational or OLAP) or other specific data sources (text file, web service, etc.). In SAP BusinessObjects BI 4.x, a connection contains the parameters used to connect to the data source to query through client tools. Because of this variety of data sources, different types of connections exist:

- ▶ The relational connections, based on the Connection Server
- ▶ The relational connections to SAP NetWeaver BW and SAS, based on the Federation Query Server
- ▶ The OLAP connections, based on OLAPClient

Connections can be created and saved locally in an IDT project or securely in the CMS repository, where they benefit from the BI platform framework. In the local project, such secured connections can be referenced through a connection shortcut. Connections based on the Connection Server and OLAPClient can be saved locally or in the CMS repository, whereas the relational connections based on the Federation Query Server can only be saved in the CMS repository.

In IDT, connections support three authentication modes: fixed credentials, credentials mapping, and, in some cases, Single Sign-on.

In addition to connections management, IDT also provides the capabilities to preview data in the data source before creating the other universe resources like data foundations and business layers.

The data foundation is the part of the Information Design Tool interface dedicated to the modeling of relational databases and is one of the components of a universe.

5 The Data Foundation

The data foundation is the first step in a relational universe building and is common to single-source and multisource universes. The data foundation is built on top of one or multiple relational connections and focuses on the entity-relationship modeling on top of relational databases dedicated to business intelligence (BI) purposes. This chapter gives guidelines, hints, and tips to write custom SQL and solve modeling issues such as loops, chasm traps, and fan traps.

The data foundation is the interface between the relational database and the business layer. The data foundation modeling requires strong relational database skills, data modeling, and SQL language skills.

The data foundation is the term for the data modeling part of the universe. The data foundation modeling is an entity-relationship model approach and doesn't favor one modeling method in particular. The main objective of the data foundation is to build a data model, including tables, views, and joins, that meets BI requirements.

A data foundation can't be directly consumed by end users because the technical information of the database isn't removed or polished, so a data foundation needs one or more business layers (see Chapter 7) exposing the database concepts (a data foundation can be consumed by multiple business layers).

Don't forget that the objective of a universe and therefore a data foundation is to be used by clients such as SAP BusinessObjects Web Intelligence, SAP Crystal Reports for Enterprise, or SAP BusinessObjects Dashboards.

So for a good data foundation design, keep in mind and apply the following guidelines:

- Insert in the data foundation only the tables that need to be added.

- Create only the joins (see Section 5.3) that are relevant for the business needs.

- Create parameters (see Section 5.9) and lists of values (see Section 5.8) if needed. Parameters and lists of values created in the data foundation are inherited in the business layer.

- If you need to introduce calculations, you should create as many derived tables (see Section 5.4) and calculated columns (see Section 5.5) as possible in the data foundation rather than adding the calculations in the business layer. Definitions in the data foundation are reusable in all business layers attached to it, which reduces the total cost of ownership and doesn't necessarily require SQL skills for the business layer designer.

- Set the join cardinalities (see Section 5.3) as much as possible. Join cardinalities are used in many scenarios by the query engine that generates SQL queries.

A universe is created by one or more persons who have database skills and business skills. So prior to creating the data foundation, you must understand the business requirements, meet the end users, and ask them questions such as the following:

- What type of information do you need to do your job?

- How do you know you're doing well?

- How does your boss know you're performing well?

- What kind of information do others ask you for?

Additional questions can be added to capture unique ad hoc requirements. For example:

- When people ask you for specific information they can't get out of a report, what types of things do they ask for?

- How do you currently do your job?

- Where is data stored, if you know?

As users answer these questions, you should record their answers in folders and objects requirements. Candidate objects (such as dimensions, attributes, or measures) can also be identified by reviewing existing BI documents.

These questions are useful to determine which tables and joins are added in the data foundation and to ascertain the structure of the business layer.

In general, a universe covers a functional domain such as finance, marketing, sales, and so on. The data needed to cover the functional domain can be stored in one database or multiple databases. In the case of the latter, a data foundation can be multisource, which means the data modeling can be created on top of multiple relational sources.

A multisource data foundation (see Chapter 6) can mix tables coming from different databases from the same Relational Database Management System (RDBMS) vendor or coming from different vendors such as SAP HANA, Oracle, Microsoft SQL Server, and so on.

5.1 Creating a Data Foundation

To create a data foundation, you need to first create a relational connection (see Chapter 4) pointing to the RDBMS where the tables are stored.

To create a data foundation, you can also select an existing relational connection in the local project; the connection can be a local connection (*.cnx*) or a shortcut to a published connection (*.cns*).

If the tables needed to build the data foundation are located on multiple databases, the data foundation must be a multisource data foundation.

Important

It's important to know at the beginning of the universe creation whether the data foundation is single-source or multisource. You cannot change the data foundation type during the universe building process or in maintenance phase.

If you need to change the data foundation type during the universe building process, you have to recreate a new data foundation and update the business layer(s) resources to take into account the data foundation change, and this process can be very costly.

The local project (see Chapter 3, Section 3.1) is where you can create data foundations. To create a data foundation, follow these steps:

1. Choose one of the following options:

    ▶ Select the menu option FILE • NEW • DATA FOUNDATION.

    ▶ Select a project or a folder, right-click, and select NEW • DATA FOUNDATION.

    ▶ Select a relational connection, right-click, and select NEW • DATA FOUNDATION.

2. In the wizard that opens, give a name to the data foundation.

3. Select the data foundation type as shown in Figure 5.1, and remember this choice can't be changed after the data foundation is created. Multisource data foundations are discussed in Chapter 6.

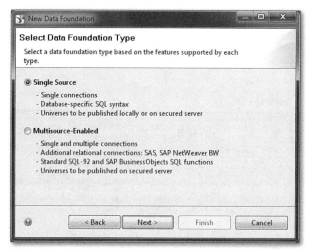

Figure 5.1 Data Foundation Creation Wizard: Selecting the Data Foundation Type

4. If you select SINGLE SOURCE, then you need to select the relational connection to be used by the universe, as shown in Figure 5.2.

    Only relational connections can be selected, and you can select either a local connection (file name suffixed by *.cnx*) or a secured connection (file name suffixed by *.cns*) that has been published in the Central Management Server (CMS) repository (see Chapter 9, Section 9.2).

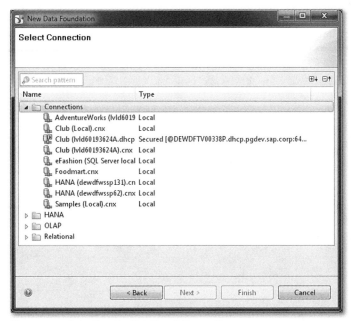

Figure 5.2 Selecting the Relational Connection

5. Click FINISH to end the wizard and create an empty data foundation.

The data foundation is saved in the file system where the local project has been created; the data foundation file, suffixed by *.dfx*, can be stored under a folder in the local project.

> **Important**
>
> To consume a published universe in the CMS repository, the relational connection must be published first, and a shortcut to the secured connection must be added in the local project. Then the data foundation must reference the secured connection so the business layer can be published.

The data foundation editor in Information Design Tool (IDT) is made of two parts: the data foundation RESOURCES pane and the data foundation modeling tool.

The data foundation RESOURCES pane is split into four parts:

▶ The CONNECTION pane where you can associate a connection to the data foundation and browse the database content

▶ The DATA FOUNDATION pane where you can view and maintain tables and joins

▶ The ALIASES AND CONTEXTS pane where you create and maintain alias tables and contexts

▶ The PARAMETERS AND LIST OF VALUES pane where you create and maintain parameters and lists of values

The data foundation modeling tool is a graphical tool where you, as a universe designer, can design the entity-relationship model as shown in Figure 5.3. This is the main part of the data foundation where you spend most of your time.

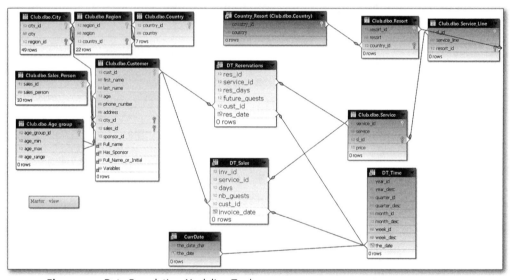

Figure 5.3 Data Foundation Modeling Tool

5.2 Identifying Tables, Columns, and Keys

After the data foundation has been created on a valid connection, the first step is to add tables to it. If the list of tables is already known, this process can be easy; however, in some circumstances, you need to browse the database catalog to identify tables and columns and view table content.

5.2.1 Database Catalog Browser

To browse the database catalog, select the CONNECTION pane and unfold the connection to see the list of schemas. Select a schema and unfold it to see the list of tables, and then select a table to see the list of columns, as shown in Figure 5.4.

Figure 5.4 Database Catalog Browser in the Data Foundation

The database catalog only displays the schemas and tables that the user authenticated in the connection is allowed to access. All tables and views already added in the data foundation have a green check mark on their icons, as shown in Figure 5.4. Tables, views, and SAP HANA views are represented with different icons, as described in Table 5.1.

Icon	Database Type
	Table
	SQL view
	SAP HANA analytic view
	SAP HANA calculation view
	SAP HANA attribute view
	SAP HANA hierarchy view
	SAP HANA table type

Table 5.1 Tables, Views, and SAP HANA Views with Associated Icons

The stored procedures aren't listed in the database catalog or supported by relational universes. Each column data type is identified by a specific icon, as described in Table 5.2.

Icon	Column Data Type
12	Numeric, decimal, money, float, integer
	Date
	Time, datetime, timestamp
AB	String, text, alphanumeric
010 101	Blob, binary, image, raw
?	Unknown

Table 5.2 List of the Column Datatypes and Associated Icons

Note
SAP HANA views are detailed in Chapter 12, Section 12.3.

5.2.2 View Table Data and Information

After you've selected a table in the database catalog browser, you can view the table information, as shown in Figure 5.5, by right-clicking on the table and selecting the option VIEW PROPERTIES.

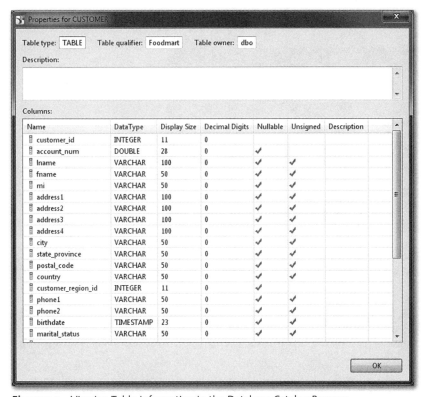

Figure 5.5 Viewing Table Information in the Database Catalog Browser

You can also obtain more information concerning the table by viewing the table content. There are two different ways to view the content of the table:

▶ Select the table, right-click, and select the option SHOW TABLE VALUES. An SQL query is generated, and the table content is displayed.

▶ Select one or more columns of the table, right-click, and select the option SHOW COLUMN VALUES. An SQL query is generated, and the column(s) content is displayed.

The result of the data preview is displayed in an editor tab, a dedicated view, or a dialog box depending on the settings defined in IDT preferences, as shown in Figure 5.6.

To set the preferences for data preview, select WINDOW • PREFERENCES; when the PREFERENCES dialog box opens, select INFORMATION DESIGN TOOL • SHOW VALUES, as shown in Figure 5.6.

Figure 5.6 Data Preview and Query Results Preferences

Note

For more information concerning the results of data view and list of values preview, see Chapter 2, Section 2.6.

5.2.3 Insert Tables in the Data Foundation

After you've identified the tables, you have to insert them in the data foundation by selecting one of the following options:

▸ Drag and drop one or multiple tables from the database catalog browser in the data foundation editor.

▸ Double-click anywhere in the data foundation schema to open the catalog browser.

▸ Select ACTIONS • INSERT • TABLES.

▸ Right-click anywhere in the data foundation schema and select INSERT • TABLES.

▶ Click the INSERT button in the toolbar above the data foundation schema and select the INSERT TABLES option.

If you've selected the second or third option in this list, a dialog box opens showing the database catalog browser. This database catalog browser offers the same capabilities that the database catalog browser does, as described in Section 5.2.1.

To insert tables, check the checkbox on the left side of the table name, as shown in Figure 5.7.

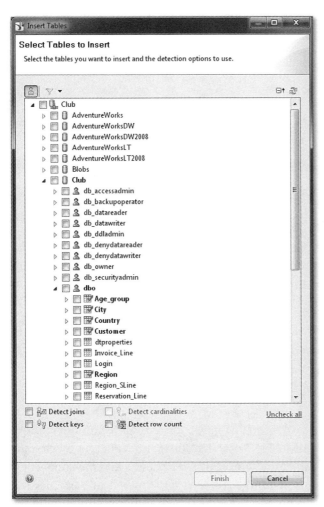

Figure 5.7 Inserting Tables in the Data Foundation

> **Caution**
>
> You can also select the entire schema. We don't recommend this because all tables belonging to this schema are checked and can be inserted. This could take a long time and generate some unwanted table aliases.

If you try to insert a table that already exists in the data foundation, IDT proposes to create an alias table (see Section 5.6.2) with a different name.

The alias table is identical to the table itself but is in fact a table duplicate in the data foundation that can be used for different purposes:

- Different meaning
- Different usage
- Different joins

5.2.4 Search and Filter

This section describes the helpers that you can use to easily find information in a data foundation. Those features are very helpful in large data foundations.

Filter Objects

You can filter the table types listed in the database catalog browser. By default, all table types are listed, and you can choose to only see the tables, views, or certain SAP HANA view types (see Chapter 12, Section 12.3).

To select one or multiple table types, click the arrow in the filter icon ( ) in the toolbar above the database catalog browser, and select the table type(s) to filter the database catalog. The appropriate object editor opens when an object in the filter list is selected.

Search in Table Names

A database catalog can be very large, so you may encounter difficulties to identify the right schema and the right tables. To search for tables, click the toggle button ( ). The filter pane is added in the CONNECTION pane below the connection content, as shown in Figure 5.8. Enter the search criteria in the text box. Click the toggle button ( ) to automatically activate wildcard characters such as "*" and "?" to search in the table names:

► "*" is used as any character whatever the value length

► "?" is used as a joker for one character

Then click the toggle button (🔍) in the filter pane to search, as shown in Figure 5.8.

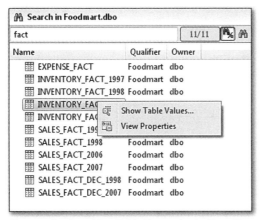

Figure 5.8 Searching Table Names in the Data Foundation

As in the database catalog browser, it's possible to view the table properties, view the table content, and also insert the tables in the data foundation with a drag-and-drop action.

5.3   Identifying Joins, Keys, and Cardinalities

After the tables and views have been added in the data foundation, you need to create the joins between the different tables, optionally define their cardinalities, and identify the keys. One of the quick ways to identify joins is to identify keys, and then use the primary keys and foreign keys that have been created by the database administrator (DBA).

5.3.1   Joins and Cardinalities

A join captures how tables are related to one another. Joins can be expressed as verbs between tables—for example, a customer "lives" in a city, an order "has" order details, a product is "built" in a country, and so on.

The join between two tables defines the role played by those two tables. A table can be joined to zero or multiple tables and a table can have multiple joins with another table, as shown in Figure 5.9. Multiple joins between two tables can be expressed in a complex SQL expression to only have one join. A join can also be defined between columns from the same table, for example, employee → manager.

A join is defined with the database SQL expressions and can also use built-in functions such as `@prompt` or `@variable`. For more information on built-in functions, see Section 5.11.

To create a join in the data foundation schema, select one of the following options:

▶ Draw a line with the mouse between two columns to join (in the same table or between different tables).

▶ Select ACTIONS • INSERT • JOIN.

▶ Click the INSERT button in the toolbar above the data foundation schema, and select INSERT JOIN.

Note
Multiple joins between the same two tables always generate an AND operator in the SQL WHERE clause.
To facilitate the maintenance of the data foundation, it's preferable to have multiple joins between two tables rather than a complex one using the AND SQL operator.

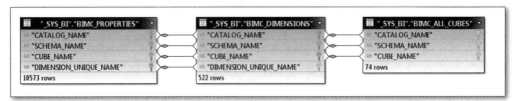

Figure 5.9 Data Foundation with Multiple Joins between Two Tables

You can set the formalism of a graphical join in IDT preferences. Select WINDOW • PREFERENCES. When the PREFERENCES dialog box opens, select INFORMATION DESIGN TOOL • DATA FOUNDATION EDITOR • APPEARANCE, as shown in Figure 5.10, and then select the JOIN LINES option.

The cardinalities are a property of the joins and explain how each table links to another.

Figure 5.10   Data Foundation Preferences Appearance

Table 5.3 describes the different cardinalities.

Cardinalities	Join Definition	Example
1 → 1	One-to-one relationship	person → age
1 → n	One-to-many relationship	country → city
n → n	Many-to-many relationship	product → shop

Table 5.3   Possible Cardinalities Used in Joins

The cardinalities are used in the following ways:

▶ By the query engine for query optimization

▶ For aggregate tables used with the aggregate awareness (see Chapter 7, Section 7.18) functionality defined in the business layer

▶ For solving loops (see Section 5.6) in the data foundation

> **Note**
>
> Defining the cardinalities in the data foundation is an optional task, but we recommend it.

5.3.2 Join Editor

To edit a join, select a join in the data foundation schema or in the DATA FOUNDA-TION pane, as shown in Figure 5.11.

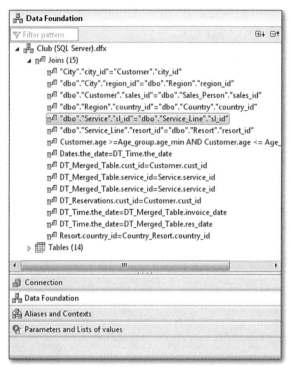

Figure 5.11 Joins List in the Data Foundation Pane

Then double-click on the join or right-click the join, and select the option EDIT JOIN. The EDIT JOIN dialog box opens, as shown in Figure 5.12.

The SQL EXPRESSION (❺) is updated according to the changes that you can do in the join editor: join operator, table columns selection, cardinalities, join type, and outer join option.

Figure 5.12 Join Editor

Join Operator

The join operator (❶ in Figure 5.12) can take the following values:

- =
- !=
- <=
- <
- >=
- >

The join operator can also take the value COMPLEX, which is set automatically when the SQL expression (❺) isn't a simple expression such as "table A"."column A" operator "table B"."column B".

Join Tables Columns

You can select a table column from one of the tables participating to the join (❷). A join can also be defined between columns from the same table—for example, employee → manager.

Join Type

You can change the join type (❸) by setting it as a shortcut join (see Section 5.6.5) and/or defining the join as an outer join (see Section 5.3.3).

SQL Editor and Validate

You can invoke the SQL editor (❹) to create the join SQL expression. (For more information on the SQL editor, see Section 5.10.) Like any resource containing an SQL expression, it's important to validate it by clicking the VALIDATE button (❹).

SQL Text Editor

The SQL text editor (❺) is where you can enter SQL or where the SQL is updated after changes in the join options. You create join SQL expressions in the text editor or use the SQL editor. A join expression can be a simple expression such as the following:

```
"table_1.column_1" = "table_2.column_2"
```

Or a complex expression:

```
"table_1.column_1" = "table_2.column_2" and "table_2.column_3" <
'value' and "table_1.column_4" in (Select distinct "column_4" from
"table_3")
```

Cardinalities

You can change the join cardinalities (❻) and choose the most appropriate cardinalities for the join from the list. A description explains how the table links to another and helps you understand how the cardinalities and outer joins are translated.

5.3.3   Join Types

Different types of joins can be used in the data foundation. The type of join always answers to a particular business need. The join cardinalities define the type of relationship between two tables and impact the SQL query generation. There are four types of joins:

▸ Inner joins

▸ Outer joins

▸ Shortcut joins

▸ Filter joins

Inner Joins

The inner joins are direct joins between two tables having one-to-one, one-to-many, or many-to-many cardinalities. In SQL, an inner join between two tables returns only rows where both tables meet the join criteria. If one of the tables has no corresponding row in the second table, its data isn't returned.

The SQL WHERE clause (ANSI SQL-92) is generated like this:

```
From "Table 1" INNER JOIN "Table 2" ON ("Table 1"."Column 1" = "Table
2"."Column 2")
```

Example
The table Country has a one-to-many relationship with the table City. The query result is:

```
USA, New York
USA, San Francisco
France, Paris
France, Marseille
```

Table 5.4 gives some examples of inner joins.

Relationship	Example	Result
1 to 1	person → age	Smith, 18
		Andrew, 25
		Brown, 42

Table 5.4   Examples of Inner Joins between Tables

Relationship	Example	Result
1 to many	country → city	USA, New York USA, San Francisco France, Paris France, Marseille
Many to many	product → shop	Perfume, Walmart Perfume, Harrods Beer, Walmart Beer, Harrods

Table 5.4 Examples of Inner Joins between Tables (Cont.)

Outer Joins

The outer joins are direct equivalents to inner joins except that at least one of the cardinalities is optional. An outer join tells the database processing the SQL query to substitute a "null" row if one of the joined tables has no corresponding row in the other table. With an outer join, information in one table that doesn't have corresponding data in the second table is returned with "blanks" in columns from the second table.

Table 5.5 describes the types of outer joins.

Outer Join Type	Example	SQL Query (ANSI SQL-92)
Left outer join	employee → department	FROM employee LEFT OUTER JOIN department ON (employee.department _id = customer.department_id
Right outer join	department → employee	FROM employee RIGHT OUTER JOIN department ON (employee.department _id = customer.department_id
Full outer join	employee → department	FROM employee FULL OUTER JOIN department ON (employee.department _id = customer.department_id

Table 5.5 Types of Outer Joins

Left Outer Join

The result of a left outer join for table X and table Y always contains all records of the left table (X), even if the WHERE condition doesn't find any record in the right table (Y). This means that if no record is found in table Y, a NULL value is returned.

Right Outer Join

The result of a right outer join for table X and table Y always contains all records of the right table (Y), even if the WHERE condition doesn't find any record in the left table (X). This means that if no record is found in table X, a NULL value is returned.

Full Outer Join

The result of a full outer join for table X and table Y is a combination of a left outer join and a right outer join. This means that if no record is found in table X or table Y, then a NULL value is returned.

> **Note**
>
> All databases support left outer joins and right outer joins, but not all of them support full outer joins.

Table 5.6 gives examples of outer joins.

Relationship	Example	Result
Left outer join	employee → department	Smith, Finance Andrew, Marketing Brown, NULL
Right outer join	department → employee	Smith, Finance Andrew, Marketing NULL, Sales
Full outer join	employee → department	Smith, Finance Andrew, Marketing Brown, NULL NULL, Sales

Table 5.6 Examples of Outer Joins between Tables

Filter Joins

The filter join is based on a single table column and is used to filter the table content. As for other join types, the SQL expression can be simple or complex and can use built-in functions.

> **Example**
>
> Here are some examples of filter joins:
> ```
> "country"."country" = 'USA'
> "country"."country" = @prompt('Select a country','A',,mono,free)
> "country"."country" in (Select "country" from "sales"."country")
> ```

To create a filter join, select a table column in the data foundation schema, right-click, and select the option INSERT FILTER. The join editor opens as shown earlier in Figure 5.12.

To delete a filter join, select a table column containing a filter in the data foundation schema, right-click, and then select DELETE FILTER.

> **Note**
>
> Because the join editor is common to all join types, you can transform a filter join in a join between two tables or transform a join between two tables into a filter join when writing the SQL expression.

Shortcut Joins

To set a join as a shortcut join, check the box SHORTCUT JOIN (refer to ❸ in Figure 5.12). A shortcut join is one of the solutions you can use to solve loops in the data foundation. They are described in Section 5.6.5.

5.3.4 Detect Joins, Keys, and Cardinalities

By default, the tables are inserted in the data foundation *without* joins and keys unless you've checked the options DETECT JOINS and DETECT KEYS, as shown earlier in Figure 5.7.

These can automatically be detected if the DETECT JOINS, DETECT KEYS, and DETECT CARDINALITIES options have been checked in the database catalog browser or in the IDT preferences.

To set the preferences for detections, select WINDOW • PREFERENCES. When the PREFERENCES dialog box opens, select INFORMATION DESIGN TOOL • DATA FOUNDATION EDITOR • DETECTIONS, as shown in Figure 5.13.

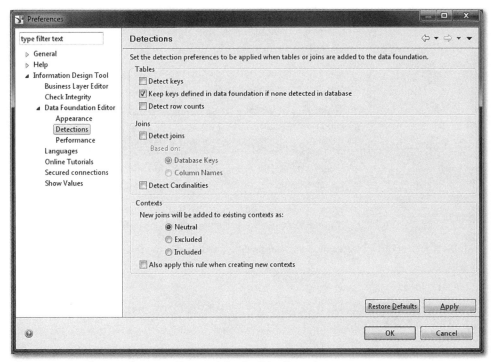

Figure 5.13 Preferences for Joins, Keys, and Cardinalities Detection

Table 5.7 describes the different ways to detect joins, cardinalities, and keys.

Detection Type	Action
Joins	Select the menu option FILE • DETECT • JOINS. If one or multiple tables are selected, the detection applies to the selected tables; otherwise, the detection applies to the entire data foundation.
	Select one or multiple tables, right-click, and then select DETECT • JOINS.
	Click the DETECT button in the toolbar above the data foundation schema and select DETECT JOINS.

Table 5.7 Options for Detecting Joins, Cardinalities, and Keys in the Data Foundation

Detection Type	Action
Keys	Select the menu option FILE • DETECT • KEYS. If one or multiple tables are selected, the detection applies to the selected tables; otherwise, the detection applies to the entire data foundation.
	Select one or multiple tables, right-click, and then select DETECT • KEYS.
	Click the DETECT button in the toolbar above the data foundation schema and select DETECT KEYS.
Cardinalities	Select FILE • DETECT • CARDINALITIES. If one or multiple joins are selected, the detection applies to the selected joins; otherwise, the detection applies to the entire data foundation.
	Select one or multiple joins, right-click, and select DETECT • CARDINALITIES.
	Click the DETECT button in the toolbar above the data foundation schema and select DETECT CARDINALITIES.

Table 5.7 Options for Detecting Joins, Cardinalities, and Keys in the Data Foundation (Cont.)

Detect Joins

As shown in Figure 5.14, there are two ways to detect joins:

▶ Database keys

▶ Column names

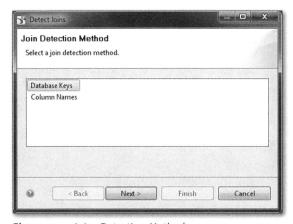

Figure 5.14 Joins Detection Methods

You can use the DATABASE KEYS detection method if the DBA has defined primary keys and foreign keys; IDT uses the keys definition to propose joins that you can accept, as shown in Figure 5.15.

You can use the COLUMN NAMES detection method when there is no key in the tables that can be used by IDT to propose joins. You can accept the list of joins proposed, as shown in Figure 5.15.

Note

We recommend that you use the DATABASE KEYS detection method whenever possible. On the other hand, it's rarely recommended that you use the COLUMN NAMES detection method because numerous joins can be proposed, and you have to review each join to accept it or not. So, in general, using this method is often more costly than manually creating joins.

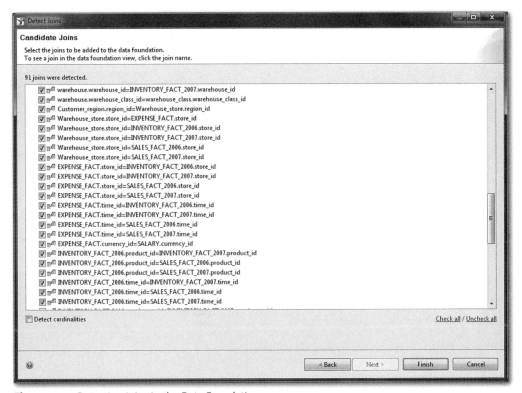

Figure 5.15 Detecting Joins in the Data Foundation

The Figure 5.15 example uses the Column Names detection method. Notice that 91 joins are proposed, and you have to unselect all joins that aren't relevant for the data foundation purpose.

Detect Cardinalities

The cardinalities detection can be done for the entire data foundation or for a selection of tables. To detect cardinalities, IDT generates SQL queries implying the tables involved in the join to figure out the cardinalities. For performance reasons, the result of the cardinalities detection may not always be correct. You should check the cardinalities detected and change any that were not set correctly.

Detect Keys

The keys detection operation browses the database catalog to detect table keys (primary keys and foreign keys). This operation isn't time consuming and can be done with no restriction.

If key columns are detected, the table's columns in the data foundation schema appear as shown in Figure 5.16:

▶ Primary key columns have a yellow key.

▶ Foreign key columns have a blue key.

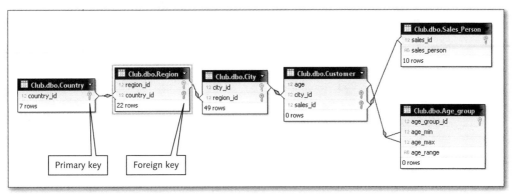

Figure 5.16 Primary Key and Foreign Key Columns

Key Columns

If the key columns have not been detected, you can manually set columns as primary keys or foreign keys. Select a table column, right-click, and select one of the following options:

▶ SET AS KEY • PRIMARY

▶ SET AS KEY • FOREIGN

▶ SET AS KEY • NO KEY

Setting key columns can be useful when you have to set the index awareness (see Chapter 7, Section 7.17) on dimensions or attributes in the business layer.

5.3.5 Joins Strategy

If there is no constraint in the data modeling and therefore most of the queries can be known in advance, the schema should be fine-tuned to decrease the number of joins and the quantity of necessary data.

To reduce the number of joins, you can either put the items that are supposed to be queried together most of the time in the same table, or you can create join indexes in the data source to bypass the normal join path from one item to another.

Where joins are optional, the type of join to use must be chosen carefully. The use of inner joins versus outer joins impacts the results of user queries. Using the wrong type of join may provide results that aren't what users expect. (For more information on join types, see Section 5.3.3.)

Always remember that outer joins may impact the query response time because outer joins always return more data than inner joins. This problem can be resolved by using aggregate aware (see Chapter 7, Section 7.18) and alias tables.

5.4   Derived Tables

The data foundation is an entity-relationship (E-R) model containing tables, views, and joins. In some cases, the data foundation defined with the available database resources may not be enough to describe the business needs, so you may have to ask for new database views. However, creating views modifies the database schema, which, as it happens, DBAs might not want to do.

To support additional business cases in the data foundation, you can create derived tables. A derived table is an SQL query that uses database resources (tables, columns, SQL views, and SQL functions) and built-in functions (see Section 5.11) such as @prompt or @variable.

The derived table looks like a physical table in the data foundation and can be used this way. A derived table can also use the @derivedtable built-in function to embed the SQL query of another derived table. Using the @derivedtable built-in function allows the reusability of SQL queries, enables the use of nested derived tables, and also avoids the need to write large SQL queries.

After they are created, derived tables offer the same capabilities that a standard table or an SQL view offers: viewing table content, viewing column(s) content, counting rows, and so on.

The derived table SELECT SQL statement is always embedded in a sub-SELECT SQL statement when used in client queries such as SAP BusinessObjects Web Intelligence, SAP Crystal Reports for Enterprise, or SAP BusinessObjects Dashboards.

Example

Consider this example of a derived table SQL expression:

```
Select city, region, country
From Club.dbo.Country INNER JOIN Club.dbo.Region ON (Club.dbo.
Region.country_id = Club.dbo.Country.country_id) INNER JOIN Club.
dbo.City ON (Club.dbo.City.region_id = Club.dbo.Region.region_id)
```

When an SAP BusinessObjects BI user selects COUNTRY and CITY in the query panel, the following SQL query is generated:

```
Select Country_Region_City.city, Country_Region_City.country
from (
Select city, region, country
From Club.dbo.Country INNER JOIN Club.dbo.Region ON (Club.dbo.
Region.country_id = Club.dbo.Country.country_id) INNER JOIN Club.
dbo.City ON (Club.dbo.City.region_id = Club.dbo.Region.region_id)
) Country_Region_City
```

There are many ways to create a derived table:

▶ Create a brand new derived table in the data foundation schema.

▶ Create a derived table from a selected table.

▶ Replace a table by a new derived table.

▶ Merge tables, SQL views, federated tables, and derived tables into a new derived table.

Let's walk through all of them now.

> **Note**
>
> A derived table always starts with the SQL statement SELECT.

5.4.1 Create a Derived Table in the Data Foundation Schema

This option lets you create a new derived table from scratch. To create a derived table, select one of the following options:

▶ Right-click anywhere in the data foundation schema, and then select INSERT • DERIVED TABLE.

▶ Select ACTIONS • INSERT • DERIVED TABLE.

▶ Click the INSERT button in the toolbar above the data foundation schema, and select INSERT DERIVED TABLE.

The derived table editor opens, as shown in Figure 5.17. You can enter the SQL expression and use the SQL editor capabilities described in Section 5.10 and Figure 5.55 in that section.

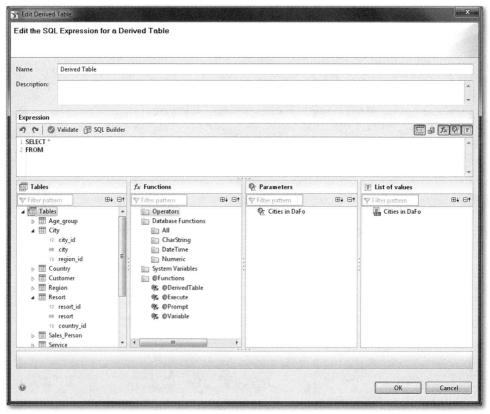

Figure 5.17 Editing a Derived Table

The derived table editor also offers the ability to use a simplified query panel (see Chapter 8) to help you in the creation of the SQL sentence. Click the button SQL BUILDER to open the panel, as shown in Figure 5.18.

The SQL builder panel is a simplified query panel and only displays the list of tables, SQL views, federated tables, and derived tables created in the data foundation. Drag and drop the columns from the tables list in the SELECTED COLUMNS pane, as shown in Figure 5.19. You can view the generated SQL by clicking the VIEW SQL button. You can view the content of the derived table by clicking the PREVIEW DATA button. (For more information on viewing data, see Chapter 2, Section 2.6.)

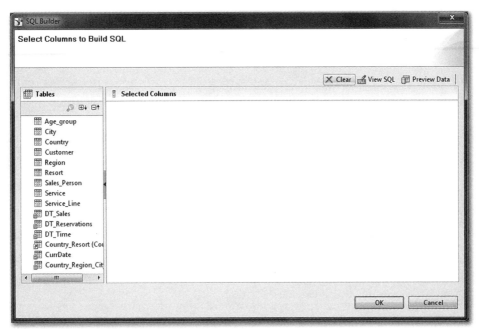

Figure 5.18 SQL Builder for Derived Tables

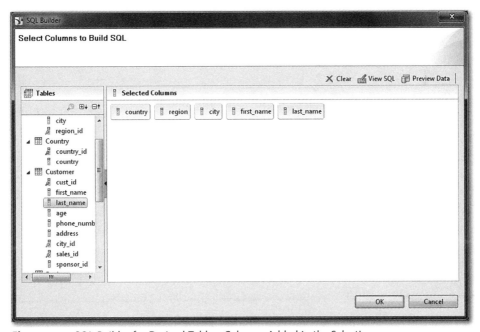

Figure 5.19 SQL Builder for Derived Tables: Columns Added in the Selection

The query engine uses the tables and joins already defined in the data foundation to generate the SQL. This query panel is only an assistant because it doesn't propose SQL transformations and filters.

After you've selected the needed columns, click OK to close the query panel. Modify the SQL in the derived table editor if needed, as shown in Figure 5.20.

Figure 5.20 Derived Table: SQL Expression Updated by SQL Builder

5.4.2   Create a Derived Table from a Selected Table

This option lets you create a new derived table from an existing table. Select a table in the data foundation schema, right-click, and then select INSERT • DERIVED TABLE.

A new derived table is created and added in the data foundation. The SQL expression is a SELECT statement, including all columns and calculated columns from the selected table as in Figure 5.21.

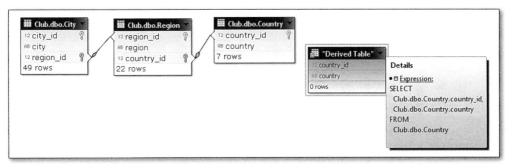

Figure 5.21   Creating a Derived Table from a Selected Table

In general, the created derived table has to be joined with other tables and, when needed, its SQL expression can be modified to capture the business needs.

5.4.3   Replace a Table with a New Derived Table

This option lets you replace an existing table with a new derived table. Select a table in the data foundation schema, right-click, and then select REPLACE BY • DERIVED TABLE. A new derived table is created and added in the data foundation. The SQL expression is a SELECT statement, including all columns and calculated columns from the selected table as shown in Figure 5.22. You're asked to choose whether the replaced table has to be removed from the data foundation. All business layer resources referencing this table need to be manually updated. The joins linked to the replaced table are cut and relinked to the new derived table, as shown in Figure 5.22.

In general, the created derived table has to be edited to modify the SQL to capture the business needs.

Before: The table "Country" is not replaced.

After: The table "Country" has been replaced by the derived table "Country Derived Table".

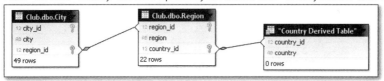

Figure 5.22 Replacing a Table with a New Derived Table

5.4.4 Merge Multiple Tables and Derived Tables in a New Derived Table

This option lets you merge multiple tables and derived tables into a new derived table. Select at least two tables in the data foundation schema, right-click, and then select MERGE.

> **Note**
>
> We recommend that you select tables that are joined together.

A new derived table is created and added in the data foundation. The SQL expression is a SELECT statement, including all columns and calculated columns from the selected tables and all included joins, as shown in Figure 5.23. You're asked to choose whether the selected tables have to be removed from the data foundation. All business layer resources referencing the selected tables need to be manually updated. The excluded joins linked to the selected tables are cut and relinked to the new derived table, as shown in Figure 5.23.

If you decide not to remove the tables that have been used to create the derived table, they remain in the data foundation with their included joins (joins between the tables used to create the derived table), but the excluded joins (joins between the tables used to create the derived table and other tables) are relinked to the new created derived table.

Figure 5.23 illustrates the merge of tables COUNTRY, REGION, CITY, and CUSTOMER in a new derived table named CUSTOMER INFO.

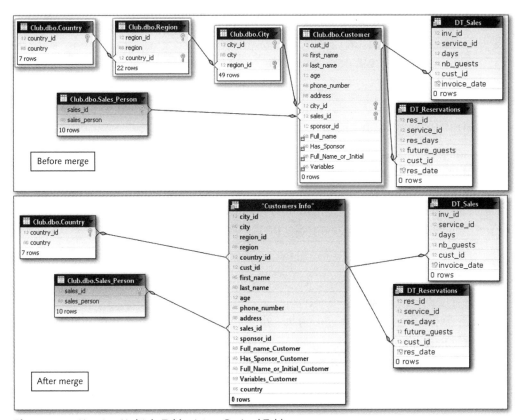

Figure 5.23 Merging Multiple Tables into a Derived Table

5.5   Calculated Columns

A data foundation can serve multiple business layers, and the person in charge of the data foundation isn't necessarily the same person in charge of the business layer.

Dimensions, attributes, or measures aren't necessarily based on a single table column and may require custom SQL. For more information on dimensions, attributes, and measures, see Chapter 7, Section 7.5, Section 7.6, and Section 7.7.

Writing derived tables (see Section 5.4) can be a good way to address custom SQL, but it's not appropriate in the case of a single calculation. Of course, the business layer offers the ability to write custom SQL in an object's definition (dimensions, attributes, or measures). But, as mentioned earlier, a data foundation is shareable, and the person in charge of the business layer may not necessarily have the required database skills.

Calculated columns are a good solution because they are virtual columns of a table defined with custom SQL.

Some calculations or filtering done at the universe or report level can be pushed down to the database level (without the need to actually modify the database). This has two advantages: Business users have less work to do (they don't need to create the calculation), and there is an improvement of performance because the database calculation engine might be faster on the database data and less data is transferred.

Writing custom SQL in calculated columns in a data foundation has multiple advantages:

- **No derived tables**
  Avoid the use of derived tables when not needed.

- **Shareability**
  SQL expressions defined in data foundations can be shared in several business layers.

- **Person focus**
  SQL is more of an IT skill than a user skill; business users can create business layers based on data foundations built by IT.

The calculated columns only use columns from the selected table, along with native database SQL functions and built-in functions such as @prompt or @variable.

To create a calculated column, select a table either in the data foundation schema or in the DATA FOUNDATION pane, right-click, and then select the option INSERT CALCULATED COLUMN.

The calculated column editor opens as shown in Figure 5.24. You can enter the SQL expression and use the SQL editor capabilities shown later in Figure 5.55 (see Section 5.10).

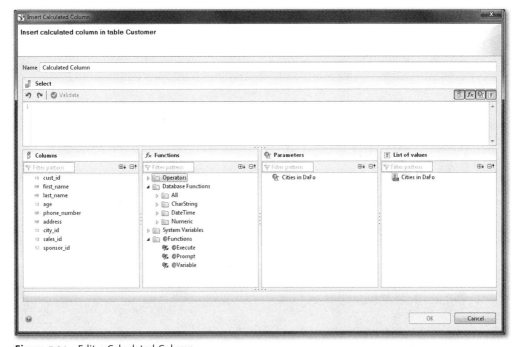

Figure 5.24 Edit a Calculated Column

Only the columns belonging to the selected table are displayed in the column editor. To validate the SQL expression, click the VALIDATE button. If you've manually added columns from other tables, the validation returns an error.

The calculated column is inserted in the table as a new column with a calculator icon added on the data type icon— , , or —as shown in Figure 5.25. A tooltip is displayed when the mouse hovers over the calculated column.

You can double-click on a calculated column to edit it, and you can right-click on a calculated column and then select DELETE to delete it. It's also possible to set a primary key or foreign key on a calculated column. (For more information on key columns, see Section 5.3.4.)

Figure 5.25 Table with Calculated Columns

The calculated column has the same capabilities that any other table column has. To use the calculated column in an SQL expression, you select it with the "table"."column" syntax. The calculated column of an SQL statement is always embedded in a sub-SELECT SQL statement when used in client tool queries.

Example

Calculated column Full_Name: "FIRST_NAME" || ' ' || "LAST_NAME"

When an end user selects FULL_NAME in the query panel, the generated SQL query is the following:

```
SELECT View__15. "Full_Name" from (SELECT ("FIRST_NAME" || ' ' ||
"LAST_NAME") AS "Full_Name" from "CLUB"."Customer") AS View__15
```

5.6 Solving Loops (Alias Tables, Contexts, Shortcut Joins)

Depending on your database schema and business requirements, you may want to introduce loops in the data foundation. A loop is said to exist when there is more than one "path" of joins between two tables. The query engine doesn't know what "path" to choose, so any loop in the data foundation must be resolved.

IDT offers assistance to detect and solve loops, so it's important to set the join cardinalities to help IDT propose the most appropriate solution.

There are many business reasons why loops exist in the data foundation, and there are many ways to solve loops. The way you solve loops depends on your business needs. A loop can be solved by using the following:

▸ Alias tables

▸ Contexts

▸ Shortcut joins

You can invoke the tool to detect the loops, to detect the potential contexts, or to detect the potential aliases. To invoke one of the tools choose one of the following options:

▸ Select ACTIONS • DETECT • LOOPS.

▸ Select ACTIONS • DETECT • ALIASES.

▸ Select ACTIONS • DETECT • CONTEXTS.

> **Note**
>
> You can use the DETECT LOOPS option in IDT to find loops, but be aware that the loop may not be detected in some situations. If the loop involves only two tables, IDT assumes that the two joins are subcomponents of a multicolumn join rather than separate relationships, so the loop isn't detected.

Consider the example shown in Figure 5.26, which is based on a simple order entry system. The boxes represent the tables, and the lines represent the joins.

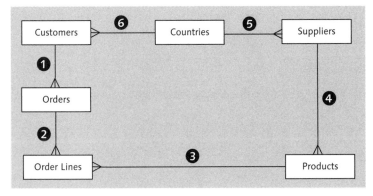

Figure 5.26 Data Foundation with a Loop

You can see that Customers place Orders, as shown by join ❶. Each order is made up of one or more Order_Lines (join ❷). Each Order_Line is for a specific Product (join ❸), and each Product is manufactured by a specific Supplier (join ❹). Each Supplier resides in a specific Country (join ❺), and each Customer resides in a specific Country as well (join ❻).

The query engine can't generate queries for objects that are part of this loop. There is more than one path from one table to another. For example, if objects in a query require information from Products and Countries, should the query engine generate SQL using joins ❹ and ❺ (Countries in which Products are made) or joins ❻, ❶, ❷, and ❸ (Countries from which Products are ordered)?

5.6.1 Resolving Loops by Eliminating Joins

Loops like this one can be resolved through the elimination of a join or the use of SQL aliases (alias tables). If possible, resolve a loop by eliminating a join so that only one path exists between any remaining objects.

Figure 5.27 shows a possible solution to solve the loop; that is, join ❻ between Countries and Customers has been removed.

> **Note**
>
> Be careful when removing a join; the remaining joins must produce query results that make sense to the users.

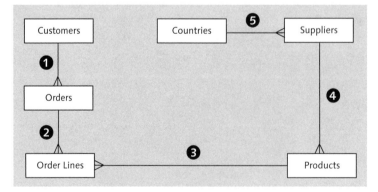

Figure 5.27 Solve a Loop by Eliminating a Join

> **Note**
>
> If the foreign key to Countries from Customers is made available as an object, and the primary key in Countries is also made available as an object, users have more than one way of retrieving the same information, each with a different meaning. The object names and the grouping of objects into folders must make it clear to the user what the result is when using each object.

5.6.2 Resolving Loops with Alias Tables

There may be times when you can't resolve a loop by removing a join. Returning to the order entry example, assume that the business situation requires country information in the context of suppliers and country information in the context of customers. The solution shown in Figure 5.27 doesn't allow the latter because the join between Countries and Customers has been removed—country information is only available for a supplier.

The previous solution doesn't support the business needs. An alternative solution is to duplicate the countries table using two aliases. An *alias* is an SQL construct designed to allow multiple instances of a table in a data foundation, which can be useful to break loops.

In the following example, two alias tables can be created: one related to customers and the other related to suppliers (see Figure 5.28).

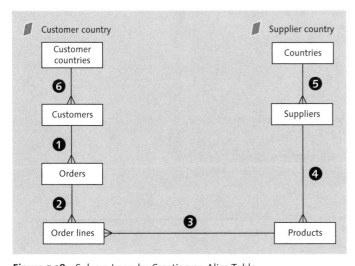

Figure 5.28 Solve a Loop by Creating an Alias Table

The alias CUSTOMER COUNTRIES is used with join ❻. The loop has been broken, but all of the required joins are still available so that COUNTRIES information is available in both contexts.

Note

Where there are loops, look for a table that is on the "one" side of multiple one-to-many relationships. This table may be a good candidate for aliasing because, in most cases, it doesn't make sense to use the table in conjunction with both the related tables. A query on those tables produces a Cartesian product (see Section 5.7) of the related rows.

Besides the ALIASES detection tool, there are different ways to create an alias table:

▸ Insert a table that already exists in the data foundation, and IDT proposes to automatically create a table alias with a different name.

▸ Select a table in the data foundation, right-click, and select the option INSERT • ALIAS TABLE.

▸ Select a table in the data foundation, and then select ACTIONS • INSERT • ALIAS.

▸ Select a table in the data foundation, click the INSERT button in the toolbar above the data foundation schema, and then select the INSERT ALIAS option.

A pop-up window asks you to choose a name for the alias table, as shown in Figure 5.29.

Figure 5.29 Creating an Alias Table in the Data Foundation

5.6.3 Resolving Loops with Contexts

Multiple paths between two tables cause ambiguity. To avoid this you can assign a path to a query context.

If you have defined contexts, when an ambiguity is found in a query, the universe does one of the following:

▸ Solves the ambiguity automatically by splitting the queries and merging data within the report when data from the two contexts is requested (split query)

▸ Gives the business user the ability to choose which path (hence, which context) to follow if the ambiguity can't be resolved automatically

Solving loops with contexts is often used when the loop includes multiple fact tables.

Figure 5.30 and Figure 5.31 show two different contexts of usage for customers and products—customers who have loaned products and customers who have bought products, respectively.

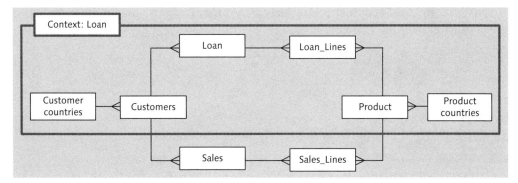

Figure 5.30 Loop with Loan Context

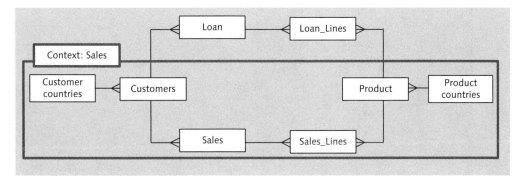

Figure 5.31 Loop with Sales Context

A context determines which method to use to solve the loop ambiguity and defines the joins that IDT must include to generate the appropriate SQL query based on the user selection.

5.6.4 Create and Edit Contexts

The context is used to solve a loop. It defines the joins that participate in the context, the joins that don't participate in the context, and the joins that are neutral.

Only the joins that participate in the loop must be set as included or excluded in a context; other joins are declared neutral. Neutral joins can be used in all queries because they aren't participating in the loop and therefore not impacting the query engine for the SQL generation.

To create or edit contexts, click the ALIASES AND CONTEXTS pane in the DATA FOUNDATION pane, as shown in Figure 5.32.

Figure 5.32 Aliases and Context Panes in the Data Foundation

If you click the VISUALIZE LOOPS button (🔍) in the LOOPS pane, all loops are displayed. Click the REFRESH button (🔁) to see if the loops are solved by contexts, alias tables, or shortcut joins, as shown in Figure 5.33.

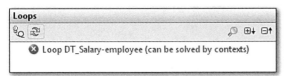

Figure 5.33 Loops Displayed in the Contexts Pane of the Data Foundation

> **Note**
>
> It's recommended to use the contexts detection tool to create contexts unless you're skilled in the manual process of context creation.

To create a context, click the 🖼 button in the toolbar above the list of aliases and contexts. Double-click on a context to make it editable, as shown in Figure 5.34.

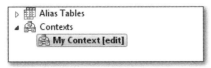

Figure 5.34 Editing a Context

Recall that a context contains joins. To include joins in a context, click on a join in the data foundation schema or in the list of joins below the data foundation schema, as shown in Figure 5.35.

A join can take three states in a context:

▶ A plus sign (➕) means that the join is included in a context.

▶ A minus sign (➖) means that the join is excluded from the context.

▶ No sign means that the join is neutral.

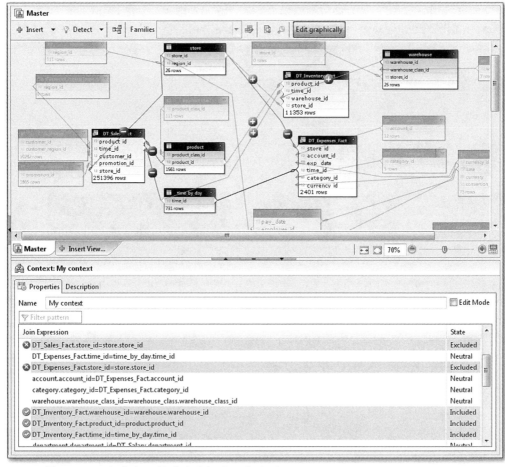

Figure 5.35 Include or Exclude Joins in a Context

To change the state of a join, click on the join, and the state changes from INCLUDED to EXCLUDED to NEUTRAL, and so on.

> **Note**
>
> It's important to set the contexts correctly and to always run the data foundation check integrity to check that all loops have been resolved and all contexts are valid.
>
> Don't forget to edit or recreate the contexts when you modify the data foundation by adding or removing joins.
>
> If the contexts aren't well defined, the query engine can generate SQL queries containing Cartesian products that lead to unwanted results and database performance degradation.

To validate the contexts, don't forget to click the CHECK INTEGRITY button ( ) after a context creation, modification, or automatic detection. (For more information on the check integrity process, see Section 5.15.)

5.6.5 Shortcut Joins

The shortcut joins are alternative join paths that universe designers can define in the data foundation wherever possible. The query engine, when generating the SQL query, looks for all possible paths and chooses the shortest one in term of joins. The shortcut joins aren't taken into account to define contexts but only to decrease the number of joins whenever possible.

In Figure 5.36, you can go from AMOUNT_SOLD to ARTICLE_ID directly without the need to join the ARTICLE_LOOKUP table. The query engine decides the fastest path based on the objects requested in the query.

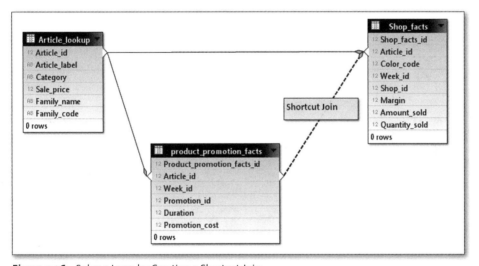

Figure 5.36 Solve a Loop by Creating a Shortcut Join

To set a join as a shortcut join, you need to check the SHORTCUT JOIN option in the join editor, as shown in Figure 5.37.

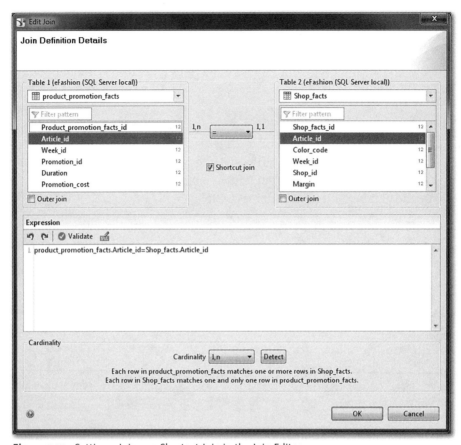

Figure 5.37 Setting a Join as a Shortcut Join in the Join Editor

5.6.6 Detection Tools

As explained in this section, there are many ways to solve loops, and IDT offers tools to help you.

Loops Detection Tool

To detect the loops, select ACTIONS • DETECT • LOOPS. The loops are displayed in the ALIASES AND CONTEXTS pane shown earlier in Figure 5.32.

Aliases Detection Tool

To detect the alias tables, use one of the following options:

- Select ACTIONS • DETECT • ALIASES.
- Click the DETECT button in the toolbar above the data foundation schema, and select the DETECT ALIASES option.
- Select the ALIASES AND CONTEXTS pane, and then click DETECT ALIASES button (🗗) in the toolbar above the list of alias tables and contexts.

The potential aliases are displayed, and you can accept or not accept the proposed aliases, as shown in Figure 5.38.

Figure 5.38 Alias Tables Detection in the Data Foundation

Note

Before accepting the creation of alias tables, check that they are useful and valid in the business representation of the universe. The aliases detection tool isn't always able to detect the appropriate aliases and can propose tables that aren't relevant and miss other tables that are relevant. Don't forget to set the join cardinalities to have a correct aliases detection.

Alias tables are inserted in the ALIAS TABLES list of the ALIASES AND CONTEXTS pane.

Contexts Detection Tool

To detect the contexts, select one of the following options:

- Select ACTIONS • DETECT • CONTEXTS.
- Select the ALIASES AND CONTEXTS pane, and then click the DETECT CONTEXTS button (🗗) in the toolbar above the list of alias tables and contexts.

The potential contexts are displayed, and you can choose whether to accept the proposed contexts, as shown in Figure 5.39.

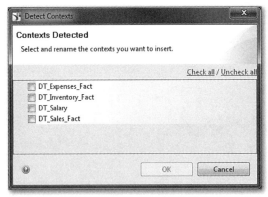

Figure 5.39 Contexts Detection in the Data Foundation

> **Notes**
>
> The alias table detection must be done before the contexts detection. Most of the time, alias tables can solve loops. If the alias tables have correctly been detected or manually created, then the contexts are also correctly detected. Don't forget to set the join cardinalities to have a correct contexts detection.

5.7 Chasm Traps and Fan Traps

In this section, you see how to solve common traps in a data foundation design and avoid incorrect query results.

5.7.1 Fan Traps

A *fan trap* is a type of join between at least three tables when a one-to-many join links a table that is also linked to another table by another one-to-many join. This type of schema is frequently used to define many-to-many joins.

The inclusion of such fanned-out one-to-many joins can cause incorrect results to be returned, especially when a query includes objects based on both tables. The incorrect results are referred to as *Cartesian products*. (For more information on joins, see Section 5.3.)

> **Note**
>
> A fan trap produces more lines than expected, and the numbers are multiplied.
>
> Tables relationships are one → many → many.

A typical example of fan trap occurs when you're using a summary table and a detail table in the same query.

Fan Trap Resolution

The query engine solves the fan trap by splitting a query into at least two queries. For the measures defined in the business layer having SQL aggregation functions, the query is split into two queries, and the results of the two queries are merged in a single result set.

> **Important**
>
> To allow the split of a query into two or more queries, check that the business layer MULTIPLE SQL STATEMENTS FOR EACH MEASURE option is activated (this is the default setting). For more information on business layer parameters, see Chapter 7, Section 7.30.

Another solution for solving a fan trap is to follow these steps:

1. Create an alias table (see Section 5.6.2) for the table that is producing the multiplication of rows.

2. Create a one-to-one join between the source table and the alias table.

3. Create a context (see Section 5.6.3) for the source table and another context for the alias table.

4. Activate the business layer option MULTIPLE SQL STATEMENTS FOR EACH MEASURE.

It's also possible to use aggregate awareness on measures to optimize the query, as described in Chapter 7, Section 7.18.

Fan Trap Example

The schema described in Figure 5.40 is a 1-N-N relationship between CUSTOMERS, ORDERS, and ORDERS_DETAIL tables.

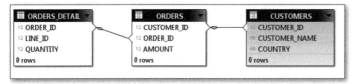

Figure 5.40 Fan Trap Schema Example

Table 5.8 describes some of the dimensions and measures defined in a business layer.

Object Name	Object Type	SQL Definition
Country	Dimension	CUSTOMERS.COUNTRY
Customer name	Dimension	CUSTOMERS.CUSTOMER_NAME
Amount	Measure	SUM(ORDERS.AMOUNT)
Quantity	Measure	SUM(ORDERS_DETAIL.QUANTITY)

Table 5.8 Dimensions and Measures Defined in the Business Layer to Illustrate a Fan-Trap Case

The user builds a query in the query panel with the following objects: Customer Name, Amount, and Quantity.

If the business layer MULTIPLE SQL STATEMENTS FOR EACH MEASURE option is activated, the correct query result is shown in Figure 5.41.

AB Customer Name	12 Amount	12 Quantity
Browne	120	16
Durant	220	70
Kleine	200	32
Martin	380	46
Schmidt	550	75
Smith	200	32

Figure 5.41 Query Result Based on a Fan Trap Schema with the Multiple SQL Statements for Each Measure Option Activated

If the business layer MULTIPLE SQL STATEMENTS FOR EACH MEASURE option isn't activated, the query result is shown in Figure 5.42.

AB Customer Name	12 Amount	12 Quantity
Browne	480	16
Durant	1240	70
Kleine	700	32
Martin	1360	46
Schmidt	2340	75
Smith	700	32

Figure 5.42 Query Result Based on a Fan Trap Schema with the Multiple SQL Statements for Each Measure Option Not Activated

5.7.2 Chasm Traps

A *chasm trap* is a type of join between at least three tables when too many-to-one joins converge to the same table. The inclusion of such joins can cause incorrect results to be returned, especially when a query includes measures based on both leaf tables. The incorrect results are referred to as Cartesian products.

> **Note**
>
> A chasm trap produces more lines than expected, and the numbers are multiplied. Tables relationships are many → one → many.

A typical example of a chasm trap occurs when you're using a dimension with two different facts tables: sales and reservations.

Chasm Trap Resolution

The query engine solves the fan trap by splitting a query into at least two queries. For measures defined in the business layer having SQL aggregation functions, the query is split into two queries, and the results of the two queries are merged in a single result set.

> **Important**
>
> To allow the split of a query into two or more queries, check that the business layer MULTIPLE SQL STATEMENTS FOR EACH MEASURE option is activated (this is the default setting).

Another solution for solving a chasm trap is to create a context (see Section 5.6.3) for each one-to-many join.

Chasm Trap Example

The schema described in Figure 5.43 is a one-to-many relationship among CUSTOM-ERS, SALES, and INVOICE_LINE tables on one side, and a one-to-many relationship among CUSTOMERS, RESERVATIONS, and RESERVATION_LINE on the other side.

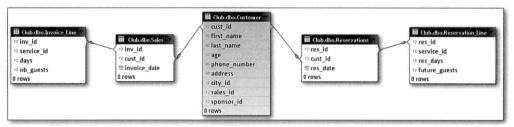

Figure 5.43 Chasm Trap Schema Example

Table 5.9 describes some of the dimensions and measures defined in a business layer.

Object Name	Object Type	SQL Definition
Customer_name	Dimension	`"Customers"."First_name" + ' ' + "Customers"."Last_name"`
Age	Dimension	`"Customers". "Age"`
Nb Days	Measure	`sum("Invoice_Line"."days")`
Nb Guests	Measure	`sum("Invoice_Line"."nb_guests")`
Nb Reservation Days	Measure	`sum("Reservation_Line"."res_days")`
Nb Reservation Guests	Measure	`sum("Reservation_Line"."future_guests")`

Table 5.9 Dimensions and Measures Defined in the Business Layer to Illustrate a Chasm-Trap Case

The user builds a query in the query panel with the following objects: Customer Name, Nb Days, and Nb Reservation Days. If the business layer MULTIPLE SQL STATEMENTS FOR EACH MEASURE option is activated, the correct query result is shown as in Figure 5.44.

AB Customer name	12 Nb Days	12 Nb Reservation Days
Adolph Durnstein	10	2
Caroline Edwards	\<Null\>	10
Christian Robert	\<Null\>	1
Christine Martin	\<Null\>	12
Erika Diemers	14	\<Null\>
George McCartney	\<Null\>	5
Hans Weimar	498	13
Hariett Keegan	\<Null\>	10
Heineke Reinman	10	4
Herbert Schultz	35	2
Isao Okumura	10	\<Null\>
Jack Swenson	8	3
Joe Larson	538	\<Null\>
John Wilson	\<Null\>	15
Jurgen Schiller	580	10
Justin Marlow	\<Null\>	3
Kenji Oneda	360	4
Luc Piaget	\<Null\>	8
Marie-Chantale Dupont	\<Null\>	14
Mariko Kamata	552	\<Null\>
Mary Jones	\<Null\>	6

Figure 5.44 Query Result Based on a Chasm Trap Schema with the Multiple SQL Statements for Each Measure Option Activated

If the business layer MULTIPLE SQL STATEMENTS FOR EACH MEASURE option isn't activated, the query result is shown as in Figure 5.45.

AB Customer name	12 Nb Days	12 Nb Reservation Days
Adolph Durnstein	10	4
Hans Weimar	1494	910
Heineke Reinman	20	8
Herbert Schultz	70	12
Jack Swenson	16	6
Jurgen Schiller	1740	700
Kenji Oneda	720	280
Masayuki Mukumoto	66	24
Satoru Kamimura	10	4
Silke Titzman	676	560
Tony Goldschmidt	35	18
William Baker	686	280

Figure 5.45 Query Result Based on a Chasm Trap Schema with the Multiple SQL Statements for Each Measure Option Not Activated

5.8   List of Values

The list of values has been introduced in IDT as an entity to be authored, shared, and reused across data foundation and business layer resources. The list of values can be created and edited in the PARAMETERS AND LIST OF VALUES pane of the data foundation editor, as shown in Figure 5.46.

All lists of values defined in the data foundation are inherited by the business layers referencing this data foundation. The inherited list of values can't be edited in the business layer.

In a data foundation, a list of values is mainly defined to be associated with a parameter or in an @prompt built-in function. The list of values can be alphabetically sorted or manually sorted. The toggle button ( ) allows filtering in the LIST OF VALUES.

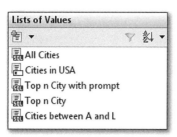

Figure 5.46   Authored List of Values in the Data Foundation

In the data foundation, only two types of list of values are available:

▶ Static list of values
▶ List of values based on custom SQL

The list of values defined in the data foundation can be used for the joins, the derived tables, and the calculated columns.

To answer specific business needs, you create a custom list of values and associate it to the parameters. You can define how the data is presented in the list and define restrictions on the amount of data and type of data returned to the list. The list of values can also be used in an @execute built-in function.

A list of values is a query that returns values. The query can be a simple query that does a Select Distinct from a table column or can be an advanced query such as returning the top ten products based on the quantity sold for year 2012. In the data foundation, the list of values is mainly used for filtering the data.

A list of values can return one or multiple columns. If the list of values returns more than one column, only one of the columns is added in the query; other columns are used as display columns. So you have to choose which column is sent to the database when used with a parameter. A list of values can be shared by different data foundation resources, and the selected column can be different from one resource to another.

Example

The list of values GEOGRAPHY is returning three columns: COUNTRY, REGION, and CITY.

The parameter SELECT A COUNTRY is referencing the list of values GEOGRAPHY, and the selected column is COUNTRY.

The parameter SELECT A CITY is referencing the list of values GEOGRAPHY, and the selected column is CITY.

For more information on the use of list of values in the business layer, see Chapter 7, Section 7.13.

Caution

Lists of values can't have the same name.

To create a list of values in the PARAMETERS AND LIST OF VALUES pane, click the 🖹 button in the toolbar above the LIST OF VALUES window, and select the TYPE of list of values to create. You can preview the content of any list of values by clicking the PREVIEW button in the list of values editor. For more information on data preview, see Chapter 2, Section 2.6.

5.8.1 Static List of Values

The values of a static list of values are stored as grid tables in the data foundation and in the business layer(s). The list of values can have from one to many columns, as shown in Figure 5.47.

You can manually create the content of the static list of values by adding the columns and values shown in Table 5.10.

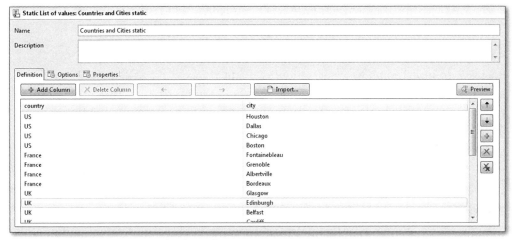

Figure 5.47 Static List of Values Editor

Button	Action
⊕ Add Column	Add columns to the list of values.
✕ Delete Column	Delete columns from the list of values.
⊕	Add values in the list of values.
✕	Remove values from the list of values.
✖	Remove all values from the list of values.
↓ ↑	Reorder values in the list of values.

Table 5.10 Static List of Values Editor Buttons

You can also automatically populate the static list of values by importing data from a text file or a *.csv* file, as shown in Figure 5.48:

1. Click the IMPORT button.

2. Select the file to import and set the different file options: DATA SEPARATOR, TEXT DELIMITER, DATE FORMAT, and FIRST ROW CONTAINS COLUMN NAMES.

The columns are automatically created and the values populated. The static list of values doesn't keep a link with the file used to populate it.

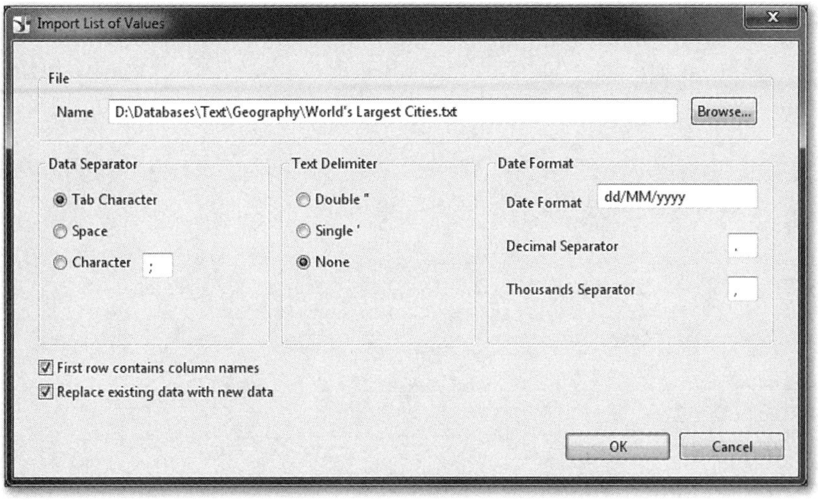

Figure 5.48 Importing a Text File to Create a Static List of Values

5.8.2 List of Values Based on Custom SQL

You can write a list of values using an SQL SELECT statement that returns one or more columns. After the SQL is written, you need to refresh the list of values structure to display the available columns, as shown in Figure 5.49. You can use the SQL assistant to edit the SQL statement.

The SQL statement can use native database functions, tables and columns, and parameters. Built-in functions such as @variable and @prompt can also be used in the SQL expression. The @execute built-in function isn't supported in an SQL list of values.

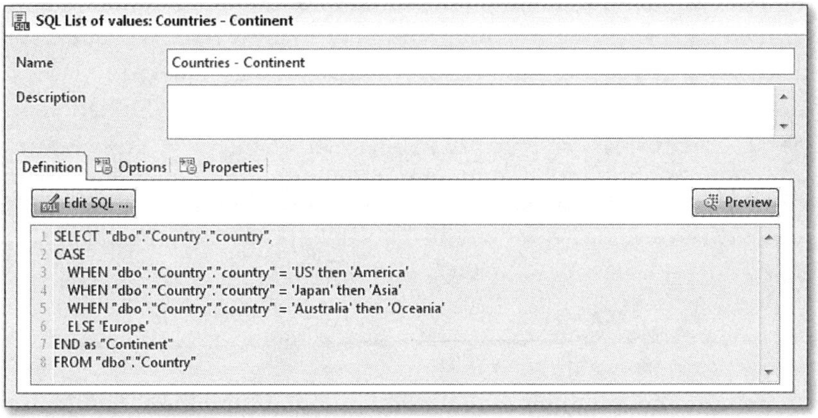

Figure 5.49 List of Values Based on a Custom SQL

215

5.8.3   List of Values Parameters and Options

At any time, you can preview the list of values content by clicking the PREVIEW button in the list of values editor, as shown in Figure 5.50.

You can set and adjust different list of values parameters. Table 5.11 displays the parameters available for the different list of values type.

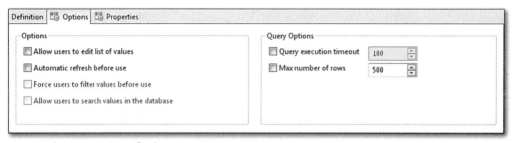

Figure 5.50   List of Values Properties

	Static List of Values Objects	List of Values Based on Custom SQL Objects
ALLOW USERS TO EDIT LIST OF VALUES	Supported	Supported
AUTOMATIC REFRESH BEFORE USE	NA	Supported

Table 5.11   List of Parameters Available for the Different List of Values

You can also restrict the maximum number of rows retrieved (MAX NUMBER OF ROWS option) and the query execution time (QUERY EXECUTION TIMEOUT option) for a list of values. Those properties are also available for a query (query properties) or for the business layer (business layer query options). For more information on query properties and business layer query options, see Chapter 7, Section 7.30.

The MAX NUMBER OF ROWS and the QUERY EXECUTION TIMEOUT options aren't available for the static list of values. For other list of values properties, see Chapter 7, Section 7.13.6.

Allow Users to Edit List of Values

If the ALLOW USERS TO EDIT LIST OF VALUES option is activated, the users can edit the list of values. The purpose of a list of values is usually to limit the set of available values to a user. If the users can edit a list of values, you no longer have control over the values they choose.

Automatic Refresh before Use

If the AUTOMATIC REFRESH BEFORE USE option is activated, the list of values is refreshed each time it's referred and used in a report. You should choose this option only if the contents of the underlying column(s) are frequently changing. This option should be used very carefully after evaluation. If this option isn't set, the list of values is refreshed first when the object is used in a user session.

5.8.4 Customize List of Values Columns

For a static list of values and custom SQL list of values, you can customize the following columns properties:

▶ COLUMN NAME

▶ DATA TYPE

▶ KEY COLUMN

▶ HIDDEN

To modify the columns properties for a list of values, click the PROPERTIES tab in the list of values editor. The DATA TYPE property can be changed like any objects of the business layer, but you should be careful when changing the data type because it might generate an error in clients such as SAP BusinessObjects Web Intelligence if the data type isn't appropriated.

If the HIDDEN option is activated, the column is hidden when the list of values is displayed to the user. This option is generally used for columns that are sent to the database such a column ID.

The KEY COLUMN property is referencing another column of the list of values. The key column is often used with the index aware setting used in a parameter or in an object. In general, a key column is often hidden from the user, so when the user see the values of the list of values, only the captions are displayed—the key column is hidden and added in the SQL script.

> **Example**
>
> The list of values GEOGRAPHY contains two columns:
>
> ▶ The column COUNTRY has the KEY COLUMN equal to COUNTRY_ID.
>
> ▶ The column COUNTRY_ID is hidden.
>
> The user only sees the COUNTRY values (USA, FRANCE, GERMANY, etc.), and the COUNTRY_ID (100, 201, 125, etc.) values are added in the SQL statement.

5.9 Parameters

Parameters were introduced in SAP BusinessObjects BI 4.0 to improve and complement the `@prompt` built-in function. The `@prompt` function is still supported, but the universe also supports this new entity that you can author, share, and reuse across the data foundation and business layer resources to prompt users. Because of this lineage, the parameter is also called a *prompt*.

The parameters can be created and edited in the PARAMETERS AND LIST OF VALUES pane of the data foundation editor, as shown in Figure 5.51. All parameters defined in the data foundation are inherited by the business layers referencing this data foundation; however, the inherited parameters can't be edited in the business layer. The parameters can be alphabetically sorted or manually sorted. You can filter the parameters using the toggle button ( ).

Figure 5.51 Authored Parameters in the Data Foundation

By definition, a parameter is a metadata that requires user answers before the query execution. As for the lists of values, the parameter or prompt is one of the features that have been fully revisited for extended capabilities, shareability, ease of creation, and maintenance.

The parameters are standalone metadata, but the @prompt functions defined in previous universe versions are supported and migrated. (For more information on universe conversion, see Chapter 13, Section 13.8.)

It's possible to create prompts without writing any code; the parameter editor provides all of the existing prompt capabilities and avoids the tedious task of writing @prompt syntax.

> **Caution**
>
> Parameters can't have the same name.

To create a parameter in the PARAMETERS AND LIST OF VALUES pane, click the button in the toolbar above the PARAMETERS section, as shown earlier in Figure 5.51.

5.9.1 Parameter Definition

After you've created a parameter, double-click it to open its editor. In the OPTIONS tab, define the parameter's characteristics and associate a list of values, as shown in Figure 5.52.

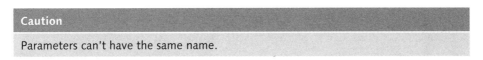

Figure 5.52 Parameters Editor with Prompt to Users Option Activated

Prompt to Users

By default, the PROMPT TO USERS option is activated, and the user has to provide answers to the parameter. If the option isn't activated, only the following options are enabled, as shown in Figure 5.53:

- ▶ SET VALUES option, which is equivalent to the SET DEFAULT VALUES option. To use this option, you must first check the PROMPT TO USERS option, associate a list of values, and uncheck the PROMPT TO USERS option.
- ▶ ALLOW MULTIPLE VALUES option.
- ▶ DATA TYPE option.

Figure 5.53 Parameters Editor: Prompt to Users Option Not Activated

5.9.2 Prompt Text

The PROMPT TEXT property is the text/question that is displayed to the user.

5.9.3 Data Type

You need to select an appropriate DATA TYPE that is the data type of the column/value(s) added to the query. For instance, in the case of index awareness (see Chapter 7, Section 7.17), the user can select country values (string), but country_id (numeric) is added to the query, so the data type is numeric.

5.9.4　Allow Multiple Values

If the ALLOW MULTIPLE VALUES option is activated, the user is authorized to select multiple values in the list of values associated with the parameter. If the option isn't activated, the user can only select one value.

5.9.5　Keep Last Values

The parameters are used in queries by all client tools that connect to the universe. When the KEEP LAST VALUES option is activated, the latest values selected during the last query refresh are displayed to the user.

5.9.6　Index Aware Prompt

If the INDEX AWARE PROMPT option is activated, the key column values of the list of values or the primary key values of the object that has a list of values are sent to the query. The INDEX AWARE PROMPT option is enabled if the SELECT ONLY FROM LIST option is activated and if one of the following criteria is met:

▶ The list of values associated to the parameter is multicolumn with a key column.

▶ The object default list of values is based on an object when a primary key has been added for this object.

5.9.7　Associated List of Values

The parameter can be associated with a list of values. To associate a list of values, click the ⟨...⟩ button on the right side of the ASSOCIATED LIST OF VALUE list box. You can select one of the lists of values created in the PARAMETERS AND LIST OF VALUES pane, as shown in Figure 5.54.

When the list of values is multicolumn, you choose which column is sent to the query. Because a list of values can be shared by multiple parameters, the same list of values can be used differently. You have to choose which list of values column is used in the context of the parameter usage.

Example

The list of values GEOGRAPHY contains two columns: COUNTRY and CITY. The parameter SELECT CITIES is linked to the list of values GEOGRAPHY and the selected column is CITY because the parameter is used in a context where cities are the data wanted by the users.

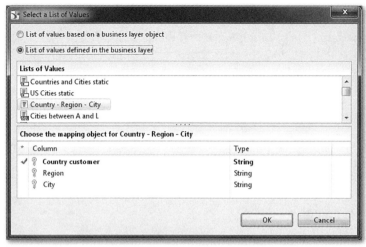

Figure 5.54 Associate a List of Values to the Parameter

5.9.8 Select Only from List

If the SELECT ONLY FROM LIST option is activated, the user is only able to select values from the list of values displayed. If the option isn't activated, the user is able to select values from the list of values or manually enter values. When this option is deactivated, the INDEX AWARE PROMPT option is disabled.

5.9.9 Set Default Values

If the SET DEFAULT VALUES option is activated, you can choose one or multiple values from the list of values associated with the parameter. To choose the values, click the [...] button on the right side of the SET DEFAULT VALUES list box. The default value is preselected in the parameter dialog box when displayed to the user. The user can then decide to keep or remove default values. The user can also select additional values or replace the default values.

5.9.10 Parameter Custom Properties

In the CUSTOM PROPERTIES tab, you can add properties and associate values to the properties. The CUSTOM PROPERTIES are purely informative and aren't used by the SAP BusinessObjects BI clients. They can be used for the documentation or for a future usage in the IDT SDK. (For more information on custom properties, see Chapter 7, Section 7.20.7.)

5.9.11 Parameters Usage

The parameters in the data foundation can be used in the following:

▶ Calculated columns

▶ Derived tables

▶ Joins

▶ Tables name

The `@prompt` function can still be used in view, calculated columns, and joins. You can use parameters in the SQL statement of derived tables, joins, or calculated columns. When used in an SQL expression, a parameter is referenced like this: `@prompt(parameter name)`.

5.10 The SQL Editor

The SQL editor is a dialog box that can help you write SQL when it's needed and particularly in the following data foundation resources:

▶ List of values based on custom SQL

▶ Derived table

▶ Calculated column

▶ Join expression

The SQL editor is also used in the business layer as described in Chapter 7, Section 7.19.1.

The SQL editor is composed of two components, as shown in Figure 5.55:

▶ The text editor pane where the SQL expression is created and edited (❶).

▶ The assistant pane, composed of the following:

　▶ The TABLES pane showing the tables and columns of the relational data source (❷).

　▶ The FUNCTIONS pane (❸), including the following:

　　– The relational databases functions: SQL expressions.

　　– The system variables such as BOUSER, DBUSER, DOCNAME, UNVNAME, and so on. System variables are always used with the `@variable` built-in function such as `@variable('BOUSER')`. (For more information on variables used in the `@variable` built-in function, see Section 5.11.4.)

- The built-in functions.

▶ The PARAMETERS pane (❹).

▶ The LIST OF VALUES pane (❺).

Each assistant component can be hidden or shown in the SQL editor. Each element of the assistant components can be added in the SQL text editor by double-clicking or using drag and drop.

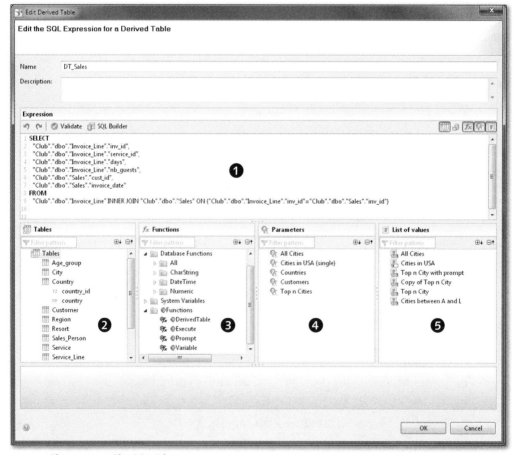

Figure 5.55 The SQL Editor

Tables and Columns

All tables and columns are listed in the TABLES pane, including derived tables, alias tables, federated tables (see Chapter 6, Section 6.4), and calculated columns. Only authorized tables are listed here.

To add one or more column values in the SQL expression, select a table column, and click the down arrow button (▼) added on the right side of the column. The values are displayed, and you can double-click or drag and drop one or more values to add them in the SQL expression, as shown in Figure 5.56.

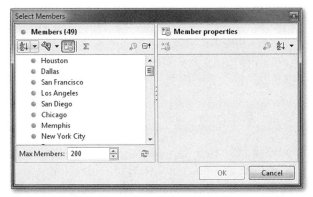

Figure 5.56 Selecting Column Values to Add in an SQL Expression

SQL Database Functions

The SQL database functions are provided by the data access parameters file (*.prm*) for the relational source used in the universe (see Chapter 4, Section 4.5.4).

SQL databases functions are available and can be used in the SQL text editor even if the connection with the relational database has not been established.

Parameters

When a parameter is added in the SQL expression, it's embedded in the @prompt built-in function.

List of Values

The list of values can be used in the @prompt built-in function or used in the @execute built-in function.

Validation

The VALIDATE button validates the SQL expression to the database. The validation works only if the connection with the database is active. (For more information on validation and check integrity, see Section 5.15.)

5.11   Built-in Functions

The built-in functions are provided by IDT to bring flexibility, reusability, and dynamicity in universe and queries. The built-in functions are only used in SQL expressions and can be entered manually or can be called from the SQL editor (see Section 5.10).

The following built-in functions can only be used in the data foundation; for built-in functions used in the business layer, see Chapter 7, Section 7.23.

5.11.1   @derivedtable

The `@derivedtable` function is only used in SQL expressions in the data foundation and is used to reference a derived table in other derived tables, joins, and calculated columns.

The syntax is `@derivedtable(<derived table name>)`, where `<derived table name>` is the name of a derived table. At query time, the `@derivedtable` function is replaced by the referenced derived table SQL expression in a sub-`SELECT` SQL statement.

Example

SQL statement for the derived table DT_Countries:

```
Select country_id, country_name, population from country
```

SQL statement for the derived table DT_Country_name *before* built-in functions resolution:

```
Select country_name from @derivedtable(DT_Countries)
```

SQL statement for the derived table DT_Country_name *after* built-in functions resolution:

```
Select A.country_name from (select country_id, country_name, popula-
tion from country) AS A
```

5.11.2   @execute

The `@execute` function is used in SQL expressions only to reference a list of values. The `@execute` function has been designed to improve performance of SQL queries, especially when the list of values definition is a complex query that includes sub-`SELECT` statements.

The list of values query is first executed, and the result of this query is pushed to the query using the `@execute` built-in function. The syntax is `@execute(<list of values name>)`, where `<list of values name>` is the name of a list of values.

Example

List of values `Best products` **SQL statement is:**

`Select product_id from (select top 5 product_id, sum(amount) from sales group by product_id having sum(quantity) > 100 order by 1)`

SQL statement *before* built-in functions resolution:

`Select product_name from products where product_id in @execute(Best products)`

SQL statement *after* built-in functions resolution:

`Select product_name from products where product_id in (10, 15, 33, 48)`

5.11.3   @prompt

The `@prompt` function is used in SQL definition to ask users to select values from a list of values or enter values that are used in query results or query filters.

The `@prompt` function can be used to define a question or to reference a parameter defined in the data foundation and can have two different syntaxes:

- **Reference a parameter**

  `@prompt(<parameter name>)`, where `<parameter name>` is the name of a parameter.

- **Message with parameters displayed to the user for value(s) selection**

  `@prompt(Message,Data_type,{List_of_values},mono|multi,free|constrained|primary_key,persistent|not_persistent,{default_values})`.

Table 5.12 describes the `@prompt` parameters and rules.

Parameter	Description
Message	The text that is displayed to the user. Must be enclosed by single quotes.
Data_type	Possible values: ▸ 'A': String data. The result of the user selection is enclosed by single quotes. ▸ 'N': Numeric data. The result of the user selection isn't enclosed by a character. ▸ 'D': Date data. The result of the user selection is enclosed by single quotes. ▸ 'DT': Date_time data. The result of the user selection is enclosed by single quotes. ▸ 'K': Data type independent. The result of the user selection isn't enclosed by a character. 'K' can be used only if the parameter primary_key key word is used. If the parameter primary_key key word is used, and the list_of_values parameter is a list of static values, then the data_type parameter can take the following values: 'A:A', 'A:N', 'A:D', 'N:A', 'N:N', 'N:D', 'D:A', 'D:N', 'D:D', and so on. The first element of the parameter is the caption data type, and the second element is the key data type.
List_of_values	This parameter is optional if the free key word is used. This parameter can reference a list of values defined in the data foundation or a list of static values: ▸ Data foundation list of values: 'list of values name' ▸ Static values: {'value 1', 'value2',…,'value n'} If the primary_key key word is used, the list_of_values parameter is static values, and the data_type parameter has two elements (e.g., 'A:A' or 'N:D'). The syntax for the static values is {'caption 1':'key 1',…,'caption n':'key n'}
Mono|multi	This parameter is optional; the default is mono. ▸ Mono: Only one value can be selected by the user. ▸ Multi: Multiple values can be selected by the user.

Table 5.12 Parameters and Options Used in an @Prompt Built-In Function

Parameter	Description
Free|constrained| primary_key	This parameter is optional; the default is free. ▶ Free: The user can select value(s) from the list or manually enter the values. ▶ Constrained: The user must select value(s) from the list. ▶ Primary_key: The user must select value(s) from the list. The user selects captions and the keys are added to the query (index awareness).
Persistent|not_persistent	This parameter is optional; the default is not_persistent. ▶ Persistent: The selected value(s) are displayed to the user the next time the prompt is displayed. The selected values are always displayed even if the prompt contains default values. ▶ Not_persistent: The selected value(s) aren't kept the next time the prompt is displayed.
Default_values	This parameter is optional. The syntax is {'value 1', 'value2',…,'value n'}. If the primary_key key word is used, the list_of_values parameter is a list of static values and the data_type parameter has two elements (e.g., 'A:A' or 'N:D'). The syntax for the default values is {'caption 1':'key 1',…,'caption n':'key n'}.

Table 5.12 Parameters and Options Used in an @Prompt Built-In Function (Cont.)

Table 5.13 lists some examples of the @prompt function used in SQL expressions.

Example	Syntax
Select one country from a list of countries with no manual entry.	@prompt('Select country', 'A', 'Customer\Country',mono,constrained)
Select multiple countries from a list of countries with possible manual entry.	@prompt('Select country', 'A', 'Customer\Country',multi,free)
Select multiple countries from a static list with selected values persisted.	@prompt('Select country', 'A', {'USA','France'},multi,constrained, persistent)

Table 5.13 Some Examples of @Prompt Definition

Example	Syntax
Select one country from a static list with index awareness activated.	`@prompt('Select country', 'A:N', {'USA':'100','France':'200'}, mono,primary_key)`
Select one country from a list of countries with index awareness activated.	`@prompt('Select country', 'K', 'Customer\ Country',mono,primary_key)`
Select one country from a static list with default values.	`@prompt('Select country', 'A', {'USA','France','Germany'}, mono,constrained,,{'USA'})`

Table 5.13 Some Examples of @Prompt Definition (Cont.)

5.11.4 @variable

The `@variable` function is used to reference system variables or user attributes in SQL expressions. The `@variable` syntax is `@variable('<variable name>')`, where `<variable name>` is the name of a variable supported by the universe out of the box or the name of a user attribute (see Chapter 10, Section 10.8). The user attributes are defined in the CMS repository.

Here is a list of some system variables that can be used in the `@variable` expression:

▶ BOUSER
The user name defined in the CMS repository and used to connect to a client such as SAP BusinessObjects Web Intelligence.

▶ DBUSER
The user name used to connect to the database.

▶ DOCNAME
The document name (e.g., an SAP BusinessObjects Web Intelligence document name).

▶ DPNAME
The data provider name (e.g., `Query 1` in an SAP BusinessObjects Web Intelligence document).

▶ UNVNAME
The universe name.

▶ PREFERRED_VIEWING_LOCALE
The user's preferred language for viewing documents.

When the @variable function is solved, the result is always enclosed by single quotes in SQL expressions. If the @variable function doesn't reference any known system variable or user attributes, it behaves like @prompt with default parameters such as @prompt('Enter a value', 'A').

5.12 Families, Comments, and Data Foundation Views

You can build large data foundations or create advanced modeling schemas that include derived tables, federated tables, calculated columns, aggregate tables, and complex joins. We generally recommend that you avoid building your data foundations too large, but this recommendation may not be practical when addressing some business requirements.

The consequence of an overly large data foundation is that it can be hard to review and maintain it. To help the maintenance and its lifecycle, the data foundation can be split into several views, commented, and include different colors for the tables.

To make building and maintaining the new data foundation easier, the following concepts have been introduced in SAP BusinessObjects BI 4.0.

5.12.1 Families

One of the features that helps you to easily maintain and understand a data foundation is the ability to change the color and font of some tables to group them by functional category (customer, product, etc.) or technical category (fact, dimension, etc.). You can create families and associate them to tables, alias tables, derived tables, or federated tables (see Chapter 6, Section 6.4).

A family can change the color and the font of the tables associated with it. You're free to create as many families as you need to give a better view and also a better understanding of the data foundation. A table can be associated to no families or one family.

To edit families, click the EDIT FAMILIES button (⊞) in the toolbar above the data foundation schema. You can edit, create, delete, import, or export families, as shown in Figure 5.57.

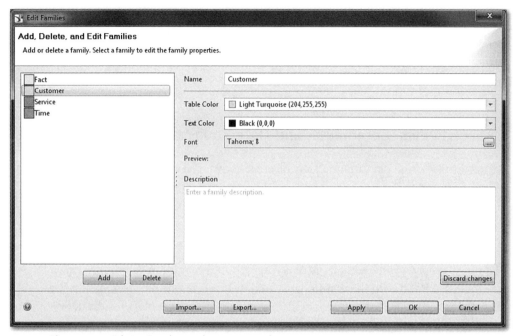

Figure 5.57 Editing Families in the Data Foundation

The family can change the table background color, the table text color, and the table text font. Families can also be imported or exported. They are stored in XML format and suffixed with *.families.xml*.

After the families have been created or edited, you can associate them with zero or multiple tables in the data foundation. To associate a family with a table, select one or several tables, alias tables, derived tables, or federated tables in the data foundation, and then select a family in the dropdown list in the toolbar above the data foundation schema, as shown in Figure 5.58.

Figure 5.58 Associating a Family with Tables

To remove the association between tables and families, select the family named No FAMILY in the dropdown list.

All selected tables are colored with the family definition, as shown in Figure 5.59. A table can be associated with a family in a given data foundation view (see Section 5.12.3) and with another family in another data foundation view.

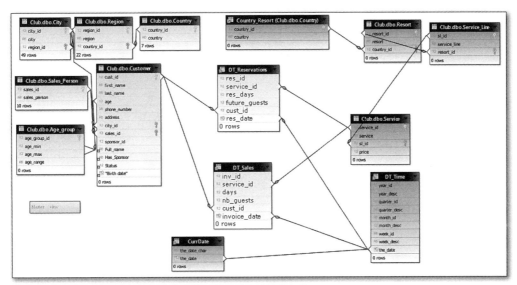

Figure 5.59 Data Foundation with Tables Associated to Families

5.12.2 Comments

Another feature that helps you to easily maintain and understand a data foundation is the ability to add comments. You can create as many comments as you want in data foundation views. Comments are linked to the data foundation and aren't linked to a particular table or join.

Comments are useful to describe the data modeling, the tables, the joins, the cardinalities, the derived tables, the alias tables, the federated tables, and so on. They are useful to describe anything that need to be commented and or anything that may not be obvious to understand for anyone that has to review or maintain the data foundation.

To create a comment, select one of the following options:

▶ Right-click anywhere in the data foundation schema, and then select INSERT • COMMENT.

▶ Select ACTIONS • INSERT • COMMENT.

▶ Click the INSERT button in the toolbar above the data foundation schema, and select INSERT COMMENT.

Enter the text in the comment text box and change the different settings if needed, as shown in Figure 5.60.

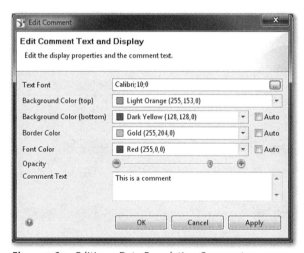

Figure 5.60 Editing a Data Foundation Comment

Comments can be edited or deleted and moved anywhere in the data foundation schema, as shown in Figure 5.61. You can also copy comments between different data foundation views.

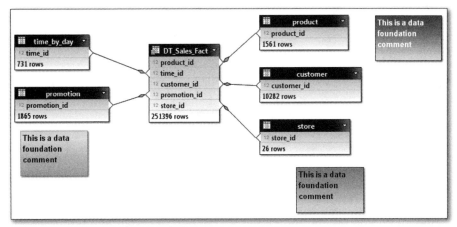

Figure 5.61 Data Foundation with Comments

To edit a comment, you can right-click on the comment and select EDIT, or you can double-click on a comment to open the editor.

5.12.3 Data Foundation View

Data foundations have been enriched with families and comments, but that's not enough to help you to manage large data foundations containing hundreds of tables. Maintaining large data foundations becomes even more difficult when they contain loops solved by contexts or aggregate tables. Data foundation *views* have been introduced to help you manage these large data foundations.

You can create as many data foundation views as you want. A data foundation view is a schema containing from zero to many tables; joins are inherited and automatically added when the tables associated with those joins are added to the data foundation views.

When a data foundation is created, a default data foundation view named Master is added. The master data foundation view can't be deleted. The master data foundation view contains all tables and joins and is the data foundation schema reference.

A data foundation view focuses on a particular aspect of the master data foundation view; the data foundation view can be functional (customers, sales, marketing, etc.) or technical (context, star schema, etc.).

In a data foundation view, you can do the following:

▶ Insert tables (see Section 5.2)

▶ Create alias tables (see Section 5.6.2)

▶ Create derived tables (see Section 5.4)

▶ Create federated tables (see Chapter 6, Section 6.4)

▶ Add joins (see Section 5.3)

▶ Create calculated columns (see Section 5.5)

All creation and insertion actions in a data foundation view are automatically propagated to the master data foundation view. New joins are also propagated to other data foundation views if the tables referenced by this new join already exist in the other data foundation views.

Some actions only impact a given data foundation view but not the master data foundation view. Actions that *do not* impact the master view include the following

▶ Remove tables, derived tables, alias tables, or federated tables. Removing tables can also remove joins if the join becomes orphan.

▶ Delete a data foundation view.

▶ Change the layout of tables and joins by moving tables, collapsing/expanding tables, zooming in/out, reorganizing tables, changing table families, and so on.

▶ Add, edit, or delete comments.

All other actions done in a given data foundation view *do* impact the master data foundation view. Here is a non-exhaustive list of actions impacting the master data foundation view:

▶ Delete a join.

▶ Delete a calculated column.

▶ Rename a table.

▶ Change the owner or the qualifier of a table.

▶ Turn a table into a derived table.

There are many ways to create a data foundation view, including the following:

▶ Right-click anywhere in the data foundation schema, and then select INSERT • DATA FOUNDATION VIEW.

▶ Click the INSERT button in the toolbar above the data foundation schema, and select INSERT VIEW.

▶ Select ACTIONS • INSERT • VIEW.

▶ Select tables in the data foundation schema, right-click, and then select INSERT • VIEW FROM SELECTION.

▶ Click the INSERT VIEW tab in the data foundation tabs below the data foundation schema, as shown in Figure 5.62.

Figure 5.62 Inserting a Data Foundation View

You can also add tables to an existing data foundation view by selecting tables from any data foundation view.

> **Note**
>
> If you delete a data foundation view, there is no impact on other data foundation views except for comments, which are deleted with the data foundation view.

If you select tables in a given data foundation view, you can create a new data foundation view based on the selection, but you can also add your selection in an existing data foundation view. After you've selected the tables, right-click, select ADD TO VIEW, and then choose one of the data foundation views, as shown in Figure 5.63. Only the data foundation views that don't contain the selected tables are displayed.

All actions available in the master data foundation view are available in all data foundation views. All data foundation views (except the master data foundation view) can be duplicated, renamed, and reordered.

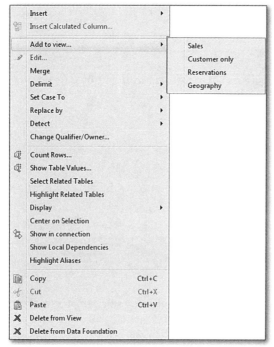

Figure 5.63 Adding Selected Tables into an Existing Data Foundation View

5.13   Data Foundation Search Panel

Recent customer feedback has highlighted that half of universes contain more than 500 resources and two-thirds of universes are updated once a month or once a quarter. The conclusion is that a universe designer has to regularly maintain large universes. In an enterprise organization, it can happen that the person who designed the universe isn't the person who maintains it.

To help you easily find information in large data foundations, a dedicated data foundation search panel feature has been introduced in SAP BusinessObjects BI 4.0. The data foundation search panel is an additional pane added on the right-hand side of the data foundation schema. To open the search panel, click the SHOW/HIDE SEARCH PANEL toggle button ( ) in the toolbar above the data foundation schema. The search panel is shown in Figure 5.64.

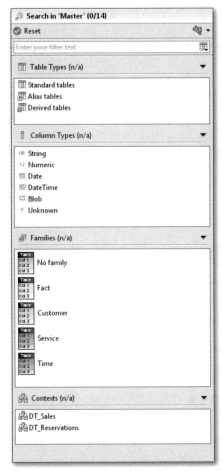

Figure 5.64 Data Foundation Search Panel

The search panel is split into five parts:

▸ Search in table names and column names: ENTER YOUR FILTER TEXT text box (see Section 5.2)

▸ TABLE TYPES

▸ COLUMN TYPES

▸ FAMILIES (see Section 5.12.1)

▸ CONTEXTS (see Section 5.6.3)

The search panel can be invoked from any data foundation view. If you select a different data foundation view while the search panel is open, the selection(s) done in the search panel are reflected in the data foundation view. By default, no selection is preset in the data foundation view when the search panel opens; all tables are grayed out.

Each selection done in the search panel highlights and selects tables in the data foundation view, and the number of tables matching the selection criteria is displayed above the search panel as shown in Figure 5.65. The different search criteria are used to select tables in a data foundation view; joins aren't selected.

If you click the RESET button, all selections are removed, and no table is selected in the data foundation view.

Figure 5.65 Number of Selected Tables in the Data Foundation Search Panel

The tables matching the different selected criteria are highlighted and selected in the data foundation view, as shown later in this chapter in Figure 5.71.

All search criteria inside the same category are combined with an OR operator, and search criteria belonging to different categories are combined with an AND operator.

Example
You've defined the following search criteria to select tables in the data foundation view:
▶ Alias tables OR derived tables
▶ AND family Sales OR family Customer
▶ AND column names contain "_id"

5.13.1 Table and Column Names Selection

You can select tables in a given data foundation view by entering full or partial table names and full or partial column names, as shown in Figure 5.66.

Figure 5.66 Search Tables: Table/Column Names Search Criteria

5.13.2 Table Types Selection

You can also select tables in a given data foundation view by selecting one or multiple table types such as STANDARD TABLES, ALIAS TABLES, DERIVED TABLES, or FEDERATED TABLES (see Chapter 6, Section 6.4), as shown in Figure 5.67. If you select ALIAS TABLES and DERIVED TABLES, the alias tables and the derived tables are selected in the data foundation view.

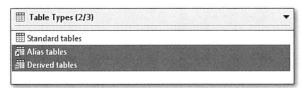

Figure 5.67 Search Tables: Table Types Search Criteria

5.13.3 Column Types Selection

You can also select tables in a given data foundation view by selecting one or multiple column data types, as shown in Figure 5.68. If you select STRING and NUMERIC, then all tables containing at least one string column or one numeric column are selected in the data foundation view.

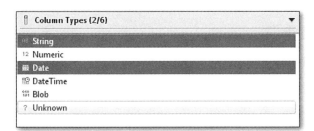

Figure 5.68 Search Tables: Column Data Types Search Criteria

5.13.4 Families Selection

You can also select tables in a given data foundation view by selecting one or multiple families as shown in Figure 5.69. If you select CUSTOMER family and TIME family, then all tables associated with those families are selected in the data foundation view. You can also select tables associated with no family by selecting the NO FAMILY family.

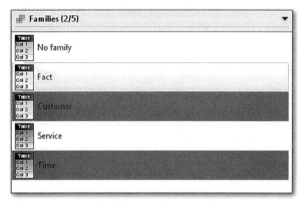

Figure 5.69 Search Tables: Families Search Criteria

5.13.5 Contexts Selection

You can also select tables in a given data foundation view by selecting one or multiple contexts in Figure 5.70. If you select the SALES context and INVENTORY context, then all tables associated with those contexts are selected in the data foundation view.

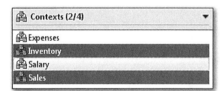

Figure 5.70 Search Tables: Contexts Search Criteria

Selecting tables belonging to one context is often an easy way to create a new data foundation view.

5.13.6 Possible Actions after Tables Selection in a Data Foundation View

After the different search criteria are entered, the number of tables matching the selected criteria is displayed above the search panel, as shown earlier in Figure 5.65. The tables are highlighted and selected in the data foundation view (see Figure 5.71).

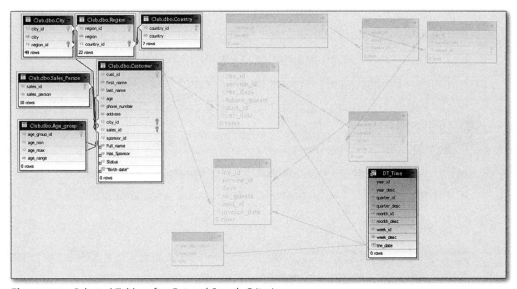

Figure 5.71 Selected Tables after Entered Search Criteria

The objective of the data foundation search panel is, of course, to find and select tables, but it's also used to perform actions on the selected tables. Several actions can be done directly in the data foundation view while the search panel is open and can also be done after the search panel is closed. The tables selected remain selected unless you do something in the data foundation schema that unselects the tables.

5.14 Data Foundation Editor

In the previous sections you discovered how to create a data foundation, insert tables and create joins, create derived tables or calculated columns, solve loops, and so on. These actions can be invoked from many places such as the data foundation schema, toolbars, menus, data foundation pane, and so on. This section summarizes all actions you can do in the data foundation, including actions that have not been mentioned in previous sections.

When working with a multisource data foundation, some additional commands and panels are available in the editor; these we discuss in Chapter 6.

The data foundation editor groups the different data foundation user interface parts to interact with the data foundation:

▶ The data foundation schema (refer to Figure 5.3)

▶ The DATA FOUNDATION pane (refer to Figure 5.11)

▶ The ALIASES AND CONTEXTS pane (refer to Figure 5.32)

▶ The PARAMETERS pane (refer to Figure 5.51) and LIST OF VALUES pane (refer to Figure 5.46)

▶ The CONNECTION pane (refer to Figure 5.4)

▶ The data foundation INSERT VIEW tab (refer to Figure 5.62)

▶ The toolbar above the data foundation schema, as shown in Figure 5.72

▶ The ACTIONS menu, as shown in Figure 5.73

Figure 5.72 Data Foundation Schema Toolbar

Figure 5.73 Actions Menu in the Data Foundation

5.14.1 Possible Actions in the Data Foundation Schema

The data foundation schema is the best place to interact with the data foundation, so it offers the most actions. If nothing is selected in the data foundation schema, the possible actions include the following:

▶ INSERT • DATA FOUNDATION VIEW

▶ INSERT • TABLES

▶ INSERT • JOIN

▶ INSERT • DERIVED TABLE

▶ INSERT • COMMENT

▶ CHECK INTEGRITY

If at least one table, alias table, derived table, or federated table is selected in the data foundation schema, the main possible actions are as listed in Table 5.14.

Action	Description and Comments
INSERT • ALIAS TABLE	This action adds a new alias table in the data foundation (see Section 5.6.2).
INSERT • DERIVED TABLE	This action adds a new derived table in the data foundation (see Section 5.4). The SQL statement of the derived tables is automatically generated.
INSERT • VIEW FROM SELECTION	This action creates a new data foundation view (see Section 5.12.3) that includes selected tables in the data foundation schema. This action is very useful when coupled with the search panel selections.
INSERT CALCULATED COLUMN	This action adds a new calculated column in the table and opens the SQL editor (see Section 5.5).
ADD TO VIEW • *<Name of View>*	This action inserts in the chosen data foundation view the selected tables in the data foundation schema. This action is very useful when coupled with the search panel selections.
MERGE	This action is only available if at least two tables are selected. This action is used for creating a derived table.

Table 5.14 Possible Actions in the Data Foundation Schema when at Least One Table is Selected

Action	Description and Comments
DELIMIT	This action adds or doesn't add a delimiter to the table names and the column names. For more information, see Section 5.14.9.
SET CASE TO	This action changes the case of table names and column names. For more information, see Section 5.14.9.
REPLACE BY • ALIAS TABLE	This action is available if only one table is selected. The selected table is replaced by an alias table and all of the joins linked to the selected table are relinked to the created alias table. The business layer isn't automatically updated, so you have to manually do the updates in the business layer.
REPLACE BY • DERIVED TABLE	This action is available if only one table is selected. The selected table is replaced by a derived table and all of the joins linked to the selected table are relinked to the created derived table. All table columns including calculated columns are included in the derived table SQL definition. The business layer isn't automatically updated, so you have to manually do the updates in the business layer.
REPLACE BY • DATABASE TABLE	This action is available if only one table is selected. The selected table is replaced by a database table. The joins linked to the selected table are relinked to the added database table, only if the column names participating to the joins are identical in the selected table and the added table. The business layer isn't automatically updated, so you have to manually do the updates in the business layer
DETECT • JOINS	This action proposes a list of potential joins between the select tables. For more information on joins detection, see Section 5.3.4.
DETECT • KEYS	This action tries to identify keys on the select tables. For more information on keys detection, see Section 5.3.4.
DETECT • ROW COUNT	This action counts the number of rows per selected table. For more information, see Section 5.14.9.

Table 5.14 Possible Actions in the Data Foundation Schema when at Least One Table is Selected (Cont.)

Action	Description and Comments
CHANGE OWNER/ QUALIFIER	This action changes the owner and the qualifier of the selected tables. For more information, see Section 5.14.9.
COUNT ROWS	This action counts the number of rows in a query involving one or multiple selected tables. For more information, see Section 5.14.9.
SHOW TABLE VALUES	This action runs a query on the selected tables and displays the results. For more information on data preview, see Section 5.16.
SELECT RELATED TABLES VALUES	This action selects tables that are joined with the selected tables. For more information, see Section 5.14.9.
HIGHLIGHT RELATED TABLES VALUES	This action highlights tables that are joined with the selected tables. For more information, see Section 5.14.9.
DISPLAY	This action changes the table's display. For more information, see Section 5.14.9.
SHOW LOCAL DEPENDENCIES	This action shows the dependencies (see Section 5.18) between resources in the data foundation.

Table 5.14 Possible Actions in the Data Foundation Schema when at Least One Table is Selected (Cont.)

If at least one join is selected in the data foundation schema, there is only one possible action: DETECT CARDINALITY. This action detects the cardinalities of the selected joins.

If a table column is selected in the data foundation schema, the possible actions are as listed in Table 5.15.

Action	Description and Comments
SET AS KEY	You can set the selected column to PRIMARY KEY, FOREIGN KEY, or NONE.
INSERT • FILTER	A filter is a filter join (see Section 5.3.3) defined on a single column.
	This join, also called a self-join, is used to filter a table, a derived table, an alias table, or a federated table.
SHOW COLUMN VALUES	This action runs a query on the selected column and displays the results.
	For more information on data preview, see Section 5.16.
PROFILE COLUMN VALUES	This action runs a query on the selected column and displays the number of occurrences per value.
	For more information on data preview, see Section 5.16.
SHOW LOCAL DEPENDENCIES	This action shows the dependencies (see Section 5.18) between resources in the data foundation.

Table 5.15 Possible Actions in the Data Foundation Schema when at Least One Column is Selected

5.14.2 Possible Actions in the Data Foundation Pane

The DATA FOUNDATION pane offers exactly the same actions available in the data foundation schema. In addition, tables and joins available in a given data foundation view are visible and selectable in the DATA FOUNDATION pane whereas other tables and joins are grayed out, as shown in Figure 5.74.

5.14.3 Possible Actions in the Aliases and Contexts Pane

In the ALIASES AND CONTEXTS pane, the list of aliases is displayed and is equivalent to the DATA FOUNDATION pane but only reduced to the list of aliases as shown in Figure 5.75. Also, the list of contexts is displayed as shown in Figure 5.75. Clicking on a context highlights the joins and tables involved in the context, and double-clicking on a context makes the selected context editable.

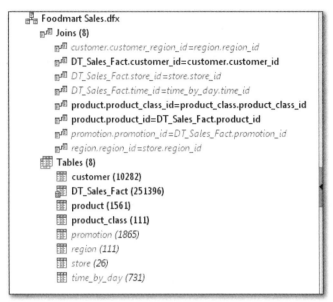

Figure 5.74 A Data Foundation View Detailed in the Data Foundation Pane

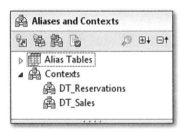

Figure 5.75 Aliases and Contexts Pane

All actions available in the data foundation schema are also available in the ALIASES AND CONTEXTS pane. A different data foundation view can be selected, and the actions performed in the panes are reflected in the data foundation view whenever possible.

5.14.4 Possible Actions in the Parameters and List of Values Pane

In the PARAMETERS pane, you can only manage parameters via create, edit, delete, duplicate, or reorder. In the LIST OF VALUES pane, you can only manage lists of values via create, edit, delete, duplicate, preview, or reorder. As for any other data foundation resources, it's also possible to show the dependencies and to run the check integrity tool.

5.14.5 Possible Actions in the Connection Pane

The CONNECTION pane offers exactly the same actions available in the data foundation schema and is focused on the connection. (For more information on connections, see Chapter 4.) You can also browse the database catalog associated with the relational connection, as shown earlier in Figure 5.4, and can run the following actions:

▸ View the list of tables and views.

▸ View a table's columns.

▸ Drag and drop a table in the data foundation schema.

▸ View a table's properties, as shown in Figure 5.76.

▸ Show table values.

▸ Show column values.

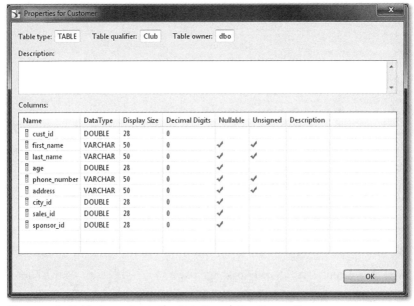

Figure 5.76 Table Properties in the Data Foundation Connection

Possible Actions in the Connection Toolbar

A toolbar in the CONNECTION pane offers additional actions, as described in Table 5.16 and shown in Figure 5.77.

Action	Description and Comments
CHANGE CONNECTION	Associate a different connection to the data foundation.
	We recommend that you do a data foundation refresh structure (see Section 5.17) to ensure that the data foundation reflects potential differences between the old and the new connections.
TEST CONNECTION	Validate the connection.
	Detailed connection information is displayed when the connection is valid, as shown in Figure 5.78.
	A detailed message error is displayed in case of an invalid connection, as shown in Figure 5.79.
SHOW QUALIFIERS AND OWNERS	Show or hide the qualifiers and owners in the database catalog browser.
	If the qualifiers and owners are hidden, only the tables belonging to the database schema defined in the connection are displayed.
FILTER	Filter the database catalog browser by selecting only tables, only views, or both.
	For SAP HANA, additional filter options are available:
	▶ Analytic view
	▶ Calculation view
	▶ Attribute view
	▶ Hierarchy view
	▶ User defined
SHOW/HIDE TABLE SEARCH	Showing the table search adds a new pane below the database catalog browser.
	For more information on search and filter in the connection, see Section 5.2.4.
REFRESH	Refresh the list of tables and views.

Table 5.16 Available Actions in the Connection Toolbar

Figure 5.77 Connection Toolbar

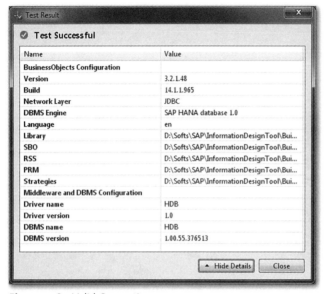

Figure 5.78 Valid Connection

Figure 5.79 Invalid Connection

5.14.6 Possible Actions in the Data Foundation Toolbar

The data foundation toolbar, as shown in Figure 5.80 and Figure 5.81, offers some of the actions available in the data foundation schema. The toolbar is above the data foundation schema and is always visible no matter which data foundation view is selected.

Figure 5.80 Data Foundation Toolbar (View 1)

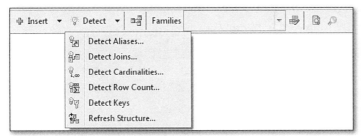

Figure 5.81 Data Foundation Toolbar (View 2)

Depending on the resources (tables, joins) selected in the data foundation schema, along with the INSERT and DETECT options/actions shown in the preceding figures, the following actions are also possible:

▶ Refresh structure (see Section 5.17)

▶ Auto arrange the tables and joins in the selected data foundation view (see Section 5.14.9)

▶ Manage families (see Section 5.12.1)

▶ Show/hide the SEARCH panel

> **Note**
>
> For more detailed information about the data foundation actions, see Section 5.14.9.

5.14.7 Possible Actions in the Data Foundation View Tab

Each data foundation view added in the data foundation can be selected from its tab as shown earlier in Figure 5.62. In addition, if you right-click on a data foundation view tab, you can do the following:

- Rename a data foundation view.

- Copy/cut and paste to duplicate a data foundation view.

- Delete a data foundation view.

- Reorder the data foundation views.

5.14.8 Possible Actions in the Actions Menu

The ACTIONS menu offers some of the actions available in the data foundation schema. Depending on the resources (tables, joins) selected in the data foundation schema, the following actions are possible:

- Change connection(s)
- Insert
  - Insert tables
  - Insert derived tables
  - Insert alias (alias table)
  - Insert join
  - Insert context
  - Insert parameter
  - Insert list of values
  - Insert view (data foundation view)
  - Insert comment
- Detect
  - Detect row count
  - Detect keys
  - Detect joins
  - Detect cardinalities
  - Detect aliases (alias table)
  - Detect contexts
  - Detect loops
- Refresh structure (see Section 5.17)
- Auto arrange the tables and joins in the selected data foundation view (see Section 5.14.9)

5.14.9 Data Foundation Actions

This section describes some of the actions that you can perform in the data foundation and its resources.

Detect Row Count

This action sends an SQL query to the database to count the number of rows for each selected table. The number of rows is displayed under the table in the data foundation schema, as shown in Figure 5.82. The number of rows is also displayed on the left-hand side of the table name enclosed in parentheses in the DATA FOUNDATION pane, as show in Figure 5.83.

Figure 5.82 Counting the Number of Rows for the Selected Tables

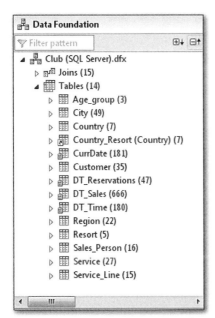

Figure 5.83 Counting the Number of Rows for the Selected Tables

Delimit

This action encloses or doesn't enclose table names and column names with double quotes. The DELIMIT action offers different choices, as shown in Figure 5.84.

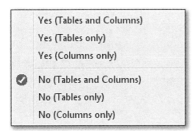

Figure 5.84 Choosing the Table Names and Column Names Delimiter

The option currently applied for the selected table is checked. The table names and column names are modified according to the selected option.

Set Case To

This action changes the table names and column names to uppercase or lowercase. The SET CASE TO action offers different choices, as shown in Figure 5.85.

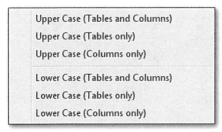

Figure 5.85 Choosing the Table Names and Column Names Case

The table names and column names are modified according to the selected option.

Change Owner/Qualifier

This action allows you to change the owner and the qualifier of the selected tables. The CHANGE OWNER/QUALIFIER action isn't available if derived tables, alias tables, or federated tables are selected. To change the owner and the qualifier for all tables in the data foundation, the best way is to use the data foundation search panel tool and select STANDARD tables. (For more information on the data foundation search panel, see Section 5.13.)

Count Rows

This action sends an SQL query to the database, including the selected tables. The generated query includes the selected tables and potentially additional tables and joins to have the selected tables included in a single SQL query.

The query is generated only if the selected tables can be joined, but it may happen that the table's selection implies other options:

▸ An error is displayed if the tables are incompatible and the contexts can't be detected.

▸ If the tables belong to different contexts, a dialog box is displayed to let you choose a context.

The number of rows returned by the query and the SQL query are displayed in a dialog box, as shown in Figure 5.86.

Figure 5.86 Counting the Number of Rows in a Query Involving Selected Tables

Select Related Tables

This action selects the tables that are directly joined to the selected tables. If you repeat the same action several times, then you can select all tables of the data foundation schema if the tables have at least one join with another.

Highlight Related Tables

This action highlights the tables that are directly joined to the selected tables as show in Figure 5.87. Other tables are grayed out.

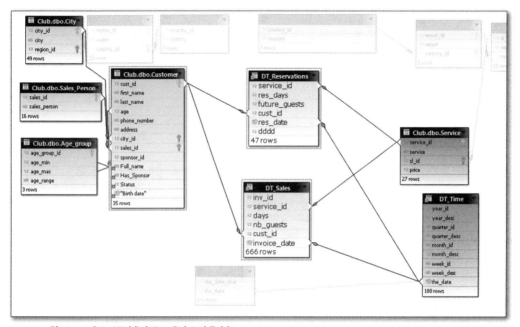

Figure 5.87 Highlighting Related Tables

Display

The DISPLAY action changes the table's display in the data foundation schema with the following possible options:

▶ COLLAPSED
No column is displayed in the table box.

▶ EXPANDED
All columns are displayed in the table box.

▶ JOINS ONLY
Only columns participating to joins are displayed in the table box.

Auto Arrange

The Auto Arrange action redraws the data foundation schema and tries to minimize the length of the different joins.

5.14.10 Data Foundation Properties

The data foundation properties are actionable in the data foundation schema as shown and discussed in Section 5.19. You can add a description or comments in the data foundation. Like almost any other universe resource, you can also add custom properties (see Chapter 7, Section 7.20.7).

The data foundation can be tuned by setting different parameters by clicking the Parameters button. In addition, you can also set SQL options (see Section 5.19) by selecting the SQL Options tab. You can also change the connection of the data foundation by clicking the button Change Connection. (For more information on relational connection, see Chapter 4, Section 4.1.)

If you change the connection, we recommend that you do a data foundation refresh structure to ensure that potential differences between the old and the new connections are reflected in the data foundation.

To see a summary of the data foundation as shown in Figure 5.88, click the Summary button.

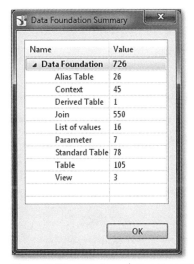

Figure 5.88 Data Foundation Summary

5.15   Checking Integrity

Before you build the business layer (see Chapter 7), it's important to ensure that the data foundation is ready to be used and doesn't contain errors in the connection or in its resources definition. You should check that the data foundation is always valid because a data foundation schema design can frequently change in the following ways:

▶ Tables and columns are deleted and renamed.

▶ New tables and columns are added.

▶ New loops are introduced.

▶ Contexts are reviewed.

▶ Derived tables are modified.

▶ Calculated columns are modified or created.

▶ Joins are modified or created.

The data foundation validation is an ongoing process because its schema can change and business requirements are constantly evolving. To validate the data foundation, you must invoke the check integrity tool. To run the check integrity tool, select one of the following options:

▶ Deselect all tables and joins, right-click anywhere in a data foundation view, and then select the CHECK INTEGRITY option.

▶ Right-click the data foundation name in the DATA FOUNDATION pane, and then select the CHECK INTEGRITY option.

▶ Click the button in the IDT toolbar.

The check integrity tool can also be individually invoked for a context, a parameter, or a list of values. To do so, right-click on the resource, and then select CHECK INTEGRITY.

The data foundation can also be validated in the business layer check integrity step.

5.15.1 Run the Check Integrity

When the CHECK INTEGRITY panel opens, the list of appropriate validation rules is displayed. You can check all or part of the validation rules, and click the CHECK INTEGRITY button to validate the data foundation resources, as shown in Figure 5.89.

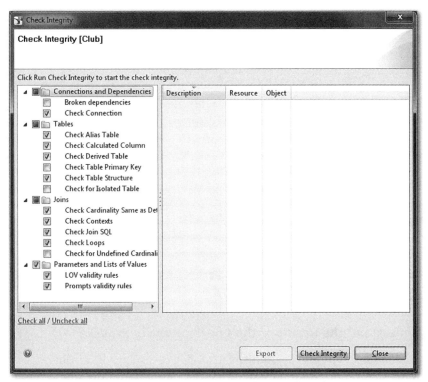

Figure 5.89 Data Foundation Check Integrity: Validation Rules Selection

Depending on the number of tables and joins and on the selected validation rules, the check integrity process can take some time. Some validation rules are more time-consuming than others, such as the CHECK CARDINALITIES rule. You can interrupt one or more processes at any time by clicking one of the red X buttons, as shown on the right side of Figure 5.90.

Figure 5.90 Data Foundation Check Integrity in Progress

5.15.2 Understand the Result of the Check Integrity Process

After the check integrity process is finished, an icon is displayed in front of each validation rule, as shown in Figure 5.91:

▶ ✅: All data foundation resources (tables, joins, list of values, etc.) have been successfully validated for this particular validation rule.

▶ ⚠: At least one resource returns a warning for this particular validation rule.

▶ ✕: At least one resource returns an error for this particular validation rule.

▶ ⓘ : At least one resource returns information for this particular validation rule.

You can export the results in a text file or a *.csv* file by clicking the EXPORT button, as shown in Figure 5.91. The results are also kept in the PROBLEMS view of IDT.

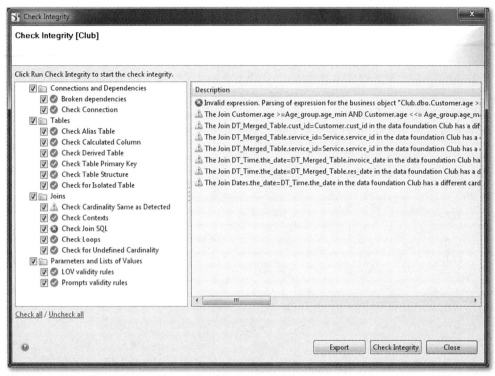

Figure 5.91 Results of the Data Foundation Check Integrity Process

5.15.3 Analyze and Fix Errors and Warnings

Warnings can be fixed, but this step isn't mandatory to make the universe consumable by the SAP BusinessObjects BI clients. On the other hand, errors *must* be fixed to avoid incorrect behavior of the universe.

To access a data foundation resource that contains an error or a warning, open the Problems view of IDT (see Figure 5.92) by selecting Window • Check Integrity Problems.

The list of errors and warnings is displayed in this view (this is a standard view of the Java Eclipse environment), and the Problems view content is always kept even if IDT is closed. The view content can be overridden with a new check integrity process or if the view content is intentionally erased. Each project resource (connection, data foundation, or business layer) open in IDT has its own Problems

263

view, so erasing or overriding the PROBLEMS view for one project resource doesn't impact other project resources.

Errors and warnings are categorized in the PROBLEMS view. To access the data foundation resource concerned by an error or a warning, double-click a row in the PROBLEMS view to open the appropriate editor as shown in Figure 5.92. If the error or warning concerns a connection resource, the editor won't open, but you can open the connection by right-clicking on it and selecting EDIT option.

Description	Resource	Path	Location	Type
⊿ ⊗ Errors (1 item)				
⊗ Invalid expression. Parsing of expression for tl	Club (SQL Ser...	IDT/Relational	Joins	Check Integrity
⊿ ⚠ Warnings (7 items)				
⚠ The Join Customer.age >=Age_group.age_m	Club (SQL Ser...	IDT/Relational	Joins	Check Integrity
⚠ The Join Dates.the_date=DT_Time.the_date ir	Club (SQL Ser...	IDT/Relational	Joins	Check Integrity
⚠ The Join DT_Merged_Table.cust_id=Custome	Club (SQL Ser...	IDT/Relational	Joins	Check Integrity
⚠ The Join DT_Merged_Table.service_id=Servic	Club (SQL Ser...	IDT/Relational	Joins	Check Integrity
⚠ The Join DT_Merged_Table.service_id=Servic	Club (SQL Ser...	IDT/Relational	Joins	Check Integrity
⚠ The Join DT_Time.the_date=DT_Merged_Tab	Club (SQL Ser...	IDT/Relational	Joins	Check Integrity

Error Log | Properties | Problems ✕ — 1 error, 7 warnings, 0 others

Figure 5.92   Selecting a Row in Problems View to Open the Appropriate Editor

Data foundation resources with errors or warnings are decorated with a wavy line, as shown in Figure 5.93. A tooltip containing the error/warning message is displayed when you hover the mouse over the concerned object, as shown in Figure 5.93.

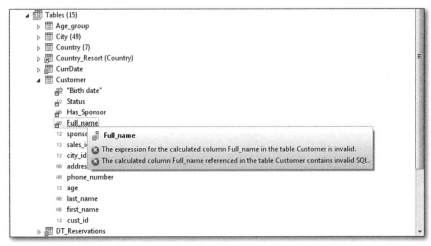

Figure 5.93   Calculated Column with an Error

5.15.4 Customize the Validation Rules

You can customize the severity of each validation rule with the values ERROR, WARNING, or INFO. To customize the validation rules, select WINDOW • PREFERENCES. When the PREFERENCES dialog box appears, select INFORMATION DESIGN TOOL • CHECK INTEGRITY, as shown in Figure 5.94.

You can change the severity of each validation rule or restore the default values for one or all validation rules. When a validation rule is checked in the PREFERENCES window, the validation rule is always checked by default when the check integrity tool is invoked. You can decide afterward to check or uncheck this validation rule.

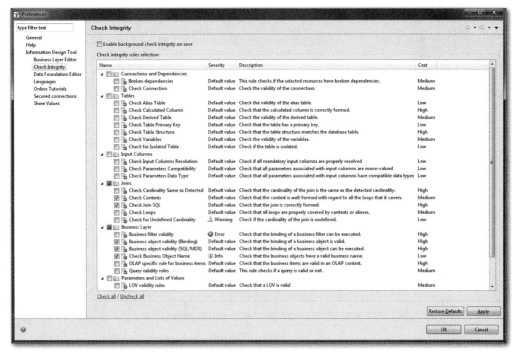

Figure 5.94 Customize the Check Integrity Validation Rules

The COST column provides information concerning the time cost when this validation rule is run.

If you activate the ENABLE BACKGROUND CHECK INTEGRITY ON SAVE option, then all validation rules that have been checked in the PREFERENCES window are executed in the background after a save operation for a connection, a data foundation, or a business layer, as shown in Figure 5.94.

5.15.5 Validation Rules Definition

Table 5.17 describes the validation rules used for the data foundation check integrity tool. Please notice that most of the validation rules can be executed only if the database connection is valid and can be established.

Validation Rule	Description
Check alias table	Check the validity of the alias table (see Section 5.6). Check whether the source table has been removed.
Check calculated column	Check that the calculated column (see Section 5.5) is correctly formed. Check that the SQL definition is correct.
Check derived table	Check the validity of the derived table (see Section 5.4). Check that the SQL definition is correct.
Check table primary key	Check that the table has a primary key (see Section 5.3).
Check input columns resolution	This validation rule only applies for a multisource data foundation (see Chapter 6).
Check parameters compatibility	This validation rule only applies for multisource data foundation.
Check parameters data type	This validation rule only applies for multisource data foundation.
Check cardinality same as detected	Check that the cardinality defined in the join is the same that the cardinality detected. Detecting cardinalities is a time-consuming process and isn't always reliable, so universe designers often manually set the cardinalities. For more information on cardinalities, see Section 5.3.
Check contexts	Check that the context (see Section 5.6) is well-formed with regard to all of the loops that it covers. Because a data foundation is frequently changing, the contexts can be impacted, and it's not obvious to know which have to be modified, created, or removed.

Table 5.17 Data Foundation Validation Rules

Validation Rule	Description
Check join SQL	Check that the join (see Section 5.3) is correctly formed. Check that the SQL definition is correct.
Check loops	Check that all loops are properly covered by contexts or aliases. Again, the changes brought in a data foundation can create new loops or remove existing loops. Sometimes it's a good solution to delete all contexts and use the automatic creation. For more information on loops, see Section 5.6.
Check for undefined cardinality	Check if the cardinality of the join is undefined. Setting join cardinalities isn't mandatory. For more information on join cardinalities, see Section 5.3.
LOV validity rules	Check that the list of values (see Section 5.8) is valid.
Prompt validity rules	Check that the @prompt function (see Section 5.11) used in a resource binding is valid.

Table 5.17 Data Foundation Validation Rules (Cont.)

5.16   Previewing Data

As for the business layer, there are many ways to see data content. Table 5.18 lists all places where you can see data content in the data foundation.

Resource	View Data
Select one or more tables	SHOW TABLE VALUES For instance, if two tables are selected, an SQL query including the tables is generated. This query can also include additional tables if the two tables aren't directly joined.
Select one or more columns	SHOW COLUMN VALUES For instance, if two columns are selected, an SQL query including the columns is built. If the two columns belong to different generated tables, the query can also include additional tables if the two tables aren't directly joined.

Table 5.18 Different Places to View Data

267

Resource	View Data
Select one column	SHOW COLUMN VALUES PROFILE COLUMN VALUES The PROFILE COLUMN VALUES query displays the distinct number of values. The result is displayed in a table, a pie chart, or a bar chart as shown in Figure 5.95.
List of values	PREVIEW Preview the content of a list of values and answer to parameters or prompts if required.

Table 5.18 Different Places to View Data (Cont.)

Figure 5.95 Profile for Column Values

You can view the content of any table or combination of tables and also any column and combination of columns at any time. You have to first select one or more tables or select one or more columns. To view the content of the selected resources, right-click and select one of the following options:

▶ SHOW TABLE VALUES

▶ SHOW COLUMN VALUES

▶ PROFILE COLUMN VALUES

In the PARAMETERS and LISTS OF VALUES panes, select a list of values, and click the button PREVIEW. You can also right-click and select PREVIEW LIST OF VALUES. The result of the data preview is displayed in an editor tab, a dedicated view, or a dialog box depending on the settings defined in IDT preferences, as shown in Figure 5.96.

To set the preferences for data preview, select WINDOW • PREFERENCES. When the PREFERENCES dialog box opens, select INFORMATION DESIGN TOOL • SHOW VALUES, as shown in Figure 5.96.

Figure 5.96 Data Preview and Query Results Preferences

For more information concerning the results of data preview and list of values preview, see Chapter 2, Section 2.6.

5.17 Data Foundation Refresh Structure

The lifecycle of a universe, and especially the lifecycle of a data foundation, is one of the important tasks that you have to manage. Because a database can change, IDT offers the ability to refresh the data foundation and take into account changes in the database such as the following:

- Table deletion
- Column deletion
- Column addition

- ▶ Column data type change
- ▶ SQL view definition change

The data foundation refresh structure doesn't take into account the following changes:

- ▶ Table addition
- ▶ Table renaming
- ▶ Column renaming

To invoke the data foundation refresh structure tool, select the ACTIONS • REFRESH STRUCTURE. The refresh structure wizard is launched, and the database catalog is analyzed to display the following:

- ▶ The tables that have been deleted (as shown in Figure 5.97). By default, the tables are removed from the data foundation, but you can decide if you want to keep them.
- ▶ The columns that have been deleted from the tables (as shown in Figure 5.98). By default, the columns are removed from the appropriate tables in the data foundation, but you can decide if you want to keep them.

Figure 5.97 Data Foundation Refresh Structure: Missing Tables

▶ The columns that have been added in tables (as shown in Figure 5.99). By default, the columns are added to the appropriate tables in the data foundation, but you can decide if you want to add them.

▶ The columns data type that have changed (as shown in Figure 5.100). By default, the columns data type are updated, but you can decide whether you want to update them.

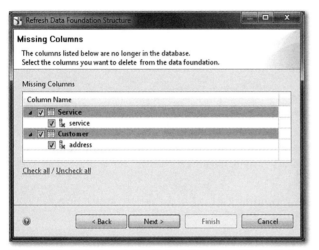

Figure 5.98 Data Foundation Refresh Structure: Missing Columns

Figure 5.99 Data Foundation Refresh Structure: New Columns

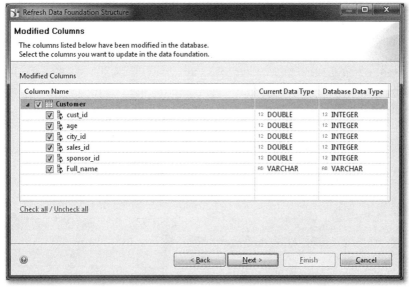

Figure 5.100 Data Foundation Refresh Structure: Modified Columns

The last wizard step shows the summary of actions that are impacting the data foundation.

5.17.1 Data Foundation Impacts after Refresh Structure

Table 5.19 describes the potential impacts and changes in the data foundation after the refresh structure.

Data Foundation Resource	Impact
Data foundation views and data foundation MASTER view	Deleted tables are removed from the data foundation. Tables with deleted columns or new columns are updated.
Derived table	Deleted tables and deleted columns can invalidate the derived table's definition.
Alias table	Alias tables referencing deleted tables are removed.

Table 5.19 Potential Data Foundation Impacts when Using the Refresh Structure

Data Foundation Resource	Impact
Calculated column	Calculated columns referencing deleted columns become invalid. A column data type change can also invalidate a calculated column.
Join	Joins referencing at least one deleted table are removed from the data foundation. Joins referencing at least one deleted column are removed from the data foundation. A filter join that includes a deleted table or a deleted column in its definition becomes invalid.

Table 5.19 Potential Data Foundation Impacts when Using the Refresh Structure (Cont.)

5.17.2 Business Layer Impacts after Refresh Structure

The business layer can also be impacted by the data foundation refresh structure. As listed in the preceding section, the data foundation resources can be modified or deleted to make a direct impact on the business layer.

There is no automatic change and update in the business layer resources, so you have to be aware that this task must be done manually. On the other hand, IDT provides several utilities and facilities to identify what resources need to be modified in the business layer:

▶ Run the check integrity tool to validate the business layer. (For more information on the business layer check integrity, see Chapter 7, Section 7.26.)

▶ Show the data foundation local dependencies (see Section 5.18) to identify the impacted business layers, then choose a business layer, and identify the impacted resources.

▶ Open a business layer and select a resource. Show the local dependencies to identify the data foundation resources impacting the business layer resource.

> **Tip**
>
> The show dependencies tool helps you identify the impacted resources and the impacting resources. So if data foundation resources have been deleted, the dependencies are also modified, and it won't be easy to identify the potential changes in the business layer beforehand. You should run the show dependencies tool prior to running the data foundation refresh structure.
>
> Because you can't run the dependencies for all resources, we recommend that you run a refresh structure to identify the deleted and modified resources but not apply the changes. Then run the dependencies for all of the resources that are supposed to be deleted to know which business layer resources are impacted.

5.18 Showing Dependencies

For a universe designer, it's important to know, understand, and estimate the impact analysis when the universe needs to be modified. Here are some questions that a universe designer has to answer:

▸ Which business layers are impacted if I modify the data foundation schema?

▸ Which dimensions, measures, and attributes are impacted if I modify a derived table definition?

▸ What are the impacted objects, parameters, and so on if I delete a list of values?

▸ What are the impacted objects if I change the definition of a calculated column?

▸ Which data foundations and business layers are impacted if I modify a connection definition?

▸ What is the impact on measures and dimensions if a column data type has changed?

▸ What are the impacted resources (connection, data foundation, and business layer) if I change the database vendor?

IDT offers a set of functionalities to help you quickly identify the impacted resources where another resource is changed in a project, in a business layer, or in a data foundation.

Let's take a look at the impact analysis between resources inside a data foundation.

To know the impacted resources, you need to select a data foundation resource (table, alias table, derived table, column, calculated column, parameter, list of values, or federated table), right-click, and select SHOW LOCAL DEPENDENCIES.

After the SHOW DEPENDENT BUSINESS LAYERS AND OBJECTS wizard opens, you have to choose one or multiple business layers sharing the same data foundation, as shown in Figure 5.101.

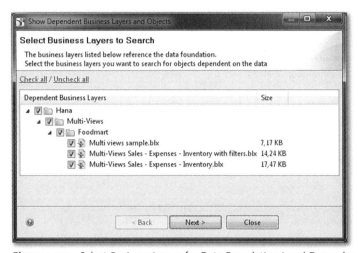

Figure 5.101 Select Business Layers for Data Foundation Local Dependencies

If the selected resource is a table (including alias tables, derived tables, and federated tables) or a column (including calculated columns), the business layer resources impacted are listed on the right-hand side of the SHOW DEPENDENT BUSINESS LAYERS AND OBJECTS dialog box. You can check or uncheck the columns on the left side to seed the list of impacted business layer resources changing, as shown in Figure 5.102.

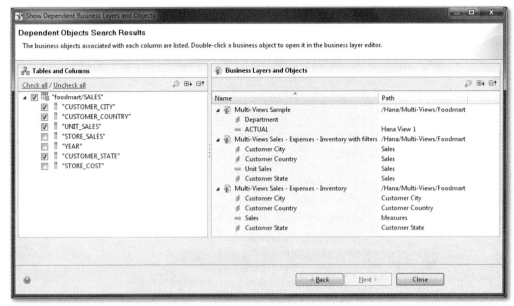

Figure 5.102 Data Foundation Impact Analysis

You can double-click on a business layer resource to open the business layer editor. If the selected resource is a list of values or a parameter, the SHOW DEPENDENT BUSINESS LAYERS AND OBJECTS dialog box is split in two parts:

▶ The DEPENDENT RESOURCES, as shown in Figure 5.103

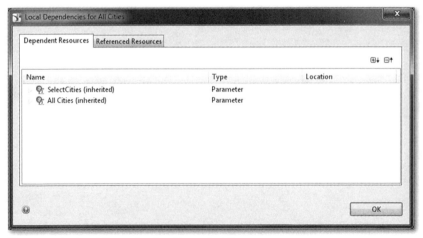

Figure 5.103 Local Dependencies: Dependent Resources

▶ The REFERENCED RESOURCES, as shown in Figure 5.104

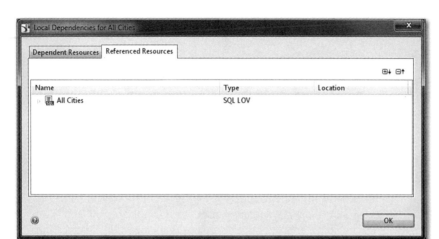

Figure 5.104 Local Dependencies: Referenced Resources

The list contains the resource name, the resource type, and the resource location (RESULT, FILTER, SELECT, WHERE, etc.). Each referenced or dependent resource can also be itself referenced by another resource or dependent of other resources; for instance, a list of values can reference a parameter in its SQL definition. Each resource can be expanded to see the other impacted resources.

5.19 Data Foundation Parameters

The data foundation behavior and hence the universe behavior can be tuned through different parameters that can impact the query generation and influence the behavior of measures, lists of values, joins, and so on. Some of the parameters are automatically set at the data foundation creation. The parameters can be added, deleted, and customized.

Data foundation parameters are only available for relational business layers (see Chapter 7). To access the data foundation SQL options, ensure that the data foundation PROPERTIES pane is visible under the data foundation schema, as shown in Figure 5.105.

Figure 5.105 Data Foundation Properties Pane

Select the data foundation root in the DATA FOUNDATION pane, select the PROPER-
TIES tab, and click the PARAMETERS button to open the QUERY SCRIPT PARAMETERS
dialog box shown in Figure 5.106.

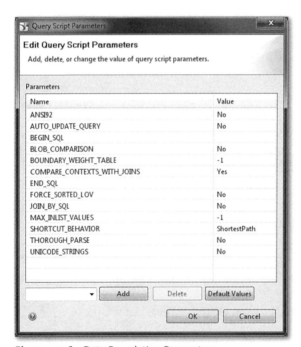

Figure 5.106 Data Foundation Parameters

Table 5.20 describes some of the data foundation parameters.

Parameter	Description
ANSI92	Values: YES/NO. Default value: No.
	This parameter is used by the query engine to generate SQL statements compliant to ANSI SQL-92.
AUTO_UPDATE_QUERY	Values: YES/NO. Default value: No.
	What happens to the query if an object isn't available for the user refreshing the query?
	If the value is No, the query is not modified and it may fail if an object is not available.
	If the value is YES, the object is removed from the query.
BEGIN_SQL	No default value.
	This placeholder can contain an SQL script and is run before the query. For instance, it can be used for setting options at the database level.
	This script can reference parameters, tables, columns, and built-in functions (see Section 5.11) such as @prompt or @variable.
BLOB_COMPARISON	Values: YES/NO. Default value: No.
	This parameter is also related to the parameter RETRIEVE DUPLICATED ROWS defined in the query panel (see Chapter 8).
	This parameter specifies whether a Select Distinct needs to be generated when a BLOB object is used in a query. If the parameter is set to YES, a Select Distinct is generated. If the parameter is set to No, the Select Distinct isn't generated even if the parameter has the RETRIEVE DUPLICATED ROWS option off.
END_SQL	No default value.
	This placeholder can contain an SQL script and is added to the end of the SQL query. For instance, in SAP HANA, the END_SQL can contain the following expression: WITH PARAMETERS ('request_flags'='USE_PARALLEL_ AGGREGATION', 'request_flags'='ANALYZE_MODEL')
FORCE_SORTED_LOV	Values: YES/NO. Default value: No.
	If the value is YES, all list of values are sorted.

Table 5.20 *Most Important Data Foundation Parameters*

Parameter	Description
INNERJOIN_IN_WHERE	Values: YES/NO. Default value: NO. This parameter concerns inner joins and only applies if no outer join is in the query. This parameter only applies if the parameter ANSI SQL-92 is set to YES. If the value is YES, the query engine generates all of the inner joins in the WHERE clause. If the value is NO, the query engine generates ANSI SQL-92 syntax for the joins in the FROM clause.
JOIN_BY_SQL	Values: YES/NO. Default value: NO. In the case of multiflow SQL statements generation, this parameter defines how the query is generated. If the value is YES and if the database permits, the multiflow SQL is generated as a single SQL statement using the JOIN_BY_ SQL function. If the value is NO, multiple SQL statements are generated.
MAX_INLIST_VALUES	Numeric value. Default value: –1. Minimum = –1; the maximum depends on the database. This parameter is used to define the maximum number of values allowed in an In list operator is used in a WHERE clause statement. If the value is equal to –1, no restriction is applied.
SELFJOIN_IN_WHERE	Values: YES/NO. Default value: NO. This parameter concerns self joins also called filter joins. This parameter only applies if the parameter ANSI92 is set to YES. If the value is YES, the query engine generates all of the self joins in the WHERE clause. If the value is NO, the query engine generates ANSI SQL-92 syntax for the joins in the FROM clause.
SHORTCUT_BEHAVIOR	Values: SHORTESTPATH/GLOBAL/SUCCESSIVE Default value: SHORTESTPATH. This parameter applies to shortcut joins (see Section 5.6.5). The SHORTESTPATH value tends to include the smaller number of tables in the query. The SUCCESSIVE value processes one shortcut join after the other. If a shortcut join removes a table that is potentially used in another shortcut join, the SUCCESSIVE parameter isn't applied.

Table 5.20 Most Important Data Foundation Parameters (Cont.)

Parameter	Description
	The GLOBAL value applies all shortcut joins. If the query result is a Cartesian product, no shortcut is applied. For more information on Cartesian products, see Section 5.7.
THOROUGH_PARSE	Values: YES/No. Default value: No. This parameter is used to specify how the query is parsed. If the value is YES, PREPARE and DESCRIBE statements are used to parse the SQL query. If the value is No, PREPARE, DESCRIBE, and EXECUTE statements are used to parse the SQL query.
UNICODE_STRINGS	Values: YES/No. Default value: No. This parameter is used to specify whether the universe can use Unicode strings or not.

Table 5.20 Most Important Data Foundation Parameters (Cont.)

The data foundation parameters help you to set universe resources behavior, whereas the SQL options are used by the query engine to use some specific data foundation features.

To access the SQL options, ensure that the data foundation PROPERTIES pane is visible under the data foundation schema as shown in Figure 5.105. Then select the data foundation root in the DATA FOUNDATION pane, and click the SQL OPTIONS tab shown in Figure 5.107.

Figure 5.107 Data Foundation SQL Options

Allow Cartesian Products

When this option is set to on, the Cartesian products are allowed in a query. Cartesian products can be generated when fan traps or chasm traps exist in the data foundation schema. (For more information on fan traps and chasm traps, see Section 5.7.)

Tip

Avoid checking the ALLOW CARTESIAN PRODUCTS option unless there is a good business reason. A Cartesian product returns all pairs between 2 tables involved in the Cartesian product. For example, if a table A contains 1,000 rows and a table B contains 100 rows, a Cartesian product between the two tables can potentially retrieve 100 × 1,000 = 100,000 rows.

Multiple SQL Statements for Each Contexts

When this option is set to on, multiple contexts can be used in a query. If this option is set to off, the error message INCOMPATIBLE OBJECTS is displayed to the user when objects coming from different contexts are selected in the query panel.

Example

A user selects the dimensions YEAR and COUNTRY, and the measures ACTUAL and BUDGET. The measures ACTUAL and BUDGET belong to two different fact tables, and a context has been created for each fact table and its related dimensions.

An SQL flow is generated per context, per fact table, and per dimension. Whenever possible, the results of the two SQL flows are merged in a single result set when the dimensions are shared by the measures.

5.20   Summary

For a relational universe, the data foundation is the most important part and is the interface between the database and the business layer. The data foundation modeling requires different skills, including SQL, entity-relationship models, and business skills.

The joins you have to create aren't only based on existing primary keys or foreign keys—they can be based, of course, on keys or tables indexes—but they are mainly created to answer business questions that end users may have to ask during the elaboration of documents in any client tools that use universes.

A data foundation can contain from tens to hundreds or thousands of tables. This requires a good understanding of the business model as well as the database structure. In the day-to-day work of a universe designer, the data foundation creation and maintenance takes a large place. A data foundation (simple or complex) can contain loops, multiple fact tables, alias tables, or derived tables. To solve the loops and potentially the chasm traps and fan traps, work closely with the business representatives that help you understand the business and make the right decisions. There are many ways to solve loops, fan traps, and chasm traps, and many ways to create custom SQL or joins.

You may have to create the data foundation and let another person create the business layer. In such situations, it's important to prepare the work and to create as much information as possible that is required for the business layer.

The business layer mainly contains dimensions, attributes, and measures. Each business layer resource can map a table column, combine multiple columns, or contain custom SQL.

Because a data foundation can be shared by multiple business layers and the business layer designer can be a different person from the data foundation designer, it's important to create the resources used by the business layer in the data foundation as much as possible. So if dimensions, attributes, or measures aren't only based on single columns but require transformations, you have to create those resources in the data foundation such as calculated columns or derived tables.

Always use the check integrity tool to validate the data foundation content. To take into account the changes in the relying database, use the refresh structure tool. Don't hesitate to preview the content of tables because this helps to check whether joins, calculated columns, and derived tables are well designed.

Before you make a change in the data foundation—either manually or through the data foundation refresh structure—remember to use the show local dependencies that can help you know in advance the impacted resources in the data foundation and the business layers.

Multisource universes can let business users access different data sources in the same query. They are based on multisource data foundations, which propose various concepts to federate real-time data coming from multiple data sources.

6   Multisource Data Foundations

With the increasing number of data sources, one challenge for a BI deployment is to gather data coming from multiple databases. In most situations, a new data mart is usually put in place to synchronize all of the information. Creating a data mart requires moving data from the various sources to the target source with a data integration process. *Integration* refers to workflows, processes, and tools to extract, transform, and load data from a source to another. The integration jobs are used to do the following:

- Retrieve the data from the various sources.
- Transform the source information into the target format.
- Synchronize the information coming from different sources so that it becomes compatible.
- Feed the data into the target data mart.
- Keep the data mart updated with the latest changes in the sources.

Setting up the data mart and the integration jobs is often expensive in terms of resources and lengthy in time. You might need a more agile approach. The federation technology provides a solution to run queries on data from multiple sources in an agile manner.

The federation technology in SAP BusinessObjects BI 4.x has been implemented in the form of multisource universes. Multisource universes are defined with multiple connections, a multisource data foundation, and a business layer.

This chapter covers the federation technology and, in particular, the multisource data foundations in SAP BusinessObjects BI 4.x. First, it presents the federation technology fundamentals, including its objectives and how it's implemented in SAP BusinessObjects BI 4.x. Then the chapter describes the multisource data foundation in Information Design Tool (IDT) and how you can use it to link tables from different data sources. Details are provided on the data foundation federated tables that have been introduced in SAP BusinessObjects BI 4.1, as well as the Data Federation Administration Tool, which you can use to administer the Federation Query Server and optimize multisource queries. The chapter concludes by presenting some tips for optimizing these queries.

> **Note**
>
> The business layer for a multisource universe is presented in Chapter 7, Section 7.28.

6.1 The Federation Technology

With federation, the data isn't moved into a single data mart, but is instead requested from the originating data sources each time it's needed for the end user query. The data retrieved is the latest in the database because no staging is necessary.

6.1.1 Merging Information from Multiple Data Sources

Whenever you need to define a project based on data from multiple sources, you have to decide between integration and a federation approach. There is no best choice valid for all scenarios; each situation requires taking into account needs and constraints that lead to the best solution in your environment.

Table 6.1 and Table 6.2 provide some hints that can be useful in choosing between integration technology and federation technology, respectively.

Criteria	Reason for Choosing Integration
Performance is a key requirement.	Query performance is faster when retrieving data from a single source where all data has been loaded. Additionally, some data preparation can already be done in the transformation process.

Table 6.1 Arguments for an Integration Technology

Criteria	Reason for Choosing Integration
You already have an integration technology in house with expert people on it.	Already having the tools and people reduces the cost of a project (companies with no such tools and people have to add a significant part of the project cost for this data movement).
The project is supposed to be used for a long time (months, years).	The return on investment is covered over a long usage period and final users might be more satisfied by the better performance.

Table 6.1 Arguments for an Integration Technology (Cont.)

Criteria	Reason for Choosing Federation
You don't have write access to the reporting database.	SAP BusinessObjects BI designers sometimes can't modify a data warehouse. Federation technology is an in-memory, virtual architecture, so no database write is needed.
The sources or target models are subject to changes.	Model changes are very expensive to take into account with an integration project. Federation models, being virtual, are less expensive to modify when the underlying model changes.
The project objectives might change, or the business requirements aren't well defined.	Because federation models can be easily changed, modifications in the final output can be made quickly.
The project is supposed to be used for a short time (weeks).	Because federation is leaner than integration, it might not be worth investing time and money in a full integration project for short-term solutions.
There is the need for real-time data.	The federation technology retrieves data in real time from the original sources; no data staging is required.

Table 6.2 Arguments for a Federation Technology

A federation technology has to be able to orchestrate in real time various queries to different data sources and aggregate the information coming from multiple places.

6.1.2 Federation Query Server

In SAP BusinessObjects BI 4.x, the server platform contains a service whose task is to federate data coming from multiple relational sources. OLAP sources, with the exception of SAP NetWeaver BW, aren't supported. This service, called the *Federation Query Server*, is used by queries generated from a universe that has been built on a data foundation defined on multiple connections. These data foundations are called *multisource-enabled data foundations* (referred to as multisource data foundations for the remainder of the book). In such data foundations, you can create joins between tables coming from different sources or build new virtual tables, called *federated tables*, which expose data from multiple sources.

Queries executed on a multisource data foundation are processed by the Federation Query Server with the following process:

1. The global query is received by the Federation Query Server. The query is defined on the multisource data foundation as a virtual model federating all sources.

2. The Federation Query Server identifies the queries that have to be sent to each physical data source.

3. The Federation Query Server generates an optimized execution plan, which describes the details and prioritized sequence of queries to be sent to each data source. The optimized plan has three main objectives:

   ▶ Extract the minimal quantity of data from each data source.

   ▶ Minimize the data movement across the network.

   ▶ Push down the execution of calculations to the data sources as much as possible.

4. The queries on each physical data source are translated in the specific database vendor syntax.

5. Queries are executed according to the optimization plan.

6. The final results are aggregated, synchronized, and sent back to the calling application.

All of the execution steps, from connecting to the data sources to optimizing and executing the queries are performed by the Federation Query Server. This means that all queries and all connections using the federation technology must go through the BI platform.

The Federation Query Server always works on the latest version of data available in the data sources. The absence of caches and of predefined data movements guarantees that the information is retrieved in real time when the client tool executes the query.

To optimize a federation project, it's important to optimize both the universe and the BI platform deployment settings. In SAP BusinessObjects BI 4.0, the Data Federation Administration Tool has been introduced to help you administer, analyze, and optimize the federation environment (see Section 6.6).

6.1.3 Supported Data Sources

The Federation Query Server supports most of the relational data sources supported by the universe. Table 4.1 in Chapter 4 summarizes the Product Availability Matrix (PAM) and lists the sources that can be used for federation.

Apart from the classic relational data sources, the Federation Query Server lets you connect to additional sources that aren't available in a single-source universe: SAP NetWeaver BW (see Chapter 12, Section 12.1.4) and SAS. When connecting to those sources, the Federation Query Server exposes a relational interface in the universe but then queries the systems with the source-specific function calls. The designer of the universe sees plain relational database schemas and works with SQL; the Federation Query Server does all of the translation to the specific calls to be done on the source systems.

Because all of the connections have to pass through the BI platform, a multisource data foundation is able to see only local shortcuts of connections published on the server.

If you need to connect to SAP NetWeaver BW or to a SAS system, you have to create a relational connection in the REPOSITORY RESOURCES view of IDT. Those connections don't appear in the list of available middleware of the LOCAL PROJECTS panel.

After your connections are created in the CMS repository, and local shortcuts are available, you can create your multisource data foundation, as described in the next section.

6.2 Multisource Data Foundations

Multisource data foundations are the resources where you model your federation project. Business layers built on top of these data foundations have just a few minor differences with respect to business layers built on top of single-source data foundations. The differences in business layers are discussed in Chapter 7, Section 7.28.

Cluster Federation
Federation of data sources used by multisource universe must not be confused with cluster federation that you can define in the Central Management Console (CMC).

6.2.1 Choosing the Data Foundation Type

In general, a multisource data foundation should be chosen only when the project being developed requires federating data from multiple sources or when it's necessary to connect to data sources not supported by a single-source universe (SAP NetWeaver BW, SAS). In all other situations, it's always better to choose the single-source data foundation.

The federation algorithms executed by the Federation Query Server introduce a performance degradation, which, even if small, isn't justified on single-source projects.

The query languages on single-source and multisource data foundation are different. Single-source data foundations require you to use the database vendor-specific SQL for defining your universe. Multisource data foundations, on the contrary, require you to use the SAP BusinessObjects SQL, a specific SQL that follows the ANSI SQL-92 syntax and proposes a fixed set of functions, as listed in Table 6.3.

Area	SQL Functions
Aggregation	SUM, AVG, MIN, MAX, COUNT
Numeric	ABS, ACOS, ASIN, ATAN, ATAN2, CEILING, COS, COT, DEGREES, EXP, FLOOR, LOG, LOG10, MOD, PI, POWER, RADIANS, RAND, ROUND, SIGN, SIN, SQRT, TAN, TRUNC

Table 6.3 Supported SQL Functions in a Multisource Data Foundation

Area	SQL Functions
Date and time	CURDATE, CURTIME, DAYNAME, DAYOFMONTH, DAYOFWEEK, DAYOFYEAR, DECREMENTDAY, HOUR, WEEK, YEAR, INCREMENTDAYS, MINUTE, MONTH, MONTHNAME, SECOND, QUARTER, NOW, TIMESTAMPADD, TIMESTAMPDIFF, TRUNC
String	ASCII, CHAR, ISLIKE, LEFTSTR, LEN, LTRIM, PERMUTE, PERMUTEGROUP, LOCATE, REPEAT, REPLACE, RPAD, RPOS, RTRIM, SPACE, SUBSTRING, TOLOWER, TOUPPER, TRIM
System and logic	DATABASE, IFELSE, NVL, USER, VALUEIFELSE
Conversion	CONVERT, CONVERTDATE, HEXATOINT, INTTOHEXA, TOBOOLEAN, TODATE, TODECIMAL, TODOUBLE, TOINTEGER, TONULL, TOSTRING, STR

Table 6.3 Supported SQL Functions in a Multisource Data Foundation (Cont.)

In a multisource data foundation, database vendor-specific SQL can be used only in a particular type of derived tables discussed later in Section 6.3.2. This constraint implies that you aren't allowed to seamlessly use SQL extensions or vendor-specific functions (e.g., analytic functions) when working with multisource universes.

6.2.2 Creating a Multisource Data Foundation

The steps to create a new multisource data foundation are the following:

- Create a new data foundation resource.
- Select the MULTISOURCE-ENABLED type.
- Select the connection(s).
- Adjust the connection information.

To create a multisource data foundation, follow these steps:

1. Select the FILE • NEW • DATA FOUNDATION command from the top menu commands or directly with by right-clicking in a project or project folder. The NEW DATA FOUNDATION dialog box opens.

2. Enter a name for the data foundation, and then click NEXT.

3. The SELECT DATA FOUNDATION TYPE panel displays. You can select to create a single-source or a multisource data foundation. This is the same panel displayed when you create a single-source data foundation (see Chapter 5, Figure 5.1).

4. Select the MULTISOURCE-ENABLED radio button, and then click NEXT. Remember that this choice isn't reversible; after the data foundation type has been chosen, you can't modify it to the other format.

5. The SELECT CONNECTIONS panel displays. You can select the connections you want to use. The connections can be modified later, and new connections can be added to an existing data foundation when needed.

The list of available connections, as shown in Figure 6.1, returns only connection shortcuts that are compatible with the federation technology and actually working on the selected server. Connections that aren't working are shown with an error message. Usually this error means that the middleware isn't properly configured on the BI platform or that the connection shortcut points to an invalid server connection.

Select the connections by clicking the checkbox in front of them, and then click NEXT.

Connection	Database Middleware	Location
SAP ERP demo.cns	SAP ERP 6 (JCO)	/BI Project/Federation
Source_1.cns	SAP HANA database 1.0 (JDB...	/BI Project/Federation
Source_2.cns	SAP HANA database 1.0 (JDB...	/BI Project/Federation
Source_3.cns	SAP HANA database 1.0 (JDB...	/BI Project/Federation
Teradata_13_1-Conn...	Teradata 13 (JDBC)	/BI Project/Federation
SQL_Server_JDBC.cns	MS SQL Server 2012 (JDBC)	/BI Project/ULM/Club
HANA_SL.cns	SAP HANA database 1.0 (JDB...	/BI Project/ULM/HANA
SQL_Server_JDBC.cns	MS SQL Server 2012 (JDBC)	/BI Project/ULM/retrieval-
NetWeaverBI .cns	Sap NW BW	/BI Project/Federation

Figure 6.1 Available Connections for a Multisource Data Foundation

6. For each connection you've selected, the DEFINE CONNECTION PROPERTIES FOR CONNECTION window displays as in Figure 6.2. In this window, you can define how the connection and its tables must appear in the multisource data foundation editor:

▶ The short name of this connection used to identify it.

▶ The color of the table headers associated to this connection.

▶ If the connection references an SAP NetWeaver BW system. Clicking the ADVANCED button allows you to automatically build the data foundation. (For more details, see Chapter 12, Section 12.1.4.)

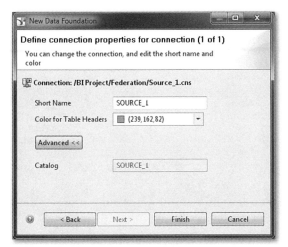

Figure 6.2 A Multisource Data Foundation Connection Properties Window

7. Click FINISH. The dialog box closes, and the data foundation is created and opened in a new editor.

6.2.3 Multisource Data Foundation Editor

The editor displaying a multisource data foundation is similar to the one displaying single-source data foundations. However, as shown in Figure 6.3, a few differences appear:

► In the left panel, the CONNECTIONS section contains the different connection shortcuts selected when creating the data foundation or added after its creation. Each connection shortcut is identified by the short name and the color you've selected for it.

► There are two additional buttons in the CONNECTIONS section toolbar:

  ► ADD NEW CONNECTION (): To add a new source to the data foundation. Click it to open the connection selection dialog box and use it as a new source in the data foundation.

  ► REMOVE CONNECTION (): To remove a source from the data foundation.

► The bottom of the left panel contains a FEDERATION LAYER section used to create federated tables (see Section 6.4).

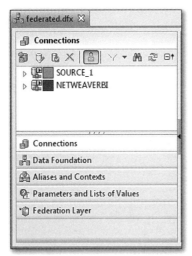

Figure 6.3 The Multisource Data Foundation Editor: Left Panel

The data foundation is now created and connected to the various data sources. The following section describes how to build some basic federation functionality in the data foundation.

6.3 Working with a Multisource Data Foundation

A multisource data foundation can be defined with the same workflow of a single-source one, with the difference that tables come from multiple connections and that the syntax is the standard ANSI SQL-92 with the SAP BusinessObjects SQL additional functions. This means that it's possible to create multisource joins and multisource derived tables with the same workflow used in single-source projects. In addition, you can also create federated tables for complex multisource manipulations. They are introduced in Section 6.4.

6.3.1 Creating Multisource Joins

After adding tables to the data foundation from the various connections, you can join them by dragging the column of a table onto the column of another table (or using Insert • Insert Join). In the example shown in Figure 6.4, the table "Resort_Info" (in the middle of the figure) is from one source, while the two other tables ("Resort" and "Sales_Person") are from another source.

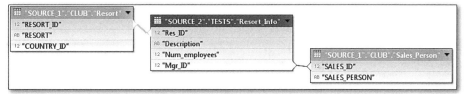

Figure 6.4 An Example of a Multisource Join

If you double-click on any of those two joins, the EDIT JOIN window pops up and shows the exact definition of the link, as shown in Figure 6.5. This window lets you create a more complex definition of the join. By using the appropriate checkboxes, you can define outer joins (right, left, full) and shortcut joins. The cardinality can be set manually, and a complex formula can be defined in the EXPRESSION text field. This SQL formula must be compliant with the SAP BusinessObjects SQL and contains only functions it supports (refer back to Table 6.3).

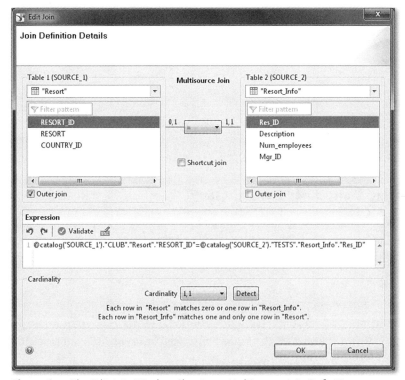

Figure 6.5 The Edit Join Window Showing a Multisource Join Definition

In the SQL formula, each table name must be prefixed by the `@catalog` built-in function with the name of the data source given when the data foundation is created (refer to Section 6.2.2). In a multisource context, this allows the system to identify exactly which database has to be referenced for the query. The `@catalog` function lets you use different data sources containing the same table names without generating a conflict.

If the database supports owner and/or qualifier, in any SQL expression involving multisource, the table name must be identified from this template:

```
@catalog(<shortname>)."<qualifier>.<owner>"."<table_name>"
```

In the example in Figure 6.4, selecting the columns "RESORT", "DESCRIPTION", and "SALES_PERSON" of the three tables and then choosing the VIEW COLUMN VALUES command returns the result by federating data from the two sources.

The following is the generated syntax:

```
SELECT Table__1."RESORT", Table__3."Description", Table__2."SALES_
PERSON"

FROM "SOURCE_1"."CLUB"."Resort" Table__1 INNER JOIN
"SOURCE_2"."TESTS"."Resort_Info"  Table__3 ON (Table__1."RESORT_
ID"=Table__3."Res_ID") INNER JOIN "SOURCE_1"."CLUB"."Sales_Person"
Table__2 ON (Table__3."Mgr_ID"=Table__2."SALES_ID")
```

In this query, the `@catalog` built-in function has been substituted with the correct data source identifier known by the Federation Query Server.

6.3.2 Creating Multisource Derived Tables

Derived tables can be used to define calculations or any data manipulation that is useful for the business usage of the information and that is too complex to define in a business object or that has to be reused in multiple business layers (see Chapter 5, Section 5.4).

In a multisource data foundation, you define a derived table differently if it queries a single source or multiple sources. This choice influences the SQL you can use in the derived table formula and how the Federation Query Server runs the resulting query, as described in the next sections.

Multisource Derived Table with Standard SQL Syntax

If your derived table is based on tables from multiple data sources, then the query is processed by the Federation Query Server. This implies some constraints in the formula to use to define the derived table:

▶ To avoid ambiguity between tables with the same name, you need to prefix table names with the `@catalog` built-in function and the short name used to identify the connection in the multisource data foundation.

▶ If the database supports owner and/or qualifier, the table name must be identified through this template:

`@catalog(<shortname>)."<qualifier>.<owner>"."<table_name>"`

▶ The SQL formula used to define the derived table must be compliant with SAP BusinessObjects SQL and contain only functions it supports (refer to Table 6.3).

The Federation Query Server can manage multisource queries and evaluate if any optimization is possible. Queries are processed, rewritten, and combined with other queries to each single source to speed up the execution.

Because the formula for multisource derived tables can be complex to write, you can use the SQL builder as much as possible to define an initial formula with the correct syntax and the correct joins. This can help you avoid errors and speed up the definition. Manual adjustments can be made to fine-tune the statement.

Single-Source Derived Table with Database-Specific Syntax

The database-specific syntax derived table is used to define derived tables on top of tables of one single source among the list of available sources in the multisource data foundation. This table allows you to use the vendor-specific database syntax (e.g., analytical functions such as ranking can be used here). In the same multisource data foundation it is possible to have many single-source derived tables, each one using the database-specific syntax of the data source.

For example, you can define a derived table that provides a standard deviation of revenue grouped by month. Because the SAP BusinessObjects SQL doesn't support any standard deviation function (see Table 6.3), this calculation can be achieved only by using a database-specific syntax derived table:

```
SELECT stddev("TESTS"."Sales"."Revenue"),"TESTS"."Sales"."MONTH"
FROM "TESTS"."Sales"
GROUP BY "TESTS"."Sales"."MONTH"
```

Because there is no ambiguity in the table name, it isn't required to use the @catalog built-in function to differentiate the tables with the same name from different data sources.

Derived tables defined with the database-specific syntax are sent to the database as is, without any processing. Their result is retrieved by the Federation Query Server and then used for the rest of the query. This happens because the Federation Query Server doesn't understand the syntax of the query and needs to delegate the whole execution to the underlying source.

Use single-source derived tables each time it's necessary to use a database-specific function that has no equivalent in the SAP BusinessObjects SQL function list. In the business layer, it is not possible to use database-specific syntax in the business objects definition.

Adding a New Derived Table

To add a derived table in a multisource data foundation, follow these steps:

1. In the data foundation toolbar, select the INSERT • INSERT DERIVED TABLE button, or right-click in the data foundation and select the INSERT • DERIVED TABLE command. The EDIT DERIVED TABLE dialog box opens, as shown in Figure 6.6.

2. To define a multisource derived table with standard SQL syntax, select the STANDARD SQL-92 radio button.

   ▶ The TABLES list is updated with the tables of the different sources, and the FUNCTIONS list is updated with the SAP BusinessObjects SQL functions.

   ▶ You can use these lists to define the SQL in the EXPRESSION text field or directly type it in the EXPRESSION text field.

   ▶ You can also use the SQL builder to generate an SQL skeleton. To do so, click the SQL BUILDER button to open it:

     – In the TABLES list, select the columns from the different sources to use in the formula.

     – Click OK to close the SQL BUILDER. An SQL skeleton text based on the selected columns is available in the EXPRESSION text field in the EDIT DERIVED TABLE window.

     – Modify the SQL to define the exact formula to use for the derived table.

Figure 6.6 Edit Derived Table Dialog Box in a Multisource Context

3. To define a single-source derived table with database-specific syntax, select the DATABASE-SPECIFIC radio button, and then select the data source onto which you want to define the table.

  ▶ The TABLES and FUNCTIONS lists are updated with the tables and the specific database functions of the source you've selected.

  ▶ In the EXPRESSION text field, enter the SQL formula to define the derived table. When defining the syntax of a single-source derived table, it isn't necessary to add the @catalog keyword to specify the source.

4. Click OK to close the EDIT DERIVED TABLE dialog box and create the derived table.

Using the SQL Builder Example

In the example in Figure 6.4 to create a derived table showing how many employees (data from "Source_2") work for a specific hotel (data from "Source_1"), use the SQL builder to get the query skeleton. As shown in Figure 6.7, select the "RESORT" and "Num_employees" columns to get the following SQL.

```
SELECT Table__1."RESORT", Table__3."Num_employees"
FROM
@catalog('SOURCE_1')."CLUB"."Resort" Table__1 INNER JOIN
@catalog('SOURCE_2')."TESTS"."Resort_Info" Table__3 ON
(Table__1."RESORT_ID"=Table__3."Res_ID")
```

This query can be then manually adjusted to fit the exact request. A Sum aggregation function is used to find the total number of employees, and the results are grouped by the resort name.

```
SELECT Table__1."RESORT", Sum(Table__3."Num_employees")
FROM
@catalog('SOURCE_1')."CLUB"."Resort" Table__1 INNER JOIN
@catalog('SOURCE_2')."TESTS"."Resort_Info" Table__3 ON
(Table__1."RESORT_ID"=Table__3."Res_ID")
GROUP BY Table__1."RESORT"
```

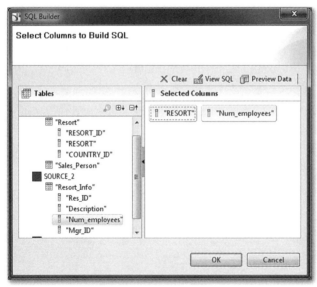

Figure 6.7 The Initial Query Created with the SQL Builder

Joins and derived tables can be used to create simple relationships and calculations between multiple sources through SQL statements. Thanks to the federated tables described in the next section, it's possible to create more elaborate relationships between tables from multiple sources.

6.4 Federated Tables

The *federated table* is a new concept introduced in SAP BusinessObjects BI 4.1. If you have an SAP BusinessObjects BI 4.0 version of the tool, the option to define and add new federated tables is not available in IDT.

6.4.1 Federated Tables Usage

Federated tables let you define complex relationships between multiple source tables in a simple and graphical manner. They allow you to cover a lot of use cases that are either too complex to define or too expensive to maintain with derived tables. Let's examine some examples where federated tables can help.

Partitioned Data

In some situations, it's necessary to have a global view of data partitioned across multiple sources. A typical example is when a large dimension is partitioned geographically, and each country office has, in its local database, the list of local customers. Another example is when a fact table is so large that not all of the information is kept in the same data warehouse. The latest information is in the data warehouse because it's used more often; older data, seldom used, is sitting in a near-line storage system both to reduce the cost and improve the performance of the main data warehouse.

A federated table can provide a single view on top of all partitions of data and can be set up to access only the necessary sources, depending on what is actually asked at runtime in the query.

Data Quality

Another use of federated tables is related to improving the quality of data at runtime. A federation technology can't fully compete against a data quality solution, but it allows you to do some basic manipulations that are applied only to the used information at runtime. For example, a federated table can put in the correct format a phone number for display when various numbers come from multiple sources in different formats. It can also be used to display error messages as results when some fields aren't matching some basic quality rules.

Optimized Data Synchronization

Federated tables can help by synchronizing data sitting in multiple sources in a single view. If a relationship can be defined between tables of various sources, it's possible to pick information where it has the most quality or where it exists to build a final table containing all pieces of information. For example, the Social Security number of a person can be found in two data sources, and you know that one of the sources has better quality data. A federated table can get the number from the more correct source by default and go to the alternate source only when the first one doesn't have the number. The use of `Case` statements provides a dynamic choice of the source.

Top-Down Models

A use case, comprehensive of all of the preceding scenarios, is when a company defines a virtual model for its data. The model is defined top down as a set of empty federated tables that aren't connected to any source. With time, sources are added, and the model starts to work. Additions of new sources don't modify the virtual model, and the newly added data is immediately available in the SAP BusinessObjects BI client tools and in existing reports. A company acquiring another company might want to add the acquired company information to the model without actually moving it into a single data warehouse. The inclusion of existing data into the virtual model is less expensive and requires a shorter project time than the actual movement of the data.

This section described the typical usage of federated tables. The next sections introduce the fundamental concepts of federated tables and the environment in which they are created: the Federation Layer editor. This editor is available only in a multisource data foundation starting with the release of SAP BusinessObjects BI 4.1.

6.4.2 Federated Table Definitions

Federated tables bring new concepts introduced in SAP BusinessObjects BI 4.1, so it's important to define them before detailing how they are implemented.

Federated Table

A federated table is a virtual table supported only in multisource data foundations. This virtual table exposes data from one or more other source tables, such as database tables coming from the different data sources on which the multisource data foundation relies. Other federated tables can also serve as source tables, but you can't create dependency loops between the federated tables.

A federated table can be created either with a top-down approach defining its schema from scratch (see Section 6.4.4), or it can be created using a source table schema as a template (see Section 6.4.5).

The federated table is defined by a set of columns, with each column being defined by the following:

- **Name**
  The column name.

- **Data type**
  The data type recognized by the Federation Query Server and returned by the column. The supported types are the ones supported by the Federation Query Server: VARCHAR, INTEGER, DOUBLE, DECIMAL, DATE, TIME, TIMESTAMP, NULL, and BIT. When used in a universe, those types are casted to the list of types supported by the data foundation, as shown in Table 6.4. The automatic match can be overridden by the universe designer in the business layer.

- **Description**
  Provides some information on the content and is very useful for documenting the project or when passing it to another person. Because you are adding a new layer of abstraction between the data and its business exposure, it is difficult for others to reverse-engineer the design. A good description takes a short time to add and simplifies the work for others.

- **Input attribute**
  If the INPUT attribute is set, then the column is an input column, which can be used when connecting to SAP ERP ABAP functions, as described in Chapter 12, Section 12.2.3.

Federation Query Server Type	Data Foundation Type
Varchar	String
Integer	Numeric
Double	Numeric
Decimal	Numeric
Date	Date
Time	DateTime
Timestamp	DateTime
Null	*Undefined*
Bit	Numeric

Table 6.4 Matching between Federation Query Server and Data Foundation Data Types

To prevent performance impact on the Federation Query Server, add only columns that are actually useful and avoid adding unnecessary columns that just increase the complexity of the schema.

One benefit of a federation project is that if a new column becomes necessary after the project has been developed, it's possible to quickly add it to the model and link it to the source data without impacting the dependent resources or requiring any additional data movement.

The federated table is a virtual table and you can define some processing on the data it exposes coming from its source tables without modifying them. This processing is done by mapping rules, pre-filters, and post-filters that are defined when you create the federated table.

Mapping Rule

When you create a federated table, *mapping rules* contain the mapping formulas that define, for each federated table column, how the data is retrieved from the source tables and transformed to be exposed through the federated table columns. This transformation is expressed through a mapping formula written in SAP

BusinessObjects SQL and containing only functions it supports (refer to Table 6.3). A mapping rule and each mapping formula can involve columns from different tables.

There are different types of mapping formulas in a federated table, depending on how the data is retrieved from the source tables and transformed to be exposed through the federated table column:

▶ **Equality**
A column is identically mapped in the federated table column.

▶ **Complex formula**
The federated table column is filled with a formula based on different source columns.

▶ **Aggregation**
The federated table column is filled with an aggregation based on different source columns.

▶ **Constant**
The federated table column is filled with a fixed value.

The data is retrieved from the sources and processed by the mapping rules only when the final user of the SAP BusinessObjects BI client tool runs or refreshes the query in real time and on the latest data into the database. The federated tables aren't storing any data; they can be considered a virtual view on top of multiple sources.

It's important to define the mapping rules so that the business requirements for data transformation are met. At the same time, you have to make sure that the rules aren't too complex to impact the performance of the query.

The mapping rules can also contain filters applied on the source data before it is queried (pre-filters) or on the data available in the federated table after the mapping formulas have been executed (post-filters).

Pre-filter

In various situations, not all of the data of a source table is needed for federation. For example, if you need only customers of a specific age group in your project, you might want to filter the source table data before this is exposed in the federated table to decrease the quantity of transferred data at its origin.

> **Data Transfers**
>
> When data appears in a federated table, it means that it has been queried and extracted from its database. To avoid extracting unnecessary data, filter the source as much as possible, and push calculations down to the source database instead of performing them in the federated model.

This filtering on the source table is done with the *pre-filter* functionality. A pre-filter is an SQL WHERE clause that is applied to the source table *before* using its data in the mapping formulas. Data eliminated by the pre-filter is never visible by the mapping formula. The pre-filter formula can only use SAP BusinessObjects SQL functions detailed earlier in Table 6.3.

Distinct Filter

If multiple records in the table contain the same values, it is possible to ask the Federation Query Server to return only one of the records. To do so, right-click the source table, and select the DISTINCT ROWS setting.

Post-Filter

A post-filter is a filter applied to a federated table after its mapping rules have been run. In some use cases, it might be necessary to filter the data of a mapping rule only after this has been calculated. For example, you might want to show in a federated table a list of customers who owe you money, and the information about purchases and payments are in two different data sources. You can build a mapping formula defining a Balance column in the federated table that takes the customer Purchase_Amount from one source and subtracts the customer Payment_Amount from the other source.

```
Balance=SourceA.Purchases_Amount-SourceB.Payments_Amount
```

And then you can filter the table to keep only customers whose Balance is positive. The post-filter formula can only use SAP BusinessObjects SQL functions detailed earlier in Table 6.3.

6.4.3   The Federation Layer Editor

The Federation Layer editor is the place where you define and edit the federated tables that gather data from multiple sources in real time. To open the editor, you have to click on the FEDERATION LAYER tab on the bottom-left part of a multisource data foundation, as shown in Figure 6.8.

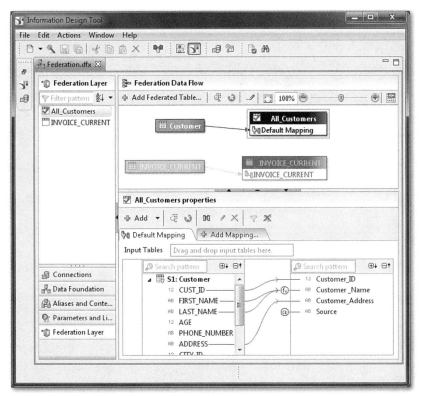

Figure 6.8 The Federation Layer Editor Interface

The editor is made of three main parts:

▸ FEDERATION LAYER panel
This left panel lists the federated tables defined in the data foundation. As shown in Figure 6.8, if those tables have a green checkmark, then they are used in the data foundation as well; if they don't have a checkmark, then they have been defined but not exposed. If you right-click on the tables, some common actions become available such as previewing data, counting the rows, or editing the definition.

▸ FEDERATION DATA FLOW panel
This top-right panel shows the dependencies between the federated tables and

the source or other federated tables that compose the sources. The information is to be regarded as a dependency map, which helps manage large federation projects.

From this panel toolbar, you can perform some high-level actions on federated tables, as described in Table 6.5.

Button	Name	Description
	ADD FEDERATED TABLE	Adds a new federated table.
	SHOW TABLE/COLUMN VALUES	Displays values returned by the selected mapping.
	VIEW ERRORS AND WARNINGS	Shows details of a problem after a check integrity has found some issues on the mapping rule. If no check integrity has been run, then this button is disabled.
	EDIT	Modifies the name and the description of the selected mapping.
	REFRESH STRUCTURE	Detects and updates the changes between the federated table and the data sources tables.
	DELETE	Deletes the selected mapping. If the federated table contains only one mapping, then the federated table is deleted as well.

Table 6.5 The Commands in the Federation Data Flow Panel Toolbar

▶ PROPERTIES panel
  When you click a federated table in the FEDERATION DATA FLOW panel, this panel at the bottom of the screen shows its mapping rules. One tab is displayed for each mapping rule. Each tab displays the source tables on the left and the federated table on the right. The two parts are connected by curved lines that represent the *mapping formulas*, which consist of the detailed syntax that transforms the source data into the data exposed in the federated table.

  The panel toolbar proposes more exhaustive actions on the federated table and its mapping rules, as described in Table 6.6.

Button	Name	Description
➕ **Add** ▾	ADD	Adds a new source table, a new pre-filter, or a new join between sources.
	SHOW TABLE/COLUMN VALUES	Shows the values of the selected item in the mapping rule editor: a column in the source table, the whole source table, or a column in the federated table.
	VIEW ERRORS AND WARNINGS	Is enabled after running a check integrity action on the mapping rule. If some errors or warnings are returned, clicking this button opens a window containing the details of the problem.
	AUTOMAP COLUMNS	Creates an automatic mapping from the source tables to the federated table. The mapping is done by checking the name of the columns and the respective order in the source and the target. It's useful mainly when creating the union of multiple tables with the same schema.
	EDIT	Changes the underlying physical table with another one when a source table is selected, or modifies the formula when a mapping formula or a column in the federated table is selected.
	DELETE	Deletes a source table title from the mapping rule when a source table title is selected. Deletes the associated mapping formula when a federated column is selected.
	EDIT POST-FILTER	Adds a new post-filter to the mapping rule or edits an existing one.
	DELETE POST-FILTER	Deletes the post-filter from the mapping rule.

Table 6.6 The Commands in the Properties Panel Toolbar

Switching Data Foundation and Federation Layer Sections

The left panel of the data foundation editor contains the CONNECTIONS section. This section is important because it contains the data sources and the tables they contain. For this reason, it must be available from both the data foundation and federation layer to include new tables.

If you are in the FEDERATION LAYER section and click on the CONNECTIONS section you remain in the Federation Layer editor but you can now see the list of all source tables, as shown in Figure 6.9. You can drag a source table into a mapping rule to make it part of a federated table definition. This workflow is described in detail in Section 6.4.6.

To get back to the DATA FOUNDATION section, click on the DATA FOUNDATION tab, and then click on the CONNECTIONS tab to add a table in the data foundation.

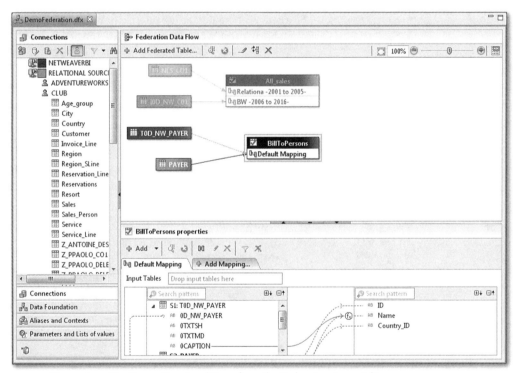

Figure 6.9 The Connection Panel Seen from the Federation Layer Editor

This section has presented the most important parts of the Federation Layer editor. The next few sections explain the workflow of creating and using federated tables in a multisource data foundation.

From the FEDERATION LAYER editor you can perform the following tasks:

▶ Create and edit the definition of a federated table.

▶ Associate source tables to a federated table.

▶ Define mapping rules to expose source table data into a federated table.

6.4.4 Creating Federated Tables from Scratch

To define a new federated table from scratch, follow these steps:

1. Click the ADD FEDERATED TABLE button (⊞) in the FEDERATION DATA FLOW panel toolbar, or right-click in this panel and select ADD FEDERATED TABLE. The table editor shown in Figure 6.10 is displayed.

2. Enter the name of the federated table in the TABLE NAME text field. You can't enter the name of an already existing federated table. Because there may be many federated tables in a project, give a self-explanatory name to the table so you can quickly grasp the table's purpose.

3. Enter a description of the table in the DESCRIPTION box at the bottom of the window. The description pops up as a tooltip when moving the mouse over the federated table, wherever it's used.

Figure 6.10 The Editor for the Definition of a Federated Table

4. To add a new column to the table, click the third button (➕) located on the right of the array. A new line is added in this array for the new column.

5. Enter the following details to define the column:
   ▶ Name, which must be unique in the federated table
   ▶ Type, which can be chosen from the DATA TYPE dropdown menu, as shown in Figure 6.11
   ▶ Description

   If you use a connection to SAP ERP, you can also define whether the column is an input column—that is, a virtual column used to pass values to a database function (see Chapter 12, Section 12.2.3). For other data sources, you should just leave the value to the default of NO INPUT.

Figure 6.11 The Available Data Types of a Federated Table

6. Repeat these steps for all columns to add. The other buttons on the right side of the dialog box can be used to modify the column order or to delete them:
   ▶ ⬆: Move the highlighted column up.
   ▶ ⬇: Move the highlighted column down.
   ▶ ✖: Delete the highlighted column.
   ▶ ✖: Delete all columns.

7. When you have defined all columns to add (see Figure 6.12 for an example of a complete federated table), click OK to create the federated table with these columns.

8. The table appears in the FEDERATION DATA FLOW panel. Hovering the mouse over it provides its description. On the bottom part of the screen, as shown in Figure 6.13, the panel of the mapping rules opens and enables you to start defining what data is exposed by this federated table.

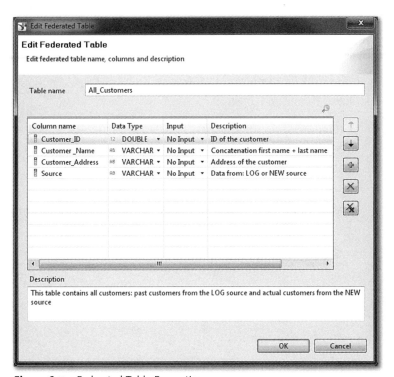

Figure 6.12 Federated Table Properties

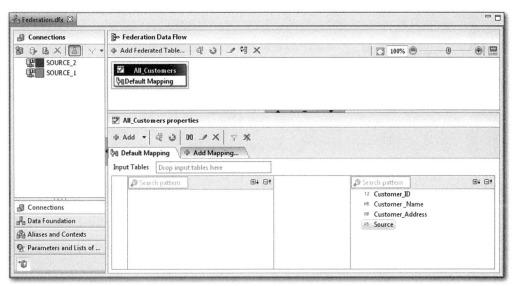

Figure 6.13 The Saved Federated Table

9. To modify the definition of the federated table, select it in the FEDERATION DATA FLOW panel, and click the EDIT icon (🖉) on the toolbar or right-click and choose EDIT.

10. Click the SAVE button (💾) in the IDT toolbar to save your federated table in the data foundation.

Once defined, the federated table can be used in the data foundation (see Section 6.4.11) but it can't be used for queries until when it has no mapping rule that associates source data to it (see Section 6.4.6).

6.4.5 Creating a Federated Table from a Source Table Template

Another way to create a federated table is by using a source table as a template and as a first input for data. To create a federated table from a source table, follow these steps:

1. Open the CONNECTION list in the Federation Layer editor as explained in Section 6.4.3.

2. From the available data sources, select a table to be used as a source table for the federated table.

3. Drag and drop it into the FEDERATION DATA FLOW panel. A new federated table is created with the same schema as the source table. A mapping rule, displayed in the PROPERTIES panel, has also been automatically created between the two tables to map identically the columns of the two tables.

> **Example**
>
> As shown in Figure 6.14, the INVOICE_CURRENT table of SOURCE_1 has been dropped in the FEDERATION DATA FLOW panel, which has created a federated table based on this source table.

As opposed to a federated table that has been created either from scratch, this new table is ready to be used because it exposes all of the data of the source table. In the first case, it's mandatory that you define a mapping rule, whereas in this case, you may optionally define or modify the mapping rule.

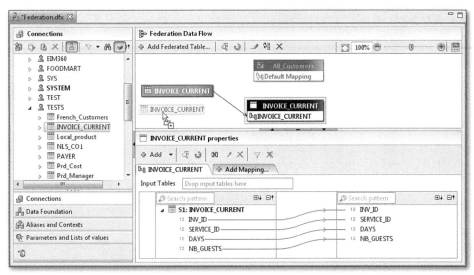

Figure 6.14 Creating a Federated Table by Dropping a Source Table

6.4.6 Defining Mapping Rules

A mapping rule is a set of mapping formulas which take as input the data from the sources and define how to expose it in each column of the federated table. In each mapping rule you have to define one mapping formula for each federated table column.

There are different types of mapping formulas, depending on how the data is retrieved from the source tables and transformed (refer to Section 6.4.2): equality, complex formula, aggregation, and constant. The icons to identify each mapping formula are described in Table 6.7.

Icon	Mapping Type
	Equality
	Complex formula
	Aggregation
	Constant

Table 6.7 Formula Description Icons

The workflow to define a mapping formula may vary depending on the type.

Adding Source Tables and Creating an Equality Mapping Formula

To create a mapping formula that identically maps columns, follow these steps:

1. Click the federated table, and the mapping rules panel opens at the bottom of the Federation Layer editor, as shown in Figure 6.15.

2. If you define your first mapping rule, you can define it in the DEFAULT MAPPING tab. Otherwise, click in the ADD MAPPING tab to add a new mapping and open a new tab for it.

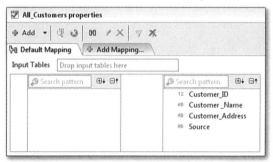

Figure 6.15 Mapping Rule Editor Ready to Accept Sources for a Federated Table

3. In the tab, the empty box on the left is used to host the source data tables; on the right part, you have the columns of the federated table that have to be mapped to the source.

4. Put some source data into the mapping rule. Drag a table from the CONNECTIONS section into the INPUT TABLES list in the PROPERTIES panel as shown in Figure 6.16, where the CUSTOMER table is dropped into the INPUT TABLES box.

5. Define a mapping formula for each target column to define how their values are computed from source tables. The simplest formula says that the source columns map as is into the federated column. You can define this equality formula simply by dragging and dropping a source column onto the federated column, as shown in Figure 6.17.

6. If you click the SHOW TABLE/COLUMNS VALUE button (⊞) to display the content of the federated table at this stage, you can check that the federated table displays all values of the source table column.

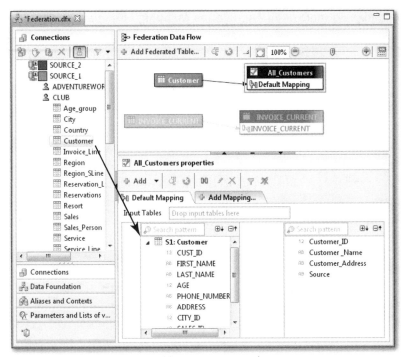

Figure 6.16 Adding a Source Table to a Mapping Rule

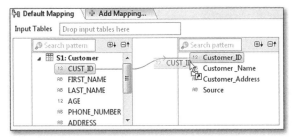

Figure 6.17 Dragging a Source Column onto the Federated Table Target Column to Create an Equality Mapping Formula

Equality Example

In the Figure 6.17 example, the federated table column CUSTOMER_ID is just exposing the data in SOURCE_1.CUST_ID by dragging the source column onto the target column. You could also map the source table ADDRESS column into the CUSTOMER_ADDRESS column.

Creating a Complex Formula or an Aggregation Mapping Formula

Mapping rule formulas can also contain more complex manipulations, such as complex formula or aggregation. To define a complex mapping rule, follow these steps:

1. Open the EDIT MAPPING FORMULA editor either by double-clicking on the target column, or by right-clicking it and selecting the EDIT MAPPING FORMULA command.

2. In this editor, enter the formula that defines the transformation between the source data and the way it's exposed in the federated table. You must use ANSI SQL-92 syntax and the SAP BusinessObjects SQL functions listed earlier in Table 6.3.

3. Click OK to save the formula and close the EDIT MAPPING FORMULA editor.

Complex Formula Example

The federated CUSTOMER_NAME column could be the concatenation of the source FIRST_NAME and LAST_NAME columns.

As shown in Figure 6.18, the formula is:

```
concat("S1"."FIRST_NAME", concat(' ',"S1"."LAST_NAME"))
```

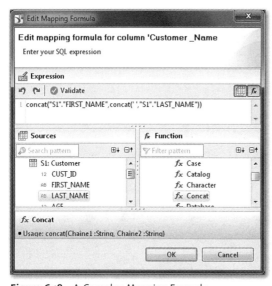

Figure 6.18 A Complex Mapping Formula

To edit the mapping formula of a column of a federated table, in the PROPERTIES panel, either double-click this column, or right-click it and select EDIT MAPPING FORMULA. In both cases, the EDIT MAPPING FORMULA dialog box opens and you can modify the mapping formula. To remove a mapping formula, in the PROPERTIES panel, right-click the column of a federated table and select the DELETE command.

Creating a Constant Mapping Formula

A federated column can also contain a constant value. To add a constant value you have to edit the mapping formula so that it contains the value. In the example, the customer list used is the list of customers coming from the actual database (the list of past customers comes from another database). You can then set the SOURCE column to the value "ACTUAL" so that in your queries you can see where the data comes from. This definition is shown in Figure 6.19.

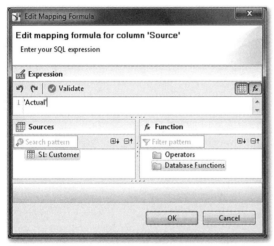

Figure 6.19   A Mapping Formula Containing a Constant Value

Quote versus Double-Quote

In the formula used to define the mapping rule, strings are surrounded by single quotes instead of the double quotes used for database elements (such as catalog names, table names, and columns). If, by mistake, you use a double quote for a string, the error message says that the system can't resolve an identifier because it searches a database element that is, in fact, the value of your string.

It's possible to combine different mapping formula types when defining federated table columns, as shown in Figure 6.20.

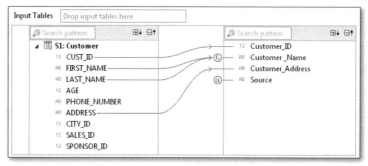

Figure 6.20   A Complete Mapping Rule

Formulas are the functionality you use when you need to transform the source data into its target format in the federated table. Sometimes, before applying the formulas or after they have been applied, you might need to filter the data as well to fine-tune your model. This can be done by defining pre-filters or post-filters.

6.4.7   Defining Pre-filters

To add a pre-filter to a source table, you have to select the source table in the mapping rules editor (in the left panel) and then either choose ADD • ADD PRE-FILTER from the toolbar (as shown in Figure 6.21) or right-click and choose ADD PRE-FILTER.

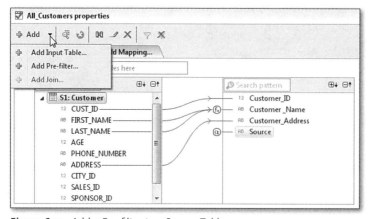

Figure 6.21   Add a Pre-filter to a Source Table

In the pre-filter editor, you can now write the clause that is applied to the table before using it. In the example, to keep only customers between 20 and 50 years old, the syntax to add to the filter is then (Figure 6.22):

```
"S1"."AGE" between 20 and 50
```

The CUSTOMER table is now displayed with a small funnel on its icon in the mapping rules editor (⊞).

The data preview of the source table (obtained by selecting the table in the mapping rules panel and clicking on the SHOW TABLE/COLUMN VALUES button) returns only customers of the appropriate age range.

Figure 6.22 Pre-filter Editor

6.4.8 Defining Post-filters

To add a post-filter, you have to click the EDIT POST-FILTER button in the toolbar, as shown in Figure 6.23.

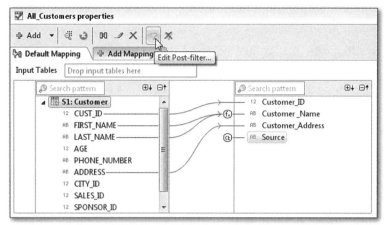

Figure 6.23 The Button to Add or Edit a Post-Filter to a Federated Table in the Mapping Rules Editor

As an example, using the table shown in Figure 6.23, you can build a post-filter to limit the results to have only customers whose name, the concatenation of first name and last name, is fewer than 15 characters.

The post-filter editor looks like the one shown in Figure 6.24. In this example, you see only one source table; however, in real-life situations, you usually have multiple tables from multiple sources.

Figure 6.24 The Post-Filter Editor

Choosing between a Pre-Filter or a Post-Filter

In the given example, the two filters can be applied either as pre-filters on the source table or post-filters on the mapping rule result. When it's possible to choose which kind of filter to apply, it's always best to create a pre-filter rather than a post-filter.

A pre-filter is always applied before any other processing of the data, so it reduces the quantity of data transferred over the network. A post-filter is generally applied after the data is transferred. The query optimization algorithms might cause the post-filter to be applied before transferring the data to decrease the network traffic and have the database do the filtering. When this happens, the final result is the same as if the filter were applied after the data transfer.

6.4.9 Defining Source Table Relationships

The previous section has shown how to build a simple mapping rule with a single table; this isn't yet a case of federation of data across multiple sources. To get data from multiple sources, you have to do the following:

▶ Drop multiple source tables in the mapping rules editor's INPUT TABLES panel

▶ Define the relationships between those tables

▶ Define which columns of the source tables are exposed in the federated table and their mapping formulas

For example, you might have information about products dispersed across multiple data sources, as shown in Figure 6.25.

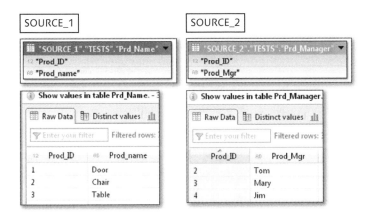

Figure 6.25 Sample Product Name and Product Manager Tables

In "SOURCE_1", which is used to manage the stock, you have a table providing the ID of the product and the name of the product. In "SOURCE_2", used by HR, you have the product ID and the name of the product manager working on that product.

The goal might be to define a single federated table showing the product ID, the name of the product, and its manager. Figure 6.26 gives an example of the resulting federated table definition. In this table, you get data from both sources making sure that the current manager is assigned to the correct product name.

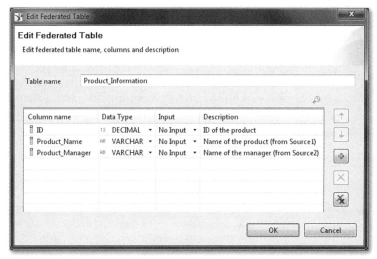

Figure 6.26 Sample Goal Federated Table

After the table is defined, you have to drag and drop both source tables into the Input Tables panel (refer to Figure 6.16) so that they can be part of the definition. After the tables are available in the source panel, you have to define the relationship between them. In the example, the product ID is the same between the two tables.

To define this relationship, you drag the Prod_ID column from one table on top of the Prod_ID column of the other table, as shown in Figure 6.27.

A curved line linking the two columns is displayed on the screen to represent the relationship. This line is called a join even if it doesn't really represent a normal join in pure SQL terms. Double-clicking on the line opens the Join Editor dialog box, which lets you modify the default equality relationship. This dialog box is similar to the one used to define data foundation joins (see Chapter 5, Section 5.3.2), but it supports only the EQUAL operator.

Figure 6.27 Creating a Source Table Relationship

Matching IDs

The join editor is used to make sure that the IDs from the various source tables match. Often an ID in one database isn't exactly mapping to an ID in another database for the same concept. In the join editor, you can, for example, change the type of an ID from number to string (or vice versa). You can also prefix or suffix the IDs with strings in order to match these IDs and link the data in the two tables.

When the relationship has been established, you can link the source columns to the federated columns by dragging and dropping them, as shown in Figure 6.17, which generates the mapping rule, as shown in Figure 6.28.

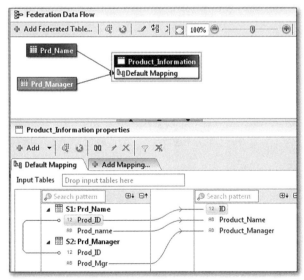

Figure 6.28 The Sample Definition of the Federated Table

In the example, the federated columns are created with an equality formula, so they display exactly the content of the source tables. If you execute a data preview on the federated table, you get the results displayed in Figure 6.29.

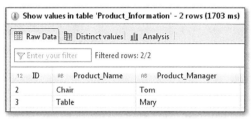

Figure 6.29 The Content of the Federated Table

Only the common products between the two sources have been kept. The relationship between the two source tables has acted as an inner join between them. This default behavior can be changed, thanks to the concept of core table.

6.4.10 Understanding Core and Non-Core Tables

A source table is a *core table* if the federated table that uses it has been defined to contain only data from rows from this source table. When multiple source tables are defined as core, then the federated table contains the intersection of their content.

The core table enables you to define exactly what records of what sources you want to see in the federated table. As a general rule, setting a table as core forces the result to contain only records that appear in that table. Setting a table as core implies that the result is going to be filtered to take out the records that aren't from that table.

In the federated table, the values that don't exist in the non-core tables are defined as `Null`. When defining the relationship, it's a best practice to avoid joining non-core tables together. A non-core table should always be joined to a core table to predict the results.

> **A Federated Table without Any Core Tables**
>
> It's possible to have no core tables in a table relationship, but this situation should be avoided. The Federation Query Server isn't pushing full outer joins so a left outer join is performed using the first table appearing in the list on the left part. This is practically the same behavior as if the first table in the list was considered a core table. To avoid confusion, it's always better to define at least one core table.

Very often, a mapping rule contains more than two tables and is connected to more than two sources. In the case of three tables (TABLE1, TABLE2, and TABLE3), the Euler-Venn set representation in Figure 6.30 shows the possible data intersections returned to the federated table.

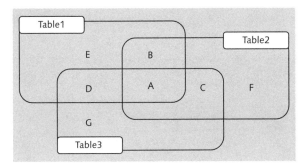

Figure 6.30 A Set Representation of the Results

If TABLE1 and TABLE3 are joined to TABLE2, then the records that appear in the federated table depend on the tables that are core or not, as displayed in Table 6.8.

Table1	Table2	Table3	What the Federated Table Contains
Core	Core	Core	A
Non-core	Core	Core	A, C
Non-core	Core	Non-core	A, B, C, F

Table 6.8 Records in the Federated Table, Depending on the Core Tables

By default, all tables are considered core when they are added as source tables to a federated table, but it's possible to modify these settings.

Setting a Table as Core

To set or unset a source table as core, right-click on it, and select (or unselect) the CORE TABLE option in the context menu, as shown in Figure 6.31.

327

Figure 6.31 Setting a Source Table as Core

Core tables are displayed with a bold font, and non-core tables are displayed with a normal font in the INPUT TABLES list in the PROPERTIES panel.

Example with Two Tables

If in the earlier Figure 6.25 example, you set the "SOURCE_1.PRD_NAME" table as core and the "SOURCE_2.PRD_MGR" table as non-core, you retrieve all records available from "SOURCE_1.PRD_NAME", with lines not existing in "SOURCE_2. PRD_MGR" set as ⟨Null⟩ (see Figure 6.32).

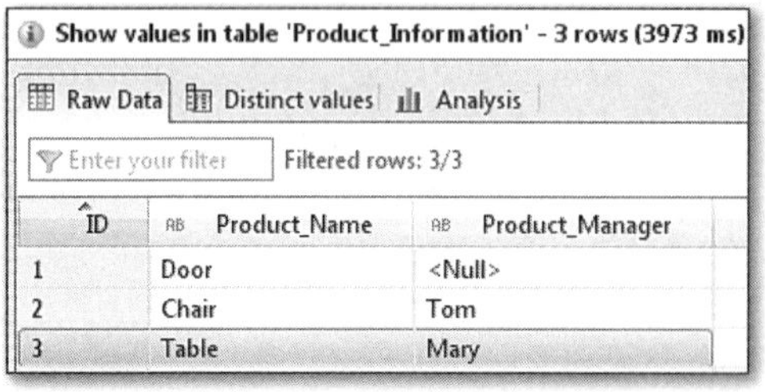

Figure 6.32 Federated Table when "SOURCE_1" is Core and "SOURCE_2" is Non-Core

If you change the core table and define the "SOURCE_1.PRD_NAME" table as non-core and the "SOURCE_2.PRD_MGR" table as core, then all records from "SOURCE_2. PRD_MGR" are retrieved, with lines not existing in "SOURCE_1.PRD_NAME" set as ⟨Null⟩ (see Figure 6.33).

> **Show values in table 'Product_Information' - 3 rows (3354 ms)**
>
> ⊞ Raw Data   🔢 Distinct values   📊 Analysis
>
> 🔽 Enter your filter   Filtered rows: 3/3

12 ID	AB Product_Name	AB Product_Manager
2	Chair	Tom
3	Table	Mary
\<Null\>	\<Null\>	Jim

Figure 6.33   Federated Table When "SOURCE_2" Is Core and "SOURCE_1" Is Non-Core

You can see that the ID for the product whose manager is Jim (information coming from the "SOURCE_2" table) is Null. This happens because the federated ID column is mapping the "SOURCE_1" table, not the "SOURCE_2" as shown earlier in Figure 6.28.

You must always be consistent when modifying the status of tables from core to non-core, making sure that the correct information is sent to the federated table. In this example, there are two options to correctly fill in the ID of the product:

▶ In the first option, the mapping to the ID column is done with the "SOURCE_2. PRD_MGR.PROD_ID" column.

▶ A second option is to check whether the value coming from "SOURCE_1" is Null. If this is the case, then the value coming from "SOURCE_2" should be used.

This is obtained by defining a complex mapping formula using the IsNull function (which is called nvl):

```
nvl("S1"."Prod_ID","S2"."Prod_ID")
```

In this formula, whenever the first value is Null, the system uses the second one. The definition is shown in Figure 6.34.

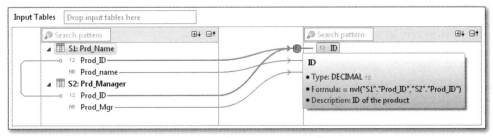

Figure 6.34   Using the IsNull Functionality in the Mapping Formula

329

The result, using either of the two options, is shown in Figure 6.35. In both cases, the ID value is returned correctly. Using the second option, the first two ID values come from "SOURCE_1", and the last value comes from "SOURCE_2".

Show values in table 'Product_Information' - 3 rows (2972

ID	Product_Name	Product_Manager
2	Chair	Tom
3	Table	Mary
4	<Null>	Jim

Figure 6.35 The Result after Making Sure That the ID Is Correctly Returned

Example with Three Tables

When adding a new table, it's important to make sure that the expected columns are returned by correctly tuning the core table settings. In the preceding example, you can have a "SOURCE_3" database containing information about the cost of each product. The example table is provided in Figure 6.36.

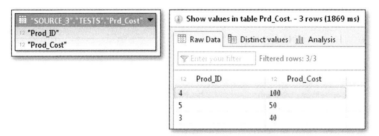

Figure 6.36 A Third Table about Product Costs

You can add the cost information to the federated table and add a mapping formula to feed this information from the "SOURCE_3" table, as shown in Figure 6.37. This table has the same relationship on "Prod_ID" as the two other tables and is linked to the "SOURCE_2" table.

The definition of the federated column ID has been modified to take into account the possibility that the value comes from the new table using the following syntax:

```
nvl(nvl("S1"."Prod_ID","S2"."Prod_ID"), "S3"."Prod_ID")
```

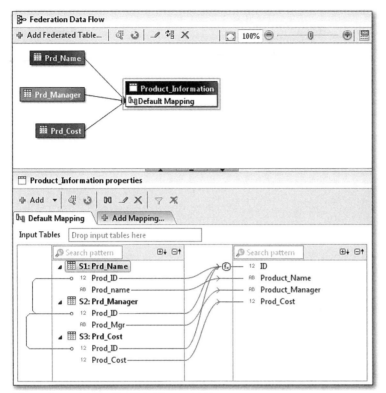

Figure 6.37 Adding the Third Source Table

The settings of core tables influence the result displayed in the federated table. Having all three tables set as core makes the federated table return the intersection of all tables' records on the "PROD_ID" (this is equivalent to an inner join between the three tables). Because the three tables have only the Prod_ID=3 in common, the result is displayed in Figure 6.38.

ID	Product_Name	Product_Manager	Prod_Cost
3	Table	Mary	40

Show values in table 'Product_Information' - 1 rows (1469 ms)

Raw Data | Distinct values | Analysis

Enter your filter | Filtered rows: 1/1

Figure 6.38 Three Tables Defined as Core

If one of the tables is set as non-core, it doesn't filter out the columns that don't belong to it, as shown in Figure 6.39.

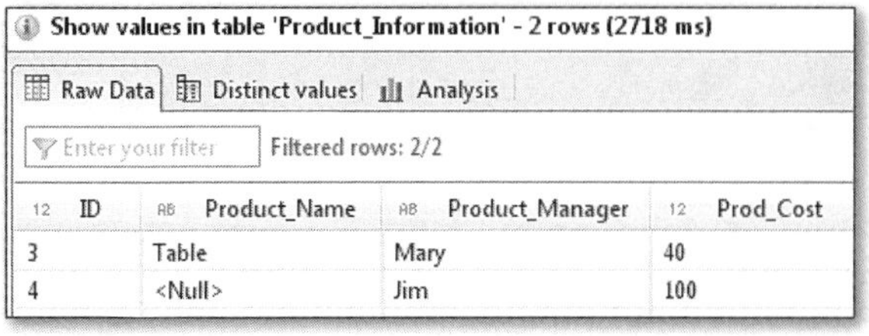

Figure 6.39 Non-Core Source_1 and Core Source_2 and Source_3

Similarly, when you set two tables as non-core, more columns appear in the result.

6.4.11 Using Federated Tables in the Data Foundation

When you've created a federated table, you need to expose it in the model the data foundation exposes; otherwise, it can't be seen by the business layer and used in an object definition.

To insert a federated table in the data foundation, follow these steps:

1. Open the DATA FOUNDATION tab.

2. In the editor, right-click and select INSERT • FEDERATED TABLE. The INSERT FEDERATED TABLE dialog box opens, listing all federated tables saved in the data foundation.

3. Select the checkbox in front of the federated tables to add, and then click OK. The dialog box closes, and the federated tables appear in the data foundation with a black background heading.

After the federated table has been added to the data foundation, it can be used as the following:

▶ A physical table that can be joined or taken as a source for a derived table or alias table

▶ A source table for objects defined in the business layer

You can use a federated table as a source table for other federated tables. The use of intermediary federated tables helps in creating complex mapping workflows. In this case, it isn't required to expose those intermediary federated tables through the data foundation.

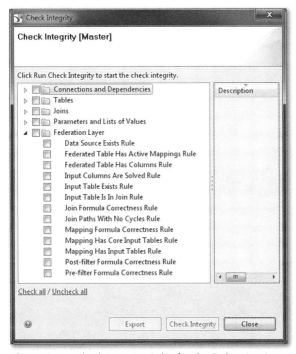

Figure 6.40 Check Integrity Rules for the Federation Layer

Thanks to the additional processing it enforces, the federated tables have many usages in different scenarios.

6.5   Multisource Scenarios

The previous sections have covered most of the theory behind the federation technology; this section describes some examples how it can be used for specific scenarios.

6.5.1   The Union Scenario

In many situations, the same kind of information is partitioned across multiple data sources. In other cases, similar information is available only at a later time in new data sources. To have a full picture of all of the data, you might want to create a union of all of the different partitions in a single virtual view.

As a practical example in a company with offices across the world, there might be multiple local databases containing the list of local customers. You might want to create a federated table showing the union of all customers.

In another example, to avoid keeping too much data in your main data warehouse, you can partition by time the facts. In the main data warehouse you keep only the past two years of transactions, and you have a secondary data warehouse containing all past facts. You can create a federated table showing values from both sources.

A Customer Story

A large company has decided to extend its international presence by acquiring smaller companies abroad, positioned on the same market segment. The business intelligence department wants to provide a global view of the financial information that takes into account each new company's data as soon as possible. The department built a virtual data model, composed of federated tables, and defined a data foundation and a universe on top of it, and then built a set of reports on this virtual model.

Each time a new company is acquired, the business intelligence department creates a new connection to the company data sources and maps the data into the existing federated tables by adding mapping rules.

The new data immediately appears in the reports without the need to change them. The reports are defined so that it's possible to see both the global view of data and the details of a specific acquired company.

In IDT, to make a union (or better, to add information to an existing federated table), you just have to add a new mapping rule. For example, you can take two customer tables coming from two different sources: a set of customers in France ("FRENCH_CUSTOMERS") and a set of customers in the United States ("US_CUST").

The definition and content of the tables are shown in Figure 6.41. You can notice that the two tables have a different format. In the "FRENCH_CUSTOMERS" list, the address is a single column; in the "US_CUST" list, the location is split in two different columns.

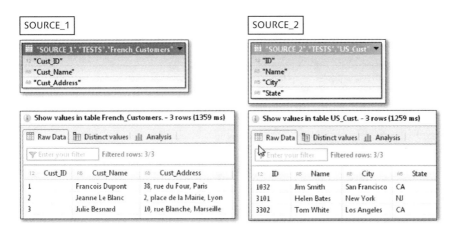

Figure 6.41 Sample Customer Table Definitions

The goal is to define a federated table that makes the virtual union of the two sources. To simplify the process, the federated table can be created using the French customer table as a template as shown in Figure 6.41. You can name the table "ALL_CUSTOMERS".

You can then add a new varchar column called "COUNTRY" to the federated table and set it to the constant value 'FRANCE', as shown in Figure 6.42.

Now it's time to create the virtual union with the table of US customers. To do so, you have to create a new mapping rule by clicking on the ADD MAPPING tab in the editor.

Mappings Added as Unions

Each mapping is added with a UNION statement to the federated table. Hence, adding a mapping is the same thing as creating a union between tables.

The benefit of the functionality is that for each mapping, you can do complex transformations of data from the sources to the federated table in a simple graphical way.

335

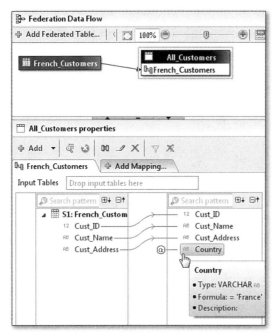

Figure 6.42   Creating a Federated Table from a Source Table Template and Adding a New Constant Column

When asked to provide a name for the mapping you can use "US_CUSTOMERS". Following the workflow shown in Figure 6.16, you can add the "US_CUST" source table to the newly created mapping rule.

You can define an equality formula to expose the ID and name of the customers in the federated table by dragging and dropping the columns from the source table to the federated one. The "COUNTRY" column can be set to "US". Since there is no single column for the address in the "US_CUSTOMERS" table, you can build one by concatenating the "CITY" and "STATE" columns, separated by a comma, using the following mapping formula for the "CUST_ADDRESS" federated column:

```
concat(concat("S1"."City",','),"S1"."State")
```

The resulting mapping rule is visible in Figure 6.43. On the FEDERATION DATA FLOW panel, you can see that the two mapping rules have been applied to the ALL_CUSTOMERS table.

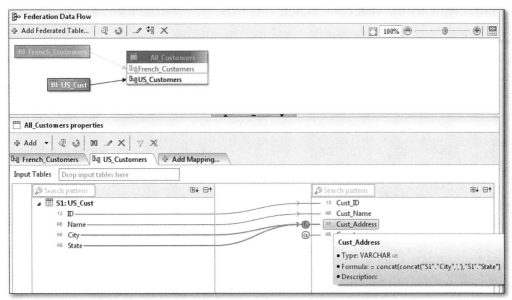

Figure 6.43 The Mapping Rule "US_Customers" for the "All_Customers" Federated Table

Viewing the data of the federated table, you can see that there is a union of the information coming from the two sources. Additionally, the "CITY" and "STATE" columns of the "US_CUSTOMERS" table have been concatenated into a single "CUST_ADDRESS" column, as shown in Figure 6.44.

Cust_ID	Cust_Name	Cust_Address	Country
1	Francois Dupont	38, rue du Four, Paris	France
2	Jeanne Le Blanc	2, place de la Mairi...	France
3	Julie Besnard	10, rue Blanche, Ma...	France
1032	Jim Smith	San Francisco,CA	US
3101	Helen Bates	New York,NJ	US
3302	Tom White	Los Angeles,CA	US

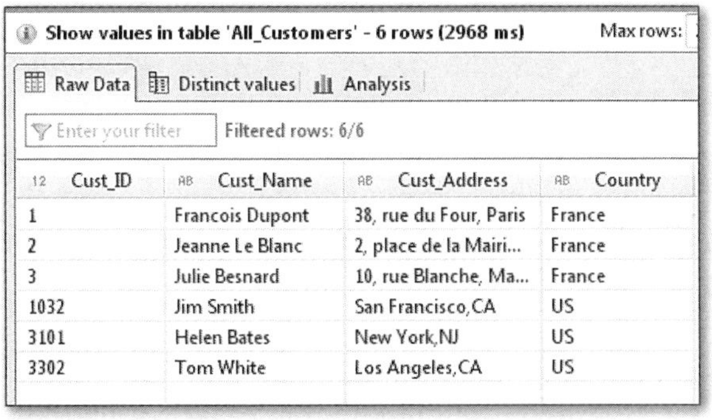

Figure 6.44 The Resulting Union of the Two Source Tables

When you query the federated table, by default the server sends requests to both sources. If you want to retrieve information only for a specific country, it's possible to make sure that the server sends a query only to the needed databases by defining a discriminatory filter on "COUNTRY".

> **Note**
>
> Section 6.7.7 and Chapter 7, Section 7.28 contain information on how to build a filter that selects the correct country and triggers the request to a single data source.

In general, if you run a query on the federated table and you specify a condition in the SQL to filter the "COUNTRY" column to "US" or to "FRANCE", the server sends the request only to the necessary source.

For example, the following query doesn't generate any request on the "FRENCH_CUSTOMER" source table:

```
Select Cust_ID from All_Customers
Where Country='US'
```

When building the rest of the data foundation and the business layer, you should take advantage of this functionality to optimize the generated queries.

In this example, each mapping rule was providing information from a single source. Nothing stops you from having multiple sources in each mapping rule for more complex manipulations of data. The next section provides some examples of mixing multiple sources in a single mapping rule.

6.5.2 The Mixed Sources Scenario

A federated table, or even a single federated column, often displays information from multiple data sources in a single record. The table relationships and the mapping formulas enable you to build complex transformations that retrieve the freshest information from the correct source at runtime. The federation technology executes the transformation rules only if they are necessary.

A typical, but simplified mixed sources scenario is the example of product information presented earlier in Section 6.4.9. In that example, the name of the product, its cost, and its manager were retrieved from different data sources and exposed in the same federated table. The example was simplified because the IDs of the products were coherent across the various data sources. Moreover, each source contained a piece of information, and there were no overlaps to choose from.

In cases different from this ideal situation, to match records from different data sources, you might use the content rather than the IDs and take advantage of overlapping information.

Matching Records

If two tables from different data sources contain product names (as shown in Figure 6.45), you can match the name instead of the ID. The "LOCAL_PRODUCT" table (from "SOURCE_2") is used in a specific department and differs from the "PRD_NAME" table (from "SOURCE_1"), which contains the company reference information.

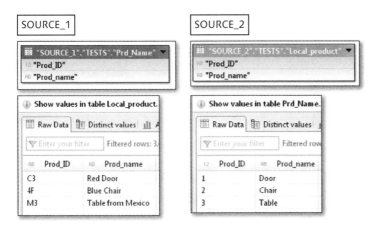

Figure 6.45 Two Tables with Different IDs that Need to Be Matched

The objective is to put in relation those two tables to build a federated table using the corporate IDs that are defined in the "PROD_NAME" table.

If two tables contain the product name, you can try to match the name instead of the ID. In this situation, sometimes you have case matching problems related to leading or trailing spaces having to do with the length of the database columns. A formula such as `Uppercase(Trim(product.name))` helps in matching the values between the two tables.

If the two tables can't be easily reconciled, you can create a new table in a database (or upload a spreadsheet on a server machine and add it as a data source to the data foundation) that defines the relationship between the IDs, such as the table depicted in Figure 6.46.

339

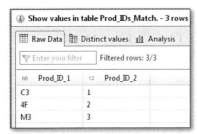

Figure 6.46 A New Table Defining the Relationship between IDs of Different Tables

This new table can be used in a mapping rule to create the correct relationship, as shown in Figure 6.47.

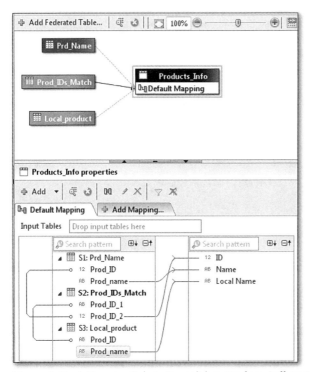

Figure 6.47 A Mapping Rule to Consolidate IDs from Different Tables via a Third Matching Table

The PROD_IDS_MATCH table is used to make sure that the IDs from the corporate and local table have a relationship. The results are shown in Figure 6.48.

A downside of this approach is that a new table has to be created and maintained when new data is added to the system. This is possible for small quantities of data but can become unmanageable for large quantities.

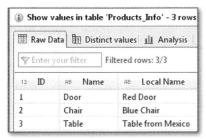

Figure 6.48 The Resulting Federated View

On the contrary, a positive effect can be seen when there are many tables with different ID systems that have to match with a corporate ID. Using such a table, you can define a column for the corporate ID, and then you have to synchronize their IDs on as many columns in as many different tables.

In this situation, it's important to make sure that only the matching ID table is defined as core to retrieve as much data as possible out of the database and, at the same time, make sure it's based on the corporate ID standards.

Overlapping Records

When working with multiple sources, you might find that you have information available in more than one place for some values. The multiple entries can be a source of problems if the values mismatch for the same record, but you can turn this situation into a benefit. You can define one source as the master source of data and use the information in the other sources only if the master is empty or not well formed.

A formula using an `IsNull` function (named `nvl` in the SAP BusinessObjects SQL syntax) lets you use the content of a second source if the first one doesn't contain a value. For example, the formula `nvl("S1"."Prod_name","S2"."Prod_name")` returns the name of the product from source `"S1"`. If this is name is `Null`, then it returns the name of the product from source `"S2"`.

By using `Case` statements and the `IfElse` statements, you can add more sophistication to the choice of the source data. Those two statements are useful with overlapping information but also solve some problems of data quality, which are covered in the next section.

6.5.3 The Data Quality Scenario

The federation technology can be used to improve the quality of the data used by the final users by putting in place some controls or quality rules at query time. Those controls can be time consuming, so it's always a best practice to guarantee the quality of the data from within the data source. In situation when it isn't possible to modify the source, and federation is available, the federation technology provides a last-minute solution for improving correctness.

The fundamental idea behind a federation data quality scenario is to use the mapping formula from the source to the federated table to make the necessary improvements in the data.

Various functions can help in the transformation of the input. Table 6.9 presents a short list of useful functions.

Function	Description
Case	Depending of the value of the input, you can set the value of the output based on a list.
IfElse	If the input verifies a condition, it returns a value; otherwise, it returns another value.
IfNull	If an input value is Null, then it returns a second input value.
Permute	Changes the format of a string into another format.
Uppercase	Turns all letters of a string to uppercase.
Lowercase	Turns all letters of a string to lowercase.
Replace	Searches for a substring in a string and replaces it with a given value.
OnlyDigits	Checks if a string contains only digits.
IsLike	Checks if a string contains a specified pattern.

Table 6.9 SQL Functions for Improving Data Quality

A complete definition of those functions can be found in the Information Design Tool User Guide available for download at *http://help.sap.com*. A couple of examples are provided here.

The Case statement lets you transform a set of values to a new set, which is supposedly easier to interpret. In the following example, the statement transforms some internal codes to a more readable and uniform format:

```
Case (S1.Product)
when 'Bike12' then ' Bike'
when 'Bike_red' then 'Bike'
when 'Fast Bike' then 'Bike'
when 'AR034K12' then 'Rollers'
when 'Ride Fast' then 'Rollers'
Else 'Other'
End
```

Depending on the value of S1.Product, the output contains the specified content.

The Permute function takes an input string and its pattern and transforms it with an output pattern. Suppose that your federated table is the union of two source tables containing date information.

▶ In S1.Table.Datefield, the dates are under the format '2013-06-10' (i.e., YYYY-MM-DD).

▶ In S2.Table.Datefield, dates are written as '10062013' (i.e., DDMMYYYY).

If your output format is 10/06/2013, you can transform both dates into DD/MM/YYYY using the functions

```
Permute(S1.Table.DateField,'YYYY-MM-DD','DD/MM/YYYY')
```

and

```
Permute(S2.Table.DateField,'DDMMYYY','DD/MM/YYYY')
```

The Permute function can be used with any string, not only dates. You set the format by repeating groups of letters which you use afterwards in the output format. For example, if you have a code for your products, you can transform it into something more readable:

```
Permute('01-JP-13-red','AA-BB-CC-DDD','product AA, color DDD, produced
in BB in 20CC')
```

This returns the following:

```
'product 01, color red, produced in JP in 2013'
```

Federating data from multiple sources is a complex task that has an impact on the performance of the queries. The remaining part of the chapter is dedicated to techniques for optimizing the execution of your queries.

The next section describes the tool used to perform some specific fine-tuning on the federation services: the Data Federation Administration Tool.

6.6   Data Federation Administration Tool

The Data Federation Administration Tool is the application used to administer, audit, and fine-tune the execution of the Federation Query Server. This tool can be used in many situations to understand where problems are in a federated query or to optimize the execution to make it as fast as possible. The following are its main capabilities:

▶ Analyze query performance and find bottlenecks

▶ Understand the query plans generated by the federation services

▶ Fine-tune the Federation Query Server settings

▶ Perform trial-and-error testing to troubleshoot issues

The following sections aren't a complete substitute for the Data Federation Administration Tool User Guide, which you can download from *http://help.sap.com*. The User Guide fully describes the tool and its parameters, but the following sections provide an overview of the tool's functionality, especially in a performance optimization context.

6.6.1   Data Federation Administration Tool User Interface

The tool is available only on the Microsoft Windows platform and is installed through the SAP BusinessObjects BI 4.x client tools installer. It can be run from the Microsoft Windows START menu, under the SAP BUSINESS INTELLIGENCE • SAP BUSINESSOBJECTS BI PLATFORM 4 CLIENT TOOLS menu.

After you've launched the tool, you first need to log in to the CMS repository using a valid account. Because the tool manages the Federation Query Server functionality, you need to log in to the CMS with a BI platform user name that belongs to the Data Federation Administrators group.

After launching the tool and providing your user information, the interface opens. As shown in Figure 6.49, the interface includes an upper area that contains five views for the different actions you can run in the Data Federation Administration Tool. They are accessed with the tabs on top. The lower space contains two views displaying the properties and, when available, the SQL information for the items selected in the views above.

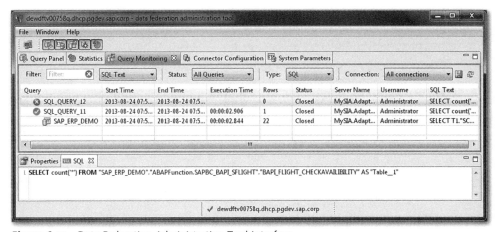

Figure 6.49 Data Federation Administration Tool Interface

The following five tabs are displayed in the upper area:

▶ The QUERY PANEL view allows you to enter an SQL statement and execute it via the Federation Query Server. During the query, you can audit the execution to show the resulting data set, the query plan, or the database statistics that influence the execution. In the query panel, you can copy an SQL statement found in the QUERY MONITORING view.

▶ The STATISTICS view shows all statistics information collected from the data sources or defined by the user. For each data source, it displays the following:

  ▶ The number of rows in a table

  ▶ The number of distinct values in a column

  ▶ The time when the statistic was calculated

  ▶ How often the data has been accessed

In this view, you can refresh the statistics information table by table.

▶ The QUERY MONITORING view presents the log of the latest queries executed by the Federation Query Server. Each line represents a different query. For multi-source queries, you can see the global federated query and all of the single-source queries generated by it.

The first column provides the name of the source onto which the query has been executed; the last column provides the SQL generated by the federation service.

▶ The CONNECTOR CONFIGURATION view shows you the list of all sources known by the Federation Query Server and, for each source, the capability it provides.

▶ Finally, the SYSTEM PARAMETERS view lets you set the values for the many sessions or system parameters that define how the Federation Query Server works. This view is very useful for fine-tuning the behavior of the system.

Query Panel

The query panel in the Data Foundation Administration Tool has nothing to do with the query panel used in IDT to query universes and described in Chapter 8.

Below these views, you have two additional tabs that provide details on the information selected on the top:

▶ The PROPERTIES tab shows detailed information about any element selected in the upper area tabs. For example, when selecting a query in the QUERY MONITORING view, you can see how much memory it has consumed, its write access on the disk, and other useful information.

▶ The SQL tab is used mainly with the QUERY MONITORING view and displays the whole SQL sentence of the query selected above. It's useful for doing a copy and paste of the SQL text.

The next section provides some information on the most typical usage of the views.

6.6.2   Query Auditing

Most of the time, the Data Federation Administration Tool is used to audit queries and find if there is a performance issue or if some part can be improved. Whenever you run a query via a multisource data foundation, the query is logged in the QUERY MONITORING view.

In the example shown in Figure 6.50, you can see that the highlighted federated query has generated three other queries on the data sources. Two source queries have returned 5 rows, a third has returned 16 rows, and the final result set (highlighted) contains only 5 rows.

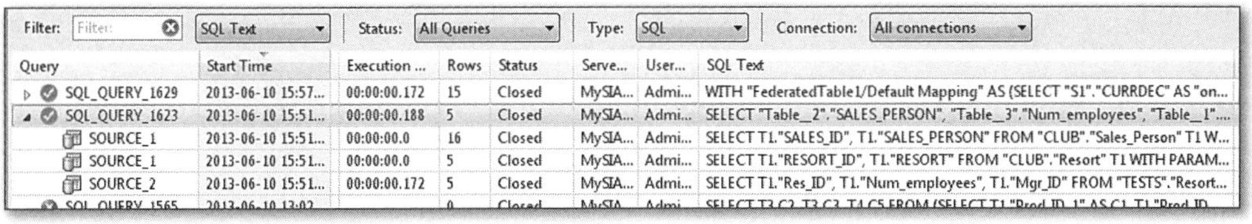

Query	Start Time	Execution ...	Rows	Status	Serve...	User...	SQL Text
▷ ⊘ SQL_QUERY_1629	2013-06-10 15:57...	00:00:00.172	15	Closed	MySIA...	Admi...	WITH "FederatedTable1/Default Mapping" AS (SELECT "S1"."CURRDEC" AS "on...
▲ ⊘ SQL_QUERY_1623	2013-06-10 15:51...	00:00:00.188	5	Closed	MySIA...	Admi...	SELECT "Table_2"."SALES_PERSON", "Table_3"."Num_employees", "Table_1"...
🗐 SOURCE_1	2013-06-10 15:51...	00:00:00.0	16	Closed	MySIA...	Admi...	SELECT T1."SALES_ID", T1."SALES_PERSON" FROM "CLUB"."Sales_Person" T1 W...
🗐 SOURCE_1	2013-06-10 15:51...	00:00:00.0	5	Closed	MySIA...	Admi...	SELECT T1."RESORT_ID", T1."RESORT" FROM "CLUB"."Resort" T1 WITH PARAM...
🗐 SOURCE_2	2013-06-10 15:51...	00:00:00.172	5	Closed	MySIA...	Admi...	SELECT T1."Res_ID", T1."Num_employees", T1."Mgr_ID" FROM "TESTS"."Resort...
⊘ SQL_QUERY_1565	2013-06-10 13:02...		0	Closed	MySIA...	Admi...	SELECT T3.C2_T3.C3_T1.C5 FROM (SELECT T1."Prod_ID_1" AS C1_T1."Prod_ID...

Figure 6.50 A Sample Output in the Query Monitoring Interface

To get more details on the query, you can select the query text from the bottom view and paste it into the query panel. In the query panel, you can do the following:

▶ Click the RUN • EXECUTE QUERY button to retrieve the data of the query.

▶ Click the RUN • EXPLAIN QUERY button to display, source by source, the columns, keys, and statistics (if available) that have been used in the definition of the query plan as shown in Figure 6.51. This information is useful because you might detect the presence of some columns that shouldn't be involved in such a query. If you see an incorrect column here, you might want to check the definition of your multisource data foundation or business layer.

▶ Click the RUN • EXPLAIN STATISTICS button to see the statistics that have influenced the execution plan, as shown in Figure 6.52. In this page, you can compute or refresh the statistics. To compute the statistics, right-click, select COMPUTE, and then choose the specific kind of computation you want to perform.

You can also override the value of statistics provided by the data source by setting a number in the USER CARDINALITY column. To have the system use the user cardinality or the source cardinality, right-click and select CURRENT CARDINALITY • USE USER CARDINALITY or USE SOURCE CARDINALITY.

Figure 6.51 The Explain Query Output

Catalogs	Last Compute...	Number Of Requests	Current Cardinality	Cardinality From Source	User Cardinality
▲ Query					
▲ SOURCE_1					
▲ CLUB					
▲ Resort	2013-06-10 16:...	10	5	5	Unset
12 RESORT_ID	2013-06-10 16:...	9	5	5	3
▲ Sales_Person	Not computed	11	Unknown	Unknown	Unset
12 SALES_ID	Not computed	10	Unknown	Unknown	Unset
▲ SOURCE_2					
▲ TESTS					
▲ Resort_Info	Not computed	12	Unknown	Unknown	Unset
12 Mgr_ID	Not computed	10	Unknown	Unknown	Unset
12 Res_ID	Not computed	9	Unknown	Unknown	Unset

Compute ▶

Current Cardinality ▶   Use User Cardinality

     Use Source Cardinality

Figure 6.52 The Statistics Output of the Query Panel

Statistics information is a very important part of the optimization techniques.

The Data Federation Administration Tool is a powerful environment to understand and fine-tune the execution of the federation services. The next sections explain how to improve performance of the federated queries with the tool and with other settings and procedures in your SAP BusinessObjects BI deployment.

6.7 Optimization Techniques

The federation technology requires the execution of complex algorithms and the movement of data across multiple sources and in the memory of the SAP Business-Objects BI platform. Projects that aren't fine-tuned might experience performance degradation. This section presents the fundamental principles and some techniques to optimize the execution of the queries.

The main objectives of the optimization techniques are the following:

- Make sure the sizing of hardware, reserved memory, and network are correct and don't present bottlenecks.
- Run calculations in memory and don't store temporary data on disks.
- Retrieve the least quantity of data from each data source.
- Move the least quantity of data across the network.
- Push calculations and filtering down to the data sources.

Those objectives can be achieved by following best practices for sizing the environment, setting the correct server parameters, calculating the database statistics, and defining a good model in federated tables and in the data foundation. The following sections provide information on those practices.

6.7.1 Preparing the Federation Query Server Environment

On the SAP BusinessObjects BI 4.x server, the federation service runs by default on an Adaptive Processing Server that hosts other services. The first optimization to apply is to create a dedicated server for federation and assign to it a good size of dedicated memory. This ensures that the federation algorithms aren't impacted by services running on the same server.

After creating the new server, you should set the appropriate amount of memory for execution. The Federation Query Server requires a minimum of 512MB of RAM to work. As a rule of thumb, you should provide the highest possible amount of memory to the server, up to the limit of 75% of the total memory of the machine.

If possible, the Federation Query Server should have its own dedicated machine into a BI platform deployment where it can consume all of the memory it requires. To define a dedicated server for data federation, follow these steps:

1. Log in to the CMC, whose URL is by default *http://<servername>:<port>/BOE/CMC*.

2. In the CMC home page, click ORGANIZE • SERVERS, or in the dropdown menu, select SERVERS to access the SERVERS tab.

3. In the panel in the right, select the DATA FEDERATION SERVICES line to display the servers already running federation services, as shown in Figure 6.53.

4. In the menu bar, select the MANAGE • NEW • NEW SERVER command to open the CREATE NEW SERVER dialog box.

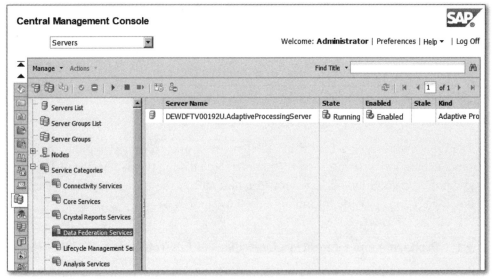

Figure 6.53 The Servers Tab in the Central Management Console

5. In the SERVICE CATEGORY dropdown menu, select DATA FEDERATION SERVICES. In the SELECT SERVICE dropdown menu, select DATA FEDERATION SERVICE, and then click NEXT.

6. In the next page that enables you to add additional services, leave DATA FEDERATION SERVICE alone in the SELECTED SERVICES list, and click NEXT.

7. Enter a name and a description for this new server in the SERVER NAME and DESCRIPTION text fields and click CREATE. The dialog box closes, and the new server is displayed in the list of servers running data federation services.

8. To set the memory it can allocate, double-click on this server. This opens its PROPERTIES dialog box.

9. In the COMMAND LINE PARAMETERS text field, find the -Xmx parameter and set the memory size to allocate, as shown in Figure 6.54.

For example, on a machine dedicated to the federation service with 4GB of RAM, you should give 3GB to this server, so you set the parameter to -Xmx3g. This 3GB is in fact the memory allocated for the Java Virtual Machine (JVM) that can distribute it to the server framework and the federation algorithms.

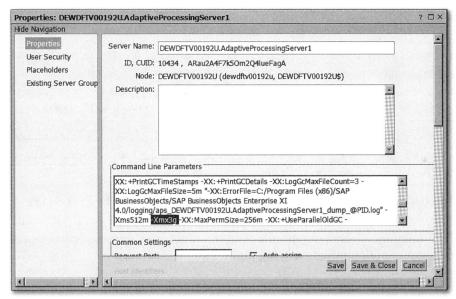

Figure 6.54 The Memory Parameter to Set in the Central Management Console

> **Note**
>
> The federation service has an internal paging system that pushes storage into the disk in case the RAM is full. This system makes sure that queries can be run without memory overflow errors but the disk manipulation has a strong negative impact on performance. Hence, RAM sizing is a key aspect to obtain a good performance. You have to make sure you have enough RAM memory to avoid the system using disk space for temporary data storage.

6.7.2 Gathering Statistics

Recall from Section 6.6.2 that the Data Federation Administration Tool enables you to provide to the query engine the statistics information for the data source. Those statistics are number of rows for a table and number of distinct values for a column.

The values are used by the optimization algorithms to decide how to perform the query. The execution plan might change a lot when running the same query with different statistics values.

The parameters to fine-tune the optimizations described in the following sections are using the computed statistics to decide the best plan. You should compute statistics at least once for a data source (or at least for some of the most often run queries on the data source). The values returned are provided directly from the database. The Data Federation Administration Tool relies on the source vendor commands to retrieve them.

In some situations, you can override the value returned by the data source because it doesn't trigger the appropriate optimization algorithm. For example, some databases don't actually return the exact statistics numbers but provide a best guess of those values. That best guess can be far from the actual content of the database.

It's a best practice to always calculate the statistics of each data source at least once. You can do this from the Data Federation Administration Tool or from the business layer of the multisource universe (as described in Chapter 7, Section 7.28).

It isn't necessary to refresh the statistics very often because the Federation Query Server is mainly interested in the relative size of tables and not in the absolute numbers. If you can safely assume that a table doesn't grow or shrink dramatically with regards to other tables, you don't need to update the values.

6.7.3 Deployment Factors Impacting the Performance

The RAM isn't the only physical parameter impacting performance because the federation technology makes heavy use of CPU power for calculations and of the network to move data between multiple systems.

A high number of CPUs (or cores) is recommended because it's possible to run multiple memory-consuming actions in parallel, one on each CPU (or core). As an initial setting, you can put the parameter MAX_CONCURRENT_MEMORY_CONSUMING_ QUERIES equal to the number of CPUs if the machine is dedicated to the federation service; this parameter is set in the Data Federation Administration Tool's SYSTEM PARAMETERS tab.

A fast network between the BI platform server and the various data sources is key for fast data transfer. It's recommended that the BI platform machine and the data sources machines be relatively "close" in terms of network. There can be multiple exchanges between the data sources and the BI platform and one single exchange of data between the BI platform and the calling client tool.

6.7.4 Optimization by Parameter Settings

You may also improve performance of the federation server by modifying its internal parameters. These parameters are set in the Data Federation Administration Tool's SYSTEM PARAMETERS tab (refer to Section 6.6.1).

Memory Distribution

In addition to the memory size reserved for the server (refer to Section 6.7.1), you should define how this memory must be distributed between various concurring actions on the server. Three main parameters define the memory distribution of the federation service:

▶ EXECUTOR_TOTAL_MEMORY
Sets the percentage of memory of the JVM dedicated to the federation service for running queries.

▶ EXECUTOR_STATIC_MEMORY
Sets the percentage of the total memory (set with the preceding parameter), which is provided at the initialization of each operator.

▶ MAX_CONCURRENT_MEMORY_CONSUMING_QUERIES
Sets how many queries can be run in parallel sharing the available memory.

For example, suppose that you've provided 4GB of RAM to the JVM using the parameter -Xmx4g dedicated to the federation services. If you set EXECUTOR_TOTAL_MEMORY to 75%, you're reserving 3GB of RAM for executing queries. Then, setting MAX_CONCURRENT_MEMORY_CONSUMING_QUERIES to 2, you're telling the system to provide space for two queries to run in parallel. If your EXECUTOR_STATIC_MEMORY is 33%, then you provide 500MB of RAM at the initiation of each query (33% of 3GB is 1GB, divided by the 2 queries, you get 500MB).

353

If you have small queries, then we advise you to increase the number of the parameter for max concurrent queries (you have enough memory to run the queries in parallel without disk paging). If you have large queries, then you should decrease the max concurrent queries (to make sure that each query is run in memory without using the disk).

Computing Query Memory Consumption

It's difficult to know how much memory is, in general, required by a system or a set of queries. It's possible to have a rough idea on a generic high-end consumption of memory with the following procedure.

Suppose that a multisource query is split by the server into subqueries (you can check this using the Data Federation Administration Tool). To have a scale of how much memory is consumed by this query, you can multiply the number of rows of the largest subquery by the sum of the sizes of the rows returned by each subquery.

For example, for a query split in two subqueries by the system:

▶ The subquery returning the largest data set returns 1,000 rows.
▶ The average sizes of the records returned by the two subqueries are 300 bytes and 500 bytes.

The calculated consumption uses about 1000 * (300 bytes + 500 bytes) = 800KB, even if usually, the real consumption is lower than this calculated value.

By studying the typical queries and returned sizes with the Data Federation Administration Tool, you can understand the typical consumption and then set the correct number of max concurrent queries and their dedicated memory.

Unions Subquery

Another useful parameter controls the time when a subquery used for unions is sent to the database for execution. By default, subqueries are sent to the databases only when the federation service is ready to use the data. This means that a database can be sitting in standby for a while instead of preparing the data for the federation services.

To start a subquery as soon as the database is ready (not waiting until the federation server is ready), you can set the parameter `Activate_multi_threaded_union_operator` to YES.

This parameter works only for scenarios when subqueries are used to union data from multiple sources. The drawback of this setting is that the federation service sends the request immediately but retrieves the data only when ready to do so.

If the database has a time-out functionality, there is the risk that the data is lost before the server retrieves it and the query fails.

6.7.5 The Semi-Join Functionality

One of the most important optimization techniques of the federation service is the ability to retrieve the least quantity of data from each data source by doing a multi-pass filtering action through an algorithm called *semi-join*. When joining data from two sources, the federation engine tries not to load all of the two data sets into the BI platform memory; instead, if possible, it makes use of the data of one of the sources to filter the data from the second one.

The semi-join is very beneficial and gets triggered when joining a large table with a small table (i.e., with a few distinct values in the joining columns).

> **Example**
>
> Suppose that you have customer names and customer IDs in one source and sales information (by customer ID) in another source, and you want to retrieve sales data for a list of customers.
>
> Using a semi-join, the federation engine retrieves from the first source the customer IDs using the customer names as a filter and then retrieves from the second source only the sales records matching the valid customer IDs.
>
> If the semi-join cannot be used, then the federation engine loads the whole list of customers and the whole sales information into memory and performs the join.

The execution of a semi-join might require the following:

- A large IN statement to be pushed to a database (and hence a long time to write the SQL sentence)
- The creation and provisioning of a temporary table
- The execution of many small SQL statements

All of those actions consume resources in the database and in the BI platform memory and have to be triggered only when they make sense.

The semi-join algorithm is useful only when there is a large decrease of information when filtering one source with data from the other source. If the decrease isn't sufficient, the algorithm might be more time-consuming than a plain in-memory join.

You can use three main parameters to fine-tune this semi-join algorithm, depending on the content of your data sources:

▶ ACTIVATE_SEMI_JOIN_RULE
This parameter is used to switch on and off the semi-join algorithm. If a database doesn't perform well with semi-joins, the functionality can be turned off (for only that connector or for the whole system).

The two following parameters have effect only if the activation parameter is set to YES.

▶ MIN_SOURCE_CARDINALITY_THRESHOLD_FOR_SEMI_JOIN_RULE
This parameter sets the minimum number of rows needed in the "large table" to trigger the semi-join algorithm. If the number of rows of the large table is smaller than this value, then the semi-join isn't applied.

You should set this parameter with the value that enables most of your large tables to be considered by the algorithm.

▶ MIN_ACTIVATION_THRESHOLD_FOR_SEMI_JOIN_RULE
This parameter sets the minimum expected reduction ratio of rows when applying the semi-join algorithm. If the federation engine expects to obtain a reduction lower than the value set here, then the semi-join algorithm isn't applied.

This parameter is the most important in fine-tuning the semi-join algorithm. Its default value is 1,000; meaning that the semi-join is applied if the expected reduction ratio of rows is at least 1,000. This setting is generally a good one. If it prevents the semi-join from being applied, you can consider decreasing the value; but for values lower than 100, you might not find a real increase of performance and might even cause a degradation.

These parameters are intended to limit the usage of the algorithm only to situations when a real increase in performance and a reduction in data traffic can be obtained. If the test associated with one of these parameters isn't passed, then the semi-join isn't applied.

Sometimes, semi-joins aren't executed because the cardinality of the tables is outside of the boundaries set in the parameters. In those situations, there is still the opportunity to have an optimization inside the database with the merge-join algorithm.

6.7.6 The Merge-Join Functionality

Another algorithm to optimize the query is the *merge-join* algorithm. The main ideas of this algorithm are to ask the database to sort the data through an `Order By` statement and to perform the join on the preordered data returned by the database.

Ordering the information enables storing less temporary data and proceeding faster with the join process. The merge-join functionality is enabled by default on databases that support the `Order By` statement

In the Data Federation Administration Tool, three main parameters fine-tune this merge-joins algorithm:

▸ `Activate_order_based_optimization_rule`
Turns on and off the merge-join optimization algorithm.

▸ `Min_store_cardinality_threshold_for_order_based_join_rule`
The minimum cardinality of the smaller table in the join.

▸ `Min_transfer_cardinality_threshold_for_merge_join_rule`
The minimum cardinality of the larger table in the join.

Apart from setting system parameters that can improve performance by triggering the embedded optimization engine, it's possible to build the data model so that some optimizations can be triggered by providing hints to the query engine at runtime. We describe one such model optimization in the next section.

6.7.7 The Source Discriminating Filter

Some queries on top of a multisource data foundation might actually only require information coming from a single source. In some situations, it's possible to tell the system exactly in which source the information is available and avoid running useless queries on all sources.

Section 6.5.1 contains an example of this functionality based on the definition of a federated table where each mapping has a hard-coded value (the country, in the example), which can be used by the system to trigger only the necessary mapping rule, and hence the necessary data source.

The same method used in this example can be applied to create more complex filters that may discriminate the source to query and optimize the resulting queries. Suppose that you've partitioned your data so that sales before the year 2010 are in "Source1", and sales from 2010 onward are in "Source2". In the two sources, you have the same exact fact table definition and the column `SalesDate` stores the information about the date of the sales transaction.

To retrieve the sales transactions between two dates, you create two date prompts `MinDate` and `MaxDate`, which return the lower and higher limit of your request, respectively.

You can define a multisource derived table with the following formula (assuming the "greater" and "lower" operators are able to compare dates):

```
Select * from Source1.Sales Where YEAR(@prompt(MinDate)<2010) and
SalesDate>=@prompt(MinDate) and SalesDate<=@Prompt(MaxDate)
Union All
Select * from Source2.Sales Where YEAR(@prompt(MaxDate)>=2010) and
SalesDate>=@prompt(MinDate) and SalesDate<=@Prompt(MaxDate)
```

When executing the derived table, the system requests the two date prompts. The sources to query are the following:

▶ "Source1" only if the maximum date is before year 2010.

▶ "Source2" only if the minimum date is in 2010 or later.

▶ If these conditions are not met, then "Source1" is used to retrieve sales before 2010 and "Source2" to retrieve sales of 2010 or later. The two result sets are then merged with the `Union` operator.

By using a similar syntax in a derived table, you make the system contact only the source which actually contains the data instead of running useless queries that return no results on all available sources.

6.8 Summary

SAP BusinessObjects BI 4.x includes federation technologies that allow you to run queries on multiple data sources through the creation of a multisource data foundation. In such data foundations, you can create the following:

▶ Joins or derived tables between tables from different data sources.

▶ Federated tables that are virtual tables whose columns can be used to map columns from tables of different data sources. Mapping rules contain formulas which define how data from the different columns are processed to fill the federated table columns. Mappings can contain complex formulas.

In all cases, formulas involving tables from different data sources must follow SAP BusinessObjects SQL.

Multisource queries are processed by the Federation Query Server running server-side. To administer, audit, and optimize this server, you can use the Data Federation Administration Tool. Optimizing multisource queries can be done through the following:

▶ Increasing allocated memory and the servers hosting the services

▶ Modifying parameters in the Data Federation Administration Tool

▶ Using SQL techniques to optimize the queries sent to data sources

After the multisource data foundation is created, you can create a business layer on top of it. The definition of the business layer on top of a multisource data foundation isn't strictly different from the design of a single-source universe.

The business layer is the part of the Information Design Tool interface dedicated to defining the business objects consumed by users in the SAP BusinessObjects BI client tools. The business layer is one of the components of a universe.

7 The Business Layer

The business layer is the last step in universe authoring before publication, security definition, and translation. A business layer is built on top of a data foundation for a relational universe and on top of an OLAP connection for a multidimensional universe.

This chapter presents the business layer that is the user interface between business users and the databases. It covers the design of the different components of a business layer and explains how a business layer takes advantage of the data foundation modeling. It details the differences between a relational business layer and a multidimensional business layer. Creating queries and the interactivity provided to the users through filters, parameters, and advanced features are also discussed. Finally, the chapter shows how to make the business layer consumable by the different SAP BusinessObjects BI client tools.

7.1 The Business Layer Objectives

The definition of a business layer has to be strongly influenced by the business users' requirements and skills. A business user should be able to open the universe interface from an SAP BusinessObjects BI client tool and quickly understand what objects are needed for the query. The business layer should contain only the objects that might be needed for answering the typical business questions and not all *possible* objects that can be defined on top of the data foundation.

The business layer is generally accessible through a query panel (additional details in Chapter 8) that exposes the concepts designed in this business layer. The business layer can be authored by a person who has business skills (finance, sales, marketing, etc.) and database language skills (SQL, MDX), as well as the ability to work closely with functional people.

Because the business layer is the part accessible to users, it's important that you hide the complexity of a database and avoid exposing technical terms as much as possible. As a universe designer, you must have a very good understanding of the business questions that the users wants to ask and also of the users' skillset in asking them. Because a business layer is a collection of objects directly usable by business users, naming objects, organizing them in folders, and placing them at the beginning or end of a folder has a huge impact on the ability of the end users to find their way in the universe.

One of the main goals of the business layer is to harmonize resources coming from different types of data sources. It means that all resources available in the business layer are valid for all kinds of data sources. This leads to a common definition and common consumption workflows in all SAP BusinessObjects BI clients. Each object corresponds to a unit of business information that can be manipulated in a query to return data.

Although the question is often asked concerning the maximum number of objects that should exist in a universe, it's difficult to provide a best practice recommendation. On one hand, reducing the number of objects to a minimum simplifies the interface but also reduces the possible queries that can be made. On the other hand, increasing the number of objects might get the final user lost trying to find what is needed and create maintenance issues for the IT team. In the industry, there are universes in production that contain up to 9,000 objects. Those huge universes are difficult to use and to maintain, but they are carefully organized by area of interest and with names that can be easily interpreted by an expert business user. In SAP BusinessObjects BI 4.0, the functionality of the business layer view enables building large universes and then exposing smaller portions of them.

When a business layer is complete, it's published to the CMS repository as a universe or locally as a local universe. A universe is a published .unx file that includes a business layer and its connection to an OLAP cube, or a business layer, its corresponding data foundation, and its relational connections. When published to the repository, the universe is available to all SAP BusinessObjects BI clients connected to the CMS.

7.2 Creating the Business Layer

The business layer is created on top of a data foundation for relational data sources and on top of an OLAP connection for OLAP sources. Relational sources include the major RDBMSs, such as Oracle, Microsoft SQL Server, Teradata, IBM DB2, SAP Sybase, and so on, and all data sources that return the query results as row sets, such as text files, Excel, XML files, Web Services, and so on. For more information on connections and supported data sources, see Chapter 4, Section 4.1.

The OLAP sources supported in SAP BusinessObjects BI 4.1 are SAP NetWeaver BW, SAP HANA, Microsoft SQL Server Analysis Services, and Oracle Hyperion Essbase.

The business layer is saved in the file system where the local project has been created, as described in Chapter 3, Section 3.1. The business layer can be stored under a folder in the local project, and the business layer file name is always suffixed by *.blx*.

> **Note**
>
> To consume a published universe in the CMS repository, the connection must be published first, and a shortcut to the secured connection must be added in the local project. Then for a relational universe, the data foundation must reference the secured connection so the business layer can be published. For a multidimensional universe, the business layer must reference the secured OLAP connection to be published.

7.2.1 OLAP Direct Access

All data sources are supported through the creation of universes that are authored, saved, and published. There is an exception for SAP NetWeaver BW and SAP HANA where you don't necessarily have to create a business layer and publish a universe.

SAP NetWeaver BW and SAP HANA are both multidimensional data sources and are self-descriptive enough for the semantic layer to understand the metadata information and make it directly consumable by users.

SAP BusinessObjects BI 4.x provides a direct access to those OLAP sources and a universe is generated on the fly (also called *transient universe*). The universe generated on the fly exists only during the user session and is not persisted. From a user point of view, there is no difference between a universe generated on the fly and an authored universe. The main difference otherwise is that there is no possibility to customize a transient universe. It is not possible to retrieve or modify a transient universe with IDT since no persisted file is created.

To enable direct access to SAP NetWeaver BW or SAP HANA, you have to create an OLAP connection (see Chapter 4, Section 4.1.3) with IDT and publish it in the CMS repository. You can also create the OLAP connection in the Central Management Console (CMC), which is the administration interface of the CMS repository. When you open an SAP BusinessObjects BI 4.x client and select the published connection, a query panel displays the multidimensional business layer mapping the OLAP cube—this is the business layer generated on the fly.

SAP NetWeaver BW direct access is supported by SAP BusinessObjects Web Intelligence, SAP Crystal Reports for Enterprise, and SAP BusinessObjects Dashboards.

SAP HANA multidimensional direct access is only supported by SAP Crystal Reports for Enterprise, as described in Chapter 12, Section 12.3.4.

The structure of the generated business layer in the multidimensional direct access is exactly the same as if it were generated for a persisted multidimensional universe as described in Section 7.2.3.

7.2.2 Business Layer Entities and Concepts

Relational business layers and multidimensional business layers share common concepts, but some of the concepts can only be used by one of the business layer types. There are plenty of concepts in the business layer spread in different categories:

- Top-level entities directly exposed to the SAP BusinessObjects BI users and directly consumable in a query and a report
- Entities used in combination with the top-level entities and mainly used to generate the query
- Concepts manipulated by the universe designer

Table 7.1 lists the business layer top-level entities that you can create or update and that are in common to the two business layers.

Entity	Business Layer Type	Icon	Description
Folder	Relational and multidimensional		A folder is an organizational concept only. The folder contains dimensions, attributes, measures, and so on.
Dimension	Relational and multidimensional		A dimension object is considered as the focus of the analysis.
Measure	Relational and multidimensional		A measure is mainly a numeric data item on which aggregation functions can be applied. A measure is aggregated by the set of dimensions composing the query.
Attribute	Relational and multidimensional		An attribute object provides descriptive data about a dimension. It's always associated with a specific dimension or with a measure.
Filter	Relational and multidimensional		A filter is a condition object that limits the data returned in a query.
List of values	Relational and multidimensional		A list of values is a list that contains the data values associated with a dimension, an attribute, or a measure.
Parameter	Relational and multidimensional		A parameter is an entity that requires user answers before the query execution.
Navigation path	Relational and multidimensional		A navigation path is a list of drillable business objects that allow a user to drill down and up on a dimension. The final user working in a client tool doesn't see the navigation path entity but, when drilling, the navigation automatically follows one of those paths.
Analysis dimension	Multidimensional		An analysis dimension is the container of the dimensions and hierarchies in a multidimensional database.

Table 7.1 Business Layer Top-Level Entities

Entity	Business Layer Type	Icon	Description
Hierarchy	Multidimensional		A hierarchy is a collection of members with one-to-many relationships and organized in levels.
Level	Multidimensional		Members in a hierarchy are organized in levels.
Calculated measures	Multidimensional		A calculated measure is a custom measure defined in the business layer.
Calculated members	Multidimensional		A calculated member is a custom member of an OLAP dimension and associated with a hierarchy.
Named sets	Multidimensional		A named set is a collection of members that can belong to one or more hierarchies. A named set can be a simple set or a complex set.

Table 7.1 Business Layer Top-Level Entities (Cont.)

The following are other objects and concepts common to the two business layer types:

▶ Index awareness (see Section 7.17)

▶ Object formatting (see Section 7.21)

▶ Business layer views (see Section 7.24)

▶ Query governors (see Section 7.30.2)

▶ Business layer parameters (see Section 7.30.1)

The following concepts are only available for the relational business layer:

▶ Aggregate awareness (see Section 7.18)

▶ Aggregate navigation (see Section 7.18.2)

In a relational or multidimensional business layer, the designer can also build queries (🗔). A query is a collection of dimensions, attributes, measures, and filters used to create an SAP BusinessObjects BI document. The query content is analyzed, and the appropriate SQL or MDX is generated. Queries built in a business layer are not exposed to the client tools and to the final users. Those queries are defined by the designer to test the business layer in the development and maintenance phase.

IDT offers different ways to secure the data and the objects in addition to the database security that is applied when a user is querying the database.

All objects authored in the business layer and exposed in the query panel can be secured in IDT, so it is possible to set security on folders, dimensions, attributes, measures, and so on. When the security is activated on a folder, all objects and subfolders belonging to that folder inherit the security rules applied to it. For more information on security on business layer resources, see Chapter 10, Section 10.2.

7.2.3 Multidimensional Business Layer Creation

A multidimensional business layer is always automatically generated from an OLAP connection by a wizard provided in IDT. The multidimensional business layer doesn't have a data foundation and the cube information is displayed as shown in Figure 7.1.

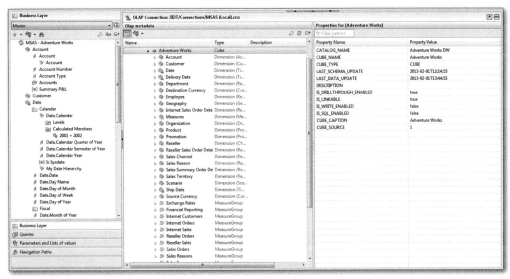

Figure 7.1 Multidimensional Business Layer Overview

You create a multidimensional business layer in the local project. There are different options for creating a new multidimensional business layer:

▶ Select menu option FILE • NEW • BUSINESS LAYER, and then select the OLAP DATA SOURCE option, as shown in Figure 7.2. Then enter a name for the business layer.

▶ Select a project in the LOCAL PROJECTS view or a folder, right-click, and select NEW • BUSINESS LAYER. Then select OLAP DATA SOURCE, as shown in Figure 7.2, and enter the name of a business layer.

▶ Select an OLAP connection in the local project, right-click, and select NEW BUSINESS LAYER. The OLAP connection can be a local connection (*.cnx*) or a shortcut to a published connection (*.cns*). A name for the business layer is automatically proposed; you can modify it.

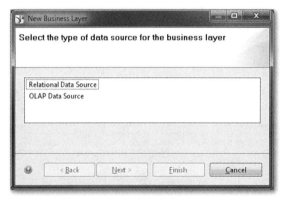

Figure 7.2 Business Layer Type Selection

After the OLAP connection is selected, two possibilities are offered depending on the OLAP connection properties:

▶ The OLAP connection used for the business layer generation is already pointing to an OLAP cube as shown in Figure 7.3.

▶ The OLAP connection used for the business layer generation is generic and is only based on an OLAP server; you have to select an OLAP cube as shown in Figure 7.3.

In both cases you also can select the options DETECT MEASURE PROJECTION FUNCTION and CREATE ATTRIBUTE FROM UNIQUE NAME, if necessary.

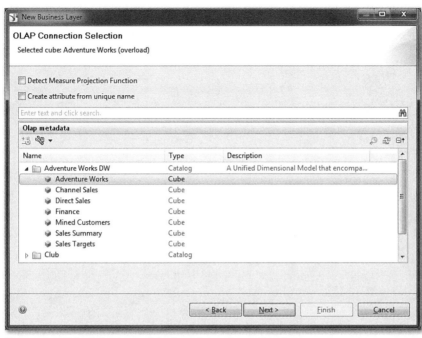

Figure 7.3 Cube Selection and Business Layer Generation Options

After the cube has been chosen, you have to choose which dimensions, hierarchies, and measures have to be generated, as shown in Figure 7.4. If the DETECT MEASURE PROJECTION FUNCTION is activated, IDT tries to get each measure aggregation function from the OLAP cube to set an appropriate projection function to the measure. If this information isn't provided by the OLAP vendor, the projection function (see Section 7.7.3) is set to DELEGATED for each measure.

If the CREATE ATTRIBUTE FROM UNIQUE NAME is activated, an attribute named TECHNICAL NAME is generated for each hierarchy.

> **Note**
>
> For multidimensional business layers, the database language used is MDX and can use database native MDX expressions.

Figure 7.4 Dimensions, Hierarchies, and Measures Selection

The MDX syntax of the attribute TECHNICAL NAME is UNIQUE_NAME. This attribute is mainly used in reports to guarantee the uniqueness of hierarchy members where duplicates exist; this attribute is a generated key by the OLAP database.

Some properties of the generated business layer depend on the underlying data source. The differences are highlighted in the next sections.

Microsoft SQL Server Analysis Services

Key performance indicators (KPIs) aren't generated in the business layer, but they can be referenced by MDX expressions in calculated members, calculated measures, or named sets. Typical MDX expressions referencing KPIs are KPITREND, KPIGOAL, KPIVALUE, and so on.

Oracle Essbase

When the business layer on top of Oracle Essbase is generated, an additional step is added to the wizard before dimensions, hierarchies, and measures are selected.

You have to choose the dimension to be used as measures. The selected dimension members are generated as measures in the business layer, as shown in Figure 7.5.

The MEASURES dimension isn't mandatory in Oracle Essbase. The MEASURES dimension is generally tagged as ACCOUNT in the Oracle Essbase outline. By default, if a dimension tagged as ACCOUNT is detected, this dimension is preselected to become the MEASURES dimension. If no dimension is tagged as ACCOUNT, then the first dimension in the list is preselected. You can decide to select a different dimension to become the MEASURES dimension.

> **Note**
>
> If the ACCOUNT dimension contains a large number of members, we recommend that you use a dimension with a smaller number of members to become the MEASURES dimension. This choice decreases the business layer generation time and reduces the size of the universe.

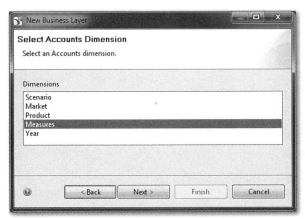

Figure 7.5 Selecting the Measures Dimension in the Oracle Essbase Business Layer Generation Wizard

The following Oracle Essbase features are partially supported in SAP Business-Objects BI 4.1:

▸ Alias tables (only the default alias table)
▸ Shared members

OLAP Generated Metadata

A multidimensional business layer is always generated, and the business layer objects map the OLAP metadata. Table 7.2 shows how the metadata maps between an OLAP source and a multidimensional business layer.

OLAP Source Metadata	Icon	Multidimensional Business Layer Objects
Dimension		Analysis dimension
Level-based hierarchy		Hierarchy
Parent-child hierarchy		Hierarchy
Hierarchy level		Level
Dimension attribute		Attribute dimension
Level attribute		Level attribute
Measure		Measure
Measure attribute		Measure attribute
Named set		Named set
Calculated member		Calculated member

Table 7.2 OLAP Metadata and Multidimensional Business Layer Objects Mapping Table

Table 7.3 describes the actions available on generated objects in a multidimensional business layer. This table only concerns generated objects because the objects that you can add afterward are fully editable.

Business Layer Objects	Available Actions
Dimension	All properties are editable.
Hierarchy	Hierarchy definition isn't editable. Other properties are editable.

Table 7.3 Available Actions on Generated Objects in a Multidimensional Business Layer

Business Layer Objects	Available Actions
Hierarchy level	Levels are only generated for level-based hierarchies. Levels of parent-child hierarchies (also called value-based hierarchies) are discovered at runtime and exposed in the query panel to be used with the member selector. Level definition isn't editable. Other properties are editable.
Dimension attribute	Dimension attribute definition and data type aren't editable. Other properties are editable.
Level attribute	Level attribute definition and data type aren't editable. Other properties are editable.
Measure	Measure definition and data type aren't editable. Other properties are editable.
Measure attribute	Measure attribute definition and data type aren't editable. Other properties are editable.
Named set	Named set definition and named set type aren't editable. Other properties are editable.

Table 7.3 Available Actions on Generated Objects in a Multidimensional Business Layer (Cont.)

7.2.4 Relational Business Layer Creation

The automatic generation of business layers on relational data sources is only partial. You should enhance and customize the business layer before publishing and consumption. The only cases where the automatically generated business layer is directly consumable by the SAP BusinessObjects BI users are the following:

▶ SAP HANA databases where a business layer can be created on top of SAP HANA views (also called SAP HANA information models).

▶ SAP NetWeaver BW InfoProviders that are only used by the Federation Query Server. This access method is available only when using multisource data foundations (see Chapter 6, Section 6.2).

For more information on universes in SAP NetWeaver BW and SAP HANA, see Chapter 12, Section 12.1 and Section 12.3.

You create a relational business layer in the local project.

There are two options for creating a relational business layer: creating it from scratch or from a data foundation. For both options, you have to give a name to the business layer. You can also define the business layer manually or have a wizard to automatically build objects and folders. The following rules apply to the objects appearing in a business layer generated automatically:

▸ Each folder represents a table and takes the table name. Special symbols and characters (such as "–" or "_") are substituted with space characters; folder names have the first letter capitalized. For example, if the table name is CALENDAR_year_Lookup, then the folder name is *Calendar Year Lookup*.

▸ Each dimension in a folder represents a column of the table and it takes the table column name with the same renaming rules applied to the folder.

A default data type is applied to the objects that are based on a single table column. An example of relational business layer and its associated data foundation are displayed in Figure 7.6.

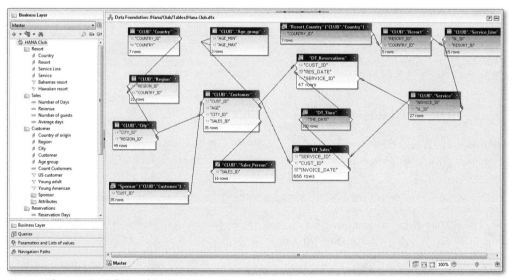

Figure 7.6 Relational Business Layer Overview

Create a Business Layer from Scratch

With this option, you create the business layer without selecting a data foundation first.

1. Select menu option FILE • NEW • BUSINESS LAYER or select a project or a folder in the LOCAL PROJECTS view, right-click, and select NEW • BUSINESS LAYER.

2. Choose RELATIONAL DATA SOURCE, as shown earlier in Figure 7.2.

3. Select a data foundation.

4. If you check AUTOMATICALLY CREATE CLASSES AND OBJECTS, the business layer is created with the following:

   ▸ A folder per table, alias table, derived table, and federated table existing in the data foundation

   ▸ A dimension per column in each respective folder

If AUTOMATICALLY CREATE CLASSES AND OBJECTS has not been activated, the business layer is created empty.

Create a Business Layer from a Data Foundation

With this option you create the business layer from a selected data foundation.

1. Select a data foundation in the local project, right-click, and select NEW BUSINESS LAYER.

2. The business layer is created with the following:

   ▸ A folder per table, alias table, derived table, and federated table existing in the data foundation

   ▸ A dimension per column in each respective folder

7.2.5   The Business Layer Editor

After the business layer is created, you can start creating/modifying objects in the business layer editor. The business layer editor in IDT is made up of two parts: the business layer objects pane and the business layer objects editor.

The business layer objects pane is split into four parts:

▸ The BUSINESS LAYER pane where you create and maintain the following:

  ▸ Folders

  ▸ Dimensions

  ▸ Attributes

- ► Measures

- ► Filters

- ► The QUERIES pane where you create and maintain queries.

- ► The PARAMETERS AND LIST OF VALUES pane where you create and maintain parameters and lists of values.

- ► The NAVIGATION PATHS pane where you create and maintain navigation paths.

The business layer objects editor displays the appropriate properties of the object you're editing. The editor self-adapts in the functions of the selected object.

7.3   Objects

You've seen that you can automatically create a business layer with its folders, dimensions, measures, and so on. This automatic creation is always used for OLAP sources because OLAP sources are self-descriptive, but the automatic creation is rarely used for relational sources because they are not as self-descriptive and are too technical to be used. Universe designers have to create business objects to make a business layer rich and comprehensive enough to be used by users. Of course, a business layer that has automatically been created by any of the wizards proposed by IDT can also be enriched.

The business layer concepts help users create reports, dashboards, analysis, and ad hoc reports. The business layer concepts directly consumable in the query panel as results objects include dimensions, hierarchies, named sets, attributes, measures, calculated members, and calculated measures. The filters are used in the query panel to filter the query and retrieve less data. Lists of values and parameters are consumable through dimensions, attributes, measures, hierarchies and filters.

Sometimes, it's hard to decide whether an object should be exposed as a measure, dimension, or attribute. For example, is the salary of an employee a dimension, an attribute, or a measure? Actually, a salary is an attribute of an employee, so it should be shown as such. A valid measure is the average salary, when you want to understand the distribution of salaries in a department, or the sum of salaries, when you want to evaluate the cost of a department. In the business layer, you can show all of those concepts: a salary attribute, an average salary measure, and a sum of salaries measures. All of those objects find the information in the same column of a table but are treated in different ways because the business layer definition associated with them is completely different.

Another important consideration on measures is that they are associated with a dimension only when running the query. When defining the measure, only the calculation method is provided, not the dimensions on which this calculation is to be performed. So, for example, the same revenue measure can be used to find the actual revenue by customer country and time or by product since the beginning of its sales. The measure definition is the same; the syntax to associate it to the specific dimensions is resolved by the system at query time only. This versatility of usage decreases the number of measure objects needed in a business layer.

It's also important to always give a brief description of the objects (dimensions, attributes, and measures) with examples if needed for users who don't understand the objects even when a good naming convention is in use.

Along with descriptions, each object in the business layer has properties that are applied in the published universe. You can define properties when you insert an object, and modify object properties at any time. Objects also have properties and options in common such as data types, lists of values, usages, states, access levels, and so on; these are detailed in Section 7.20.

Generic SQL Expressions

For relational business layers, SQL is the database language used to define the business layer objects. You can use generic SQL expressions provided by the JDBC and ODBC drivers or database native SQL expressions.

We recommend using the generic SQL expressions provided by the JDBC and ODBC drivers as much as possible, as listed in Table 7.4. They don't cover all use cases, so universe designers generally use database native SQL expressions. If you have to do a universe conversion from one relational database to another, all expressions used in the business layer and in the data foundation must be translated in the target database SQL, if, of course, there are equivalent expressions in the target database. The available generic SQL functions are provided by the data access parameters file (*.prm*) for each relational source used in the universe (see Chapter 4, Section 4.5.4).

Area	SQL Functions
Numeric	{fn cot()}, {fn mod()}, {fn abs()}, {fn acos()}, {fn asin()}, {fn atan()}, {fn atan2()}, {fn cos()}, {fn ceiling()}, {fn exp()}, {fn floor()}, {fn log()}, {fn pi()}, {fn rand()}, {fn sign()}, {fn sin()}, {fn sqrt()}, {fn tan()}
Date and time	{fn dayofmonth()}, {fn dayofweek()}, {fn dayofyear()}, {fn month()}, {fn week()}, {fn year()}, {fn CURDATE()}
String	{fn length()}, {fn locate()}, {fn concat()}, {fn left()}, {fn right()}, {fn ascii()}, {fn ltrim()}, {fn rtrim()}, {fn lcase()}, {fn rcase()}, {fn repeat()}, {fn substring()}

Table 7.4 JDBC and ODBC Generic SQL Functions

7.4   Folders

A folder (also called class in the Universe Design Tool) is an organizational concept only; a folder doesn't handle data definition. The objective of a folder is to organize dimensions, attributes, measures, analysis dimensions, hierarchies, and filters to help users find the business objects they need. A folder can also contain subfolders; there is no limit on the number of folders or subfolders. Note that folders with the same parent (folder or business layer root) can't have the same name.

To create a folder, select the business layer root or another folder in the BUSINESS LAYER pane, and then choose one of the following options:

▶ Right-click and select NEW • FOLDER.

▶ Click the INSERT OBJECT button (➕) in the BUSINESS LAYER section toolbar and select FOLDER.

A folder isn't used in a query definition but can be dragged and dropped in the query panel. All of its associated objects are added in the query results pane.

The folder editor displays its content, including subfolders, as shown in Figure 7.7. This gives an overview of the folder content and the objects usage.

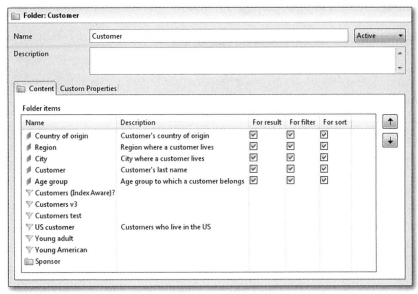

Figure 7.7 Folder Editor

7.5 Dimensions

A dimension is generally considered as the focus of the analysis. A dimension can be an object—such as country, customer, or year—that is the basis for analysis in a report, analysis, or dashboard. The dimensions typically retrieve alphanumeric data (customer names, country names, zip codes, age, etc.) or dates (years, quarters, reservation dates, etc.).

The dimensions can be used as results and/or as filters in a query defined with IDT or in a query panel used by SAP BusinessObjects BI clients.

The dimensions can also be used in filters, lists of values, and navigation paths, as well as be referenced by other dimensions, attributes, or measures.

The dimensions are used as grouping sets for the measures used in queries, but dimensions can also be queried without any measures. Note that dimensions belonging to the same folder or the business layer root can't have the same name.

To create a dimension, select the business layer root or a folder in the BUSINESS LAYER pane, and then choose one of the following options:

- ▶ Right-click, and select NEW • DIMENSION.
- ▶ Click the INSERT OBJECT button (➕) in the BUSINESS LAYER section toolbar and select DIMENSION.

After the dimension is created, your next steps depend on whether it is for a relational business layer or a multidimensional business layer:

- ▶ For a relational business layer, click the SQL DEFINITION tab and then enter the definition in the SELECT text box, or click the SQL ASSISTANT button to open the SQL editor (see Section 7.19.1), as shown in Figure 7.8.
- ▶ For a multidimensional business layer, click the MDX DEFINITION tab, and then enter the definition in the EXPRESSION text box or click the MDX ASSISTANT button to open the MDX editor (see Section 7.19.2), as shown in Figure 7.9. It's also mandatory to associate a hierarchy to the newly created dimension, as shown in Figure 7.9.

In a relational business layer, you can also create dimensions by dragging and dropping a table or a column from the data foundation view into the BUSINESS LAYER pane. The dimension is added in the place where you dropped the table or the column.

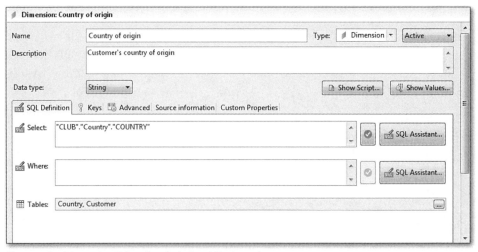

Figure 7.8 Dimension Editor in a Relational Business Layer

To create multiple dimensions at once, you can drag and drop a table from the data foundation view on a folder or an object in the BUSINESS LAYER pane. A folder (with table name) and dimensions (with table name + column name) is added in the place where you dropped the table. The naming convention is applied, and the folder is a subfolder if added under another folder.

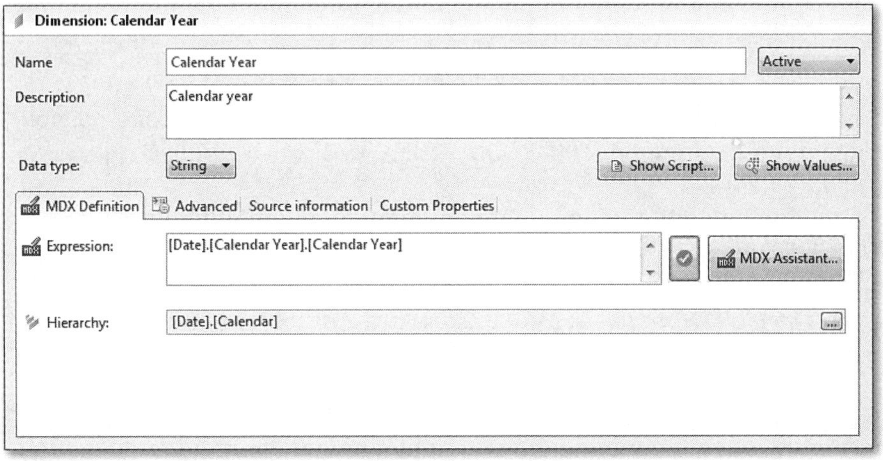

Figure 7.9 Dimension Editor in a Multidimensional Business Layer

For relational business layers, another object such as an attribute or measure can be changed into a dimension.

To change another object into a dimension, choose one of the following options:

▶ In the object editor, select DIMENSION in the TYPE combo box.

▶ In the BUSINESS LAYER pane, select an object, right-click, and select TURN INTO DIMENSION.

To be valid, a dimension needs to have a definition that you have to specify in the SELECT text box in the dimension editor.

For a relational business layer, the dimension definition is an SQL expression using column definition and eventually additional SQL expressions.

▶ For relational and multidimensional business layers, the dimension definition is added to the SELECT clause when used in the RESULTS pane of the query panel.

▶ For a relational business layer, the dimension filter is added to the WHERE clause when used in the FILTERS pane of the query panel.

For the multidimensional business layer, the dimension definition is an MDX expression using cube dimensions, hierarchies, or measures definitions and additional MDX expressions. The dimension is always associated with a hierarchy.

7.5.1 Dimension Definition: SELECT Clause

In the dimension editor, you enter the dimension definition in the SELECT text box. Alternatively, you can invoke the SQL editor (refer to Figure 7.8) for a relational business layer, or invoke the MDX editor (refer to Figure 7.9) for a multidimensional business layer.

In a relational business layer, a dimension is generally a one-to-one mapping with a table column or a calculated column defined in the data foundation. But a dimension can also use SQL expressions to transform the data in something that can be directly used in a query.

The following are examples of custom SQL expressions used in a dimension definition:

► The dimension "CUSTOMER NAME" is the concatenation of two table columns: "CUSTOMER FIRST NAME" and "CUSTOMER LAST NAME".

► The dimension "YEAR" is an SQL expression extracting the year from the table column "ORDER DATE".

► The dimension "GENDER" is the first character of the table column "SOCIAL SECURITY NUMBER".

For a multidimensional business layer, if the dimension is used in the FILTER pane of the query panel, the expression can be added in the query in different places of the MDX statement depending on the number of dimension values the user uses to filter the query.

IDT also provides built-in functions described in Section 7.23 that can be used in dimension definition but also in attributes, measures, filters, named sets, calculated members, and calculated measures definition:

▶ @select

▶ @where

▶ @variable

▶ @prompt

The @where built-in function can be used in a filter expression, or can be used in the WHERE definition of a dimension, attribute, or measure.

Using the @variable and the @prompt built-in functions make the content of the dimension dynamic when used in a query. Users have to answer the question proposed by the @prompt definition at query time. The variable name used in the @variable definition is replaced by its value at query time (e.g., @variable('PREFERRED_VIEW-ING_LOCALE') is replaced by 'fr_FR').

> ### Example
>
> Examples of dimensions using the @prompt and the @variable functions include the following:
>
> ▶ Ask the user to enter a numeric value as a percentage: @prompt('Enter a percentage','N',,mono,constrained)
>
> ▶ Ask the user to select one column out of the two proposed columns: @prompt('Select the time dimension', 'A:K', {'Year':'DT_Time.year_desc','Month':'DT_Time.month_desc'}, Mono,Primary_key)
>
> ▶ Ask the user to choose one of the values displayed by the parameter: @prompt(MyParameter)
>
> ▶ Display the current user connected to the CMS repository when running the query: @variable('BOUser')

The dimensions can be used in queries but also in lists of values, filters, navigation paths, and other dimensions. To reference an existing dimension in another dimension expression, it's recommended to use the built-in @select function.

The main advantage of using the @select function is that a dimension can be referenced in multiple places in the business layer and in different folders. That means that only one definition of the dimension has to be maintained because all dimensions using the @select function inherit the referenced dimension definition.

For multidimensional business layers, we recommend that you use the `@select` function when defining objects to guarantee the validity of those objects after a refresh structure of the multidimensional business layer (see Section 7.29).

The `@select` function can be used by itself, can be combined with any other SQL or MDX function, or can be used with another IDT predefined function.

The `@select` function is solved at runtime by the query engine. The syntax of the `@select` function is `@select(<folder name[\folder name]\object name>)` where `<folder name\[folder name]\object name>` specifies the full path of another object in the business layer. For more information on the `@select` built-in function, see Section 7.23.4.

> **Tip**
>
> If you drag and drop a dimension, attribute, or measure from the BUSINESS LAYER pane into a SELECT text box (that is, an EXPRESSION text box for multidimensional objects) or a WHERE text box, the `@select` function referencing the business layer object is added in the object definition at the cursor position in the text box.

7.5.2 Dimension Definition: WHERE Clause

In the dimension editor, you can also enter a filter definition in the WHERE text box as shown earlier in Figure 7.8, or you can invoke the SQL editor to create it. This step is optional and is only used for filtering the query. The WHERE text box respects the same rules as the SELECT text box and uses the same built-in functions and SQL expressions. The WHERE text box is only available for relational business layers.

When a dimension is used in the query results, the WHERE definition is added in the `WHERE` clause of the SQL statement and is applied to the entire query.

> **Note**
>
> The WHERE definition of an object (dimension, attribute, or measure) is always added in the SQL statement if the business object is used in a query.
>
> If you always need to filter the query, you can use the WHERE definition; if you only need to filter the query for particular cases, it's preferable to create filters that are used on demand.

7.5.3   Validation

When the dimension is created, it's important to validate the expression using the VALIDATE button in the SQL editor or in the MDX editor. The SQL editor and the MDX editor provide a wide set of database functions, operators, and business layer objects to help create the dimension definition.

The validation is also available by clicking the VALIDATE button (✓) in the SELECT text box or in the WHERE text box. For more information on object validation and check integrity, see Section 7.26.

The dimension data type can be inherited from the column if the dimension has been automatically created or changed into a dimension from another object. The data type can of course be modified, and the dimension validation takes into account the SQL expression or MDX expression and the data type to validate the definition.

7.5.4   Extra Tables

In the relational business layer, when the dimension definition is created in the SELECT box, the tables associated with the dimension definition are added to the EXTRA TABLES list.

> **Note**
>
> If the dimension definition only contains a constant, the @prompt or the @variable function, a table reference needs to be added manually in the EXTRA TABLES list used by this dimension. If you don't add a reference, the dimension definition is set as invalid during the validation operation.

It can be useful for certain use cases to force the query to use more tables than the tables used by the dimension in the query. To add a table, click the [...] button to the right of the combo box tables shown in Figure 7.8. The list of potential extra tables shows up in Figure 7.10. The tables are added in the FROM clause of the SQL statement. A dimension definition needs at least one table referenced in the tables list.

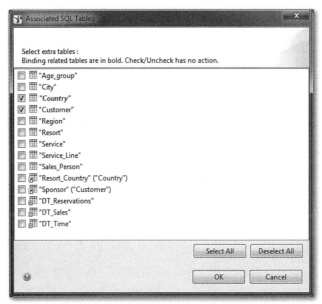

Figure 7.10 Extra Tables Selection for a Relational Business Layer

---

Example

Let's assume the following schema: the table "COUNTRY" is joined to the table "REGION" that is joined to the table "CITY" that is joined to the table "CUSTOMER". The dimension "COUNTRY" is referencing the table "COUNTRY".

You can build a report displaying the list of countries. If you want to build a report that only displays the countries that have customers, you can add the table "CUSTOMER" in the list of tables of the "COUNTRY" dimension, as shown in Figure 7.10. The table "CUSTOMER" is then always added to the query when "COUNTRY" is requested (with a FROM clause), and only the countries having customers are retrieved in the report.

The generated SQL script includes all tables that are joined between "COUNTRY" and "CUSTOMER":

```
Select Table__3."COUNTRY"

From "CLUB"."Country" Table__3 INNER JOIN "CLUB"."Region" Table__5
ON (Table__3."COUNTRY_ID" = Table__5."COUNTRY_ID")

INNER JOIN "CLUB"."City" Table__2 ON (Table__5."REGION_ID" =
Table__2."REGION_ID")

INNER JOIN "CLUB"."Customer" Table__4 ON (Table__2."CITY_ID" =
Table__4."CITY_ID")
```

7.5.5 Preview Data and List of Values

After the dimension definition has been created and validated, you can view the content of the dimension. For more information on dimension preview data, see Section 7.25.1.

When a dimension is created, a default list of values is associated with the dimension, and the list of values definition is based on the dimension definition. You can choose a different list of values from the lists of values that have been created in the business layer. It's also possible to not associate a list of values with the dimension.

The list of values associated with a dimension is used for filtering the dimension at runtime. If no list of values has been associated with the dimension, you can filter the dimensions, but the user has to manually enter dimension value(s) for filtering. For more information on associating a list of values to a dimension, see Section 7.13.

7.6 Attributes

An attribute object (also called details in the Universe Design Tool) provides descriptive data about a dimension object (or attribute of a dimension). It's always associated with a specific dimension object. An attribute is something that tells you more about a dimension.

In general, you set an object as an attribute of a dimension when there is a one-to-one relationship with its dimension. For example, you may have a dimension called "CUSTOMER" and related attributes such as "PHONE NUMBER" and "SS NUMBER", or you may have a "PRODUCT" dimension and related attributes such as "PACKAGING", "COLOR", and so on.

The attributes can be used as results and/or as filters in a query defined with IDT or in a query panel.

The attributes can also be used in filters, lists of values, and be referenced by other dimensions, attributes, or measures. However, an attribute object can't be used in drilldown analysis (navigation paths).

The attributes are always associated with dimensions or measures. A typical example of an attribute associated with a measure is the currency or the unit; this is mainly used by the SAP NetWeaver BW and SAP HANA data sources. However, you can associate any attribute with a measure. Note that attributes belonging to the same dimension can't have the same name.

Warning

A dimension or a measure is expected to have one and only one value for a specific attribute. This constraint can be described as a one-to-one cardinality between a dimension or a measure and their attributes. There is no check integrity in IDT to check the cardinality between a dimension and its attributes. It's up to you to define the relationships correctly. For example:

▸ Country can be an attribute of city because a city has one and only one country.

▸ City can't be an attribute of country because a country has more than one city.

If a dimension and its attribute are used in an SAP BusinessObjects Web Intelligence query, SAP BusinessObjects Web Intelligence assumes that there is a one-to-one cardinality between the dimension and its attribute. So if that's not the case, the attribute data displayed in the report is #MULTIVALUE.

To create an attribute, select a dimension, measure, or a hierarchy in the BUSINESS LAYER pane, and then choose one of the following options:

▸ Right-click, and select NEW • ATTRIBUTE.

▸ Click the INSERT OBJECT button (➕) in the BUSINESS LAYER section toolbar and select ATTRIBUTE.

After the attribute is created:

▸ For a relational business layer, click the SQL DEFINITION tab, and then enter the definition in the SELECT text box, or click the SQL ASSISTANT button to open the SQL editor, as shown in Figure 7.11.

▸ For a multidimensional business layer, click the MDX DEFINITION tab, and then enter the definition in the EXPRESSION text box, or click the MDX ASSISTANT button to open the MDX editor, as shown in Figure 7.12 in the next section.

In relational business layers, dimension and measure objects can be changed into attributes. To change an object into an attribute, choose one of the following options:

▸ In the object editor, select ATTRIBUTE in the TYPE combo box.

▸ In the BUSINESS LAYER pane, select an object, right-click, and select TURN INTO ATTRIBUTE.

Figure 7.11 Attribute Editor in a Relational Business Layer

> **Note**
>
> Attributes can't be used in navigation paths. Be careful when creating an attribute or changing a dimension into an attribute because the cardinality between the dimension and the attribute isn't checked by IDT.

7.6.1 Attribute Definition: SELECT Clause and WHERE Clause

As for dimensions, the attributes definition uses SQL or MDX expressions to transform the data into something that can be directly used in a query.

An attribute must have a definition (SELECT) and can have a filter definition (WHERE), as shown earlier in Figure 7.11. The attribute editor has the same capabilities as the dimension editor, and the same rules apply.

In a multidimensional business layer, the attributes are automatically generated, but a number of limited attributes can be manually created concerning the database syntax.

For a multidimensional business layer, the following possible attribute definitions can be used (see Figure 7.12):

▶ MEMBER_UNIQUE_NAME

▶ MEMBER_NAME

▶ MEMBER_CAPTION

▶ MEMBER_VALUE

Some of these listed attributes aren't supported by all of the OLAP databases. The attributes used in a query as results don't participate in the measures aggregation.

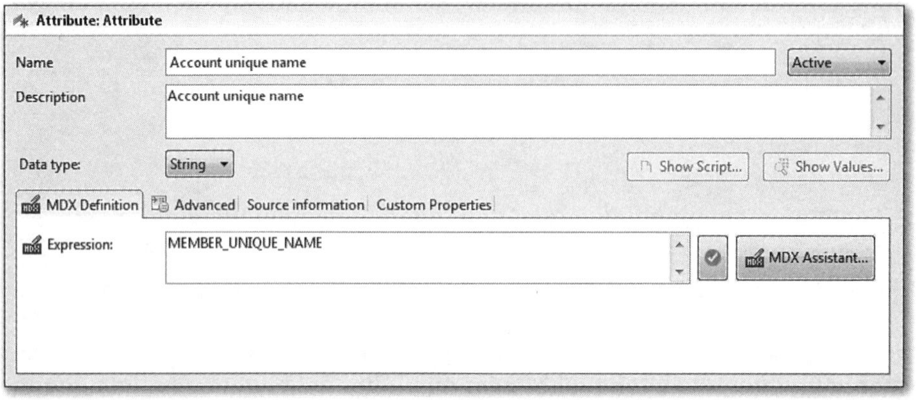

Figure 7.12 Attribute Editor in a Multidimensional Business Layer

The attribute definition can be filled by entering an SQL expression that does or does not use built-in functions (see Section 7.23) such as `@select`, `@variable`, or `@prompt`. The attributes used in a query as results participate in the measures aggregation as grouping sets.

7.6.2 Preview Data and List of Values

After the attribute definition has been created and validated, you can view the content of the attribute. When an attribute is created, a default list of values is associated with the attribute, and the list of values definition is based on the attribute definition. You can choose a different list of values from the list of values that has been created in the business layer. It's also possible to not associate a list of values to the attribute.

The list of values associated with an attribute is used for filtering the attribute at runtime. If no list of values has been associated with the attribute, the user can filter the attributes manually by entering attribute values in a prompt.

7.6.3   Attribute Validation and Other Properties

Like other objects, it's important to validate the attribute expression using the VALIDATE button in the SQL editor or in the MDX editor. For more information on object validation and check integrity, see Section 7.26. You can also reference additional tables to an attribute in the TABLES text box.

The attribute data type (see Section 7.20.1) can be inherited from the table column if the attribute has been automatically created or changed into an attribute from another object.

The data type can, of course, be modified, and the attribute validation takes into account the SQL or MDX expression and the data type to validate the definition.

7.7   Measures and Calculated Measures

A measure object is mainly derived from one of the following aggregate functions: `Count`, `Sum`, `Min` (Minimum), `Max` (Maximum), or `Avg` (Average). Measures are mainly numeric data items on which aggregation functions can be applied. Having numeric measures with an aggregation function isn't mandatory, you can define measures without aggregation function and you can also have nonnumeric measures. Examples of measures include revenue, quantity, number of orders, unit price, average sales price, discount percentage, and so on.

The measures can be used as results and/or as filters in a query defined with IDT or in a query panel used by client tools.

The measures can also be used in filters and lists of values, as well as be referenced by other dimensions, attributes, or measures. Measures can't be used in navigation paths.

Like dimensions and attributes, a measure definition uses SQL language for relational data sources and MDX language for OLAP data sources.

For the relational sources, a measure definition can be based on one or multiple columns and can also use built-in functions such as `@select`, `@variable`, or `@prompt`. Measures belonging to the same folder or the business layer root can't have the same name.

> **Note**
>
> In the relational sources, each measure should be defined with an SQL aggregation function. This isn't mandatory, but it's highly recommended.
>
> If at least one measure used in the query results has an SQL aggregation function, the SQL generated query adds a GROUP BY expression for all dimensions included in the query results.
>
> If no measure used in the query results has an SQL aggregation function, the SQL generated query retrieves the details for all objects in the query, and the measure is considered as a dimension by the relational database

For OLAP sources, a new measure manually added in the business layer is also called a calculated measure and is always associated with the dimension [Measures].

> **Note**
>
> A calculated measure created in a multidimensional business layer is generated in the MDX query as the following:
>
> WITH MEMBER [Measures].[My measure] AS 'My measure definition'

To create a measure, select the business layer root or a folder in the BUSINESS LAYER pane, and then choose one of the following options:

▶ Right-click and select NEW • MEASURE.

▶ Click the INSERT OBJECT button (➕) in the BUSINESS LAYER section toolbar and select MEASURE.

After the measure is created:

▶ For a relational business layer, click the SQL DEFINITION tab and then enter the definition in the SELECT text box, or click the SQL ASSISTANT button to open the SQL editor, as shown in Figure 7.13.

▶ For a multidimensional business layer, click the MDX DEFINITION tab and then enter the definition in the EXPRESSION text box, or click the MDX ASSISTANT button to open the MDX editor, as shown in Figure 7.14.

An OLAP calculated measure has the same capabilities and properties as a calculated member (see Section 7.8).

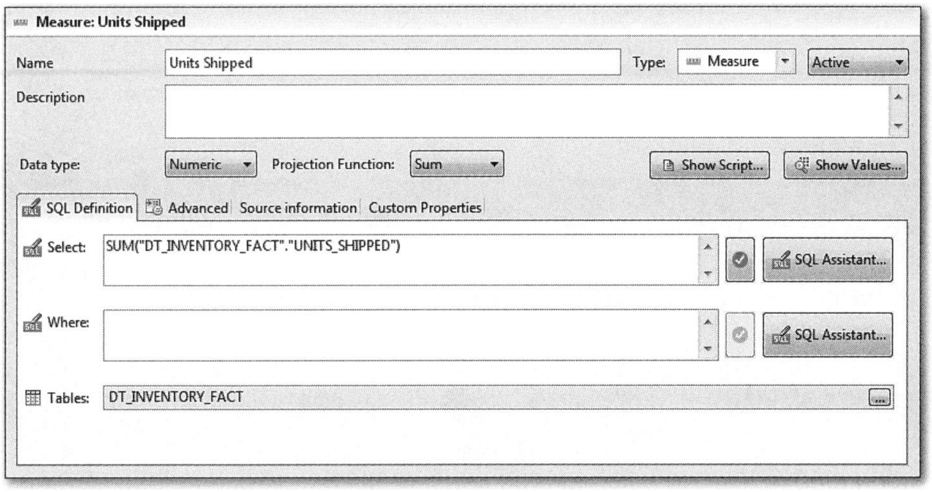

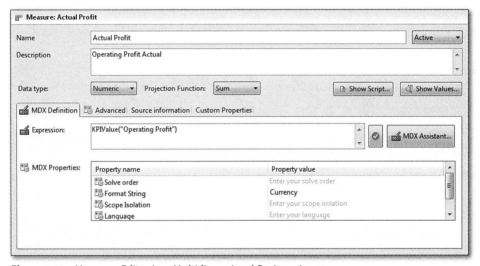

Figure 7.13 Measures Editor in a Relational Business Layer

Figure 7.14 Measures Editor in a Multidimensional Business Layer

For the relational business layers, another object such as an attribute or dimension can be changed into a measure. To change an object into a dimension, choose one of the following options:

▶ In the object editor, select MEASURE in the TYPE combo box.

▶ In the BUSINESS LAYER pane, select an object, right-click, select TURN INTO MEA-SURE WITH AGGREGATION FUNCTION, and then select an aggregation function.

When turning a dimension or an attribute into a measure with an aggregation function, a list of SQL aggregation functions is displayed depending on the object data type. Table 7.5 shows the possible aggregation functions depending on the object data type.

Object Data Type	Aggregation Function					
	Sum	Min	Max	Count	Average	None
Blob	N/A	N/A	N/A	N/A	N/A	Possible
Boolean	N/A	N/A	N/A	N/A	N/A	Possible
Date	N/A	Possible	Possible	Possible	N/A	Possible
Date Time	N/A	Possible	Possible	Possible	N/A	Possible
Long Text	N/A	Possible	Possible	Possible	N/A	Possible
Numeric	Possible	Possible	Possible	Possible	Possible	Possible
String	N/A	Possible	Possible	Possible	N/A	Possible

Table 7.5 Data Types and SQL Aggregations Functions Mapping Table

When an object is turned into a measure with an SQL aggregation function, the SQL aggregation function is added in the SQL expression of the object definition.

Example

The following object has a string data type and is turned into a measure with the COUNT aggregation function:

▶ SQL definition before: "CUSTOMERS"."COUNTRY"
▶ SQL definition after: COUNT("CUSTOMERS"."COUNTRY")

The following object has a numeric data type and is turned into a measure with the SUM aggregation function:

▶ SQL definition before: "SALES"."QUANTITY"
▶ SQL definition after: SUM("SALES"."QUANTITY")

The following object has a date data type and is turned into a measure with the NONE aggregation function:

▶ SQL definition before: "SALES"."ORDER_DATE"
▶ SQL definition after: "SALES"."ORDER_DATE"

The latter object becomes a measure in the business layer but is treated as a dimension in an SQL query.

7.7.1 Measure Definition: SELECT Clause and WHERE Clause

As for dimensions, the measures definition uses SQL or MDX expressions to transform the data into something that can be directly used in a query. A measure must have a definition (SELECT) and can have a filter definition (WHERE), as shown earlier in Figure 7.13. The measure editor has the same capabilities as the dimension editor, and the same rules apply.

> **Note**
>
> The WHERE definition of a measure is always added in the SQL statement if the business object is used in a query.
>
> As opposed to the dimensions and attributes where the WHERE definition filters the entire query, the measure WHERE definition only filters the concerned measure.
>
> So in the case you have added in a query 2 measures with at least one containing a WHERE definition, 2 SQL flows are generated. An SQL flow is generated per filtered measure, the SQL flows are combined with a full outer join operator, and the results are merged in a single result set.

In a multidimensional business layer, the measures are automatically generated, but the calculated measures can be manually created respecting the database syntax, as shown earlier in Figure 7.14.

The measure definition can be filled by entering an SQL expression that does or does not use a built-in function such as @select, @variable, or @prompt.

The measures used in a query as results are aggregated by the database respecting the SQL aggregation function if the latter has been filled.

7.7.2 Preview Data and List of Values

After the measure definition has been created and validated, you can view the content of the measure.

> **Note**
>
> When previewing the content of a measure, the SQL aggregation function is applied, and the aggregated measure value is displayed. For an OLAP source, the total for the measure is displayed.

When the measure is created, no list of values is associated with the measure. A list of values can be automatically associated with the measure if a dimension or an attribute has been changed into a measure because the attribute or the dimension already had a list of values. You can associate a default list of values or a list of values created in the business layer.

Note

Generally, it's not recommended to associate a list of values with a measure because measures often have SQL aggregation functions, and the list of values only returns one value such as the "sum of revenue" or the "count of customers."

You can associate a list of values to a measure that has no SQL aggregation function, for instance, for measures such as "% OBJECTIVE", "PERCENTAGE", and so on.

7.7.3   Projection Function

The measures aggregations are always computed by the relying database, and the result of a query, including dimensions, attributes, and measures, is sent to the SAP BusinessObjects BI client. The SAP BusinessObjects BI client displays the query result in charts, tables, and other graphical elements. All clients consume the results returned by the database.

SAP BusinessObjects Web Intelligence is also able to store the query results in a local report cache (also called a *microcube*). The microcube is in fact a cache and a calculation engine; the main microcube capabilities are local aggregations, calculations, data transformations, and data merges.

SAP BusinessObjects Web Intelligence is able to locally aggregate the results of a query if only part of the query is used in a table or a chart. To aggregate locally, SAP BusinessObjects Web Intelligence needs to know the aggregation function associated with the measure to re-aggregate it with the dimensions used in a table or a chart.

The aggregation function used by SAP BusinessObjects Web Intelligence is called a *projection function*. To associate a projection function to the measure, select one of the Table 7.6 values from the PROJECTION FUNCTION combo box in the measure editor, as shown in Figure 7.15.

Projection Function	Description
AVERAGE	Computes the average of all values in the context of the report. SAP BusinessObjects Web Intelligence performs the aggregation locally for this measure.
COUNT	Computes the count of all values in the context of the report. SAP BusinessObjects Web Intelligence performs the aggregation locally for this measure.
DELEGATED	When this aggregation function has been set, the value #TOREFRESH is displayed in the document instead of the measure aggregation value. It means that the user needs to refresh the query to have the measure aggregation computed by the database. The query is then updated, and a new statement (SQL or MDX) is generated containing only the dimensions and measures used in the table/chart. A hidden grouping set column is then added for all SQL/MDX statements to help the microcube displaying the appropriate results. The database, *not* SAP BusinessObjects Web Intelligence, performs the aggregation for this measure.
MAX	Computes the maximum of all values in the context of the report. SAP BusinessObjects Web Intelligence performs the aggregation locally for this measure.
MIN	Computes the minimum of all values in the context of the report. SAP BusinessObjects Web Intelligence performs the aggregation locally for this measure.
NONE	No aggregation is done for this measure.
SUM	Computes the sum of all values in the context of the report. SAP BusinessObjects Web Intelligence performs the aggregation locally for this measure.

Table 7.6 Projection Functions Description

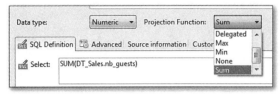

Figure 7.15 Setting a Measure Projection Function

SAP BusinessObjects Web Intelligence users can create as many tables/charts as they want with a single query result. The aggregation function defined for the measures applies, and the result of the aggregation is displayed in the tables/charts.

For the relational business layers, it's recommended to apply the projection functions listed in Table 7.7 to have correct results.

SQL Aggregation Function	Projection Function
SUM	SUM
MIN	MIN
MAX	MAX
COUNT	SUM or DELEGATED
AVG	DELEGATED

Table 7.7 SQL Aggregation Functions and Projection Functions Recommendations

The measure projection function is available for relational business layers and multidimensional business layers. For the multidimensional business layer, it's always recommended to use the DELEGATED projection function unless the database measure aggregation is known.

Example

An SAP BusinessObjects Web Intelligence user has selected the following objects in the query panel: "YEAR", "PRODUCT", and "REVENUE", where "REVENUE" is the measure. The "REVENUE" projection function is set to DELEGATED.

The generated SQL query is listed here:

```
Select "Year", "Product", Sum("Revenue") From "Fact_table" Group By
"Year", "Product"
```

After running the query, the user creates a table that only displays "YEAR" and "REVENUE". The value #TOREFRESH is displayed in the "REVENUE" cells.

When the user refreshes the query, the "Revenue" values computed by the database are displayed, and the generated SQL query is as shown here:

```
Select 0 as GID, "Year", NULL, Sum("Revenue") From "Fact_table"
Group By "Year", "Product"
Union
Select 1 as GID, "Year", "Product", Sum("Revenue") From "Fact_table"
Group By "Year", "Product"
```

GID is the hidden column used by the microcube.

The value #TOREFRESH is replaced by the "Revenue" value computed by the database.

7.7.4 Measure Validation and Other Properties

Like other objects, it's important to validate the measure expression using the VALIDATE button in the SQL editor or in the MDX editor. For more information on object validation and check integrity, see Section 7.26. You can also reference additional tables to a measure in the TABLES text box.

The measure data type can be inherited from the table column if the measure has been automatically created or changed into a measure from another object.

> **Note**
>
> It's not mandatory that measures have a numeric data type, but all measures with an SQL aggregation function must have a numeric data type.

The data type can of course be modified, and the measure validation takes into account the SQL or MDX expression and the data type to validate the definition.

7.8 Calculated Members

Calculated members are only available for multidimensional business layers. These calculated members are members of an OLAP dimension and associated with a hierarchy. They are based on a combination of cube data, numbers, arithmetic operators, OLAP functions and built-in functions such as @prompt or @select, as described in Section 7.23.

The calculated member values are calculated by the database and not by the client. The calculated members based on members of the [Measure] dimension are also called calculated measures and can be created as measures in the business layer as described in Section 7.7.

The calculated members can be used as results in a query defined with IDT or in a query panel used by SAP BusinessObjects BI clients. They can only be used in the member selector of the query panel, as described in Chapter 8. Note that calculated members belonging to the same hierarchy can't have the same name.

A calculated member is an MDX expression that can use OLAP database functions, built-in functions, and business layer objects.

Example

The calculated members are generally used to do calculations between members of the same hierarchy:

▶ Semester 1 definition: [Time].[Quarter 1] + [Time].[Quarter 2]
▶ Semester 2 definition: [Time].[Quarter 3] + [Time].[Quarter 4]

It's generally recommended to use the @select built-in functions as much as possible to ensure that the definition remains valid after a business layer refresh structure (see Section 7.29).

To create a calculated member, select a hierarchy in the BUSINESS LAYER pane, and then choose one of the following options:

▶ Right-click, and select NEW • CALCULATED MEMBER.
▶ Click the INSERT OBJECT button (🛖) in the BUSINESS LAYER section toolbar and select CALCULATED MEMBER.

After the calculated member is created, you can enter the calculated member definition or click the MDX ASSISTANT button to open the MDX editor, as shown in Figure 7.16.

A calculated member must always be associated with a hierarchy. To associate the calculated member to a hierarchy, click the ▦ button in the right side of the HIERARCHY text box, and select a hierarchy from the list of hierarchies, as shown in

Figure 7.17. When a hierarchy is selected, the calculated member is moved under the chosen hierarchy in the business layer.

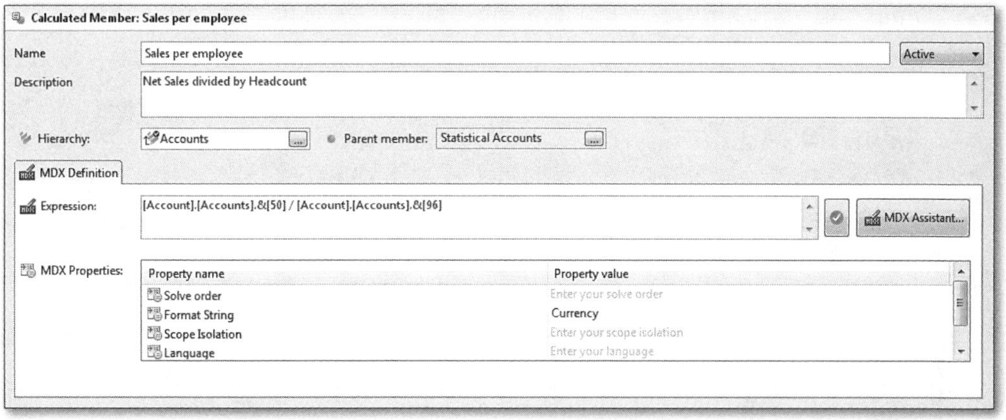

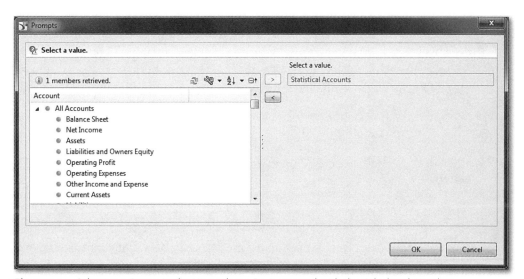

Figure 7.16   Calculated Member Editor

Some databases such as Microsoft SQL Server Analysis Services support the ability to associate the calculated member with a parent in the hierarchy. To do so, click the [...] button in the right side of the PARENT MEMBER text box button, and select a member in the chosen hierarchy.

Figure 7.17   Selecting a Parent in the Hierarchy to Be Associated with the Calculated Member

If a calculated member is associated with a parent in the hierarchy, it appears under the parent in the chosen hierarchy displayed in a client such as SAP BusinessObjects Web Intelligence. If the calculated member isn't associated with a parent, it appears under the chosen hierarchy root member displayed in an SAP BusinessObjects BI client.

> **Note**
>
> A calculated member created in a multidimensional business layer is generated in the MDX query as the following:
> ```
> WITH MEMBER [Hierarchy].[My member] AS 'My member definition'
> WITH MEMBER [Dimension.hierarchy].[My member] AS 'My member
> definition'
> ```

A calculated member or a calculated measure also has additional properties that can be set: Solve Order, Format String, Scope Isolation, and Language. They are editable in the calculated member editor in the MDX Properties text box, as shown earlier in Figure 7.16.

7.8.1 Solve Order

The Solve order property is an integer that determines the order in which dimensions, members, calculated members, custom rollups, and calculated cells are evaluated and calculated. The Solve order property proceeds from the highest to the lowest level. It is mainly used when a calculated member definition is using other calculated members or calculated measures. In such cases, the Solve order property helps to determine the order of calculations.

7.8.2 Format String

The Format String property determines the output format of the calculated member.

7.8.3 Scope Isolation

When an MDX script contains calculated members, by default the calculated members are resolved before any session-scoped calculations are resolved and before any query-defined calculations are resolved.

The behavior allows generic client applications to work with cubes that contain complex calculations without having to take into account the specific implementation of the calculations. However, in certain scenarios, you might want to execute session-scoped or query-scoped calculated members before certain calculations in the cube. To accomplish this, use the SCOPE ISOLATION property.

7.8.4 Language

The LANGUAGE property is the LANGUAGE CODE ID used for the calculated member. The default value is 1033 for the United States. For more information on the LANGUAGE property, navigate to the Microsoft KB article at *http://support.microsoft. com/kb/950598*.

> **Example**
>
> The calculated member '2001 + 2002' is the sum of years 2001 and 2002, with SOLVE ORDER = 5, FORMAT STRING = #, LANGUAGE = EN, and SCOPE ISOLATION = CUBE.
>
> The generated MDX script of the calculated member looks like this:
>
> ```
> WITH MEMBER [Date].[Calendar].[2001 + 2002] AS '[Date].
> [Calendar].[Calendar Year].&[2001] + [Date].[Calendar].[Calendar
> Year].&[2001]', SOLVE_ORDER = 5, SCOPE_ISOLATION = CUBE, FORMAT_
> STRING = '#', LANGUAGE = 1033
> ```

7.9   Named Sets

Named sets are only available for multidimensional business layers. A named set is a set of hierarchy members. You can create named sets by combining cube data, numbers, arithmetic operators, OLAP functions, and built-in functions such as @prompt or @select, as described in Section 7.23. The named sets can only be used with the member selector.

A named set is an MDX expression than can use OLAP database functions, built-in functions, and business layer objects. A named set can be a simple expression such as a list of products or a complex query such as the top ten customers that bought $50,000 of entertainment products for the year 2012.

It's generally recommended to use the `@select` function as much as possible to ensure that the definition remains valid after a business layer refresh structure.

The named sets can be used as results in a query defined with IDT, or in a query panel used by SAP BusinessObjects BI clients. Note that named sets belonging to the same hierarchy or the same analysis dimension can't have the same name.

To create a named set, select a hierarchy, an analysis dimension, a folder, or the business layer root in the BUSINESS LAYER pane, and then choose one of the following options:

▶ Right-click, and select NEW • NAMED SET.

▶ Click the INSERT OBJECT button (➕) in the BUSINESS LAYER section toolbar and select NAMED SET.

The named set is created, and the editor opens, as shown in Figure 7.18.

A named set is always associated with a hierarchy, but no relationship is necessary between the selected hierarchy and the members composing the named set. To associate the named set to a hierarchy, click the BROWSE button (⬚) in the right side of the HIERARCHY text box button, and select a hierarchy from the list of hierarchies, as shown in Figure 7.18.

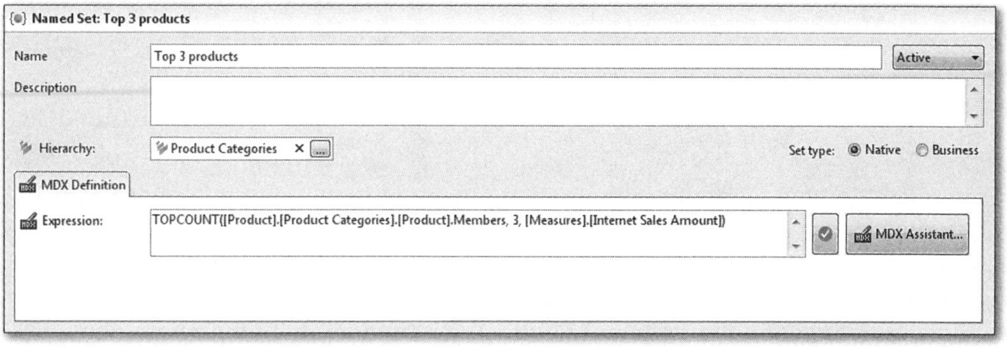

Figure 7.18 Native Named Set with MDX Definition

> **Example**
>
> Let's assume you create a named set with a collection of members coming from the product hierarchy and associate it to the time hierarchy. If you create an MDX query that mixes the product hierarchy and the named set associated with the time hierarchy, the query returns an error because you can't have members coming from the same hierarchy (product) into two different hierarchies (product and time).

Before entering the named set definition, you have to choose the named set type:

▶ NATIVE

▶ BUSINESS

If the named set type is NATIVE, you can enter the named set definition or click the MDX ASSISTANT button to open the MDX editor, as shown earlier in Figure 7.18.

If the named set type is BUSINESS, you have to click the EDIT ITEMS button to pick members from the selected hierarchy. You can use the member selector and use OLAP style family selection, as shown in Figure 7.19.

> **Note**
>
> A named set can mix members coming from different hierarchies, but you have to respect the database constraints and use the CROSSJOIN operator to mix the members from the different hierarchies.
>
> A named set created in a multidimensional business layer is generated in the MDX query like this:
>
> ```
> WITH SET [My Set] AS 'My named set definition'
> ```

Figure 7.19 Business Named Set with Selected Members

Example

Create a named set "My Products" and set its type as Business. Select the products "Bikes" and "Accessories".

The named set generated in an MDX query looks like this:

```
WITH SET [My Products] AS '{ [Product].[Product Categories].
[Category].&[4], [Product].[Product Categories].[Category].&[1] }'
```

7.10   Analysis Dimensions

Analysis dimensions are only available for multidimensional business layers. The analysis dimensions are OLAP dimensions that are automatically created when the multidimensional business layer is generated. An analysis dimension is the container of dimensions and hierarchies; the hierarchies contain levels and attributes.

An analysis dimension doesn't have a definition using the MDX language. An analysis dimension is an OLAP dimension holding one or multiples dimensions, hierarchies, hierarchy levels, and attributes. Note that analysis dimensions can't have the same name.

To create an analysis dimension, select the business layer root in the Business Layer pane, and then do one of the following:

▶ Right-click, and select New • Analysis Dimension.

▶ Click the Insert object button (➕) in the Business Layer section toolbar and select Analysis Dimension.

An analysis dimension has a TYPE that can be selected in the analysis dimension editor from the following list, as shown in Figure 7.20:

▶ STANDARD

▶ TIME

▶ GEOGRAPHY

▶ CUSTOMER

▶ PRODUCT

▶ ORGANIZATION

▶ EMPLOYEE

▶ CURRENCY

▶ CHANNEL

Only the TIME type has an impact on the potential MDX expressions that can be used with the hierarchies and dimensions belonging to this analysis dimension. Typically MDX functions such as `PERIODSTODATE`, `YTD`, `QTD`, `MTD`, `OPENINGPERIOD`, `CLOSINGPERIOD`, `PARALLELPERIOD`, `LAG`, `LEAD`, and so on can be used with TIME analysis dimensions. Other types are purely informative and behave like the STANDARD type. An analysis dimension can have a default hierarchy specified in the analysis dimension editor.

An analysis dimension must always have an associated KEY ATTRIBUTE, as shown in Figure 7.20. The KEY ATTRIBUTE is always one of the attributes associated with the analysis dimension.

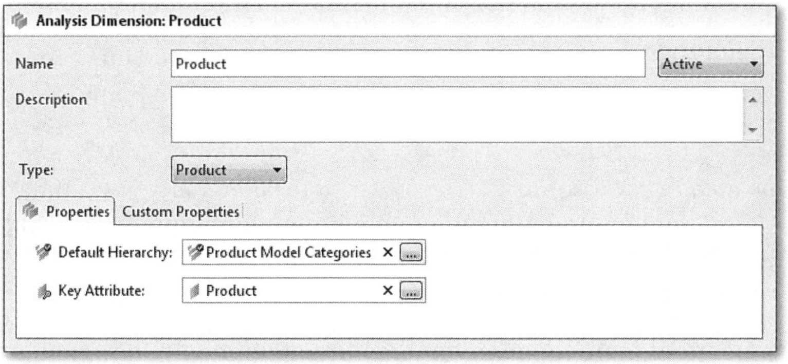

Figure 7.20 Analysis Dimension Editor

7.11   Hierarchies

Hierarchies are only available for multidimensional business layers. The hierarchies are created within OLAP dimensions. A hierarchy is a collection of members with one-to-many relationships and organized in levels. Each hierarchy member has only one parent and zero to many children. There are two main categories of hierarchies:

► Level-based hierarchies

► Parent-child hierarchies (also called value-based hierarchies)

7.11.1   Level-Based Hierarchies

Level-based hierarchies contain levels with meaningful names such as Year, Quarter, Month, Product, Customer, and so on. Level-based hierarchies are generally defined on top of slowly changing dimensions. Typical slowly changing dimensions are Geography, Customer, or Product.

Users can use the member selector to pick members in the hierarchy; select members using OLAP-style family selection such as children, descendants, and so on; or select hierarchy levels.

7.11.2   Parent-Child or Value-Based Hierarchies

Parent-child hierarchies or value-based hierarchies contain levels with names that have no business meaning such as Level1, Level2, and so on. Some OLAP databases such as SAP NetWeaver BW offer the ability to name some levels. Typical parent-child hierarchies are human resources and accounts. The depth of this type of hierarchy is frequently changing, which is why the levels can't be named. In an HR hierarchy, employees report to managers and belong to a level depth (1, 2, 3, n). The level depth can change if an employee is promoted or if an employee is moving in the organization with a new manager.

Users can use the member selector to pick members in the hierarchy; select members using OLAP-style family selection such as children, descendants, and so on; or select hierarchy levels.

7.11.3 Hierarchy Creation

Only level-based hierarchies can be created in a business layer. Hierarchies belonging to the same analysis dimension can't have the same name.

> **Note**
>
> Hierarchies are not navigation paths. The hierarchy is the OLAP concept used in business layers, whereas the navigation path is the new name for the concept of hierarchy in the Universe Design Tool. In IDT, hierarchies are available on OLAP sources and map the very same OLAP concept; navigation paths are a set of relationships that can be used when drilling from one object to another.

To create a hierarchy, select an analysis dimension, a folder, or the business layer root in the BUSINESS LAYER pane, and then choose one of the following options:

▶ Right-click, and select NEW • HIERARCHY.

▶ Click the INSERT OBJECT button (➕) in the BUSINESS LAYER section toolbar and select HIERARCHY.

After the hierarchy is created, you can enter the hierarchy definition or click the MDX ASSISTANT button to open the MDX editor (see Section 7.19.2), as shown in Figure 7.21.

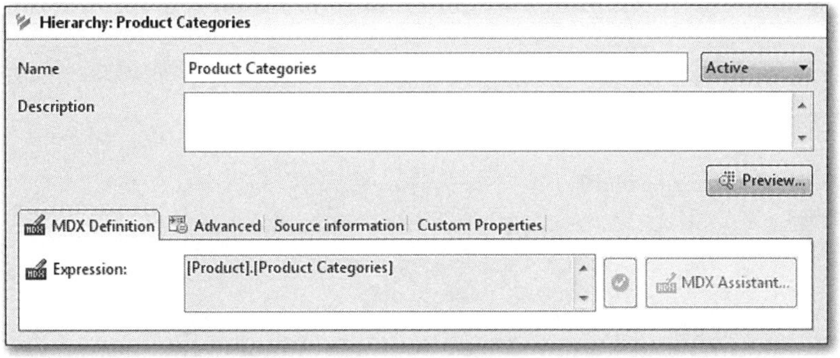

Figure 7.21 Hierarchy Editor

The MDX definition of a hierarchy must always be based on a hierarchy existing in the OLAP cube. It's generally recommended to use the @select built-in function as much as possible to ensure that the definition remains valid after a business layer refresh structure.

The hierarchies can be used as results and/or filters in a query defined with IDT or in a query panel used by SAP BusinessObjects BI clients.

Hierarchies can be selected in the member selector as described in Chapter 8, Section 8.2.1.

Example

Hierarchy "PRODUCT CATEGORY": `[Product].[Product Categories]`

7.12   Levels

Levels are only available for multidimensional business layers. A hierarchy is a collection of members having one-to-many relationships and organized in levels. The levels can only be created for level-based hierarchies. Note that levels belonging to the same hierarchy can't have the same name.

To create a level, select a hierarchy in the BUSINESS LAYER pane, and then choose one of the following options:

▶ Right-click and select NEW • LEVEL.

▶ Click the INSERT OBJECT button (➕) in the BUSINESS LAYER section toolbar and select LEVEL.

After the level is created, you can enter the level definition or click the MDX ASSISTANT button to open the MDX editor, as shown in Figure 7.22.

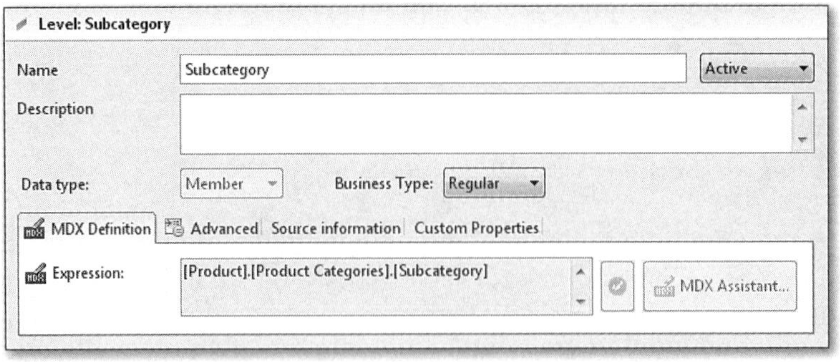

Figure 7.22   Level Editor

The MDX definition of a level must always be a hierarchy level existing in the OLAP cube. The level definition must have a relationship with the hierarchy where the level has been created.

It's generally recommended to use the built-in @select function as much as possible to ensure that the definition remains valid after a business layer refresh structure.

A level business type can be associated with the level in the level editor; by default, a new level is created with the REGULAR level business type. The available level business types are listed here:

- REGULAR
- TEXT
- UNIT
- TIME UNIT
- CURRENCY
- YEAR
- SEMESTER
- QUARTER
- MONTH
- WEEK
- DAY

The levels can be used as results in a query defined with IDT or in a query panel used by SAP BusinessObjects BI clients. Levels can be selected in the member selector.

Example

Level "SUBCATEGORY": `[Product].[Product Categories].[Subcategory]`

7.13 List of Values

The list of values was introduced in IDT as entities to be authored, shared, and reused across data foundation and business layer objects.

The list of values can be created and edited in the PARAMETERS and LIST OF VALUES pane of the business layer editor, as shown in Figure 7.23.

If the data foundation contains lists of values, they are inherited in the business layer in read-only mode with the notation "(INHERITED)".

The list of values can be alphabetically sorted or manually sorted. The SHOW/HIDE toggle button ( ) allows filtering in the list of values.

Figure 7.23 Authored List of Values in the Business Layer

A list of values is a list that contains the data values associated with a dimension, an attribute, or a measure. The list of values allows users to select from a pick list when the list of values associated with objects is used to filter a query. You determine the lists of values to associate with the objects via the object properties.

Because users can select condition values from a list of values, they don't need to enter conditions manually and therefore don't need to memorize lists of key codes or know the context of values usage.

You can therefore create custom lists of values to answer specific business needs and associate them with objects or parameters. You can define how the data is presented in the list and define restrictions on the amount of data and type of data returned to the list.

A list of values can be a query that returns values and can be a simple SQL sentence such as `Select Distinct` from a table column or a dimension. It can also be an advanced query such as returning the top ten products based on the quantity sold for year 2012.

A list of values can return one or multiple columns and can be flat or hierarchical. If the list of values returns more than one column, only one of the columns is used in the object list of values. Other columns are used as display columns, so you have to select which column is selected when used with an object, a parameter, and so on. A list of values can be shared by different objects, and the selected columns can be different from one object to another.

> **Example**
>
> The following are examples of lists of values:
>
> ▶ The list of values "GEOGRAPHY" returns three columns: "COUNTRY", "REGION", and "CITY".
>
> ▶ The object "COUNTRY" references the list of values "GEOGRAPHY", and the selected column is "COUNTRY".
>
> ▶ The object "CITY" references the list of values "GEOGRAPHY", and the selected column is "CITY".

The list of values can be used in multiple places in a data foundation and a business layer; they can have different types. A list of values can be associated with an object, a parameter, or a filter, or it can be used in an SQL expression.

The lists of values created in the data foundation (see Chapter 5) are inherited by all business layers based on that data foundation. These lists of values can't be edited in the business layer. Note that lists of values can't have the same name. Table 7.8 shows the different list of values types and where they can be used.

	List of Values Based on Business Layer Objects	Static List of Values Objects	List of Values Based on Custom SQL Objects
Data Foundation			
Join	N/A	Supported	Supported
Calculated column	N/A	Supported	Supported
Derived table	N/A	Supported	Supported
Parameter	N/A	Supported	Supported

Table 7.8 Values Types and Usage

	List of Values Based on Business Layer Objects	Static List of Values Objects	List of Values Based on Custom SQL Objects
Relational Business Layer			
Dimension	Supported	Supported	Supported
Attribute	Supported	Supported	Supported
Measure	Supported	Supported	Supported
Parameter	Supported	Supported	Supported
Filter	Supported	Supported	Supported
List of values	N/A	N/A	N/A
Multidimensional Business Layer			
Dimension	Supported	Supported	N/A
Attribute	Supported	Supported	N/A
Measure	Supported	Supported	N/A
Named set	N/A	N/A	N/A
Calculated member	N/A	N/A	N/A
Analysis dimension	N/A	N/A	N/A
Hierarchy	Supported	Supported	N/A
Level	Supported	Supported	N/A
Filter	N/A	N/A	N/A
List of values	N/A	N/A	N/A

Table 7.8 Values Types and Usage (Cont.)

To create a list of values in the PARAMETERS and LIST OF VALUES pane, click the ⊞ ▾ button in the toolbar above the LIST OF VALUES window, and select the TYPE of list of values to create. You can preview the content of any list of values by clicking the PREVIEW button in the list of values editor.

7.13.1 List of Values Based on Business Layer Objects

When the LIST OF VALUES BASED ON BUSINESS LAYER OBJECTS option has been selected, you have to choose between the two lists of values subtypes:

▶ LIST OF VALUES BASED ON THE QUERY PANEL

▶ LIST OF VALUES BASED ON A CUSTOM HIERARCHY

Select the appropriate option before entering the list of values definition.

7.13.2 List of Values Based on the Query Panel

This list of values is based on business layer objects and is editable in the query panel, as shown in Figure 7.24.

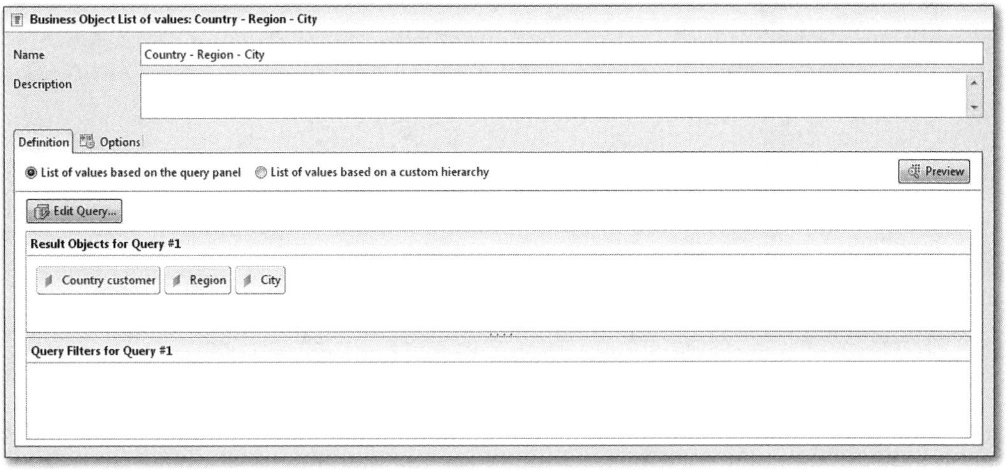

Figure 7.24 List of Values Based on the Query Panel Editor

The query panel used for list of values offers the same capabilities as the query panel used to create a query (described in Chapter 8). To define the list of values query, click the EDIT QUERY button.

When designing this list of values, you can also use hidden objects in the list of values definition. A hidden object is an object where the object state is equal to HIDDEN. For more information on object states, see Section 7.20.6.

415

You can create a list of values that includes hidden objects for different reasons; the hidden objects aren't exposed to the user in the query panel but can be handled by the business layer object's list of values or the business filters.

You can select the different objects in the QUERY RESULTS pane and then add objects or filters in the QUERY FILTERS pane when necessary.

The query to build the list of values can also include the query panel features such as subquery, ranking, or combined query (UNION, INTERSECTION, MINUS).

7.13.3 List of Values Based on a Custom Hierarchy

A list of values can be created on a custom hierarchy of business layer dimensions. The hierarchy obtained is a level-based hierarchy where the business layer dimensions are the hierarchy levels, as shown in Figure 7.25.

When designing this list of values, you can also use the hidden objects in the list of values definition. As stated earlier, a hidden object is an object where the object state is equal to HIDDEN.

To add levels to the list of values, click the ADD DIMENSION button. Then select one or more dimensions in the business layer to add into the hierarchical list of values. To remove levels to the list of values, click the DELETE button. To move levels up or down in the list of values, click the up and down arrows (↑ or ↓).

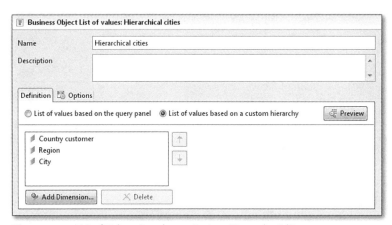

Figure 7.25 List of Values Based on a Custom Hierarchy Editor

7.13.4 Static List of Values

The values of static lists of values are stored as grid tables in the business layer or the data foundation. The list of values can have from one to many columns, as shown in Figure 7.26. You can manually create the content of the static list of values by adding columns and values, as shown in Table 7.9.

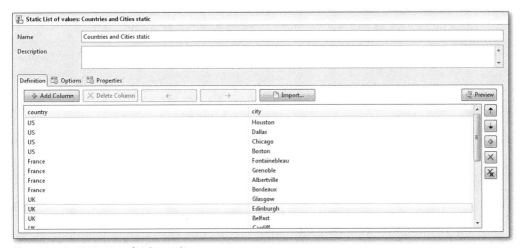

Figure 7.26 Static List of Values Editor

Button	Action
Add Column	Add columns to the list of values.
Delete Column	Delete columns from the list of values.
(+)	Add values in the list of values.
(×)	Remove values from the list of values.
(×)	Remove all values from the list of values.
(↓) (↑)	Reorder values in the list of values.

Table 7.9 Commands in the Static List of Values Editor

You can also automatically populate the static list of values by importing data from a text file or a *.csv* file, as shown in Figure 7.27:

- ▶ Click the IMPORT button.
- ▶ Select the file to import, and set the different file options: DATA SEPARATOR, TEXT DELIMITER, DATE FORMAT, and FIRST ROW CONTAINS COLUMN NAMES.

The columns are automatically created and the values populated. The static list of values doesn't maintain a link with the file used to populate it.

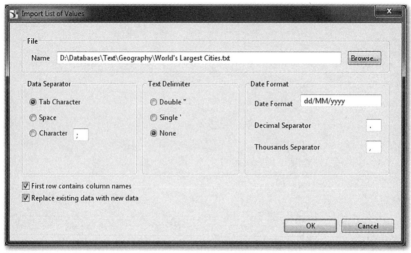

Figure 7.27 Importing a Text File to Create a Static List of Values

7.13.5 List of Values Based on Custom SQL

You can write a list of values using an SQL SELECT statement that returns one or more columns. This list of values type isn't available for multidimensional business layers.

After the SQL is written, you need to refresh the list of values structure to display the available columns, as shown in Figure 7.28. You can use the SQL assistant (see Section 7.19.1) to edit the SQL statement.

The SQL expression can use native database functions, tables and columns, business layer objects and parameters. Built-in functions described in Section 7.23 such as `@select` and `@prompt` can also be used in the SQL expression. The `@execute` built-in function isn't supported in an SQL list of values.

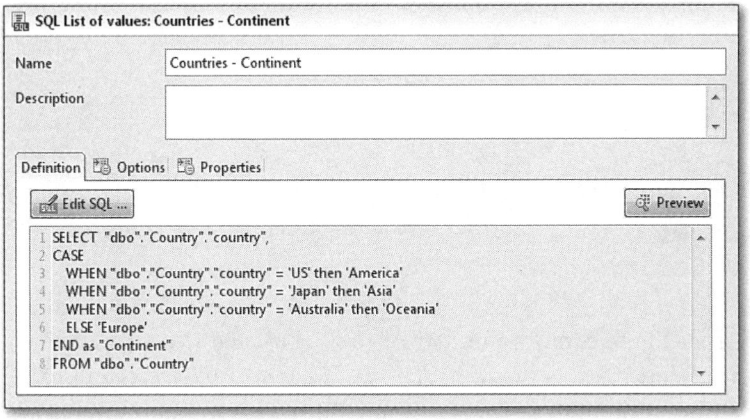

Figure 7.28 List of Values Based on a Custom SQL

7.13.6 List of Values Parameters and Options

At any time, you can preview the list of values content by clicking the PREVIEW button in the list of values editor, as shown in Figure 7.29.

You can set and adjust different list of values parameters as well. Table 7.10 displays the parameters available for the different list of values type.

Figure 7.29 List of Values Properties

	List of Values Based on Business Layer Objects	Static List of Values Objects	List of Values Based on Custom SQL Objects
ALLOW USERS TO EDIT LIST OF VALUES	Supported	Supported	Supported
AUTOMATIC REFRESH BEFORE USE	Supported	NA	Supported
FORCE USERS TO FILTER VALUES BEFORE USE	Supported	NA	NA
ALLOW USERS TO SEARCH VALUES IN THE DATABASE	Supported	NA	NA

Table 7.10 Different Lists of Values Types

You can also restrict the maximum number of rows retrieved (MAX NUMBER OF ROWS option) and the query execution time (QUERY EXECUTION TIMEOUT option) for a list of values. Those properties are also available for a query (query properties) or for the universe (business layer query options). For more information on query properties and business layer query options, see Section 7.30.

The MAX NUMBER OF ROWS and the QUERY EXECUTION TIMEOUT options aren't available for *static lists of values*. These options are grayed out for the business object's list of values because they are inherited from the query options that have been used to create the list of values.

For *default lists of values* associated with objects, the options are inherited from the business layer options.

Allow Users to Edit List of Values

If the ALLOW USERS TO EDIT LIST OF VALUES option is activated, the users can edit the list of values. The purpose of a list of values is usually to limit the set of available values to a user. If the users can edit a list of values, you no longer have control over the values they choose.

Automatic Refresh before Use

If the AUTOMATIC REFRESH BEFORE USE option is activated, the list of values is refreshed each time it's referred to and used in a report. You should choose this option only if contents of underlying column(s) are frequently changing. This option should be used very carefully after evaluation. If this option isn't set, the list of values is refreshed first when the object is used in a user session.

Force Users to Filter Values before Use

If the FORCE USERS TO FILTER VALUES BEFORE USE option is activated, the user running a query using this list of values is required to enter search criteria before getting filtered values for the list of values. Only the values that match the search criteria are returned in the list of values, as shown in Figure 7.30. The following characters are used to define the matching criteria:

► "*": Matches any number of characters, even zero characters.

► "?": Matches exactly one character.

► "\": Escapes the next character, allowing you to search for a wild card character.

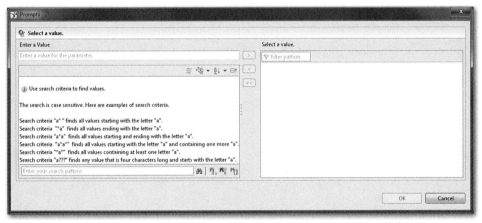

Figure 7.30 List of Values Used in a Query with the Force Users to Filter Values before Use Option Activated

Allow Users to Search Values in the Database

If the ALLOW USERS TO SEARCH VALUES IN THE DATABASE option is activated, the user running a query using this list of values can search for a value in the database. This option is useful when the user performs a search on partial list of values results. It's recommended to set this option for large lists of values.

When a list of values is used in a query, this option forces the user to enter search criteria prior to selecting values from the list of values. Users can use wild card characters "*" and "?" to filter the values in the database:

▶ "*" is used as any character whatever the value length.

▶ "?" is used as a wild card for one character.

If the list of values is multicolumn with a KEY COLUMN, the user can specify if the search applies on the name or on the key. The user can also activate the MATCH CASE option.

7.13.7 Customize List of Values Columns

For static lists of values and custom SQL lists of values, you can customize the following columns properties:

▶ COLUMN NAME

▶ DATA TYPE

▶ KEY COLUMN

▶ HIDDEN

To modify the list of values column properties, click the PROPERTIES tab in the list of values editor. The DATA TYPE property can be changed like any objects of the business layer, but be careful when changing the data type because it might generate an error in clients such as SAP BusinessObjects Web Intelligence if the data type isn't appropriated.

If the HIDDEN option is activated, the column is hidden when the list of values is displayed to the user. This option is generally used for columns that are sent to the database, such as a column ID.

The KEY COLUMN property is referencing another column of the list of values. The KEY COLUMN is often used with index aware setting in a parameter or in an object. In general, a KEY COLUMN is often hidden from the user, so when the user sees the values of the list of values, only the captions are displayed. The KEY COLUMN is hidden and added in the SQL script or MDX script.

Example

The following are examples of multicolumn lists of values with a key column set to hidden. The user can see the caption column values and the key column values are added to the query:

- The list of values "GEOGRAPHY" contains two columns: "COUNTRY" and "COUNTRY_ID".
- The column "COUNTRY" has the KEY COLUMN equal to "COUNTRY_ID".
- The column "COUNTRY_ID" is hidden.
- The user only sees the "COUNTRY" values (USA, FRANCE, GERMANY, etc.), and the "COUNTRY_ID" (100, 201, 125, etc.) values are added in the SQL statement.

7.14 Parameters

The parameters have been introduced in SAP BusinessObjects BI 4.0 to improve and complement the built-in @prompt function (see Section 7.23.3). The @prompt function is still supported, but the universe also supports this new entity you can author, share, and reuse across the data foundation and business layer objects to prompt users. Because of this lineage, the parameter is also called a prompt. The parameters can be created and edited in the PARAMETERS AND LIST OF VALUES pane of the business layer editor, as shown in Figure 7.31.

If the data foundation contains parameters, they are inherited in the business layer in read-only mode with the notation "(INHERITED)". The parameters can be alphabetically sorted or manually sorted. The toggle button ( ) allows you to filter the parameters.

Figure 7.31 Authored Parameters in the Business Layer

By definition, a parameter is a metadata that requires user answers before the query execution. As for the lists of values (see Section 7.13), the parameter (also called a *prompt*) is one of the features that has been fully revisited for extended capabilities, shareability, and ease of creation and maintenance.

The parameters are standalone metadata, but the `@prompt` function defined in previous universe versions is supported and migrated. For more information on universe conversion, see Chapter 13, Section 13.8.

You can now create prompts without writing any code; the parameter editor provides all of the existing prompt capabilities but avoids the tedious task to write the `@prompt` syntax. Note that parameters can't have the same name.

To create a parameter in the PARAMETERS and LIST OF VALUES pane, click the INSERT PARAMETER button (🦊) in the toolbar of the PARAMETERS section, as shown earlier in Figure 7.31.

7.14.1 Parameter Definition

In the OPTIONS tab, you define the parameters characteristics and associate a list of values, as shown in Figure 7.32.

Figure 7.32 Parameters Editor with the Prompt to Users Option Activated

By default, the PROMPT TO USERS option is activated and the user has to provide answers to the parameter. If the option isn't activated, only the following options are enabled, as shown in Figure 7.33:

▶ The SET VALUES combo box that is equivalent to the SET DEFAULT VALUES option. To use this option, you must first check the PROMPT TO USERS option, associate a list of values, and then uncheck the PROMPT TO USERS option.

▶ The ALLOW MULTIPLE VALUES option.

▶ The DATA TYPE option.

Figure 7.33 Parameters Editor: Prompt to Users Option Not Activated

7.14.2 Prompt Text

The PROMPT TEXT property is the text/question that is displayed to the user.

7.14.3 Data Type

You need to select an appropriate DATA TYPE that is the data type of the column/value(s) added to the query. For instance, in the case of index awareness as described in Section 7.17, the user can select "COUNTRY" values (string) but "COUNTRY_ID" (numeric) is added to the query. So the data type is numeric.

7.14.4 Allow Multiple Values

If the ALLOW MULTIPLE VALUES option is activated, the user is authorized to select multiple values in the list of values associated with the parameter. If the option isn't activated, the user can only select one value.

7.14.5 Keep Last Values

The parameters are used in queries by clients such as SAP BusinessObjects Web Intelligence, SAP Crystal Reports for Enterprise, or SAP BusinessObjects Dashboards.

When the KEEP LAST VALUES option is activated, the latest values selected during the last query refresh are displayed to the user.

7.14.6 Index Aware Prompt

If the INDEX AWARE PROMPT option is activated, the key column values of the list of values or the primary key values of the object that has a list of values are sent to the query. The INDEX AWARE PROMPT option is enabled if the SELECT ONLY FROM LIST option is activated and if one of the following criteria is met:

- The list of values associated with the parameter is multicolumn with a key column.

- The object default list of values is based on an object when a primary key has been added for this object.

7.14.7 Associated List of Values

The parameter can be associated with a list of values (see Figure 7.34). To associate a list of values, click the ⬛ button to the right of the ASSOCIATED LIST OF VALUE list box. You can select from the following:

- A dimension or an attribute that has a list of values

- A list of values created in the PARAMETERS and LIST OF VALUES pane

When the list of values is multicolumn, you choose which column is sent to the query. Because a list of values can be shared by multiple objects or parameters, the same list of values can be used differently. You have to choose which list of values column is used in the context of the parameter usage.

Example

Let's look at some examples of associated lists of values:
- The list of values "GEOGRAPHY" contains two columns: "COUNTRY" and "CITY".
- The parameter "SELECT CITIES" is linked to the list of values "GEOGRAPHY", and the selected column is "CITY" because the parameter is used in a context where cities reflect the data wanted by the users.

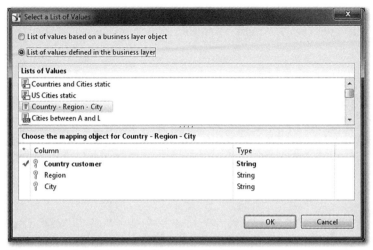

Figure 7.34 Associate a List of Values to the Parameter

The list of values created in the Parameters and List of Values pane, displayed in Figure 7.34, are filtered to match the parameter Data Type.

7.14.8 Select Only From List

If the Select only from list option is activated, the user is only able to select values from the list of values displayed. If the option isn't activated, the user is able to select values from the list of values or manually enter values. When this option is deactivated, the Index aware prompt option is disabled.

7.14.9 Set Default Values

If the Set default values option is activated, you can choose one or multiple values from the list of values associated with the parameter. To choose the values, click the [...] button to the right of the Set default values list box. The default value is preselected in the parameter dialog box when displayed to the user. The user can then decide to keep or remove default values. The user can also select additional values or replace the default values.

7.14.10 Parameter Custom Properties

In the Custom Properties tab, you can add properties and associate values to the properties. The *custom properties* are purely informative and aren't used by the SAP

BusinessObjects BI clients. They can be used for documentation or for a future usage in the semantic layer Java SDK. For more information on custom properties, see Section 7.20.7.

7.14.11 Dependent Parameters

You can define the dependencies between parameters in the business layer at design time. Defining parameter dependencies in the business layer is very useful when you want to force (or constrain) users to first answer one or more parameters before solving the others. A parameter can depend on several parameters, and several parameters can depend on the same parameter.

Creating logical parameter dependencies can be a complex workflow because it forces you to correctly define the associated list of values with the concerned parameters. For instance, the parameter "Country" depends directly on the parameter "Product." The parameter "Country" depends indirectly on the parameter "Promotion" because the parameter "Product" depends directly on the parameter "Promotion."

Example

In the business layer, you've created three different parameters associated with their three respective lists of values:

▶ "Country" parameter is associated with the "Country" list of values.

▶ "Region" parameter is associated with the "Region" list of values.

▶ "City" parameter is associated with the "City" list of values.

The user must first answer to the "Country" parameter, then to the "Region" parameter, and finally to the "City" parameter.

To create a dependency between the parameters "Country," "Region," and "City," edit the list of values, and make the following modifications.

▶ "Country" list of values: No modification.

▶ "Region" list of values: Add a filter in the WHERE text box such as `Country = @prompt(Country)`.

▶ "City" list of values: Add a filter in the WHERE text box such as `Region = @prompt(Region)`.

The parameter dependencies are now created.

When the parameters are consumed in the query, the parameters dependency appears as in Figure 7.35.

Figure 7.35 Parameters Dependencies Processing in a Query

7.14.12 Parameters Usage

The parameters can be used in the following:

▶ Dimensions, attributes, measures, calculated members, named sets, hierarchies, and levels definition (SQL or MDX expression) or WHERE (filter) definition

▶ Filters

▶ Calculated columns

▶ Derived tables

▶ Lists of values based on business objects

▶ List of values based on custom SQL

▶ Joins

▶ Tables name

▶ Business layer queries

▶ SAP BusinessObjects BI clients queries (SAP BusinessObjects Web Intelligence, SAP Crystal Reports for Enterprise, SAP BusinessObjects Dashboards)

The @prompt built-in function can still be used in objects definition, filters definition, derived tables, calculated columns, and joins.

You can use parameters in the binding expressions of business layer objects (SELECT and WHERE elements objects) or data foundation resources (derived tables, calculated columns, joins, etc.)

When used in MDX or SQL expressions, a parameter is referenced like this: @prompt(parameter name).

7.14.13 Mandatory and Optional Parameters

The parameters can be mandatory or optional, which means that the user answer is also mandatory or optional. This option isn't associated with the parameter definition but is associated to the following objects using the parameters:

▶ Business filters

▶ Business layer queries

▶ Lists of values based on business objects

To summarize, the parameters can be optional if they are used in the query panel, as shown in Figure 7.36. If a parameter is used in an SQL or MDX expression, the user answer is always mandatory.

Figure 7.36 Setting Parameter Answers as Optional

7.14.14 Parameter Dialog Box

When a parameter is used in a query, the user must answer the parameters. The parameter can be set as mandatory or optional in the query where the parameter is used. The parameter default values or the latest selected values are already preselected.

The selectable values displayed to the user can be:

▸ Refreshed

▸ Sorted

▸ Displayed by NAME, KEY, NAME AND KEY, or KEY AND NAME

▸ Searched if the list of values search option has been activated

7.15 Filters and Mandatory Filters

A filter is a condition object that limits the data returned in a query. The filters can be inserted into the QUERY FILTERS pane in the query panel to be applied to the query.

There are two types of filters:

▸ **Native filters**
The native filters are defined with an SQL expression and added in the WHERE clause on the SQL query. The native filters are only available with relational business layers.

▸ **Business filters**
The business filters are defined by creating and combining conditions on dimensions, attributes, hierarchies, or measures in the business layer. The business filters definitions are created within the query panel as described in Chapter 8.

The business filters are easier to create and maintain than native filters and they can become optional when a parameter (see Section 7.14) is used in their definition. Another objective is to have a better filters management and make them less opaque. The filters can be reused in many places such as an object's list of values, queries, and so on. Note that filters belonging to the same folder or the business layer root can't have the same name.

To create a filter, select the business layer root or another folder in the BUSINESS LAYER pane, and then choose one of the following options:

▶ Right-click, and select NEW • FILTER.

▶ Click the INSERT OBJECT button (➕) in the BUSINESS LAYER section toolbar and select FILTER.

After the filter has been created, select the filter type: NATIVE or BUSINESS. If you've selected the NATIVE type, click the SQL ASSISTANT button to open the SQL editor (see Section 7.19.1) and then use table columns, business layer objects, and database functions to create the filter definition, as shown in Figure 7.37.

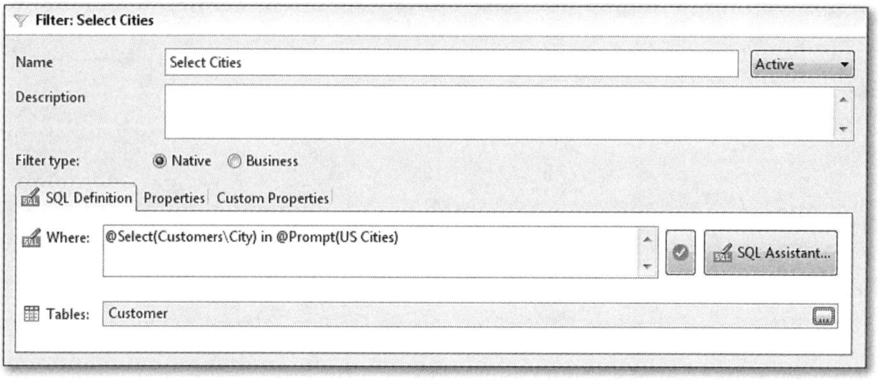

Figure 7.37 Native Filter

If you've selected the BUSINESS type, click the EDIT FILTER button to open the query panel, and then use business layer objects, operators, and values/parameters to create the filter definition, as shown in Figure 7.38.

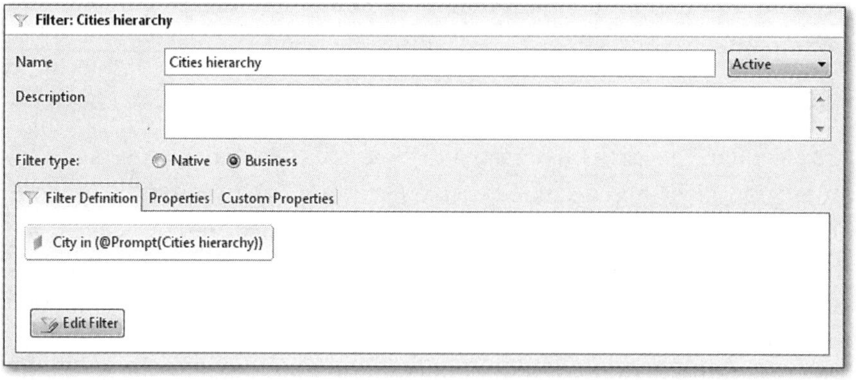

Figure 7.38 Business Filter

7.15.1 Native Filter Validation and Extra Tables

Like other objects, it's important to validate the native filter expression using the VALIDATE button in the SQL editor. You can also reference additional tables to native filters in the TABLES text box.

7.15.2 Filter Properties

By default, a filter is an object that can be used by a user in the query panel. The filter you create helps the user to filter a query such as the following:

- Current period
- List of products in promotion
- Revenue greater than $100,000
- Cities of USA
- People married with at least two children

Users can use and combine multiple filters in the query and also create their own filters in the query panel. In some cases, you (or the DBA) might want to automatically add filters to the query without asking the users to do it. There are different ways to add filters in a query:

- Add a filter on a table in the data foundation (see Chapter 5, Section 5.3.3).
- Add a WHERE expression to an object (see Section 7.5.2, Section 7.6.1, and Section 7.7.1).
- Create mandatory filters in the business layer (detailed in this section).
- Define security profiles in the universe (see Chapter 10, Section 10.4 and Section 10.5).

Mandatory Filters in the Business Layer

You can force a filter to become mandatory. A mandatory filter is automatically added to the query; it is not visible and cannot be selected in the query panel. To make the filter mandatory, click the PROPERTIES pane of the filter editor and check USE FILTER AS MANDATORY IN QUERY, as shown in Figure 7.39.

A mandatory filter can apply to the entire universe (APPLY ON UNIVERSE option) or apply to the folder and subfolders where the filter is seating (APPLY ON FOLDER option).

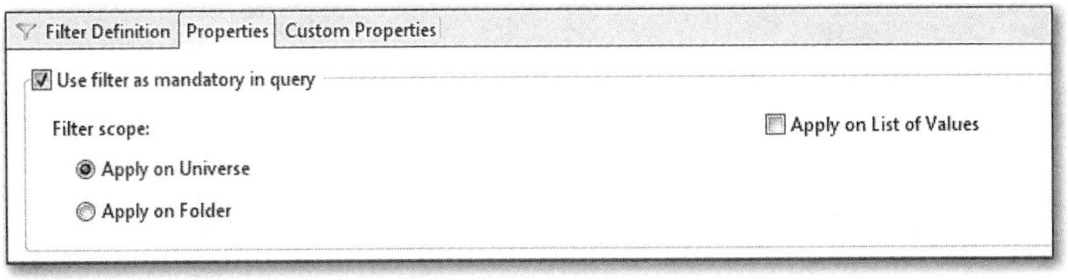

Figure 7.39 Filter Properties

Apply on Universe Option

If the APPLY ON UNIVERSE option has been activated, the filter is always added to the query whatever the objects used in the query. This type of mandatory filter behaves like SAP NetWeaver BW variables or SAP HANA variables. Like a filter, a mandatory filter can contain a parameter or a prompt. (For more information on universes on SAP HANA and SAP NetWeaver BW, see Chapter 12.)

Example 1

You want users to query the database only between 10 a.m. and 5 p.m. The filter defined in SQL (using SAP HANA SQL syntax) is shown here:

```
TO_DOUBLE(TO_VARCHAR(Now(), 'HH24mmss') between '100000' and
'170000'
```

The filter is automatically added to any query, and the query returns results only if the time period is valid.

Example 2

The authorized users are defined in a database table, and users have to answer a prompt to provide their user name.

The filter SQL expression is shown here:

```
"Table"."Username" = @prompt('Enter user name','A',,mono,free)
```

The filter is automatically added to any query, and each user has to provide his or her user name to run the query.

Apply on Folder Option

If the APPLY ON FOLDER option has been activated, the filter is added to the query if at least one object belonging to the same folder or subfolder of the filter is added to the query in the RESULTS pane or in the FILTERS pane. This type of mandatory filter is useful when you want to filter a query in certain use cases.

> **Example**
>
> You want users to select a date when order detail objects are added to the query. To avoid a query returning too many rows, a folder is created with objects defining the order details, and a mandatory filter is added in the same folder. The mandatory filter definition contains a parameter that forces the user to select a date or a period that guarantees a result with an acceptable number of rows and an acceptable performance.

Apply on List of Values Option

The APPLY ON LIST OF VALUES option is available for all mandatory filter types. When this option is activated, all lists of values are impacted by the mandatory filter.

This option can be useful in certain use cases, but we recommend that you use this option with caution because the result of a query can be unexpected, and, in some cases, the mandatory filter can introduce loops in the list of values query.

> **Warning**
>
> The business layer contains a list of values based on countries and a mandatory filter containing a parameter that forces users to select a country.
>
> If you activate APPLY ON LIST OF VALUES for the country mandatory filter, then a loop is generated to the list of values if the mandatory filter and the list of values reference the same object.

7.16 Navigation Paths

A navigation path is an object that defines the drilldown path used by SAP Business-Objects BI clients and especially SAP BusinessObjects Web Intelligence. A navigation path is a list of drillable business objects that allows a user to drill down and up on a dimension.

The navigation path was previously named hierarchy in the Universe Design Tool, so it's important to differentiate between a hierarchy and a navigation path. A *hierarchy*, described in Section 7.11, is a collection of members where members have relationships between them, for instance, a level-based hierarchy or a parent-child hierarchy. A *navigation path* is a drilldown path between dimensions that may have no strict relationship in the data source but which have a business relationship.

Note

A hierarchy can be a level-based hierarchy such as Year → Quarter → Month → Date.

A hierarchy can be a parent-child hierarchy such as Manager → Employee.

A navigation path allows a user to drill from a dimension to another dimension such as Year → Product → Country → Quarter.

A navigation path provides drill capabilities also known as "drill through" mode in the OLAP world. The navigation paths can only contain visible dimensions. There are two types of navigation paths: default and custom.

Custom navigation paths can't have the same name. Custom and default navigation paths are both available in the SAP BusinessObjects BI clients, and users can decide which one to use during drilldown operations.

If two or more navigation paths share dimensions but follow different dimensions at the lower end, the users are asked to select a drill path during drilldown operations in SAP BusinessObjects Web Intelligence. The navigation paths can be created and edited in the NAVIGATION PATHS pane of the business layer editor.

7.16.1 Default Navigation Paths

The default navigation paths can't be created or edited; they are inherited from the folder content defined in the business layer.

A default navigation path is created by analysis dimensions, as described in Section 7.10, or by folder/subfolder (see Section 7.4) containing at least one visible dimension. The default navigation paths contain all visible dimensions of a given folder or an analysis dimension, as shown in Figure 7.40.

Figure 7.40 Default Navigation Paths

Example

The business layer contains the following objects:

▶ Folder 1

   ▶ Dimension 1

   ▶ Measure 1

▶ Folder 2

   ▶ Dimension 2

   ▶ Dimension 3

▶ Folder 3

   ▶ Measure 2

   ▶ Measure 3

The following is the default navigation path:

▶ Folder 1

   ▶ Dimension 1

> ► Folder 2
> > ► Dimension 2
> > ► Dimension 3

7.16.2 Custom Navigation Paths

A custom navigation path has the same rules as a default navigation path but can be created and edited and can contain dimensions belonging to different analysis dimensions, folders, or subfolders. To allow more flexibility in report analysis using drill operations, it's recommended to create custom navigation paths.

To create a custom navigation path, you have to select the CUSTOM option in the navigation path editor and click the 🏗 button in the toolbar, as shown in Figure 7.41. On the right side of the custom navigation path editor, you can add, edit, and move dimensions.

Figure 7.41 Custom Navigation Paths

7.17   Index Awareness

In a relational business layer, the index awareness is the ability to take advantage of the key columns to do the following:

▶ Use the indexes to improve query performance.

▶ Reduce the number of tables and joins used in the query.

▶ Avoid confusion between duplicates by taking the uniqueness of values in lists of values into account.

The objects in the business layer are based on table columns that are meaningful for querying data. For example, a product object retrieves the product caption in the product column of the products table. The product caption is obviously useful for reporting and analysis purposes, whereas the key isn't meaningful for the user. For performance reasons, it might be useful to use the key rather than the caption because the key is unique, and often indexes are created on top of key columns.

For other reasons, many cities in a country may have the same name but a different ZIP code, so when the user selects a city in a list of values, it's crucial to select the correct city. The ZIP code is sent to the database rather than the city name.

When you set up index awareness, you define which table columns are keys for the dimensions and attributes in the business layer. There are two types of index awareness in a universe:

▶ Primary key

▶ Foreign key

To create the index awareness, click the dimension or attribute to open the editor, select the KEYS tab, and then click the ADD KEY button. Choose PRIMARY KEY or FOREIGN KEY under KEY TYPE, enter the index awareness definition (under SELECT), and optionally enter the index awareness filter (under WHERE), as shown in Figure 7.42.

You can invoke the SQL editor by clicking the ▨ button for each of the definitions. Change the index awareness data type if needed.

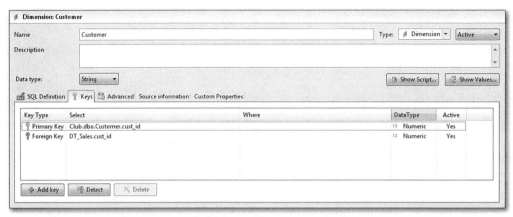

Figure 7.42 Index Awareness Definition in Dimensions or Attributes

7.17.1 Primary Key

The PRIMARY KEY index awareness defined on objects uses the index value instead of the actual value of an object. The query thus uses the key value. This helps the database perform better. When an object with index awareness defined is used in a query filter through its list of values, the users can select the object value, but only the key is used in the query to remove confusion with duplicates that can return unwanted results.

> **Example**
>
> The table "GEOGRAPHY" contains three columns—"COUNTRY", "CITY", "CITY_ID"—with the following values, respectively:
>
> ▶ USA, PARIS, 101
>
> ▶ FRANCE, PARIS, 222
>
> When the query is filtered on the "CITY" list of values, the user can choose PARIS in USA or PARIS in FRANCE, and then the appropriate "CITY_ID" is added to the query.

7.17.2 Foreign Key

The FOREIGN KEY index awareness defined on the objects filters the data without the need of a join in the query. Suppose you need to build a report that has a filter on the dimensions table. In the absence of index awareness, the query engine uses dimension values, which requires a join between the fact table and the dimension table. However, if you apply foreign key index awareness, the query engine applies a filter directly in the fact table using the foreign key index, avoiding join between the dimension table and the fact table. However, the foreign key index awareness requires object values to be unique if the same value is represented by a different key.

Example

Without foreign key index awareness, four tables, three joins, WHERE on label:

```
Select Region.region, Customer.last_name
From Country INNER JOIN Region ON (Country.country_id = Region.
country_id)
INNER JOIN City ON (City.region_id = Region.region_id)
INNER JOIN Customer ON (City.city_id = Customer.city_id)
Where Country.country = 'France'
```

With foreign key index awareness, three tables, two joins, WHERE on key:

```
Select Region.region, Customer.last_name
From Customer INNER JOIN City ON (City.city_id = Customer.city_id)
INNER JOIN Region ON (City.region_id = Region.region_id)
Where Region.country_id = 2
```

7.18 Aggregate Awareness

Aggregate awareness is a feature that was introduced in the universes a long time ago and was designed to dynamically define a measure on top of the most appropriate aggregated tables in the data warehouse. When this feature was designed, RDBMS vendors weren't able to provide capabilities to address this need in business intelligence and particularly to rewrite SQL queries.

The aggregate navigation feature of universes is designed to take advantage of preaggregated tables. By preaggregating measures, query users can get more immediate responses to high-level queries.

To address aggregate navigation, a built-in function named @aggregate_aware (see Section 7.23.1) can be used in SQL expressions in objects definition. The function tries to get the data from the highest aggregation level and goes to a more detailed level if this isn't possible (because the query is asking for detailed dimensions).

The aggregate awareness techniques accelerate queries by processing fewer facts and aggregating fewer rows. Users build a query by selecting the dimensions, attributes, and measures, and then the query engine analyzes the scope of the query and generates the appropriate SQL to target the right fact tables (aggregate tables or detailed fact tables).

Implementing aggregate awareness has several steps, some done at the database level and others in the universe design. The DBA must set up and fill the summary tables as desired. The appropriate objects have to be set up as "aggregate aware." The tedious part is defining the incompatibilities between objects and setting up the contexts to set aggregate navigation.

The `@aggregate_aware` built-in function is mainly used in measures definitions, but in some particular cases, it can also be used in dimensions and attributes definitions.

7.18.1 The Aggregate Aware Process

Table 7.11 describes the different steps to create aggregate navigation in a universe.

Aggregate Navigation Steps	Comments
Add aggregate tables in the data foundation.	In general, aggregate tables aren't joined with other tables.
Select objects that will be aggregate aware.	For each object, enter the SQL definition `@aggregate_aware(<expression 1>, <expression 2>,…,<expression n>)` where `<expression_n>` is the name of a column and its table in the database.
Determine incompatibilities, that is, discover which aggregate tables and objects can't be used in the same query.	This feature is available by clicking the menu ACTIONS • SET AGGREGATION NAVIGATION in the business layer editor.

Table 7.11 Steps to Define Aggregate Navigation

7.18.2 Aggregate Navigation Incompatibility

To set aggregation navigation compatibility, you have to compare one row from an aggregate table against every object in the business layer:

▶ If the object is at the same level of aggregation or higher, it's *compatible* with the aggregate table.

▸ If the object is at a lower level of aggregation, it's *incompatible*.

▸ If the object has nothing to do with the aggregate table, it's *incompatible*.

After you've selected ACTIONS • SET AGGREGATION NAVIGATION in the business layer editor, the aggregate navigation dialog box opens. You can select each aggregate table on the left side of the dialog box and check each business layer object that is incompatible with this aggregate table.

It's important to set join cardinalities in the data foundation when using aggregate navigation. If you've correctly set the join cardinalities, the best way to set aggregate navigation is to let IDT do it for you by clicking the DETECT INCOMPATIBILITY button in the dialog box, as shown in Figure 7.43.

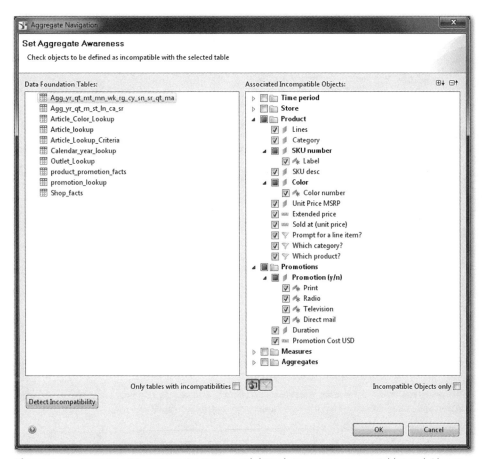

Figure 7.43 Aggregate Navigation: Set Incompatibilities between Aggregate Tables and Objects

7.18.3 Aggregate Navigation Set on Measures

In the following data foundation example, there are two fact tables (PRODUCT_PROMO-TION_FACTS and SHOP_FACTS) and two aggregate tables derived from the SHOP_FACTS table: `Agg_yr_qt_mt_mn_wk_rg_cy_sn_sr_qt_ma` and `Agg_yr_qt_rn_st_ln_ca_sr`.

The fact tables and the aggregate tables are displayed in their respective box, as shown in Figure 7.44.

In the business layer, the SQL definition of sales revenue measure is the following:

```
@aggregate_aware(sum(Agg_yr_qt_rn_st_ln_ca_sr.Sales_revenue), sum(Agg_
yr_qt_mt_mn_wk_rg_cy_sn_sr_qt_ma.Sales_revenue), sum(Shop_facts.Amount_
sold)
```

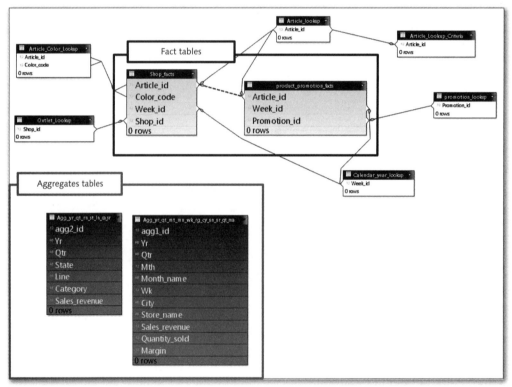

Figure 7.44 Data Foundation with Fact Tables and Aggregate Tables

The @aggregate_aware function syntax contains a definition for each aggregate table and fact table. The detailed fact table is added in the last position of the @aggregate_aware expression.

When the user selects objects in the query panel, the definition of each aggregate-aware object is analyzed, and the appropriate SQL definition is used in the SQL query to target the right aggregate table or fact table.

7.18.4 Aggregate Navigation Set on Dimensions

The @aggregate_aware function can also be used to dynamically define a dimension on the most appropriate table at query time. In the following data foundation example, there are three tables containing the measures and the dimensions, and they are considered cubes. They contain different measures and share some dimensions, but they aren't joined, as shown in Figure 7.45.

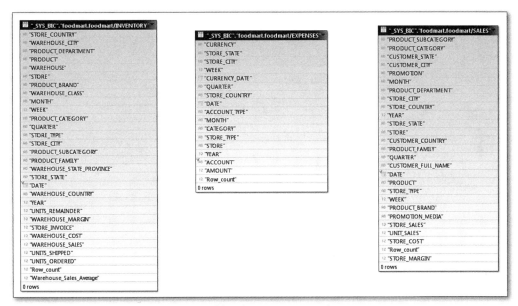

Figure 7.45 Data Foundation with Fact Tables That Are Not Joined

In that example, each dimension definition contains the @aggregate_aware function with a mapping to each respective dimension in the table.

If there is no corresponding column for the dimension in a given table, the NULL placeholder is used in place of a table column definition as described in Table 7.12, which is an excerpt of the data foundation shown in Figure 7.45.

	INVENTORY	SALES	EXPENSES
Dimension	YEAR	YEAR	YEAR
Dimension	PRODUCT	PRODUCT	
Dimension	WAREHOUSE		
Dimension			ACCOUNT
Measure		UNIT_SALES	
Measure			AMOUNT
Measure	UNITS_SHIPPED		

Table 7.12 Excerpt of a Multifacts Data Foundation

It's important to set the NULL placeholder because the query engine generates SQL that takes into account the number of columns defined in the @aggregate_aware expression, and then the query result is well balanced.

Based on the columns mapping defined in Table 7.12, the following are the dimensions definition:

▶ YEAR: @aggregate_aware(INVENTORY.YEAR, SALES.YEAR, EXPENSES.YEAR)

▶ PRODUCT: @aggregate_aware(INVENTORY.PRODUCT, SALES.PRODUCT, NULL)

▶ WAREHOUSE: @aggregate_aware(INVENTORY.WAREHOUSE, NULL)

▶ ACCOUNT: @aggregate_aware(EXPENSES.ACCOUNT, NULL)

If a user adds an object in the query filter, the query engine removes it from the generated SQL query if the definition of this object is equal to NULL.

This feature has been used in SAP BusinessObjects BI 4.1 to support data foundations containing multiple SAP HANA views. For more information on universes on SAP HANA, see Chapter 12, Section 12.3.

7.19   SQL and MDX Editors

This section describes how to use the SQL editor and the MDX editor in the business layer knowing that they can also be used in the data foundation (see Chapter 5) or in the objects security definition (see Chapter 10).

The SQL editor is used to write SQL expressions for relational data sources, whereas the MDX editor is used to write MDX expressions for OLAP data sources.

7.19.1   The SQL Editor

The SQL editor is a dialog box that can assist you in writing SQL as needed and particularly for the following business layer objects:

▶ Dimension definition and where definition

▶ Attribute definition and where definition

▶ Measure definition and where definition

▶ Native filter definition

▶ List of values based on custom SQL

It's also used in the data foundation, when you define joins, derived tables or calculated columns, as described in Chapter 5, Section 5.10.

The SQL editor is composed of two components, as shown in Figure 7.46:

▶ The text editor pane (❶) where the SQL expression is created and edited.

▶ The assistant pane, which is composed of the following:

  ▶ The TABLES pane with tables and columns of the relational data source (❷).

  ▶ The FUNCTIONS pane (❸):

    – The relational databases functions: SQL expressions.

    – The system variables such as BOUSER, DBUSER, DOCNAME, UNVNAME, and so on. System variables, described in Section 7.23.5, are always used with the @ variable built-in function, such as @variable('BOUSER').

    – The built-in functions.

  ▶ The BUSINESS LAYER pane (❹) with dimension, attribute, measure, and filter objects.

▶ The PARAMETERS pane (**❺**).

▶ The LIST OF VALUES pane (**❻**).

Each assistant component can be hidden or shown in the SQL editor. Each element of the assistant components can be added in the SQL text editor by double-clicking or using drag and drop.

Figure 7.46 The SQL Editor

Tables and Columns

All tables and columns are listed in the pane, including derived tables, alias tables, federated tables, and calculated columns. Only authorized tables are listed here.

To add one or more column values in the SQL expression, select a table column, and click the ⊙ button added on the right side of the column. The values are displayed, and you can double-click or drag and drop one or more values to add them in the SQL expression, as shown in Figure 7.47.

Figure 7.47 Selecting Column Values to Add in the SQL Expression

SQL Database Functions

The SQL database functions are provided by the data access parameters file (*.prm*) for the relational source used in the universe (see Chapter 4, Section 4.5.4).

SQL databases functions are available and can be used in the SQL text editor even if the connection with the relational database has not been established.

Business Layer Objects

The business layer objects can be used in SQL expressions using the built-in @select function (see Section 7.23.4) for dimensions, attributes, and measures, and the built-in @where function (see Section 7.23.6) for filters.

When a business layer object (dimension, attribute, or measure) is added in the SQL expression, it's embedded in the built-in @select function.

Parameters

When a parameter (see Section 7.14) is added in the SQL expression, it's embedded in the built-in @prompt function (see Section 7.23.3).

List of Values

The business layer list of values (see Section 7.13) can be used in the built-in @prompt function or used in the built-in @execute function (see Section 7.23.2).

Validation

The VALIDATE button validates the SQL expression to the database. The validation works only if the connection with the database is active. For more information on validation and check integrity, see Section 7.26.

7.19.2 The MDX Editor

The MDX editor is a dialog box that can help you write MDX as needed and especially help with creating new multidimensional objects such as the following:

▶ Dimension definition

▶ Attribute definition

▶ Measure definition

▶ Named set definition

▶ Calculated member definition

▶ Hierarchy definition

▶ Level definition

The MDX editor is composed of two components, as shown in Figure 7.48:

▶ The text editor pane (❶) where the MDX expression is created and edited.

▶ The assistant pane composed of the following:

  ▶ The OLAP METADATA pane (❷).

  ▶ The FUNCTIONS pane (❸), including the following:

    – The OLAP databases functions: MDX expressions.

    – The system variables such as BOUSER, DBUSER, DOCNAME, UNVNAME, and so on. System variables are always used with the @variable built-in function, such as @variable('BOUSER').

    – The built-in functions.

  ▶ The BUSINESS LAYER pane (❹) with dimension, attribute, measure, hierarchy, calculated member, named set, and filter objects.

  ▶ The PARAMETERS pane (❺).

  ▶ The LIST OF VALUES pane (❻).

Each assistant component can be hidden or shown in the MDX editor. Each element of the assistant components can be added in the MDX text editor by using double-click or drag and drop.

Figure 7.48 MDX Editor

OLAP Cube Metadata

The dimensions, measures, attributes, hierarchies, levels, calculated members, and named sets are displayed in the OLAP METADATA pane. The cube metadata can be used in MDX expressions as well as members.

To add one or more members in the MDX expression, select a hierarchy, level, dimension, or attribute, and click the ⊙ button on the right side of the metadata. The members are displayed, and you can double-click or drag and drop one or more members to add them in the MDX expression, as shown in Figure 7.49.

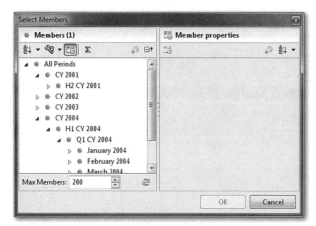

Figure 7.49 Selecting OLAP Cube Members to Add in an MDX Expression

MDX Database Functions

The MDX database functions are provided by the OLAP data sources: Microsoft SQL Server Analysis Services and Oracle Essbase. The MDX database functions are available and can be used in the MDX text editor only if the connection with the OLAP database has been established.

Business Layer Objects

The business layer objects can be used in MDX expressions using the @select built-in function for dimensions, attributes, measures, hierarchies, levels, calculated members, and named sets, and the @where built-in function for filters.

When a business layer object (dimension, attribute, measure, hierarchy, level, named set, or calculated member) is added in the MDX expression, it's embedded in the @select built-in function. For more information on built-in functions, see Section 7.23.

Parameters

When a parameter is added in the MDX expression, it's embedded in the @prompt built-in function.

List of Values

The business layer list of values can be used in the @prompt built-in function.

Validation

The VALIDATE button validates the MDX expression to the database. The validation works only if the connection with the database is active.

7.20   Object Common Properties

All objects, both relational and multidimensional, share properties that you can set. Some of the properties directly impact the query, whereas other properties are purely informative.

7.20.1   Data Types

All dimensions, attributes, measures, and calculated members have a data type. The data type can be automatically derived from the table column or the OLAP metadata during the business layer generation process. It can also be automatically detected if a table column is dragged and dropped in the business layer or when a dimension or an attribute is turned into a measure.

A business layer object definition can also contain calculated expressions, using SQL or MDX language, and based on one or multiple table columns or OLAP metadata.

The list of values columns and the parameters also have a data type. For a parameter, the data type is inherited from the list of values definition but can be changed. For static lists of values and list of values based on custom SQL, you can change the data type for each column composing the list of values. It's important that you set the correct data type. If the data type isn't correctly set, a warning or an error can be displayed during the object validation. More important, if the data type is incorrect, SAP BusinessObjects BI clients may return errors during the query execution.

For the relational business layers, the data type of objects based on a single table column is automatically deduced from the column data type, as shown in Table 7.13.

Data Foundation Column Data Type	Business Layer Object Data Type
BIGINT	Numeric
BINARY	Blob
BIT	Numeric

Table 7.13   Business Layer Objects and Columns Data Types Mapping

Data Foundation Column Data Type	Business Layer Object Data Type
CHAR	String
DATE	Date
DECIMAL	Numeric
DOUBLE	Numeric
FLOAT	Numeric
INTEGER	Numeric
LONBINARY	Blob
LONGVARCHAR	Long Text
NUMERIC	Numeric
REAL	Numeric
SMALLINT	Numeric
TIME	DateTime
TIMESTAMP	DateTime
TINYINT	Numeric
UNDEFINED	String
VARBINARY	Blob
VARCHAR	String
XML	String
OTHER	*Undefined*

Table 7.13 Business Layer Objects and Columns Data Types Mapping (Cont.)

7.20.2 List of Values

A list of values can be associated with dimensions, attributes, and measures. When dimensions and attributes are created, they have a default list of values, whereas new measures don't have a default list of values. The calculated members and the named sets don't have associated list of values. The default list of values is based on the object definition.

Lists of values (see Section 7.13) available in the PARAMETERS and LIST OF VALUES pane can be associated with an object. To associate a list of values with an object, click the object in the BUSINESS LAYER pane to open the object editor. In the object editor, click the ADVANCED tab, and then check or uncheck the ASSOCIATE LIST OF VALUES checkbox. When associating a list of values, the default [DEFAULT] list of values is associated with the object.

To select another list of values, click the ⟨...⟩ button on the right side of the LIST OF VALUES text box. All lists of values are displayed, so you can then select the desired list of values to associate with the object, as shown in Figure 7.50.

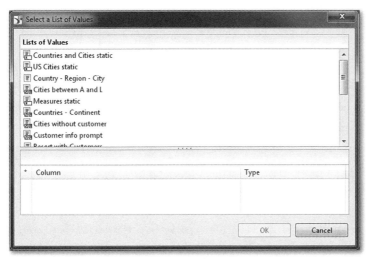

Figure 7.50 Associating a Custom List of Values to an Object

If the selected list of values has been defined with more than one column, you have to select which column applies to the object. Because a list of values can be shared by multiple objects or parameters, the same list of values can be used differently. You have to choose which list of values column is used in the context of the object.

Example
A custom list of values COUNTRY/REGION/CITY contains three columns: COUNTRY, REGION, and CITY.

The custom list of values COUNTRY/REGION/CITY is associated with the dimension CITY, and the selected column is CITY. |

The objects can be used as query filters in the query panel, and the associated list of values can then be used when the filter definition is based on a list of values or a new prompt created in the query panel.

List of Values Properties

When a default list of values is associated with an object, you can set and adjust the list of values parameters. Those parameters are the same as for a list of values created in the business layer:

▶ ALLOW USERS TO EDIT LIST OF VALUES

▶ AUTOMATIC REFRESH BEFORE USE

▶ FORCE USERS TO FILTER VALUES BEFORE USE

▶ ALLOW USERS TO SEARCH VALUES IN THE DATABASE

If the list of values associated with the object is created in the business layer, the list of values parameters are inherited and can't be overridden.

7.20.3 Access Level

There are many ways to set security on business layer objects. One of the ways to set security is to set an access level security for the following objects:

▶ Dimensions

▶ Attributes

▶ Measures

▶ Hierarchies

▶ Levels

From the less restrictive to the more restrictive, the following are possible access level types:

▶ PUBLIC

▶ CONTROLLED

▶ RESTRICTED

▶ CONFIDENTIAL

▶ PRIVATE

User profiles are defined in the CMS repository and are applied to the universes when used in an SAP BusinessObjects BI client. Depending on the level of authorization defined for the connected user, objects are visible or hidden.

By default, the access level is set to PUBLIC for any new created object. To set a particular access level to an object, select the object in the BUSINESS LAYER pane, and then click the ADVANCED pane of the object editor.

If an object is assigned to PUBLIC access, then all users can have access to this object. If an object is assigned to CONFIDENTIAL access, users that have been granted to CONFIDENTIAL or higher levels of security (PRIVATE) can see and use this object.

If a user edits a query previously created by another user, some objects can be removed if the user has an access level lower than the object's access level. This might happen if the user who previously created the query had more rights than the current user.

7.20.4 Usage

The business layer objects can be used in queries for different purposes. There are three ways to use an object in the query panel, as shown in Figure 7.51:

► RESULTS

► CONDITIONS

► SORT

The object usage concerns dimensions, attributes, measures, hierarchies, and levels.

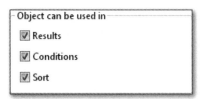

Figure 7.51 Potential Objects Usage in the Query Panel

By default, the three options are activated for any new created object. To change an object usage, select the object in the BUSINESS LAYER pane, and then click the ADVANCED pane of the object editor:

- If RESULTS option is activated, the user can select the object and add it in the RESULTS OBJECTS pane of the query panel described in Chapter 8.

- If CONDITIONS option is activated, the user can select the object and add it in the QUERY FILTERS pane of the query panel.

- If SORT option is activated, the user can add a sort on this object in the RESULTS OBJECTS pane of the query panel. There is no obligation to put this object in the query results.

If a user edits a query previously created, some objects can be removed from the RESULTS OBJECTS, QUERY FILTERS, or SORT options if the object usage has been modified.

7.20.5 Source Information

The universes can be automatically generated from third-party tools such as ETL, CASE tools, or any modeling tool. The SOURCE INFORMATION pane in the object editor contains information concerning the source of that generated object in the three text boxes described in Table 7.14.

Source Information Property	Description
TECHNICAL INFORMATION	If the source information concerns an object, then it can contain information on the table(s) and column(s).
	If the source information concerns the business layer, then it can contain the database information or any other useful information.
MAPPING	This information can contain the formula, the SQL expression, or any other information explaining the object definition.
LINEAGE	This information is mainly provided by ETL or CASE tools. It contains information on the source used to create the database, the tables, and the columns.

Table 7.14 Source Information Description

The TECHNICAL INFORMATION, the MAPPING, and the LINEAGE text boxes are editable for the following business layer objects: dimensions, attributes, measures, hierarchies, and levels.

SAP Data Services is able to generate relational universes (*.unv*) created with the Universe Design Tool and automatically fill the source information properties. Source information properties are kept in the new universe (*.unx*) after universe (*.unv*) migration with IDT. (For more information on universe conversion, see Chapter 13, Section 13.8.)

The SOURCE INFORMATION pane is only used by the people designing the universes. The source information isn't passed to the clients.

7.20.6 State

All objects except lists of values, parameters, and navigation paths can take three states. The object state determines whether an object can be used or not in queries, lists of values, or referenced by other objects.

Active

When the object state is active, the object is visible in the query panel. This is the default state, so any new object created has the active state.

Hidden

When the object state is hidden, the object is valid but not available in the query panel (used by other objects as a hidden object).

If a folder state is equal to hidden, all objects belonging to this folder are also hidden by inheritance. If a dimension state or a measure state is equal to hidden, all attributes belonging to this dimension or measure are also hidden by inheritance.

Hidden objects can be referenced in the definition of other objects using the @select built-in function (*see* Section 7.23.4).

Hidden objects can also be used by lists of values based on a custom hierarchy, lists of values based on the query panel, or business filters.

> **Note**
>
> A query built in IDT or in an SAP BusinessObjects BI client such as SAP BusinessObjects Web Intelligence, SAP Crystal Reports for Enterprise, or SAP BusinessObjects Dashboards contains active objects.

If you've set some objects state to hidden, when the user edits the query, those objects are removed from the query, and a message is displayed to the user explaining that some objects have been removed from the query.

Deprecated

A deprecated object isn't valid and therefore is hidden to the users. Another use case is when the table column no longer exists in the table, but you want to keep the object referencing this column for possible future usage. Another possible use case is when an object is invalid or incomplete, but you want to publish the universe and review this object later.

If a folder state is equal to deprecated, all objects belonging to this folder are also deprecated by inheritance. If a dimension state or a measure state is equal to deprecated, all attributes belonging to this dimension or measure are also deprecated by inheritance.

Deprecated objects can be referenced in the definition of other objects using the built-in function `@select`, but unlike hidden objects, the objects referencing deprecated objects are invalid. Objects with deprecated states aren't available for queries.

> **Note**
>
> If you've set some objects states to deprecated, when the user edits the query, those objects are removed from the query, and a message is displayed to the user explaining that some objects have been removed from the query.
>
> It's not a common use case to set a folder as deprecated because it means that all objects belonging to the folder are also deprecated.

7.20.7 Custom Properties

The custom properties are available for internal use only and aren't passed to the SAP BusinessObjects BI clients. When an object is created, the custom properties are empty, and you can create and edit as many custom properties per object as you need. The objective of custom properties is to let partners, OEMs, and customers add documentation or any valuable information to the objects.

With the semantic layer Java SDK, you can add/edit/remove custom properties. To create custom properties, select the object in the BUSINESS LAYER pane, and then click the Custom Properties pane of the object editor. Click the Add button to add a custom property. Each custom property can be renamed and its value changed.

The custom properties are available for the following:

▸ Business layers
▸ Folders
▸ Analysis dimensions
▸ Dimensions
▸ Attributes
▸ Measures
▸ Hierarchies
▸ Levels
▸ Named sets
▸ Calculated members
▸ Filters
▸ Parameters
▸ Lists of values

7.21   Object Formatting

All objects except folders, analysis dimensions, named sets, and filters have a display format. A default display format is always associated with each object depending on its data type.

7.21.1   Display Format

To associate a display format to an object, click the object in the Business Layer pane to open the object editor. In the object editor, click the Advanced tab, and then click the Create Display Format button. The list of predefined display formats and custom display formats appears. Select a display format in the list, or create a custom display format and select it, as shown in Figure 7.52.

The display format is applied to the object by a client such as SAP BusinessObjects Web Intelligence, SAP Crystal Reports for Enterprise, or SAP BusinessObjects Dashboards.

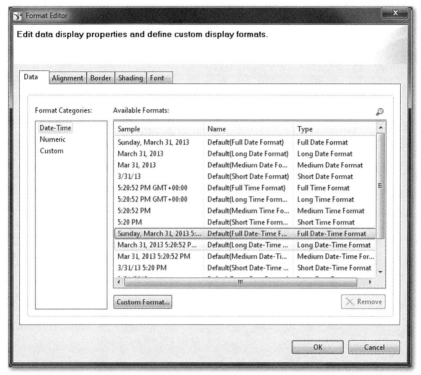

Figure 7.52 Associating a Display Format to an Object

By default, the display format is applied as defined for the object data type. If you need to display the content of the object as an HTML string or a hyperlink, check either HTML or HYPERLINK.

Example

In a relational business layer, the dimension "COUNTRY_MAP" definition is 'http://maps.google.com/maps?q=' + "Geography"."Country".

The dimension definition contains a link to Google Maps and the country value, so the object format is set as a hyperlink.

7.21.2 Custom Format

If a display format isn't in the list of predefined display formats, a custom display format can be created and associated with an object.

The custom display formats are mainly used for numeric, date, and time data types. It's very unusual to create a custom display format for string data types.

To create a custom display format, select an object in the BUSINESS LAYER pane, right-click, and select CREATE DISPLAY FORMAT. The display format dialog box allows you to change the following format properties, as shown in Figure 7.52:

- ► DATA
- ► ALIGNMENT
- ► BORDER
- ► SHADING
- ► FONT

The display format is used with SAP BusinessObjects BI clients, but only the data properties are taken into account in SAP BusinessObjects BI 4.x, so don't spend time customizing the alignment, border, shading, and font properties.

The data properties concern the display of the object values, as shown in Figure 7.53:

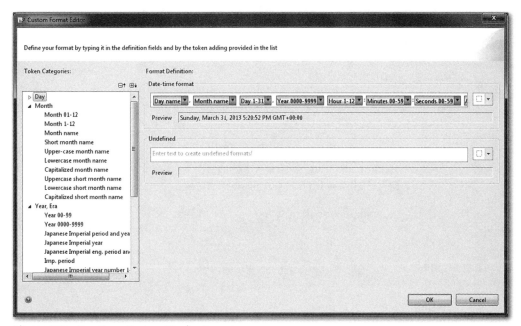

Figure 7.53 Creating a Custom Display Format

- Numeric formatting, such as decimal symbol, currency, minus sign, thousands separator, zeros, number of decimals, and so on

- Date and time formatting, such as year, quarter, month, week, day, day of week, day of month, hour, minute, second, and so on

7.21.3 Database Format

The database format is only enabled for objects with the date data type. This format can be modified in the DATABASE FORMAT text box of the ADVANCED tab of the object editor.

The database format is by default based on the regional settings defined in the Microsoft Windows Control Panel but you can modify to define the date format to use when sending a request to the database.

7.22 Business Layer Queries

It's important for you to validate the universe. The validation concerns the business layer, the data foundation, and the data content. When you validate the business layer, the data foundation is also validated. More importantly, the validation isn't a solitary exercise but needs to be conducted with people representing the different business areas covered by the universe.

IDT enables you to create as many queries as needed for the universe validation. The queries created and saved with the business layer are only used with IDT.

All queries are displayed in the QUERIES tab in the BUSINESS LAYER pane and can be edited, renamed, deleted, sorted, duplicated, and executed. The SHOW/HIDE toggle button ( ) allows filtering in the list of queries, as shown in Figure 7.54.

The queries are available for all universes types and can be used to do the following:

- Check the object's definition.

- Validate with business users the accuracy of dimensions, attributes, and measures.

- Do non-regression testing.

- Check whether some objects are broken after a data source change or a CMS repository change (promotion).

▶ Analyze universe and database performance (benchmarks).

▶ Validate query generation, that is, check that the joins, contexts, and other data foundation features have been correctly defined.

Figure 7.54 List of Queries in the Business Layer

To build queries, click the QUERIES tab in the BUSINESS LAYER pane. Then click the button in the upper toolbar to open the query panel.

A query designed with the query panel in IDT supports the same features as other clients such as SAP BusinessObjects Web Intelligence, SAP Crystal Reports for Enterprise, or SAP BusinessObjects Dashboards.

To execute a query without editing, select the query, and then click the EXECUTE QUERY button in the query editor. The query result is displayed in an editor tab, a dedicated view, or a dialog box depending on the settings defined in IDT preferences (see Chapter 2, Section 2.5, and Figure 7.59, later in this chapter).

If the query contains parameters (see Section 7.14) or @prompt (see Section 7.23.3) in the business layer objects definition, you're prompted to select values from the list of values or enter values manually depending on the parameter definition. Your answer can also be mandatory or optional. (For more information on the results of a query, see Chapter 2, Section 2.6.)

When the designer selects a query, the query editor displays the definition of the query (name, description, results, and filters), as shown in Figure 7.55.

Query: Margin	
Name	Margin ☐ Hidden
Description	Period to period comparison normalized per day

🗗 Edit Query 　 ⊞ Execute query

Result Objects for Query #1

✓ Accounts	✓ Date.Calendar	▚ Amount Fmt	▚ Nb of Days Fmt	▚ Avg per day Fmt
● Gross Margin	*fx* Children of Q1 CY 2003			
fx Children of Gross Margin	1 items			
▤ Cost as % of Sales				
3 items				

▚ Avg per day Prior Period Fmt	▚ Avg per day PTP pct Change Fmt

Query Filters for Query #1

Figure 7.55　Query Editor

If an object has been deleted in the business layer, the ⊗ icon replaces the object icon in the query as shown in Figure 7.56. The query can't be executed as is and needs to be edited to fix the problems.

⬦ Quarter	⬦ Country customer	⬦ Region	⬦ Year	⊗ Services\Resort	▥ Nb Guests	⊗ Sales\Nb Days

Figure 7.56　Query Containing Deleted Objects

7.23　Built-in Functions

The built-in functions are provided by IDT to bring flexibility, reusability, and dynamicity in universes and queries. The built-in functions are only used in SQL expressions and MDX expressions and can be entered manually or called from the SQL editor (see Section 7.19.1) or MDX editor (see Section 7.19.2).

The following built-in functions can only be used in the business layer; for built-in functions that can be used in the data foundation, *see* Chapter 5, Section 5.11.

7.23.1 @aggregate_aware

The `@aggregate_aware` function is used in SQL expressions mainly to define a single SQL expression for measures belonging to multiple fact tables. This function is only used for the aggregate awareness feature, and the syntax is `@aggregate_aware(<table_1.column_1>, <table_2.column_2>, <table_3.column_3>,…, <table_n.column_n>)` where `<table_n.column_n>` is the name of a column and its table in the database.

When the `@aggregate_aware` function is solved at query time, only one table column is added to the generated SQL depending on the dimension, attributes, and measures selected by the user in the query panel. (For more information on aggregate awareness, *see* Section 7.18.)

7.23.2 @execute

The `@execute` function is used in SQL expressions to reference lists of values. The `@execute` function has been designed to improve performance of SQL queries, especially when the list of values definition is a complex query, including sub-`Select` statements.

The list of values (*see* Section 7.13) query is executed first, and the result of this query is pushed to the query using the `@execute` built-in function. The syntax is `@execute(<list of values name>)` where `<list of values name>` is the name of a list of values.

Example

The list of values "Best products" SQL statement is shown here:

```
Select product_id from (select top 5 product_id, sum(amount) from
sales group by product_id having sum(quantity) > 100 order by 2)
```

The SQL statement *before* built-in functions resolution:

```
Select product_name from products where product_id in @execute(Best
products)
```

The SQL statement *after* built-in functions resolution:

```
Select product_name from products where product_id in (10, 22, 15,
33, 48)
```

7.23.3 @prompt

The `@prompt` function is used in SQL or MDX definitions to ask users to select values from a list of values or enter values that are used in query results or query filters.

The `@prompt` function can be used to define a question or to reference a parameter defined in the business layer and can have two different syntaxes:

- ▶ Reference a parameter: `@prompt(<parameter name>)` **where** `<parameter name>` is the name of a parameter.

- ▶ Message with parameters displayed to the user for value(s) selection: `@prompt(Message,Data_type,{List_of_values},mono|multi,free|constraine d|primary_key,persistent|not_persistent,{default_values})`.

Table 7.15 describes the `@prompt` parameters and rules.

Parameter	Description
`Message`	The text that is displayed to the user. Must be enclosed by single quotes.
`Data_type`	Possible values: ▶ `'A'` for string data. The result of the user selection is enclosed by single quotes. ▶ `'N'` for numeric data. The result of the user selection isn't enclosed by a character. ▶ `'D'` for date data. The result of the user selection is enclosed by single quotes. ▶ `'DT'` for date/time data. The result of the user selection is enclosed by single quotes. ▶ `'K'` is data type independent. The result of the user selection isn't enclosed by a character. `'K'` can be used only if the parameter `primary_key` key word is used.

Table 7.15 @prompt Parameters Definition

Parameter	Description
	If the parameter `primary_key` key word is used, and the `list_of_values` parameter is a list of static values, then the `data_type` parameter can take the following values: `'A:A'`, `'A:N'`, `'A:D'`, `'N:A'`, `'N:N'`, `'N:D'`, `'D:A'`, `'D:N'`, `'D:D'`, and so on. The first element of the parameter is the caption data type, and the second element is the key data type. Note that for `@prompt` used in an MDX expression, the result of the user selection isn't enclosed by a character, whatever the data type.
`List_of_values`	This parameter is optional if the `free` key word is used. This parameter can reference a list of values, a business layer object, or a list of static values: ▶ Object: `'folder\object name'` ▶ List of values: `'list of values name'` ▶ Static values: `{'value 1', 'value2',…,'value n'}` If the parameter `primary_key` key word is used, the `list_of_values` parameter is a list of static values, and the `data_type` parameter has two elements (for example, `'A:A'` or `'N:D'`), then the syntax for the static values is `{'caption 1':'key 1',…,'caption n':'key n'}`.
`Mono|multi`	This parameter is optional; the default is `mono`. ▶ `Mono`: Only one value can be selected by the user. ▶ `Multi`: Multiple values can be selected by the user.
`Free|constrained |primary_key`	This parameter is optional; the default is `free`. ▶ `Free`: The user can select value(s) from the list or manually enter the values. ▶ `Constrained`: The user must select value(s) from the list. ▶ `Primary_key`: The user must select value(s) from the list. The user selects captions and the keys are added to the query (index awareness). For more information on index awareness, see Section 7.17.

Table 7.15 @prompt Parameters Definition (Cont.)

Parameter	Description
Persistent|not_ persistent	This parameter is optional, the default is not_persistent. ▶ Persistent: The selected value(s) are displayed to the user the next time the prompt is displayed. The selected values are always displayed even if the prompt contains default values. ▶ not_persistent: The selected value(s) aren't kept the next time the prompt is displayed.
Default_values	This parameter is optional. The syntax is {'value 1', 'value2',…,'value n'}. If the parameter primary_key key word is used, the list_of_values parameter is a list of static values, and data_type parameter has two elements (for example, 'A:A' or 'N:D'), then the syntax for the default values is {'caption 1':'key 1',…,'caption n':'key n'}.

Table 7.15 @prompt Parameters Definition (Cont.)

Table 7.16 lists some examples of the @prompt function used in SQL expressions.

Example	Syntax
Select one country from a list of countries with no manual entry.	@prompt('Select country', 'A', 'Customer\Country',mono,constrained)
Select multiple countries from a list of countries with possible manual entry.	@prompt('Select country', 'A', 'Customer\Country',multi,free)
Select multiple countries from a static list with selected values persisted.	@prompt('Select country', 'A', {'USA','France'},multi,constrained, persistent)
Select one country from a static list with index awareness activated.	@prompt('Select country', 'A:N', {'USA':'100','France':'200'}, mono,primary_key)
Select one country from a list of countries with index awareness activated.	@prompt('Select country', 'K', 'Customer\Country',mono,primary_key)

Table 7.16 Examples of @prompt in Objects Definition

Example	Syntax
Select one country from a static list with default values.	`@prompt('Select country', 'A', {'USA','France','Germany'},mono, constrained,,{'USA'})`

Table 7.16 Examples of @prompt in Objects Definition (Cont.)

7.23.4 @select

The `@select` function is used to reference a business layer object definition: SQL or MDX expression. The main advantage of the `@select` built-in function is that the definition of an object can be defined once and referenced in multiple places in the business layer.

The `@select` function can be used solely or coupled with other SQL/MDX expressions or other built-in functions. The `@select` function can be used in the following object definitions:

▶ Dimensions

▶ Attributes

▶ Measures and calculated measures

▶ Hierarchies

▶ Levels

▶ Named sets

▶ Calculated members

The `@select` function syntax is `@select(<folder name[\folder name]\object name>)` where `<folder name[\folder name]\object name>` is an object's (dimension, attribute, or measure) full path defined in the business layer.

Table 7.17 lists some examples of the `@select` function used in SQL expressions.

Object	Definition
Customer country	`"country"."country_name"`
Sales	`"fact"."sales"`
Costs	`"fact"."costs"`

Table 7.17 Examples of @select in Objects Definition

Object	Definition
Order date	`"Time"."order_date"`
Product country	`@select(Customer\Country)`
Margin	`@select(Facts\Sales) - @select(Facts\Costs)`
Order year	`Year(@select(Time\Order date)`

Table 7.17 Examples of @select in Objects Definition (Cont.)

Note

If the `@select` references an object that has been deleted, the object becomes invalid, and the `@select` syntax in the object definition is `@select([Unknown Reference])`.

7.23.5 @variable

The `@variable` function is used to reference system variables or user attributes in SQL or MDX expressions. The `@variable` syntax is `@variable('<variable name>')` where `<variable name>` is the name of a variable supported by the universe out of the box or the name of a user attribute (see Chapter 10, Section 10.8).

The user attributes are defined in the CMS repository.

Here is a list of some system variables that can be used in the `@variable` expression:

▶ BOUSER
The user name defined in the CMS repository and used to connect to a client such as SAP BusinessObjects Web Intelligence.

▶ DBUSER
The user name used to connect to the database.

▶ DOCNAME
The document name (e.g., an SAP BusinessObjects Web Intelligence document name).

▶ DPNAME
The data provider name (e.g., "Query 1" in an SAP BusinessObjects Web Intelligence document).

▶ UNVNAME

The universe name.

▶ PREFERRED_VIEWING_LOCALE

The user's preferred language for viewing documents.

When the @variable function is solved, the result is always enclosed by single quotes in SQL expressions and not enclosed by a character in MDX expressions.

If the @variable function doesn't reference any known system variable or user attributes, it behaves like @prompt with default parameters, for example, @prompt('Enter a value', 'A').

7.23.6 @where

The @where function is used to reference the WHERE definition of other business layer objects in SQL expressions. The @where syntax is @where(folder name[\folder name]\object name) where <folder name[\folder name]\object name> is an object's (dimension, attribute, or measure) full path defined in the business layer.

The @where function is only available for relational business layers and can only be used in WHERE definitions of the following:

▶ Dimensions

▶ Attributes

▶ Measures

▶ Native filters

7.24 Business Layer Views

Customer feedback has highlighted that a noteworthy number of universes can contain from hundreds to thousands of objects. So it's difficult for the BI users to find the information they need in such large universes. For IT people, one of the solutions to avoid big universes is to split a universe into multiple smaller universes, but this adds additional maintenance costs because several objects can be shared by multiple universes.

To address this use case, IDT offers the capability to create business layer views that are consumed as universes. A business layer view is in fact a universe view that behaves like a universe but only exposes part of the business layer objects.

You can create as many business layer views as needed and apply authorizations to those views as described in Chapter 10. Some users may be authorized to access only one or more business layer views.

By default, when the business layer is created, a default business layer view is created: the MASTER business layer view. The MASTER business layer view can't be deleted.

A business layer view only exposes the list of objects available in the business layer. In a business layer view, you can't do the following:

▶ Rename objects

▶ Add/delete/rename folders

▶ Reorganize the business layer structure

▶ Change object formatting

To create a business layer view, select the BUSINESS LAYER pane, and then click the 🔳 button in the toolbar above the business layer content. When the business layer view editor opens, click the NEW button to create a business layer view, as shown in Figure 7.57.

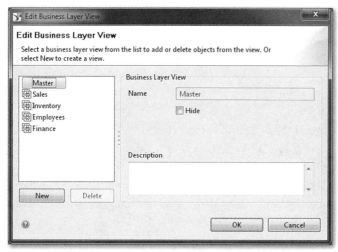

Figure 7.57 Creating a Business Layer View

After the business layer view is created, you can select the folders, dimensions, measures, attributes, hierarchies, levels, and so on that are part of the business layer view. When you do so, all depending objects are also selected. Each object can be selected or deselected individually, as shown in Figure 7.58.

All objects are displayed in the business layer view, including hidden and deprecated objects. When new objects are created in the business layer, they aren't automatically added in the business layer views even if the folder parent of the object has been selected in one of the business views. For more information on object states, see Section 7.20.6.

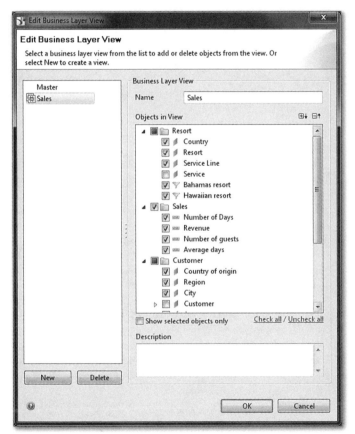

Figure 7.58 Business Layer View Editor

7.25 Business Layer Functionalities

The business layer is where you define the business concepts. A business layer can contain large number of objects; at some point you may want to easily search for objects, change the definition of a group of objects, move them, view data, and manage their lifecycle.

This section covers the different tasks you face when building a business layer.

7.25.1 Preview Data

As for the data foundation, there are many ways to see data content and query results. Table 7.18 lists all of the places where you can see data content.

Resource	View Data
Hierarchy (multidimensional business layer only)	PREVIEW LIST OF VALUES: Hierarchical tree with drill operations. SHOW VALUES: Hierarchical list.
Level (level-based hierarchy only)	PREVIEW LIST OF VALUES: Hierarchical tree with drill operations.
Attribute	SHOW VALUES: Show the data content of the attribute. PREVIEW LIST OF VALUES: This action is equivalent to the list of values PREVIEW ACTION.
Dimension	SHOW VALUES: Show the data content of the dimension. PREVIEW LIST OF VALUES: This action is equivalent to the list of values PREVIEW ACTION.
Measure	SHOW VALUES: Show the data content of the measure. For a relational business layer, the SQL aggregation function is applied, meaning that most of the time, only one row is retrieved. For a multidimensional business layer, the total aggregation is applied by the OLAP cube, meaning also that only one row is retrieved. PREVIEW LIST OF VALUES: This action is equivalent to the list of values PREVIEW ACTION.
List of values	PREVIEW: Preview the content of a list of values and answer to parameters or prompts if required.

Table 7.18 Available Actions for Previewing Data

Resource	View Data
Data foundation: tables, derived tables, federated tables, and alias tables	SHOW TABLE VALUES: For instance, if two tables are selected, an SQL query including the tables is generated. This query can also include additional tables if the two tables aren't directly joined.
Data foundation: columns, calculated columns	SHOW COLUMN VALUES: For instance, if two columns are selected, an SQL query including the columns is built. If the two columns belong to different generated tables, the query can also include additional tables if the two tables aren't directly joined. PROFILE COLUMN VALUES: This is enabled only if one column is selected and displays the distinct number of values of the selected column. The result is displayed in a table, a pie chart, or a bar chart.

Table 7.18 Available Actions for Previewing Data (Cont.)

You can view the content of any object in the business layer at any time and in multiple ways. You first have to select a dimension, attribute, measure, or hierarchy to open the object editor. To view the content of an object, click the SHOW VALUES button in the object editor, or right-click the object in the BUSINESS LAYER pane, and select SHOW VALUES. To view the content of the list of values associated with the object, right-click the object in the BUSINESS LAYER pane, and select PREVIEW LIST OF VALUES. THE PREVIEW LIST OF VALUES menu is only available if a list of values has been defined for the object.

The SHOW VALUES option and the PREVIEW LIST OF VALUES option are different:

▶ SHOW VALUES displays the content of the object based on its definition and its filter.

▶ PREVIEW LIST OF VALUES displays the content of the list of values associated with the object. The list of values definition can be different from the object definition.

The result of the data preview is displayed in an editor tab, a dedicated view, or a dialog box, depending on the settings defined in IDT preferences, as shown in Figure 7.59.

To set the preferences for data preview, select WINDOW • PREFERENCES. When the PREFERENCES dialog box appears, select INFORMATION DESIGN TOOL • SHOW VALUES, as shown in Figure 7.59.

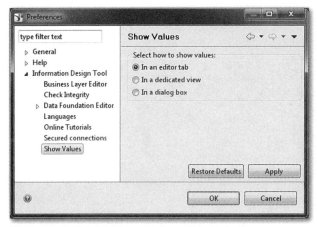

Figure 7.59 Data Preview and Query Results Preferences

> **Note**
>
> For more information concerning the results of data preview and list of values preview, see Chapter 2, Section 2.6.

You can also show the generated SQL script or the generated MDX script when the object is used in a query. Click the SHOW SCRIPT button in the object editor, or right-click the object in the BUSINESS LAYER pane, and select SHOW QUERY SCRIPT.

The generated SQL statement contains the SQL definition of the object (SELECT) and the table(s) used (FROM) as shown in Figure 7.60. Extra tables (see Section 7.5.4) are added to the FROM clause as well as the tables referenced in the object definition. Finally, a potential WHERE clause is added if the following are true:

▸ More than one table is referenced in the object definition or in the EXTRA TABLES list.

▸ One of the tables referenced in the object definition contains a filter join (see Chapter 5, Section 5.3.3) defined in the data foundation.

▶ For multidimensional business layers, the generated MDX statement contains the MDX definition of the object included in an MDX query statement.

Figure 7.60 Show Query Script

7.25.2 Search, Filter, Show, and Hide

The business layer editor offers the ability to search for objects and to filter object types. In addition, IDT offers you the ability to only show objects visible in the query panel.

For multidimensional business layers, you may also want to see the unique name of OLAP metadata.

Filter Objects

You can search and filter objects in the BUSINESS LAYER pane. To activate the FILTER pane, click the toggle button (🔍) in the toolbar above BUSINESS LAYER. The FILTER pane is added in the BUSINESS LAYER pane below the business layer content shown in Figure 7.61.

By default, the filter list is empty, and no object is selected. You can select one or more objects in the dropdown list to filter the content of the business layer. The list of objects is added in the filter list in flat mode, as shown in Figure 7.61; the business layer organization isn't respected in the filter list.

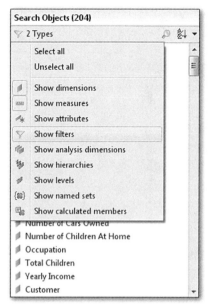

Figure 7.61 Business Layer Filter List

The appropriate object editor opens when an object returned in the list is selected. Most of the actions available in the business layer content are also available in the filter list by right-clicking:

▶ Data preview

▶ Change object state

▶ Change data type

▶ Change and apply a format

▶ Change access level

▶ Turn an object into another object: dimension into attribute, dimension into measure, and so on

Search in Objects

Because the business layer can be very large, you may want to search objects in the business layer. To search objects by their name, click the magnifying glass button (🔍) to open a small text editor and enter search criteria. The search criteria can contain wild card characters "*" and "?" to search in the object's name:

- "*" is used as any character whatever the value length.

- "?" is used as a wild card for one character.

The first occurrence of objects matching the search criteria is highlighted in the business layer. If you press the [Enter] key, the next occurrence of objects is highlighted. The occurrence number and the number of occurrences is displayed in the right side of the text box (e.g., "3/5" for the third occurrence over five occurrences).

Show/Hide Objects

Because a business layer can contain ACTIVE, HIDDEN, and DEPRECATED objects, IDT offers the ability to keep only ACTIVE objects visible. With this option you can only focus on objects that are visible the query panel.

By default all objects are visible. To set only ACTIVE objects visible, click the DISPLAY OPTIONS button (🖐) in the BUSINESS LAYER section toolbar, and select HIDE NON-ACTIVE OBJECTS. To show all objects in the business layer, select SHOW ALL OBJECTS.

For more information about objects state, see Section 7.20.6.

Display Name and Unique Name

The metadata created in OLAP databases always have a name and a unique name. When the multidimensional business layer is generated, all the OLAP metadata are generated, included their properties.

By default, only the name is displayed in the business layer because it is the business term that is used by the users in the BI clients. You may want for some reasons see the unique name of the generated objects. IDT offers the ability to see the name, the unique name, or both name and unique name in the business layer object name that has been generated.

To change the business object name, click the DISPLAY OPTIONS button (🖐) in the toolbar above BUSINESS LAYER, and select either DISPLAY NAME, DISPLAY UNIQUE NAME, or DISPLAY BOTH NAME AND UNIQUE NAME.

It is also possible to see the name and/or the unique name of objects when using the member selector (see Chapter 8, Section 8.2.1) in the query panel.

7.25.3 Find and Replace

IDT also offers the ability to explore the business layer content to find text contained in an object's name, definition (SQL or MDX), and WHERE clause (SQL). You can also do mass renaming in an object's name, definition (SQL or MDX), or WHERE clause (SQL).

Only objects available in the business layer content can be searched. Parameters, lists of values, navigation paths, named sets, and queries can't be searched.

To search objects, click the toggle button (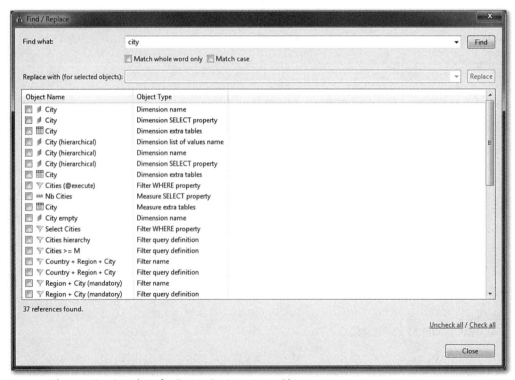) in the IDT toolbar. Enter the search criteria, and click the SEARCH button, as shown in Figure 7.62. Select the MATCH WHOLE WORD ONLY and MATCH CASE options if needed, and use wild card characters "*" and "?" to search in the objects name and definition.

Figure 7.62 Searching for Text in Business Layer Objects

The list of objects is then displayed in the FIND/REPLACE dialog box. The appropriate object icon is displayed as well as the object element concerned by the search operation: object name, object SELECT property, object WHERE clause. An object can be listed more than once if more than one object property is concerned, as shown in Figure 7.62.

To replace strings in object properties, enter the text in the REPLACE WITH text box, select the objects, and click the REPLACE button, as shown in Figure 7.63. All object properties that have been updated are removed from the search list.

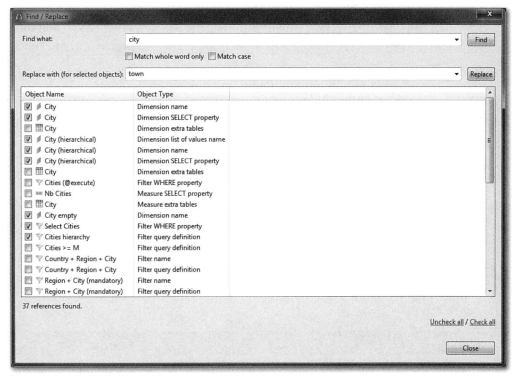

Figure 7.63 Replacing Text in Business Layer Objects

7.25.4 Business Layer Lifecycle Functionalities

Repetitive tasks are common, so limiting the number of these tasks is really helpful. IDT offers a large set of features dedicated to making your day-to-day job easier.

The business layer editor offers many features to create, edit, find, copy, or change objects. Most of those features are accessible in a dedicated toolbar above the different panes or by right-clicking.

Change the Data Foundation

One of the actions you may take is to associate another data foundation to the relational business layer. To change the data foundation, choose one of the following options in the BUSINESS LAYER pane:

▶ Select ACTIONS • CHANGE DATA FOUNDATION.

▶ Select the business layer root in the BUSINESS LAYER pane, then select the PROPERTIES tab, and click the CHANGE DATA FOUNDATION button.

▶ Make the data foundation schema visible in the business layer editor, and then click the ▣ button to the right of the data foundation name, as shown in Figure 7.64.

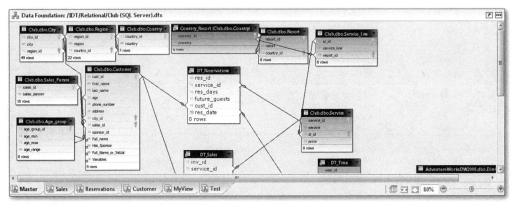

Figure 7.64 Changing the Data Foundation of a Business Layer

Note

After a data foundation change, it's highly recommended to run the check integrity (see Section 7.26) on the entire business layer to ensure that all resources remain valid.

Change the OLAP Connection or Change the OLAP Cube

For multidimensional business layers, you can change the OLAP connection (see Chapter 4, Section 4.1.3) or change the OLAP cube. To change the connection, choose one of the following options in the BUSINESS LAYER pane:

▶ Select the menu ACTIONS • CHANGE CONNECTION.

- ▶ Select the business layer root in the BUSINESS LAYER pane, then select the PROP-ERTIES tab, and click the CHANGE OLAP CONNECTION button.

- ▶ Make the OLAP connection frame visible in the business layer editor, and then click the ▥ button to the right of the connection.

You can change the OLAP cube, the OLAP connection, or both, as shown in Figure 7.65.

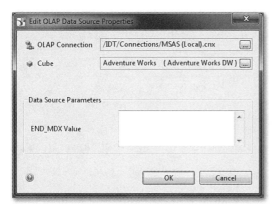

Figure 7.65 Changing the OLAP Connection and/or OLAP Cube

Organize the Business Layer

You can change the order of objects (dimensions, attributes, measures, etc.), lists of values, parameters, queries, and custom navigation paths in the business layer. Multiple objects of the same type can be moved in the business layer content: move multiple dimensions, multiple measures, multiple folders, and so on. List of values, parameters, queries and navigation paths can be also moved but only one at a time.

Lists of values, parameters, and queries can also be alphabetically sorted, whereas business layer objects can't because that might break the business layer presentation.

Of course, it's always possible to group objects in folders or subfolders, to hide some objects (in general, the technical one), to associate attributes to dimensions or measures, to mix dimensions and measures in a same folder, and so on.

Mass Changes

One of the main universe designer tasks is to do mass updates, changes, copies, and so on. IDT offers a large set of functionalities dedicated to mass changes, which are accessible by right-clicking:

- Select multiple heterogeneous objects and copy them in the same folder or a different folder.
- Select multiple heterogeneous objects and delete them.
- Select multiple heterogeneous objects and change their object state, access level, data type (not available for folders and filters), and so on.
- Turn multiple homogeneous objects into different objects: dimensions, attributes, or measures.
- Select multiple measures and change their projection function.
- Select multiple heterogeneous objects, edit, and apply a custom display format.
- Select multiple heterogeneous objects to view the data (not available for filters). A query mixing the selected objects is generated and run.
- Select multiple heterogeneous objects to view the generated SQL script or MDX script (not available for filters).

7.26 Check Integrity

When designing the universe, you've created the data foundation resources and the business layer resources and you've validated each resource individually (although this isn't a mandatory step). Before publishing the business layer, including its data foundation for relational business layers, the most important task is to ensure that the published universe is ready to be used by users and doesn't contain errors in the connection (see Chapter 4), data foundation (see Chapter 5), and business layer.

To validate the universe, you must invoke the check integrity tool. The check integrity tool can be run for a given object, for a folder and its content, or for the entire business layer:

▶ To run the check integrity tool for a given object, select an object (dimension, attribute, measure, etc.), a parameter, a list of values, or a query in the business layer, right-click it, and select CHECK INTEGRITY.

▶ To run the check integrity tool for a list of objects, select a folder in the business layer, right-click it, and select CHECK INTEGRITY.

▶ To run the check integrity tool for the entire business layer, select multiple objects, right-click it, and select CHECK INTEGRITY. You can also select the business layer root, and then click the CHECK INTEGRITY button (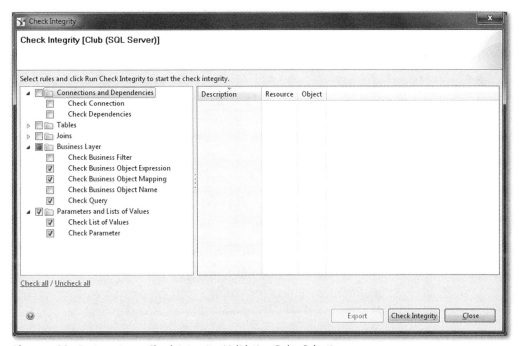) in the IDT toolbar.

7.26.1 Run the Check Integrity

The CHECK INTEGRITY dialog box opens, and the list of appropriate validation rules is displayed. Depending on the objects selected in the business layer, the validation rules can be different. When the check integrity concerns the entire business layer, the proposed validation rules include business layer validation rules and also data foundation and connection validation rules, as shown in Figure 7.66.

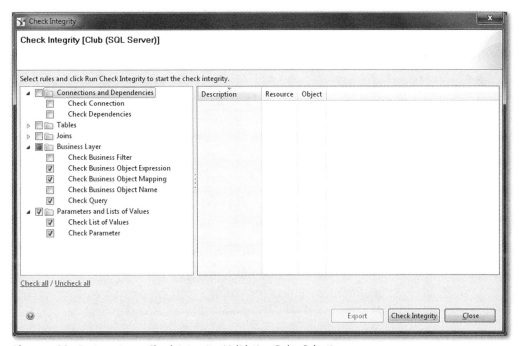

Figure 7.66 Business Layer Check Integrity: Validation Rules Selection

You can check all or part of the validation rules and click the CHECK INTEGRITY button to start the business layer resources validation, as shown in Figure 7.67.

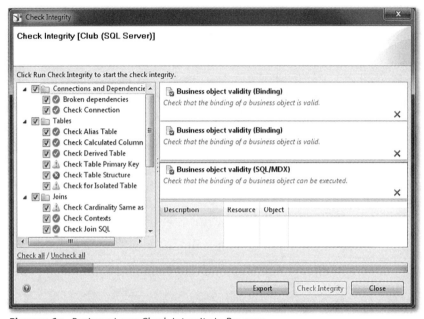

Figure 7.67 Business Layer Check Integrity in Progress

The check integrity process can be a long process depending on the size of the business layer (number of objects) and the size of the data foundation (number of tables, number of joins). You can interrupt at any time one or more processes by clicking one of the red buttons (✖).

7.26.2 Understand the Result of the Check Integrity Process

After the check integrity process is finished, an icon is displayed in front of each validation rules as shown in Figure 7.68:

▶ ✔: All resources (tables, joins, dimensions, measures, lists of values, etc.) have been successfully validated for this particular validation rule.

▶ ⚠: At least one resource returns a warning for this particular validation rule.

▶ ✖: At least one resource returns an error for this particular validation rule.

▶ ⓘ: At least one resource returns information for this particular validation rule.

To keep the result of the check integrity, you can export it in a text file or a *.csv* file by clicking the EXPORT button shown in Figure 7.68. The check integrity result is also kept in the PROBLEMS view of IDT.

Figure 7.68 Results of the Business Layer Check Integrity Process

7.26.3 Analyze and Fix Errors and Warnings

Warnings can be fixed, but this isn't mandatory to make the universe consumable by the SAP BusinessObjects BI clients. On the other hand, errors *must* be fixed to avoid incorrect behavior of the universe.

To access a business layer resource that contains an error or a warning, open the PROBLEMS view (see Figure 7.69) by selecting WINDOW • CHECK INTEGRITY PROBLEMS. The list of errors and warnings is displayed in this view, and the PROBLEMS view content is always kept even if IDT is closed. The view content can be overridden with a new check integrity process or if the view content is intentionally erased. Each project resource (connection, data foundation, or business layer) open in IDT has its own PROBLEMS view; erasing or overriding the PROBLEMS view for one project resource doesn't impact other project resources.

Errors and warning are categorized in the PROBLEMS view. To access the business layer resource concerned by an error or a warning, double-click a row in the PROBLEMS view to open the appropriate editor as shown in Figure 7.69. If the error or warning concerns a connection resource or a data foundation resource, the appropriate editor doesn't open. You should run the check integrity for each component of the universe separately in this order:

1. Connection

2. Data foundation

3. Business layer

Description	Resource	Path	Location	Type
▲ ⊗ Errors (3 items)				
⊗ The business object has a duplicate name. (Parent path : Services).	Club (SQL Server).blx	IDT/Relational	Services\Resort	Check Integrity
⊗ The business object has a duplicate name. (Parent path : Services).	Club (SQL Server).blx	IDT/Relational	Services\Resort	Check Integrity
⊗ The connection Club is invalid: com.microsoft.sqlserver.jdbc.SQLServerDriver.	Club (SQL Server).blx	IDT/Relational	Unknown	Check Integrity
▲ ⚠ Warnings (8 items)				
⚠ Table DimCustomer is missing a primary key.	Club (SQL Server).blx	IDT/Relational	Tables	Check Integrity
⚠ Table DimCustomer is not joined to any other table.	Club (SQL Server).blx	IDT/Relational	Tables	Check Integrity
⚠ Table DT_Countries is not joined to any other table.	Club (SQL Server).blx	IDT/Relational	Tables	Check Integrity
⚠ Table DT_Country_Name is not joined to any other table.	Club (SQL Server).blx	IDT/Relational	Tables	Check Integrity
⚠ The data type of parameter My Cities is empty, unknown, or different from the data type of the list-of-values column.	Club (SQL Server).blx	IDT/Relational	Unknown	Check Integrity
⚠ The default values for the prompt are empty.	Club (SQL Server).blx	IDT/Relational	Unknown	Check Integrity
⚠ The selected column in the list of values associated with the parameter "Cities hierarchy" is invalid.	Club (SQL Server).blx	IDT/Relational	Unknown	Check Integrity
⚠ The selected column in the list of values associated with the parameter "Country-Region-City" is invalid.	Club (SQL Server).blx	IDT/Relational	Unknown	Check Integrity

Figure 7.69 Selecting a Row in the Problems View to Open the Editor

All objects with errors or warnings are shown in the business layer with a line under them, as shown in Figure 7.70. A tooltip containing the error/warning message is displayed when you put the mouse pointer over the object.

Figure 7.70 Dimension with an Error

7.26.4 Customize the Validation Rules

You can customize the severity of each validation rule. The severity can take the following values:

▶ Error

▶ Warning

▶ Info

To customize the validation rules, select WINDOW • PREFERENCES. When the PREFERENCES dialog box is open, select INFORMATION DESIGN TOOL • CHECK INTEGRITY, as shown in Figure 7.71.

You can change the severity of each validation rule or restore the default values for one or all validation rules. When a validation rule is checked in the PREFERENCES window, the validation rule is always checked by default when the check integrity tool is invoked. You can decide afterwards to check or uncheck this validation rule.

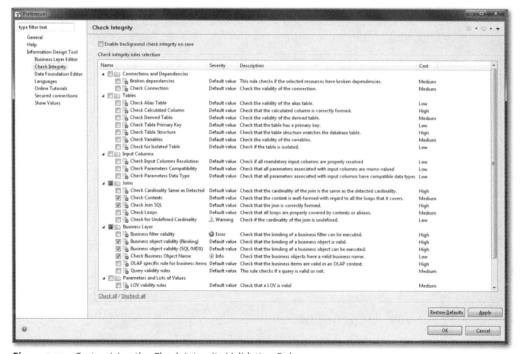

Figure 7.71 Customizing the Check Integrity Validation Rules

The Cost column gives estimate information concerning the time cost when this validation rule is run. If you activate the ENABLE BACKGROUND CHECK INTEGRITY ON SAVE option, then all validation rules that have been checked in the PREFERENCES window are executed in the background after a save operation for a connection, a data foundation, or a business layer.

7.26.5 Validation Rules Definition

Table 7.19 describes the validation rules used for the business layer check integrity. Most of the validation rules can be executed only if the database connection is valid and can be established.

Validation Rule	Description
Business filter validity	Check that the business filter binding can be executed on the database.
Business object validity (binding)	Check that the object binding (SELECT and WHERE expressions) is valid. For instance, if the binding is using built-in functions (see Section 7.23), check that the syntax is correct.
Business object validity (SQL/MDX)	Check that the object binding (SELECT and WHERE expressions) can be executed on the database.
Check business object name	Check that the business object name is valid.
OLAP-specific rules for business items	Check that the business items are valid in a multidimensional business layer.
Query validity rules	Check that the query is valid. For instance, check that the query references existing objects.
LOV validity rules	Check that the list of values is valid.
Prompt validity rules	Check that the @prompt used in an object binding is valid.

Table 7.19 Check Integrity Rules for the Business Layer

7.27 Show Dependencies

For a universe designer, it's important to know, understand, and estimate the impact analysis when the universe needs to be modified. Here are questions that you, as a universe designer, may have to answer:

- What dimensions, measures, and attributes are impacted if I modify a derived table definition?

- What objects, queries, parameters, and so on are impacted if I delete a list of values?

- What objects, queries, lists of values, and so on are impacted if I modify a filter definition?

- What data foundations and business layers are impacted if I modify a connection definition?

IDT offers a set of functionalities to help you quickly know the impacted resources where another resource is changed in the project or inside a business layer or a data foundation. This section covers the impact analysis between resources inside a business layer.

> **Note**
>
> For more information on showing dependencies in a project, see Chapter 3, Section 3.2.5.
> For more information on showing dependencies in a data foundation, see Chapter 5, Section 5.18.

To know the impacted resources, you need to select a business layer resource (dimension, measure, attribute, parameter, list of values, query, etc.), right click it, and select SHOW LOCAL DEPENDENCIES.

The SHOW LOCAL DEPENDENCIES dialog box is split in two parts:

- The dependent resources (see Figure 7.72)

- The referenced resources (see Figure 7.73)

The list contains the resource name, the resource type, and the resource location (RESULT, FILTER, SELECT, WHERE, etc.). Each referenced or dependent resource can also be itself referenced by another resource or dependent of other resources. So each resource can be expanded to see the other impacted resources, which gives the full scope of impacted resources, as shown in Figure 7.72 and Figure 7.73.

Double-clicking on a business layer resource opens the appropriate editor. Double-clicking on a data foundation resource (table, column, calculated column, derived table, federated table, or alias table) highlights this resource in the data foundation view of the business layer editor.

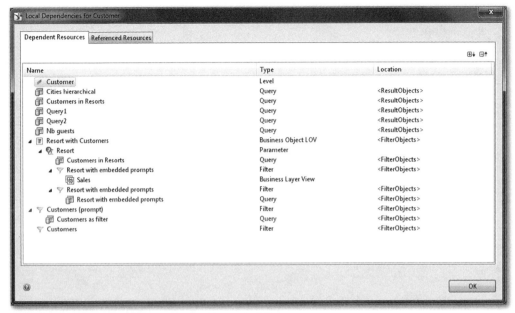

Figure 7.72 Local Dependencies: Dependent Resources

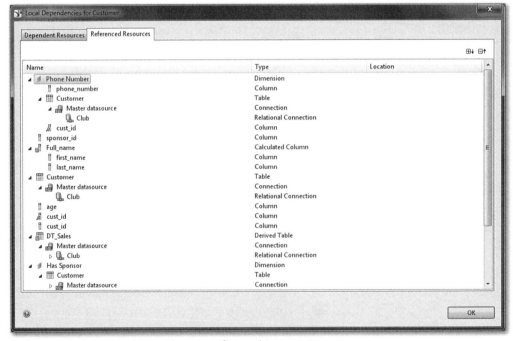

Figure 7.73 Local Dependencies: Referenced Resources

7.28 Business Layers Built on Multisource Data Foundations

Business layers built on top of multisource data foundations aren't essentially different from any other business layers built on a single-source data foundation; the same development principles and the same functionality apply. The only noteworthy difference is that the objects have to be defined using the SAP BusinessObjects SQL, which follows the ANSI SQL-92 syntax and proposes a fixed set of functions listed in Table 6.3 of Chapter 6.

The Federation Query Server translates the multisource query into multiple database calls using the vendor-specific language. The list of SQL functions is very rich and covers most of the functionality available in vendor-specific syntaxes.

If a multisource derived table or federated table with a discriminating field was created in the data foundation, as shown in Chapter 6, you can build a filter that enables the choice of the appropriate data source. This filter just lets a user select from one or many values of the discriminating field via a list of values built on it.

Example of a Discriminating Filter

Let's return to an example in Chapter 6, Section 6.7. A federated table might have a YEAR field that discriminates the source of data. In the business layer, you can build a list of values selecting all distinct years from the federated table, create a prompt on that list of values, and define a business filter where the YEAR field is chosen with the prompt. If the YEAR field points to a specific data source, the Federation Query Server only queries that source.

In the example provided in Chapter 6, Section 6.5.1, the discriminating filter lets the business user select a specific COUNTRY to choose from.

A business layer built on top of a multisource data foundation provides an additional action that gathers various statistics of the used data sources. This action can be used to optimize the performance of the queries at runtime.

To gather the statistics, it's necessary to open the business layer by right-clicking on the business layer name and selecting COMPUTE STATISTICS, as shown in Figure 7.74.

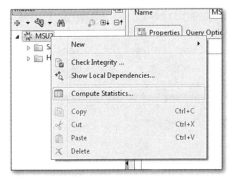

Figure 7.74 The Compute Statistics Command in the Context Menu

IDT now provides a list of suggested statistics to gather. This list is built based on the sources, tables, and fields actually used by the business layer. As shown in Figure 7.75, the user can accept the default list or can modify it at will.

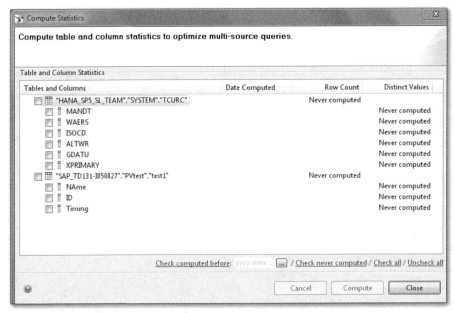

Figure 7.75 Possible Statistics to Gather

Running the statistics, the information is sent to the query server, which uses it the next time a query is executed. No other particular functionality makes a business layer built on a multisource data foundation different from the other relational business layers. The business user, connecting to the universe via an SAP Business-Objects BI client, doesn't actually know that the universe built from that business layer is generating multisource queries.

7.29   Multidimensional Business Layer Refresh Structure

Multidimensional business layers (see Section 7.2) are business layers built on top of OLAP cubes and can be enriched like relational business layers.

All universes can be impacted by databases changes. For relational universes, IDT captures these potential changes in the data foundation using the refresh structure tool as described in Chapter 5, Section 5.17.

For multidimensional universes, the refresh structure feature is available in the business layer. To refresh the structure of the multidimensional business layer, select ACTION • REFRESH STRUCTURE. You can check the following options in the Refresh Structure wizard shown in Figure 7.76.

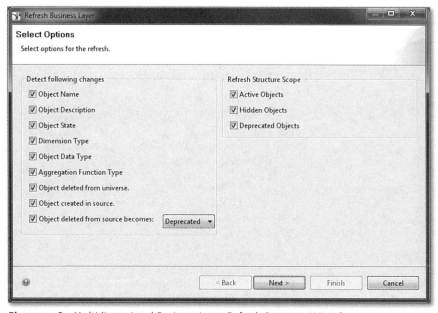

Figure 7.76   Multidimensional Business Layer Refresh Structure Wizard

All business layer objects that have been automatically generated keep the source information of the OLAP cube. Only the generated resources are updated during the refresh structure operation. All resources manually created aren't directly impacted by the refresh structure, so it's recommended to use the `@select` (*see* Section 7.23.4) built-in function in the definition of manually created objects to ensure that they are impacted by the refresh structure.

Table 7.20 describes the refresh structure wizard options:

Option	Description
OBJECT NAME	If the option is activated, the business layer object name is updated with the name of the OLAP metadata.
OBJECT DESCRIPTION	If the option is activated, the business layer resource description is updated with the description of the OLAP metadata.
OBJECT STATE	If the option is activated, the business layer object state (see Section 7.20.6) is set to ACTIVE only if the OLAP metadata still exist in the OLAP cube.
DIMENSION TYPE	If the option is activated, the original OLAP metadata type is applied. If you've turned a dimension into an attribute, the object becomes a dimension again.
OBJECT DATA TYPE	If the option is activated, the original OLAP metadata data type is applied.
AGGREGATION FUNCTION TYPE	If the option is activated, the original aggregation function is applied in the measure projection function (see Section 7.7.3). This option applies only in the OLAP database, which is able to provide this information.
OBJECT DELETED FROM UNIVERSE	When you delete a generated object from a multidimensional business layer, the information is kept in the business layer. If the option is activated, deleted objects are regenerated.
OBJECT CREATED IN SOURCE	If the option is activated, all new OLAP metadata are generated in the business layer.

Table 7.20 Business Layer Refresh Structure Options

Option	Description
OBJECT DELETED FROM SOURCE BECOMES	If the option is activated, OLAP metadata that no longer exist in the OLAP source are deleted or deprecated based on the choice set in the combo box associated with the option, as shown in Figure 7.76.
REFRESH STRUCTURE SCOPE	You can also check only active, hidden, and/or deprecated objects that are impacted by the refresh structure.

Table 7.20 Business Layer Refresh Structure Options (Cont.)

After the options are selected, click NEXT to run the refresh structure. After the refresh structure process is finished, the list of actions is listed in the wizard shown in Figure 7.77.

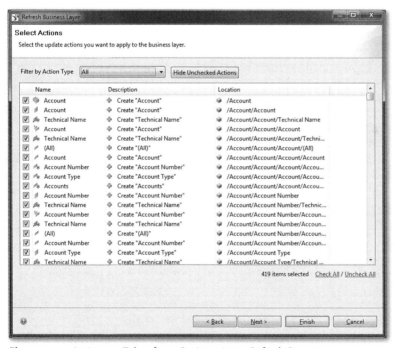

Figure 7.77 Actions to Take after a Business Layer Refresh Structure

To filter the actions, you can choose ALL, CREATE, DEPRECATE, MODIFY (DATA TYPE), or REGENERATE from the FILTER BY ACTION TYPE dropdown list. Finally, you can decide to check or uncheck actions to update the business layer; all actions are checked by default.

In the next wizard step, the list of actions you've selected can be saved in a file for future analysis.

> **Note**
>
> After the refresh structure of the business layer, it's highly recommended to run a check integrity on the entire business layer to ensure that all resources remain valid. This task is important because the business layer can contain resources that have been manually created.

7.30 Business Layer Parameters and Query Governors

Before publication, you need to adjust business layer parameters and define query governors.

7.30.1 Business Layer Parameters

The business layer behavior and hence the universe behavior can be tuned through different parameters that can impact the query generation and influence behaviors for measures, lists of values, queries, and so on. Some of the parameters are automatically generated at the business layer creation. The business layer parameters are only available for relational business layers and can be added, deleted, and customized.

To access the business layer parameters list, select the business layer root in the BUSINESS LAYER pane, select the PROPERTIES tab, and click PARAMETERS, as shown in Figure 7.78.

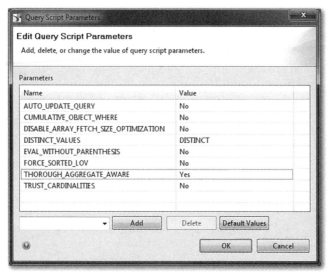

Figure 7.78 Customizing the Business Layer Parameters

Table 7.21 describes some of the business layer parameters.

Parameter	Description
AUTO_UPDATE_QUERY	Values: YES/NO. Default value: No. What happens to the query if an object isn't available for the user refreshing the query? If the value is No, the query isn't modified and it may fail if an object is not available. If the value is YES, the object is removed from the query.
BEGIN_SQL	No default value. This placeholder can contain an SQL script that is run before the query. For instance, it can be used for settings options at the database level. This script can reference parameters, tables, columns, dimensions, attributes, measures, and built-in functions (see Section 7.23) such as @prompt or @variable.

Table 7.21 Main Business Layer Parameters

Parameter	Description
CUMULATIVE_OBJECT_WHERE	Values: Yes/No. Default value: No. It concerns only filtered objects (objects with a Where definition). If the value is No, the filter is combined with the object condition. If the value is Yes, the filter is combined in the Where clause of the main query.
DISABLE_ARRAY_FETCH_SIZE_OPTIMIZATION	Values: Yes/No. Default value: No. The query engine is able to optimize the arrays of data to be returned without taking into account the array fetch default value. If the value is No, all queries take advantage of this optimization. If the value is Yes, the array fetch value is taken into account.
END_SQL	No default value. This placeholder can contain an SQL script and is added at the end of the query. For instance, in SAP HANA, the END_SQL can contain the following expression: WITH PARAMETERS ('request_flags'='USE_PARALLEL_AGGREGATION', 'request_flags'='ANALYZE_MODEL').
EVAL_WITHOUT_PARENTHESIS	Values: Yes/No. Default value: No. By default, the @select built-in function used in objects definition is replaced by the object SQL expression embedded within parentheses. If the value is No, parentheses are added around the SQL expression. If the value is Yes, parentheses are removed from the SQL expression.
FORCE_SORTED_LOV	Values: Yes/No. Default value: No. If the value is No, the list of values query isn't sorted. If the value is Yes, the list of values query is sorted.

Table 7.21 Main Business Layer Parameters (Cont.)

Parameter	Description
JOIN_BY_SQL	Values: YES/NO. Default value: No.
	This option depends on database capabilities supporting the JOIN_BY_SQL function. This function is used to combine multiple SQL flows into a single one.
	If the value is No, multiple SQL statements aren't combined and are generated separately.
	If the value is YES, multiple SQL statements are combined using the JOIN_BY_SQL function.
TRUST_CARDINALITIES	Values: YES/NO. Default value: No.
	This option is used in case of inflated results (see Chapter 5, Section 5.7).
	If the value is No, there is no optimization in the SQL generation.
	If the value is YES, all conditions inflating a measure not used in the query results are generated as subqueries.

Table 7.21 Main Business Layer Parameters (Cont.)

7.30.2 Query Governors

The business layer parameters help you set universe resource behavior; whereas the query governors help you define the universe query user rights. To access the business layer query governors, select the business layer root in the BUSINESS LAYER pane, and then select the QUERY OPTIONS tab.

The relational business layers have more options (as shown in Figure 7.79) than the multidimensional business layers (as shown in Figure 7.80).

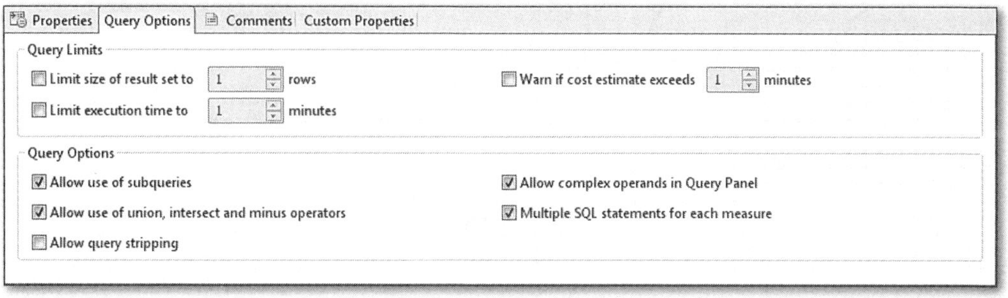

Figure 7.79 Query Governors for Relational Business Layers

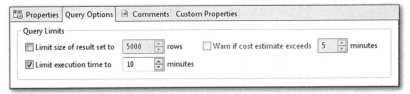

Figure 7.80 Query Governors for Multidimensional Business Layers

The query governors are organized in two categories: query limits and query options.

Query Limits

The query limits are the options dedicated to restrict the number of rows returned by a query or to limit the execution time of a query. When a business layer is created, the following option values are applied:

▶ LIMIT SIZE OF RESULT SET: 5,000 rows

▶ LIMIT EXECUTION TIME: 10 minutes

You can override the values or deactivate the options so that no restriction is applied.

The WARN IF COST ESTIMATE EXCEEDS option can be used to warn the user that a given query exceeds a certain time. Each query run within SAP BusinessObjects BI clients keeps the latest execution time. This information is reused to give an estimate time to the user. Of course, this is just an estimate, and the query can depend on potential parameters or SAP variables that can influence the query time.

The LIMIT SIZE OF RESULT SET and LIMIT EXECUTION TIME options can be overridden by users in the client tool query panel. Users can only provide a lower value than the one defined for the option.

> **Example**
>
> The LIMIT SIZE OF RESULT SET option has been set to 10,000 rows and the LIMIT EXECU-TION TIME option has been set to 5 minutes.
>
> Users can change the value of the two options and provide a value lower than 10,000 for the first option and lower than 5 for the second option.

If one of the limits is reached during the query execution, it means that not all query rows have been retrieved for the data source. For example, an SAP Business-Objects Web Intelligence user is informed that the query did not return all rows with a warning icon in the report status bar.

Query Options

The QUERY OPTIONS (only available with relational business layers) define the scope of query capabilities that a user is able to build with the query panel, as listed in Table 7.22.

Option	Description
ALLOW USE OF SUBQUERIES	When this option is activated, the user is able to add a subquery to a filter. To add a subquery in the query panel, the user has to click the button in the FILTER pane of the query panel.
ALLOW USE OF UNION, INTERSECT AND MINUS OPERATORS	When this option is activated, the user is able to add a UNION, INTERSECTION, or MINUS query to the initial query. To add such an operator in the query panel, the user has to click the button in the query panel toolbar.
ALLOW COMPLEX OPERANDS IN QUERY PANEL	When this option is activated, the operators BOTH and EXCEPT are available for filter operators in the FILTER pane of the query panel.
MULTIPLE SQL STATEMENTS FOR EACH MEASURE	When this option is activated: ▶ An SQL flow is generated per group of measures belonging to the same fact table. ▶ An SQL flow is generated per measure having an SQL statement in its WHERE definition. ▶ The results of multiple SQL flows are combined with a FULL OUTER JOIN operator, and the results are merged in a single result set.
ALLOW QUERY STRIPPING	The objective of query stripping is to optimize the database performance by reducing the number of objects used in a query, which reduces the data volume retrieved from the database. It has been introduced for SAP BusinessObjects Web Intelligence, initially for SAP NetWeaver BW support. Starting with SAP BusinessObjects BI 4.1, it has been extended to all OLAP sources and relational sources.

Table 7.22 Business Layer Query Options

Option	Description
	Once the option has been enabled in the business layer, it must also be set in the query properties of an SAP BusinessObjects Web Intelligence document as shown in Figure 7.81.
	When the QUERY STRIPPING option is activated, the query is regenerated to take into account only the dimensions, attributes, and measures actually used in the document. All objects that are used in the query panel (RESULTS pane) but not consumed are removed. Objects only used in the query panel FILTER pane are kept even if they aren't in the RESULTS pane.
	Because the query is regenerated, this can impact the SQL FROM and WHERE clauses and potentially the contexts; this is why this option can be set by the universe designer who is the person who can decide if this option can be used safely.

Table 7.22 Business Layer Query Options (Cont.)

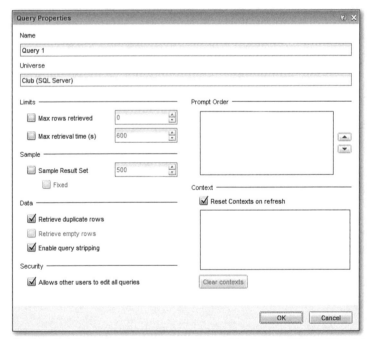

Figure 7.81 Query Stripping Option Set in an SAP BusinessObjects Web Intelligence Query

7.31 Recommendations for Building a Business Layer

A universe is made of three main components; because the business layer is the interface between end users and IT, it's important to polish the design of the business layer and adopt standards. Standards for the components of a universe help guarantee consistency and stability in the final product. If the enterprise has a data administrator, that person should be involved in the standard selection process.

You can specify standards for the following:

- Universe names
- Object definition
- Names for simple objects
- Names for complex objects
- Names for aggregate objects
- Folder names
- Alias names
- Filter names
- List of values names
- Parameters names
- Help text

First you have to identify candidate objects as dimensions, attributes, or measures to facilitate slice-and-dice analysis. You can also plan for drilldown and drillup analysis by identifying navigation paths. The measures projection function used by SAP BusinessObjects Web Intelligence is also important and can improve performance.

You can also define the appropriate rights to be applied to business layer resources such as the following:

- Set appropriate access level to the objects.
- Create business layer views.
- Hide technical objects that you don't want to be used in queries.
- Define objects security.

Always provide the needed information and the right information to the end users by ensuring you do the following:

▶ Always provide a description for dimensions, attributes, measures, and filters.

▶ Create filters with accurate names.

▶ Create parameters with the right operator and the right list of values.

▶ Provide different lists of values to help users better filter their queries.

You can organize the business layer, reuse objects, and reuse object definitions using the @select built-in function. Don't create too large of business layers! 500 distinct objects is often a maximum acceptable for end users. Create business layer views to break the business layer in small parts or create smaller business layers based on the same data foundation.

Always use the check integrity tool to validate the business layer before publication. To always have an up-to-date business layer, use the refresh structure tool for multidimensional business layers.

Once published, universes can be accessed by many users in different departments of the enterprise. Different roles, authorizations and security profiles need be created and granted to users and groups, as described in Chapter 10.

In worldwide companies, there's often more than one language for users to access Enterprise data and BI documents. In that case, universes—but also BI documents—need to be translated in the appropriate languages that users are expected to read and understand, as described in Chapter 11.

7.32   Summary

In the universe definition, the business layer is the universe interface that exposes the underlying technical models to end users through meaningful objects name. The business layer can be relational (single-source or multisource) or multidimensional.

In the business layer, the different objects are organized as a tree folder:

▶ For relational and multidimensional universes: folders, dimensions, attributes and measures

▶ For multidimensional universes: Calculated members, named sets, analysis dimensions, hierarchies and levels

▶ Parameters, lists of values, and filters

▶ Navigation path, index awareness, and aggregation awareness

The business layer supports views to organize its objects and built-in functions that can be called in SQL or MDX expressions that define the objects.

Information Design Tool allows you to define the business layer, its objects, and their properties. It also proposes some helpers like the SQL/MDX editors, the check integrity tool, the dependencies analysis, and the refresh structure for multidimensional universes.

Before publishing the universe, you need to check its parameters and the query governors that define the limit for queries created from the published universe.

The query panel enables users to define sophisticated questions on the data source with simple drag-and-drop actions on objects representing business concepts. Information Design Tool provides a query panel for testing business layers and published universes.

8   Universe Query Panel

The query panel is the typical user interface proposed by SAP BusinessObjects BI tools to access data from a universe. The objective of the query panel is to provide a graphical representation of a query that lets business users deal with simple and complex concepts in an easy and consistent manner.

By simple drag-and-drop actions of objects defined in the universe, a business user can create a query and run it against the data sources; the query script is automatically generated by the semantic layer technology based on the information available in a universe.

In SAP BusinessObjects BI 4.1, SAP BusinessObjects Web Intelligence and SAP Crystal Reports for Enterprise have their own versions of the query panel that support all semantic layer capabilities. Simplified versions of the query panel are available in SAP BusinessObjects Dashboards, SAP Lumira, SAP Predictive Analysis, and SAP BusinessObjects Explorer. Information Design Tool (IDT) also includes a complete query panel and lets the designer of a universe test and validate the model during its development.

This chapter presents the functionalities of the IDT query panel and how to use it to create simple or complex queries. These queries can be useful to run detailed tests on an ongoing project and understand the possible challenges for a business user when using the universe.

8.1   The Query Panel Interface

To create powerful queries and take advantage of its capabilities, you first need to identify how to launch the query panel and the different subpanels and controls it contains.

8.1.1   Launching the Query Panel

In IDT, the query panel can be started from three different locations:

▶ In the business layer editor, in the QUERIES section toolbar, by clicking the INSERT QUERY button (🔲)

▶ In the REPOSITORY RESOURCES view, by right-clicking on a universe and selecting the RUN QUERY command in the context menu

▶ In the SECURITY EDITOR, by right-clicking on a universe and selecting the RUN QUERY command in the context menu

In all three cases, the same query panel opens, except that when you run a query from the business layer editor, no security is applied; only the database security is applied with the credentials and authentication mode defined in the connection. However, if you run the query from the REPOSITORY RESOURCES or the SECURITY EDITOR views, in complement of the database security, the security rights and profiles are applied for the account used to open the session to the CMS repository in IDT.

8.1.2   Query Panel Parts

The query panel is a graphical component that opens in a dedicated window, as shown in Figure 8.1.

It's made of several subpanels. On the left, two panels can be displayed:

▶ UNIVERSES
This panel is always displayed because it contains the universe list of objects and folders. You select these objects to add in the query results or filters from this panel. On the top of this panel, you can select the universe view to display from a dropdown, if any has been defined in the business layer and if your security allows you to see them. By default, the master view is selected.

▶ COMBINED QUERIES
In this panel, you add and manage combined queries.

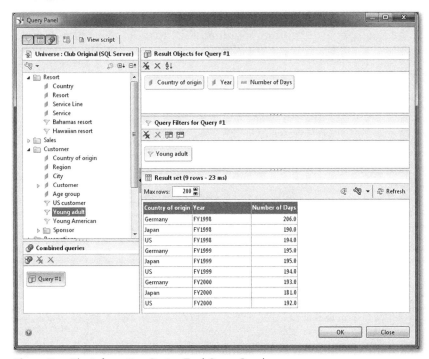

Figure 8.1 The Information Design Tool Query Panel

On the right, three panels are displayed by default:

▶ RESULTS OBJECTS
In this panel, you add the objects from the universe to retrieve in the query. The object order is used to display the corresponding result columns in the DATA PREVIEW panel.

▶ QUERY FILTERS
In this panel, you add and define the filters to apply to the query to filter the result data set.

▶ DATA PREVIEW
In this panel, the query result data set is displayed after you've run it.

If the query panel has been launched from the business layer editor, then it has two buttons:

▶ OK

This button is used to close the query panel and save the current query. If you've created a new one, then this new query is added in the list of business layer predefined queries and you can edit its properties (name, description). Otherwise, if the query was an existing one, then this query is updated with your changes.

▶ CLOSE

This button is used to close the query panel without saving any changes.

If the query panel has been launched from the SECURITY EDITOR or the REPOSITORY RESOURCES view, then only the CLOSE button is displayed to close the query panel.

8.1.3 Query Panel Toolbars

The query panel contains several toolbars, one main toolbar used to show or hide some other parts or open additional dialog boxes, and one for each part where you build and run the query. The buttons on these toolbars are described in Table 8.1.

Toolbar	Button	Description
Main		Click (SHOW/HIDE) FILTER PANEL to show or hide the FILTER panel.
Main		Click (SHOW/HIDE) DATA PREVIEW PANEL to show or hide the DATA PREVIEW panel.
Main		Click (SHOW/HIDE) COMBINED QUERIES PANEL to show or hide the COMBINED QUERIES panel.
Main		Click QUERY PROPERTIES to open the QUERY PROPERTIES dialog box (see Section 8.4).
Main		Click VIEW SCRIPT to open the QUERY SCRIPT VIEWER, where you can display the generated query (e.g., SQL or MDX) to be sent to the data source(s) or to modify it (see Section 8.5.4).
Combined Queries		Click INSERT COMBINED QUERY to add a new query and combine it with the existing ones. This button is disabled for multidimensional universes.

Table 8.1 Query Panel Toolbar Buttons

Toolbar	Button	Description
Combined Queries		Click REMOVE ALL COMBINED QUERIES to remove all queries from the COMBINED QUERIES panel and add an empty default one.
Combined Queries		Click REMOVE SELECTED COMBINED QUERY to remove the selected query from the COMBINED QUERIES panel.
Result Objects		Click REMOVE ALL RESULT OBJECTS to empty the RESULT OBJECTS panel and remove all objects from it.
Result Objects		Click REMOVE SELECTED RESULT OBJECTS to remove the selected objects from the RESULT OBJECTS panel.
Result Objects		Click SORT DIALOG to open the SORT dialog box (see Section 8.2.3).
Filters		Click REMOVE ALL FILTERS to empty the QUERY FILTERS panel and remove all filters from it.
Filters		Click REMOVE SELECTED FILTERS to remove the selected filters from the QUERY FILTERS panel.
Filters		Click ADD SUBQUERY to add a subquery in the QUERY FILTERS panel (see Section 8.5.1). This button is enabled only if the data sources support subqueries. This button is disabled for multidimensional universes.
Filters		Click ADD RANKING to add a ranking filter in the QUERY FILTERS panel (see Section 8.5.2). This button is enabled only if the data sources support ranking. This button is disabled for multidimensional universes.
Data Preview	200	The MAX ROWS text field is where you can set the maximum number of rows to display in the data preview.
Data Preview		Click ADVANCED PREVIEW to open a DATA PREVIEW dialog box (see Chapter 2, Section 2.6) where you can display and analyze the query result set.
Data Preview		The RESULT SET DISPLAY OPTIONS button opens a dropdown menu where you can define how a result set is displayed: ▸ FLAT LAYOUT lists all fields of each record. ▸ HIERARCHICAL LAYOUT groups fields with the same value in the same cell.

Table 8.1 Query Panel Toolbar Buttons (Cont.)

Toolbar	Button	Description
Data Preview	⟳	Click REFRESH to run the query the first time or to refresh it afterwards.

Table 8.1 Query Panel Toolbar Buttons (Cont.)

8.2 Creating Queries

Based on the universe abstraction, the query panel allows you to quickly create queries, add filters to them, and sort the resulting data set.

8.2.1 Selecting the Result Objects

In the query panel, the RESULT OBJECTS panel is where you enter the objects that are used to generate the list of data to retrieve from the data source (in general the SELECT statement on relational sources). The order of objects in the RESULT OBJECTS panel defines the order in which the result columns are displayed in the DATA PREVIEW panel. From the UNIVERSE panel, select an object (except predefined filters) to use in the query and drag and drop it in this RESULT OBJECTS panel. Instead of drag and drop, you can also double-click an object to add it in the RESULT OBJECTS at the end of the selected objects list.

If you add a folder, all objects in this folder (except predefined filters) are added to the RESULT OBJECTS panel. If you add an attribute object, the dimension or measure associated with the attribute is also added to the RESULT OBJECTS panel.

When the RESULT OBJECTS panel contains at least one object, you can click the REFRESH button to run the query. The result set is then displayed in the DATA PREVIEW panel. Predefined filters can't be selected in the RESULT OBJECTS panel and must be added to the QUERY FILTERS panel (see Section 8.2.2).

Member Selector

Multidimensional universes contain richer metadata that you can select in the RESULT OBJECTS panel, including the hierarchy. This object lets you choose the members you want to display in the result set. The choice of members affects only the display of the data, not the calculations or the filtering. For example, if you choose to display the revenue of "US" and of its child "California", then the revenue of "US" takes into account all states—it's not filtered on the California state only. To filter the revenue, it's necessary to work in the QUERY FILTERS panel, as shown in the next section.

When you add a hierarchy in the RESULT OBJECTS panel, it retrieves its default member by default. You may explicitly define the members to query by using the MEMBER SELECTOR dialog box, which can be opened by clicking the downward arrow on the right of a hierarchy object, as shown in Figure 8.2.

Figure 8.2 Level-Based and Parent-Child Hierarchies

As shown in Figure 8.3, the MEMBER SELECTOR contains three tabs, depending on how you define the members to add in the query.

Figure 8.3 The Multidimensional Member Selector

Let's look at each of those now.

Members Tab

Directly choose which members to display in the result. You can directly check each needed member. Use the toolbar icons or right-click a member to use operators that automatically add or exclude other members based on those selected. The possible operators appearing in the menu are described in Table 8.2.

Operator	Description
SELF	Adds the selected member.
CHILDREN	Adds all children members of the selected member (one level down).
DESCENDANTS	Adds all members who descend from the selected member (all levels down).
DESCENDANTS UNTIL NAMED LEVEL	Adds all members who descend from the selected member to a specific level. For level-based hierarchies, the level is defined by its name. For parent-child hierarchies, the level name is its position (e.g., LEVEL 01, LEVEL 02, etc.).
DESCENDANTS UNTIL...	Adds all members that descend from the selected member to a specified number of levels below.
PARENT	Adds the parent of the selected member (one level up). This option is not available with SAP direct access on SAP NetWeaver BW based on a BICS connection.
ANCESTORS	Adds all members from which the selected member descends. This option is not available with SAP direct access on SAP NetWeaver BW based on a BICS connection.
SIBLINGS	Adds all members at the same level and with the same parent of the selected member. This option is not available with SAP direct access on SAP NetWeaver BW based on a BICS connection.

Table 8.2 Member Selection Operators

Operator	Description
EXCLUDE	Excludes members from the selection; this command opens a submenu, letting you choose the operator (among CHILDREN, DESCENDANTS, PARENT, ANCESTORS, and SIBLINGS) to use to compute the members to exclude.
	This option is not available with SAP direct access on SAP NetWeaver BW based on a BICS connection.
SELECT ALL MEMBERS	Adds all the members of the hierarchy.
	To use this selection, click the SELECT dropdown button (⊞ ▾) in the MEMBER SELECTOR toolbar and click SELECT ALL MEMBERS.
SELECT ALL MEMBERS UNTIL NAMED LEVEL	Adds all the members that descend from the hierarchy root member(s) to a specified number of levels below.
	To use this selection, click the SELECT dropdown button (⊞ ▾) in the MEMBER SELECTOR toolbar and click SELECT ALL MEMBERS UNTIL NAMED LEVEL.
SELECT ALL MEMBERS UNTIL …	Adds all the members that descend from the hierarchy root member(s) to a specified number of levels below.
	To use this selection, click the SELECT dropdown button (⊞ ▾) in the MEMBER SELECTOR toolbar and click SELECT ALL MEMBERS UNTIL…
SELECT NONE	Deselect all the members of the hierarchy. This option removes all members selected with the option starting by SELECT ALL MEMBERS…
	To use this selection, click the SELECT dropdown button (⊞ ▾) in the MEMBER SELECTOR toolbar and click SELECT NONE.

Table 8.2 Member Selection Operators (Cont.)

Metadata Tab

The METADATA pane offers the possibility to select hierarchy levels, named sets, and calculated members. You can choose the levels, the named sets, and the calculated members to display in the result, as shown in Figure 8.4. The list of named sets contains the named sets you have created in the business layer and the named sets that have been created in the OLAP cube—mainly for Microsoft SQL Server Analysis Services.

Figure 8.4 Metadata Tab of the Member Selector

Prompt Tab

Define a prompt (and its text) asking to choose the members when clicking REFRESH. The prompt appears before running the query. The prompt member selection removes all the selections you have added in the MEMBERS and METADATA panes. As shown in Figure 8.5, you can define some properties for this prompt:

▶ ENABLE PROMPT: Enable or disable this prompt.

▶ PROMPT TEXT: Define the text to display in the prompt.

▶ KEEP LAST VALUES SELECTED: Keep the same selected members when the query is refreshed again.

▶ SET DEFAULT VALUES: Define default members selected in the prompt. To modify these members, click the EDIT button.

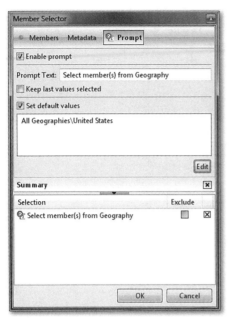

Figure 8.5 Prompt Tab of the Member Selector

When the prompt is displayed to let the user choose members, the member selector only offers the ability to check members (member picker). The OLAP-style family selection (children, descendants, and so on) is not possible in the prompted member selection.

Member Selector Toolbar

The MEMBER SELECTOR toolbar allows you to search for members, select members, sort members, change the members' name display, and show the member selection.

▶ **Search for members**

To search for members, click the SEARCH button () to open the search dialog box, as shown in Figure 8.6 This button is enabled only if the list of values associated to the hierarchies has the ALLOW USERS TO SEARCH VALUES IN THE DATABASE option activated (see Chapter 7, Section 7.13.6).

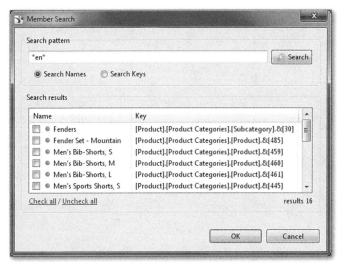

Figure 8.6 Searching for Members in the Member Selector

Only the values that match the search criteria are returned in member search dialog box. The following characters are used to define the matching criteria:

▶ "*": Matches any number of characters, even zero characters.

▶ "?": Matches exactly one character.

You can search for member names (select SEARCH NAMES option) or member unique names (select SEARCH KEYS option). You can check the members and click OK to add them in the current member selection. You can search for members several times to add members in the selection.

▶ **Member selection**
When you click the SELECT dropdown button (⊞ ▾) you can select different member selection options (described in Table 8.2):

  ▶ SELECT ALL MEMBERS

  ▶ SELECT NONE

  ▶ SELECT ALL MEMBERS UNTIL NAMED LEVEL

  ▶ SELECT ALL MEMBERS UNTIL…

▶ **Display name and/or unique name**
You can change the members name display by clicking the MEMBER DISPLAY OPTIONS dropdown button (🖐 ▾), and select one of the following options:

- DISPLAY NAME (e.g., `Accessories`)

- DISPLAY UNIQUE NAME (e.g., `[Product].[Product Model Categories].[Cat-egory].&[4]`)

- DISPLAY NAME AND UNIQUE NAME (e.g., `Accessories [Product].[Product Model Categories].[Category].&[4]`)

- UNIQUE NAME AND DISPLAY NAME (e.g., `[Product].[Product Model Catego-ries].[Category].&[4] Accessories`)

▶ **Sort members**

By default the hierarchy members are displayed in the database order. But it is possible to sort the members of a hierarchy by clicking the SORT ORDER drop-down button ($\frac{A}{Z}\downarrow$ ▾), and select one of the following options:

- NO SORT (DATABASE ORDER): Restore the default members' display.

- SORT ASCENDING: The members are sorted in ascending mode. The sort applies for all members with the same parent and thus for the whole hierarchy.

- SORT DESCENDING: The members are sorted in descending mode. The sort applies for all members with the same parent and thus for the whole hierarchy.

▶ **Show the member selection**

The selected members can be directly selected or indirectly selected by using OLAP-style family selection (described in Table 8.2) and levels selection. To view all the selected members you can unfold members in the hierarchy or click the EXPAND TREE TO SHOW SELECTIONS button (⊞) that expands the hierarchy to make all selected members visible in the member selector panel.

Summary

The selections you have added in the MEMBERS and METADATA panes are reflected in the MEMBER SELECTION pane above the SUMMARY section. If you unfold the hierarchies, the members, that have been indirectly selected by the metadata selection or the OLAP-style selection (children, descendants, and so on), are checked, as shown in Figure 8.7.

Figure 8.7 Member Selector Summary

The SUMMARY section of the MEMBER SELECTOR displays the currently selected members (see Figure 8.7). From this section, you can do the following:

▶ Directly delete a selection by clicking the X in the column in the right.

▶ Exclude the selected members from the list of members to query, by selecting the checkbox in the EXCLUDE column.

▶ Delete the entire selection by clicking the [✖] button on the right side of SUMMARY text.

When you've defined your member selection, click OK to close the MEMBER SELECTOR. In the RESULT OBJECTS panel, the hierarchy object is updated with the selected members.

In multidimensional universes, the MEMBER SELECTOR can be used only to select members to display. It doesn't really filter the data, which is done through query filters you can define for both relational and multidimensional universes.

8.2.2 Applying Filters to the Query

When a query is run, its results can be filtered by using a predefined filter defined in the universe or by creating new filters from universe objects. Filtering occurs by defining a condition based on an object of the universe. If the condition isn't met, then the retrieved row isn't added to the result data set. In practice, when you run the query, the filter defined in the query panel is converted into the corresponding SQL or MDX clause and is appended to the query script to be run against the database.

The operators you can use in filters are listed in Table 8.3, which also defines for each operator its number of operands, whether it's supported in a subquery, and whether it supports the ANY and ALL operators (see Section 8.5.1). Some operators aren't available if the underlying data source doesn't support them or if the data type to the filter doesn't support them.

Filters can be defined for both relational and multidimensional universes, but for multidimensional universes:

▶ BOTH and EXCEPT operators are not supported whatever the object type used in the filter.

▶ If the filter applies to a hierarchy, then only a limited number of operators are supported: EQUAL, NOT EQUAL, IN LIST, NOT IN LIST, MATCHES PATTERN, and DIFFERENT FROM PATTERN.

▶ If the filter applies to a hierarchy level, then MATCHES PATTERN and DIFFERENT FROM PATTERN operators are not supported.

Operator	Operands Number	Subquery	Any, All
EQUAL	1	Yes	No
NOT EQUAL	1	Yes	Yes
IN LIST	1 (list)	Yes	No
NOT IN LIST	1 (list)	Yes	No
BETWEEN	2	No	N/A
NOT BETWEEN	2	No	N/A
GREATER	1	Yes	Yes
GREATER OR EQUAL	1	Yes	Yes
LESS	1	Yes	Yes
LESS OR EQUAL	1	Yes	Yes
MATCHES PATTERN	1	No	N/A
DIFFERENT FROM PATTERN	1	No	N/A

Table 8.3 Filter Operators

Operator	Operands Number	Subquery	Any, All
BOTH	2	No	N/A
EXCEPT	1	No	N/A
IS NULL	0	No	N/A
IS NOT NULL	0	No	N/A

Table 8.3 Filter Operators (Cont.)

When defining the filter, you can use different operand types:

► CONSTANT
This value is used each time the query is refreshed (until changed again in the filter definition).

  ► It's also possible to enter a variable using the `@variable` function. The variables values are automatically computed and substituted in the query text at run time.

  ► Strings don't need to be surrounded by quotes.

  ► For the MATCHES PATTERN and DIFFERENT FROM PATTERN operators, the character to use for the mask pattern is the percent symbol ("%") for relational universes and no character for multidimensional universes.

  ► For the LIST and IN LIST operators, there is only one operand where you enter the list of values separated by a semicolon (";").

► LIST OF VALUES
You can choose the value from a dialog box showing the list of values associated to the object to filter. After the choice is made, the value is used each time the query is refreshed (until changed again in the filter definition).

► OBJECT
The values for the filter are retrieved from the values of another object. This retrieval is dynamic and is done each time the query is refreshed. For example, you can filter the object "Customer" by making sure it appears in another object called "Top Customer", which has been defined in the universe. The "Top Customer" object is evaluated each time the query is run, so the filtering is dynamic.

The OBJECT option is not available for multidimensional universes.

▶ PROMPT

The operand to use in the filter is prompted each time the query is run. The prompt can be based on the filtering object, or you can reuse a parameter (prompt) previously defined in the universe.

To add a predefined filter to a query, from the UNIVERSE panel, select the filter and drag and drop it in the QUERY FILTERS panel.

To create and add a new filter to a query, follow these steps:

1. From the UNIVERSE panel, select an object and drag and drop it in the QUERY FILTERS panel to use in the query. You can also select an object from the RESULT OBJECTS panel and drag and drop it in the QUERY FILTERS panel; the object is added in the QUERY FILTERS panel and also kept in the RESULT OBJECTS panel.

2. Select the operator from the dropdown list. The supported operators are listed in Table 8.3, but this list may change depending on the capabilities of the underlying data source and on the selected object. Based on the chosen operator, the number of operands is updated.

3. For each operand (if any), select in the dropdown list the operand type, as shown in Figure 8.8. If you've chosen:

   ▶ CONSTANT, then, in the text field, enter the value to use. You may also enter the `@variable` function.

   ▶ LIST OF VALUES, then the PROMPTS dialog box opens, where you can select the values used for the filters (see Section 8.3.3).

   ▶ OBJECT, then from the UNIVERSE panel, select an object to use as an operand, and drag and drop it in the DROP AN OBJECT box.

   ▶ PROMPT, then the EDIT PROMPT dialog box opens, where you can define the options for this prompt (see Section 8.3.2).

Figure 8.8 Value Selection Methods

4. You can combine multiple filters together by dragging and dropping predefined filters or universe objects to create new filters. By default, filters are combined with an AND operator as shown in Figure 8.9.

Figure 8.9 Two Combined Filters

5. To change the operator, double-click it: the operator swaps from AND to OR and vice versa. Multidimensional universes only support the AND operator.

6. When adding new objects or filters to create complex filter, if you drop the object or filter on top of another, this creates a combined filter aggregated with the AND operator between the new filter and the existing one, as shown in Figure 8.10.

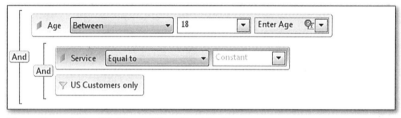

Figure 8.10 A Possible Three-Filters Combination

7. After dropping the objects in the panel, the various filters can be reorganized by moving them up and down with the mouse to obtain the correct combination.

8. Complete your query, and click REFRESH to run it.

8.2.3 Sorting Result Objects

In relational universes, a result set can be ordered by selecting objects to use as sort criteria. These objects may belong to the list of query objects, but it's not mandatory.

For a single-source universe, the sort is delegated to the underlying database by adding the Order By clause to the generated query. If the universe is multisource, then the Federation Query Server can sort the data itself if the underlying database doesn't support it.

To sort the result set, follow these steps:

1. In the RESULT OBJECTS panel toolbar, click the SORT button (⅍↓) to open the SORT dialog box, as shown in Figure 8.11.

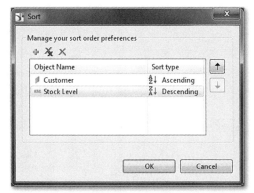

Figure 8.11 Sort Dialog Box

2. In this dialog box, click the INSERT SORT OBJECT button to open a dialog box where you can select the object to use to sort the result set. The object is displayed in the OBJECT NAME list.

3. In the SORT TYPE column, select ASCENDING or DESCENDING depending on how to sort the values.

4. If you have several objects for sorting, you can use the arrow buttons to raise or lower the order in which the sort is applied; the one on top of the list is applied first.

5. Click OK to close the SORT dialog box. If the sort is applied on an object that belongs to the list of objects in the RESULT OBJECTS panel, then the object is tagged with an A (for ascending sort) or Z (for descending sort) icon, as shown in Figure 8.12.

6. Complete your query, and click REFRESH to run it.

Figure 8.12 Objects Used to Sort Result Sets

8.3   Setting and Answering Prompts

Some queries require you to choose a context or to provide answers to prompts. When this happens, the query panel requests your feedback by showing pop-up windows. The choice of context and the answers to prompts are hence resolved before actually running the query.

This section describes the various types of prompt interfaces that can be defined and surfaced by the query panel.

8.3.1   Choosing Contexts

When you run a query for the first time, if the objects selected in the query panel don't prescribe a specific universe context (see Chapter 5, Section 5.6.3), the prompt interface is displayed to ask you to make a context choice, as shown in Figure 8.13.

Figure 8.13   Context Choice Prompt

When one context is selected in the window, all incompatible contexts are disabled. The prompt interface for the choice of a context is generated by the query panel itself and can't be customized. The choice is, by default, kept in the query definition the next time you run it. To change a context, you have to reset it in the QUERY PROPERTIES panel, as described in Section 8.4.

8.3.2   Customizing a Prompt in the Query Filters

When you create a filter, you can define one operand of the filter to be prompted to the user when the query is run. In the EDIT PROMPT dialog box shown in Figure 8.14, you can choose to either create a new prompt or reuse a parameter defined in the universe. All the operand's properties are then inherited from this universe parameter.

Figure 8.14 Edit Prompt Dialog Box

To create a new prompt, follow these steps:

1. In the EDIT PROMPT dialog box, select the NEW PROMPT radio button, as shown in Figure 8.14.
2. Set the prompt properties, as listed in Table 8.4.
3. Click OK to save your choices.

Property	Description
PROMPT WITH LIST OF VALUES	The prompt lets the user choose the value from the list of values associated with the filtered object. This option is enabled only if a list of values is associated to the filtered object.
SELECT ONLY FROM LIST	The choice of the answer is restricted to values that appear in the list of values. It's not possible to type another value in the text field. This option is enabled only if a list of values is associated to the filtered object.

Table 8.4 The Prompt Properties

Property	Description
KEEP LAST VALUES	After the first query refresh, the chosen values are kept in the query definition and are applied by default. To modify them, you have to choose new values.
OPTIONAL PROMPT	When this option is checked, the query can be executed even if you don't provide an answer for this prompt. When no answer is provided, the filter associated with the prompt is removed from the query.
SET DEFAULT VALUES	You can associate a default value to the prompt. This can simplify the workflow when running the query.

Table 8.4 The Prompt Properties (Cont.)

To reuse a parameter already defined in the universe, follow these steps:

1. In the EDIT PROMPT dialog box, select the USE UNIVERSE PARAMETERS radio button, as shown in Figure 8.15.

2. Select a parameter from the list of parameters already defined in the universe.

3. To use the selected universe parameter as an optional prompt, click the corresponding checkbox.

4. Click OK to save your choices.

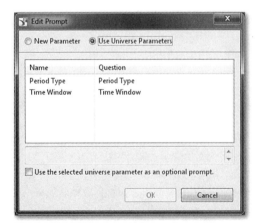

Figure 8.15 Selecting a Universe Parameter

8.3.3 Answering a Prompt

When the query is run, the prompts are presented in the following sequence:

1. Choice of the context (if necessary to run the query)

2. Universe and query prompts

The choice of the context is done in its own dialog box (refer to Section 8.3.1). The context choice appears first as its answer might impact the following list of prompts.

The universe and query prompts are all displayed in the same dialog box. This box shows:

▶ Prompts defined in filters (refer to Section 8.3.2)

▶ Objects parameters defined in the universe and used in an object definition or a filter

▶ Prompts entered through the @prompt function

If the same prompt (same question text, same data type, etc.) is used in different locations, then it's asked only once, and the answer is used for all objects, prompts, and parameters that need it.

The interface of the prompt window is shown in Figure 8.16. This interface can vary depending on the settings of the prompt's properties. On the left panel, the PROMPT SUMMARY area shows all of the prompts that have to be answered before running the query. Prompts with a green checkmark (✅) are answered and prompts with a red star (∗) are mandatory.

Figure 8.16 An Example of the Prompt User Interface

In some situations, a prompt requires another prompt to be answered before being enabled. For example, in a geographical query, you might have a prompt asking for the country and a second prompt proposing a list of values containing only the regions for the chosen country. The two prompts are said to be *cascading*. As shown in Figure 8.17, an arrow highlights which prompts are cascading and the prompt resolution is automatically requested in the correct order.

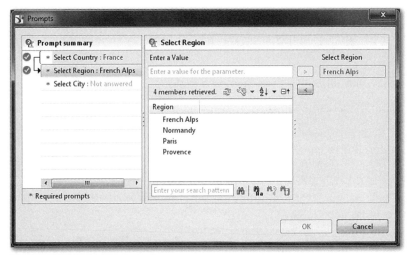

Figure 8.17 Cascading Prompts

The right panel is specific for each prompt. In this example, it displays a SELECT COUNTRY prompt. The ENTER A VALUE text box is available for adding values manually. This box is available only if the property SELECT ONLY FROM LIST is unchecked. Below the prompt, you see the list of values associated with the filtered object (or the universe prompt). Values in the list can be searched with the search box at the bottom. This list of values appears only if the PROMPT WITH LIST OF VALUES property is set.

To create cascading prompts also known as dependent parameters, refer to Chapter 7, Section 7.14.11.

If the list of values is hierarchical, then you can choose values from any level of the hierarchy as shown in Figure 8.18. A hierarchical prompt is defined with a list of values based on a custom hierarchy as discussed in Chapter 7, Section 7.13.

Figure 8.18 A Hierarchical List of Values

The panel on the far right contains the values passed to the prompt. To pass a value, add it in the text box or select it from the list, and then click on the ADD button (>).

You're allowed to pass a single value for filter operators that require a single entry of the operand (e.g., EQUAL TO, NOT EQUAL TO, LESS THAN, LESS THAN OR EQUAL TO, GREATER THAN, or GREATER THAN OR EQUAL TO). For operators accepting multiple entries, you can enter a list (e.g., IN).

Search for Values

For prompts based on list of values, you can search for values retrieved and cached in the BI platform or search for values in the database.

Only the values that match the search criteria are returned in member search dialog box. The following characters are used to define the matching criteria:

▶ "*": Matches any number of characters, even zero characters.

▶ "?": Matches exactly one character.

Click the 🔍 button to search for values in the cache or click the 🔍 button to search for values in the database. Search for values database button is enabled only if the list of values associated to the filtered object has the ALLOW USERS TO SEARCH VALUES IN THE DATABASE option activated (see Chapter 7, Section 7.13.6).

You can also click the MATCH CASE button (🔍ₐ) and SEARCH IN KEY toggle button (🔍). If the SEARCH IN KEY button is pressed, the values are searched in the primary key associated to the object (see Chapter 7, Section 7.17) for relational universes, or in the unique name for multidimensional universes.

After you've selected the values to pass for all of the prompts, click OK to run the query. The execution of the query depends on some properties that are described in the next section.

8.4 Setting the Query Properties

The QUERY PROPERTIES panel, launched from the button in the top toolbar, lets you fine-tune the execution of the defined query. The panel for relational universes is shown in Figure 8.19 and the panel for multidimensional universes is shown in Figure 8.20.

Figure 8.19 The Query Properties Panel for Relational Universes

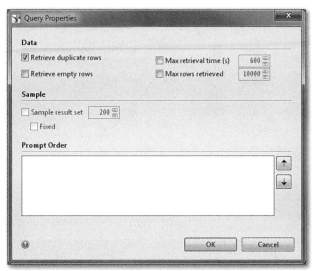

Figure 8.20 The Query Properties Panel for Multidimensional Universes

The properties you can set in the panel are described in Table 8.5.

Property	Description
RETRIEVE DUPLICATE ROWS	Checked by default; the query retrieves identical rows each time they appear. If this is unchecked, only distinct rows are retrieved. This action is an equivalent of adding a DISTINCT in an SQL statement.
RETRIEVE EMPTY ROWS	Available only for multidimensional universes. If checked, it retrieves rows even if there is no data associated with the intersection of the dimensions chosen in the result set.
MAX RETRIEVAL TIME(S)	Limits the time the queries can run. This value overrides the value set in the universe. Users can only provide a lower value than the one defined for the option in the universe.
MAX ROWS RETRIEVED	Limits the number of rows retrieved from the sources. This value overrides the value set in the universe. Users can only provide a lower value than the one defined for the option in the universe.

Table 8.5 Query Properties

Property	Description
SAMPLE RESULT SET	Available only for data sources supporting a sampling technique. It returns a sample of data. The size of the sample is defined in the numeric control. Checking the FIXED box (if supported by the data source) tells the system to retrieve the sample on the first query but then always use the same values when refreshing the query.
RESET CONTEXTS ON REFRESH	After a context has been chosen in a query, it remains in memory by default. This control lets you clear the context memory or request to enter the context choice each time the query is refreshed. This control is useful only on queries with contexts.
PROMPT ORDER	The control lets you specify the order in which prompts have to be presented to the end user when running the query. This control only applies to the prompts added in the QUERY FILTER pane and does not apply on business layer predefined filters that contain prompts.

Table 8.5 Query Properties (Cont.)

The query properties can strongly modify the result of a query, so it's important to verify that the default or the modified values are correct for the query to be run.

The information provided in the previous sections covers the majority of use cases for the query panel. In some situations, it's necessary to create more complex query statements that involve subqueries or the combination of multiple queries. The next section explains how to generate advanced query sentences.

8.5   Advanced Functionalities

We've already described the basic functionality of the query panel in the preceding sections. When dealing with complex queries, however, the usual interface might not be sufficient to build the requested statement. Four advanced functionalities enable you to go further in the definition of the query:

▸ Subquery filters
▸ Ranking filters

▸ Combined queries

▸ Custom SQL

The next few sections cover those functionalities.

8.5.1 Adding a Subquery Filter

A subquery filter is used to filter the dimensions of the data set without filtering the measures.

Example

A sales manager wants to retrieve the customer names and their global amount spent, limiting the customer list to those who purchased product A. By just adding the product A as a global filter, the amount spent represents only the amount spent for that product. By using a subquery, the manager can filter the customers who have purchased product A and then calculate the global amount spent on all products.

This filter is available only for relational universes:

▸ If the universe is single-source, then it's available only if the underlying data source of the universe supports subquery statements.

▸ If the universe is multisource, then it's always enforced by the Federation Query Server.

The list of operators supported in a subquery is listed in Table 8.3. As shown in the table, for some operators, you can afterward choose the ANY operator to select the object if the filter is valid for at least one object in the operand list, or you can choose ALL operator to select the object if the filter is valid for all objects in the operand list.

To add a subquery filter, follow these steps:

1. In the QUERY FILTERS panel toolbar, click the ADD SUBQUERY button (🖫) to add a subquery object, as shown in Figure 8.21.

Figure 8.21 The Subquery Filter Interface

2. From the UNIVERSE panel, select the dimension or the attribute to be filtered in the subquery, and drag and drop it in the DIMENSIONS boxes. You can use the same dimension/attribute or two different dimensions/attributes in the two DIMENSIONS boxes.

3. In the dropdown list, select the operator to use to filter the dimension.

4. If the selected operator supports the ALL or ANY option, then the ALL/ANY dropdown list is displayed. Select the option to apply.

5. From the UNIVERSE panel, select an object to use in the subquery filtering statement, and drag and drop it in the WHERE section of the subquery filter. Edit the filter as described in Section 8.2.2 to define the condition to apply. Note that adding an object in the WHERE section is optional.

6. Complete your query, and click REFRESH to run it.

In the Figure 8.22 example, the query returns the sales amounts by CUSTOMER NAME and RESORT, but the subquery limits the customers list to those who, globally, have an amount bigger than 100,000. In the result set, customer "KAMATA" is returned with an amount of 80368 spent in one resort, which means that "KAMATA" globally has spent more than 100,000 in all of the resorts.

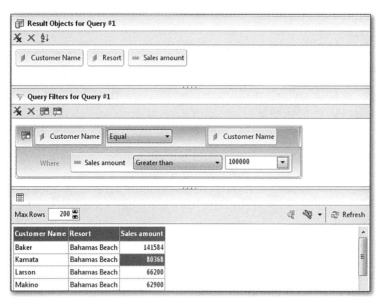

Figure 8.22 An Example of a Query Filtered with a Subquery

Subquery filters can be combined with normal filters and other subquery filters, with AND and OR operators. They can also be rearranged by moving them up and down in the interface as described in Section 8.2.2.

8.5.2 Adding a Ranking Filter

A ranking filter lets you retrieve only the top or bottom values of a dimension based on a specific measure value. This capability isn't supported in multisource or multidimensional universes. It's enabled for single-source universes only if the data source onto which the universe is built supports the ranking capability.

To build a ranking filter, follow these steps:

1. Click the ADD RANKING button (⬚) to add a ranking filter object in the QUERY FILTERS panel, as shown in Figure 8.23.

Figure 8.23 Ranking Filter Interface

2. In the first dropdown list, select a TOP or BOTTOM ranking.

3. Set the CONSTANT number of rows to return, or set it as a PROMPT to be asked when running the query. If you've selected a prompt, see Section 8.3.2.

4. From the UNIVERSE panel, select a dimension or an attribute on which the ranking is done, and drag and drop it in the DIMENSION box.

5. From the UNIVERSE panel, select a measure object on which the ranking is based, and drag and drop it in the MEASURE box.

6. Complete your query, and click REFRESH to run it.

As an example, Figure 8.24 shows a ranking filter returning the overall top three customers ranked by their sales amount.

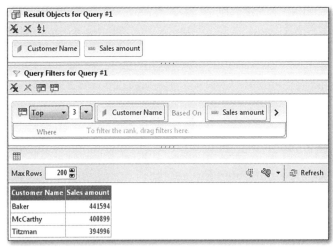

Figure 8.24 A Simple Ranking Example

Through ranking, it's also possible to create more complex requests, such as partitioning:

1. After you've defined your ranking object, as described previously, click the arrow on the right to expand the ranking object and display the RANKED BY box.

2. From the UNIVERSE panel, select a dimension or an attribute to partition the result, and drag and drop it in this RANKED BY box.

3. From the UNIVERSE panel, select an object to filter the result, and drag and drop it in the WHERE section of the ranking filter. Edit the filter as described in Section 8.2.2 to define the condition to apply.

4. Complete your query, and click REFRESH to run it.

For example, Figure 8.25 shows the top two customers for each country based on their expenses on HOTEL SUITE. The sales amount appearing in the result set is the global sales amount; it's not limited to HOTEL SUITE.

Ranking filters can be combined with normal filters and with subquery filters using the AND and OR operators.

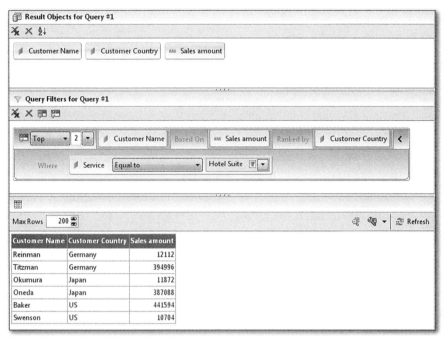

Figure 8.25 A Sophisticated Ranking Example

8.5.3 Using Combined Queries

In the query panel, you can run multiple queries and combine their results to get another result set. This enables you to create unions or intersections of query results or to subtract from one query the results of another query.

The following are the possible operators:

▶ UNION
The final result set is the union of the two result sets. Duplicate rows aren't displayed multiple times.

▶ MINUS
The content of the second query is taken away from the first query.

▶ INTERSECTION
Only the records appearing in both queries are kept in the final result set.

Union Example

A database has a list of customers partitioned by region: there is a West Customers table and an East Customers table. In the universe, two objects have been defined: one for West Customers, and another for East Customers.

To create a report showing revenue for all customers, you can define a query returning revenue for the West Customers and combine it, using the UNION operator, with a query returning revenue for the East Customers.

To combine queries, follow these steps:

1. In the QUERY PANEL toolbar, click the (SHOW/HIDE) COMBINED QUERIES PANEL toggle button (🔗) to open the COMBINED QUERIES panel, located below the universe outline.

2. By default, this panel already contains the first query. Click the INSERT COMBINED QUERY button (🔗) to add a new query, which, by default, contains the same objects as those in the RESULT OBJECTS panel. You can change the objects, but all queries must have the same number of objects, and the same object types must be found at the same position.

3. By default, when a new query is added, it's added to the current top root operator. If there isn't yet any operator, it's UNION. Double-click it to change it to MINUS, INTERSECT (for INTERSECTION), or UNION.

4. Drag and drop a query to modify its position and level in the tree of operations and create various combinations, as shown in Figure 8.26. In this example, the QUERY #2 result set is removed from the QUERY #3 result set. The remaining data is then united with the QUERY #1 result set.

5. Click REFRESH to run your query.

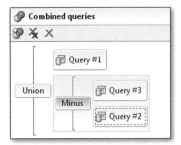

Figure 8.26 A Complex Combination of Queries

8.5.4 Setting a Custom Query Script

In some very complex scenarios, the graphical definition of the query can't express exactly the requested question. In those situations, it's possible to explicitly enter the query sentence to run against the data sources. This option is available only on relational universes using SQL as a query language. The text can be changed at will with the restriction that the query has to return the same number of fields and with the same type in the order appearing in the graphical interface.

To enter custom SQL in the query panel, follow these steps:

1. Click the VIEW SCRIPT button (📄) on the QUERY PANEL toolbar to open the QUERY SCRIPT VIEWER dialog box, as shown in Figure 8.27. This dialog box shows the query automatically generated from the objects that have been selected in the query panel through drag and drop.

2. Select the USE CUSTOM QUERY SCRIPT radio button to modify the SQL in the [QUERY] SCRIPT text field and adapt it to your needs making sure that the number of returned objects and their type hasn't changed.

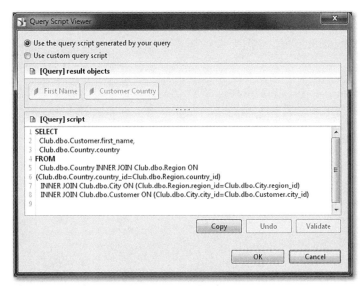

Figure 8.27 The Query Script Viewer Window

3. When the text has been modified, you can check if its syntax is correct by clicking the VALIDATE button.

4. Click OK to save the query you've entered. This query is run when you click REFRESH in the query panel. If you change the selected objects in the query panel, the query you have typed is automatically replaced by the new objects selection.

For multidimensional universes it is possible to view the MDX script that is sent to the database; click the VIEW SCRIPT button (🗒) on the QUERY PANEL toolbar to open the QUERY SCRIPT VIEWER dialog box. Note that the MDX can't be modified.

You can copy the SQL or the MDX from the QUERY SCRIPT VIEWER dialog box to paste it in the SHOW VALUES tab of the relational connection or in the QUERY tab of the OLAP connection respectively; then run the query (see Chapter 4, Section 4.7).

8.6 Summary

The query panel is a graphical user interface component implemented by client tools to connect to the semantic layer interface and expose a universe abstraction. The query panel is common to relational and multidimensional universes.

For testing purposes, IDT implements a version of the query panel that supports all semantic layer capabilities.

The query panel allows you to simply and interactively create and run queries to a data source by dragging and dropping objects from a universe built on that source.

The queries you can create in the query panel can contain filters, prompts, or advanced capabilities such as subqueries, ranking filters, combined queries, and custom SQL.

The Query Panel can be run from a universe already published in a CMS repository or in a business layer editor to test a universe before you publish it, as described in the next chapter.

The publishing step is necessary to create a universe that can be consumed by client tools either locally or in a CMS repository. Retrieval is the reverse operation that extracts resources from a published universe.

9 Publishing and Retrieving Universes

After the resources that make the universe have been authored in your local project, you must merge them into one single artifact—the universe—that can be then consumed by SAP BusinessObjects Business Intelligence (BI) 4.x client tools. This mandatory step, called *publication*, has several objectives:

▸ **Expose only the business layer part of the universe that is meaningful to users.**
Underlying artifacts such as data foundations or connectivities must remain technical details that are hidden behind the business layer.

▸ **Separate the authoring and consumption spaces.**
You can continue to work on the data foundation and business layer without impacting the published universes and the reports that use them. Client tools continue to access the universes in the consumption space, as they are doing for universes created by the Universe Design Tool.

The consumption space where a universe is published can be either the local file system (where it's accessible only by SAP BusinessObjects Web Intelligence Rich Client) or, most often, the *Universes* folder in a CMS repository, where it can take advantage of the BI platform framework.

The reverse operation, universe *retrieval*, extracts resources (data foundation, business layer, connection, or connection shortcut) from a published universe to edit them in Information Design Tool (IDT).

This chapter describes these two operations. Section 9.1 and Section 9.2 cover universe publication into a local folder and a CMS repository, respectively. Section 9.3 and Section 9.4 teach you how to retrieve a universe from a local folder and a CMS repository, respectively, and describe the related security implications. Finally, Section 9.5 details the workflows in IDT to publish and retrieve universes.

9.1 Publishing a Universe Locally

As shown in previous chapters, creating a universe is done by authoring several resources and then merging these resources to generate the actual universe that can be used by client tools. This last step, called *publication*, is mandatory and can be done to generate the universe locally on your file system. In this case, the following resources are required to make the universe:

▶ If the universe is relational, the required resources are one—and only one—local connection, a data foundation based on this connection, and a relational business layer based on this data foundation, as shown in Figure 9.1.

▶ If the universe is multidimensional, the required resources are an OLAP connection and a business layer based on it, as shown in Figure 9.2.

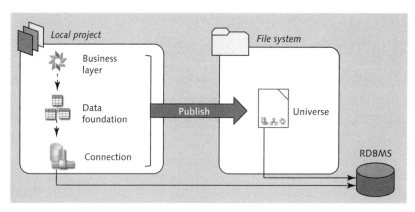

Figure 9.1 Relational Universe Published Locally

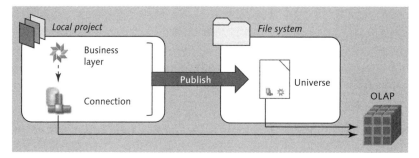

Figure 9.2 Multidimensional Universe Published Locally

The universe published locally contains a copy of these resources. Thus, it's self-sufficient because it contains all requested parameters to be consumed by client tools. You can copy, mail, or share this universe file.

You may continue to work on the resources in your local project without impacting the published universe. Changes aren't propagated to the published universe unless you republish it. IDT makes the difference between authoring and consumption workflows.

To stop a universe from being published, you actually have to delete it from the local file system where you've published it and where the tools expect to find it. The published universe is named from the business layer's name suffixed with the *.unx* file extension.

From the same resources, you can publish the universe in several folders:

▶ Republishing a universe in the same folder removes and replaces the previous universe.

▶ Publishing the universe in another folder creates a new version of this universe. IDT doesn't keep the log of these published universes, and there is no link between these published universes and the resources in the local project.

9.1.1 Connection

To publish a relational universe locally, the data foundation or business layer must rely on a local connection. When the universe is generated, this connection is directly embedded inside it. When the universe queries the data source, it retrieves the data source parameters from this connection. Communication with the data source is then done through local middleware.

You can't publish locally a multisource universe or a relational universe that queries an SAP NetWeaver BW or SAS system. These universes require a Federation Query Server and thus need to be published on a CMS repository to have access to this server. Therefore, the only possible universes that can be published locally are the relational single-source universe and multidimensional universe.

9.1.2 Security

When the universe is published locally, you can't define Central Management Console (CMC) rights or security profiles (see Chapter 10) because they must be defined in the CMS repository. Thus no security applies to the universe. The only security that can apply is the one defined for the user to access database.

In IDT the universe can be seen as an archive that contains the resources you've merged to create it. When you publish a universe locally, you actually copy a version of these resources into the universe file.

Since the connection and the database parameters that define the universe are saved in the published file, it's recommended that you publish a universe into a CMS repository rather than on the file system because the CMS offers a better protection.

9.1.3 Web Intelligence Rich Client

The only client tool that can consume and query a local universe is SAP BusinessObjects Web Intelligence Rich Client. For example, on Windows 7, SAP BusinessObjects Web Intelligence looks for universes located by default in the *C:\Users\<username>\AppData\Roaming\SAP BusinessObjects\SAP BusinessObjects Enterprise XI 4.0\Universes* folder. You can modify this folder in the WEB INTELLIGENCE OPTIONS dialog box shown in Figure 9.3.

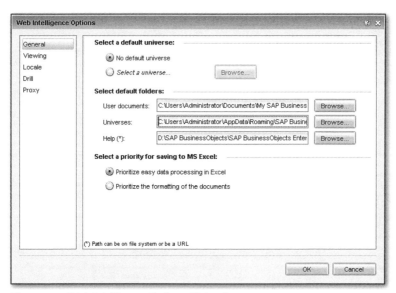

Figure 9.3 Web Intelligence Options Dialog Box

When you create an SAP BusinessObjects Web Intelligence document based on a universe, the following list of available universes is displayed, as shown in Figure 9.4:

▸ The local universes located in this folder.

▸ The universes published in this CMS repository, if a session to a CMS repository has been opened. In this case, the FOLDER column contains the cluster name with the folder containing the universe.

Both universes created by the Universe Design Tool and IDT are listed. Universe names created with IDT are suffixed with the *.unx* extension.

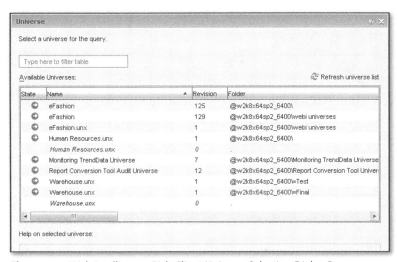

Figure 9.4 Web Intelligence Rich Client Universe Selection Dialog Box

When SAP BusinessObjects Web Intelligence Rich Client uses a local universe to create or refresh a document, it uses only the resources saved in the local universe, such as the connection, without referencing any other resources.

Using local universe is limited because it can only be consumed by SAP Business-Objects Web Intelligence running on the machine containing the folder, unless you've shared this folder on the network. Furthermore, you can't set security on this universe. To overcome these restrictions, you may publish it in a CMS repository, as described in the next section.

9.2 Publishing a Universe in a CMS Repository

In SAP BusinessObjects BI 4.x, the CMS repository is the central location where corporate BI resources (universes, reports, etc.) are shared among the different users of the SAP BusinessObjects BI system (see Chapter 3, Section 3.3). Publishing a universe into a CMS repository is very similar to a local publication. But contrary to a local universe, a universe published into a CMS repository can take advantage of the BI platform framework, including system and database authentication (Single Sign-On), security, secured connection, and so on.

You need the following resources to publish a universe:

- If the universe is relational and single-source, you need a relational connection shortcut, a data foundation based on this shortcut, and a business layer created on this data foundation, as shown in Figure 9.5.

- If the universe is relational and multisource, you need one or several relational connection shortcuts, a data foundation based on those shortcuts, and a business layer created on this data foundation, as shown in Figure 9.6.

- If the universe is multidimensional, you need an OLAP connection shortcut and a business layer created on this shortcut, as shown in Figure 9.7.

When the universe is published, it contains a copy of these resources. You may continue to modify these original authored resources without impacting the published universe. To take into consideration these changes, you need to republish the universe.

To prevent access to this universe, you must delete it from the CMS repository or set security onto it (see Chapter 10).

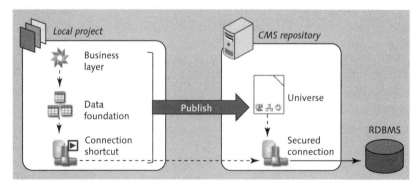

Figure 9.5 Relational Universe Published in a CMS Repository

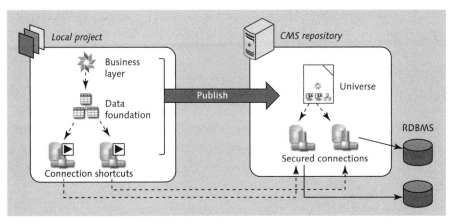

Figure 9.6 Multisource Relational Universe Published in a CMS Repository

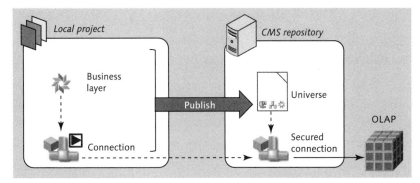

Figure 9.7 Multidimensional Universe Published in a CMS Repository

In the CMS repository, the published universe is named from the business layer's name followed by the *.unx* extension to differentiate it from a universe exported by the Universe Design Tool that doesn't have this extension.

Publication is done in a CMS repository in the *Universes* folder or one of its sub-folders. After the universe is published, client tools can access this universe and generate reports from it. The universe uses the connection shortcut(s) to identify the secured connections to use and thus query the data source(s) they reference.

9.2.1 Connection Shortcut

To publish a universe in a CMS repository, the universe must refer to a connection shortcut pointing to a connection in the same CMS repository. You can't publish a universe in a CMS repository if the business layer is still based on a local connection or a shortcut to a connection saved in another CMS repository.

If your data foundation and business layer relies on a local connection, you first need to link this resource to connections stored in the CMS repository, by following these steps:

1. If the connection hasn't yet been published in the CMS repository, publish it in the CMS repository (see Chapter 4, Section 4.6.3).

2. Create a connection shortcut that references this secured connection (see Chapter 4, Section 4.6.4).

3. Link your resources to this connection shortcut:

   ▶ For a relational business layer, link your data foundation to this shortcut (see Chapter 5, Section 5.14). If the universe is based on a multisource data foundation, by design, when you create the data foundation, you use secure connections and enter connection shortcuts.

   ▶ For a multidimensional universe, link the business layer to the OLAP connection shortcut (see Chapter 7, Section 7.25).

The universe can only be published in the CMS repository where the secured connections are located.

9.2.2 CMS Repository

To publish a universe in a CMS repository, you must be connected to this repository and have the following rights granted (see Chapter 10, Section 10.1):

▶ LOG ON TO THE DESIGNER AND VIEW THIS OBJECT IN THE CMC and PUBLISH UNIVERSES IDT rights

▶ ADD OBJECTS TO THE FOLDER right for the universe destination folder

The owner of the published universe is the user used to open the session in IDT.

In the CMS repository, as for any object, a published universe is identified by the following:

▶ **ID**
   The ID of the universe in a cluster. In the same cluster, all objects are linked with this ID because it's guaranteed to be unique in that cluster.

▶ **Cluster Unique Identifier (CUID)**
When it's generated, this CUID is statistically unique in the world. The CUID is used each time you want to promote some object from one system to another.

When you publish a universe, if you overwrite an existing universe, the new universe takes the ID and CUID of the universe it overwrites.

It's possible to save the same universe in different CMS repositories, as long as you reconnect the corresponding data foundation or business layer to shortcuts to secured connections saved in those CMS repositories before publishing the universe.

In a CMS repository, a universe can be consumed by most SAP BusinessObjects BI 4.x client tools: SAP BusinessObjects Web Intelligence, SAP BusinessObjects Explorer, SAP Crystal Reports for Enterprise, SAP BusinessObjects Dashboards, SAP Lumira, SAP Predictive Analysis, and so on.

After the universe is published in the CMS, you can take advantage of the CMS framework. For example, you can define security for this universe to set the users who can access and use this universe or filter the metadata and data they can access (see Chapter 10). If the processing is done on the server side, then it uses the engines running on the server and the drivers and middleware installed server-side.

9.2.3 Managing Published Universes

Most administration tasks are done in the Central Management Console (CMC). This SAP BusinessObjects BI 4.x administration tool is available through a web browser at the following default URL: *http://<servername>:<port>/BOE/CMC*.

In the CMC, the UNIVERSES tab lists all universes published in the CMS repository, by both IDT and the Universe Design Tool, as shown in Figure 9.8. The universes have different icons (for IDT and for the Universe Design Tool). Furthermore, the universes created by IDT have the *.unx* extension, and their type in the TYPE column is UNIVERSE (INFORMATION DESIGN TOOL).

From the UNIVERSES tab, you can perform some tasks not available in IDT:

▶ Move a universe in another folder.

▶ Display universe properties (ID, CUID, etc.).

▶ Set universe security rights and assign object access levels (see Chapter 10, Section 10.1).

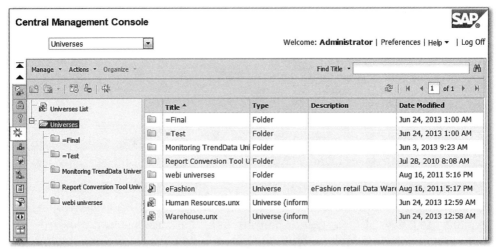

Figure 9.8 Universes Tab in the Central Management Console

Some other tasks aren't available in the CMC and must be done in IDT, either directly (see Section 9.5.3) or indirectly:

▶ To copy a universe, republish it in another folder.

▶ To change its connection(s), change them in its data foundation or business layer and republish the universe.

▶ To manage and assign security profiles, open the Security Editor (see Chapter 10, Section 10.3).

You can also run a query on top of the published universe in the IDT query panel (see Section 9.5.3).

9.3 Retrieving a Local Universe

After you've authored and published your universe, you keep its authored resources as a reference. The published universes are considered artifacts generated from these resources. In some situations, however, you don't have access to the authored resources but only to the published universe. For example, you may have lost the authored resources, or the universe may have been published or sent to you by another designer who did not share the data foundation and business layer with you.

To recover from these situations and be able to edit the universe, it's possible to extract from a published universe the different resources used to create it. This step, called *universe retrieval*, can be used to edit a universe if you don't have the resources used to create it. Retrieving a universe can be seen as the reverse workflow of publication.

A universe can be retrieved either from the local file system or from a CMS repository. Both workflows look similar. Let's review the local retrieval to compare it with retrieving a universe from a CMS repository in Section 9.4.

9.3.1 Retrieved Resources

When you retrieve a local universe, a copy of the resources used to generate it, which are saved in its file, is extracted from it and saved in a local project. If the universe is relational, the resources include its relational connection, data foundation, and business layer, as shown in Figure 9.9. If the universe is multidimensional, the resources include its OLAP connection and business layer, as shown in Figure 9.10. Only single-source universes can be published locally. Thus, retrieving a local universe can only return one connection.

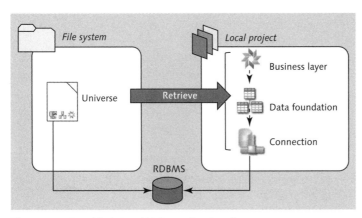

Figure 9.9 Local Relational Universe Retrieved

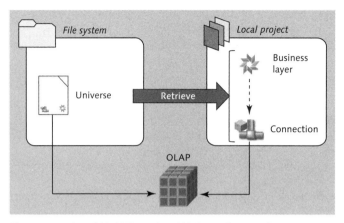

Figure 9.10 Local Multidimensional Universe Retrieved

Once retrieved, you can re-edit and republish these resources into a universe either locally or in another folder in the CMS repository. Retrieving a universe doesn't modify or delete it from the local folder where it has been published. The universe remains available for consumption. You can edit the retrieved resources without impacting this universe, unless you republish it.

9.3.2 Folder

When you retrieve a universe, to avoid conflict with resources that may already exist in the local project, its resources are retrieved and saved in a specific folder created in a local project or one of its folders. The name of this created folder is *retrieval-<date>-<time>*. When a universe is retrieved, the retrieved resources have no link with the source universe they have been retrieved from.

Retrieving a universe isn't a task that should be carried out often, and should only be considered as a recovery facility. If you retrieve universes too often, you may end up with too many retrieval folders in your local projects because a new folder is created at each retrieval.

9.4 Retrieving a Universe from the CMS Repository

Retrieving a universe from a CMS repository is similar to retrieving it from the local file system in two ways. It creates a copy of its resources in a local project in a local folder called *retrieval-<date>-<time>* and it also doesn't modify the published universe. This one remains available for consumption while you're editing its retrieved resources.

The main differences with the retrieval of a universe published locally are the connection shortcut and security.

9.4.1 Connection Shortcuts

When you retrieve a universe from a CMS repository, a copy of the resources used to publish it are retrieved from the universe and are re-created in your local project:

▶ If the universe is relational and single-source, the retrieval creates a local shortcut to the relational connection saved in the CMS repository that the universe queries, its data foundation, and its business layer, as shown in Figure 9.11.

▶ If the universe is relational and multisource, the retrieval creates shortcuts to the relational connections saved in the CMS repository that the universe queries, its data foundation, and its business layer, as shown in Figure 9.12.

▶ If the universe is multidimensional, the retrieval creates a shortcut to the OLAP connection saved in the CMS repository that the universe queries and its business layer, as shown in Figure 9.13.

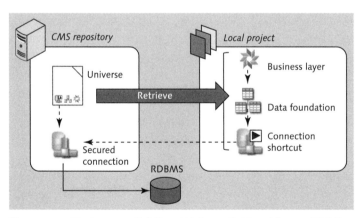

Figure 9.11 Single-source Relational Universe Retrieved from a CMS Repository

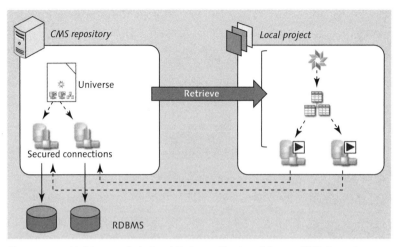

Figure 9.12 Multisource Relational Universe Retrieved from a CMS Repository

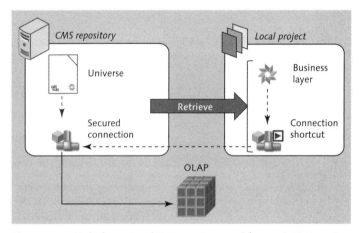

Figure 9.13 Multidimensional Universe Retrieved from a CMS Repository

The connection shortcuts are used to reference the secured connections in the CMS repository. These connections are not retrieved automatically because they contain sensitive details such as server names, user names and passwords.

Once retrieved, it's possible to attach a data foundation or a multidimensional business layer to another connection shortcut or connection. You may then refresh the data foundation or business layer to make sure it's properly synchronized with the data source.

9.4.2 Security

To retrieve a universe from a CMS repository, you must be connected to this CMS repository and have the following rights granted (see Chapter 10, Section 10.1):

▶ IDT right: Retrieve universes

▶ Universe right: Retrieve universe to retrieve the corresponding universe

▶ Universe right: Save for all users to remove the security from the authored resources

When you create a business layer or a data foundation in a local project, the business layers or data foundations aren't secured, and anyone can open them in IDT. But when you retrieve universes from a CMS repository, by default, the data foundation and business layer created in the local project are secured:

▶ They contain the cluster ID from where they have been retrieved.

▶ To open them in IDT, you first need to be authenticated to this cluster. If a session to this CMS is already open, it's used by default to authenticate to this CMS repository.

If you don't authenticate to the source CMS repository, then you can't open the resource editor, and an error message is displayed, as shown in Figure 9.14.

Figure 9.14 Incorrect Authentication Error Message

Once authenticated, however, you can run any action on the resources, except the ones involving the secured connection shortcut(s) used by the data foundation or the business layer because you still need to authenticate to the CMS repository to get access to these secured connections.

To avoid having to authenticate to use these retrieved resources, follow these two steps:

▶ When you retrieve the universe, select the SAVE FOR ALL USERS option. This removes the data foundation and business layer security, so you don't need to authenticate to open them.

▶ Once retrieved, you may link your resources to local connection(s) instead of the connection shortcut(s).

When IDT starts, it opens the editors from your previous session. If one of these editors were used to display a data foundation or business layer retrieved from a CMS repository and not saved for all users, then, during IDT startup, you're prompted to authenticate to this CMS repository.

Authentication

If they aren't saved for all users, a retrieved data foundation and business layer can only be opened if you authenticate to the source CMS repository. If you've uninstalled your SAP BusinessObjects BI 4.x deployment, you're no longer able to open these resources. To avoid this situation, before uninstalling your cluster, you should either retrieve your universe again with the SAVE FOR ALL USERS option, or use Promotion Management in the CMC to back up your universe in a LCMBIAR file. You can then re-export to a new reinstalled cluster later.

9.5 Information Design Tool Workflows

After you've authored the different resources in your local project, you use IDT to generate and publish the universe locally or in a CMS repository. IDT is also used to retrieve universes to create a local copy of their resources.

The following sections detail these workflows, as well as some information related to universe management in the CMS repository.

9.5.1 Publishing a Universe Locally

To publish a universe locally in the file system, follow these steps:

1. Make sure the authored resources use only one local connection.

2. In the LOCAL PROJECTS view, right-click the business layer of the universe to publish, and select PUBLISH • TO A LOCAL FOLDER. The PUBLISH UNIVERSE dialog box opens.

3. If you want to scan the data foundation and business layer looking for errors through integrity check (see Chapter 5, Section 5.15 and Chapter 7, Section 7.26):

   ▶ Select the rules to check in the left pane by clicking their checkboxes. You may also click the CHECK ALL or UNCHECK ALL links to select or unselect all of these rules.

   ▶ Click CHECK INTEGRITY to start the scan. After it's completed, any found error and warning is displayed in the dialog box, as shown in Figure 9.15.

   ▶ When you've reviewed these messages, if needed, click CANCEL to cancel the publication and make any appropriate changes.

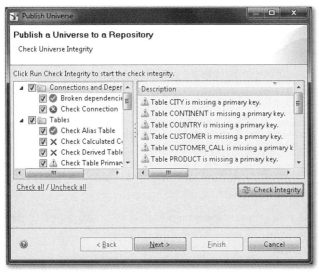

Figure 9.15 Check Integrity

4. Click NEXT to enter the destination folder for the universe.

5. In the FOLDER PATH text field, click the [...] button to open the BROWSE FOR FOLDER dialog box.

6. Navigate to the destination folder, and click OK to close the dialog box.

7. Click FINISH to publish the universe. After the universe is published, a success message is displayed.

8. Click CLOSE to close the PUBLISH UNIVERSE dialog box.

9.5.2   Publishing a Universe in a CMS Repository

Before publishing a universe in a CMS repository, make sure its resources depend on secured connection(s) saved in this CMS repository. Then, to publish it in the CMS repository, follow these steps:

1. Select the business layer in the LOCAL PROJECTS view.

2. Right-click this business layer, and select PUBLISH • TO A REPOSITORY.

3. If a session to this CMS repository is already open, then it's used to connect to this CMS repository. Otherwise, the OPEN SESSION dialog box opens. Use it to open a session to the CMS repository where the universe must be published (see Chapter 3, Section 3.4).

4. The PUBLISH UNIVERSE dialog box opens. To scan the data foundation and business layer looking for errors through the integrity check (see Chapter 5, Section 5.15 and Chapter 7, Section 7.26):

   ▶ Select the rules to check in the left pane by clicking their checkboxes. You may also click the CHECK ALL or UNCHECK ALL links to select or unselect all of these rules.

   ▶ Click CHECK INTEGRITY to start the scan. After it's completed, any found error and warning is displayed in the dialog box.

   ▶ When you've reviewed these messages, if needed, click CANCEL to cancel the publication and make any appropriate changes.

5. Click NEXT to open the CMS repository browser, and select the destination folder for the universe.

6. Click FINISH to publish the universe. After the universe is published, a success message is displayed.

7. Click CLOSE to close the PUBLISH UNIVERSE dialog box. If the universe doesn't display in the REPOSITORY RESOURCES view, click REFRESH (📲) in its toolbar.

You can also publish a universe in a CMS repository through drag and drop by following these steps:

1. Open the REPOSITORY RESOURCES and LOCAL PROJECTS views side by side in the IDT interface.

2. In the REPOSITORY RESOURCES view, open the CMS repository where the universe must be published.

3. In the LOCAL PROJECTS view, select the business layer of the universe to publish.

4. Drag and drop it in the REPOSITORY RESOURCES view in the destination folder for the universe. The PUBLISH UNIVERSE dialog box opens.

5. As in the previous workflow, you may scan the data foundation and business layer to look for errors before publishing the universe. Select the rules to run, and click CHECK INTEGRITY.

6. Click FINISH to publish the universe in the selected folder.

9.5.3 Managing Universes Published in a CMS Repository

After a universe has been published in the CMS repository, the REPOSITORY RESOURCES view provides some capabilities to interact and administrate the universe. The right-click context menu contains the following commands for the universe:

▶ CHECK INTEGRITY
Runs the rules to check the validity of the universe to publish (see Chapter 5, Section 5.15 and Chapter 7, Section 7.26).

▶ RUN QUERY
Launches the query panel (see Chapter 8) on the published universe to run a query. Security that applies to the account used to open the session is taken into consideration (see Chapter 10, Section 10.9).

▶ RETRIEVE UNIVERSE
Retrieves the universe (see Section 9.4).

▶ RENAME UNIVERSE
Renames the universe name in the CMS repository.

▶ MIGRATE TO SAP HANA and POST-MIGRATION
Manages the universe conversion into a universe for SAP HANA (see Chapter 12, Section 12.4).

▶ DELETE UNIVERSE
Deletes the universe.

9.5.4 Show Repository Dependencies

A data foundation or a business layer can be used to generate several universes in the same CMS repository. To keep track of all of these universes, you may look for dependencies between one data foundation or business layer and the universes of a CMS repository. To do so, follow these steps:

1. Select a data foundation or a business layer in the LOCAL PROJECTS view.

2. Right-click this resource and select SHOW REPOSITORY DEPENDENCIES.

3. In the SHOW REPOSITORY DEPENDENCIES dialog box in Figure 9.16, select or open a session to the CMS repository in which you want to look for the universes. The dialog box then displays the list of universes where the selected resource has contributed.

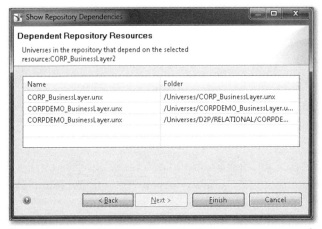

Figure 9.16 List of Universes Found in Show Repository Dependencies

This result list may return more universes than the selected resource has actually generated, especially if a resource has been copied:

▸ If you copy a resource, then a repository search for this copy or the original resource returns the universes published from both resources.

▸ If you retrieve a universe from a CMS repository, then the retrieved resources are also considered as copies of the original resources. A repository search also returns universes published from both resources.

9.5.5 Retrieving a Local Universe

To retrieve a local universe, follow these steps:

1. In the LOCAL PROJECTS view, select the local destination project or folder for the retrieved universe resources.

2. To open the RETRIEVE UNIVERSE dialog box, as shown in Figure 9.17, select FILE • RETRIEVE A PUBLISHED UNIVERSE • FROM A LOCAL FOLDER, or right-click the project or folder and select RETRIEVE A PUBLISHED UNIVERSE • FROM A LOCAL FOLDER.

Figure 9.17   Retrieve Universe Dialog Box for a Local Universe

3. In the FILE PATH text field, enter the universe full path or click the [...] button to open the file system browser and select the universe to retrieve.

4. Click FINISH to create the *retrieval-<date>-<time>* folder in the selected project or folder, retrieve the universe, and save its connection, data foundation (if the universe is relational), and business layer in this folder. The retrieved business layer opens in its editor.

9.5.6   Retrieving a Universe from a CMS Repository

To retrieve a universe from a CMS repository, follow these steps:

1. In the REPOSITORY RESOURCES view, open a session to the CMS repository containing the universe to retrieve.

2. Navigate in the *Universes* folder and its subfolders to select the universe to retrieve.

3. Right-click the universe, and select the RETRIEVE UNIVERSE command.

4. In the SELECT A LOCAL PROJECT dialog box, select a local project or a folder, as shown in Figure 9.18.

5. To remove security from the generated resources, select the SAVE FOR ALL USERS checkbox; otherwise, keep it unchecked.

6. Click OK to create the *retrieval-<date>-<time>* folder in the selected project or folder, retrieve the universe, and save its connection shortcut(s), data foundation (if the universe is relational), and business layer in this folder. The retrieved business layer opens in its editor.

Figure 9.18 Local Project Selection

You may also retrieve a universe by following these steps:

1. In the LOCAL PROJECTS view, select the local destination project or folder for the retrieved universe resources.

2. In the FILE menu, select the RETRIEVE A PUBLISHED UNIVERSE • FROM A REPOSITORY command or right-click the project or folder, and in the context menu, select the RETRIEVE A PUBLISHED UNIVERSE • FROM A REPOSITORY command.

3. In the RETRIEVE UNIVERSE dialog box, create a session to the CMS repository containing the universe to retrieve or open a predefined one (see Chapter 3, Section 3.4).

4. In the *Universes* folder, navigate into the folder tree to select the universe to retrieve, as shown in Figure 9.19.

5. To remove security from the generated resources, select the SAVE FOR ALL USERS checkbox; otherwise, keep it unchecked.

6. Click FINISH to create the *retrieval-<date>-<time>* folder in the selected project or folder, retrieve the universe, and save its connection shortcut(s), data foundation (if the universe is relational), and business layer in this folder. The retrieved business layer opens in its editor.

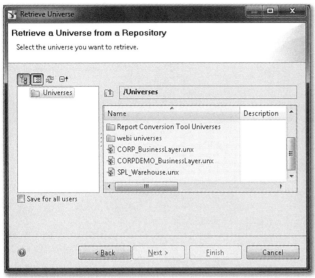

Figure 9.19 Universe Selection in a CMS Repository

9.6 Summary

Publishing is the mandatory step to create a universe from its authored resources and make it available to client tools for consumption. A universe can be published either locally or in a CMS repository:

▶ Published locally, the universe can be based on only one local connection. It doesn't enforce security and can only be used by SAP BusinessObjects Web Intelligence Rich Client.

▶ Published in a CMS repository, the universe must be based on one or more secured connections from this CMS repository. It enforces the BI platform security and can be used by most client tools of the SAP BusinessObjects BI 4.x suite.

Universe retrieval is the reverse operation: It extracts the resources from the published universe and saves them in a local project for further authoring. To open a data foundation and business layer retrieved from a secured universe, you must by default authenticate to the source CMS repository. You can remove this authentication by saving the resources for all users when retrieving the universe.

Because universes can be used to centralize access to data sources, they also propose some security capabilities to control access to these data sources.

10 Securing Universes

The SAP BusinessObjects Business Intelligence (BI) 4.x client tools are intended to be deployed on top of enterprise databases and data warehouses. By nature, these databases contain enterprise operational data that may be sensitive. In this context, security is a must-have requirement because it ensures that unauthorized persons can't see data they aren't permitted to see, don't perform an action they aren't allowed to take, or don't corrupt data they have been able to access.

To secure a universe, it must be published in the Central Management Server (CMS) repository, where it can take advantage of the following security concepts:

- *Security rights*, enforced by the SAP BusinessObjects BI 4.x platform.
- *Object access level*, defined for objects of the business layer.
- *Security profiles*, which can be seen as the evolution of the Universe Design Tool's access restrictions. Security profiles define security at two different levels:
  - A *data security profile* handles security related to database schemas, connections, and some universe parameters.
  - A *business security profile* secures objects defined in the business layer. For multidimensional universes, it also includes connection replacement.
- *User attributes*, which allow you to create new variables for the `@variable` function.

In the next few sections, we cover these security concepts, beginning with security rights and then moving on to the object access level and the various security profiles and user attributes.

10.1 Rights

When using Information Design Tool (IDT) and resources that are stored in the CMS repository, it's possible to define rights that control what actions users can do with these resources. For this purpose, semantic layer resources enforce the rights framework provided by the BI platform. The following objects in the CMS repository support general rights enforced by the platform, but they can also support specific rights:

- **Information Design Tool**
  To define rights for the IDT application itself. This application supports specific rights.

- **Universe (Information Design Tool)**
  To define rights for universes created by IDT. These universes support specific rights.

- **Relational connection**
  To define rights for relational connections created by the Universe Design Tool and IDT (see Chapter 4, Section 4.1.1). These connections support specific rights.

- **Data Federator Data Source**
  To define rights for relational connections to SAP NetWeaver Business Warehouse (BW) and SAS enforced by the Federation Query Server and created in IDT (see Chapter 4, Section 4.1.2). These data sources support specific rights.

- **OLAP connection**
  To define rights for OLAP connections created in IDT and the Central Management Console (CMC) (see Chapter 4, Section 4.1.3).

Note

In the CMC, the Connection InfoObject isn't used for connections created in IDT, but for connections created in SAP Crystal Reports Business View Manager.

10.1.1 Information Design Tool Rights

The IDT application leverages only the rights related to a CMS repository when a session to this CMS repository has been opened. This session can only be opened if you have the application's Log on to the Designer and view this object in the CMC right granted for this repository. When several sessions are opened in parallel, the rights that apply are the ones computed for the account used to open the session used to access the resource. Once connected to a CMS repository, IDT enforces the specific rights discussed in the following subsections.

Administer Security Profiles

This right allows you to use the Security Editor to create, administer, and assign universe data and business security profiles.

Compute Statistics

This right allows you to launch the Statistics Management dialog box used to select tables and columns to calculate and publish the statistics used by Federation Query Server for multisource universes or universes based on a relational connection to SAP NetWeaver BW or SAS, as described in Chapter 6, Section 6.7.

Create, Modify, or Delete Connections

This right allows you to create a connection or publish a local connection into a CMS repository. It also allows you to administer secured connections in this CMS repository. To create a secured connection, you also need the Add objects to the folder right granted for the connection folder where the connection is created. To edit a secured connection, you also need the Edit objects right for this connection and the Delete objects right to delete it.

Publish Universes

This right allows you to publish a universe in the CMS repository. To publish a universe, you also need the Add objects to the folder right for the folder where the universe is published, and the data foundation or business layer must be based on a connection shortcut that references a connection in the CMS repository.

Retrieve Universes

This right allows you to retrieve a universe from a CMS repository to edit locally its data foundation (if any) and business layer. To retrieve a universe, you must also have the RETRIEVE UNIVERSE right for this universe.

Save for All Users

This right allows you to retrieve the corresponding data foundation (if any) and business layer from a universe published in the CMS and save them locally as unsecured resources. To save a universe for all users, you also need to have the IDT RETRIEVE UNIVERSES and the universe RETRIEVE UNIVERSE rights.

Share Projects

This right allows you to create shared projects and to synchronize objects in these shared projects.

10.1.2 Universe Rights

In IDT, when you edit a universe through its data foundation or its business layer, no security rights apply. But when you merge these resources to publish the universe in the CMS repository, the rights described next apply to the generated universe. These rights apply only in IDT, except CREATE AND EDIT QUERIES BASED ON THE UNIVERSE and DATA ACCESS, which impact the client tools that consume the universe.

If the universe was already published, when you republish it and replace the previous universe, the previously assigned rights are kept: the users and groups to which they were assigned and their values.

Assign Security Profiles

This right allows you to assign or unassign this universe's security profiles to a user or a group. To connect to the Security Editor, you also must have the ADMINISTER SECURITY PROFILES right.

Create and Edit Queries Based on the Universe

This right allows you to create or edit queries based on this universe. It's enforced both in IDT and in client tools that support these universes. This right is useful if you want your users to be able to refresh reports based on this universe but without being able to create new queries.

If the right is denied, you can't run a query based on this universe, whether from the IDT REPOSITORY RESOURCES view, the Security Editor, or any client tools that consume this universe.

Data Access

This right allows you to query data through this universe. This right secures data only and doesn't cover metadata. If the right is denied in IDT, you can't query data from this published universe.

In client tools that may support universe created with IDT, any workflows that retrieve data through this universe fail. For example, in SAP BusinessObjects Web Intelligence or SAP Crystal Reports for Enterprise, when you try to create a new document from this universe, after you have created your query with the query panel and try to run it, an error message is displayed.

Edit Security Profiles

This right allows you to create, edit, or delete data or business security profiles and modify aggregation options. To connect to the Security Editor, you must also have the ADMINISTER SECURITY PROFILES right.

Retrieve Universe

This right allows you to retrieve a universe from a CMS repository and edit its data foundation (if any) and business layer locally. To retrieve a universe, you must also have the IDT's RETRIEVE UNIVERSES right granted.

10.1.3 Relational Connection Rights

This connection is created in IDT. It supports the following specific rights.

Data Access

This right allows you to retrieve data from the data source defined in this connection. However, it doesn't prevent reading metadata from the database (such as the database model). If the right is denied, any workflow that needs to query data from the database referenced by the connection fails, both in metadata design tools and client tools. For example, in IDT, any workflow that queries data from the database fails, such as seeing the table's value or running a query through a universe based on this connection. Identically, running a query through a universe based on this connection in SAP BusinessObjects Web Intelligence also fails.

Download Connection Locally

This right allows the tools running on the desktop to retrieve all of the connection parameters from the CMS repository. (See also Chapter 4, Section 4.4.3 for more details.) If the right is denied, the different tools can retrieve only a subset of the connection parameters. For any request to the database, they no longer use local middleware, but they need to contact the Connection Server hosted on the server. The Connection Server then runs the request and returns the result to the client tools. Thus, the connection's most sensitive parameters (user name, password) remain on the CMS repository and aren't stored on the client machine. Consider these potential impacts for these desktop tools:

- In the SAP BusinessObjects Web Intelligence Rich Client, the connection parameters can't be downloaded on the cache. Thus, in the SAP BusinessObjects Web Intelligence Rich Client, in offline mode, it's no longer possible to run a query based on a universe that is based on this connection.
- In IDT:
  - Only the parameters that aren't considered sensible are displayed: connectivity type, network layer, authentication mode, and connection configuration parameters (see Chapter 4, Section 4.5.1 and Section 4.5.2).
  - In the connection's editor, the EDIT and CHANGE DRIVER buttons are disabled, preventing you from editing this connection.

10.1.4 OLAP Connection Rights

The OLAP Connection InfoObject type is the connection used by IDT, SAP direct access (supported by SAP BusinessObjects Web Intelligence, SAP Crystal Reports for Enterprise, and SAP BusinessObjects Dashboards) and SAP BusinessObjects Analysis, edition for OLAP. It doesn't support specific rights.

10.1.5 Data Federator Data Source Rights

This InfoObject is used for relational connections to SAP NetWeaver BW or SAS, created in IDT and based on the Federation Query Server. It can be used only with universes created in IDT. It supports general rights and one specific right, described next.

Data Access

This right allows you to retrieve data from the database defined in this connection. As for relational connections described in Section 10.1.3, if this right is denied, then any workflow that needs access to the database referenced by the connection fails, both in metadata design tools and client tools.

10.2 Object Access Level

You can also assign access levels to objects of universes created with IDT. An access level is a property that can be set to objects that define the business layer:

► For a relational universe, these objects are dimensions, measures, and attributes.

► For a multidimensional universe, these objects are dimensions, attributes, measures, calculated measures, filters, hierarchies, and named sets.

The access level defines the object level of confidentiality. It can take the following values, in increasing order of confidentiality:

► Public (the default value and the least confidential)

► Controlled

► Restricted

► Confidential

► Private (the most confidential)

These access levels can be set in the ADVANCED tab of the object editor, as shown in Figure 10.1.

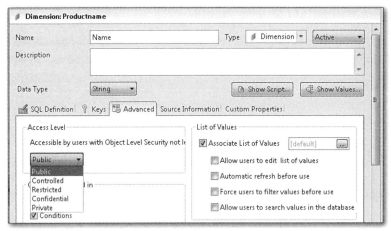

Figure 10.1 Object Access Level Definition

To enforce the access levels of these objects, you need to publish your universe in a CMS repository (see Chapter 9, Section 9.2). In the CMC, a user or a group can be assigned any of these access levels for a universe or a universe folder: Public, Controlled, Restricted, Confidential, or Private. These access levels are similar to the ones you can set to universe objects. A user can see only objects of the universe whose access levels are lower than or equal to his own access level.

> **Example**
>
> A user who has been assigned the Restricted access level for a universe can see only Public, Controlled, and Restricted objects of this universe.

If an object is denied through an object access level, it means two things:

▶ In the query panel, this object isn't exposed by the universe.

▶ A query containing this object fails, and no data is retrieved from the database. The user can edit the query to remove the object and run the query.

If an access level is explicitly assigned to a user for a universe, this access level is used without taking the inherited ones into consideration.

10.3   Security Profiles

In IDT, data security profiles and business security profiles are extensions of the Universe Design Tool's access restrictions. Security profiles can be seen as a superset of access restrictions:

- The concepts are similar, and access restrictions can be mapped into data and business security profiles. However, security profiles offer some new capabilities.

- You can create data security profiles only for relational universes, whereas you can create business security profiles for both relational and multidimensional universes, as shown in Figure 10.2 and Figure 10.3.

This section details common characteristics of security profiles; Section 10.4 and Section 10.5 focus on data and business security profiles, respectively.

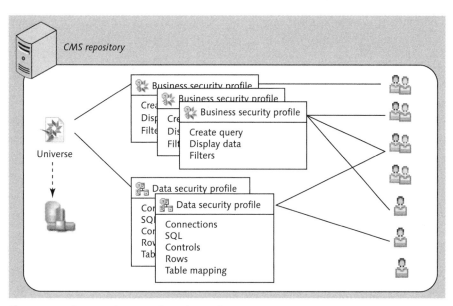

Figure 10.2   Security Overview for Relational Universe

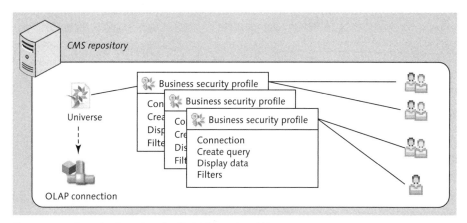

Figure 10.3 Security Overview for Multidimensional Universe

10.3.1 Assigned Users and Groups

Data and business security profiles can only be created after the universe has been published in a CMS repository. By default, no data security profiles and no business security profiles are created for this universe or assigned to users or groups. The universe isn't considered secured, and no security profile applies.

You can secure the universe by creating data and business security profiles and by assigning them to users or groups. Remember that a data or business security profile assigned to a user applies to the *user*, and a data or business security profile assigned to a group applies to *all users and groups* it contains.

A data or business security profile can be attached to only one universe and applies only to this universe. You can assign several security profiles to the same user or group.

In the CMS repository, security profiles are created and stored as InfoObjects linked to the universe they secure. They are also linked to the users and groups they are assigned to. Thus, these security profiles and their assigned users and groups aren't changed if the universe is modified and republished.

Identically, a change in a data or business security profile definition doesn't modify its assigned users or groups.

To compute the list of security profiles that apply to a user, this user must be given the VIEW OBJECTS right for all groups from which he can inherit security profiles. If a user can't see the groups he belongs to, he can't get the list of security profiles that apply to him.

10.3.2 Consumption

After the effective data and business security profiles that must apply to a user have been computed from aggregation options, they must be applied. In IDT, security profiles apply depending on how you run a query:

▶ In authoring mode, when you run a query directly from the business layer editor, data and business security profiles do not apply.

▶ IDT allows you to run secured queries (see Section 10.9). When you run a query on top of a published universe from the REPOSITORY RESOURCES or SECURITY EDITOR views, the query takes into consideration the data and business security profiles that apply to the user whose account has been used to open the CMS session.

When a client tool uses a universe to query data from a database, security profiles are applied for any request to the database at query time:

▶ During the query itself

▶ When retrieving a list of values, if the table on which the rows restriction is based is involved in the computation of the list of values

10.4 Data Security Profiles

Data security profiles can be created only for relational universes. It isn't possible to create them for multidimensional universes.

In IDT, relational universes rely on a data foundation that is the database abstraction used by universes. Data foundation concepts are secured by data security profiles that cover almost the same concepts and behaviors as the Universe Design Tool's access restrictions, except object access restrictions, whose equivalent is supported by the business security profile (see Section 10.5). The following are the data security profiles, which appear as tabs in Figure 10.4:

▶ CONNECTIONS data security profile

▶ CONTROLS data security profile

▶ SQL data security profile

▶ Rows data security profile

▶ TABLES data security profile

Figure 10.4 Data Security Profile Dialog Box

Furthermore, they have been adapted to take multisource universes into consideration.

> **Warning!**
>
> The Rows and TABLES data security profiles do not apply if the user has directly edited the generated SQL, for example, in SAP BusinessObjects Web Intelligence. For this reason, it's important to secure the ability to edit SQL in SAP BusinessObjects Web Intelligence through the QUERY SCRIPT: ENABLE EDITING right or the document EDIT SCRIPT right.

10.4.1 Connections

The CONNECTIONS data security profile is used to define alternate secured connections for a user. With this security profile, you can select a connection for a user from the *Connections* folder or subfolders in the CMS repository that replaces the default universe connection. When this user runs a query on top of the universe, the connection defined at the data security profile is used instead of the one defined by default for this universe.

If the universe is a multisource universe, the CONNECTIONS data security profile allows the replacement of each individual, used connection. To select the replacement connection, you must be connected and authenticated to the CMS repository. Thus, CMS rights apply to you; that is, you can see only the connections for which you have the VIEW OBJECTS right granted.

> **Warning!**
>
> When assigning a CONNECTIONS data security profile to a user or a group, you should check that the user or group is granted the connection security rights needed to query the database with this replacement connection.

Only relational connections can be selected as alternate connections. A connection can be replaced only by a connection of the same type:

- Only a relational connection to SAP NetWeaver BW can replace a relational connection to SAP NetWeaver BW (see Chapter 4, Section 4.1.2).

- Only a relational connection to SAS data source can replace a relational connection to SAS (see Chapter 4, Section 4.1.2).

- A relational connection of another type can be replaced by any relational connections *except* by a relational connection to SAP NetWeaver BW or SAS. However, we do not recommend that you replace a connection to SAP HANA with any relational connection of another type and vice-versa because of some SAP HANA specificities, such as SAP HANA variables and input parameters (*see* Chapter 12, Section 12.3.3).

When this security profile is applied, any query is sent to the database referenced by the replacement connection instead of the original connection. This can be useful to prevent a user from seeing a database and the data it contains. To do so, follow these steps to use a CONNECTIONS data security profile:

1. In your database, create another schema with the same structure as the original database, and fill it with sample data.

2. Create a connection to this new database containing sample data.

3. For a universe that uses the connection to the original database, create a CONNECTIONS data security profile to replace this source connection by this new connection.

4. Assign this CONNECTIONS data security profile to the user or user group.

When the user creates a query on top of this universe, then the query is sent to the database containing the sample data. This sample data set is returned, instead of the actual data from the original database.

The databases referenced by the two connections must have the same structure. This isn't checked when the CONNECTIONS data security profile is created. But at query time, an error is raised if the query references tables or columns that aren't found in the replacement database.

10.4.2 Controls

In relational universes, the CONTROLS data security profile is used to override some parameters defined at the universe level. Users and groups who have been assigned this CONTROLS data security profile use these parameters instead of the ones defined in the universe.

These parameters are related to time-outs and limits when retrieving data from databases:

▶ Limit size of result set to

▶ Limit execution time to

▶ Warn if cost estimates exceed

These parameters are typically used to secure the reporting servers and make sure they do not freeze by limiting the set of data they have to handle. In the universe, these parameters are defined in the business layer (see Chapter 7, Section 7.30).

This data security profile can be used to define some conservative values for a universe to prevent most users from downgrading the system but extend these limits for a specific set of users.

10.4.3 SQL

The SQL data security profile is used to override some parameters defined at the universe level. Users and groups who have been assigned this SQL data security profile use these parameters instead of the ones defined at the universe level. These parameters are related to the operations that are allowed when generating the SQL query:

- ▶ Allow use of subqueries
- ▶ Allow use of union, intersect, and minus operators
- ▶ Allow complex operands in query panel
- ▶ Multiple SQL statements for each context
- ▶ Multiple SQL statements for each measure
- ▶ Allow Cartesian products

In the universe, these parameters are defined in the business layer (see Chapter 7, Section 7.30), except for the MULTIPLE SQL STATEMENTS FOR EACH CONTEXT and ALLOW CARTESIAN PRODUCTS parameters, which are defined in the data foundation (see Chapter 5, Section 5.19).

10.4.4 Rows

Rows data security profiles are the most used security profiles. They are used to associate a WHERE clause you can specify to a conditional table. This table can be any table from the universe's data foundation, including alias, derived, and federated table.

If no Rows data security profile is defined for any user, no WHERE clause is added to the queries generated. The data retrieved by the query aren't filtered. If a Rows data security profile is assigned to a user and if the SQL query to retrieve data contains the conditional table secured by the Rows data security profile, then this WHERE clause is added to the query when the query is generated. The data retrieved by the queries are filtered by this clause, and only data that comply with this filter are seen by the user. Other users who don't have any Rows data security profile assigned continue to see data without the filter applied.

A table named Customer contains the column Country. To allow users to access only data for customers whose country is France, you may create a Rows data security profile, based on the Customer table and with the following WHERE clause:

```
Where Customer.Country = 'France'
```

This security is widely used to secure universes because the SQL request that can be used in the WHERE clause can be very flexible and very complex:

▶ It supports IDT built-in functions, such as @variable that also supports user attributes (see Section 10.8).

▶ It can reference and query another table containing some security definition.

In a multisource universe, the WHERE clause can reference tables in any databases used in it.

A Rows data security profile triggered by a table isn't triggered by a derived or an alias table created from this table (see Chapter 5, Section 5.4 and Section 5.6). If needed, the row restriction must be re-created on any alias or derived table based on this table.

Example

In the previous example, if you create a Premium_Customer table derived from the Customer table, then the Rows data security profile created for the Customer table isn't applied if the query contains the Premium_Customer table. You need to explicitly re-create the same Rows data security profile on the Premium_Customer table.

10.4.5 Tables

TABLES data security profiles allow you to define a replacement table instead of a table defined in the data foundation. When a query is run against the database, any occurrence of this table is replaced by the replacement table in the generated SQL. The original table can be an alias table but not a derived table.

When you define the replacement table, you must give the name of an actual table. You can't enter an expression (based on @variable, for example) for the name of this replacement table.

You can't select an alias table as a replacement table or select a derived table as a source or replacement table. To set the owner and qualifier of the table, you must explicitly enter them as such and not as part of the table name. In a multisource universe, the replacement table can be a table from any database used by the multisource universe. You can also use a federated table as a replacement table by explicitly typing its name in the DEFINE REPLACEMENT TABLE dialog box, since it is not proposed in the table selection dialog box.

TABLES data security profiles can be used to prevent a user or a user group from seeing a table and the data it contains. To do so, follow these steps:

1. Create a table in your database with the same structure as the original table, and fill it with sample data.

2. For a universe using this table, create a TABLES data security profile to replace the source table by this sample table.

3. Assign this TABLES data security profile to a user or a group.

When the user creates a query that contains this table, then the table is replaced by the replacement table, and the system returns sample data from the replacement table instead of actual data.

> **Warning!**
>
> As for the ROWS data security profile, a TABLES data security profile doesn't apply if the query contains an alias or a derived table created from the source table rather than the source table itself.

10.5   Business Security Profiles

Business security profiles are another type of security enforced by relational and multidimensional universes. Although similar to data security profiles, business security profiles secure different concepts in the business layer. As shown in Figure 10.5, there are a few different business security profile types:

▶ CONNECTION
This business security profile is available only to multidimensional universes. It's equivalent to the CONNECTIONS data security profile that applies to relational universes (see Section 10.4.1).

▶ CREATE QUERY
To grant or deny business layer views, objects, and folders in the query panel.

▶ DISPLAY DATA
To grant or deny objects that can actually query data from the data source.

▶ FILTERS
To filter data returned by the query:

    ▶ For a relational universe, data are filtered by a predefined condition.

    ▶ For a multidimensional universe, data are filtered by a hierarchy member set.

Figure 10.5 Business Security Profile Dialog Box

DISPLAY DATA and FILTERS business security profiles actually secure the data retrieved from the database, whereas a CREATE QUERY business security profile secures the metadata in the query panel.

With business security profiles, displaying an object in the query panel can be secured independently of retrieving data from the same object. Thus, such scenarios are possible:

▶ A designer is allowed to create a query, but isn't allowed to query the data behind.

▸ A user is allowed to refresh data in reports, but isn't allowed to select this object in the query panel, for example, to create new queries with this object.

In the next sections, we detail each type of business security profile and how it can be used.

10.5.1 Connection

The CONNECTION business security profile is available only for multidimensional universes. As for the CONNECTIONS data security profile (see Section 10.4.1), it's used to define alternate secured connections for a user. When this user runs a query on top of the universe, the connection defined at the business security profile is used instead of the one defined by default for this universe.

Only OLAP connections can be selected as alternate connections. A connection can be replaced only by a connection of the same type. Furthermore, the replacement can only work with a connection that specifies a cube (see Chapter 4, Section 4.1.3). When creating the business security profile, it's possible to select any OLAP connection, but when applied, if the replacement connection doesn't specify a cube, an error message is raised. If the replacement connection defines a cube, then this cube is used for the query.

To select the replacement connection, you must be connected and authenticated to the CMS repository. Thus, CMS rights apply to you, so you can see only the connections for which you have the VIEW OBJECTS right granted.

> **Warning!**
>
> When assigning a CONNECTIONS data security profile to a user or a group, you should check that the user or group is granted the connection security rights they need to query the database with this replacement connection.

CONNECTION business security profile can also be used when, for performance reasons, the data are stored in different cubes. For example, if you use geography, then data for a country can be saved in a cube and data for another country in another cube. By defining CONNECTION business security profiles, you can assign a cube, and thus the data of a country, to the corresponding users.

10.5.2 Create Query

This business security profile secures the business layer views and objects users are allowed to use when they create a query in the query panel.

Authoring

When you create a CREATE QUERY business security profile, you can independently secure two levels:

▶ **View**
Defines whether a business layer view is displayed in the query panel's view list and whether the user can select it. You can explicitly grant or explicitly deny any view (including the master view).

  ▶ You can also define whether all views are by default denied or granted through the ALL VIEWS shortcut.

  ▶ If the master view is defined as hidden, then it can't be selected in the business security profile (it isn't displayed in the view list).

▶ **Object**
Defines whether an object is displayed in the query panel and whether a user can select it to create a query. You can explicitly grant or explicitly deny any object of the business layer (dimension, attribute, measure, filter, named set, folder, analysis dimension, hierarchy, etc.) except level and calculated member.

  ▶ It isn't possible to secure an individual level. All levels must be granted or denied as a whole through the hierarchy.

  ▶ You can also define whether all objects are by default denied or granted through the ALL OBJECTS shortcut.

  ▶ You can select hidden and deprecated objects. However, if the object is hidden or deprecated, then it isn't displayed in the query panel, even if it has been granted by a business security profile.

All objects and views available in the business layer can be selected in the CREATE QUERY business security profile. There is no security applied to check whether the user is allowed to see and select them in the definition of a business security profile.

Default Values

If no CREATE QUERY business security profile is assigned to any user or group, then no create query security is applied. Users can see all objects and all views in the query panel for this universe. If a CREATE QUERY business security profile is assigned to a user, all views become denied to this user by default. Then you can explicitly grant some views in the CREATE QUERY business security profile.

By default, because all views are denied when a business security profile is created, the user can't see the objects in these views. But if a view is granted, then all objects it contains are granted by default: A user is allowed to see all of them, except the ones you may explicitly deny in the CREATE QUERY business security profile.

Other users who do not have any CREATE QUERY business security profile that applies to them (directly assigned or inherited) keep seeing all objects and views in the query panel.

> **Warning!**
>
> When you create a business security profile, it's important to grant some objects and views for both CREATE QUERY and DISPLAY DATA business security profiles. By default, this new business security profile denies all objects and all views. Thus, unless this is the expected behavior, any user and group assigned this business security profile sees an empty query panel and can't retrieve data from the database.

In a CREATE QUERY business security profile, a value set to ALL VIEWS defines the default value for all views. This value can be explicitly modified for other views:

▶ If in the same CREATE QUERY business security profile, ALL VIEWS is granted and some views are denied, then this security profile grants all views except the ones explicitly denied.

▶ If in the same CREATE QUERY business security profile, ALL VIEWS is denied and some views are granted, then this security profile denies all views except the ones explicitly granted.

In a CREATE QUERY business security profile, a value set to ALL OBJECTS defines the default value for all objects. This value can be explicitly modified for other objects:

▶ If in the same CREATE QUERY business security profile, ALL OBJECTS is granted and some objects are denied, then this security profile grants all objects except the ones explicitly denied. However, if these objects are containers, the objects they contain are also denied and aren't displayed in the query panel.

▶ If in the same CREATE QUERY business security profile, ALL OBJECTS is denied and some objects are granted, then this security profile denies all objects except the ones explicitly granted. However, to grant an object, you need to explicitly grant its parent objects through to the root folder as well.

Example

A business layer contains the following folder hierarchy: FOLDER1 • FOLDER2 • MYDIMENSION.

If ALL OBJECTS is denied, then to grant MYDIMENSION, you need to explicitly grant the two folders and the object:

▶ FOLDER1

▶ FOLDER1 • FOLDER2

▶ FOLDER1 • FOLDER2 • MYDIMENSION

If ALL OBJECTS is granted, then by denying FOLDER1, you also deny all of the objects it contains (FOLDER2 and MYDIMENSION).

Using ALL VIEWS or ALL OBJECTS avoids selecting explicitly all views or all objects. Furthermore, if the list of views or objects evolves, ALL VIEWS and ALL OBJECTS dynamically cover them.

Query Panel Impact

The CREATE QUERY business security profile impacts only the query panel and the views and objects it displays. The list of views available in the query panel is computed using the aggregation option because several CREATE QUERY business security profiles may set different values for this view. Each view is considered independently:

▶ If the value aggregated from all security profiles is granted, then the view is displayed in the query panel.

▶ If this aggregated value is denied, then the view isn't displayed.

▶ If this aggregated value isn't defined, then it's also considered denied, and it isn't displayed.

▶ If all views are denied, then the user isn't authorized to see any view—and, indirectly, any object—in the query panel. The list of objects available in the query panel is also computed using the aggregation option.

- If the value aggregated from all security profiles is granted, then the object is displayed in the views that contain this object, if all its parent folders to the root folder are also granted. If one of its parents is effectively denied, then the object isn't displayed.

- If this aggregated value is denied or not defined, then the object isn't displayed in the views that contain it.

As a consequence, the following scenarios arise after the aggregation of all CREATE QUERY business security profiles:

- In a view, an object is displayed if any of the following is true:
  - It belongs to this view.
  - It's effectively granted.
  - It isn't hidden or deprecated in the business layer.
  - All of its parent objects through to the root folder are also effectively granted.

- An object isn't displayed if one of its parents is denied.

- If a container is set as denied, all objects and subcontainers below are denied, whatever their status.

- An object granted in a view isn't necessarily displayed in all views.

10.5.3 Display Data

The CREATE QUERY business security profile shown in the previous section secures the views and objects in the business layer that the user can see in the query panel. A DISPLAY DATA business security profile secures the actual data retrieved by the query.

The philosophy behind a DISPLAY DATA business security profile is similar to that of a CREATE QUERY business security profile, both in authoring workflows, default values, aggregation rules, and effectively granted objects computation.

Authoring

When creating a DISPLAY DATA business security profile, you can grant or deny objects of the business layer that retrieve data:

▶ **Single objects**
Dimensions, attributes, measures, calculated measures, and named sets, but not levels and calculated members.

▶ **Containers that may contain single objects or other containers**
Folders, dimensions, measures, analysis dimensions, and hierarchies.

You can also explicitly set no status, explicitly grant a status, or explicitly deny a status to ALL OBJECTS (itself a shortcut to represent all objects).

All objects from the business layer that return data can be selected in the DISPLAY DATA business security profile. There is no security applied to check whether the user is allowed to see and select them in the definition of a DISPLAY DATA business security profile.

Default Values

If no DISPLAY DATA business security profile is defined for any user, no security is applied, and users can see data from all objects. If a DISPLAY DATA business security profile is assigned to a user, then all objects become, by default, denied to this user, except the ones granted in the DISPLAY DATA business security profile. An empty DISPLAY DATA business security profile denies all objects by default.

In a DISPLAY DATA business security profile, a value set to ALL OBJECTS defines the default value for all objects. This value can be explicitly modified for other objects:

▶ If, in the DISPLAY DATA business security profile, ALL OBJECTS is granted and some objects are denied, then this security profile grants all objects except the ones explicitly denied. However, if these objects are containers, the objects they contain are also denied and aren't displayed in the query panel.

▶ If, in the same DISPLAY DATA business security profile, ALL OBJECTS is denied and some objects are granted, then this security profile denies all objects except the ones explicitly granted. However, to grant an object, you need to explicitly grant its parent objects to the root folder as well.

Consumption

If an object is included in a query, then this object can actually query data if, after the aggregation of all business security profiles, the object is effectively granted and all of the object's parent objects through to the root folder are effectively granted.

As a consequence, after aggregation of all DISPLAY DATA business security profiles:

▸ An object isn't displayed if one of its parents is denied (an object can't have more rights than its parents).

▸ If a container is set as denied, all objects and subcontainers below are denied, whatever their status.

In SAP BusinessObjects Web Intelligence, refreshing a document containing an object denied by security may lead to some unexpected behaviors because removing an object from the query may modify the document structure. The AUTO_ UPDATE_QUERY parameter, defined in the data foundation or the business layer (see Chapter 5, Section 5.19, and Chapter 7, Section 7.30), is used to define how to manage the refresh of a document based on a universe with an object denied by a display data business security profile:

▸ If this parameter is set to NO, then the query isn't executed, the report isn't displayed, and an error message is displayed.

▸ If this parameter is set to YES, then the report is refreshed, but the object isn't taken into consideration:

  ▸ The object is removed from the query definition, as well as predefined filters, calculated measures, and variables depending on it.

  ▸ Data corresponding to this object are no longer retrieved from the database and are thus removed from the report.

▸ If this parameter is defined both in the data foundation and the business layer, then the value defined in the business layer takes priority.

10.5.4 Filters (Relational Universe)

With a FILTERS business security profile, you can filter data retrieved from relational universes through a filter defined with objects from the business layer.

Authoring

A FILTERS business security profile can be seen as the equivalent of the ROWS data security profile but defined at the business layer level. Instead of explicitly writing the WHERE clause to apply, it's defined using a business filter similar to the one that can be created in the business layer (see Chapter 7, Section 7.15). This business filter can be created using the same user interface as the one used in the query panel. For this reason, it can enforce the same filters capabilities:

- You can select any object (measure, dimension, or attribute) available in the business layer, except the objects whose state is hidden.

- You can use any operator (equal, not equal, in list, etc.) supported by business filters on these objects. Furthermore, you can also use subqueries.

- The filters operand can be a constant, a list of values, or an object. But it can't be a prompt. For a constant, it can use the `@variable` operator and user attributes (see Section 10.8).

- This filter is created in the FILTERS business security profile; it isn't possible to reuse a filter created in the business layer. This filter is attached to this security profile and is accessible only from it. If the business security profile is deleted, this filter is deleted as well.

- Native filters, expressed with an SQL expression, aren't supported in the FILTERS business security profile.

Query

Compared to a Rows data security profile that applies only if a table is used in a query, a FILTERS business security profile always applies at query time, regardless of the objects selected in the query. If no FILTERS business security profile is assigned or inherited by a user, no business filter is applied to the data retrieved by queries. If a FILTERS business security profile applies to a user, then the business filter is converted into a `WHERE` clause. The `WHERE` clause is added to the query sent to the database. Thus, data retrieved by the query are filtered by the business filter, and only data that comply with this filter are returned.

No business filter is applied to other users who do not have any assigned or inherited FILTERS business security profiles.

10.5.5 Filters (Multidimensional Universe)

Multidimensional universes do not support the same FILTERS business security profiles as just described. They support another FILTERS business security profiles type that takes advantage of the multidimensional universe.

Authoring

For multidimensional universes, the FILTERS business security profile is used to grant or deny members of a multidimensional hierarchy. When you define such a FILTERS business security profile, you create a newly named set that defines the granted members. This named set is created in the FILTERS business security profile. It's attached to this security profile and is accessible only from it. Additionally, you can't reuse this named set outside this security profile, and if the business security profile is deleted, this named set is deleted as well.

Only business named sets can be used in the definition of a business security profile. These named sets are similar to the member sets you can create in the query panel when you select members in a hierarchy because both workflows use the same member selector. Specifically, the member selector supports the selection of members in a hierarchy through level selection, which selects all members in the selected levels, and the explicit selection of members. To select these members, you can also use the multidimensional operators listed in Table 8.2 in Chapter 8.

Query

In the query panel, when you create the query, the member selector doesn't take FILTERS security profiles into consideration. Thus, all members are displayed when you select hierarchy members, even if some are denied through FILTERS business security profiles.

But FILTERS business security profiles are applied at query time. If no FILTERS business security profile is assigned to you, then you can see all members of the hierarchy if you select it in your query. Otherwise, the effective FILTERS business security profile defines the members you can see in the hierarchy if it's added to the query. The corresponding MDX code to filter the hierarchy with the effective FILTERS business security profile is generated and added to the query sent to the database. In practice, the MDX intersects the member set defined by the effective FILTERS business security profile with the member set returned by the hierarchy.

Depending on the database, the default member returned by a hierarchy can be the first member or a specific member defined as the default member, which is often ALL MEMBERS. This member intersects with the member set defined in the effective FILTERS business security profile to guarantee that users can't see the members they aren't allowed to see.

If the member set defined by the effective security profile contains selected members other than the default member, the intersection returns an empty set, and the resulting query returns no value. To avoid this, when you select a hierarchy in a query, you should explicitly select all or some members in this hierarchy.

For example, a FILTERS business security profile grants AMER and EMEA members in the Geography hierarchy, whose default member is the ALL MEMBERS member.

If you use the Geography hierarchy in a query but don't select any member, then the hierarchy returns the default member and its intersection with the named set defined in the FILTERS business security profile as empty, as shown in the top half of Figure 10.6.

If in the Geography hierarchy, however, you explicitly select several members, including AMER and EMEA, then the intersection with the named set defined in the FILTERS business security profile returns AMER and EMEA members, as shown in the bottom half of Figure 10.6.

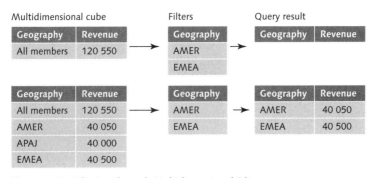

Figure 10.6 Filtering through Multidimensional Filters

For the same reason, if you want to add a prompt to select the values of the hierarchy to query, it's better to add it in the hierarchy member selector rather than adding a specific filter based on a prompt on this hierarchy. If the hierarchy isn't selected in the query, the filter isn't applied.

10.6 Security Profiles Aggregation

Several data and/or business security profiles of the same universe can be applied to the same user. Several different cases can occur, as shown in Figure 10.7:

▶ **Parent-child (❶)**

The user belongs to a group. Both the user and the groups are assigned a data and/or business security profile.

▶ **Multiple parents (❷)**

The user belongs to different groups that are assigned a data and/or business security profile.

▶ **Multiple assignments (❸)**

Several data and/or business security profiles are assigned to the same user or group.

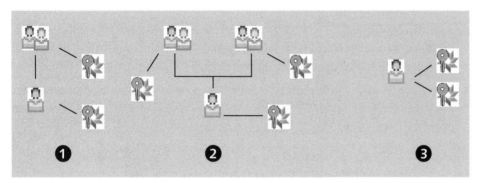

Figure 10.7 Various Aggregation Cases

These aggregation rules depend on the data security profile and the business security profile type. When a security profile type supports several aggregation options, you can select one to define how security profiles are aggregated. There are two main aggregation methods:

▶ Priority, defined for data security profiles or business security profiles

▶ AND, ANDOR, or OR algorithms and their adaptations

10.6.1 Priority Aggregation

You can define two security priorities—one for data security profile aggregation and one for business security profile aggregation. This priority is absolute and applies to all data security profiles or business security profiles. To define this priority, you order all data security profiles and all business security profiles, starting from the one with the highest priority to the one with the lowest priority.

For security profile types aggregated by priority, when several security profiles conflict, the one to apply is always the one with the higher priority, even if one or several data security profiles are directly assigned to the user.

10.6.2 AND, ANDOR, and OR Aggregation

The AND, ANDOR, and OR algorithms, also respectively called very restrictive, moderately restrictive, and less restrictive algorithms, are three generic algorithms that can be used to aggregate security profiles. They follow the same workflows, but depending on the security profiles type, two specific operators are used to aggregate them:

- ▶ A restrictive one, which returns a value for the two security profiles that enforces the higher security level. Depending on the security profile's type, the actual operator to apply is AND, MIN, or intersection.

- ▶ A permissive one, which returns a value for the two security profiles that enforces the lower security level. Depending on the security profile's type, the actual operator to apply is OR, MIN, or union.

When a security profile aggregation supports the AND, ANDOR, and OR algorithms, you can select one of these algorithms that define how these operators are combined in inheritance.

To compute the effective value of any parameter modified by a security profile, the following scenarios apply:

- ▶ In parent-child (profiles inherited from one parent to a child) or multiple-assignment (profiles assigned to the same user or group) cases:
  - ▶ If you've selected very restrictive (AND) or moderately restrictive (ANDOR), then the aggregation operator is the restrictive one.
  - ▶ If you've selected less restrictive (OR), then the aggregation operator is the permissive one.
- ▶ In multiple parents (profiles that aggregate from different groups at same level) cases:
  - ▶ If you've selected very restrictive (AND), then the aggregation operator is the restrictive one.
  - ▶ If you've selected moderately restrictive (ANDOR) or less restrictive (OR), then the aggregation operator is the permissive one.

Example

In the example depicted in Figure 10.8 (**❶**), if R(X) is the function that returns the value set for the parameter by the security profile assigned to the user or group X, and AND represents the restrictive operator, whereas OR is the permissive operator, then, the aggregated security is the following:

- ▶ R(U) AND R(G$_1$) AND R(G$_2$) if you have selected very restrictive (AND).
- ▶ R(U) AND [R(G$_1$) OR R(G$_2$)] if you have selected moderately restrictive (ANDOR).
- ▶ R(U) OR R(G$_1$) OR R(G$_2$) if you have selected less restrictive (OR).

In the example depicted in Figure 10.8 (**❷**), if you've selected moderately restrictive (ANDOR), then the resulting security is aggregated into the following:

- ▶ R(U) AND [(R(G$_1$) AND (R(G$_{11}$) OR R(G$_{12}$))) OR (R(G$_2$) AND R(G$_{21}$))]

Very restrictive (AND) (respectively, less restrictive (OR)) aggregation is computed by using the AND (respectively, OR) operator only.

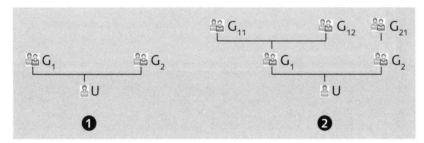

Figure 10.8 Inheritance Examples

10.6.3 Supported Aggregations

Table 10.1 shows for each security profile, whether it supports priority aggregation or AND, ANDOR, and OR aggregation.

Security Profile	Supported Aggregation(s)
CONNECTIONS data security profile	The replacement connection that applies is the one defined by the data security profile with the highest priority. For multisource universes, each replacement connection is computed independently of the other connections.

Table 10.1 Supported Aggregations for Security Profiles

Security Profile	Supported Aggregation(s)

CONTROLS data security profile and SQL data security profile	CONTROLS and SQL data security profiles share the same aggregation option: the one you choose is common to both.
	
	The following are the possible aggregation options for these data security profiles:
	
	▶ Priority: The value of the parameter in the data security profile with the highest priority is used. This is the default aggregation option.
	
	▶ The very restrictive (AND), moderately restrictive (ANDOR), and less restrictive (OR) algorithms. In these algorithms, to aggregate a parameter covered in two CONTROLS data security profiles:
	
	  ▶ If the parameter is similar in both security profiles, then the aggregated parameter also has the same value.
	
	  ▶ If the parameter is enabled in one security profile and disabled in the other one, then the aggregated parameter is enabled if the aggregation is permissive or disabled if the aggregation is restrictive.
	
	To aggregate a parameter covered in two SQL data security profiles:
	
	  ▶ If the parameter is disabled in both security profiles, then the aggregated parameter is also disabled.
	
	  ▶ If the parameter is enabled in both security profiles, then the aggregated parameter is also enabled. The value for the parameter is the smaller value for a restrictive aggregation and the greater value for a permissive aggregation.
	
	  ▶ If the parameter is enabled in one security profile and disabled in the other, then the aggregated parameter is also enabled if the aggregation is restrictive and disabled if the aggregation is permissive.

Rows data security profile	The possible options to aggregate the Rows data security profile triggered by the same table are the very restrictive (AND), moderately restrictive (ANDOR), and less restrictive (OR) algorithms. In the generated query, the following operators that aggregate the WHERE clauses:

Table 10.1 Supported Aggregations for Security Profiles (Cont.)

Security Profile	Supported Aggregation(s)
	▶ The AND operator, for the restrictive one ▶ The OR operator, for the permissive one After the clauses that apply to the same table are aggregated, they are aggregated with an AND operator.
TABLES data security profile	If one table is overloaded by several TABLES data security profiles, then the replacement table to apply is the one defined by the data security profile with the higher priority. In a universe, several tables can be secured by a TABLES data security profile. In this case, each replacement table is computed independently of the other tables.
CONNECTION business security profile	The replacement connection that applies is the one defined by the business security profile with the highest priority.
CREATE QUERY business security profile and DISPLAY DATA business security profile	CREATE QUERY and DISPLAY DATA business security profiles share the same aggregation option: the one you choose is common to both. The possible aggregation options for these business security profiles are the very restrictive (AND)—the default, moderately restrictive (ANDOR), and less restrictive (OR) algorithms. These algorithms use two operators: ▶ Objects and views intersection, for the restrictive aggregation (AND): An object or a view is granted if it's granted in both security profiles to aggregate or if it's granted in one but not specified in the other. ▶ Objects and views union, for the permissive aggregation (OR): An object or a view is granted if it's granted in one of the security profiles to aggregate or if it's granted in one but not specified in the other.
FILTERS business security profile (relational universe)	The possible aggregation options for these business security profiles are the very restrictive (AND)—the default, moderately restrictive (ANDOR), and less restrictive (OR) algorithms.

Table 10.1 Supported Aggregations for Security Profiles (Cont.)

Security Profile	Supported Aggregation(s)
	In these algorithms, the resulting `WHERE` clause generated from the filters are aggregated with the following: ▸ An `AND` operator for the restrictive aggregation ▸ An `OR` operator for the permissive aggregation
FILTERS business security profile (multidimensional universe)	The possible aggregation options for these business security profiles are the very restrictive (AND)—the default, moderately restrictive (ANDOR), and less restrictive (OR) algorithms. These algorithms use these operators: ▸ Member set intersection, for the restrictive aggregation (`AND`): The resulting filter contains the members that are granted in both filters. ▸ Member set union, for the permissive aggregation (`OR`): The resulting filter contains the members that are granted in either of the filters.

Table 10.1 Supported Aggregations for Security Profiles (Cont.)

Rows data security profiles and FILTERS business security profiles both generate a `WHERE` clause to filter the query. If both a Rows data security profile and a FILTERS business security profile are applied, these two resulting `WHERE` clauses are aggregated with the `AND` operator.

10.7 Managing Security Profiles in Information Design Tool

In IDT, both the data and business security profiles described in the previous sections are managed in the Security Editor. The Security Editor is dedicated to security administrators who can manage security and focus on their security tasks without having to handle universe edition. It clearly separates the tasks and the two corresponding user personas and is secured by security rights (see Section 10.1).

The Security Editor also provides an overview of all universes and users/groups in the CMS repository displays the security applied to security profiles explicitly assigned, inherited, and security that actually applies.

To open the Security Editor in IDT, follow these steps:

1. In the menu bar, select WINDOW • SECURITY EDITOR or in the toolbar; click the SECURITY EDITOR button (⬚).

2. Provide the valid credentials to open a session to a CMS.

3. If the ADMINISTER SECURITY PROFILES right is granted to you, then the Security Editor appears as a tab in the IDT window, as shown in Figure 10.9.

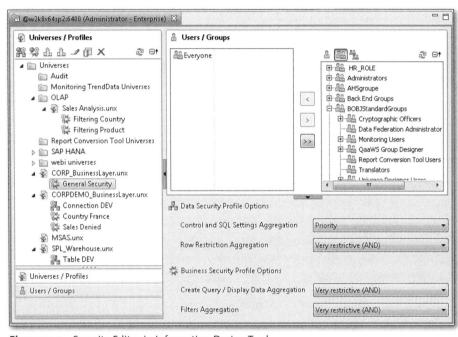

Figure 10.9 Security Editor in Information Design Tool

Once connected to the Security Editor, you can perform the following tasks for security profiles administration:

▶ Create, edit, and delete security profiles.

▶ Assign, unassign, and show assigned security profiles.

▶ Set security profile aggregation options and priorities.

▶ Show security profile inheritance or aggregated security profiles.

▶ Display them using universe-centric or user-centric views:

▸ The *universe-centric view* is more oriented to security profile administration. It's more appropriate for the tasks where the starting point is the universe and its security profiles: administering them or assigning them to principals.

▸ The *user-centric view* is more oriented to display the security profiles assigned to a principal.

▸ Check integrity.

▸ Run a secured query, as described in Section 10.9.

Several views displaying Security Editor connected to different CMS repositories can be opened in parallel. In this case, there is one tab for each Security Editor.

By default, any changes done in the Security Editor aren't committed in the CMS repository and are kept in memory by IDT. The SECURITY EDITOR tab indicates any outstanding changes; in this case, an asterisk (*) prefixes the cluster name, as shown in Figure 10.10.

Figure 10.10 Outstanding Changes in the Security Editor

These changes are saved when you explicitly save these changes by clicking SAVE (🖫) in the toolbar, or you close the Security Editor, and you're asked to save or not to save these changes.

When you save these changes, all modified universe security (security profiles, assigned users and groups, data security profiles priority, aggregation options) are updated in the CMS repository. If several designers work on the same universe on their own machines, the last save with the Security Editor overwrites any previous saves. We recommend that you save your work on a regular basis to avoid losing it.

10.8 User Attributes

The @variable function is a useful way to personalize a universe (see Chapter 5, Section 5.11 and Chapter 7, Section 7.23.5) and secure it. However, the list of variables attached to a CMS session and supported by default is limited; the most-used variable is BOUSER. To extend this list, you can take advantage of user attributes.

10.8.1 Defining User Attributes

Through this new feature supported by IDT, you can define new variables for users defined in the CMS repository. When you define these user attributes, you also define how these attributes must get their value for each user. These values can be explicitly set in the CMS repository for each user. In this case, the user attribute is called Enterprise.

They can also be retrieved from an LDAP, Active Directory, or SAP NetWeaver BW system used by the CMS for authentication. By using an external system, you can benefit and reuse attributes already contained in this external system.

To define a user attribute that retrieves values from an external system, your CMS system must first have been configured to support authentication to this external system (LDAP, Active Directory, and SAP).

When you define the user attribute, you need to give the name of the attribute in the external system that must be used to retrieve the values from the external system. Furthermore, you need to enable this capability both globally for this authentication mode and for each individual user.

User attributes can be defined in the CMC in the USER ATTRIBUTE MANAGEMENT tab. To add some values for Enterprise user attributes to a user, you must have the ADD OR EDIT USER ATTRIBUTES right for this user. For each user, its user attributes can also be seen in the CMC, when you edit the user's properties.

10.8.2 Using User Attributes

In IDT, you can use user attributes in any script definition where you can use the @variable function:

- In a join or an object (dimension, attribute, measure) definition
- In a list of values definition
- In a derived table or calculated column definition
- In a Rows data security profile
- In a relational filter or in a relational FILTERS business security profile

When using @variable, you must provide the user attribute internal name. This internal name is given in the CMC when you define it; it's the name of the user attribute prefixed by SI_.

> **Example**
>
> To use a user attribute called COUNTRY, you need to use the expression:
> @variable('SI_COUNTRY').

10.8.3 User Attributes Substitution

In the universe, user attributes used in @variable functions are replaced by their values for the connected user when the query is sent to the database. These user attribute values are retrieved from the CMS repository when the user logs on to the CMS repository. If you forget to prefix the user attribute with SI_, then the user attribute is seen as an unknown variable and is prompted to the user at query time. An unknown variable is considered as an @prompt with default behavior: a free entry and a single value.

10.9 Running a Secured Query

When you're defining security on your universe, you might find it useful to test it. This can be done from the Security Editor or the REPOSITORY RESOURCES view. Indeed, these panels take into consideration the VIEW OBJECTS, DATA ACCESS, and CREATE AND EDIT QUERY ON TOP OF THE UNIVERSE security rights.

When the query is run, the data result set is filtered by the aggregated data security profile and business security profile that apply to the user logged on to the Security Editor or the REPOSITORY RESOURCES view.

To test your universe's security, follow these steps:

1. If you're running the query from the Security Editor, click SAVE in the toolbar to save any outstanding changes and take them into consideration in the query.

2. In the Security Editor or in the REPOSITORY RESOURCES view, select a published universe, right-click, and select RUN QUERY. The query panel opens. It takes into consideration the object access level and aggregated business security profile that apply to the logged on user:

   ▶ The objects denied through object access level aren't displayed.

   ▶ The views and objects denied by the CREATE QUERY business security profile aren't displayed.

3. Create a query by selecting objects in the pane containing the universe objects and by moving them into the RESULT OBJECTS FOR QUERY pane.

4. Click REFRESH to run the query. The query takes into consideration the security that applies to the logged on user:

   ▶ Data is retrieved from databases referenced by replacement connections defined by data or business security profiles.

   ▶ Data is retrieved from replacement tables defined in the TABLES data security profile.

   ▶ Data is filtered by aggregated ROWS data security profiles and FILTERS business security profiles.

   ▶ Only objects granted by DISPLAY DATA business security profiles and objects access levels can return a data set.

   ▶ Parameters defined by CONTROLS and SQL data security profiles apply.

   ▶ User attributes, as any other variables, are substituted.

5. Click CLOSE to close the query panel.

Query Run from Business Layer Editor

Security applies only on a universe published in a CMS repository. When you edit a business layer, you can also run a query on top of this business layer. This query isn't protected by any data, by business security profiles, or by any right except the connection rights if this business layer still refers to a secured connection saved in the CMS repository.

10.10 Summary

Once published in a CMS repository, universes can centralize security definitions and control access to the database and the data it contains. The different security features they enforce include the following:

▶ Security rights defined in the CMS repository are used for Information Design Tool, universes, connections, or data sources.

▶ Object access levels define confidentiality level for objects and users.

▶ Data security profiles support previous access restriction's security concepts but have been adapted to support multisource universes.

▶ Business security profiles secure the business layer content.

User attributes provide the ability to define dynamic variables that can be explicitly set in the CMS repository or can be retrieved from an SAP, LDAP, or Active Directory system. These attributes, as any other variables supported by `@variable`, can be used to personalize joins, objects, filters, or security profile definitions.

In IDT, security profiles are defined through a dedicated panel, the Security Editor, which also allows you to run queries that enforce these security features.

To support a multilingual deployment, universes can be translated using the Translation Management Tool. The preferred viewing locale can be retrieved using a variable, and the OLAP connection may use a dynamic locale.

11 Working in Multilingual Environments

In worldwide deployment, multilingualism is often mandatory. This requirement must satisfy two constraints:

▶ **Functional**
The same documents, reports, or dashboards must be available in different languages to target different regions and audiences.

▶ **Technical**
Its implementation must be done without increasing the maintenance cost. For example, a solution where the documents are duplicated in the different languages isn't optimal from a maintenance point of view.

The framework to put in place to address such multilingual deployments goes beyond the SAP BusinessObjects BI client tools. It includes the processes to translate the documents and validate the translations, the infrastructure (databases, portals, translation tools, etc.), and the people—typically the translators.

This chapter explains how the semantic layer supports multilingualism and how it can fit into such a framework. Section 11.1 defines several language and locale concepts, especially the preferred viewing locale, that is, the locale the user selects to display the BI content. This preferred viewing locale is supported through all SAP BusinessObjects BI 4.x.

Section 11.2 introduces the Translation Management Tool, which is used in SAP BusinessObjects BI 4.x to translate different resources. Some of its basic workflows are explained to describe universe translation.

In Information Design Tool (IDT), the universe is generated from its data foundation and business layer. Section 11.3 introduces some specific workflows for translating universe metadata when needed. Section 11.4 presents the techniques to return multilingual data through relational universes.

Finally, this chapter concludes in Section 11.5 with multidimensional universes and how they query multilingual metadata and data from OLAP databases.

11.1 Languages and Locales

Before describing how universes manage multilingualism, it's important to first define what languages and locales cover.

11.1.1 Language

A language is a system shared by a group of people for spoken and written communication (e.g., English, French, German, Chinese, etc.).

11.1.2 Locale

A language can be used in different countries around the world. However, the cultural background may impact the usage of this language in different ways, including the following:

▶ Vocabulary (although vocabulary should be common and shared by all people speaking it)

▶ Sorting rules

▶ Units of measure, especially currency

▶ Formatting of date, time, and numbers

For SAP BusinessObjects BI client tools, such differences need to be taken into account to display data in a format that the reader can expect to accurately understand. To grasp these differences, *locales* are defined as the association of a language, a country, and the set of rules that differentiate their use of the language. For example, English is spoken in different countries and has a variety of associated locales: English (Australia), English (Canada), English (Ireland), English (Philippines), English (South Africa), English (United Kingdom), English (United States), and so on.

11.1.3 Dominant Locale

From the previous definition of the locales, it seems logical to classify the locales by their language. Unfortunately, it's not that simple because some languages can be completely different depending on the countries where they are used. This is the case, for example, for simplified Chinese and traditional Chinese which are spoken in different countries.

Thus, using the language to define similarities between locales isn't appropriate. For this reason, another way to sort the locales is to use the dominant locale, which can be defined as a locale whose vocabulary can be a reference for other locales. For example, the English (United States) dominant locale is the reference for all other English locales.

As another example, Chinese (China) is the dominant locale for Chinese (Singapore) and corresponds to the simplified Chinese, whereas Chinese (Taiwan) is the dominant locale for Chinese (Hong Kong SAR China) and Chinese (Macao SAR China) and corresponds to traditional Chinese.

The list of locales supported by SAP BusinessObjects BI 4.x and their dominant locales are listed as a reference in the Translation Management Tool User Guide.

11.1.4 Product Language

The product language is the language you select to display the menus, toolbars, buttons, texts, messages, and so on of your user interface. This language can only be chosen among the language packs you install during product setup.

To change the product language in IDT, you have to open the PREFERENCES dialog box from the WINDOW • PREFERENCES menu. Then set the language in the INFORMATION DESIGN TOOL • LANGUAGES • PRODUCT LANGUAGES list, as shown in Figure 11.1.

Product locale is independent of the locale of the document content.

Figure 11.1 Information Design Tool Languages Preferences Panel

11.1.5 Preferred Viewing Locale

All SAP BusinessObjects BI 4.x client tools (SAP BusinessObjects Web Intelligence, SAP Crystal Reports for Enterprise, SAP BusinessObjects Dashboards, etc.) use the *preferred viewing locale* to manage multilingualism.

This locale is the one chosen by the user to display report content:

- Report title and text
- Data and metadata
- Dates, times, numbers, and currencies with the proper format

The preferred viewing locale is independent from the product locale because you may work with a user interface that is always displayed in a product locale, but modify your preferred viewing locale to display the same report in a different locale. The preferred viewing locale is stored in the CMS repository. For a standalone component, this locale may be stored locally on the machine. This locale can be set in two ways:

- In SAP BusinessObjects Web Intelligence Rich Client, use the LOCALE • PREFERRED VIEWING LOCALE dropdown menu in the OPTIONS dialog box, as shown in Figure 11.2.

▶ In the SAP BusinessObjects BI Launch Pad, use the LOCALES AND TIME ZONE •
PREFERRED VIEWING LOCALE dropdown menu in the OPTIONS dialog box.

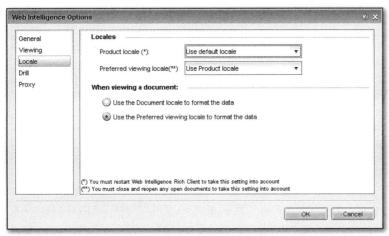

Figure 11.2 SAP BusinessObjects Web Intelligence Locales Options Panel

Since IDT is a design tool and not a client tool, during metadata authoring, it displays
only the original metadata content—also called original content locale (see Section
11.2.1)—without its translation. You can however define a preferred viewing locale
to check a universe's behavior when used for reporting.

As shown earlier in Figure 11.1, this locale can be set in the PREFERENCES dialog
box, called from the INFORMATION DESIGN TOOL • LANGUAGES • PREFERRED VIEWING
LOCALE dropdown menu. The dominant preferred viewing locale is the dominant
locale of the user's preferred viewing locale.

11.2   Translation Management Tool

To translate the metadata of a universe created in IDT, you must use the Transla-
tion Management Tool. This tool, installed with the SAP BusinessObjects BI 4.x
client tools installer, is used to translate local resources or resources saved in the
CMS repository: SAP BusinessObjects Web Intelligence documents, SAP Business-
Objects BI Launch Pad dashboards, universes created with the Universe Design
Tool and IDT, and so on.

This section is a short overview of this tool. It presents some workflows but doesn't cover all of them and can't substitute the official guide of the tool.

11.2.1 Locales in the Translation Management Tool

In its translation workflows, the Translation Management Tool identifies four different locales:

▶ **Original content locale**
This is a fake locale because it contains the resource content as it was created by its designer. It's not associated with any real locale and is intended to be translated in other locales that can be displayed to users.

▶ **Available locales**
These are the different locales in which the resource is translated. The translations of the resource in these available locales are usually stored in the resource file.

▶ **Visible locales**
These locales are a subset of the available locales and are available for consumption. A locale is visible when the translations of this locale are exposed to make them available to client tools.

▶ **Fallback locale**
This locale is the one displayed if a translatable item isn't available in the user's preferred viewing locale; the locale is either not visible or the property has not been translated.

To reduce the translation effort, you may translate only the dominant locales—for example: English (United States), French (France), and Spanish (Spain). If the user's preferred viewing locale isn't available in the resource, then SAP BusinessObjects BI products first try to display the resource in the user's dominant preferred viewing locale. If it is also not visible, then they display the fallback locale.

11.2.2 Translation Management Tool

The Translation Management Tool can translate two types of properties: strings (simple texts) and numbers, dates, and times, whose format can be defined per locale. For each resource to translate, the Translation Management Tool opens an editor containing the matrix shown in Figure 11.3.

The first column of this matrix displays the resource, its objects, and their properties to translate (strings and formats). This column can be organized hierarchically by clicking the CATEGORY VIEW tab, or through a list by clicking the LIST VIEW tab.

The second column, ORIGINAL CONTENT LANGUAGE, contains the original content locale (see Section 11.2.1)—that is, the resource properties as they were set at creation time.

The other columns contain the translations with one column being assigned to each locale. This list of locales is managed in the LANGUAGE MANAGEMENT view (see Section 11.2.6). Each row contains a resource string or format that can be translated. Thus, a cell contains the translation of the property of its row in the locale of its column.

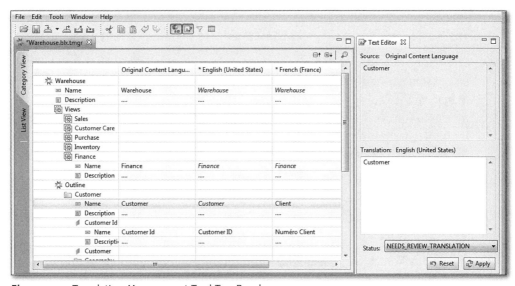

Figure 11.3 Translation Management Tool Top Panels

11.2.3 Resources in the CMS Repository

The Translation Management Tool can work in two modes:

▶ **Standalone mode**
No security is requested. In this mode, you can import translation metadata and export them back only for local and unsecured resources.

▶ **Connected to a CMS repository**
You must first authenticate the Translation Management Tool to the CMS repository using one of the supported authentication modes: Enterprise, Active Directory, or LDAP.

In this mode, you can open any object from the CMS repository that can be translated and for which you're granted the TRANSLATE OBJECTS right. Even in connected mode, you can't translate secured resources saved locally if they have not been saved with the SAVE FOR ALL USERS option (see Chapter 9, Section 9.4).

To translate a resource in the CMS repository, you must check that the Translation Server is enabled and started. During the translation, this server is used to exchange the properties to translate and their translation with the Translation Management Tool.

11.2.4 Translation Status in the Translation Management Tool

Translation is a process that may need iterations between the different stakeholders: designers, business users, technical writers, and translators. The Translation Management Tool supports status information to keep track of which stage in the translation process a translatable item is in. The status values are inspired from the XML Localization Interchange File Format (XLIFF) standard. In the Translation Management Tool, these values are sorted into two categories. Table 11.1 details both categories and their statuses.

Category	Status
Needs Translation	▶ NEW ▶ NEEDS_L10N ▶ NEEDS_TRANSLATION ▶ NEEDS_ADAPTATION
Translation Visible	▶ NEEDS_REVIEW_TRANSLATION ▶ NEEDS_REVIEW_ADAPTATION ▶ NEEDS_REVIEW_L10N ▶ TRANSLATED ▶ SIGNED_OFF ▶ FINAL

Table 11.1 Translation Category and Statuses

> **L10N**
>
> In the status names, L10N is used as an abbreviation for localization. Ten is the number of letters between the first and last letter.

For each translatable string or format and for each locale, you can set one status; this gives you the status of the translation of this property in this locale. The category is used to define whether the translation of one specific data in one locale must be visible. When its status is in the NEEDS TRANSLATION category, it's not displayed to users because the translation is considered as still in progress. When its status is in the TRANSLATION VISIBLE category, then it's considered as done and can be displayed to a user that uses this locale.

11.2.5 Running the Translation Management Tool

The Translation Management Tool is a generic tool used to translate any resources in SAP BusinessObjects BI 4.x, so its translation workflows are generic and apply to all resources. Section 11.3 describes the specificities of translating semantic layer resources.

To translate a resource from a CMS repository, follow these steps:

1. Launch the Translation Management Tool.

2. In the USER IDENTIFICATION dialog box, enter the login parameters to connect to the corresponding CMS repository and open a session.

3. After the Translation Management Tool is open, select the FILE • IMPORT STRINGS TO TRANSLATE FROM • SYSTEM REPOSITORY command, or in the toolbar, click the IMPORT STRINGS TO TRANSLATE FROM dropdown button (⤓), and select the SYSTEM REPOSITORY command. The IMPORT TMGR FILE FROM CMS dialog box opens, as shown in Figure 11.4.

4. Select the resource to translate in the right panel, and then click the ADD button. The name of the resource appears in the bottom panel.

5. Click FINISH to close the dialog box, retrieve the strings and formats to translate from the selected resource, and display them in an editor.

6. Translate the strings and formats, as explained in Section 11.2.6.

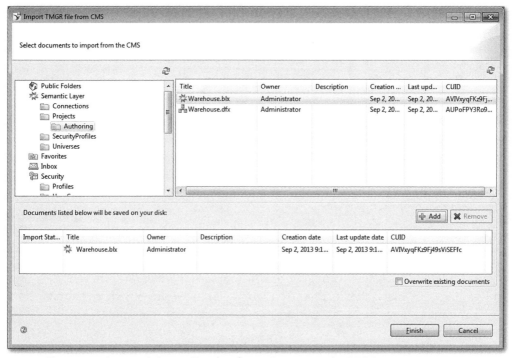

Figure 11.4 Imports Strings to Translate from a Resource in the CMS Repository

7. When the resource has been translated, you must export back the added translations into the original resource in the CMS repository. To do so, select the FILE • EXPORT TRANSLATED STRINGS command (<img>).

To translate a local resource, follow these steps:

1. Launch the Translation Management Tool.

2. In the USER IDENTIFICATION dialog box, enter the login parameters to connect to a CMS repository and open a session. You may also simply select the STAND-ALONE authentication.

3. After the Translation Management Tool is open, select the FILE • IMPORT STRINGS TO TRANSLATE FROM • LOCAL FOLDER command, or in the toolbar, click the IMPORT STRINGS TO TRANSLATE FROM dropdown button (<img>), and select the LOCAL FOLDER command. The OPEN dialog box opens.

4. Select the file to translate, and then click OPEN.

5. In the OPEN dialog box that displays, select the resource to translate, click OPEN to close the OPEN dialog box, retrieve the strings and formats to translate from the selected resource, and display them in an editor.

6. Translate the strings and formats as explained in the next section.

7. When the resource has been translated, you must export back the translation into the local original resource. To do so, select the FILE • EXPORT TRANSLATED STRINGS command, or in the toolbar, click the EXPORT TRANSLATED STRINGS button (⬆️).

11.2.6 Translating Properties in the Translation Management Tool

After you've retrieved the strings and formats to translate, you can translate them by following these steps:

1. In the LANGUAGE MANAGEMENT view (see Figure 11.5), select a locale in the left panel. This panel contains all locales supported by SAP BusinessObjects BI 4.x.

2. Click the button with a right arrow (▶) to move the selected locale into the SELECTED LANGUAGES panel. The column with this locale is added in the editor containing the strings and formats to translate.

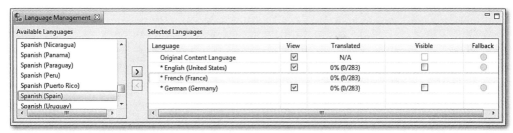

Figure 11.5 Translation Management Tool Language Management Panel

3. Click a cell in the matrix displayed in the resource editor. If the row contains a string to translate, type the translation for the string in the corresponding locale.

   If the row contains a format, right-click the cell and select a predefined format in the context menu. To set a different format, in the context menu, select OTHER FORMATS (FORMAT EDITOR) to open the FORMAT EDITOR where you can define your own format.

4. Right-click this cell and select CHANGE STATUS. In the CHANGE STATUS dialog box shown in Figure 11.6, select a translation status in the STATUS dropdown menu,

and then click OK. The cell font is modified depending on the translation status category:

▶ The cell font is bold, blue, and italicized if the translation status is NEW.

▶ The cell font is blue and italicized if the translation status is in the NEEDS TRANSLATION category and different from NEW.

▶ The cell font is black and regular if the status is in the TRANSLATION VISIBLE category.

Figure 11.6 The Change Status Dialog Box

You may alternatively type the translation and set the translation status in the TEXT EDITOR view, and then click the APPLY button.

5. Repeat these steps for each string and format to translate for each language.

6. To set a locale as visible, in the LANGUAGE MANAGEMENT view, click the checkbox in the VISIBLE column for this locale.

7. To set one of the visible columns as the fallback locale, click the radio button in the FALLBACK column for this locale.

8. Save the translated strings and formats in the original resource, as described in Section 11.2.5.

11.3 Translating Universe Metadata

Universe metadata must also be translated to be displayed in the user's preferred viewing locale in the query panel or in reports. Because universes in IDT are generated from a data foundation and a business layer, there are specific workflows for their translation.

11.3.1   Universe Translation Workflow

The translation of a universe created with IDT requires an additional step due to its authoring and publishing workflows. Translation is also considered as an authoring step. Thus, you don't directly translate a published universe but rather the data foundation and business layer that make it.

Furthermore, the data foundation and business layer can be used by several universes. Translating the resources that are used by multiple universes avoids translating each universe.

Just as you can't directly edit a published universe, you also can't directly translate a universe. You must first retrieve the universe to get and translate its resources (see Chapter 9, Section 9.3 and Section 9.4). For a relational universe, you must retrieve and translate the data foundation and business layer; for a multidimensional universe, you must retrieve and translate the business layer.

If the universe has been published in the CMS repository, you must select the SAVE FOR ALL USERS option when you retrieve the universe (see Chapter 9, Section 9.4) because the Translation Management Tool can't translate secured resources. When the universe is retrieved, the translation metadata (translated strings, visible and available locales, etc.) are saved into the generated business layer and data foundation.

The Translation Management Tool can translate resources located in a local or shared project. To translate a local data foundation or business layer, you must retrieve the strings to translate from its file saved in the folder associated to the local project (see Chapter 3, Section 3.1.1).

The data foundation and business layer can be saved in the CMS repository in shared projects. To translate them, select them in the IMPORT TMG FROM CMS dialog box. Then, in the left panel, open the SEMANTIC LAYER • PROJECTS folder, and select the shared project containing the resources to translate, which are then displayed in the right panel.

The rest of the translation workflows are described in Section 11.2.5 and Section 11.2.6. The properties that can be translated in the data foundation and business layers are listed in Section 11.3.3 and Section 11.3.4, respectively.

11.3.2 Publishing Universe

When these resources are translated, you can use them to generate a multilingual universe. If the translated resources are stored in a local project, you can publish the universe directly. But if the translated resources are stored in a shared project, you first need to resynchronize your local project to get the latest version that contains the translations and then publish the universe.

> **Locales Availability**
>
> Before publishing a universe, make sure in the Translation Management Tool that the locales are set as VISIBLE and the translation status for each string is in the TRANSLATION VISIBLE category; otherwise, these locales and translations aren't exposed in the published universe.

When a relational universe is published, its data foundation and its business layer are merged together to generate the published universe.

- The fallback locale of the universe is the one defined for the business layer, if any. If no fallback locale has been defined for the business layer, then the universe fallback locale is the one defined for the data foundation. Otherwise, the universe has no fallback locale.

- The available locales of the universe are the union of the data foundation locales and the business layer locales.

- Its visible locales are the union of the data foundation locales and the business layer locales. Visible locales may be different between business layer and data foundation. If a locale is visible for the data foundation and not for the business layer or vice versa then the fallback algorithm is used to find the translations that are available. This isn't supposed to be a normal situation because in a correct translation, both data foundation and business layer are expected to have the same set of visible and fallback locales.

- Its translations (and their statuses) are the unions of the business layer and data foundation translations.

A multidimensional universe is made of a single business layer so there are no possible conflicts. The translations and the translation parameters (fallback locale and available locales) of the published universe are the ones defined in its business layer level.

After the universe is translated and published, the translated metadata are displayed in the client tools that request them in a specific locale, assuming this locale has been translated and that the translations have been assigned a status in the TRANS-LATION VISIBLE category.

11.3.3 Data Foundation Translatable Properties

In a relational universe, the data foundation is the technical layer that isn't exposed through the universe. Thus, few objects of the data foundation can actually be translated. These objects are listed in Table 11.2.

For each object, this table defines the following:

▶ **Object**
The object to translate.

▶ **Property**
The object property that can be translated.

▶ **Type**
The translation type, either a string for simple text, or a format for number, date, or time.

▶ **Used**
If the property is actually exposed.

Object	Property	Type	Used
Context	Name	String	Yes
	Description	String	Yes
Parameter	Name	String	No
	Description	String	No
	Question	String	Yes

Table 11.2 Data Foundation Translatable Items

For the business layer, a similar table is listed in Section 11.3.4.

11.3.4 Business Layer Translatable Properties

Just as was shown for the data foundation, Table 11.3 lists which objects and properties in the business layer can be translated. Compared to the data foundation, most objects of the business layer are exposed through the query panel and thus must be translated.

Object	Property	Type	Used
Business layer, view, hierarchy, folder, analysis dimension, level, named set, filter	Name	String	Yes
	Description	String	Yes
Dimension, measure, attribute	Name	String	Yes
	Description	String	Yes
	Format	Number or date/time format	Yes
Parameter	Name	String	No
	Description	String	Yes
	Question	String	Yes
Predefined query	Name	String	No
	Description	String	No

Table 11.3 Business Layer Translatable Items

Although they can be translated, some properties aren't exposed in SAP Business-Objects BI 4.x for the moment. This is the case, for example, for predefined queries that can be defined in IDT and used in this tool only. For consistency, you can translate them, even if these translations aren't yet exploited.

When the universe is published, the business layer name becomes the published universe name, and its description becomes the published universe description.

11.4   Multilingual Data in Relational Universes

Besides the universe metadata, users expect to see the data they retrieve in their language, assuming their data source contains it. Usually, this is done by translating in all languages to support the strings stored in the database. These translations are themselves stored in the database.

Except for some data sources that also propose applicative content (SAP ERP, relational access to SAP NetWeaver BW or SAP HANA—all described in Chapter 12), relational data sources don't support multilingual data out of the box. It's usually implemented by using some database schema patterns designed for multilingualism.

This section first describes some of these patterns. Then it explains how relational universes can retrieve a user's preferred viewing locale and how it can be used in universes to query multilingual data.

11.4.1   Multilingual Patterns in Relational Database

When it comes to storing multilingual data in a relational data source, the database designer must define the model that best fits the functional and multilingual requirements. Most often, the chosen model follows one of these patterns:

- Translated data stored in different rows
- Translated data stored in different columns
- Translated data stored in different tables
- Translated data stored in different databases

Language-Specific Rows

In the *language-specific rows* pattern, all strings and their translations are stored in the same table. As shown in Figure 11.7, one column of the table contains a label that is used to identify in which language the data is stored in the row. The labels used to identify the locales aren't necessarily standard. The database designer may have defined them.

PRODUCT

ID	LANG	ProdName
E451	EN	Digital camera
E452	EN	Flat screen TV
E451	FR	Appareil photo digital
E452	FR	Téléviseur écran plat
...	...	...

Figure 11.7 Language-Specific Rows Example

SAP ERP

This model is used internally by SAP ERP to store multilingual data.

Language-Specific Columns

In the *language-specific columns* model, translated strings or data are stored in the same table with one column being used per language. As shown in Figure 11.8, the name of the column identifies the locale of the data in the column.

PRODUCT

ID	ProdName_FR	ProdName_EN	ProdName_DE	...
E451	Appareil photo digital	Digital camera	...	...
E452	Téléviseur écran plat	Flat screen TV	...	...
..	...	...	...	...

Figure 11.8 Language-Specific Columns Example

Language-Specific Tables

In the *language-specific tables* model, translated strings or data are stored in different tables. As shown in Figure 11.9, one table is used per language (here, English and French). These tables must have the same structure (same column names and types) so processing may be independent of the table and, thus, of the language. This model is less common than the two previous ones.

PRODUCT_EN

ID	ProductName
E451	Digital camera
E452	Flat screen TV
...	...

PRODUCT_FR

ID	ProductName
E451	Appareil photo digital
E452	Téléviseur écran plat
...	...

Figure 11.9 Language-Specific Tables Example

Language-Specific Databases

In the *language-specific databases* model, translated strings or data are stored in different databases; one database is used for one language. These databases must have the same schema (tables, columns, etc.) and security so processing may be independent of the database and, thus, of the language.

Mixed Model

You can combine the different previous techniques to create other patterns for multilingual use in a *mixed model*. For example, a possible model may rely on two tables:

▶ A first table, the data reference table, contains the data stored in rows or columns, and an ID to reference the translations.

▶ A second table, the data dictionary table, contains this ID and their translations.

This model is only one of the possible combinations to store multilingual data. But in all cases, retrieving it in the correct locale can be done only if the preferred viewing locale is available. This information can be retrieved with the built-in `@variable` function.

11.4.2 Retrieving a Locale in a Universe with @Variable

A universe created on one of the previous multilingual patterns can be used to return data in a user's preferred viewing locale only if it's given this preferred viewing locale. One option to pass it is to explicitly ask the user at runtime through the built-in function `@prompt`. This solution isn't the most efficient because it requires the user to fill the prompt each time a query is executed. This was the only available option until the availability of the preferred viewing locale in `@variable`.

In IDT, the `@variable` function supports two variables that are useful for multilingual processing:

▶ PREFERRED_VIEWING_LOCALE

This variable returns the user's preferred viewing locale.

▶ DOMINANT_PREFERRED_VIEWING_LOCALE

This variable returns the dominant locale of the user's preferred viewing locale.

The values returned by these variables follow the template

⟨*language*⟩_⟨*country*⟩

where ⟨*language*⟩ is the language name in the ISO 639-1 standard, and ⟨*country*⟩ is the country name in the ISO 3166 standard. For example: en_GB, fr_FR, and so on.

These variables can be used in any SQL expression defined in the data foundation or business layer: join formula, derived table formula, object SELECT or WHERE clauses, and so on. Thanks to these variables, you can create a dynamic behavior that enables the universe to deal with multilingual data.

11.4.3 Using @Variable in Different Patterns

Thanks to the @variable function, resolving multilingual queries on the different models presented in Section 11.4.1 is done by using some techniques. We look into those next.

Language-Specific Rows

In the model where a translation and the locale are stored in rows, retrieving the data in a specific locale can be done by filtering the rows with a WHERE clause based on the locale name. The WHERE clause can be defined in different locations:

▶ In a filter join defined on the table (see Chapter 5, Section 5.3.3)

▶ In the definition of a derived table based on this table (see Chapter 5, Section 5.4)

▶ In the WHERE clause of an object based on the table (see Chapter 7, Section 7.5.2)

▶ In a mandatory filter defined in the business layer (see Chapter 7, Section 7.15)

The main difficulty is to compare the value returned by the @variable function and the value actually stored in the table to identify the language. Some string manipulation may be needed with SQL functions such as Upper, Substring, and others.

In the example in Figure 11.7, the SQL clause that can be used in the table join, derived table, or object is the following:

```
Where LANG = Upper ( Substring ( @variable

               ( 'DOMINANT_PREFERRED_VIEWING_LOCALE' ), 1, 2) )
```

Language-Specific Columns

In a model where different columns are used to store different languages, retrieving translated content in a user's locale can be done by creating a derived table whose formula dynamically defines the table content in the user's preferred viewing locale.

This derived table has a column dynamically mapped to the column containing the translations in the user's language. The switch to the correct column is done by a Union operator and a WHERE clause that checks each different locale.

In the example in Figure 11.8, the derived table is created from the following formula:

```
Select ID, ProdName_EN AS Name FROM PRODUCT_NAME Where
 @variable('DOMINANT_PREFERRED_VIEWING_LOCALE') = 'en_US'
Union
Select ID, ProdName_FR FROM PRODUCT_NAME Where
 @variable('DOMINANT_PREFERRED_VIEWING_LOCALE') = 'fr_FR'
Union
Select ID, ProdName_DE FROM PRODUCT_NAME Where
 @variable('DOMINANT_PREFERRED_VIEWING_LOCALE') = 'de_DE'
```

This derived table has only two columns: ID and Name. If the user's dominant preferred viewing locale is en_US, then the Name column is mapped with the ProdName _EN column that contains the English translations. Only the WHERE clause of the first SELECT statement is valid. Other SELECT statements do not return any row because the locale does not fit the value returned by @variable.

The advantage of using the dominant preferred viewing locale is that it covers all locales that depend on this dominant locale—in this case, en_UK, en_CA, and so on. In the same example, if the user-dominant preferred viewing locale is fr_FR, then the Name column is mapped with the ProdName_FR column that contains the French translations. In the business layer, you can define an object that queries the Name column of the derived table.

Language-Specific Tables

If the translations are stored in different tables, then the same technique shown previously for the language-specific columns pattern can be used. But in this case, the column of the derived table isn't mapped to different columns of the table containing all translations but to the columns of different tables.

In the Figure 11.9 example, the derived table is created with the following formula:

```
Select ID, ProductName AS ProductName FROM PRODUCT_EN Where
  @variable('DOMINANT_PREFERRED_VIEWING_LOCALE') = 'en_US'
Union
Select ID, ProductName FROM PRODUCT_FR Where
  @variable('DOMINANT_PREFERRED_VIEWING_LOCALE') = 'fr_FR'
Union
Select ID, ProductName FROM PRODUCT_DE Where
  @variable('DOMINANT_PREFERRED_VIEWING_LOCALE') = 'de_DE'
```

In the business layer, you can define an object that queries the Name column of the derived table.

11.5 Multilingual and Multidimensional Universes

As opposed to relational databases, OLAP databases natively support multilingualism: Both their metadata and data can be translated and stored in the databases. This is the case for the OLAP databases supported by IDT that aren't in an SAP system: Microsoft SQL Server Analysis Services and Oracle Hyperion Essbase.

This native support leads to new behaviors in the way the semantic layer manages multilingualism for these data sources, both for their metadata and their data.

SAP NetWeaver BW and SAP HANA

SAP NetWeaver BW and SAP HANA also support natively multilingualism, but the semantic layer does not automatically supporting them unless using SAP direct access (see Chapter 12).

11.5.1 Metadata

In IDT when you create a connection to Microsoft SQL Server Analysis Services and Oracle Hyperion Essbase OLAP databases, you set a locale, as shown in Figure 11.10. The only access proposed by the semantic layer to these databases is through an automatically generated multidimensional universe.

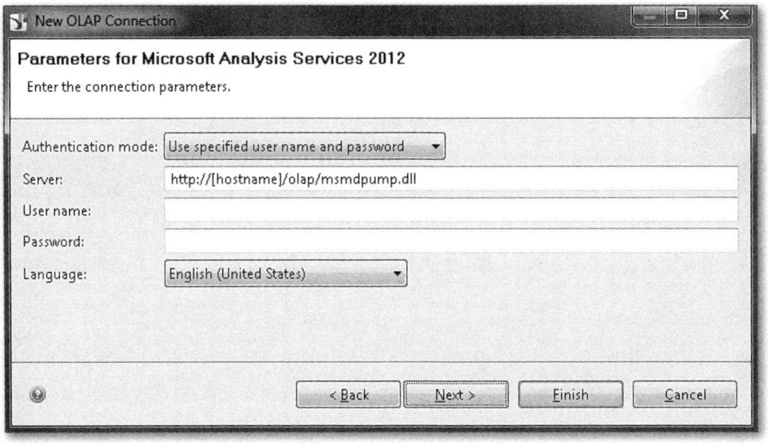

Figure 11.10   Language Setting in the OLAP Connection Editor

When the business layer is created, it retrieves only the object names in the locale defined in the OLAP connection. If the database content isn't available in the locale requested by the client tool, then the returned content is managed by the OLAP data source: Microsoft SQL Server Analysis Services returns the fallback locale content, and Oracle Hyperion Essbase returns the default labels defined in the default alias table.

The retrieved names become the business layer original content locale (see Section 11.2.1). This content is static. If you change the locale defined in the connection, then the business layer isn't modified, unless you explicitly refresh the business layer from the database (see Chapter 7, Section 7.29). The locale isn't impacted by the user's preferred viewing locale change unless you explicitly translate the business layer in the Translation Management Tool.

11.5.2 Data

When the client tools query these databases through this multidimensional universe, the data is returned in the locale corresponding to the user's preferred viewing locale. The locale given at the connection creation isn't taken into consideration. If data isn't available in the locale requested by the client tool, then the OLAP data source returns this data in the OLAP data source fallback locale, or using the default alias table in the case of Oracle Hyperion Essbase.

11.6 Summary

In a global enterprise deployment, a BI solution is expected to support multilingual requirements. SAP BusinessObjects BI 4.x addresses these requirements through the user's preferred viewing locale, which defines in which locale report content must be displayed.

The semantic layer also supports this preferred viewing locale. Data foundation and business layer metadata can be translated in the Translation Management Tool. When the published universe is used, the metadata is then displayed in the user's preferred viewing locale in the various client tools.

Additionally, the `@variable` function supports the `PREFERRED_VIEWING_LOCALE` and `DOMINANT_PREFERRED_VIEWING_LOCALE` variables, which can be used in the SQL query to filter data from relational databases. OLAP connections can dynamically query data and metadata in the user's preferred viewing locale.

SAP ERP, SAP NetWeaver BW, and SAP HANA are different sources of enterprise data used by SAP customers. Information Design Tool can be used to connect the SAP BusinessObjects BI 4.x client tools to these data sources.

12 Connecting to SAP ERP, SAP NetWeaver BW, and SAP HANA

The SAP portfolio contains three systems that are now widely used for company day-to-day operations:

▶ **SAP ERP**
This is the SAP suite for enterprise operations (finance, human resources, production, sales, services, etc.). Because these ERP modules contain most of the data from a company, it can be useful to query them directly.

▶ **SAP NetWeaver Business Warehouse (SAP NetWeaver BW)**
This is the SAP data warehousing, analytical, and client tools solution before the Business Objects acquisition. Customers who have deployed it can now use it as a data source for reporting with the SAP BusinessObjects BI toolset.

▶ **SAP HANA**
This is the new SAP in-memory database and application platform.

The semantic layer is the common interface used by most SAP BusinessObjects BI 4.1 client tools to connect and query data from these systems, using specific technologies optimized for each data source.

This chapter provides an overview of these access methods, with a focus on the connections and universes you can create in Information Design Tool (IDT). First the chapter presents the OLAP and relational connections you can create to SAP NetWeaver BW and the universe you can create on the relational one. Section 12.2 covers the relational connection to SAP ERP that can be used in a single-source or multisource universe. Section 12.3 details the relational connection and universe you can create to SAP HANA and the OLAP connection it supports for direct access. Finally, the chapter concludes in Section 12.4 with the wizard that converts a universe pointing to a non-SAP relational database to a universe pointing to SAP HANA.

12.1 Access to SAP NetWeaver BW

SAP NetWeaver BW is a mature system widely used for reporting in the SAP landscape. To use it as a data source in IDT, you need to know some specifics about its connection:

▶ SAP NetWeaver BW can be accessed through different interfaces, relational or multidimensional, that don't support the same capabilities.

▶ Specific parameters are required to connect to the SAP NetWeaver BW system.

▶ The semantic layer offers a multidimensional direct access or a relational universe access, and you have to choose the one you need.

The following sections provide information on those access methods and finally explain some general recommendations about performance of a universe on SAP NetWeaver BW.

12.1.1 SAP NetWeaver BW Interfaces

SAP BusinessObjects BI 4.x client tools access SAP NetWeaver BW with three main technologies:

▶ **Business Intelligence Consumer Services (BICS)**
This SAP technology enables you to connect client tools to OLAP sources providing a multidimensional view.

▶ **SQL**
This is the relational database query language.

▶ **MDX**
This is the OLAP database query language.

Business Intelligence Consumer Services

BICS is the recommended access method for SAP NetWeaver BW. The BICS interface enables client tools to keep most of the functionality of the SAP NetWeaver BW system. It typically exposes full Business Explorer (BEx) query concepts, such as hierarchies, restricted key figures, exception aggregations, and so on.

The BICS-based connectivity is used by the following products:

- SAP BusinessObjects Analysis, edition for Office
- SAP BusinessObjects Analysis, edition for OLAP
- SAP BusinessObjects Design Studio
- SAP BusinessObjects Web Intelligence
- SAP Crystal Reports for Enterprise
- SAP BusinessObjects Dashboards

In those applications, it's possible to access the result of a BEx query directly without any additional modeling step, except the creation of the OLAP connection to SAP NetWeaver BW that can be done in IDT as described in Section 12.1.3 or in the Central Management Console (CMC). This access is called *SAP direct access* because it doesn't require you to build a universe on top of a BEx query (see Chapter 7, Section 7.2.1).

SQL

The SQL access provides a relational interface to SAP NetWeaver BW that exposes various types of InfoProviders as relational structures. This interface, called the *SQL façade* or *federation façade*, is only used by the Federation Query Server to build relational universes on top of SAP NetWeaver BW. Such universes can be used to federate SAP NetWeaver BW data with data coming from other sources. This access method is available only when using multisource data foundations (see Chapter 6, Section 6.2).

The relational interface reduces the functionalities available when querying the model. As an example, hierarchies or restricted key figures defined in SAP NetWeaver BW aren't visible through the façade. The façade doesn't expose BEx queries but the SAP BW NetWeaver InfoProviders listed in Table 12.3.

The client tools supporting the SQL universe access to SAP NetWeaver BW are all those supporting universes created with IDT. The steps to create a relational universe on SAP NetWeaver BW are the same as creating any multisource universe:

- Creating the relational connection (see Section 12.1.4 for details on the SAP relational connection definition)
- Creating the multisource data foundation (see Chapter 6)

- ▸ Creating the business layer (see Chapter 7)
- ▸ Publishing the universe (see Chapter 9)

IDT can automatically create the data foundation and the business layer. Information on how the resources are created can be found in Section 12.1.5 and Section 12.1.6. You may also manually generate them to better control their creation (see Section 12.1.7).

MDX

The MDX access provides a multidimensional access to InfoProviders and BEx queries. This interface is less functional and less performing than the BICS interface. This access is used by universes created with the Universe Design Tool, but not by universes created with IDT; for this reason, it's not covered in this book.

SAP Direct Access versus Universe

It's recommended to use the BICS connection to BEx query as the main access method to SAP NetWeaver BW. The BICS access reduces the cost of ownership because no additional modeling is required, preserves more SAP NetWeaver BW functionality, and gives a more performing access to the system.

The relational façade access via a universe should be used only to merge data from several sources. Even if not recommended, it can be used also to customize objects or to add another security layer.

12.1.2 Connection Parameters to SAP NetWeaver BW

To create a connection—either relational or OLAP—to access the SAP NetWeaver BW system, you must provide the parameters listed in Table 12.1.

Parameter Name	Parameter Description
Authentication Mode	The authentication mode is one of three supported: Fixed Credentials, Credentials Mapping, or Single Sign-On (see Chapter 4, Section 4.3).
Client	This parameter is made of the three numbers that identify the SAP system client.

Table 12.1 Common Parameters to Create a Connection to SAP NetWeaver BW

Parameter Name	Parameter Description
USER NAME	If the authentication is done with fixed credentials, then set the user account and password used to connect to the SAP NetWeaver BW system.
PASSWORD	
LANGUAGE	If the SAVE LANGUAGE option has been selected, then this is the locale to use to retrieve data from the SAP system.
SAVE LANGUAGE	If this option isn't selected, then this is the language to use to retrieve data from the SAP system set dynamically with the user's preferred viewing locale (see Chapter 11, Section 11.1). If this option is selected, then the locale to retrieve data is always the one defined in the LANGUAGE parameter.
SYSTEM ID	This parameter is made of the three letters that identify the SAP NetWeaver BW system name.
SERVER TYPE	This is one choice among APPLICATION SERVER and MESSAGE SERVER.
SERVER NAME	If your SAP ERP system has been defined as Application Server, then you must fill in its server name and system number, a number between "00" and "99".
SYSTEM NUMBER	
SERVER NAME	If your SAP ERP system has been defined as Message Server, you need to provide the application server name and its group name.
GROUP NAME	

Table 12.1 Common Parameters to Create a Connection to SAP NetWeaver BW (Cont.)

Message Server

To access SAP NetWeaver BW through a message server, you need to add the following line to the *C:\WINDOWS\system32\drivers\etc\services* file on the machine hosting the application:

`sapms<SystemID> 3601/tcp`

In this line, `sapms` means SAP message server, `<SystemID>` is the System ID of the server to connect, and `3601/tcp` is the default TCP port used for communication.

The parameters listed in Table 12.1 are common to relational and OLAP connections. Additional parameters for relational connections are listed in Section 12.1.4. Additional parameters for the OLAP connection are described in the next section.

12.1.3 Creating an SAP NetWeaver BW OLAP Connection

The OLAP connection to the SAP NetWeaver BW system is also called the BICS connection because it's based on the BICS interface. As for other OLAP connections, the SAP NetWeaver BW OLAP connection can give more or fewer choices to the end user by referring to one of the following:

▶ **A BEx query on an InfoProvider on the server**
This connection can query only this BEx query.

▶ **An InfoProvider on the server**
This connection can connect to any BEx query created on this InfoProvider. Before using this connection in client tools, the user must select the BEx query to use.

▶ **The SAP NetWeaver BW server**
This connection can query any BEx query created on the SAP NetWeaver BW server. Before using this connection in client tools, the user must select the InfoProvider and the BEx query to use.

Tools such as SAP BusinessObjects Analysis for OLAP, SAP BusinessObjects Analysis for Office, and SAP Design Studio can access InfoProviders—not only BEx queries—from this connection.

Roles

For security reasons, you must assign a role for all accounts in the SAP system whose credentials can be used to authenticate to the SAP NetWeaver BW system through the OLAP connection. This role must contain at least the following authorizations:

▶ S_RFC
Authorization check for remote function call (RFC) access.

▶ S_DATASET
Authorizations for accessing files.

▶ S_USER_GROUP
Authorization for user master maintenance.

If necessary, ask your SAP NetWeaver BW administrator to assign your users these rights.

Information Design Tool Workflow

The OLAP connection to SAP NetWeaver BW can be created and published using IDT. The general definition and publication workflows are described in detail in Chapter 4, Section 4.6; this section deals specifically with connections to SAP NetWeaver BW.

To create an OLAP connection to an SAP NetWeaver BW system, follow these steps:

1. From the LOCAL PROJECTS or the REPOSITORY RESOURCES view, run the OLAP connection wizard.

2. The connection wizard opens. Enter a name for the connection, then click NEXT.

3. In the list of drivers shown in Figure 12.1, select SAP BUSINESSOBJECTS BI 7.X • SAP BICS CLIENT driver, and then click NEXT.

Figure 12.1 Supported OLAP Connections to SAP Systems

The connection parameters panel is displayed as shown in Figure 12.2.

Figure 12.2 The SAP NetWeaver BW OLAP Connection Parameters

4. Enter the required parameters, as described in Table 12.1, to connect to the SAP system, and then click NEXT.

5. In the CUBE SELECTION panel shown in Figure 12.3, you can select the SAP NetWeaver BW connection to reference:

   ▶ The SAP NetWeaver BW server, by selecting the DO NOT SPECIFY A CUBE IN THE CONNECTION radio button

   ▶ An InfoProvider, by selecting the SPECIFY A CUBE IN THE CONNECTION radio button, and by selecting it (⬤) in the OLAP METADATA tree list

   ▶ A BEx query, by selecting the SPECIFY A CUBE IN THE CONNECTION radio button, and by selecting it (⬛) in the OLAP METADATA tree list

Figure 12.3 Choosing a BEx Query or Leaving the Choice to the Final User

6. Click FINISH to create the connection. Depending on your starting point, the connection appears in the LOCAL PROJECTS or REPOSITORY RESOURCES view.

7. If the connection is created in a local project, you may publish it to the Central Management Server (CMS) repository to make it available to all SAP BusinessObjects BI tools that support the SAP direct access (refer to Section 12.1.1).

The tools can use this connection to run queries to the SAP NetWeaver BW, without needing to build a universe. To federate data from SAP NetWeaver BW with data from other sources, you can define a relational universe on top of a relational connection.

12.1.4 Creating a Relational Connection to SAP NetWeaver BW

Relational connections to SAP NetWeaver BW can be defined only from the REPOSITORY RESOURCES panel. The driver proposed is used only by the Federation Query Server that runs on the BI platform, so there is no connectivity on the local machine. The driver is the standard SAP Java Connector (JCo), which is installed along with the SAP BusinessObjects BI server.

Roles

SAP NetWeaver BW security requires you to assign a role for all accounts in the SAP system whose credentials can be used to authenticate to the SAP NetWeaver BW system through the relational connection. This role must contain at least the following authorizations:

▶ S_RFC: Authorization check for RFC access

▶ S_RS_ADMWB: Data Warehousing Workbench—Objects

▶ S_RS_AUTH: SAP BusinessObjects BI Analysis Authorizations in Role

▶ S_RS_ICUBE: Data Warehousing Workbench—InfoCube

▶ S_RS_IOBJ: Data Warehousing Workbench—InfoObject

▶ S_RS_ISET: Data Warehousing Workbench—InfoSet

▶ S_RS_MPRO: Data Warehousing Workbench—MultiProvider

▶ S_RS_ODSO: Data Warehousing Workbench—DataStore Object

If necessary, ask your SAP NetWeaver BW administrator to assign your users these rights.

Connection Parameters

To create the relational connection, you need to provide the same parameters of the BICS connection (refer to Table 12.1) plus some optional additional parameters listed in Table 12.2.

To benefit from SAP NetWeaver BW load-balancing capabilities, it's possible to manually set these optional parameters that the SAP NetWeaver BW server can use to exchange information with the SAP BusinessObjects BI platform server. Starting with SAP BusinessObjects BI 4.1, these parameters can be set in IDT when creating the connection. In SAP BusinessObjects BI 4.0, these parameters are set in the Data Federation Administration Tool (see Chapter 6, Section 6.6).

Parameter Name	Parameter Description
programIDMapping	Defines the program IDs for the callback that SAP NetWeaver BW uses to contact the SAP BusinessObjects BI platform. The IDs are provided as a list of mappings: "server name = program ID". This list is formatted as a string containing key/values separated by a semicolon (;). The key represents the SAP BusinessObjects BI platform service name, and the value represents the name of an RFC destination created on SAP NetWeaver BW.
	If this property isn't manually set, then the Federation Query Server automatically sets an auto-generated RFC destination. In case of conflict, the system can generate up to 10 different RFC destinations. After this pool of 10 is used, the connection between SAP NetWeaver BW and the SAP BusinessObjects BI platform is no longer possible. Consequently, we strongly suggest that you manually enter the complete mapping for all servers and RFC destinations.
	Examples:
	`MySIA.AdaptiveProcessingServer=RFC1`
	`MySIA.DFServer1=RFC1;MySIA.DFServer2=RFC2;`
gatewayHostname	The name of the machine hosting the SAP NetWeaver BW gateway.
	Example:
	`gatewayHostname=server.mycompany.corp`
	If not specified, an RFC is executed to let SAP NetWeaver BW choose the value.

Table 12.2 Parameters to Create the Relational Connection to SAP NetWeaver BW

Parameter Name	Parameter Description
gatewayServiceName	The name or port number of the SAP NetWeaver BW gateway service. Examples: gatewayServiceName=sap50 gatewayServiceName=3350 If not specified, an RFC is executed to let SAP NetWeaver BW choose this value.

Table 12.2 Parameters to Create the Relational Connection to SAP NetWeaver BW (Cont.)

Supported InfoProviders

The relational connection to SAP NetWeaver BW points to an InfoProvider that is exposed by the SQL façade as a relational schema. The supported InfoProviders are listed in Table 12.3.

Type	InfoProvider
CUBE	InfoCube
ODSO	DSO
VIRT	VirtualProvider
MPRO	MultiProvider

Table 12.3 Supported InfoProviders in a Relational Connection to SAP NetWeaver BW

Information Design Tool Workflow

To create a relational connection to SAP NetWeaver BW, follow these steps:

1. From the Repository Resources view, run the relational connection wizard.

2. Enter a name for the connection, and click Next.

3. In the list of available drivers, select SAP NetWeaver BW • SAP Java Connector, as shown in Figure 12.4, and then click Next.

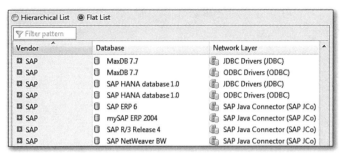

Figure 12.4 The Supported Relational Connections to SAP Systems

The connection parameters panel is displayed, as shown in Figure 12.5.

4. Enter the required parameters to connect to the SAP system, as described earlier in Table 12.1 and Table 12.2, and then click NEXT.

Figure 12.5 The SAP NetWeaver BW Relational Connection Parameters

5. Click TEST CONNECTION to validate the connection parameters. If the connection is valid, the INFOPROVIDER text field becomes enabled.

6. Click the 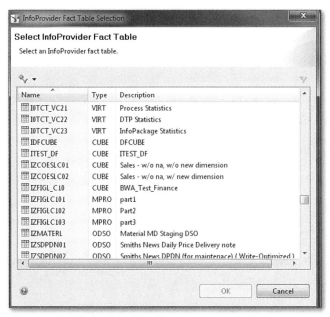 button in the INFOPROVIDER text field to open the SELECT INFO-PROVIDER FACT TABLE dialog box. The dialog box displays the possible InfoProviders you can select on this system, as shown in Figure 12.6. The different InfoProviders types available are listed in Table 12.3, earlier in this chapter.

Figure 12.6 InfoProvider Selection

7. Select one InfoProvider from the list, and click OK.

8. Click FINISH to close the connection wizard and create the connection. The connection opens in an editor and is listed in the REPOSITORY RESOURCES view.

9. Create a connection shortcut to this connection (as described in Chapter 4, Section 4.6.4).

After you've created the connection to the SAP NetWeaver BW system and its shortcut, you should build a multisource data foundation. Single-source data foundations don't support the SAP NetWeaver BW relational connection.

12.1.5 Creating a Multisource Data Foundation Automatically

In the local project containing the shortcut to the SAP NetWeaver BW relational connection, you can add a new multisource data foundation.

1. Create a new data foundation and select type MULTISOURCE-ENABLED (as described in Chapter 6, Section 6.2.2).

2. In the panel where you select the sources for the data foundation, choose the connection shortcut(s) to be used by the universe. At least one shortcut must reference a secured connection to an SAP NetWeaver BW system. Click NEXT.

3. For each selected connection, you may set additional properties in the DEFINE CONNECTION PROPERTIES FOR CONNECTION panel.

   If the connection is to SAP NetWeaver BW, click on the ADVANCED button to display advanced parameters and check that the AUTOMATICALLY CREATE TABLES AND JOINS checkbox is selected, as shown in Figure 12.7. With this setting, tables and joins are automatically created from the InfoProvider referenced by the connection.

Figure 12.7 Settings to Automatically Create the Data Foundation

4. Click FINISH to close the dialog box and create the data foundation and automatically generate the tables and joins.

The resulting data foundation is a star schema containing three types of tables whose name starts with a different prefix, as described in Table 12.4. The names of the tables' columns are the technical names appearing in the definition of the InfoProvider.

Type	Prefix	Description
Fact table	I	A single fact table containing the facts information of the InfoProvider (e.g., IOD_NW_01)
Dimension table	D	Multiple tables describing the InfoProvider master data (e.g., D0CALYEAR)
Text table	T	Multiple tables mapping to the InfoProvider text tables (e.g., T0CALMONTH)

Table 12.4 Table Types Appearing in a Data Foundation Based on SAP NetWeaver BW

The algorithm automatically creates alias tables so that the same information can be used in multiple places without creating loops.

After the data foundation has been saved, it can be used to build a business layer.

12.1.6 Creating a Business Layer Automatically

You can build a new business layer in the local project as described in Chapter 7, Section 7.2.4. In the business layer creation wizard, when you select a data foundation based on an SAP NetWeaver BW connection, IDT proposes by default to automatically create the business objects. If you keep this option, the business layer is created and filled with objects created out of the information available in the InfoProvider referenced by the connection. Each object of the InfoProvider may generate one or several objects in the business layer. The rules to create these objects are described in Table 12.5.

InfoProvider Object	Business Layer Object
Dimension	A folder. Example: In Figure 12.8, the CUSTOMER folder.
Characteristic	A dimension object pointing to the I-table and various attribute objects pointing to the T-tables.

Table 12.5 Objects Defined from an InfoProvider

InfoProvider Object	Business Layer Object
	Example: In Figure 12.8, the VERSION (SAP NW DEMO) dimension and its attributes VERSION (SAP NW DEMO) (SHORT DESCRIPTION), VERSION (SAP NW DEMO)(MEDIUM DESCRIPTION), and VERSION (SAP NW DEMO)(HEADING).
Key figure	A measure.
	Example: In Figure 12.8, the NUMBER OF DOCUMENTS (SAP NW DEMO) measure.
Key figure with unit or currency	A folder with a measure and dimensions representing the units.
	Example: In Figure 12.8, the folder OPEN ORDER QUANTITY IN BASE UNIT (SAP NW DEMO) and the measure and three dimensions it contains.

Table 12.5 Objects Defined from an InfoProvider (Cont.)

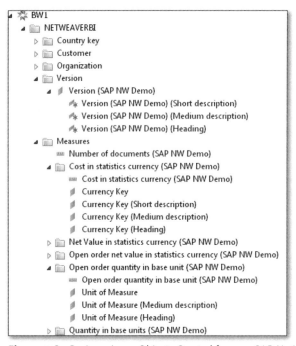

Figure 12.8 Business Layer Objects Created from an SAP NetWeaver BW InfoProvider

After the business layer has been saved, you can publish it to generate a universe.

12.1.7 Creating a Data Foundation and a Business Layer Manually

Creating the data foundation and business layer automatically is a quick way to retrieve all of the available information from the SAP NetWeaver BW InfoProvider and to generate a universe from scratch without doing any customization. However, in various situations, it can be more appropriate to create the universe manually and to tailor it to the final users' needs:

▶ You need only a subset of the information stored in the InfoProvider. Adding only the necessary fact, dimension, and text tables in the data foundation saves extra work and simplifies the project.

▶ You don't need to expose all objects that can be created from the data foundation. Exposing only the necessary objects in the business layer simplifies the usage for the business user.

▶ You federate the data of SAP NetWeaver BW with data from other systems. The default joins in the data foundation might not match the federated model and you should build your federated tables and multisource joins respecting some business requirements.

▶ You have multiple fact tables and you need to define contexts. Because the dimension objects are defined by default on the fact table, they get excluded from a query if the fact table isn't in the context. In this case, you should manually define the objects on the dimension or text tables.

To avoid the automatic generation of the data foundation, you should disable the default behavior in the data foundation creation wizard. To do so, unselect the AUTOMATICALLY CREATE TABLES AND JOINS checkbox in the ADVANCED tab shown earlier in Figure 12.7. After the empty data foundation has been created, you must manually add the tables and define the joins.

You should also disable the automatic generation of the business layer and manually define the objects from the data foundation tables. To do so, in the business layer creation wizard, unselected the AUTOMATICALLY CREATE CLASSES AND OBJECTS checkbox. Then, if you create objects by dragging data foundation items onto the business layer panel, the rules described in Section 12.1.6 don't apply, and the objects creation follows the standard behavior:

▶ Tables generate folders; the folder name is the table name.

▶ Table columns generate dimensions; the dimension name is the table column name.

12.1.8 SAP NetWeaver BW Relational Universe Performance

The relational façade to SAP NetWeaver BW doesn't provide access to the physical tables but provides a logical view of an InfoProvider in relational terms. This means that the underlying system doesn't behave in all situations like a plain relational database, and some limitations apply.

For example, the façade doesn't perform joins in SAP NetWeaver BW, so when you're running a query joining two tables in the universe, the data has to be fully retrieved, and the join is performed in the SAP BusinessObjects BI server memory. The performance of a relational universe on SAP NetWeaver BW is then very sensitive to the kind of queries executed.

The following are some best practices when creating a relational universe on SAP NetWeaver BW:

▶ Use only the necessary number of tables.

▶ Use the minimum number of joins (e.g., dimensions can be defined on the fact table).

▶ Filter the data at the SAP NetWeaver BW level before exposing it in the universe.

▶ Do most of the calculations and data manipulation within SAP NetWeaver BW instead of in the universe objects.

12.2 Access to SAP ERP

The SAP BusinessObjects BI 4.0 SP4 release introduced a relational connection to SAP ERP. This connection supports the main releases of the SAP ERP technology (SAP R/3 release 4, MySAP ERP 2004, SAP ERP 6). To minimize the impact on the SAP ERP system and avoid reducing its performance, the connection doesn't read the physical tables of the system but queries some artifacts that are meant for viewing data: ABAP functions, InfoSets, and SAP queries.

This connection can be used to create a universe, either single-source or multisource. The two solutions provide slightly different functionality, which is discussed in the following sections.

Creating a universe on an SAP ERP system follows the same process already described of creating the connection, the data foundation, and the business layer, and then publishing the universe for the BI client tools.

12.2.1 SAP ERP Connection Parameters

As for SAP NetWeaver BW, some specific parameters are required to connect to an SAP ERP system. These parameters are described in Table 12.6.

Parameter	Description
AUTHENTICATION MODE	The authentication mode is one of three supported: FIXED CREDENTIALS, CREDENTIALS MAPPING, or SINGLE SIGN-ON (see Chapter 4, Section 4.3).
CLIENT	This parameter is made of the three numbers that identify the SAP system client.
USER NAME PASSWORD	If the authentication mode is fixed credentials, then this is the user account and password used to connect to the SAP ERP system.
LANGUAGE	If the SAVE LANGUAGE option has been selected, then this is the locale to use to retrieve data from the SAP system.
SAVE LANGUAGE	If this option isn't selected, then the language to use to retrieve data from the SAP system is dynamic and is computed from the user's preferred viewing locale (see Chapter 11, Section 11.1). If this option is selected, then the locale to retrieve data is always the one defined in the LANGUAGE parameter.
SYSTEM ID	This parameter comprises three letters that identify the SAP system name.
SERVER TYPE	This is one choice among APPLICATION SERVER and MESSAGE SERVER.
SERVER NAME SYSTEM NUMBER	If your SAP ERP system has been defined as APPLICATION SERVER, then you must fill in its server name and system number, a number between "00" and "99".
SERVER NAME GROUP NAME	If your SAP ERP system has been defined as MESSAGE SERVER, you need to provide the application server name and its group name.

Table 12.6 Parameters to Connect to SAP ERP

In addition to these mandatory parameters, it's possible to set optional parameters when creating the connection. The optional parameters specific to SAP ERP are described in Table 12.7; the other parameters are the usual ones for a relational connection and they are described in Chapter 4, Section 4.5.2.

Parameter	Description
FUNCTION NAME WILDCARD	The parameter filters the functions to be displayed in the catalog by matching their name with the defined value. Wildcards can be used for the matching. The example "client*" in Figure 12.10 limits the functions to those whose name starts with the string "client".
MAP TABLE PARAMETERS INTO INPUT COLUMNS	SAP ABAP functions may contain input and output parameters that have the form of a structure (an ordered list of fields). They are called table parameters. If this option is checked, then table parameters are used both as input values (in input columns) and output values (tables). If the option is unchecked, then the table parameters are considered only output. Information on input columns can be found in Section 12.2.3.
MAP SELECTION FIELD INTO TABLE COLUMNS	SAP queries and InfoSets may contain optional inputs called selection fields, which are used to filter the data. If this parameter is checked, those inputs are mapped to optional input columns; if the parameter is unchecked, those inputs are ignored.
ARRAY FETCH SIZE	Doesn't apply to the SAP ERP connection. All data is retrieved in a single fetch.

Table 12.7 Optional Parameters for SAP ERP

12.2.2 Creating a Relational Connection to SAP ERP

The connection to SAP ERP is a relational connection that can be created from the LOCAL PROJECTS view or the REPOSITORY RESOURCES view. The middleware is the standard SAP Java Connector (JCo), which is installed with the SAP Business-Objects BI 4.x client tools or server installer. If the data foundation is chosen as multisource, then it's necessary to publish the connection to the server and use a local shortcut as discussed in Chapter 6, Section 6.1.3.

The workflow to create a relational connection for SAP ERP is similar to the one described in Chapter 4, Section 4.6:

1. From the LOCAL PROJECTS or the REPOSITORY RESOURCES view, run the relational connection wizard.

2. Enter a name for the connection, and then click NEXT.

3. In the list of supported drivers, choose the version of your SAP ERP from SAP ERP 6, MYSAP ERP 2004, and SAP R/3 RELEASE 4, as shown earlier in Figure 12.4. Click NEXT.

4. The connection parameters panel is displayed, as shown in Figure 12.9. To connect to the SAP system, enter the required parameters, as described previously in Table 12.6. Click NEXT.

Figure 12.9 Parameters of an SAP ERP Connection

5. You can then set the optional parameters of the connection described in Table 12.7 and visible in Figure 12.10.

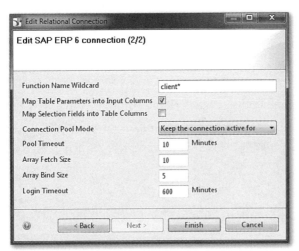

Figure 12.10 Connection Parameters Page

After the definition is complete, you should save the connection locally or publish it on the server and keep a local shortcut pointing to it. After you've created the connection to the SAP ERP system, you may use it and create a data foundation on it.

12.2.3 Data Foundation on SAP ERP

Because there are functional differences between a single-source and multisource data foundation on SAP ERP, the next sections treat the two versions separately. In general, it's better to use a single-source data foundation because it returns data faster than a multisource data foundation. The use of a multisource data foundation has to be kept for scenarios where the functionalities of a single-source data foundation aren't sufficient.

The main differences between the two architectures are that in a single-source data foundation:

▸ Joins are automatically detected with primary key and foreign key relationships between columns defined in the SAP ERP system. It's not possible to manually define a join.

▸ Column filters aren't allowed.

▸ Calculated columns aren't allowed.

▸ The SQL syntax is limited to Sum, Avg, Min, Max, and Count.

A multisource data foundation doesn't have those constraints.

In both single-source and multisource data foundations, the tables representing the SAP ERP artifacts still show some common functionality. Because the tables' records are exposed through InfoSets, SAP queries, and ABAP functions, they might contain *import*, *export*, or *changing parameters*, which are the equivalent of input or output parameters of a function. The imports sometimes require input information to let the table return any value. Those parameters are mapped into input columns in the data foundation tables.

Input Columns

An input column is a column that requires a value, which is sent to the database to display the content of the table. An input column is the equivalent of an input parameter for a stored procedure:

▶ If the parameter is mandatory, then a mandatory input column is created—its icon in the table has a red dot (AB)—as shown in Figure 12.11.

▶ If the parameter is optional, then an optional input column is created. An optional input column influences the result of the table but isn't strictly necessary to return the data. Its icon in the table has a yellow triangle (AB).

All input columns defined over import parameters of the SAP ERP system are automatically prefixed by the "-IMPORT_" string.

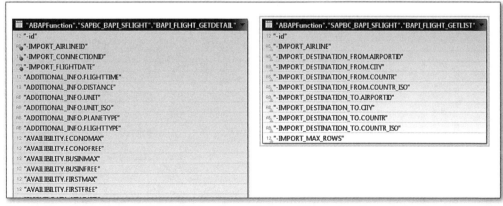

Figure 12.11 Tables Representing ABAP Functions with Import Parameters Shown as Input Columns

There are three ways to assign a value to the input columns. To choose this assignment, right-click the table or the column and select EDIT INPUT COLUMNS. A pop-up window appears letting you choose the resolution method, as shown in Figure 12.12.

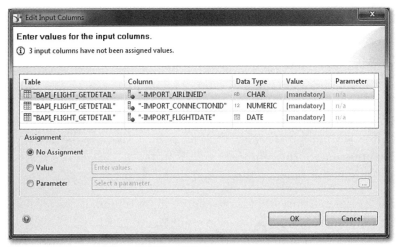

Figure 12.12 Input Columns Settings Window

The choice of the assignment method is described in Table 12.8.

Assignment	Description
NO ASSIGNMENT	No value is passed by default to the input column.
	For optional input columns, this can be a valid choice to let the system deal with the situation (the input is optional, so there should be no error).
	Alternatively, if this column is joined with a column from another table, then the values of the join are passed one by one to the input column. An example of this workflow is described in Section 12.2.5.
VALUE	A fixed value is passed to the input column. This value is a constant and is passed each time the table is called.
PARAMETER	A parameter (a prompt) is associated to the input column. When the table is called, the prompt interface is displayed and asks the end user to provide some information.
	The prompt must return a single value.

Table 12.8 Assignment Mode of an Input Column

Input columns are part of the common functionalities between single-source and multisource data foundations. The following section explains the specific functionality found in a single-source data foundation.

12.2.4 Single-Source Data Foundations on SAP ERP

In a single-source data foundation built on SAP ERP, you can't define the joins manually between tables. Joins are found by detecting the primary key and foreign key relationships between the SAP ERP artifacts. If there is no key relationship defined in the SAP ERP system, no joins are created.

To create the joins between the various tables, follow these steps:

1. Add to the data foundation the tables you need for your project.

2. From the data foundation top panel, select the command DETECT • DETECT KEYS. Make sure no table is selected to perform the detection across all tables. All of the primary keys and foreign keys of the tables appearing in the data foundation are found and displayed.

3. From the same menu command, choose the DETECT • DETECT JOINS to find the possible joins between tables.

4. The DETECT JOINS dialog box is displayed as shown in Figure 12.13. Select the DATABASE KEYS join detection method.

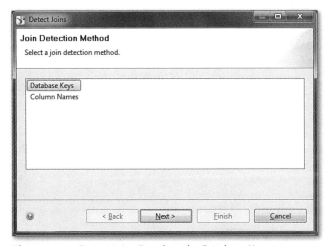

Figure 12.13 Detect Joins Based on the Database Keys

5. In the CANDIDATE JOINS window, click the checkbox in front of the joins to add as shown in Figure 12.14, and then click FINISH.

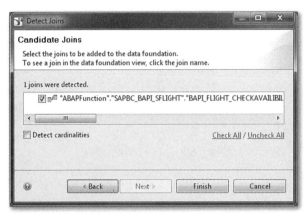

Figure 12.14 Candidate Join Selection

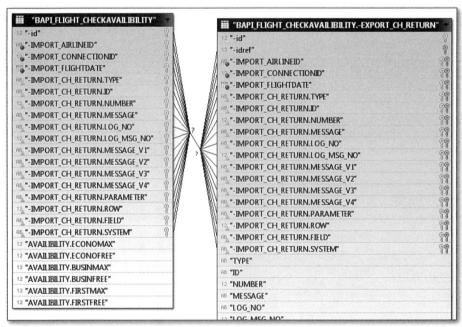

Figure 12.15 Autodetected Join

The joins are now added to the data foundation as shown in Figure 12.15. Note that instead of linking the fields one by one, a complex join is created to link multiple fields between them. This automatic join detection is very useful when working with groups of related ABAP functions. The SAP ERP system may require values to be passed between functions; those dependencies are exposed as joins in the data foundation.

When all tables and joins are added to the data foundation, and all input columns values assignments have been resolved, you can build the business layer.

The next section describes the functionalities of a multisource data foundation built on an SAP ERP connection.

12.2.5 Multisource-Enabled Data Foundations on SAP ERP

Multisource data foundations give you more freedom in the definition of the data model built on an SAP ERP connection. It's possible to manually create joins between any kind of artifacts (e.g., join an InfoSet with an ABAP function) and, obviously, join SAP ERP information with data coming from any other supported source.

As shown earlier in Section 12.1.8, a performance impact has to be expected when the federation services manage the queries and perform multisource activities.

A multisource data foundation on an SAP ERP connection permits to show how to pass a set of values to an input column with a join as suggested in Table 12.8. As an example, the SAP ERP standard demo ABAP function CHECKAVAILABILITY, available in the model SAPBC_BAPI_SFLIGHT, contains three mandatory input parameters asking for an airline ID, a flight ID, and a flight date. This ABAP function returns the number of free places of a flight after receiving the correct input values. If you have a table containing the list of flights, you can join it to the ABAP function to provide the whole list and retrieve the free places on all aircrafts. In the example, the InfoSet "BCS1" contains such a list and, as shown in Figure 12.16, it can be joined to the ABAP function input columns.

You have to make sure that the assignment method of all input columns is set to NO ASSIGNMENT.

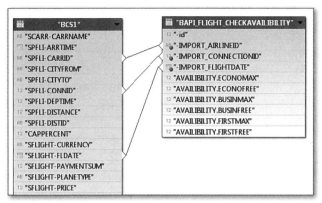

Figure 12.16 A Join to Input Columns Used to Pass Parameters

After the joins have been created, you can already run a simple query by selecting a few fields from the InfoSet and from the ABAP function tables in the data foundation. If the joins are correctly set, and if both tables contain data, the query returns data from both of them. In the example shown in Figure 12.17, the first two columns come from the InfoSet, and the last two columns come from the ABAP function.

(i) Show values in ERP_Multi-source. - 13 rows (3475 ms)			
▦ Raw Data ▦ Distinct values ⅉ Analysis			
▽ Enter your filter Filtered rows: 13/13			

AB SCARR-CARRNAME	12 SPFLI-CONNID	12 AVAILABILITY.ECONOFREE	12 AVAILABILITY.BUSINFREE
Air Canada	820	308	19
Air France	820	318	19
Lufthansa	400	346	0
Lufthansa	454	348	0
Lufthansa	455	219	0
Lufthansa	455	190	0
Lufthansa	2402	200	0

Figure 12.17 A Query between an InfoSet and an ABAP Function with an Assignment of Input Columns by Join

Multisource data foundations built on an SAP ERP system support SAP Business-Objects SQL based on ANSI SQL-92 syntax and on the functions listed in Table 6.3 of Chapter 6.

The ERP ABAP functions, InfoSets, and SAP queries can also be used as sources for federated tables.

12.2.6 Business Layers on an SAP ERP-Based Data Foundation

Creating a business layer on top of an SAP ERP-based data foundation isn't different from creating it on other sources. The customization of objects or the creation of new objects is quite restricted in a single-source universe because of the limited SQL syntax exposed on the SAP ERP system (refer to Section 12.2.3). On the multisource data foundation, the syntax is larger but, because the database can't process the functions, all computations are performed in the memory of the SAP BusinessObjects BI 4.x server.

When creating the business layer automatically or when manually dragging and dropping table fields from the data foundation onto the business layer panel, objects are automatically created. Their name is the description of the table field, and their description is the name of the table field. As shown in Figure 12.18, these NAME and DESCRIPTION fields are reversed because the names of the fields are technical and often not meaningful to business users. On the other hand, the description of the field is a good business name for the information.

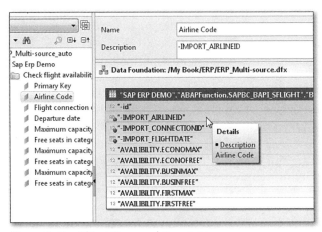

Figure 12.18 Object Name and Description

The business layer is now ready to be saved and published as a universe for consumption.

12.3 Access to SAP HANA

SAP HANA is an in-memory database with row storage and columnar storage for the tables. SAP HANA is both an RDBMS and an OLAP engine. To take advantage of SAP HANA performance, it is recommended to use its in-memory capabilities and the columns storage for the database tables.

In SAP HANA, designers have to create *information models* on top of the physical tables to take advantage of all its performance. The information models, also called SAP HANA views, column views, or SAP HANA cubes are of three main types:

▸ **Attribute views**
Define the dimensions of the model (e.g., product, time, geography).

▸ **Analytic views**
Define the measures of the model and their relationships to the dimensions. An analytic view is based on a single fact table.

▸ **Calculation views**
Combine several analytic views and other calculation views. Calculation views can contain calculated attributes, calculated measures, and complex calculations defined with a script language.

SAP HANA views are business oriented and contain dimensions, attributes, measures, and hierarchies. Client tools should access only analytic views, calculation views, and tables. All SAP HANA views are designed with the administrative and modeling tool of SAP HANA called SAP HANA Studio.

SAP ERP and SAP NetWeaver BW on SAP HANA

As an application platform, SAP HANA can run and host SAP ERP and SAP NetWeaver BW. In these cases, you access SAP ERP or SAP NetWeaver BW as if they were hosted on any other system and apply the workflows described earlier in Section 12.1 and Section 12.2, without considering the SAP HANA access described in this section.

With SAP BusinessObjects BI 4.1, the semantic layer and hence the universes built with IDT have evolved to support the new capabilities of the latest SAP HANA versions. The semantic layer offers two ways to access SAP HANA:

▸ A relational access through authored relational universes using SQL. The following sections describe the creation of a universe on top of SAP HANA views.

For SAP HANA, IDT also proposes a wizard to automatically generate the data foundation and the business layer on top of SAP HANA views.

▶ A multidimensional access through a direct access using the MDX query language.

Note

To fully take advantage of the in-memory processing and the performance, SAP recommends accessing SAP HANA through the SAP HANA views rather than a direct access to its tables. It is also possible to create a universe on top of the SAP HANA tables, as any universe built on top of other relational databases.

Accessing SAP HANA views introduces some constraints. For SAP BusinessObjects Web Intelligence, additional constraints related to variables and input parameters exist. Both are described in Section 12.3.3.

12.3.1 Creating a Universe on SAP HANA Views

This section describes how to build universes on top of SAP HANA views, not SAP HANA tables. The steps for creating this relational universe are the same as creating any relational universe: you have to manually create a relational connection to the SAP HANA system, create a new data foundation and add SAP HANA views in it. Finally, the business layer can be automatically generated before being published to generate the universe.

Creating a Relational Connection to SAP HANA

The workflow to create a relational connection for SAP HANA is similar to the one described in Chapter 4, Section 4.6:

1. From the LOCAL PROJECTS or the REPOSITORY RESOURCES view, run the relational connection wizard.

2. Enter a name for the connection, and then click NEXT.

3. In the list of supported drivers, select SAP • SAP HANA DATABASE 1.0 • JDBC or ODBC, as shown earlier in Figure 12.4. Click NEXT.

4. The connection parameters panel is displayed, as shown in Figure 12.19.

5. Enter the required parameters to connect to the SAP HANA system. Click NEXT.

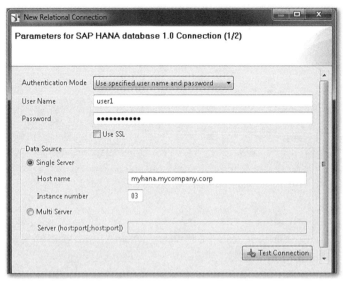

Figure 12.19 Adding the SAP HANA Connection Information

Parameters	Description
AUTHENTICATION MODE	The authentication mode is one of the three supported: FIXED CREDENTIALS, CREDENTIALS MAPPING, or SINGLE SIGN-ON (see Chapter 4, Section 4.3).
USER NAME PASSWORD	If AUTHENTICATION MODE is FIXED CREDENTIALS, then this is the user account and password used to connect to the SAP HANA system.
USE SSL	Use the SSL protocol to connect to the SAP HANA server.
DATA SOURCE	Select either SINGLE SERVER if your SAP HANA system is made of only one server or MULTI SERVER if it has failover and runs several servers.
HOST NAME	If you've selected the SINGLE SERVER option, then enter the SAP HANA host name.
INSTANCE NUMBER	If you've selected the SINGLE SERVER option, then enter the 2-digit SAP HANA instance number.
SERVER	If you've selected the MULTI SERVER option, then enter the list of server hosts and ports separated by a semicolon. Example: `myserver1:30115;myserver2:30115`

Table 12.9 Parameters to Create the Relational Connection to SAP HANA

6. Click the TEST CONNECTION button to make sure the definition is correct, and then click FINISH to create the connection.

> **SAP HANA Instance Number and SAP HANA Port Number**
>
> The SAP HANA port can be computed from its instance number. The port is "3<instance>15" where <instance> is the two-digit instance number. For example: instance 02 has the port number 30215.

After the relational connection to SAP HANA has been created, there are two different ways to create a relational universe on top of SAP HANA views:

▸ Create a data foundation, and add one or multiple SAP HANA views. Then automatically generate the business layer.

▸ Use the universe wizard to automatically generate the data foundation and the business layer, as described in Section 12.3.2.

Create the Data Foundation

Select an existing SAP HANA relational connection in the local project; the connection can be a local connection *(.cnx)* or a shortcut to a published connection *(.cns).*

To create a data foundation, choose one of the following options in the local project:

▸ Select the menu option FILE • NEW • DATA FOUNDATION.

▸ Select a project or a folder, right-click, and select NEW • DATA FOUNDATION.

▸ Select an SAP HANA relational connection, right-click, and select NEW • DATA FOUNDATION.

In the data foundation editor, you have to browse the SAP HANA catalog and open the schema _SYS_BIC. By default, the schema _SYS_BIC is the schema where the SAP HANA views are stored after they've been activated with SAP HANA Studio. An example of SAP HANA views in the connection catalog browser is shown in Figure 12.20.

A universe is usually built on top of analytic views (🗗) or calculation views (🗒).

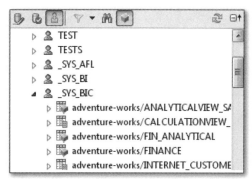

Figure 12.20 List of SAP HANA Views in the Catalog Browser

Select one or more SAP HANA views and then insert them in the data foundation. The SAP HANA views are seen as database tables but are identified with different icons as described in Chapter 5, Section 5.2.1.

By default, the SAP HANA views are filtered to only show the ones that are consumable by the SAP BusinessObjects BI clients. The FILTER INFORMATION MODELS toggle button (🌑) is pushed by default and if you release it, all SAP HANA views are displayed included those that SAP doesn't recommend to access as they are defined for internal usage.

In general, it's common to only add one SAP HANA view per data foundation. An SAP HANA view is self-descriptive and is equivalent to an OLAP cube. You can add more than one SAP HANA view in the data foundation, but you have to avoid creating joins between the different SAP HANA views.

> **Note**
>
> SAP doesn't recommend creating joins between SAP HANA views and other SAP HANA views, tables, and SQL views because it may have an impact on the query performance.

If you need to merge dimensions and attributes coming from two or more SAP HANA views, then you should not create the data foundation manually but instead use the wizard that automatically creates both the data foundation and business layer as described in Section 12.3.2.

You can view the content of the SAP HANA view like any other database table. If the SAP HANA view contains variables and/or input parameters, you're prompted to provide an answer for each variable and input parameter. SAP HANA variables and input parameters are detected and automatically added in the data foundation. Hidden prompts are added to surface the SAP HANA variables and input parameters.

Hidden parameters can't be seen in the list of available parameters in the data foundation and in the business layer. However the list of input parameters and variables is visible in the data foundation in the VARIABLES tab under the data foundation schema, as shown in Figure 12.21.

Name	Mandatory	Type		Value Attribute	Selection Type	Multiple Entries	Default Value	Description	Data Type
CUST_TYPE_PAR	Yes	AB	String		Single Value	No		Customer Type	Input Parameters
CUSTOMER_VAR	No	AB	String	CUSTOMID	Interval	No		Customers	Variable
VAR_COUNTRY	No	AB	String	COUNTRY	Single Value	No		Country	Variable

Table: crossprojecthana.sflight/SBOOK_CALCVIEW_PARAMETERS_VARIABLES

Properties · Columns · Variables

Figure 12.21 SAP HANA Variables and Input Parameters in the Data Foundation

When you refresh the structure of the data the variables and input parameters are updated at the same time as the SAP HANA views structure.

Although the parameters aren't visible, they can be used in an SQL definition of calculated columns, derived tables, or list of values definition as described in Section 12.3.3.

Create the Business Layer

After the data foundation has been created as shown in Figure 12.22, validated, and saved, you can generate the business layer.

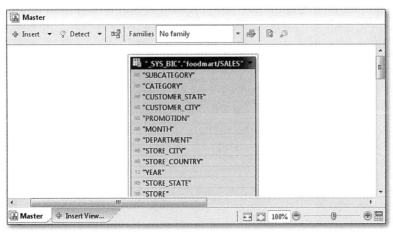

Figure 12.22 Data Foundation with One SAP HANA View

As already explained, an SAP HANA view is self-descriptive and is equivalent to an OLAP cube, so you don't have to manually create the dimensions, attributes, and measures in the business layer because they have already been defined in the SAP HANA view.

Select the data foundation created in the local project, right-click, and select New Business Layer.

The business layer is automatically created with the following:

▸ A folder per dimension or per hierarchy defined in the SAP HANA view

▸ A dimension per attribute defined in the SAP HANA view

▸ A measure per measure defined in the SAP HANA view

▸ A measure attribute per unit/currency associated to a measure defined in the SAP HANA view

Attributes associated to dimensions are created in the business layer for the following situations:

▸ Key attribute in the SAP HANA view

▸ Related attributes associated to other attributes in the SAP HANA view

The hierarchies created in SAP HANA views aren't generated in the relational business layer; instead, the hierarchy is generated as a folder and its levels are generated as dimensions.

All SAP HANA views metadata set as Hidden in the SAP HANA views aren't generated in the business layer. All objects created in the business layer are named with the caption defined for each SAP HANA view metadata. The business layer visible in Figure 12.23 is now ready to be saved and published as a universe for consumption.

If you modify the data foundation and add more SAP HANA views, the business layer isn't automatically updated. If you drag and drop the new SAP HANA view(s) in the business layer structure, a new folder is added (named with the SAP HANA view name), and a dimension is created per SAP HANA view metadata. The automatic business layer object's creation isn't applied in that case.

Figure 12.23 Business Layer Created from an SAP HANA Data Foundation

12.3.2 Creating a Data Foundation and a Business Layer Automatically

SAP BusinessObjects BI 4.1 offers the ability to automatically create a data foundation and a business layer from a selection of one or more SAP HANA views. Sometimes, a single SAP HANA view can't answer all business questions of the user, so it might be necessary to ask the IT department to build a new information model. The universe wizard provides an alternative.

Starting with SAP BusinessObjects BI 4.1, in IDT, you have a wizard to automatically create universes on multiple SAP HANA views so that users have more chances to find the information to answer the questions they ask. This technology doesn't impact SAP HANA performance.

This solution is unique because it provides the ability to mix multiple SAP HANA views in a single result without requiring the creation of a new view. This functionality also offers the ability to merge common dimensions coming from different SAP HANA views in a single dimension in the business layer.

Generate the Data Foundation and the Business Layer

The local project is the place where you create the data foundation and the business layer. To automatically generate the data foundation and the business layer, follow these steps:

1. Select a project or a folder in the local project, right-click, and select NEW • SAP HANA BUSINESS LAYER.

2. Give a name to the data foundation and the business layer, as shown in Figure 12.24.

3. Click NEXT, and select an existing SAP HANA relational connection from the list that pops up. The listed connections are all local connections (*.cnx*).

Figure 12.24 Entering a Name for the Data Foundation and the Business Layer

4. Browse the SAP HANA connection catalog browser, select one or more SAP HANA views, and then click FINISH, as shown in Figure 12.25. Only the allowed SAP HANA views can be selected.

Figure 12.25 Select One or Several SAP HANA Views

The wizard automatically generates the data foundation and the business layer. The business layer is generated with the same rules described earlier.

The Data Foundation Content

The data foundation contains all of the SAP HANA views you've selected, but they aren't joined. Each SAP HANA view is accessed by a distinct SQL flow to guarantee the query performance. Common dimensions and attributes are mapped by single objects; for instance, even if "Country" exists in more than one SAP HANA view, "Country" is created as a single business object in the business layer.

The user experience is exactly the same as on any other universe. A business user selects the dimensions, attributes, and measures in the query panel, one or more SQL flows are generated, and the query results are displayed in a single result set.

To allow the generation of multiple SQL flows, the wizard automatically generates a join filter associated to a context per SAP HANA view in the data foundation, as shown in Figure 12.26.

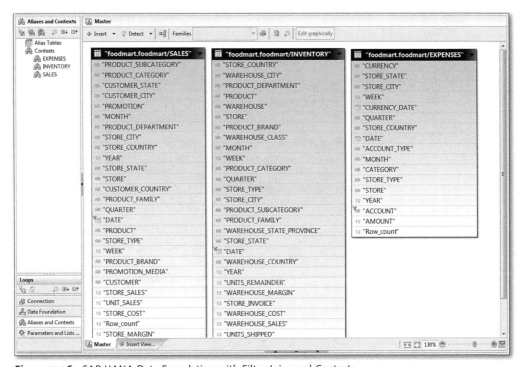

Figure 12.26 SAP HANA Data Foundation with Filter Joins and Contexts

The Business Layer Content

The generated business layer contains all attributes, dimensions, and measures enabled in the SAP HANA view. If there are common dimensions or attributes in the selected SAP HANA views, only one object is created. The object SQL definition has multiple bindings—one for each SAP HANA view where it appears. To allow an object to have multiple SQL bindings, the wizard uses the `@aggregate_aware` function (described in Chapter 7, Section 7.23.1). The `@aggregate_aware` function is used to dynamically switch from one SAP HANA view to another SAP HANA view depending on the query context. Users select dimensions, attributes, and measures from the business layer and therefore force the query engine to choose one SAP HANA view or another.

The goal of this solution is to allow users to query multiple SAP HANA views at once. The `@aggregate_aware` function is used with the contexts defined in the data foundation to generate multiple SQL flows. This solution always returns the result of different SQL queries into a single result set.

> **Note**
>
> For more information on aggregate awareness and aggregate navigation, see Chapter 7, Section 7.18.

As all dimensions aren't common to the selected SAP HANA views, the `@aggregate_aware` function needs to create a balanced query. To do so, all dimensions have a corresponding binding in an SAP HANA view, even if they don't appear in a given SAP HANA view. To satisfy this requirement, a `NULL` placeholder is used in place of an SQL definition when a dimension doesn't exist in a given SAP HANA view.

Table 12.10 gives an example of dimensions and measures mapping in the business layer.

Object Type	Object Name	SQL Definition
Dimension	Year	`@aggregate_aware(SALES.YEAR, INVENTORY.YEAR, EXPENSES.YEAR)`
Dimension	Quarter	`@aggregate_aware(SALES.QUARTER, EXPENSES.QUARTER, NULL)`
Dimension	Product	`@aggregate_aware(SALES.PRODUCT, INVENTORY.YEAR, NULL)`

Table 12.10 An Example of Defining Objects on Multiple Views

Object Type	Object Name	SQL Definition
Dimension	Category	`@aggregate_aware(EXPENSES.CATEGORY, NULL)`
Dimension	Country	`@aggregate_aware(SALES.COUNTRY, NULL)`
Dimension	Warehouse	`@aggregate_aware(INVENTORY.WAREHOUSE, NULL)`
Measure	Revenue	`Sum(SALES.REVENUE)`
Measure	Quantity	`Sum(INVENTORY.QUANTITY)`
Measure	Amount	`Sum(EXPENSES.AMOUNT)`

Table 12.10 An Example of Defining Objects on Multiple Views (Cont.)

The business layer visible in Figure 12.27 is now ready to be saved and published as a universe for consumption.

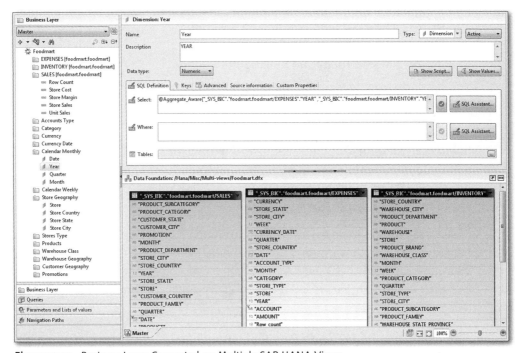

Figure 12.27 Business Layer Generated on Multiple SAP HANA Views

If you modify the data foundation and add more SAP HANA views, the business layer isn't automatically updated. The recommendation is to execute the automatic generation wizard again to build a new universe. If you want to manually update an existing data foundation and business layer, you have to follow these steps:

1. Create a filter join in each SAP HANA view.

2. Create a context for each filter join.

3. Modify the `@aggregate_aware` SQL expression for each existing dimension.

4. Define the SQL expression for each new dimension while using the `@aggregate_aware` function and the `NULL` placeholder appropriately.

5. Modify the aggregate navigation.

12.3.3 SAP HANA Views: Recommendations and Constraints

The data foundation built on top of one or more SAP HANA views has the same capabilities as any other data foundation built on top of database tables. However, SAP HANA views have some specificities to consider.

General Recommendations and Constraints

You can customize the data foundation by creating calculated columns or derived tables. Calculated columns may impact SAP HANA performance and can be created only on SAP HANA calculation views.

If you have to manually build a derived table from an SAP HANA view, you have to include all of the required SAP HANA variables and input parameters in the SQL definition. IDT provides an automatic way to create a derived table that includes SAP HANA variables and input parameters.

Even if it's possible to do so, SAP doesn't recommend creating joins between SAP HANA views and other resources because it may impact the query performance. You can create joins between tables or SQL views and define a context for each SAP HANA view to isolate it and force the query engine to generate a specific SQL query for it.

When querying SAP HANA views some constraints have to be taken into account, including the variables and input parameters in the SQL definition. Some general constraints apply when querying an SAP HANA analytic view:

▶ The query should not demand custom SQL expressions such as string concatenation, substring, and so on.

▶ The query should not demand calculation expressions such as: +, −, *, /, and so on.

▶ Each measure created in the business layer must include an SQL aggregation function: SUM, MIN, MAX, or COUNT.

▶ If the query doesn't contain a measure but only dimensions and attributes, then the SQL query must start with Select Distinct.

These constraints don't apply to universes connecting to SAP HANA calculation views. The query engine takes into account all SAP HANA views constraints and restrictions and generates the appropriate SQL when building a query in the business layer, previewing data on an SAP HANA view or previewing data on an SAP HANA view column.

Access Constraint for SAP BusinessObjects Web Intelligence 4.1

With SAP BusinessObjects BI 4.1, only SAP Crystal Reports for Enterprise and SAP BusinessObjects Dashboards fully support automatically generated universes that contain SAP HANA variables and input parameters.

For SAP BusinessObjects Web Intelligence, it's necessary to customize the universe whenever a variable or input parameter is found in a view. The universe customization consists in creating a derived table per SAP HANA view in the data foundation and then defining the business layer objects on those tables. The derived table should explicitly expose in its definition the variables and input parameters of the SAP HANA view.

Variables are used to filter the SAP HANA view; they should be added to the WHERE clause of the SQL statement.

Input parameters are used in calculated attributes formulas, calculated measures formulas, and currency conversion; they should be added in the PLACEHOLDER clause after the FROM clause of the SQL statement as follows: From myview 'PLACEHOLDER' = ('$$MY_INPUT_PARAM_1$$', 'User answer'). The variable and input parameters behave like the parameters for the @prompt function; that is, they require user answers before the query execution.

IDT enables you to automatically generate a derived table by selecting an SAP HANA view in the data foundation, right-clicking, and choosing INSERT • DERIVED TABLE, as described in Chapter 5, Section 5.4.1.

When inserting a derived table from an SAP HANA view, the generated SQL takes into account the input parameters and the variables. The SQL syntax makes reference to hidden parameters using the `@prompt` function.

Example

Here is an example of a generated derived table containing SAP HANA variables and input parameters:

```
Select Table__7."CARRID", Table__7."CONNID", Table__7."FLDATE",
Table__7."CUSTOMID", Table__7."CUSTTYPE", Table__7."LOCCURKEY",
Table__7."COUNTRY", Table__7."LOCCURAM" From "_SYS_BIC"." sflight/
SBOOK_CALCVIEW" ('PLACEHOLDER' = ('$$CUST_TYPE_PAR$$', @Prompt(Hana
Variable sflight/SBOOK_CALCVIEW/CUST_TYPE_PAR))) Table__7 Where (
Table__7."CUSTOMID" @Prompt(Hana Variable sflight/SBOOK_CALCVIEW) )
AND ( Table__7."COUNTRY" = @Prompt(Hana Variable sflight/SBOOK_CAL-
CVIEW/VAR_COUNTRY) )
```

SAP BusinessObjects Web Intelligence 4.1 doesn't support those hidden parameters, so you have to replace their occurrence in the derived table `PLACEHOLDER` and `WHERE` clauses. The hidden parameters can be replaced by explicit parameters you define in the business layer or by setting hard-coded values.

Note

SAP HANA variables and input parameters referenced in derived tables always require a mandatory answer even if they have been defined as optional in the SAP HANA view.

Internationalization

Relational universes don't support out-of-the-box text metadata translated created in SAP HANA views. As for any relational universe, the business layer object texts need to be translated with the Translation Management Tool, which is delivered with SAP BusinessObjects BI 4.1 (see Chapter 11, Section 11.2). The Translation Management Tool supports the XLIFF standard in import and export mode just like the SAP HANA Repository Translation Tool.

For the multilingual data, the user's preferred viewing locale (see Chapter 11, Section 11.1) is passed to SAP HANA for Java Database Connectivity (JDBC) connection only.

12.3.4 Creating a Multidimensional Access on SAP HANA

SAP BusinessObjects BI 4.1 provides a direct dimensional access to SAP HANA. With this technology, SAP HANA views can be exposed directly without the need to define a universe on them. Only a connection has to be defined and published. The client tools use that connection to connect to an SAP HANA view, and a query panel opens exactly as if a universe was available.

This technology is actually building a universe on the fly, which isn't persisted and exists only during the client session. From an end user's point of view, there is no difference between the direct access and an authored multidimensional universe. The SAP HANA direct access supports and displays the SAP HANA hierarchies, variables, and input parameters.

As of SAP BusinessObjects BI 4.1, only SAP Crystal Reports for Enterprise supports the SAP HANA direct access. SAP BusinessObjects Web Intelligence and SAP BusinessObjects Dashboards don't support this access method yet. To connect them to SAP HANA, you have to build a relational universe.

To enable the direct access to an entire SAP HANA system or to one of its views, you first have to create an SAP HANA OLAP connection. The steps to follow are similar to the ones to create an OLAP connection:

1. From the LOCAL PROJECTS or the REPOSITORY RESOURCES view, run the OLAP connection wizard.

2. Enter a name for the connection, and then click NEXT.

3. In the list of drivers shown earlier in Figure 12.1, select the SAP • SAP HANA • SAP HANA CLIENT driver, and then click NEXT. The connection parameters panel displays, as shown in Figure 12.28.

4. Enter the required parameters, as described in Table 12.11, to connect to the SAP system, and then click NEXT.

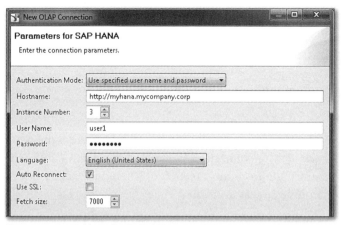

Figure 12.28 Adding the SAP HANA OLAP Connection Information

Parameters	Description
AUTHENTICATION MODE	The authentication mode is one of three supported: FIXED CREDENTIALS, CREDENTIALS MAPPING, or SINGLE SIGN-ON (see Chapter 4, Section 4.3).
HOSTNAME	The name or IP address of the machine onto which SAP HANA is running.
INSTANCE NUMBER	The two-digit number of the SAP HANA instance.
USER NAME	If AUTHENTICATION MODE is FIXED CREDENTIALS, then this is the user account and password used to connect to the SAP HANA system.
PASSWORD	
LANGUAGE	The default language to be used when connecting to SAP HANA.
AUTO RECONNECT	If true, allows the session to stay open with SAP HANA, even after a long inactivity time.
USE SSL	Use the SSL protocol to connect to the SAP HANA server. On Windows operating systems, when you configure the data source name (DSN) in the ODBC Data Source Administrator, select the SSL option.
FETCH SIZE	Defines the number of rows of data retrieved per bucket.

Table 12.11 Parameters to Create the OLAP Connection to SAP HANA

5. In the CUBE SELECTION panel, you can select the connection to reference the following:

   ▶ The whole SAP HANA system, by selecting the DO NOT SPECIFY A CUBE IN THE CONNECTION radio button.

   ▶ One of its views, by selecting the SPECIFY A CUBE IN THE CONNECTION radio button, and by selecting it (🔵) in the OLAP METADATA tree list.

6. Click FINISH to close the wizard and create the connection. Depending on your starting point, the connection appears in the LOCAL PROJECTS or REPOSITORY RESOURCES view.

7. If the connection is created in a local project, you have to publish it to the CMS repository to share it with the SAP BusinessObjects BI tools that support the direct access from the CMS repository.

You can also create the OLAP connection in the Central Management Console (CMC), which is the administration interface of the CMS repository.

Client tools that support the direct access automatically display the connection when browsing for possible data sources. If the connection enables access to the whole SAP HANA system, then the client tools user needs to select the view to query before creating a report.

The OLAP direct access technology on SAP HANA is very similar to the one offered for SAP NetWeaver BW as described in Chapter 7, Section 7.2.1.

Internationalization

The locale defined in the OLAP connection is always overridden by SAP Crystal Reports for Enterprise. The language used for the translation is the preferred viewing locale defined in SAP Crystal Reports for Enterprise.

12.4   Migrating a Universe to SAP HANA

Starting with the SAP BusinessObjects BI 4.1 release, IDT contains a wizard to migrate a relational single-source universe created in IDT and based on a non-SAP HANA database to a universe based on SAP HANA. As of SAP BusinessObjects BI 4.1, the supported databases are Oracle, Microsoft SQL Server, Teradata, and SAP Sybase ASE.

This wizard is called the Universe Migration Landscape tool and has to be explicitly selected during the SAP BusinessObjects BI 4.1 client tools installation because it's not installed by default. The tool performs the following actions:

▶ Creates a new data foundation and business layer based on the information of the original universe

▶ Points the new resources to an SAP HANA connection

▶ Converts the SQL used in objects definition to comply with the SQL supported by SAP HANA

▶ Publishes the new universe on SAP HANA in the CMS repository

▶ Creates copies of the SAP BusinessObjects Web Intelligence and SAP Crystal Reports for Enterprise documents that were pointing to the original universe and points them to the new universe on SAP HANA

The tool expects to find on SAP HANA the same schema used in the data foundation on the original database. Table names must match up to the catalog and owner names. You must have previously created the schema on SAP HANA (and optionally moved the data). If the tables aren't found, the tool returns an error and a script that can be used in SAP Data Services 4.1 to automatically create the schema on SAP HANA and move the data.

SAP Data Services 4.1 is an extract-transform-load (ETL) tool that can be used to move data from one source to another. If you've installed the application on the SAP BusinessObjects BI platform, the script generated by the Universe Landscape Migration wizard can be directly used to generate the schema in SAP HANA and move the data from the source database. You can also create the schema and move the data in other ways, but you need to make sure that the table names match on the original system and in SAP HANA.

The migration process starts from a relational universe created with IDT on a non-SAP database and published in the CMS repository. To migrate this universe, follow these steps:

1. In the REPOSITORY RESOURCES view, select a relational universe based on a supported data source, right-click it, and select the MIGRATE TO SAP HANA command (▶🗒) to start the SAP HANA MIGRATION wizard.

2. The wizard retrieves the published universe in a local project named MIGRATION. If this project doesn't exist, the wizard creates it.

In the wizard's CONNECTIONS page, shown in Figure 12.29, select an SAP HANA connection published in a CMS repository or a connection shortcut to this connection. You can click the REPOSITORY CONNECTIONS button (⊞) to select this connection from the server, or you can click the three dots in the CONNECTION text field to select a local connection shortcut. This connection is the target source for the new universe.

Figure 12.29 Choice of the Target SAP HANA Connection

3. Click NEXT. The MIGRATION PREVIEW page opens and shows the result of the analysis of the content on the SAP HANA system.

4. If some tables used in the source universe are missing in SAP HANA, the REP-LICATE TABLES button appears, as shown in Figure 12.30.

   It's mandatory that all tables used in the source universe are created in SAP HANA; otherwise, the migration can't succeed, and it's not worth continuing the wizard as further steps return errors.

5. From this step onward, an EXPORT REPORT button appears. You can click the button to generate a report in PDF format of all the actions performed by the tool on the migration process.

   If you've installed SAP Data Services 4.1, click the REPLICATE TABLES button to open a dialog box that displays a script; you can copy it and use it in SAP Data Services 4.1 to create the missing tables and transfer their data in SAP HANA. Alternatively, create the tables with other methods (manually or with other tools). Once all tables are in SAP HANA, restart the wizard and repeat the previous steps.

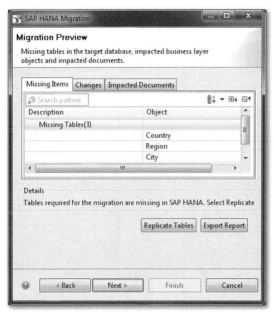

Figure 12.30 Migration Preview Page

6. If all tables are found in SAP HANA, in the MIGRATION PREVIEW page, the CHANGES tab shows the necessary changes to perform in the object syntax, if any, and the IMPACTED DOCUMENTS tab shows the documents that use this source universe.

7. Click NEXT to start the migration. The new data foundation and business layer are built on the SAP HANA connection, and the syntax of the objects, if necessary, is translated to the SAP HANA SQL.

8. The SUMMARY OF MIGRATED UNIVERSE page opens telling which changes have been performed. Click NEXT to publish the universe on the server.

9. When the universe has been published on the server, the wizard displays the list of SAP BusinessObjects Web Intelligence and SAP Crystal Reports for Enterprise documents saved in the CMS repository and using the original universe as shown in Figure 12.31.

10. Select some reports by checking the checkbox in front of them, and then click NEXT to create a copy of the selected reports and change their source to the generated universe connected to SAP HANA.

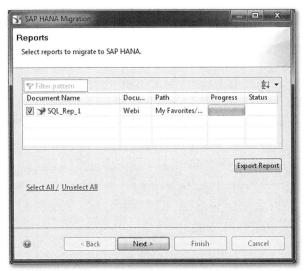

Figure 12.31 List of Reports That Can Be Migrated

11. The SUMMARY OF MIGRATED REPORTS shows the result of the migration for the selected reports. Click FINISH to close the wizard.

If some errors occur during the execution, the wizard can be launched again. If errors occur in the reports migration, you can right-click the newly created universe on SAP HANA and select the command POST MIGRATION to run only the report migration part of the wizard.

12.5 Summary

The semantic layer and universe technologies can be used to connect SAP Business-Objects BI tools to SAP data sources such as SAP ERP, SAP NetWeaver BW, and SAP HANA. The semantic layer technology provides multiple ways to connect to those systems:

▶ OLAP connection to SAP NetWeaver BW, for SAP direct access from client tools

▶ Relational connection to SAP NetWeaver BW, used in multisource universes

▶ Relational connection to SAP ERP, used in single-source or multisource universes

- ▶ Relational connection to SAP HANA, used in single-source or multisource universes

- ▶ OLAP connection to SAP HANA, for a direct access to SAP HANA

Finally, the Universe Landscape Migration plug-in for IDT allows you to migrate a universe based on other databases to a universe based on SAP HANA. The plug-in can also migrate the reports based on the source universe and point them to the generated universe.

The semantic layer technology is continuously evolving, mainly around the support of SAP HANA, and provides new capabilities to access these data sources with each new release.

The Universe Design Tool and Information Design Tool share many concepts. However, you must take some differences into consideration when converting universes.

13   Comparing the Universe Design Tool and Information Design Tool

Previous chapters have described the different capabilities of Information Design Tool (IDT). IDT is the successor of the Universe Design Tool, so most concepts are common to both tools, and IDT can be seen as a superset of the Universe Design Tool. However, there are some slight differences you need to know about when converting a universe created with the Universe Design Tool to the new universe format if you expect the converted universe to behave like the original one. This chapter compares the two tools on different topics:

▸ The main workflows and capabilities

▸ The connections created by the two tools

▸ The data foundation and the database schema made of tables, joins, and so on

▸ The business layer and its classes/folders and objects

▸ The prompts/parameters and lists of values

▸ The security proposed by the two tools

▸ Some usability differences

Finally, the chapter describes how a universe is converted and how to perform this conversion in IDT.

13.1   General

Table 13.1 describes the main differences between the Universe Design Tool and IDT.

Universe Design Tool	Information Design Tool
Generates universe (*.unv*) that can be consumed by the following: ▸ SAP BusinessObjects Web Intelligence ▸ SAP Crystal Reports 2013 ▸ SAP BusinessObjects Explorer ▸ Query as a Web Service ▸ SAP BusinessObjects Live Office, through SAP BusinessObjects Web Intelligence and Query as a Web Service ▸ SAP BusinessObjects Dashboard, through Query as a Web Service ▸ SAP Lumira ▸ SAP Predictive Analysis	Generates universe (*.unx*) that can be consumed by the following: ▸ SAP BusinessObjects Web Intelligence ▸ SAP Crystal Reports for Enterprise ▸ SAP BusinessObjects Explorer (relational only) ▸ SAP BusinessObjects Dashboards ▸ SAP Lumira (relational only) ▸ SAP Predictive Analysis (relational only)
Doesn't differ between authoring and consumption resources; the only supported file is the universe that can be saved locally or exported to the Central Management Server (CMS) repository.	Separates the authoring and consumption workflows. For authoring, the data foundation and business layer are saved in a local project. For consumption, the universe can be published locally or in the CMS repository.
You connect to the CMS repository in the USER AUTHENTICATION dialog box. You can open only one session at a time. Before opening a new session, you must close the previous one.	You can access several CMS repositories simultaneously. All sessions are managed in a single location, the REPOSITORY RESOURCES view, where you can define and save predefined sessions.
Doesn't have collaboration mode.	Supports designers' collaboration and resource synchronization in shared projects.
Supports linked universes.	Doesn't support linked universes.
Doesn't support custom user attributes.	Supports custom user attributes (as of SAP BusinessObjects BI 4.0 SP4).

Table 13.1 Workflow Comparison

Universe Design Tool	Information Design Tool
Can display values for only one table or one column at a time. The values are displayed in columns.	Uses a common SHOW VALUES editor to display data from connections, tables, columns, query results, and so on. This editor can display values for several tables or columns. It proposes an advanced graphical display with a large number of supported charts and filtering capabilities that can be used to profile data.
Supports metadata exchange to automatically create universes from third-party databases models or export universes to these models.	Doesn't support metadata exchange.
Can't convert a universe based on a relational source into a universe based on SAP HANA.	Supports the conversion of a universe based on another database to a universe based on SAP HANA (as of SAP BusinessObjects BI 4.1).
Proposes a Software Development Kit (SDK) that covers all Universe Design Tool capabilities.	As of SAP BusinessObjects BI 4.1, it proposes an SDK that supports only simple workflows. Since its first release in SAP BusinessObjects BI 4.0 SP4, this SDK has been updated with new methods in SAP BusinessObjects BI 4.0 SP5 and SAP BusinessObjects BI 4.1.

Table 13.1 Workflow Comparison (Cont.)

13.2 Connections

Table 13.2 compares the different connections supported by the Universe Design Tool and IDT.

Universe Design Tool	Information Design Tool
Supports two local connection types: ▶ Personal: Can be used only on the computer on which it was created. ▶ Shared: Created locally on the computer but can be used by all users.	Supports only one local connection, the one you create in a local project.
Supports a secured connection, which is the connection created in the CMS repository.	Supports a secured connection, which is the connection created in the CMS repository. To reference a secured connection, you must use a connection shortcut.
Supports relational connections based on Connection Server and in common with IDT (interoperability).	Supports relational connections based on Connection Server and in common with the Universe Design Tool (interoperability).
Supports SAP NetWeaver BW and SAS relational connections through SAP BusinessObjects Data Federator XI 3.0.	Multisource data foundation supports SAP NetWeaver BW or SAS relational connections based on the Federation Query Server. These connections can only be created in the CMS repository. It isn't possible to create them locally. Supports also OLAP connection to SAP NetWeaver BW.
Supports OLAP connections based on Connection Server created in the Universe Design Tool.	Doesn't support OLAP connections based on Connection Server created in the Universe Design Tool.
Doesn't support OLAP connections created in IDT or CMC.	Supports OLAP connections created in IDT or CMC. These connections can be used for multidimensional universes or direct access (for SAP systems).
Supports connections based on stored procedures and Java beans.	Doesn't support connections based on stored procedures and Java beans.

Table 13.2 Connection Support Comparison

Universe Design Tool	Information Design Tool
Supports connections created in SAP BusinessObjects Data Federator XI 3.0.	Doesn't support connections created in SAP BusinessObjects Data Federator XI 3.0, but supports multisource data foundations (as of SAP BusinessObjects BI 4.0) and federated tables (as of starting from SAP BusinessObjects BI 4.1).
Doesn't support new connectivity supported by Connection Server.	Supports new connectivity types: Hadoop, Web Service, OData, and so on.
Supports the use of @variable in connection parameters.	Doesn't support the use of @variable in connection parameters, except if used in the BEGIN_SQL parameter, which can be set in the data foundation or in the business layer.
Relational connection, for which you have the DOWNLOAD CONNECTION LOCALLY right granted, uses local middleware.	Allows you to choose either local or server middleware to use a relational connection for which you have the DOWNLOAD CONNECTION LOCALLY right granted.
Can't copy a local connection into the CMS repository.	Can publish a local connection into the CMS repository and copy its parameters in this newly created secured connection.
You can navigate in the database structure but not in the database data.	In the connection editor, you can navigate in the database structure and use the SHOW VALUES view to preview, filter, and analyze data, and then display the data using charts.
You can send SQL queries to the database, but they are only validated and no data is returned. You can't send direct MDX queries.	You can run custom SQL queries directly to a relational database or run custom MDX queries directly to an OLAP database.

Table 13.2 Connection Support Comparison (Cont.)

13.3   Data Foundation

In the Universe Design Tool, the data foundation doesn't exist, but it can be seen as the database schema—the set of tables and joins—used in the universe. Table 13.3 compares the concepts supported by the Universe Design Tool for this underlying model and data foundation created for relational universes in IDT.

Universe Design Tool	Information Design Tool
The database schema can only be used in one universe, unless you duplicate it.	A data foundation can be reused by several different business layers and, therefore, by several universes.
Displays the database schema as a whole.	Supports data foundation views.
Doesn't support table grouping and colors.	Supports families to organize tables and assign them a color.
Doesn't support calculated columns.	Supports calculated columns.
Defines context by explicitly adding all joins that may contribute to the context.	Defines contexts by adding only the necessary joins. It's no longer mandatory to explicitly include or exclude all data foundation joins.
Generates only single-source universes. Multisource is supported through a connection created in SAP Business-Objects Data Federator XI 3.0.	Supports relational multisource data foundations.
Doesn't support tables that query different data sources, unless they are defined in SAP BusinessObjects Data Federator XI 3.0.	Supports federated tables (as of SAP BusinessObjects BI 4.1).
Can show the tables used by an object or the objects depending on a table.	Can show full dependencies between business layers, data foundations, objects, tables, and columns.
Supports strategies.	Doesn't support strategies.

Table 13.3   Data Foundation Comparison

Universe Design Tool	Information Design Tool
Doesn't search text on the tables, joins, and so on.	Proposes an advanced search where you can also select the table and column types, views, and families to search.
N/A	Proposes enhanced capabilities for ease of use: merge tables, highlight related tables, data foundation overview while zooming, comments, and so on.

Table 13.3 Data Foundation Comparison (Cont.)

13.4 Business Layer

In the Universe Design Tool, the business layer doesn't exist, but it can be seen as the set of objects exposed by the universe to client tools. In the business layer, IDT proposes new concepts compared to the classes and objects supported in the Universe Design Tool. Table 13.4 lists these IDT enhancements.

Universe Design Tool	Information Design Tool
Supports relational objects: dimensions, details, and measures organized in classes.	Supports the same relational objects that have been renamed into dimensions, attributes, and measures. These objects are organized in folders.
Supports a flat representation of OLAP universe through the relational objects: dimensions, details, and measures. Supports calculated measures with restrictions.	Supports multidimensional business layer and multidimensional objects: hierarchies, levels, calculated members, calculated measures, analysis dimensions, and named sets. Supports full MDX expressions in these multidimensional objects.
Doesn't take advantage of multidimensionality of hierarchies in OLAP universes	Proposes a MEMBER SELECTOR dialog box to select members in a multidimensional hierarchy and use OLAP operators.

Table 13.4 Business Layer Comparison

Universe Design Tool	Information Design Tool
In an OLAP-generated universe, the objects can be edited.	In a multidimensional business layer created from an OLAP data source, the generated objects, especially the query that defines the object, can't be modified. However, you may add new objects to the business layer.
A WHERE clause can be added to an object in an OLAP universe.	It is not possible to add a WHERE clause to an object in a multidimensional universe.
Only four object types are supported: character, date, long text, and number.	More object types are supported: Boolean, date, date/time, long text, numeric, and string. Binary large objects ("blobs") are also supported, but no client tools can take advantage of them at this time.
A folder name is unique in a universe.	A folder name is unique only under its parent folder.
An object can have the Active or Hidden states.	An object can have the Active, Hidden, or Deprecated states.
Doesn't support measure details.	Supports measure attributes.
Doesn't support custom properties, except through the SDK.	Supports custom properties for the business layer, dimensions, attributes, measures, filters, folders, and parameters.
Classes and objects are exposed as a whole in the universe.	Supports business layer views that may contain subset of folders and objects. Views can be used in the business layer editor and also in the query panel.
Classes and objects depend on the database schema on which they have been created.	It's possible to change the data foundation on which a business layer relies.
Filters in relational universes are defined with an SQL expression.	Supports also business filters, where the condition is expressed based on objects of the business layer.
Filters in OLAP universes are defined with an XML expression.	Business filters are the only filters supported in multidimensional universes.

Table 13.4 Business Layer Comparison (Cont.)

Universe Design Tool	Information Design Tool
Supports user object (also called user defined object), used only by SAP BusinessObjects Desktop Intelligence.	Does not support user object.
Universes are translated directly in the Translation Management Tool.	The data foundation and business layer are translated in the Translation Management Tool before publishing the universe.
Can't save queries.	Supports predefined queries; you can create, save, and run queries in the business layer.
Support OLAP universes created on SAP NetWeaver BW InfoProvider or BEx query.	Doesn't support multidimensional universes created on an SAP NetWeaver BW connection, but supports relational universes created on SAP NetWeaver BW InfoProviders. Client tools can directly query SAP BEx queries.
Relational universes support hierarchies.	Hierarchies have been renamed as navigation paths.
The search in based only on object names.	Also proposes an advanced search based on object types.

Table 13.4 Business Layer Comparison (Cont.)

13.5   List of Values and Parameters

Among IDT changes, the list of values, prompts, and renamed parameters have been completely redesigned to offer new capabilities and easier usability. Table 13.5 lists these enhancements.

Universe Design Tool	Information Design Tool
Lists of values are only defined in an object, which can have only one list of values associated.	Lists of values are defined in a data foundation or a business layer. Their editor contains a dedicated panel to manage these lists of values.

Table 13.5 List of Values and Prompt Comparison

Universe Design Tool	Information Design Tool
A list of values can only be used in the object where it's defined. It isn't possible to use the same list of values for several objects.	The same list of values isn't limited to a single object. It's global to the data foundation or business layer where it's defined. It can be reused by several objects, prompts, or filters.

Supports only lists of values defined from the following:
▸ An object's values (by default)
▸ The query panel
	Supports list of values defined from the following:
	▸ An object values (except if it's defined in a data foundation). Object values can be retrieved from the following:
	  ▸ The query panel
	  ▸ A custom hierarchy
	▸ A static list
	▸ An SQL expression

Uses an object to attach a list of values to a prompt or a filter.	Can directly attach a list of values to a prompt, a parameter, a filter, or an object.
If the list of values is defined with several columns, only the first column is used to return values.	If the list of values is defined with several columns, you can define which column returns values. Furthermore, if the list of values is re-used in several places, you can select for each case a different column to use.
Supports cascading lists of values.	Supports cascading and hierarchical lists of values.
Can't use lists of values content in an SQL script.	Supports the @execute function to return the list of values content in an SQL script.
Prompts are expressed using the @prompt built-in function.	Supports the same @prompt function but also a new object called parameter. Parameters are also used to prompt values, but are simpler to create, richer, and can be reused.

Table 13.5 List of Values and Prompt Comparison (Cont.)

Universe Design Tool	Information Design Tool
In the @prompt function, the object is identified by its parent name and its name.	In the @prompt function, the object is identified by its full parent path and its name.
Prompts are identified by the question prompted to the user.	Parameters are identified by a name that can be different from the question prompted to the user. They can also have a description.
Prompts can only be answered by the user (prompt to user).	Supports parameters prompted to users and also parameters with preset values.
Proposes a wizard to create @prompt expressions.	The wizard is no longer available to generate @prompt expressions. The editor is available to create parameters only.
Supports cascading prompts.	Supports cascading and hierarchical parameter dependencies.
The @prompt function supports alphanumeric, numeric, and date prompt.	The @prompt function supports alphanumeric, numeric, date types, and K-prompts, which return a not-quoted string to give more flexibility when concatenating strings in an expression.
Using a key to compare values is named the PRIMARY KEY option.	Supports the same option, but it has been renamed as INDEX AWARE PROMPT.
Only OLAP universe supports optional prompts.	Relational and multidimensional universes support optional prompts used in business filters.

Table 13.5 List of Values and Prompt Comparison (Cont.)

13.6 Security

In IDT, security profiles are the equivalent of the Universe Design Tool access restrictions. However, they have been extended. Let's see how they can compare with one another, in terms of their functional behavior and aggregation as well as their user interface.

13.6.1 Access Restrictions and Security Profiles (Relational Universe)

In IDT, access restrictions have been replaced and extended by data security profiles and business security profiles. Table 13.6 points out the differences between the two concepts for a relational universe.

Universe Design Tool	Information Design Tool
Supports access restrictions to secure universes: CONNECTION, SQL, CONTROLS, OBJECTS, ROWS, and TABLE MAPPING.	Supports data and business security profiles: ▶ CONNECTIONS, SQL, CONTROLS, ROWS, and TABLES data security profiles are the equivalent of CONNECTION, SQL, CONTROLS, ROWS, and TABLE MAPPING access restrictions. ▶ CREATE QUERY and DISPLAY DATA business security profiles are the equivalent of objects access restriction. The first secures objects and views in the query panel, whereas the second secures objects that retrieve data. They have been adapted to also support multisource universes. The FILTERS business security profile can also be used to filter data but through conditions expressed on business layer objects. Such a filter is always applied to the query, while a ROWS data security profile is added only if its conditional table is used in the query.
Supports the LIMIT SIZE OF LONG TEXT OBJECTS TO parameter in controls access restriction.	Doesn't support this parameter anymore in the CONTROLS data security profile. Other parameters are equivalent.
Supports the WARN CARTESIAN PRODUCT option in the SQL access restriction.	Doesn't support this option anymore in the SQL data security profile.
OBJECTS access restriction is used to deny objects. By default, a user can see all objects and classes in the universe, except the ones denied by the OBJECTS access restriction.	Uses the CREATE QUERY and DISPLAY DATA business security profiles to grant or deny objects. When a data security profile is assigned to a user, all objects and views are, by default, denied to him. CREATE QUERY and DISPLAY DATA business security profiles are used to grant or deny objects or views.

Table 13.6 Relational Universe Security Comparison

Universe Design Tool	Information Design Tool
Rows access restriction doesn't support an alias table or derived table as the conditional table.	Supports an alias table and derived table as the conditional table for the Rows data security profile (as of SAP BusinessObjects BI 4.0 SP4).
Supports an alias table as the source or replacement table in the TABLE MAPPING access restriction.	Supports an alias table as the source table only in the TABLES data security profile (as of SAP BusinessObjects BI 4.0 SP4).
Supports free text for the name of the replacement table in the TABLE MAPPING access restriction.	Supports only the data foundation table as a replacement table in the TABLES data security profile. It's no longer possible to type free text as the replacement table, and thus define the dynamic table (using @prompt or @variable).
Supports @variable use in the Rows access restriction. It can substitute for predefined parameters.	Supports @variable use in the Rows data security profile and FILTERS business security profile. It can substitute for predefined parameters or custom user attributes.

Table 13.6 Relational Universe Security Comparison (Cont.)

13.6.2 Access Restrictions and Security Profiles (OLAP Universe)

In the Universe Design Tool, the access restrictions you can define for an OLAP universe are a limited subset of the access restrictions types supported by relational universes. Indeed, they secure generic database concepts without being specific to relational databases: connection, controls, and objects.

IDT doesn't convert the OLAP universes created with the Universe Design Tool. However, the multidimensional universes created in IDT can be secured by business security profiles. Table 13.7 compares the security concepts enforced by the two tools.

Universe Design Tool	Information Design Tool
Supports the CONNECTION access restriction.	Supports the CONNECTION business security profile for multidimensional universes (as of SAP BusinessObjects BI 4.1).

Table 13.7 OLAP and Multidimensional Universe Security Comparison

Universe Design Tool	Information Design Tool
Supports the CONTROLS access restriction.	Doesn't support the query parameters replacement.
Supports the OBJECTS access restriction to secure universe objects.	Supports business security profiles: ▶ CREATE QUERY, to secure the business layer objects and views ▶ DISPLAY DATA, to secure the objects to query data
OBJECTS access restriction is used to deny objects. By default, a user can see all objects and classes in the universe, except the ones denied by the objects access restrictions that apply to him.	CREATE QUERY and DISPLAY DATA business security profiles can be used to grant or deny objects. The first secures objects and views in the query panel, whereas the second secures objects that retrieve data. By default, a user can see all objects and views in the universe. But if a business security profile applies to him, then all objects and views are denied to him. You can then use these business security profiles to grant or deny the user universe objects and views.
Can't filter data returned by an OLAP universe.	The FILTERS business security profile can secure hierarchies members.

Table 13.7 OLAP and Multidimensional Universe Security Comparison (Cont.)

13.6.3 Aggregation

In addition to the differences in the access restriction and security profiles behavior, IDT offers more options to aggregate security profiles. These differences are listed in Table 13.8.

Universe Design Tool	Information Design Tool
Only one access restriction can be assigned to a user or a group.	Several data and business security profiles can be assigned to a user or a group.
Defines access restriction priority through groups.	Defines priority at the security profile level.

Table 13.8 Security Aggregation Comparison

Universe Design Tool	Information Design Tool
For access restriction aggregated by priority, the value defined is the one assigned to the user, if any. Otherwise, the access restriction is applied to the group with the highest priority.	For security profiles aggregated by priority, the value to apply is always the one defined in the data security profile with the highest priority among the ones that apply to the user.
CONTROLS and SQL access restrictions can only be aggregated through the group priority.	CONTROLS and SQL data security profiles can be aggregated through the data security profiles' priority and also through the AND, ANDOR, or OR algorithms.
OBJECTS access restrictions can only be aggregated with the AND operator.	The CREATE QUERY business security profile and DISPLAY DATA business security profile can independently be aggregated through the AND, ANDOR, or OR algorithms.
Rows access restrictions can be aggregated through the AND or ANDOR algorithms.	Rows data security profiles can be aggregated through the AND, ANDOR, or OR algorithms
Doesn't support security filters based on objects.	The FILTERS business security profiles for relational or multidimensional universes can be aggregated through the AND, ANDOR, or OR algorithms. For relational universes, the WHERE clauses are merged using AND or OR operators. For multidimensional universes, the hierarchy members used to query data is computed though the union or intersection operators.

Table 13.8 Security Aggregation Comparison (Cont.)

13.6.4 Security Editor

IDT proposes the SECURITY EDITOR which is dedicated to creating, editing, assigning, and managing security profiles. This editor is more complete and offers more capabilities than the security management dialog box you can use in the Universe Design Tool. The main differences between the two tools are listed in Table 13.9.

Universe Design Tool	Information Design Tool
Must import the universe to edit its access restrictions and the user(s) and/or group(s) they are assigned to.	Can edit a universe security profiles and the user(s) and/or group(s) they are assigned to without importing it.
Can display and manage the access restrictions of only one universe at a time.	Displays in the SECURITY EDITOR an overview of all universes in the CMS repository and all of their security profiles. Furthermore, the SECURITY EDITOR can display all universes that have security profiles explicitly assigned to a user or a group.
Can't run secured queries.	Can run a query from a universe published in the CMS repository. Security assigned to the connected user applies.
Can't display inherited security profiles.	Can display security profiles inherited by a user or a group.

Table 13.9 Security Editor Comparison

13.6.5 Central Management Console Rights

Both applications can benefit from the BI platform framework and define some security rights. These rights slightly differ, as described next.

Application Rights

The authoring workflows in the Universe Design Tool and IDT are different. This affects the specific rights supported by the two tools. Table 13.10 compares and shows the equivalencies between these rights.

Universe Design Tool	Information Design Tool
APPLY UNIVERSE CONSTRAINTS	ADMINISTER SECURITY PROFILES
N/A	PUBLISH UNIVERSES
N/A	RETRIEVE UNIVERSES
CREATE, MODIFY, OR DELETE CONNECTIONS	CREATE, MODIFY, OR DELETE CONNECTIONS

Table 13.10 Application-Specific Rights Comparison

Universe Design Tool	Information Design Tool
CHECK UNIVERSE INTEGRITY	N/A
REFRESH STRUCTURE WINDOW	N/A
USE TABLE BROWSER	N/A
LINK UNIVERSE	N/A
N/A	USE SHARED PROJECTS
N/A	SAVE FOR ALL USERS
N/A	COMPUTE STATISTICS

Table 13.10 Application-Specific Rights Comparison (Cont.)

Universe Rights

The specific design rights for universes created in IDT and the Universe Design Tool differ. Table 13.11 compares and shows the equivalencies between these rights.

Universe Design Tool	Information Design Tool
CREATE AND EDIT QUERIES BASED ON UNIVERSE	CREATE AND EDIT QUERIES BASED ON THE UNIVERSE
EDIT ACCESS RESTRICTIONS	EDIT SECURITY PROFILES
	ASSIGN SECURITY PROFILES
DATA ACCESS	DATA ACCESS
UNLOCK UNIVERSE	N/A
NEW LIST OF VALUES	N/A
PRINT UNIVERSE	N/A
SHOW TABLE OR OBJECT VALUES	N/A
N/A	RETRIEVE UNIVERSE

Table 13.11 Universe-Specific Rights Comparison

13.6.6 Connection Rights

In the Universe Design Tool, relational universes are created on top of relational connections that are also supported by IDT. During conversion in the CMS repository, these connections aren't converted, and their general and custom rights are similarly enforced in the two tools.

OLAP connections created in the Universe Design Tool aren't supported by IDT, and there is no conversion path between these connections and the OLAP ones supported by IDT.

13.7 Miscellaneous

In addition to the functional changes described previously, IDT also presents some differences in usability and its framework compared to the Universe Design Tool. These main changes are listed in Table 13.12.

Universe Design Tool	Information Design Tool
Has only one menu bar and toolbar.	Displays in the menu bar and toolbar only the main commands. Most commands are contextual and displayed in each editor and view toolbar.
Supports a SCAN AND REPAIR command.	Supports the CHECK INTEGRITY command you can run on different locations to validate the following: ▸ A data foundation or business layer, before saving or publishing them ▸ A published universe and its security Each rule result status can be categorized as an error, a warning, or information.
Copying objects between two universes works perfectly.	We don't recommend that you copy objects between two data foundations or business layers because it may lead to erroneous results.
Can create .pdf reports that document the universe.	Can create .pdf, .html, or .txt reports that document the business layer or data foundation.
Supports a split screen for the tables and joins schema.	Doesn't support a split screen, but different editors can be organized and displayed side by side.
Supports only online help.	Supports online help, context help, cheat sheets, and a WELCOME page.

Table 13.12 Additional Differences

Universe Design Tool	Information Design Tool
Supports the options to change the shape of join endpoints.	Doesn't propose to modify the shape of joins endpoints, but the PREFERENCES dialog box proposes several other appearance options, such as the join lines style.
Can automatically save an edited universe.	Doesn't support auto-save for resources.
Supports password changes.	Doesn't support password changes, except if you must change it when you first log in to the CMS repository.
Supports passwords to protect universe read and write.	Doesn't support passwords to read and write the universe in IDT. If retrieved from a CMS repository, the authoring resources can be protected by authenticating against the CMS repository.

Table 13.12 Additional Differences (Cont.)

Even with this list of differences, universes created in both tools remain similar and answer the same objectives and requirements. Universes created with IDT propose more capabilities than universes created with the Universe Design Tool, which brings universe conversion to the table. Conversion of the universes created in the Universe Design Tool to the IDT format is a straightforward process.

13.8 Universe Conversion

IDT can convert a universe created with the Universe Design Tool to save it in the new file format supported by IDT. You may also use the semantic layer Java SDK to run this conversion, especially if you have a large number of universes to convert, because IDT can only convert one universe at a time.

This section first lists the universes that can be converted or not before describing how this conversion differs between local and secured universes, especially for connections. The universe conversion is covered next, including the specific case of linked universes. Finally, the section ends by describing the security conversion: rights, access restrictions, and object access levels.

13.8.1 Universe Conversion Scope

The following universes created in the Universe Design Tool can't be converted because IDT doesn't support them:

▶ Relational universes based on a stored procedure or on a Java bean.

▶ Relational universes based on an SAP BusinessObjects Data Federator XI 3.0 connection.

▶ OLAP universes based on an OLAP connection created with the Universe Design Tool. Only relational universes can be converted, and the remainder of this section focuses only on relational universe.

▶ OLAP connections created in the Universe Design Tool aren't converted because OLAP universes aren't converted by IDT.

Oracle OLAP 9i and Oracle OLAP 10g
Relational universes based on a relational connection to Oracle OLAP 9i and Oracle OLAP 10g can be converted by IDT, but they use hints in the joins between tables that are not supported in IDT data foundation, so queries on the converted universe fail.

Universe conversion generates a relational universe that complies with the different layers in IDT. The converted universe contains the three resources described in previous chapters:

▶ Connection or connection shortcut in case of a secured universe

▶ Data foundation

▶ Business layer

If the universe is a secured universe saved in the CMS repository, its security is converted as well. Security in IDT reuses and extends the Universe Design Tool's security, so the conversion is done with respect to the original universe's security.

SAP BusinessObjects Web Intelligence Change Source
Converting a universe doesn't change the reports that use it. For example, SAP BusinessObjects Web Intelligence supports universes created with both tools. After the universe conversion, you need to explicitly change the original universe used by Web Intelligence documents so they can access the converted universe. Otherwise, they keep consuming the universe created with the Universe Design Tool.

13.8.2 Local versus Secured Universe Conversion

IDT can convert both local relational universes and universes saved in the CMS repository. If the universe is local, then the conversion also generates the different resources in a local project. The relational personal or shared connection used by the source universe is converted into the equivalent local connection in IDT. The same parameters are used to recreate the local connection embedded in the converted universe, as shown in Figure 13.1.

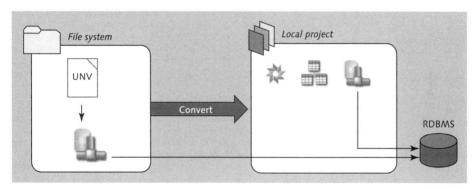

Figure 13.1 Local Universe Conversion

You can republish the generated resources to generate a local *.unx* universe that can be consumed by client tools.

In a local conversion, there are no access restrictions or security rights to convert. A local conversion can convert universes created in previous releases (SAP Business-Objects XI R2 or SAP BusinessObjects XI 3.x), whereas a secured conversion must have a universe created or upgraded in a CMS repository of a SAP BusinessObjects BI 4.x system.

If the universe is secured, then the conversion generates the converted universe in the same CMS repository. This universe reuses the same secured relational connection used by the source universe, as shown in Figure 13.2. The generated universe contains a connection shortcut to this secured connection.

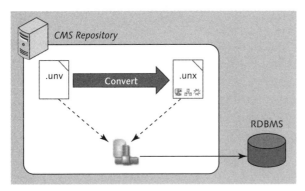

Figure 13.2 Secured Universe Conversion

The conversion of the universe itself is done through the creation of the data foundation and business layer. These resources are converted in the same manner in a local conversion or a conversion in the CMS repository.

13.8.3 Data Foundation and Business Layer

When a universe is converted, the created data foundation and business layer are defined to behave as in the original universe. A single-source data foundation is created for the converted universe. As shown in Chapter 5, Section 5.1, this data foundation can't be enabled for multisource. The database schema used in the universe is recreated in this data foundation. The tables, including alias and derived tables, their columns, the joins that link them, and the contexts are recreated in this data foundation with the same properties. This data foundation contains only one view—the master view. The conversion also creates a business layer that relies on this data foundation.

The converted business layer is created with only one business layer view. The objects (dimensions, measures, details, filters) and classes from source universe are converted in the converted business layer as objects (dimensions, measures, attributes, filters) and folders with the same properties: name, description, SELECT and WHERE clauses, extra tables, translations, and so on. These objects are organized in the same folders in which the corresponding objects are organized in the source universe.

Prompts can be either converted as @prompt or as parameter objects. You select this option in the conversion wizard (see Section 13.9).

Lists of values associated with objects are converted as explicit lists of values based on business layer objects in the business layer. These new lists of values are based on the query panel and are attached to their corresponding objects. But lists of values using custom SQL are converted into list of values based on business layer objects with custom SQL.

Universe parameters are converted and set either in the data foundation or in the business layer, depending on the place where they were defined in the original universe.

13.8.4 Linked Universe

Linked universes used in the Universe Design Tool to reference a *core universe* in a *derived universe* are no longer supported in IDT, but they can be converted by IDT. During the conversion, the core universe is explicitly copied in the converted derived universe, as shown in Figure 13.3.

The converted universes are still working and expose the same list of objects as the source universe. The dynamic link provided by the core universe is no longer provided in the converted universes, so you can't make changes in the core that are inherited by all derived universes. Such changes must be explicitly made in every converted universe.

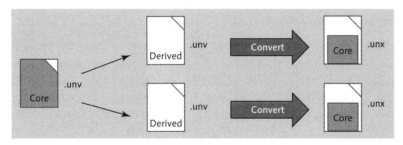

Figure 13.3 Linked Universes Conversion

Although their behaviors are different, reusability can also be achieved in IDT by doing the following:

▶ Sharing a data foundation with several business layers

▶ Creating one single universe with the following:

► The folders and objects of the core universe and its derived universes

► Several business layer views, one for each derived universe, each view containing the objects and folders of this derived universe before the conversion

13.8.5 Universe Rights Conversion

When a secured universe is converted, its security rights settings are also converted to secure as identically as possible the converted universe. Its rights access levels and advanced security rights settings are recreated and assigned to the converted universe for the same groups and users.

Because the rights differ between the two universe types, a mapping is done between them during conversion:

► The value for all general CREATE AND EDIT QUERIES BASED ON THIS UNIVERSE and DATA ACCESS rights are identically set.

► The EDIT ACCESS RESTRICTIONS right is no longer supported by IDT, but its value is set to EDIT SECURITY PROFILES and ASSIGN SECURITY PROFILES rights.

► The following rights are no longer supported by IDT, thus their values aren't kept during conversion: UNLOCK UNIVERSE, NEW LIST OF VALUES, PRINT UNIVERSE, and SHOW TABLE OR OBJECT VALUES.

13.8.6 Access Restriction Conversion

The security defined in IDT is a super-set of the security set in the Universe Design Tool and the access restriction conversion is done by mapping its parameters to equivalent security profiles. However, the slight differences between access restrictions and security profiles require some adaptation during the conversion phase to get the same behavior applied to the converted universe as in the original universe.

For each universe to convert, each access restriction generates one or several data security profiles and/or a business security profile. By default, a Universe Design Tool access restriction is converted into a data security profile and assigned to the same user and group. The name of this data security profile is the name of the access restriction. The definition of this data security profile is directly retrieved from the access restriction definition (connection, controls, SQL, rows, and table mapping security).

In IDT, however, priority is no longer defined at the group level but at the data security profile level. If the access restriction is assigned to more than one user or group, and if this conversion doesn't allow the converted security to properly reflect the same security as in the source universe, then the access restriction is converted into several data security profiles, one for each user or group.

The names of these data security profiles are the names of the access restriction followed by the user or group names: *<Access Restriction Name>_<user or group name>*. The definitions of these data security profiles are all identical and are directly retrieved from the access restriction definitions (connection, controls, SQL, rows, and table mapping security). These data security profiles are assigned to the same users and groups as their corresponding access restrictions and are prioritized using the group priority in the Universe Design Tool.

If the access restriction defines the objects access restriction, then a business security profile is created and attached to the converted universe. This business security profile has the same name as the access restriction, and it defines both CREATE QUERY and DISPLAY DATA business security profiles to deny the same objects denied in the objects access restriction:

▶ In CREATE QUERY, the master view is granted and all objects and classes denied in the access restriction are denied in the security profile.

▶ In DISPLAY DATA, the ALL OBJECTS shortcut is granted to grant all objects by default. Furthermore, all objects and classes denied in the access restriction are also denied in the security profile.

This business security profile is assigned to the same users and groups as the access restriction.

13.8.7 Access Restriction Aggregation Option Conversion

When the universe is converted, its aggregation options are converted with these rules:

▶ The CONTROLS and SQL data security profile aggregation option is set to PRIORITY because it's the only one available for controls and SQL access restriction.

▶ The ROWS data security profile aggregation option is defined from the value of the original universe rows access restriction aggregation option:

> ▸ VERY RESTRICTIVE (AND) if it's AND

> ▸ MODERATELY RESTRICTIVE (ANDOR) if it's ANDOR

▸ The CREATE QUERY and DISPLAY DATA business security profile aggregation option is set to VERY RESTRICTIVE (AND) because it's the only one available for the objects access restriction aggregation option in the Universe Design Tool.

▸ The FILTERS business security profile aggregation mode is set to VERY RESTRICTIVE (AND).

13.8.8 Object Access Level

The Universe Design Tool supports object access level for any business objects defined in a universe (measure, dimension, and detail). IDT also supports them for any business objects defined in a business layer of a universe (measure, dimension, attribute, etc.).

The different access levels are identical for both tools: public, controlled, restricted, confidential, and private. The user access level you define in the CMC can be identically defined for a universe defined with the Universe Design Tool or a universe defined with IDT. User access levels inherited by a user from the groups the user belongs to are also aggregated identically in the Universe Design Tool and IDT.

When a universe is converted, object access levels that are object properties are converted as well. The user access levels defined for this universe are also recreated for the converted universe, for the same user(s) and group(s).

13.9 Converting Universes in Information Design Tool

Universe conversion can be run from IDT. This process converts both local universes and universes saved in the CMS repository. We describe both workflows in the next sections.

13.9.1 Converting a Local Universe

To convert a local universe, follow these steps:

1. In the menu bar, select FILE • CONVERT UNIVERSE to open the CONVERT .unv UNIVERSE dialog box.

2. Click the Select .unv Universe from the Local File System button () to select the universe to convert:

   ▶ In the Open dialog box, navigate in the file system to select the universe to convert, and then click OK.

   ▶ The dialog box closes and the universe name to convert is displayed in the Select the .unv Universe to Convert text field. As shown in Figure 13.4, the dialog box is updated. Enter the destination folder for the converted resources.

Figure 13.4 Convert a .UNV Universe Dialog Box for a Local Conversion

3. Click the Browse button () located near the Destination Local Project Folder text field to select the destination folder:

   ▶ In the Select Local Project dialog box, select a project or a folder in a local project, and then click OK.

   ▶ The Select Local Project dialog box closes, and the selected project or folder is displayed in the Destination Local Project Folder text field.

4. To convert the @prompt expressions as parameter objects, select the Automatically convert @Prompt expressions into universe named parameters checkbox.

5. Click OK to start the conversion. The converted connection, data foundation, and business layer are generated in the selected folder or project.

13.9.2 Converting a Secured Universe

The conversion of a secured universe is quite similar to a local universe; except the security that is converted with the universe. Before starting the conversion, make sure you have the ADD OBJECTS TO FOLDER right for the destination folder so you can create the converted universe. Then, to convert a secured universe, follow these steps:

1. In the menu bar, select FILE • CONVERT UNIVERSE to open the CONVERT .UNV UNIVERSE dialog box.

2. Click the SELECT .UNV UNIVERSE FROM A REPOSITORY button (⌨) to select the universe to convert:

   ▶ In the OPEN SESSION dialog box, create a new session or open a predefined one (see Chapter 3, Section 3.4), and then click OK.

   ▶ In the universe browser dialog box, navigate in the *Universes* folder in the CMS repository, select the universe to convert, and click OK.

   ▶ The dialog box closes, and the universe name to convert is displayed in the SELECT .UNV UNIVERSE TO CONVERT text field.

3. Click the BROWSE button (⌨) located near the DESTINATION REPOSITORY FOLDER text field to enter the destination folder:

   ▶ In the universe browser dialog box, navigate in the *Universes* folder in the CMS repository, select the destination folder, and then click OK.

   ▶ The dialog box closes, and the folder name is displayed in the DESTINATION REPOSITORY FOLDER text field.

4. You may optionally choose to retrieve the converted universe after the conversion is done:

   ▶ Click the BROWSE button (⌨) near the DESTINATION LOCAL PROJECT FOLDER text field to open the SELECT LOCAL PROJECT dialog box.

   ▶ Select the project or a folder in a local project, and then click OK.

   ▶ The SELECT LOCAL PROJECT dialog box closes, and the selected project and folder are displayed in the DESTINATION LOCAL PROJECT FOLDER text field, as shown in Figure 13.5.

   ▶ To remove security from the extracted resources (see Chapter 9, Section 9.4), select the SAVE FOR ALL USERS checkbox.

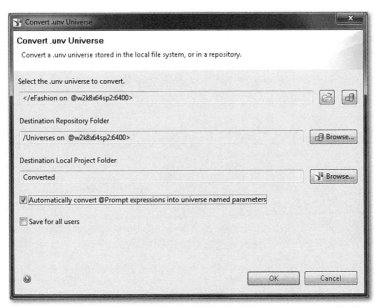

Figure 13.5 Convert a .UNV Universe Dialog Box for a Conversion in the Repository

5. To convert `@prompt` expressions as parameter objects, select the AUTOMATICALLY CONVERT @PROMPT EXPRESSIONS INTO UNIVERSE NAMED PARAMETERS checkbox.

6. Click OK to start the conversion. The converted universe is generated in the selected folder in the CMS repository. It has the same name as the original, except for its *.unv* extension that is replaced by *.unx*. If you've opted to retrieve the converted universe at the same time, its resources are also generated in the local project folder you've selected.

To convert a secured universe, you can also directly right-click the universe in the REPOSITORY RESOURCES view. The CONVERT .UNV UNIVERSE dialog box opens, where you can define the same options previously described.

13.10 Summary

Information Design Tool is the Universe Design Tool successor, and it proposes several major changes and enhancements: in the workflows, in the authoring resources, and in their capabilities. Some features, however, aren't identically supported, and some are not supported at all. For this reason, assessing the features you use is important if you plan to move your existing universes created with the Universe Design Tool to universes compatible with IDT.

When you're ready to convert, you can use IDT to run this conversion. IDT can convert both local and secured universe. In the latter case, security is converted as well.

The Authors

Christian Ah-Soon has worked for SAP BusinessObjects for 14 years as a program manager on transversal areas like administration, security, internationalization, installation, and SDK. For SAP BusinessObjects BI 4.x, he worked on the semantic layer team as a product owner for Information Design Tool.

He is a co-author of *SAP BusinessObjects BI Security* (SAP PRESS, 2013).

Christian holds a Ph.D. in computer science and graduated from TELECOM Nancy.

Photograph by Philippe Cuvillier

Didier Mazoué is an expert product manager in the SAP BusinessObjects BI organization. He joined Business Objects in 2000 as an expert sales consultant in French operations, where he focused on helping close large deals involving data warehousing and OLAP.

In 2005 Didier joined the product group as senior program manager, moved to Voyager in 2006, and then to the semantic layer area as product manager. Didier is a product expert in business intelligence, data modeling, OLAP, and RDBMS.

Before joining SAP BusinessObjects, Didier held several positions in the software industry as developer, project leader, support engineer, and sales consultant.

Photograph by Alain Somvang

Pierpaolo Vezzosi is director of solution management in the SAP BusinessObjects organization. He joined Business Objects in 2000 as a technology alliances manager to develop the company relationship with key technological partners and monitor innovating trends. In 2004, Pierpaolo helped develop Business Objects' offshore activities in India. In 2006 he moved to product management.

He is currently responsible for the solution management of SAP BusinessObjects BI 4 on top of SAP HANA and for the overall semantic layer technology.

Pierpaolo holds a master's degree in aeronautics and space engineering.

Photograph by Alain Somvang

Index

D

T

■ Learn how to run SAP
BusinessObjects BI tools on top of
SAP data

■ Understand your data
connectivity options for integration

■ Get up to speed on SAP BO
Design Studio and SAP Lumira

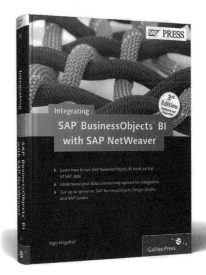

Ingo Hilgefort

Integrating SAP BusinessObjects BI with SAP NetWeaver

You know what SAP's business intelligence solutions can do for a business—
now make it happen. With this detailed, click-by-click guide, learn how to get
the SAP BI tools talking to SAP NetWeaver. From data connectivity to creating
reports, this latest edition contains updates for release 4.1, including coverage
of the newest solutions: SAP Lumira and SAP BusinessObjects Design Studio.

approx. 545 pp., 3. edition, 79,95 Euro / US$ 79.95
ISBN 978-1-59229-923-2, Nov 2013
www.sap-press.com

Galileo Press

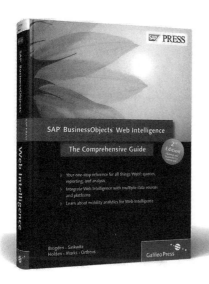

■ Your one-stop reference for all things WebI: queries, reporting, and analysis

■ Integrate Web Intelligence with multiple data sources and platforms

■ Learn about mobility analytics for Web Intelligence

■ 2nd edition updated and expanded for release 4.0

Jim Brogden, Heather Sinkwitz, Mac Holden, Dallas Marks, Gabriel Orthous

SAP BusinessObjects Web Intelligence

The Comprehensive Guide

Revolutionize your company's data presentation with SAP BusinessObjects Web Intelligence 4.0 with new flexibility and functionalities. This comprehensive guide will help you build a foundational understanding of WebI by beginning with the fundamentals; or you can jump straight into the advanced discussions that are new to the latest release, including advanced charting, advanced formula writing, and report scheduling and distribution.

591 pp., 2. edition 2012, 79,95 Euro / US$ 79.95
ISBN 978-1-59229-430-5
www.sap-press.com

■ Learn how to size, install, and configure a system that will best meet your needs

■ Master the daily tasks that are necessary to keep an SAP BusinessObjects BI system up and running

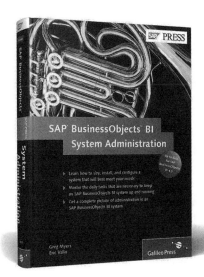

Greg Myers, Eric Vallo

SAP BusinessObjects BI System Administration

A system administrator's job isn't easy. When stuff works, no one notices. When stuff breaks, suddenly everyone knows your name. Your most important task, then—for your users and for you—is to set up your system right the first time, and to keep it running effectively. With this book, do just that. Guided by step-by-step instructions and screenshots, you'll learn how to perform the most common administration tasks in an SAP BusinessObjects system, and also get acquainted with the vital changes in the 4.0 SP4 release.

472 pp., 2012, 69,95 Euro / US$ 69.95
ISBN 978-1-59229-404-6
www.sap-press.com

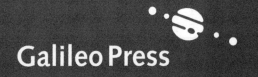

Galileo Press

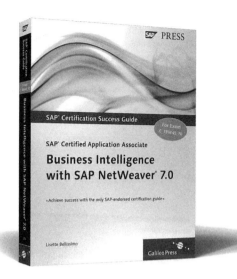

■ Aligned to the SAP Global Certification Program

■ Ensures certification success for the SAP Certified Application Associate- Business Intelligence with SAP NetWeaver 7.0 exam (C_TBW45_70)

■ Only SAP-endorsed certification guide

Lisette Bellissimo

SAP Certified Application Associate — Business Intelligence with SAP NetWeaver 7.0

This book serves as a supplementary guide for anyone taking SAP Education to help them prepare for and pass the SAP Certified Application Associate – Business Intelligence with SAP NetWeaver (7.0) exam. The content of the book is mapped to the specific exam objectives to help you prepare for the exam. It provides practice questions and answers for each topic.

318 pp., 2010, 69,95 Euro / US$ 69.95
ISBN 978-1-59229-353-7
www.sap-press.com